Proceedings in Parliament 1626

Volume III: House of Commons

The preparation of this volume was made possible in part
by a grant from the
National Endowment for the Humanities,
an independent federal agency.

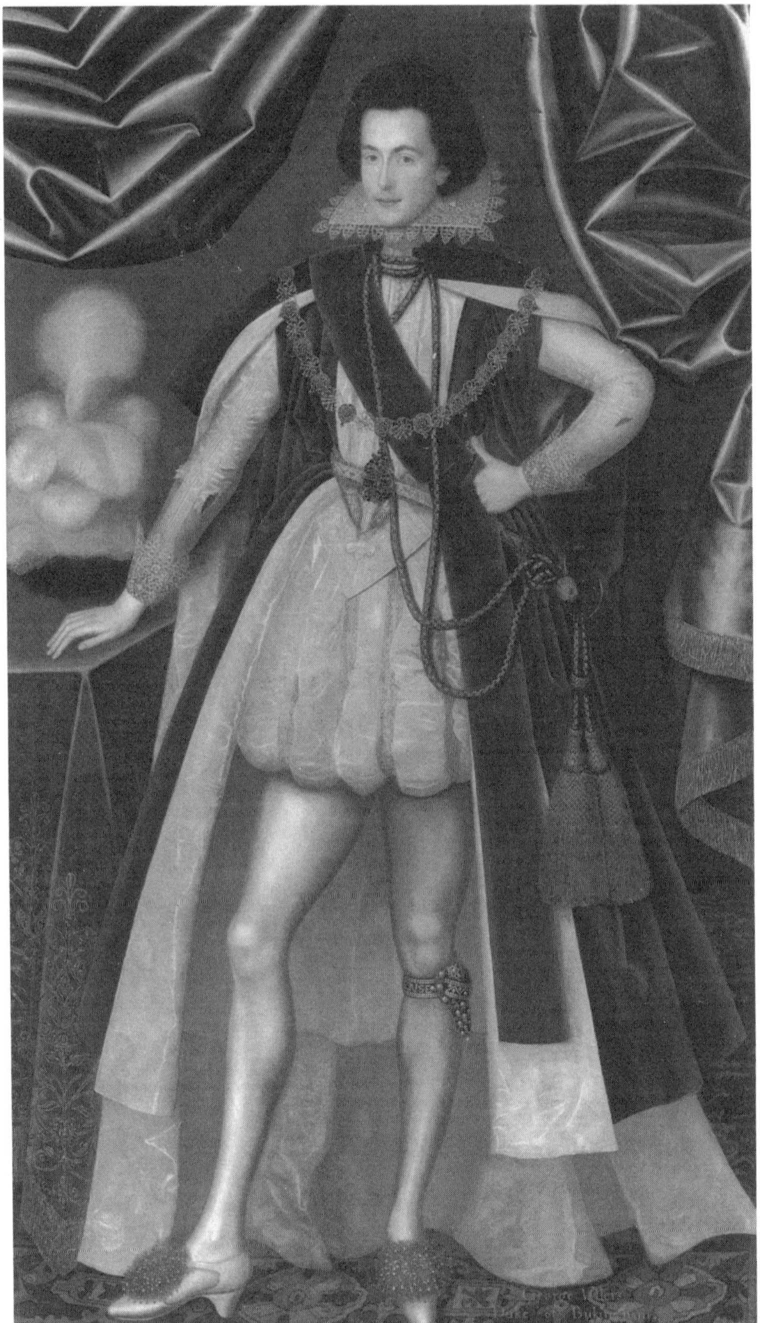

GEORGE VILLIERS, FIRST DUKE OF BUCKINGHAM
Portrait attributed to William Larkin
National Portrait Gallery, London

Proceedings in Parliament
1626

Volume III: House of Commons

Edited by
William B. Bidwell and Maija Jansson

The Yale Center for Parliamentary History
David E. Underdown, Director

New Haven and London Yale University Press

Library of Congress CCN: 90–71244
ISBN: 1–58046–004–6

Distributed worldwide by the University of Rochester Press:

P.O. Box 41026
Rochester, NY
14604-4126
USA

or

P.O. Box 9
Woodbridge, Suffolk
IP12 3DF
United Kingdom

This book is printed in the United States of America

Set in Baskerville Roman types by The Composing Room of Michigan, Inc., Grand Rapids, Michigan. Printed in the United States of America by Thomson-Shore, Inc., Dexter, Michigan.

The paper in this book meets the guidelines for permanence and durability of the Committee on Production Guidelines for Book Longevity of the Council on Library Resources.

CONTENTS

Volume III: House of Commons

Order of Business Monday, 17 April 1626

Committee on the bill for making void a decree in the Exchequer Chamber made in behalf of Sir Francis **Neale** against Sir Edward **Fisher** to meet on Thursday [20 April]	3, *7/3
Subcommittee for examining the **causes of causes** to meet tomorrow	3, 5, *20/3
Subcommittee for examining whether **inexperienced commanders** have been employed: to meet on Wednesday [19 April]	3, 5, 10, *18/3
Committee for considering **Heaman's** complaint and such other **defects in shipping,** victuals, munition, etc., to meet on Wednesday [19 April]	3, 5, *3/3
Committee on **Willes's** petition and the **Dover** business to meet next Monday [24 April]	3, *8/3
Sir Eubule Thelwall: presents complaints against the **Bishop of Bangor**	3, 5, 10, *26/4; 27/4; 29/4; 3/5; 5/5; 6/5; 22/5; 24/5; 25/5; 15/6
Complaints against the Bishop of Bangor: read and referred to the committee of **religion**	3, 5, 10
Warrants to be issued for witnesses in the Bishop of Bangor's case	3
Committee on the bill for the settling of certain **marshlands** by the name of the Isle of **Canvey** to meet on Wednesday [19 April]	3, *21/3
Committee on the bill against the transportation of **ordnance** to meet on Wednesday [19 April]	3, *13/2
Committee on the bill for the making of the **arms** of the kingdom more serviceable to meet on Wednesday [19 April]	3, *20/3
John Haynes: more complaints from **merchants** trading in **France** concerning **seizure of their goods** and the restraint of Protestant religion	3, 5, 11, *18/2
Sir John Eliot	5
Sir Dudley Digges	5
Committee of the whole House on the causes of the evils of the **King's estate** and **state of the kingdom** to meet tomorrow	3, *24/2
Ordered: engrossed bills to be read tomorrow	3
Report from the committee of religion: concerning Richard **Montagu** (John Pym)	3, 5, 11, *20/2
Christopher Wandesford	9
Sir George More	9
Sir Thomas Hoby	9
Sir John Eliot	9
John Pym	10
Sir James Perrot	10
Mr. Rolle	10
Sir Humphrey May (Chancellor Duchy)	10
Thomas Wentworth	10
Edward Whitby	10
Sir Nathaniel Rich	10
Ordered: further debate and resolution concerning Montagu deferred until Thursday [20 April]; Montagu to have notice and to be heard if he wishes	4, 10
Subcommittee for considering Montagu's books is to be a committee for drawing up interrogatories to be ministered unto Montagu; three members added	4, 10

MONDAY, 17 APRIL 1626

I. JOURNAL OF THE HOUSE OF COMMONS

[CJ 845; p. 18]
Lunae, 17[1] *Aprilis, 2 Caroli Regis*

Sir Edward Fisher's bill, *sine die,* Thursday next, 2 clock.

The subcommittee for finding out the cause of causes, tomorrow, 2 clock in the afternoon, in the Star Chamber.

The subcommittee for employment of unexperienced commanders, on Wednesday next, Exchequer Chamber.

The committee for Heaman's ship, at the same time and place.

The committee for the ships of Dover,[2] this day 7night, in the Star Chamber.

SIR EUBULE THELWALL tenders divers articles against the Bishop of Bangor; which read.[3]

This committed to the committee for religion to be examined. A warrant from the Speaker for witnesses, such as Sir Eubule Thelwall shall tender to Mr. Speaker.

Committee for Canvey Island, this day 7night.

Transportation of ordnance, Wednesday next, Exchequer Court.

Bill of arms, and for finding arms, Wednesday next, Star Chamber.

[p. 19] MR. HAYNES reports further proceedings of the French against our English ships and men.[4]

Ordered, the committee[5] of the whole House for evils, causes, and remedies to sit tomorrow morning; and the engrossed bills to be read tomorrow, at 8 clock.

MR. PYM reports the business concerning Montagu his books:[6]

1. MS: *18.*

2. This is presumably the committee that was appointed to consider Mark Willes's petition and the Dover business, see HofC, 8 March, OB.

3. For some of the complaints against Lewis Bayly, Bishop of Bangor, see Whitelocke and Rich, below. Copies of the "informations" delivered in by Thelwall are included in several manuscript collections of "separates" of parliamentary materials for 1626, e.g., Lansd. 491, f. 155v and Tanner 72, f. 93. Although witnesses were examined, the House did not reach a resolution on this matter before the dissolution on 15 June. Following the dissolution, John Griffith, who sat in 1626 as MP for Caernarvonshire, petitioned the King for a present proceeding against the Bishop, annexing to his petition a catalog of twenty-one crimes that he stated had been charged against Bangor in the Commons and had been proved by many witnesses. For Griffith's petition, see SP 16/30:8. A copy of the articles against the Bishop is among Griffith's papers, see HMC, *5th Report, Appendix,* pp. 417–418. For further business concerning Bayly, see also, HofC, 5 May, OB.

4. Concerning earlier complaints about the French, see HofC, 17 February, n. 20; and 22 February, nn. 7 and 11. For more recent complaints, see SP 16/22:89, 95, 106. See also, Sir Dudley Carleton's report to the House on his diplomatic mission to France, 18 April, OB.

5. *select* is crossed out in the MS preceding *committee* and *for preparing of the heads of the conference with the Lords about the French business* is crossed out after *committee* and *of the whole House for evils, causes, and remedies* is inserted. Concerning the select committee, see Eliot's speech in Whitelocke, below, following Haynes's report.

6. Pym is reporting from the committee of religion rather than from the subcommittee for considering Montagu's books appointed on 6 March, see Whitelocke, below. For a fuller account of Pym's report, see SP 16/25:10, printed in S. R. Gardiner, *Debates in the House of Commons in 1625* (London: Camden Society, 1873), pp. 179–186. Montagu's books referred to in Pym's report are: *Appello Caesarem: a just Appeale from two unjust Informers* (*STC,* no. 18030); *A Gagg for the New Gospell? No: A New Gagg for an Old Goose* (*STC,* no. 18038), and *A Treatise of the Invocation of Saints* (a revision of his *Immediate Address unto God Alone*) (*STC,* no. 18039). The proceedings in the House were known to Montagu, see his letter to Richard Neile, Bishop of Durham, Surtees Society, Vol. 52, pt. I, pp. 87–88.

1. The motives to the committee's care in this business.

2. The heads of the charge, with the aggravations.

3. The proofs of every head.

4. The opinion of the committee concerning the whole matter.

1. The writ;[7] 2ly, care of God's religion; 3, precedents of other states in the like kind in respect of the dangerous consequences by these distempers[8] which commonly, if not presently suppressed, increase and grow; 4, precedents of our parliaments in like cases, and of the 2 last parliaments in this particular.[9]

1. That Montagu has disturbed our Church, contrary to the doctrine thereof published in 39 Articles, 1562, and contrary to the *Book of Homilies,* both confirmed by parliament.[10]

2. That in these books divers matters tending to sedition by setting the King against the people and the people one against another.

3. That the whole scope of this book is to discountenance the true profession of the religion here established, and[11] so to draw the people to popery, and reconcile them to the Church of Rome.

That he[12] contraries the doctrine of the Church of England in 6 points:

1. Concerning the Church of Rome/[13]

[p. 20] That the committee fully of opinion Montagu stands convicted[14] of all the three heads of the charge and that, as a public offender against the peace of our Church he should, by this House, be presented to the Lords, there to receive punishment according to his demerits.

Upon question,[15] to defer the further debate and resolution of this business concerning his books until Thursday morning next, and he to have notice thereof that he may be then heard in the House, if he will. This notice to be given him by Mr. Serjeant.

2ly, upon question, a select committee to consider of interrogatories to be ministered unto him by Mr. Speaker.

This to be done by the subcommittee appointed by the committee for religion to consider of his books,[16] with addition of Sir Thomas Hoby, Sir Nathaniel Rich, and Mr. Whitaker: 4 clock this afternoon, in the Treasury Chamber.[17]

And this committee also to consider and report their opinions to the House, what they think fittest to be done for prevention of danger by further writing in this business.

II. DIARY OF BULSTRODE WHITELOCKE, ESQ., DD. 12.21, CAMBRIDGE UNIVERSITY LIBRARY

[f. 132v]

17 April[18]

7. I.e., the writ of summons to parliament; see below, n. 22.

8. *misdemeanors* is crossed out in the MS preceding *distempers.*

9. For action against Montagu in the parliaments of 1624 and 1625, see *CJ,* I, 704, 788, and *PP 1625,* pp. 330–344.

10. The thirty-nine Articles put forth by the Church of England in 1562 were revised by Convocation and sanctioned by act of parliament in 1571 (*SR,* 13 Eliz. I, c. 12). For the *Book of Homilies,* see *Sermons, or Homilies, appointed to be read in Churches in the time of Queen Elizabeth . . . to which are added, the Articles of Religion; the Constitutions and Canons Ecclesiastical* (London, 1817).

11. *the opening a way* is crossed out in the MS following *and* and is replaced with *so to draw the people.*

12. Printed edition: *the.*

13. The lower half of this page is blank in the MS. For the remainder of Pym's report, see Whitelocke, below.

14. MS: *convinced.*

15. *these books contain* is crossed out in the MS following *question.*

16. I.e., the subcommittee appointed on 6 March.

17. For notes of the afternoon meeting of this committee, taken by Henry Sherfield, see App., II, C.

18. *Martii* is crossed out in the MS and *April* is inserted.

The committees of causes of causes, and for employment of unexperienced commanders, and for Heaman's complaint, and for/

SIR EUBULE THELWALL presents divers complaints against the Bishop of Bangor,[19] accusing him of simony, contracting to pay £600 to one Mr. Ramsey, £400 whereof he paid. And perjury he is accused of. And branded for incontinency. A woman being in labor said that the Bishop was the father of her child, which before justices of the peace she afterwards affirmed, viz., that he got her with child. Licensed a man to marry his wife's sister's daughter. He bestows his livings upon unable and unworthy men, as a Frenchman, Scotchmen, and others, other that understand not the language, besides a sexton, decayed tradesman, footman and groom, apparitors. He takes and extorts money to repair his cathedral church and yet suffers it to go to ruin. He/

Both in the pulpit and in other places he gives very foul language, calling/

He is a common striker of men and women. He has granted protection to 12 dissolute and vile persons.

[f. 133] This complaint committed to the committee of religion.

MR. HAYNES. Many complaints out of the west countries for new arrests in France, and great calamities daily befalling the merchants, and restraint of the Protestants' religion. These are mysteries of state. Desires the House to take consideration of the miseries of the merchants.

SIR JOHN ELIOT. If there be a cause found of the restraint of religion, we may punish and redress that, though the restraint we cannot. A committee was formerly appointed to consider of some heads for a conference with the Lords,[20] which may likewise prepare heads for this too.

SIR DUDLEY DIGGES. That it may be first debated in the whole House.

MR. PYM reports from the committee of religion the proceedings in the case of Mr. Montagu.[21] By the words of the writ *ecclesiae Anglicanae*/[22]

God commands we should mark diligently those that cause divisions in the Church. Tho/

The spreading of/

The constant practice of parliament in like cases, especially in 21 and the last parliament.[23] In 21 [*Jac.*] the House commended the articles against Montagu to the Archbishop. 1 *Car.*, we found the business worse. The House sent again to the Archbishop of Canterbury. Resolved by question, 1 *Car.*, that Mr. Montagu had committed a great contempt against this House by setting out his last book, and a committee appointed to draw heads for a conference with the Lords about it. The committee/

Nor with the truth or falsehood of the doctrine, but only the matter of fact and the disturbance which he has made in the Church.

[f. 133v] 1. Mr. Montagu disturbed the Church and published doctrine contrary to the 39 Articles (confirmed 13 *Eliz.*), 1562, *et*

19. See above, n. 3.

20. I.e., the committee for considering heads of a conference with the Lords on the merchants trading in France, appointed on 17 March. See OB.

21. See above, n. 6.

22. I.e., the words in the writ of summons to parliament, which are: *Pro quibusdam arduis urgentibus negotiis, nos, statum et defensionem regni nostri Angliae, et ecclesiae Anglicanae concernentibus quoddam parliamentum nostrum apud,* etc. Coke, *Fourth Inst.*, p. 9, and see the forms of writs printed in Elsynge, *Parliaments*, pp. 67–68.

23. See above, n. 9. Many of the points regarding Montagu's books had been discussed in 1625 and would again be raised in 1628. The editors refer readers to *PP 1625*, pp. 330–334, 336–340 and *CD 1628*, III, 26 and 28 April (see OBs), and ibid., IV, 11 June (see OB).

contrary to the *Book of Homilies.*[24] 2. In his books contained divers passages apt to make sedition. 3. The whole frame of the book so made as [to] discourage men from the religion now established and invite them to a reconciliation with the see of Rome.

[1st point:]

1. I am to use his 3 books.[25]

2. Concerning the Church of Rome, doctrine of [*blank*] England taken out of the 2d part of the homily of the gifts of the Holy Ghost. 50[26] page of his *Gagg;* 139 p. of the *Appeal;* 28 Article and 25 Article.[27]

3. Controversies. 31 Article concerning masses, affirmative. M[ontagu's] *Gagg,* 14 page, negative.[28]

4. Concerning images. Homily against idolatry, 1 part. 300[29] p., *Gagg:* we agree that images may be used.[30]

5. Concerning saints to be peculiar patrons of some countries. Homily against idolatry, 1 part. *Invocation [of] Saints,* 107 page in the margin and following.[31]

6. Concerning the falling away from grace. 17 Article, a const[ancy]/[32]

30 p., *Appeal,* Mr. Montagu perverted this Article's words and sense, and by his [f. 134] interpretation sets the doctrine of England against the doctrine of the Church of Ireland, in the 38 Article.[33] By this doctrine he sets the Church of England in opposition to the reformed churches beyond seas. In Dort/[34]

24. See above, n. 10.

25. For the three books, see above, n. 6.

26. MS: *15.*

27. *Homilies,* pp. 434–435: "The true church is a universal congregation or fellowship of God's faithful and elect people, built upon the foundation of the apostles and prophets . . . .Now, if you will compare this with the Church of Rome . . . the state thereof [is] so far wide from the nature of the true church that nothing can be more. For, neither are they built upon the foundation of the apostles and prophets . . . ".

Gagg, p. 50: "this present-day Roman church . . . knows and cherishes its bond with that ancient church which is without question the Church of Christ. It cannot be, therefore, anything other than and different from that church . . . ".

Appeal, p. 139: "The Church of Rome is, and ever was a true Church since it was a Church".

See also Articles 25 and 28 of the 39 Articles, regarding transubstantiation and the sacraments practiced in the Roman church.

28. Article 31 of the 29 Articles: "the sacrifices of masses . . . were blasphemous fables and dangerous deceits".

Gagg, p. 14: "The controverted points are of a larger and an inferior alloy: of them a man may be ignorant, without any danger of his soul at all. A man may resolve or oppose this way, or that way, without peril of perishing forever".

29. MS: *30.*

30. *Homilies,* pp. 165–166: "we see they [images] teach no good lesson, neither of God nor godliness, but all error and wickedness".

Gagg, pp. 300–301: "Images have three uses assigned by your schools . . . . *Institutionem rudium: Commonefactionem historiae: et Excitationem devotionis,* you and we also give unto them".

31. *Homilies,* p. 206: "What, I pray you, be such saints with us, to whom we attribute the defense of certain countries, spoiling God of his due honor herein, but *dii tutelares* of the gentiles' idolaters?"

Invocation of Saints, pp. 107–108: "some saint or saints departed may have more special care of, interest in, charge over some men or man, country or countries, than is used ordinarily or others commonly have by usual disposition . . . .Examples hereof are frequent and many. Saint George is accounted the patron of England . . . ".

32. Article 17 of the 39 Articles: "God . . . has constantly decreed by his counsel, secret to us, to deliver from curse and damnation those whom he has chosen in Christ out of mankind, and to bring them by Christ to everlasing salvation".

33. On p. 30 of the *Appeal,* in referring to Article 16, concerning falling from grace, Montagu misquotes the wording of the article, and concludes: "possible, but not certain or necessary". The Articles of Ireland (*STC,* no. 14260) were drawn and agreed to by the Convocation of the Irish clergy held in Dublin in 1615 and were signed by Lord Deputy Chichester by order from King James in his name. See Richard Mant, *History of the Church of Ireland* (London, 1840), I, 382–388.

34. I.e., the Synod of Dort, 1619. On the Synod, see Thomas Fuller, *The Church History of Britain* (London, 1837), III, 274–279; *PP 1625,* p. 337, nn. 54, 55.

Falsifies the conference at Hampton Court.[35] Contradicts himself in 32 p. of his *Appeal,* 260 p.[36] of the *Appeal.*[37]

By this, appears Mr. Montagu has disturbed the Church of England by teaching.

2nd point is sedition charged against him:

3 propositions: 1. M[ontagu] does draw together in one collective name of Puritans the greatest part of the King's true subjects. 2. Divers crimes laid to their charge, and endeavors to bring the King into jealousy with them. 3. By divers odious terms endeavors to bring them into hate and scorn with the rest of the people. 3[38] p., *Appeal,* brings that name on those who subscribe or on those that hold the doctrine of/[39]

111 p. of the *Appeal,* to the bishops he extends that name of Puritans.[40] 114 p. of the *Appeal*/[41]

Lays to their charge crimes antipathizing to kings and princes. 114 p., *Appeal;* 136 p., *Appeal;* 3 p.,[42] *Appeal;* 12[43] p., *Appeal;* 44 p., *Appeal.*[44]

By divers aspersions and provocations endeavors to bring them into contempt and/

291[45] p., *Appeal;* 271[46] p., *Appeal;* and in other places.

[f. 134v] 3rd point, the frame and model of his books tending to discourage men from the Protestant religion and to reconcile them to the see of Rome consequently.

23 Eliz., to strive to reconcile men to the see of Rome is made treason.[47]

5 heads:

1. By the matters in difference between us and the Church of Rome. Of 47 positions he has left but 9 in controversy by be/

He leaves no rule in his differences which may/

35. *Appeal,* p. 30: "but challenged it was [Article 16] in the sense as unsound at the conference of Hampton Court by those that were petitioners against the doctrine and discipline established in the Church of England".

36. MS: *160.*

37. On p. 32 of the *Appeal,* Montagu refers to the *Book of Homilies* as "approved and justified in parliament in Queen Elizabeth's days . . . ", but on p. 260 he states that the homilies are "not as the public dogmatical resolutions confirmed of the Church of England".

38. MS: *30.*

39. The *Appeal,* p. 3: " . . . they seldom or never talk of any misbeing, misordering, misdemeaning, in any point or case, but that ever and anon, directly or upon the by, they can lend a lash unto, or pinch upon the credit of authority, though most sacred, that great *cordolium* and mote-in-the-eye unto popular irregularity and puritanical parity, the idol of our Godly brethren". See Matt. 7:3–4. See also, *CD 1628,* IV, nn. 25 and 27.

40. *Appeal,* p. 111: "whereunto the Puritans and schismatics themselves, at least the wiser and subtler sort of them, come off roundly now, for ends best known amongst themselves, remaining *quod erant, quoad doctrinam & tantum non in episcopatu puritani*".

41. *Appeal,* p. 114: "For wheras the Puritans were wont to be shrouded under the covert of the Church of England . . . Montagu . . . to the good service of his Majesty and the Church, has disbanded them from their shelter, taken them off from colluding under the Church's protection, and sent them to their own home".

42. *Appeal,* p. 114: "such a potent overweening faction as they [puritans] are". Ibid., p. 136: "for they may be many, a strong, potent, prevailing party that thus opine and run a course to themselves in their own tenets, against or beside public, enacted, and authorized doctrine". Ibid., p. 3: "It is unknown not [*sic*] authority, that puritanical self-conceit and presumption will square law and gospel too according unto that untoward lesbian rule of their own private spirit and special opinion: and dare challenge any authority . . . . These informers . . . are two grandees of the faction".

43. MS: *12. Appeal,* p. 42: "Those classical projects . . . of the zealous brethren . . . aim at anarchy, popular confusion; dangerous indeed to prince and people".

44. *Appeal,* p. 44: "that so through foreign doctrine, being infused secretly and instilled cunningly and pretended craftily to be the Church's, at length you may wind-in with foreign discipline also . . . ".

45. MS: *191. Appeal,* p. 291: "the devil bred you up in a faction".

46. MS: *27. Appeal,* p. 271: "For we live with Puritans and opposite factionists that have the cross of Christ in as great contempt and despite as ever had Julian or any pagan".

47. *SR,* 23 Eliz. I, c. 1.

54[48] p., *Appeal,* that the imputations of them against us too true; 83[49] p., *Appeal,* ours against them but bugbears.

2. By countenancing some superstitious practices of the Church of Rome, as using the cross, etc. That an indissoluble constriction is between the understanding and the actions.

3. By his opinions concerning the Church of Rome and the Pope: says the interpretation of Anselm is good and proper.[50]

4. By his opinions concerning the divines of the Romanists and of our Church.[51]

68[52] p., *Gagg.*

Mr. Montagu but the executor of a project given to the King of Spain by one Campanella, 25 book.[53] Gondomar was here when this book a broaching.[54]

The papists are allowed to read Mr. Montagu's book.

These books of M[ontagu] dishonorable to King *Jac.,* teaching that doctrine which he wrote against, and he contradicts King *Jac. in terminis. Bertius,*[55] *De Apostasia Sanctorum,* held a liar by [f. 135] King James; Mr. Montagu uphold[s] the doctrine of Bertius.[56]

Discredits the assembly of Dort as much as in him lies.[57]

M[ontagu] says he never heard a persuasive argument that the Pope is Antichrist.[58]

2nd aggravation: the scurvy and railing terms that he uses against divines. 2 p., *Appeal;* 3 p., *Appeal,* Puritans the hornets' nests of men; 16 p., *Appeal;* 121 p., *Appeal;* 122 p., *Appeal;* 304 p., *Appeal;* 223, 142 p., *Appeal.*[59]

48. MS: *4. Appeal,* p. 54: "I brought no inferences to press you withal; such as are commonly and odiously made against you by opposites . . . whose virulent invectives and strange, though too true, imputations I like not".

49. MS: *38.* On p. 83 of the *Appeal,* Montagu states that the Puritans proclaim that the clerics of the Church of Rome, "are enemies professed unto the grace of Christ . . . and that we must forever, upon pain of damnation (strange bugbears and *terriculamenta*) dissent from them in this as in all things else".

50. *Gagg,* p. 29: "I could interpret St. Anselm well enough . . . [controversy] could not be put over more fitly to any one man by the Church representative in a council than unto the Pope, first bishop of Christendom: of greatest, not absolute, power amongst bishops".

51. Cf. *PP 1625,* p. 332 and n. 15.

52. MS: *86.* The account of Pym's report in SP 16/25:10 (see above, n. 6) suggests that the reference is to Montagu's comments, occurring on p. 68 of the *Gagg,* which seem to deny that Queen Elizabeth was head of the Church.

53. Concerning the book by Thomas Campanella, written about 1600 and first published in 1620, see *CD 1628,* IV, 240 n. 37.

54. Diego Sarmiento de Acuña, Count of Gondomar, was Spanish ambassador to England from 1613 to 1621.

55. MS: *Persius.* Concerning Petrus Bertius and his censure by King James, see *PP 1625,* p. 337 n. 53; and p. 342 n. 100.

56. MS: *Persius.* Concerning Montagu's support of the opinions of Jacobus Arminius and his student, Bertius, see *PP 1625,* p. 337 n. 52.

57. Concerning Montagu's attitude toward the Synod of Dort, see *PP 1625,* p. 331 n. 8; and p. 337 n. 54.

58. On the differences between King James and Montagu concerning Antichrist, see *PP 1625,* p. 331, n. 11.

59. A number of Whitelocke's page references concerning the second "aggravation" are inaccurate, but the correct references are difficult to identify because no page numbers are given in the other extant accounts of this section of the report. SP 16/25:10 (see above, n. 6): "classical, hornets' nests, cheverelized consciences, liars, thieves, rebels, quicksilver, and many other like or worse". Combined, the information from Whitelocke and SP 16/25:10 results in the following list of citations.

Appeal, p. 2: "they may wilfully mistake his meaning . . . . Or lastly, they may well enough be guilty of misreporting his words". Ibid., p. 3: "such malcontent malingers . . . . they are two grandees of the faction; as great and turbulent as most be in the diocese of Norwich". Ibid., p. 6: "stir the hornets' nests of men affected otherways . . . . some classical resolutions of the brethren". Ibid., p. 16: "Such illuminates are our classical brethren". Ibid., pp. 22–23: "I appeal unto your own, though never so much cheverelized consciences, my good calumniators". Ibid., p. 112: "Men of moving, violent, quicksilver, gunpowder spirits". Ibid., p. 142: "if yourselves and such halfers in opinions, *omnium horarum homines* for your private ends, would openly avow what covertly you conceal". Ibid., p. 191: "these great masters in Israel, liars against their own knowledge". Ibid., p. 223: "Be papists with me, or rebels without me". Ibid., p. 304: "with puritanical quicksilver spirits".

3rd aggravation: that he does disgrace and despise the learned divines of our Church and of the reformed churches. 51 p., *Appeal;*[60] 173 p., *Appeal;* 270[61] p., *Appeal;* 72 p., *Appeal.*[62] Touches Doctor Hall for his sermon.[63] Touches Doctor Prideaux.[64] Talks of Calvinism and Genevanism.[65]

4th aggravation: his detestable profaneness and scoffing at preaching, meditations, lecturers. 8 p., *Appeal;* 136 p., *Appeal.*[66] 139 p.[67]; 88 p.; the crying Abba father; saint-seeming, Bible-bearing, hypocritical Puritan.[68]

The committee convict Mr. Montagu of publishing doctrine contrary to the doctrine of the Homilies and Articles.[69] That in his books are passages apt to move sedition. By the course in his books he discourages men from this Church and invites to the Romish, by seeking to reconcile us to the Romish see. And thought fit that he be by the Commons House of parliament accused to the Lords to have judgment.

[f. 135v] MR. WANDESFORD.[70] That we should not proceed to a resolution before we have heard Mr. Montagu, but pray a conference *super totam materiam.*

SIR GEORGE MORE. That we should resolve these things before we pray a conference.

SIR THOMAS HOBY. That a day may be set for judgment herein, whereof he may have notice to answer if he will.

SIR JOHN ELIOT. I am of opinion with those that hold M[ontagu] a delinquent and worthy of the greatest punishment that can be inflicted on him. *In foro conscientiae* I have already judged, but in this court he is not yet ready to be judged. *Audi alteram partem. Qui inauditi et indefensi tamquam innocentes*

60. On p. 51 of the *Appeal,* Montagu terms Calvinism, "the founder of your fancies".

61. MS: *170. Appeal,* p. 270: "M. Perkins in his *Problem,* though he fain would puritanize it, and so goes on, hanging hoof against hoof".

62. *Appeal,* pp. 71–72: "through the opinion of the great worth and learning that they had of the then professor [William Whitaker], a thorough man every way upon your side, and an earnest promoter of the novel opinions against other learned divines".

63. Montagu's remark in the *Appeal,* pp. 291–292, that "It was no blessed speech, in my opinion; but unworthy to be heard in an open pulpit and published in print, *Maledicti Pacifici*", appears to refer to the sermon of Joseph Hall, Dean of Worcester, given before King James at Theobalds on 19 September 1624 entitled, "The True Peace-Maker" (*STC,* no. 12715). In 1624 Hall also published his *No Peace with Rome.* See his *Works* (*STC,* no. 12635), pp. 625–664.

64. John Prideaux, Regius Professor of Divinity at Oxford, is not mentioned by name in the *Appeal,* however Montagu's statement that "Everyone that prates, reads, lectures, preaches, or professes must not look to have his *Theses, Lectiones, Harangues* or discourses taken as the dictates or doctrines of our church" (*Appeal,* p. 49), appears to be a reference to Prideaux and the publication in 1625 of his *Lectiones Novem de Totidem Religionis Capitibus Praecipue hoc Tempore Controversis prout Publice Habebantur* (*STC,* no. 20356).

65. Montagu refers to the "Calvinists" numerous times in the *Appeal;* for "Genevanism", see p. 72.

66. *Appeal,* p. 8: "I disclaim, as incompetent, popular cantonings of dismembered Scripture and private interpretations of enforced Scripture. I will not be put over unto classical decisions nor, that idol of some men's reformation, unto any prophetical determinations in private conventicles after lectures". Ibid., p. 136: "and run a course to themselves in their own tenets against or beside public enacted and authorized doctrine".

67. MS: *39. Appeal,* p. 139: "and so leave my friends and Informers to chew the cud upon it, as they do after lectures".

68. *Appeal,* p. 88: "in their sermons, lectures, and pulpits they brawl at the shadow of their own fancies, as dogs bark at the moon". Ibid., 213: "And whatsoever you may resolve for your crying Abba Father, *secundum praesentem justitiam,* I crave pardon". Ibid., p. 43: "There is never a saint-seeming and Bible-bearing hypocritical Puritan in the pack, a better patriot every way, than the man that has delivered such dangerous errors".

69. See above, n. 10.

70. *Resolved, that the books of Mr. Montagu do* is crossed out in the MS preceding *Mr. Wandesford.* Without identifying the speakers by name, the following debate and orders in the House are summarzied in SP 16/25:10 (see above, n. 6).

pereunt. In our last proceedings in this case we [took] especial care not to meddle with those things that do concern doctrine, but matters of policy and contempt, which was only done.[71] I am not of opinion that we should judge him in those things which concern religion, but desire help. But set a day for judgment in the other matters whereof he to have notice.

MR. PYM. That the committee have done nothing but what is contained in the instructions at Oxford, and only present matter of fact.[72]

SIR JAMES PERROT. Against praying a conference with the Lords. But refer the examination of the book to some learned divines.

MR. ROLLE. 1 *Eliz. Book of Common Prayer* established by act of parliament and indictments are usually upon it.[73] And in 13 *Eliz.*/[74]

But we should not proceed till we have heard him.

[f. 136] CHANCELLOR[75] DUCHY. It is fit to have a day or 2 for every man to inform his own conscience whether that which is said be so or not. And set down a day for judgment, whereof Mr. Montagu may have notice.

MR. WENTWORTH. Resembles it.

MR. WHITBY. He that cried, "Adam, where art thou?",[76] knew very well what he had done. Never known that a man was transmitted to the Lords unheard here.

SIR NATHANIEL RICH. That there may be a day appointed for resolution hereof and Mr. Montagu to have notice of it. In the meantime a committee may be appointed to draw some interrogatories for the Speaker to be ministered unto him.

Ordered, that on Thursday next the House shall further debate this business and he to have notice of it to answer for himself if he will. And the subcommittee appointed by the committee of religion to draw interrogatories to be ministered by the Speaker to Mr. Montagu. The Serjeant to give him notice.

SIR ROBERT HARLEY. That we may entreat the King that there may be no more writing in this case until he have heard what we shall say against him.

This motion referred to the consideration of the former committee that consider of the interrogatories.[77]

III. DIARY OF SIR NATHANIEL RICH, HIST. COLLECT. 143, HLRO

[f. 75]

April 17, Monday[78]

Committee for unexperienced captains employed in the late service. Exchequer Chamber, on Wednesday next.

SIR EUBULE THELWALL exhibits complaints against the Bishop of Bangor. 1, for giving of money for his bishopric contrary to his oath: he gave £400; 2, that he did

71. On this matter, see the consideration of the Montagu business by the House on 7 and 9 July and 2 August 1625 (*PP 1625*, OBs, and pp. 518 and 533).

72. On 7 July 1625, a committee was appointed to set down in writing the particulars against Montagu, and the House resolved "at their next meeting, to enter into a particular examination of such parts of the said books as tend to sedition and the general disturbance of the peace of the Church and commonwealth". *PP 1625*, p. 335; and see ibid., pp. 338, 344, 518.

73. *SR*, 1 Eliz. I, c. 2.

74. The reference may be to *SR*, 13 Eliz. I, c. 2, which recites the statute of 5 Eliz. I, c. 1, against those who attribute any jurisdiction, authority, or preeminence to the see of Rome; or to *SR*, 13 Eliz. I, c. 12, concerning subscription to the Articles of Religion.

75. *Exchequer* is crossed out in the MS preceding *Duchy*.

76. Gen. 3:9.

77. *articles* is crossed out in the MS and replaced with *interrogatories*. Concerning the (sub)committee, see above, nn. 16 and 17.

78. MS: *16*.

voluntarily take an oath that he would never make a lease, etc., which after he did; 3, that he has had 4 or 5 wives which might have been a means to keep him from incontinency,[79] and yet branded with that sin for a maid got with child in his house. That he did license a man to marry his wife's sister's daughter. That he bestows his livings upon unworthy men.

MR. HAYNES. That the embargo in France goes on worse and worse. No assemblies of religion in France,[80] either French or English, to be on pain of death. That this may be a grievance, and for trade.

MR. PYM his report of Montagu: I am commanded to report to this House the cause of Mr. Montagu, a man long known to be a disturber of the peace of Church and state. Motives: 1, the writ;[81] 2ly, the commandment of God to mark them that are seditious, etc., especially belonging to law makers; 3, the observation of the wisdom of states. The world to be made of atoms, a speculation but this applied to a truth. 4. The constant practice of parliaments, especially of the 2 last parliaments: 1st in [*illegible*] 21 *Jac.*, in the parliament, the *Gagg* complained of and commended to my Lord of Canterbury. [f. 75v] 1 *Caroli*, his *Appeal*, which was indeed from the parliament, the whole frame and composition of this book.

1. First, contradictions against the doctrine of the Church of England. 1, concerning the Church of Rome are [taken out of] the 2d homily of the gifts of the Holy Ghost: the state of the Church of Rome has nothing in [it] of a true Church. *Gagg*, 50 *et Appeal*, 139.[82] The Church of Rome is not built on the foundation of doctrine of the apostles. 2ly, in the same homily, the Church of Rome is not built/

The third, concerning the points, controverted points: he says it is a true Church but not sound.[83] The 4th, concerning images: homily against idolatry, 1st part.[84] Observation: speaks as if he were possessed with the whole spirit of the Church of England.[85] 5, that saints are peculiar patrons of some countries.[86]

In those he sets article against article, church against church, and himself against himself.

Sedition:

1, calls the greater part of the King's subjects Puritans; 2, labors to make them odious; 3, and labors to breed hatred from one subject to another. He may perhaps avoid the penalty of treason, but the commonwealth shall not be free from the mischief.

79. Bayly did not actually have four or five wives; the "separates" (see above, n. 3) indicate that the charge was that he had been incontinent, or adulterous, four or five times. See HofC, 22 February, f. 48.

80. I.e., no assemblies of Protestants were allowed in France. Concerning the complaints against the French, see above, n. 4.

81. See above, n. 22.

82. MS: *109*. See above, n. 27.

83. *Appeal*, p. 113: "I am absolutely persuaded, and shall be till I see cause to the contrary, that the Church of Rome is a *true*, though not a *sound* church of Christ".

84. See above, n. 30.

85. I.e., in his use of the term "we", see above, n. 30.

86. See above, n. 31.

ORDER OF BUSINESS TUESDAY, 18 APRIL 1626

Upon question: committee of the whole House for **evils, causes, and remedies** shall sit this afternoon 15, 18, *24/2

[*Afternoon*]

[*Committee of the Whole House: Christopher Wandesford in the chair*]

Report from the subcommittee for examining if there has been unnecessary staying of ships (Sir Edward Spencer) 18

Resolved: the taking of money by the Lord Admiral from the **East India Company** was an undue exacting and extorting 19, *20/4

TUESDAY, 18 APRIL 1626

I. JOURNAL OF THE HOUSE OF COMMONS

[CJ 845; p. 20]
Martis, 18[1] *Aprilis, 2 Caroli Regis*

Lord Abergavenny's bill, Wednesday next, 2 clock. Mr. Bysshe, Sir J. Perrot, Sir Neville Poole, added to the committee.

Bill for seacoal, Wednesday next.

L. 1a. An act for relief of cloth workers and dyers.

Ward's bill, Thursday next, former place.[2]

Bill of concealments, Thursday next, former place.

Bill of administrations, Wednesday next, former place.

Clerk of the market; upon Friday next, in the former place.

L. 1a. An act concerning appropriations and vicarages.

L. 3a. An act/[3]
Upon question, passed.

L. 3a. Citations. Upon question, passed.

MR. VICE CHAMBERLAIN. That his Majesty has given leave and commanded him to lay open the proceedings in the French treaties and negotiations concerning the embargo in France.[4]

1. 3 points in charge to them upon their embassage: 1, to demand the sending home of our ships;[5] 2, to procure the peace of the Protestants;[6] [3,] to engage the King, if possible, in the wars of Germany.[7]

For the 1st, no negative answer, but some delay. Promise of the King's ship,[8] which lent only in courtesy; but for the 7 merchant ships: hired for 16 months.[9] To this they replied: these ships were lent, as also the Dutch ships were,[10] against the common enemy for the service against Genoa; and therefore the using them against the Rochellers an abuse. That the French yielded to send home our ships; and they having paid their men (in the ships in mutiny for pay) they are to be brought to the Isle of Wight, and we are thither to send ships to carry the Frenchmen back.

2. For the peace of the Protestants, a work of great difficulty. Great enemies to them. Their wants thought **[CJ 846]** great, both in money and all other provisions. Wants also on the King's part who had 115,000 men in pay. A good peace for the Protestants not to be hoped for at the present; but if a war, that certainly bad in the beginning. Thought therefore best for them to submit

1. *19* is crossed out in the MS and *18* is inserted.

2. This is presumably the meeting for the committee on the bill to enable James Ward, alias Farmor, to sell certain lands. The bill was read the first time on 17 March; we find no record of its second reading and commitment. Henry Pelham made the committee report on the bill on 4 May, see OB.

3. Marginal note: "Dorset".

4. Sir Dudley Carleton, Vice Chamberlain, had recently returned from the embassy to France undertaken with the Earl of Holland in January to mediate peace between the crown and the Huguenots. For their instructions, see SP 78/76, f. 192 (printed in Rymer, *Foedera,* VIII, pt. 1, pp. 182–184. See also, SP 78/76, f. 294, and Gardiner, *History of England,* VI, 39–48, 50–55.

5. I.e., the *Vanguard* and seven English merchant ships loaned to the French. See HofC, 27 February, n. 20; and HofL, 13 May, pp. 425–439.

6. I.e., between the French King and the Protestants of France.

7. See above, n. 4, regarding the King's instructions to Carleton and Holland for their mission, dated from Hampton Court, 30 December 1625.

8. Printed edition: *ships.* The ship referred to is the *Vanguard.*

9. Concerning the terms of the contract between the French crown and the English merchants, see the testimony of Mr. Moyer, master of the *Industry,* at the subcommittee for examining causes of causes, HofC, 23 March, and n. 26; and HofL, 13 May, p. 435, n. 118.

10. Concerning the loan of Dutch ships to France, see Gardiner, *History of England,* V, 302, 305.

themselves for the present, especially [with] the clergy of France offering a great supply for a cruel prosecution of them.[11]

Queen mother[12] a great furtherer of this peace.

This peace good for the rest of the Protestants, but for Rochelle not so good; but yet with some promises of hopes for afterwards. This joyous to the Protestants in general, who had appointed a general fast for procuring a peace, which peace procured the next day after the general fast.[13]

3. The French, for the German war, seemed more forward than we; but the instructions being now to draw the French King into the league and confederation made at the Hague with King of Denmark, Sweden, and the Low Countries, he promised the effects of the confederation, but would not enter into it.[14]

That the French King being now sent unto by our King to renew the league made 1610,[15] which they most willingly yielded to; but then happened the embargo in France. Their merchants much complained upon the stay of their ships here. Hereupon our ambassadors gave the reasons of the stay of their ships here.[16] Hereupon the King promised enlargement of our goods, and this at last granted under the Great Seal, though crossed not only by clamors of the French, but much more by such who had been lately naturalized in Calais. This command interrupted a while by those of Rouen, upon pretense of their privilege; but fortified by a new commission.

The treaty of 1610 at last confirmed; wherein one clause that though wars, yet the merchants to have 3 months time to withdraw their goods.

That the French King has promised to march towards Germany, with 25,000 men, so as we would not leave them alone.

[p. 22] For this they offered assurance by merchants for a certain sum of money for 1 year, for the present, with assurance for 3 years more, so we would do the like.

They offered to join for restitution of the Palatinate, and of other dispossessed princes in Germany, but no further.

That now all rests upon the King's answer to the French upon this their proposition; and the King rests upon the parliament.

MR. CHANCELLOR OF THE EXCHEQUER delivers a message from his Majesty to revive his message last week about his Majesty's supply,[17] viz., that his Majesty had considered and advised of our remonstrance delivered him before Easter,[18] but finding the affairs of Christendom/

Upon question, no question to be now made for prefixing Thursday 7night for entering into consideration [of] the King's message.

Upon question, the committee for evils, causes, and remedies shall sit this afternoon.

11. Regarding the position of the French clergy, see Gardiner, *History of England,* VI, 51.

12. I.e., Marie de Medici, mother of Louis XIII.

13. The agreement between the French crown and the Protestant deputies was announced at Fontainebleau on 27 January 1626. See SP 78/77, f. 88 and Gardiner, *History of England,* VI, 51–55.

14. Concerning the instructions to Carleton and Holland, see above, n. 7. Regarding the Treaty of the Hague, signed on 29 November 1625, see HofC 30 March, nn. 15 and 23.

15. For the ratification of the treaty of defensive alliance between England and France agreed to in August 1610, see Rymer, *Foedera,* VII, pt. 2, 171–175.

16. For a list of French ships taken by the English, see SP 78/76, ff. 298–299.

17. I.e., the message delivered to the House by the Chancellor of the Exchequer, Sir Richard Weston, on 13 April, see OB.

18. I.e., the remonstrance presented to the King on 5 April, see OB.

II. DIARY OF BULSTRODE WHITELOCKE, ESQ., DD. 12.21, CAMBRIDGE UNIVERSITY LIBRARY

[f. 136v]

18 April

MR. NOY. To the bill concerning citations. 47 E. 3, complaint in parliament against citations *quorum nomina.*[19] Fame is when a thing is raised abroad among the people and the cry of it comes to the ears of the judge.[20]

MR. ROLLE. The 1st part of this bill grounded upon a canon in 1 *Jac.*[21]

MR. WENTWORTH. Fame is that which is spoken by the greater part of men where it is raised. That which is spoken by the fewer part is but a rumor.

SIR THOMAS HOBY. Popish recusants have been brought to the sessions only by fame.

SIR HENRY MARTEN. If the ordinary proceed against any man upon fame, the party may appeal from him to the Arches where if it do not appear that the fame is by the greater part of the parish, the accused shall have good damages.

MR. BANKES. A bill read after engrossing cannot be recommitted,[22] and objections against it then ought to be very weighty. Common voice and fame is a good ground to arrest a man upon suspicion of treason or felony, but there must be 2 cautions or restrictions: 1, that such a fact as felony or treason must be done; 2, it must be done in the same county where the fame is raised. If a man call one thief and an action is brought against him for it, if the def[endant] say that common fame is so, it is not sufficient and no justification.

MR. SELDEN.[23] By the bill concerning citations we shall not deprive the ecclesiastical courts of any jurisdiction that they now have, but only reduce them to that which anciently was their course and practice. [f. 137] By the general canon law there are 3 ways of proceeding in the spiritual courts: by accusation, denunciation, inquisition. *Register et Natura Brevium* writes that no ordinary should call before him any man *ex officio.*[24]

SIR DUDLEY CARLETON. That I asked leave, which was graciously granted by his Majesty, to relate unto you our knowledge concerning his negotiations in France, and I shall show you the points of our employments, the proceedings of our employment, and the success thereof.[25]

SIR DUDLEY DIGGES interrupts him here. Moves that we may go to a committee to hear Sir Dudley Carleton, he not being required by the House to relate anything of those businesses.

19. *Rot. Parl.*, 47 E. III, no. 21.

20. "Common fame", or "fama" is a term of art used by Bracton (*De Legibus Angliae, Lib.* 3, f. 143), and defined by Sir Edward Coke as follows: "When treason and felony is committed and the common fame and voice is that A is guilty, it is lawful for any man that suspects him to apprehend him". Coke, *Second Inst.*, p. 51. Littleton says, on 22 April, below, that there was "a great difference between common fame and rumor. The general voice is common fame".

21. See HofC, 21 March, n. 26.

22. The bill concerning citations had been ordered engrossed following the committee report on 21 March (see OB). Concerning the question of recommiting a bill after it is engrossed, see Hakewill, *Manner How Statutes are Enacted,* pp. 151–152. "After a bill has been committed and is reported it ought . . . to be dashed or engrossed; and yet when the matter is of importance it is sometimes for special reasons suffered. But then usually the recommitment is to the same committees".

23. *Doctor Eden* is crossed out in the MS preceding *Mr. Selden.*

24. The point is less clear in Fitzherbert. See *The New Natura Brevium* (London, 1686), pp. 144–145.

25. See above, n. 4.

CHANCELLOR EXCHEQUER. [*Blank*] gave commandment that he should deliver his knowledge concerning those negotiations wherein he was employed, for the satisfaction of the House.

SIR DUDLEY CARLETON. The best way to let you know the chief points wherewith we were charged out of this kingdom and the proceeding/

3 points specially in charge:[26] 1, to demand restitution of our ships; 2, to procure the peace of the Protestants;[27] 3, to engage the French King, if it were possible, in the war in Germany.[28]

To the first we had no denial but a delayed answer. They alleged as an abuse/

It was concluded we should have restitution of our ships, but protracted it till the 2nd point was concluded. Which being [f. 137v] done, the peace concluded. The French mariners refused to come over the seas with our ships for want of pay. That the ships should be sent away 15 April; the resolution that they should be brought to the Isle of Wight. About this time we are to expect the restitution of them and we to send ships for the carrying back of the French mariners. If they come not, it is a fallacy in the French and no neglect in us. I cannot conceive any such sudden alteration that the King's ship should be made admiral.

The concluding the peace was a matter very difficult. The King of France had 115,000 men in pay at that time, but wanted money. His men more willing to go against the Protestants than any other. Though a good peace could not be made, yet considering the Protestants' disadvantages, it was thought fit to submit themselves to the King. The Queen mother,[29] a woman of much better temper than a Queen mother of that house, was very forward for the peace. The Rochellers lost 2 ships at sea and 2 islands.[30] According as he should be satisfied in their proceedings and see their intentions, the King of France promised to hear the Protestants. [f. 138] Those of the religion were much joyed with this peace concluded the day after the general fast in France.[31] A business concluded in a pavilion in the same house where we lay.

The French always seemed more forward in the war of Germany than ourselves. The French King presented himself as one that would perform the effects of our confederation.[32]

2 incidents and accidents of our negotiation. 1. The renewing of an ancient confederation *anno* 1610.[33] The French King and his counselors embraced it very willingly. 2. The merchants' goods seized. We agreed if they would release the ships and goods of our merchants, we would agree to the renewing of the treaties in 1610. Their complaint for the delay of justice here. We allege in their excuse/

The King of France gave us a satisfactory answer, that we should be/

Divers since were naturalized in Calais. The King of France made an order for the release of the seizures, which was sent to Rouen but the high court there continued the arrest till they had answered the King's orders. [f. 138v] The French King agreed to ratify the treaty in 1610 and sent down a commission to the court of parlement in Rouen by 4 Masters of his Requests and to all other places where was any seizure, with

26. See above, n. 5.
27. See above, n. 6.
28. See above, n. 7.
29. See above, n. 12.
30. I.e., the islands of Ré and Oleron.
31. See above, n. 13.
32. MS: *consideration.* Concerning the confederation formed at the Hague, see above, n. 14.
33. See above, n. 15.

commandment that all the English goods should be free. Which I presume had such effect that the good[s] are released.

That they would march towards Germany with an army of 25,000 men, with condition that they should not be alone in that war but that we would really show ourselves in it. That he could not now conclude anything because the E/

The English had neither commission nor money in their purses for this business. They dismissed us with very good honor. The[y] would be content to join for the restitution of the Palatinate and some other princes in Germany but no further. What answer the King will return to the French consists much upon the proceedings in parliament.

SIR JOHN ELIOT. Delivered at Oxford in the presence of the King and parliament that the peace for the Protestants was generally established and a war proclaimed by the King of France against the Spanish in Italy.[34] Moves we may go to the charge.

[f. 139] [SIR RICHARD WESTON.] I am commanded by his Majesty to say something to you and to revive the message sent on Thursday.[35] I doubt not but all men are satisfied with the care of his Majesty and the wisdom and fidelity of the ambassadors and the felicity of their employments. Repeats the King's message.

CHANCELLOR DUCHY. I never knew message brought from the King but either we presently took it into consideration or appointed a day for it. Moves we appoint a day for the consideration of this message.

MR. GOODWIN. That we should go on to the committee.

CHANCELLOR EXCHEQUER. That we may proceed with all respect unto the King's counsels and examples and endeavor to give him satisfaction.[36] Fortitude of words are good things and come from a good affection, but they neither set forth ships nor raise men and are but an alarum.

MR. KIRTON. That we should set no day now for the consideration of the King's message but go on with our grievances, which will be the way to give the King satisfaction.

SIR DUDLEY CARLETON. The Dunkirkers have built a fort to secure the navy within and keeping out an enemy. So that now whereas but 3 or 4 ships could come forth at once and might be kept in by a few, as was in '88, now a great many ships may come forth together.

[f. 139v] Resolved, that there shall be no question whether Thursday sennight shall be the day to take his Majesty's message into further consideration.

Ordered, that the grand committee for evils, causes, and remedies shall sit this afternoon.

Pomeridiem
[*Committee of the Whole House*]

Mr. Wandesford takes the chair for evils, causes, and remedies.

Sir Edward Spencer reports from the committee to consider what ships have been unnecessarily stayed of merchants.[37] 5 March [1624], a stay of ships of the East India Company of 4 ships and 2 pinnaces; stayed till the voyage was almost lost.[38] A

34. See Sir John Coke's speech to both Houses on 4 August 1625, *PP 1625,* pp. 135, 388, 536.

35. See above, n. 17.

36. *Quoties volui et noluisses* is crossed out in the MS following *satisfaction.* See the account in Rich, below.

37. For the appointment of this subcommittee, see HofC, 20 March, OB.

38. For more detailed accounts and annotation concerning the matter of the East India Company and the Duke of Buckingham, Lord Admiral, see the sixth charge in the articles of impeachment against Buckingham (HofL, 15 May, 467–468) and Buckingham's response to that charge (HofL, 8 June, pp. 573–575). See also, the report from this committee of the whole House, HofC, 20 April, OB and HofL, 13 May, pp. 420–425.

question before for the Admiral's tenths and some delivered in the Admiral's behalf. It was resolved by 2 civil lawyers that there was no law for the Admiral's tenth in reprises.[39] £2,000 was given to the Admiral's wife for this business.[40] 1623, a rumor that the East Indian ships had taken a great prize at Hormuz. The King called for the Admiral's rights. The Admiral stood upon his right and said the ships should not be released unless the company would compound with him for it. After, the Company compounded for £10,000 for the release of the ships. *Julii* 1623.[41] The Lords House of Parliament made an order for the stay of some ships of the East Indian Company upon Lord Admiral's motion in the Lords House of Parliament that, there being want of shipping for the present occasions and defense of the kingdom, that he might have the reputation and authority of the parliament to stay some ships of the East India Company thereof, his pretense only upon a secret claim or duty owing him for reprises taken at Hormuz which the company denied him. Divers capitulations for composition for the release of the ships, and when £10,000 was agreed to be given the Duke for the release, he again in the Lords House moved for the crossing of the former order, which was granted. King James interposed himself for bringing about this composition and £10,000 more himself, but the Admiral gave his acquittance for the £10,000 which he had. The Company had a pardon of the King, who said he would leave them to the [*illegible*].

Resolved, that the taking of the money by the Lord Admiral in this manner from the East Indian Company was an undue exacting and extorting.[42]

III. DIARY OF SIR NATHANIEL RICH, HIST. COLLECT. 143, HLRO

[f. 76]

[18 April 1626]

SIR D. CARLETON. He has his Majesty's leave. Troubled how to digest this matter for his own memory and for the clear understanding of this House for/

3 points in charge: 1, to demand restitution of ships; 2, procure peace of Protestants in France; 3, to engage the French King in the war of Germany.

The first proposed first and was never denied but delayed. Because lent of courtesy, could not be denied.[43] The merchants' ships being hired for 16 months they could not, they said, be justly demanded.[44] The ships, being 7, furnished to pursue the common enemy. They, as the States' ships,[45] were first desired and lent for that purpose; but the Rochellers, taking part with Soubise, they were employed against them. Concluded the ships should be restored, but protracted this till they saw the 2nd point of peace of the Protestants. This being concluded, 3 direct orders sent for delivery of the ships. The admiral hereon

39. Concerning the opinions given by the two civil lawyers—Dr. Steward (either Nicholas or Richard) and Dr. Richard Zouche—see the court minutes of the East India Company, 18 February 1624, printed in Gardiner, *Impeachment*, pp. 84–87, and summarized in *CSPC, East Indies, 1622–1624*, pp. 247–248.

40. Regarding the payment of the £2,000, see Gardiner, *Impeachment*, pp. 72–73, 87; and see *CSPC, East Indies, 1622–1624*, p. 125.

41. *5 April 1624* is crossed out in the MS following *Julii 1623*. The meaning of these dates is unclear. In July 1623 the company had agreed to pay £2,000 to the Duke (see above, n. 40). It was not until the beginning of March 1624 that the Lords approved the stay of the Company's ships. The sum the Company was to pay the Duke was settled at the beginning of April, and on 5 April the Duke moved the Lords to release the ships and countermand the order for their stay (*LJ*, III, 290). See also, Gardiner, *Impeachment*, pp. 89–90, 118–126.

42. *to the disturbance of trade* is crossed out in the MS following *extorting*.

43. See above, n. 8.

44. See above, n. 9.

45. See above, n. 10.

gave way but the mariners and soldiers mutinied till they were paid this; the ambassador pressing a device to stay the ships. The money sent, order given that they should come away the 15 of this month, brought to the Isle of Wight, and we are to provide ships to carry back their men. If this be altered it is unknown, neither does he believe any alteration.

For the peace of the Protestants it was a matter intricate and full of difficulty because main enemies, and they poor and in want of money, men, victuals. This was conceived by their enemy, and [f. 76v] sorry that their friends must confess it to be so. French had at that time 150 thousand[46] in pay, etc. They found they could not have a very good peace, but a worse war. For by land they were wont to have great supplies of the rutters out of Germany. Therefore fittest to make peace; especially the clergy, being assembled, did send an offer of a powerful supply of money to root out the Protestants.[47] The Queen mother interposed and placed the peace in the breasts of the English ambassadors. H. 4, he only kept word with them; and all the conditions of [the] peace of Montpellier renewed at Fontainebleau.[48] All these except that concerning Rochelle were yielded unto. The Protestants confessed they had in 14/

The Rochellers have lost their ships and 2 islands in which were 2 forts,[49] and to demolish the fort by the town[50] must be the work not of an embassage but of a battery. But would hereafter be more willing to harken unto it. With these conditions the Protestants were well satisfied and much joyed, attributed it to God's blessings and, having 3 months before had a general fast for a peace, this peace was concluded the next day after the peace [*sic*] and much joy expressed in visiting the pavilion under which it was made.

The continuance of this peace will much depend on that of Germany which is the 3d part. The French seemed forward in it but in a several nature. But they pressing to come [f. 77] into the last league for the liberties of Germany; but the French King would perform the effects of confederation, but long ere he concluded because of divers accidents. First, one that proceeded from hence. One was the renewing of an ancient confederation, 1610, which confederation does bear that the renewing be within a year demanded after the decease of one king. But the next was the seizing of our ships contrary to that treaty. *Etiamsi justa sit causa.* They desired the whole restoring of that treaty but first pressed to lay open the cause of the stay of our ships, which were: 1, that they came from St. Lucas when there was an embargo of all French goods and ships; 2, these ships set out by the new admiralty which has undertaken the convoy of all ships between Spain and Flanders,[51] notwithstanding all enmity.

Hereupon the King answered that our embargo should be discharged, but delayed. Yet at last the King yielded a discharge under the Great Seal which was carried to Rouen. Yet they held it off till they had written their answer to the King. But the King renewed his command and against this there is commonly no gainsay-

46. *115,000* according to CJ and Whitelocke.

47. See above, n. 11.

48. The Treaty of Fontainebleau (see above, n. 13) renewed provisions of the Treaty of Montpellier that had been signed by representatives of Louis XIII and the French Protestants on 19 October 1622 and which, in turn, had confirmed the Edict of Nantes promulgated by Henry IV in 1598. See D. Parker, *La Rochelle and the French Monarchy* (London: Royal Historical Society, 1980), p. 13, n. 4.

49. See above, n. 30.

50. I.e., Fort Louis, which commanded the entrance to the port of Rochelle.

51. Concerning the creation of Spain's *Almirantazgo* or "new admiralty", see HofC, 8 June, p. 572, n. 30.

ing, and the English ambassador had leave to frame the commission which he offers to read to this House. Thus, the French King yielded to ratify the treaty of 1610 with addition that if [f. 77v] war between the 2 crowns the merchants shall have 3 months time to convey away their goods. And if now the French do not discharge our ships we may say they are *foedi fragi,* and that must introduce another business.

I only owe you now an account of one point concerning the war of Germany. They professing that they will be confederate in effect in this, that they will march towards Germany with an army of 25,000 men, so that we will not desert that cause. And promised a supply of money for one year and wanted your assurance by merchants for 3 years. Demanded what commission they had to engage our King with merchants to assure it that the King of England/

The English have neither commission nor money, and the want of money can tell better than I where this sticks. This discussed with all honor and good treatment all the while we were there. The French will join as far as the restitution of the Palatinate and other dispossessed princes. But the point is what answer we will return for maintaining the war on the King's part.

[f. 78] SIR JOHN ELIOT. I do much admire the sufficiency of that honorable person from whom we have received an exquisite narration of his employment but will make some observations out of it conducing to the present business. His message divided into 3 parts. [1.] His employment, divided also into 3 parts: 1, restoring the ships; 2, peace for Protestants; 3, to draw that King into the general league.

2. His proceeding in that employment. 3ly. The success.

Touching the restitution of the ships, it was concluded it should be about this time, and if that not done they were *foedi fragi.*

Observes that at Oxford it was delivered that there was then a peace established for the Protestants in France and a war proclaimed against Spain by the French.[52]

SIR RICHARD WESTON. He is commanded by the King to revive his former message which will come, he thinks, seasonably now he has acquainted [you] with these particulars. They have left all perfected which the ambassador had in charge, the King having taken care thus to cease the intemperance of rumor, which is not now spoken to interrupt any the business of the House.

The message this: That his Majesty had considered of the remonstrance of this House but,[53] finding that the affairs of Christendom will not admit new answer or the replies, the King resolves to forbear and does expect that we lay aside all other occasions and enable him to maintain those great actions which he has undertaken by our advice. The time of the year admonishes us that a delay is denial, and therefore prays [f. 78v] to proceed to make him safe.

SIR HUMPHREY MAY. We have heard a renewed message, and the order of the House either to give answer presently or else to appoint a time to take it into our consideration.

MR. GOODWIN. We have received a message from a most gracious King. As there is in him an increasing merit, so doubts not but that there will be like affection in us to supply him. But thinks fit to take time to consider of it.

SIR RICHARD WESTON. That his Majesty may see his message is valued. The necessities are great, consider what a king is that speaks unto us, one that is ready to follow the advice. Proceed so that we may encour-

52. See above, n. 34.

53. See above, n. 18.

age him so to do still. *Quoties volui et noluisses.* Fortitude of words do only awaken an enemy, they do not build forts, etc.

MR. KIRTON. To give all due respect to his Majesty but let us be first enabled.

SIR G. MORE speaks for the honor of the House. We have showed more love and duty already in bounty. We resolved to give a new supply before the old be paid, but fit to appoint a time.

SIR T. HOBY. To go a parliamentary fashion and that/

SIR G. GORING. That we may not go less with his Majesty than with others. Thinks the King cannot take this well at our hands.

MR. SPENCER. Thursday come sevennight.

MR. CORYTON. To do it when we have considered of our grievances.

SIR T. PUCKERING. The question is what answer to give to the message. The King desires no answer, but we shall better satisfy him by action than word. [f. 79] And that we should go on with these things which hinder, i.e., our grievances not answered.

MR. WENTWORTH moves for a day certain to consider of the King's message. To keep his Majesty's heart sweetened to us will be a ready way to obtain the relief of our grievances. The affairs of Germany/

SIR WILLIAM STRODE moves for Thursday come sevennight.

MR. CREW. To return a present answer to the King that we are about that which we hope will bring supply to his Majesty.

MR. LITTLETON. All our hearts for the King's service, which will be disadvantaged if we give before our grievances answered. But that we will do, that which may make the French say *ils Angloys avoyt et pouvoir et argent* [*sic*].

SIR D. CARLETON thinks a day to be appointed: 1st, to make it appear that as he did not neglect our remonstrance so not we his message; 2nd, observe the use of this House that no matter is left *sine die*. We have entered into an offensive war against the most puissant monarch, an inveterate enemy to our religion and state. Marquis Spinola lately the admiral of the Narrow Seas.[54]

54. Ambrogio Spinola, the Spanish general who, at the beginning of 1626, was made an admiral and put in charge of enlarging the fleet at Dunkirk. *CSPV 1625–1626*, pp. 273, 335.

Order of Business Wednesday, 19 April 1626

WEDNESDAY, 19 APRIL 1626

I. JOURNAL OF THE HOUSE OF COMMONS

[CJ 846; p. 22]
Mercurii, 19[1] *Aprilis, 2 Caroli Regis*

The election for the University of Oxford to be referred to the committee for privileges.[2]

L. 1a. Dale.[3]

Bill for outlawries,[4] Tuesday next, 2 clock, Court Wards.

MR. SHERFIELD reports from the committee concerning interrogatories to Mr. Montagu.[5] He offered the interrogatories in writing.[6] That they have prepared a frame of a petition[7] to his Majesty to hinder any further printing of his books till the parliament[8] have taken order for his books. This to be sent by Mr. Vice Chamberlain, Chancellor Duchy, and Sir James Fullerton, and Mr. Secretary Coke.

Ordered upon question.

[p. 23] Sir Robert Howard's business to be proceeded in here upon Friday next.[9]

L. 3a. An act for the further reformation of sundry abuses committed on the Lord's day, commonly called Sunday.

Upon question, passed.[10]

II. DIARY OF BULSTRODE WHITELOCKE, ESQ., DD. 12.21, CAMBRIDGE UNIVERSITY LIBRARY

[f. 140]

19 April

MR. SHERFIELD reports from the committee the interrogatories prepared to be asked of Mr. Montagu by the Speaker, which were 6 (upon each of his books two), and a course for stay of printing any more. 1. Whether or no he did write the book called the *Appeal*. 2. Whether it were published by him or by his consent. The same questions to be asked upon his other 2

1. *20* is crossed out in the MS and *19* is inserted.

2. On 4 April, Sir Francis Stewart had requested direction from the House regarding his eligibility to sit for the University of Oxford. See HofC, 4 April, n. 2.

3. Grosvenor (see 1 May, below) identifies this as a bill for restoring to Dame Elizabeth Dale the sum of £1,930 that she claimed was taken from her late husband, Sir Thomas Dale, in an adventure in the East Indies. Sir Thomas had died in India in the summer of 1619 and since then Dame Elizabeth had tried in various ways, including a petition to the House of Commons in 1624, to recover the money from the East India Company. See *CSPC, East Indies,* volumes for 1617–1629, Indexes, *sub* Dale, Sir Thomas; and see *CJ*, I, 700, 708 and SP 14/148:7, 164:4.

4. It is not clear which bill is referred to here. The bill previously called the "bill for outlawries" was to relieve creditors, reform abuses of undersheriffs, and limit their fees upon outlawries; it was second read and committed on 1 March and reported, amended, and ordered engrossed on 10 March. It would have been unusual for a further committee meeting to be scheduled for it. Two other bills committed earlier this session also dealt with outlawries: the bill to make the lands of persons outlawed for debt subject and liable to extents, committed on 27 March; and the bill for the abridging the number of unskillful attorneys and to prevent forfeitures by secret outlawries, committed on 23 March and reported 4 May. See Table of Bills, App., II, A.

5. I.e., the committee formed from a subcommittee of religion by order of the House on 17 April. See HofC, 17 April, nn. 16 and 17.

6. For the content of the questions, see Sherfield's report in Whitelocke, below; and see the notes of the committee meeting on the afternoon of 17 April, App., II, C.

7. *message* is crossed out in the MS and *petition* is inserted. For the wording of the proposed petition, see the notes of the committee meeting, App., II, C. And for the report from the messengers named below, see HofC, 20 April, OB.

8. *this House* is crossed out in the MS and *parliament* is inserted.

9. On 21 March the House had ordered that some MPs and others be questioned for their proceedings against Sir Robert Howard. See HofC, 21 March, OB.

10. *L.3a. An act for the better venting of dyed, dressed, and mingled, colored cloths, kerseys, new draperies, and other manufactures made of wool, into parts beyond the seas* is crossed out in the MS following *passed.* Whitelocke, below, states that the bill was read by the Clerk's mistake for it had already received its third reading and been passed by the House on 25 March.

books.[11] And the committee think fit that Mr. Vice Chamberlain and Secretary Coke recommend the humble desire of this House unto the King that he will be pleased to command that no other books be set forth by him until some order be taken with the books now in question of his.

SIR DUDLEY CARLETON desires to be spared for that it is thought Mr. Montagu is publishing a reply to the book lately set forth by his kinsman, Bishop Carleton.[12] It may be thought he is too desirous for the hindering of the reply against his kinsman.

But he is not excused.

[*Committee of the Whole House*]

Mr. Wandesford takes the chair.

Mr. Kirton. That the prejudice and loss come to the Lady Elizabeth[13] and her children is a great cause of our evils. We have entered into/

The cause of the Queen of Bohemia's misfortune and ill success, as he was told by one Mr. Gresley[14] who heard it from the Lord of Bristol, is the Duke of Buckingham. The ill success in the negotiation for the recovery of the Palatinate may be justly attributed to the Duke of Buckingham's fault.

Sir Dudley Digges. That the losses of the Lady and the disherison of that posterity is a great cause of the diminution of our honor and reputation. But it is hard to find out the cause thereof. That said out of the gallery is but *auditus ex auditu*. Cannot tell what to think of the sending for Mr. Gresley presently.

Mr. Malet desires to know if the House will allow him now in this case to speak of the [f. 140v] general question of common fame.[15]

Non allocatur.

Resolved by question, that Mr. Gresley shall be sent for. And he is presently sent for.

Upon a motion to prepare some questions to be asked of Mr. Gresley, Mr. Kirton reads what his meaning is, what Mr. Gresley told him, viz., that the ill success in the negotiation for the recovery of the Palatinate may be justly attributed to be the Duke of Buckingham's fault.

Mr. Kirton asking him what/

Mr. Gresley brought in. Being asked, says that some speeches passed between him and Mr. Kirton, whom he told he had acquainted his Lordship about a letter which my Lord Duke read, whereby an aspersion was laid up[on] the Lord of Bristol.[16] That he told Mr. Kirton that he heard his Lordship say that if he might be heard he doubted not but to make it appear that the ill success in the negotiation [*blank*] Palatinate may be attributed to my Lord of Buckingham's fault.

Chancellor Duchy. The ancient parliamentary way to reject any petition or information whereto a man will not set his hand. Seconds motions that Mr. Gresley may set down under his hand what passed between him and his Lordship.

11. I.e., the *Gagg* and *Invocation of Saints*, see HofC, 17 April, n. 6.

12. I.e., George Carleton, Bishop of Chichester, who in 1626 published *An Examination of those Things wherein the Author of the Late "Appeale" Holds the Doctrines of the Church of the Pelagians and Arminians to be the Doctrines of the Church of England* (*STC*, no. 4633).

13. I.e., Elizabeth of Bohemia, Electress Palatine.

14. I.e., Walsingham Gresley, steward to John Digby, Earl of Bristol.

15. Concerning the question of common fame, see HofC, 18 April, n. 20.

16. Gresley is presumably referring to the letter from the King to Bristol, dated 20 January 1626, that was brought in by Buckingham and read in the Upper House on 30 March (p. 226). Concerning the conflict between Bristol and Buckingham, see HofL, 22 March, p. 192, n. 5; and also, HofL, 19 April, 1, 6, 19 May, and 8 June, OBs.

Mr. Gresley, brought in again, repeats what he said before, which was that he speaking with his Lordship, the Lord of Bristol, told him what he heard of the aspersions laid upon him by the Duke in the Upper House [that] some thought the[17] hindrance of the recovery of the Palatinate was by his treaties. And that Lord of Bristol said that if he might be heard he doubted not but to make it appear that the ill successes in/

Mr. Gresley, brought in again, brings in writing what he said before, which was read. That he told Lord Bristol that upon the Duke of Buckingham's aspersions upon him in the Upper House it was thought by many that the recovery of the Palatinate was hindered by his treaties. And the Lord Bristol said that if he might be heard he doubted not but to make it appear that the ill successes in the negotiations/

[f. 141] Mr. Speaker takes his chair.

SIR JOHN STRANGWAYS[18] moves for a day next Friday for Sir Robert Howard's business.

SIR JOHN ELIOT. That it may be declined for a time.

Bill for the venting cloths. Read the 4th time by the Clerk's mistake, which was very extraordinary, the bill having been passed before.[19]

During the time of the session the records of the court are in the breast of those that sit to amend them as they shall see cause.[20]

17. MS: *the he.*

18. *Eliot* is crossed out in the MS and *Strangways* is inserted.

19. See above, n. 10.

20. This sentence appears to be Whitelocke's own comment that bills, etc., were generally kept in the hands of the committee chairmen, etc., until they were ready for engrossing.

Order of Business Thursday, 20 April 1626

THURSDAY, 20 APRIL 1626

I. JOURNAL OF THE HOUSE OF COMMONS

[CJ 846; p. 23]
Jovis, 20 Aprilis, 2 Caroli Regis

Skipwith's bill, Thursday[1] next week,[2] 2 clock.

Lord Morley's bill, Friday next, with addition of Mr. Ashton.

Sir James Altham's bill, Saturday next, 2 clock.

L. 1a. Wolstenholme.[3]

MR. MALET reports the Lord Abergavenny his bill. Thought fit by the committee to pass without any alteration.

MR. WANDESFORD reports from the committee for the cause of causes.

That the East India Company, after the service in taking in Hormuz, presented the Duchess (the Duke being then in Spain) with £2,000.[4] Upon the Duke's return, a suit in the Admiral Court against the Company but at whose instance[5] *non constant.* That after, Secretary Coke pressed the Company for the Lord Admiral's rights. The Company thereupon, advising[6] with Dr. Steward and Dr. Zouche, they, upon consideration, advised them there was no due to the Lord Admiral.

That the Duke afterwards moved the Lords House for stay of the[7] Company's ships, upon pretense of staying them for defense of the kingdom. Hereupon the ships stayed *5 Martii.*

That the Duke being moved by Sir Robert Mansell for their release, he answered they were not stayed by him but by the Lords in parliament; yet gave way for their falling down to Tilbury.[8]

That being after moved for their discharge, he told them plainly they should not be discharged till they had compounded with him. That *15 Martii* the King's advocate in the East India Court demanded £15,000 for goods piratically taken.[9] That 5 or 6,000 £ were refused; consultation amongst them to give over their Company, [p.24] but the loss of their journey importing them, they offered £10,000, which with scorn refused.[10] Thereupon seeing it could be no otherwise, and the staying of their ships then would lose their journey, they agreed to give 20 thousand pounds; whereof they paid £10,000 to the Duke to his own use, the other £10,000 they paid also to one of the Duke's servants, and afterwards took a pardon.

That the King did nothing in it, but only made demands for his own right, telling them he was no tyrant king but would leave all to the law; where the Duke used pretenses of stay by parliament for his own private.

That the Duke, if he had had right, might have had remedy (though the ships had gone away) for his own right; where, if the ships had been stayed but 4 or 5 days longer the whole voyage for that year had been lost. This resembled to the case of the Lord of Middlesex, for the 2500 pounds.[11]

1. MS: *Thursday day.* Concerning this bill, see HofC, 6 March, n. 3.

2. *Saturday next* is crossed out in the MS and *Thursday day next week* is inserted.

3. We have been unable to identify this bill, which received no further reading in this session.

4. For the consideration of the East India business in the committee of the whole, see HofC, 18 April, OB. Regarding Buckingham and the money, see 18 April, nn. 38 and 40. See also, HofL, 13 May, pp. 420–425.

5. Printed edition: *instant.*

6. Printed edition: *advised.* Concerning Drs. Steward and Zouche, see HofC, 18 April, n. 39.

7. MS: *these.*

8. See Gardiner, *Impeachment,* pp. 89–90.

9. See Gardiner, *Impeachment,* pp. 111–113, 113–114.

10. See Gardiner, *Impeachment,* pp. 115–116.

11. For the charge in the parliament of 1624 against Lionel Cranfield, Earl of Middlesex, for taking bribes from the customs farmers, see *LJ,* III, 350–361, 380.

That the committee resolved, upon question, the money taken by the Lord Admiral in this manner was an undue exaction and extortion from the merchants of the East India Company.

MR. SECRETARY COKE. That he being Master of the Requests, the King commanded him to speak with the East India Company to know whether they would compound the business or stand upon the law. That they chose to stand upon the law.[12] That all the goods taken, if they proved piratical, were forfeited to the King, though granted under the Great Seal to the Lord Admiral.

Upon question, that the money taken by the Lord Admiral in this manner was an undue exacting and extorting money from the East India Company.

[CJ 847] MR. CHANCELLOR delivers a message from his Majesty: That he called this parliament for assistance.[13]

Upon question, the House to be presently turned into a committee, to consider what fit to be done concerning this message of his Majesty.

[p. 25] MR. HERBERT reports to the House (Mr. Speaker taking his chair for that purpose) the resolution of the grand committee, which was ordered thus: that we should proceed in the business in hand concerning the Duke of Buckingham, forenoon and afternoon, setting all other businesses aside till that be done; to the intent we may, upon Tuesday[14] next, proceed to the consideration of his Majesty's message for supply.

Upon question, the engrossed bills passed the House to be sent up to the Lords tomorrow morning. To be sent up by Mr. Vice Chamberlain.

Upon question, the House to proceed in the great business in hand concerning the Duke of Buckingham, forenoon and afternoon, setting all other business aside not conducing to that till that be done; to the intent we may, by Tuesday next, proceed to the consideration of satisfaction to his Majesty's message for supply.

MR. VICE CHAMBERLAIN. That he and the rest of the messengers yesterday, concerning restraint of Mr. Montagu his further writing books, delivered the message to his Majesty. That his Majesty not slightly passed over the message, but questioned whether we here examined the doctrine, or no. Wherein being satisfied, his Majesty, upon deliberation, signified his dislike of Mr. Montagu his writings. That the doctrine of the books he would refer to the Convocation House and would, in future, take special care for the examination of all books which should be printed, for avoiding any matter of sedition, etc.

Viz., the 4 privy councillors, and Sir J. Fullerton, to relate to his Majesty the proceedings of the House this day.[15]

Jovis, 20 Aprilis, 2 Caroli Regis
Post meridiem

SIR D. DIGGES moves that the subcommittee now about the business of Rochelle may

12. Concerning Coke's role, see *CSPC, East Indies, 1622–1624,* p. 271.

13. For the message, see Whitelocke, below, and BL Add. 22,474, f. 39, printed at the end of this day's proceedings.

14. *Friday* is crossed out in the MS preceding *Tuesday.*

15. The four privy councillors referred to are presumably the same three who had been sent as messengers to the King the preceding day (Sir Dudley Carleton, Vice Chamberlain; Sir Humphrey May, Chancellor of the Duchy; and Sir John Coke, Secretary), plus Sir Richard Weston, Chancellor of the Exchequer, who delivered the message this day. However, two other privy councillors also sat in the House in 1626: Sir John Suckling, Comptroller of the Household, and Sir Robert Naunton, Master of the Wards.

sit,[16] notwithstanding the sitting of the House; and resolved accordingly.

The committee for evils, causes, and remedies, to sit presently.

II. DIARY OF BULSTRODE WHITELOCKE, ESQ., DD. 12.21, CAMBRIDGE UNIVERSITY LIBRARY

[f. 141]

April 20

MR. MALET reports the bill for assurance of the jointure of the wife of [Sir Thomas] Neville, son and heir of the Lord Abergavenny.

MR. WANDESFORD reports for the committee of evils, causes, and remedies, the resolution of that committee about the Admiral's stay of the East Indian Company.[17]

SIR ROBERT MANSELL. The reason of establishing the East Indian Company was to draw experience upon our nation that if we fell out with the Spaniard we might know how to deal with him in those parts.

SECRETARY COKE. That he received a commandment from the King and a little book of the charges against the East Indian Company.[18] That they had taken, as was conceived, by way of piracy to the value of £100,000. That he should acquaint them with the particulars and know if they would end this by composition or a legal course. They answered they would proceed in a legal course, which answer he returned and did no more in the business.

Resolved by the House, that the taking of money from the East Indian Company by the Lord Admiral in the manner declared by the committee was an undue exacting and extorting.

[f. 141v] CHANCELLOR EXCHEQUER.[19] That he called this parliament to consult of the weighty affairs of this kingdom, and having entered into a fatherly conference/

His Majesty cannot tell/

Should breed a fear or jealousy of him that he means to precipitate your counsels.

His Majesty knows that he has deserved a right and perfect understanding between him and his people and is confident that it will always be so/

[f. 142] Has con/

That finding you have not only laid aside the consideration of his late message[20] and fallen into other businesses that must necessarily cause much expense of time/

His Majesty except he may receive from you within 4 or 5 days such a satisfaction as might be agreeable to his designs and proportionable to the great actions wherein we have engaged him, both the time of the year and occurrences [*blank*] will force him to new counsels. As his Majesty intends when/

His Majesty expects you prefer his business before others.

The King protested very earnestly that if the time and [*blank*] did not [*blank*] he would expect/

MR. WANDESFORD moves that we may resolve ourselves into a grand committee to take consideration of this message.

Resolved accordingly.

[*Committee of the Whole House*]

Mr. Herbert takes the chair.

Mr. Glanville desires the message may be repeated.

Sir Dudley Digges. If we may go on I doubt not but before the day required by

16. A subcommittee of the committee for examining the causes of causes, appointed on 20 March, that first met on 23 March, see OB.

17. See Wandesford's report in the CJ, above.

18. See above, n. 12.

19. For a more complete account of the message, see BL Add. 22,474, f. 39, printed at the end of this day's proceedings.

20. I.e., the message delivered to the House by the Chancellor on 13 April and revived by a further message on 18 April.

the King we shall really answer the King and give him satisfaction.

Chancellor Duchy. They were thought the wisest men of [*blank*] that always/

I shall ever think them the wisest men of the people[21] that will be ever ready to please the King. Moves we set Tuesday for a day for consideration of this business.

[f. 142v] Sir Peter Heyman. The King would know within 4 or 5 days what we will give. For the time, we shall do our endeavors to bring our business about by that time. That we should wait the setting of a day, but go on with the businesses of greatest moment as speedily as we may.

Upon mistakes of some speaking, Chancellor Exchequer repeats the point of the King's message again.

Sir Thomas Hoby. That within these 4 or 5 day[s] we apply ourselves to the greatest grievance we have and send that to the King or the Lords. And then appoint a day for consideration of this business.

Sir Dudley Carleton. For a man to keep himself to the point and not to recite what has been formerly spoken is a good ground in all councils. How unwillingly the King came to this message I, being present, can witness. The point is to show how this is a time which cannot be protracted nor endure any longer delay. The necessity of the present occasion may be divided into three parts: matter of negotiation, action, preparation. The French King is ready to join with his Majesty in the affairs of Germany;[22] charged to know of our King what he will do in it.

The man is now in court who must/

The answer is whether our King will on his part do that which is convenient, whereby the French King may see that the war shall not lie on his shoulders wholly. We have it by commission under the King of France's hand that our merchants shall have their goods, that the Protestants shall have their peace. [f. 143] As soon as the word that we will make our King safe at home and feared abroad came into France, they went to give us satisfaction; but when the ambassador here wrote that this was but a gallantry and that there was no good correspondence between King and people/[23]

There is at this day a prince come from the King of Denmark to the Hague and expects hourly when some blessed message from hence.[24]

The/

In place of 40,000 men that are now for us with the King of Denmark, upon the first mutiny will be all against us, being mercenary men.

The case in the Low Countries will admit no longer delay. At this time the King of Spain is providing a fleet of 200 sail with flat bottoms purposely to come hither or to Ireland, as is conceived. 300 of our best cannoneers gotten by corruption from us. And many of our shipwrights gotten from Genoa to Dunkirk. What the other councils are, I do not know. Be they what they will, they are of necessity. What other princes have done in the like cases all do know. *Horret animus, etc.,* not speak of them. In Bohemia to this day they examine what was the cause of the/

Prince of Orange was wont to say/

Things past may be blamed and shamed, but not remedied. [f. 143v] Those of Prague had money enough but lost the op-

21. *kingdom* is crossed out in the MS preceding *people*.

22. See Carleton's report on his embassy to France, HofC, 18 April, OB.

23. Carleton may be referring to the Marquis de Blainville, French ambassador to England, who had recently had his final audience with Charles and was about to depart for France. See *CSPV 1625–1626*, pp. 391–392, 397–398.

24. Carleton is referring to John Ernest, Duke of Saxe-Weimar. See HofC, 30 March, n. 14.

portunity of their money by formality of their proceeding. It is now necessary/

Agrees with the motion for Tuesday next.

Sir Dudley Digges. That Sir Dudley Carleton is a stranger in Israel. He knows not our reasons here.[25] There is a necessity in Ireland, too.

From whence comes all these necessities? There is a great fault, a chief fault, I/

Too much confidence in foreign negotiations, which grew from too much power, perhaps, given to subjects, to one subject. Had we been let alone, the kingdom had been sufficiently defended by this time.

Sir Edwin Sandys. In all assemblies when men are in difference of judgment, by long arguing they will be all of one opinion if they differ not in the ends. In the end we all agree, which is his Majesty's service and the good of our country; and after our arguing I doubt not but we shall grow to an *unanime* resolution. The difficulty of pi/

The great foresight of the difficulty of the work. The better part of the businesses abroad must be paid by this small and not very rich island. The 3 subsidies and 3 fifteens,[26] in regard of all the businesses in Germany, etc., in as much as nothing. [f. 144] A retrospection to the monies formerly given, another reason of difficulty. The 2 subsidies were but given to the King at his coming to the Crown by way of due.[27] Little appears what has been the effect of the 3 subsidies in 21 [*Jac.*],[28] as is the *vox populi*. We would clear the/

A pressing necessity of the King and present time. The King comes not, as I have heard language in this House: I will have my business first, and subjects ought in duty to obey him. But the King comes with a most mild and gracious language.[29] That we should hold on our course in our grievances, especially with those that have brought the kingdom into this distress. And withal upon Tuesday peremptorily enter into the consideration of the King's business for supplying him.

Sir Robert Mansell. It is more than high time that we should be in action. Is it a time when we should be in action to make demand for preparation? What should be the reason of this we are in hand to lay open? That which now should be for preparation I hope is for a year or 2 hence. If it fall out otherwise, we must lay open the faults and help to supply. When the time comes I shall speak much for the aggravation of these faults and improvidence. That we spend no more time in these interruptions, but as soon as is possible fix a day for satisfying the King's demands.

Chancellor Exchequer.[30] The reason why the King sent unto us now was because we had laid aside the message formerly sent and let it go without a day.[31] [f. 144v] If we set not a day for this message, I fear it will leave a very ill understanding with the King of the proceedings of this House.

Sir John Eliot. Hearing this repetition, I cannot think there is a right understanding with the King of our hearts, of our proceedings; and they are misreported to him. Though that already given be more than nothing, yet I confess it is too little. We shall find means more honorable. There is a

25. Cf. Luke 24:18. This was the first parliament to which Carleton had been elected since 1604, and he had only recently taken his seat following his return from France.

26. I.e., the supply already voted by the House. See HofC, 27 March, OB.

27. *SR*, I Car. I, c. 6.

28. *SR*, 21 Jac., I, c. 33.

29. *We ought to give satisfaction to this House that* is crossed out in the MS following *language*.

30. *Mr. Wandesford* is crossed out in the MS preceding *Chancellor Exchequer*.

31. See above, n. 20.

great grievance, too great a one. The treasure, laws, persons, actions of the kingdom, the kingdom itself suffers under the too great power of one man. The abuses, errors, faults of one great man will be ready very suddenly to be presented, and whereof we shall clear our hands by Saturday, if there be not further interruptions. That if we do not give the particular time moved, it is because we hope to come to the business required sooner.

Mr. Long. If we set a day I am afraid of interruptions among ourselves, not from the King.

Upon Sir Dudley Digges's motion, ordered to proceed in the great business in hand concerning the Duke of Buckingham, forenoon and afternoon, and lay aside all other businesses until this be done, to the intent that by Tuesday we may be ready to fall into consideration of his Majesty's message this day sent. And some are [to be] appointed by the House to acquaint the King with this day's proceeding.

The Speaker takes his chair.

MR. HERBERT reports the resolution of the committee.

Ordered, to send up the engrossed bills to the Lords tomorrow, and appointed the messengers.

[f. 145] SIR DUDLEY CARLETON reports from the King that he, hearing our message concerning the inhibiting Mr. Montagu's publishing of any more books until his books now in question be sufficiently examined by this House and such order therein taken as shall be fit, the King first expressing his dislike of Mr. Montagu's books. That for the matter of the doctrine, he was resolved to refer it to the consideration of the Convocation House. In the interim and hereafter before any of his books go to the press, he will have them so well looked into that, if they contain any matter of sedition or false doctrine, they shall not be published.

The resolution of the committee upon the King's message reported by Mr. Herbert is confirmed by the House.

Pomeridiem

[*Committee of the Whole House*]

Mr. Wandesford takes the chair.

Sir John Eliot reports from the committee for causes of causes. Consists on 3 particulars: 1. For the intercepting, unnecessary exhausting, and misemploying/[32]

2. The buying and selling of offices and places of judicature.[33] 3. Sending and delivering of our ships to the French, which were employed against Rochelle.[34] The ships about March was twelvemonth were pressed for the King's service, shortly after released. It was pretended they should be employed against Genoa. These ships had certain conditions drawn up. Without consent of the owners the ships went to Dieppe. In the public and general articles was: they were to serve the French King against any prince or state whatsoever except the King of Great Britain [f. 145v] and were to take into their ships to them what number the French King would appoint.[35] But the

32. I.e., of the King's revenue. This was the sixth cause resolved on by the House, see HofC, 25 March, and Eliot's report on 21 April. See also, HofL, 15 May, pp. 452–457.

33. This was the seventh cause resolved on by the House, see HofC, 25 March, and Eliot's report on 21 April. See also, HofL, 13 May, p. 409.

34. This was the eighth cause resolved on by the House, see HofC, 25 March. Concerning the ships loaned to France, see HofC, 27 February, n. 20; and see also, HofL, 13 May, pp. 425–439, and 15 May, pp. 446–451.

35. See the articles, printed in Gardiner, *Impeachment*, pp. 158–162.

Duke told them that they should not let come aboard more men than they could master. When they came to Dieppe the French Admiral told them they were to go against Rochelle, offering to put into the ships to them more men than they could master. Of all the ships there, there was not one that would be drawn to accept of this service though to some of the principals jewels and pensions very large were offered them. Upon this refusal they kept themselves possessors of their ships and returned to the Downs. Some of them came to court and acquainted Lord Duke and Lord Conway with what was put on them at Dieppe. Not long after, by a letter of the 10 of June [*sic*][36] of Lord Conway's, came a command for their return to Dieppe and to put themselves into the King of France's service and to receive aboard what number of men the French would put aboard. Captain Pennington, the Admiral, told the rest of the captains this, who said they could not presume that it was the will of the King that they should deliver their ships or take in men of France so that they should not be masters of their own ships and without security.[37] The 3 ambassadors proffered themselves to be bound for their King. The merchants [f. 146] thought this not fit security; so did the Duke in private tell them. A security was drawn up in French as it had been by the ambassadors offered. The merchants, understanding by interpreter, would not accept this security. While the interpreter was seeking, the Duke commanded one of them in private that if this security liked them not, they should return to Dieppe, and if there they had not security to their minds, they should keep their ships. The merchants returned to Dieppe, where they for/

Mr. Nicholas, the Duke's secretary, persuaded, threatened. The merchants sent to Monsieur Effiat certain cautions. In case they should have security for delivering up their ships; yet conceiving themselves subject to the law here, they desired to have a discharge under the Great Seal of England. Nicholas again treated with the merchants and expressed that he was commanded by the Duke to know their resolutions whether upon Lord Conway's letters and the security at Rochester agreed to by the Duke they would deliver up their ships. If they would, he would see they should be safe. Merchants in writing set down that for the security they accepted it not nor would now receive it, but had [f. 146v] security of their own which was money to be put into the Chamberlain of London's hands. Mr. Nicholas threatened that if they should not deliver up their ship it was as much as their lives were worth. The merchants considered if the[y] did deliver their ship up they were in danger of being hanged at home, if they did not that they/

2 of the ships resolved to retire to the Downs and thence ran away to the Low Countries. This 28 *Julii*. Not long after was drawn a new command from hence that Captain Pennington should deliver over his ship and require the rest to do so too to the French; and if they refused he should force them, even to sinking. The committee observed here that before the 28 of *Julii* the intent of employing[38] of our ships against Rochelle was taken notice of by our state. Pennington told the merchants of this command. They weighed anchors to be gone.

36. See the letter of 10 July 1625 from Secretary Conway to Captain Pennington, printed in Gardiner, *Impeachment*, pp. 228–229.

37. See the letter from the captains to Secretary Conway, 11 July 1625, printed in Gardiner, *Impeachment*, pp. 229–231. See also, ibid., pp. 235–291, and see the account of the subcommittee, HofC, 23 March, OB.

38. *pretense of going* is crossed out in the MS and *intent of employing* is inserted.

Pennington shot at them. Whereupon coming back, being in a necessity, they agreed to conditions propounded and security to them, and delivering up their ships, brought their persons home. [f. 147] The merchants, asked by the committee, said that Mr. Nicholas had for his reward of the French a diamond ring and a diamond hatband.

Lord St. John puts him in mind of 2 things. One, that [*blank*], in a letter of the Lord Duke's was/

That he would endeavor to serve the Marquis Effiat's turn with the ships.

Resolved to determine this before Sir John Eliot go on with his report.

Sir Dudley Digges. When Queen Elizabeth had 3 treaties on foot with France,[39] as an offensive and defensive league, a secret treaty against the greatness of the House of Austria, and a marriage, Rochelle being besieged, no ships were sent thither by that Queen but some of the west country relieved the town. It may be a fault that the Duke did not prevent nor hinder the sending of the ships to Rochelle.

Sir Robert Mansell. That in this case my Lord of Buckingham is in fault from the beginning to the ending. If I had counselled him, he should rather have died in prison than have given way to the sending of these ships.

Resolved to defer the determination of this business till Mr. Nicholas be heard.

Sir John Hippisley undertakes to bring him hither by tomorrow morning, 7 a clock.

III. MESSAGE FROM THE KING, ADD. 22, 474, p. 39, BRITISH LIBRARY

The 20th day of April being Thursday, his Majesty did again by a message sent by Sir Richard Weston put the House of Commons in mind of augmenting and perfecting their supply, as follows.

Sir Richard Weston to the House of Commons, 20 April 1626:

The King has often moved us by messages for the expediting and speeding of the great and weighty affairs, but nothing has proceeded but loss of time. He has likewise of late called upon us by a message to that purpose which we have laid by without setting about it a day, and have gone on with other business. His Majesty can no longer use his wonted patience but if we grow not to a resolution within these 4 or 5 days to give him such satisfaction as may concur and be proportionable to the weight of his design, his Majesty must be driven to change his counsels. His Majesty intends not hereby to prevent your just grievances or his giving you satisfaction therein but that the other should be first done and preferred as most necessary, and afterwards he will give you as much time as the season will permit. But if you shall not do this his Majesty will give you no longer time, he will endure no longer delay, nor recede from what he now sends unto you.

39. Digges's references are to c. 1572–1573 when Elizabeth was considering marriage with the Duke of Alençon. The Treaty of Blois was signed on 19 April 1572, and private English ships under Count de Montgomery went to assist Rochelle. See *CSPF 1572–1574,* Index *sub* Alençon; Blois; Montgomery, Count; Rochelle. See also *CSPV 1558–1580,* p. 485.

Order of Business Friday, 21 April 1626

I. Journal of the House of Commons,	38
II. Whitelocke,	38–43

Sir Dudley Digges: moves for a committee to consider the business concerning the **Duke of Buckingham** [*see below*]	38, *22/4; 24/4; 25/4; 26/4; 27/4; 28/4; 29/4; 2/5; 3/5; 6/5; 8/5; 9/5; 10/5; 9/6; 10/6; 13/6; 14/6
Committee of 12 for considering the business concerning the Duke of Buckingham: appointed	38, 39
Committee for framing a petition to the King for the **presentment** of **recusants** to meet this afternoon; all that will come to have voice; MPs for Kent to be present	38, *21/2
[*Committee of the Whole House: Christopher Wandesford in the chair*]	
Edward Nicholas is brought in to the committee of the whole on the **evils, causes, and remedies:** testifies concerning the **ships** loaned to **France**	39, *24/2; 23/3
Sir Robert Mansell	39
Sir John Eliot	39
Roger Matthew	40
Sir Dudley Digges	40
Sir James Bagg	40
Sir John Coke (Secretary)	40
John Selden	40
Sir Humphrey May (Chancellor Duchy)	40
Sir John Eliot	40
Resolved: the Duke of Buckingham is the cause of the delivery of the ships to France	40
[*End: Committee of the whole House*]	
Report from the committee of the whole House (Christopher Wandesford)	38, 40
[*Committee of the Whole House: Christopher Wandesford in the chair*]	
Report from the subcommittee for examining the **causes of causes** concerning the **sale of places of judicature** (Sir John Eliot)	40, *20/3; 22/4
Sir George Hastings	41
Thomas Fotherley	41
Resolutions concerning the sale of places of judicature	41
Report from the subcommittee for examining the causes of causes concerning the intercepting, exhausting, and **misemploying of the King's revenue** (Sir John Eliot)	41, *22/4
Sir Walter Erle	42
Sir Robert Pye	43
Sir Henry Mildmay is brought in to the committee of the whole: testifies concerning sale of the office of Master of the Wards	43
The matter of the sale of the office of Master of the Wards is laid by and no question passed	43
Thomas Fotherley	43
Resolutions concerning the misemploying of the King's revenue	43
[*End: Committee of the Whole House*]	
[*Afternoon*]	
Report from the committee of 12 considering the business concerning the **Duke of Buckingham** (John Glanville): moves that the House resolve concerning the matter of common fame [*see above*]	38, 43
Resolved: House to consider the matter of common fame tomorrow; lawyers to attend with precedents	38, 43

FRIDAY, 21 APRIL 1626

I. JOURNAL OF THE HOUSE OF COMMONS

[CJ 847; p. 26]
Veneris, 21 Aprilis, 2 Caroli Regis

SIR D. DIGGES moves for a subcommittee to consider of the state of the great business now in hand, and to reduce it into form; and to search for, and make use of, and apply precedents for it; and to present those things to the House, with their opinions. The number to be 12, besides those which have the chairs at committees.[1]

[col. 1]
Mr. [Christopher] Wandesford
Mr. [Edward] Whitby
Sir John Eliot
Mr. Herbert

[col. 2]
Mr. [John] Pym
Sir Thomas Hoby
Sir D[udley] Digges
Mr. [John] Selden

[col. 3]
Mr. [Christopher] Sherland
Sir W[alter] Erle
Mr. [John] Glanville
Sir Thomas Lake

This committee to meet at 1 clock this afternoon, in Court of Wards, and then to adjourn themselves at their pleasure.[2]

The committee for presenting recusants enlarged by appointing that all that will come to have voice.

The knights and burgesses of Kent, whose presentments of recusants are found defective, to be present at the said committee, which is appointed to meet at 5 of the clock this afternoon.

The bill for the sabbath/[3]

MR. WANDESFORD reports from the committee for evils, causes, and remedies, the resolution of the committee; viz., that the Duke the cause of the delivery of our ships unto the French, which were employed against Rochelle.

Veneris, 21 Aprilis, 2 Caroli Regis
Post meridiem

MR. GLANVILLE moves from the select committee, this day appointed, that they desire the House will resolve whether common fame a ground for this House to proceed upon,[4] because it conduces much to the business now in hand. And that notice hereof may be taken by the House, to be debated and resolved tomorrow morning.

Upon question, this resolved; and the lawyers required to attend with the precedents they have searched.

A warrant to the officers to bring the records.

II. DIARY OF BULSTRODE WHITELOCKE, ESQ., DD. 12.21, CAMBRIDGE UNIVERSITY LIBRARY

[f. 147v]

April 21

1. Following *committees* there are twelve names of MPs that are crossed out and rewritten in the committee list, below. In compiling the list four new names (Christopher Wandesford, Edward Whitby, Mr. Herbert, and John Pym) were substituted for four of the crossed-out names (Mr. Littleton, Sir Benjamin Rudyard, Sir Miles Fleetwood, and Sir John Strangways). Although there is no order noted concerning Digges's motion that "chairs at committees" be named to this committee, all four of the latter group were chairmen of important committees during this session: Wandesford chaired the committee of the whole on the evils, causes, and remedies; Whitby, the standing committee of the whole on grievances; Herbert, several ad hoc committees of the whole including that on the remonstrance; and Pym, the standing committee of the whole on religion.

2. *has power to agree of the time and place for their 1st meeting* is crossed out in the MS and *to meet at 1 clock this afternoon in Court of Wards and then to adjourn themselves at their pleasure* is inserted.

3. The meaning of this incomplete entry is unclear. The bill for the Lord's day was one of the five engrossed bills which, according to the House's order of 20 April (see OB), were sent up to the Lords this day (see HofL, 21 April, OB).

4. Regarding common fame, see HofC, 18 April, n. 20.

A select committee appointed of 12 to consider of the businesses concerning the Duke of Buckingham and to reduce it into form and search and prepare such precedents as they shall think fit, and present the whole matter with their opinions.

[*Committee of the Whole House*]

Mr. Wandesford takes his chair.

Mr. Nicholas, brought in and asked,[5] says [1,] that he was at Rochester when the Duke and the ambassadors of France were there, but heard not what the Duke said to the merchants but as the merchants told him. 2. That he went into France about July with Monsieur Effiat. That he had no promise of reward for his service in that business. 3. That he was sent by Lord Admiral. He knows not whether the King knew of his going or not. Lord Admiral gave him directions what to do, only his commission when he went was verbal. What the directions are he prays to be excused for telling till he has leave, for my Lord Duke told him they were matters of state. That the directions were partly in writing, partly by word of mouth, chiefly by mouth. The directions in writing sent to him when Captain Pennington came over about the beginning of August, *stilo Angliae,* as he remembers.[6] That he carried a draft of the security for the merchants' ships and for the King, which was offered at Rochester which he received from the ambassadors being there. That the directions in writing explained those he had by[7] word of mouth. [f. 148] He knows [not] whether the merchants consented to that security or no. That he desired the merchants at Dieppe to consider of the King's pleasure signified to them by the Lord Conway's letters. That he used no menacing words to the merchants nor told them that it would be as much as their lives were worth if they refused to deliver their ships, and went not so far with them as the letter went. That he had a diamond ring and a hatband of diamonds to the value of 100 marks from the ambassador, but he knows not for what service. That he required from the merchants no more of the merchants than he conceived he had instructions to do. That some things which he required of them was in writing and something not. That he tendered that to the merchants which is in writing brought in to the committee. That he thinks there were some letters written by Lord Buckingham to Monsieur Effiat, but what they were he knows not.

Sir Robert Mansell. Never any prince of England took the ships and men of English merchants to serve a foreign state without their own consents. This sending away of the ships is so dangerous a precedent that those that had a hand in it should have an exemplary punishment. No redemption of Lord Admiral's fault in that he did not oppose nor give counsel against this.

Sir John Eliot. I have observed a new wisdom in this House in this, that the faults of private men shall be shadowed under secrets of state. The intention of the state was not to deliver over these ships but to serve against the public enemy in the public cause. [f. 148v] In this a weakness to the state, a dishonor to the King, a prejudice to private men, the merchants, and an abuse of the parliament. I hold Lord Duke guilty of all these.

5. Nicholas, the Lord Admiral's secretary, had been ordered to be brought in to the committee of the whole on the preceding day (see HofC, 20 April, OB). Concerning Nicholas's part in this business, see HofL, 13 May, pp. 431–437, and see the correspondence printed in Gardiner, *Impeachment,* pp. 139–302.

6. Concerning Nicholas's directions, see the correspondence printed in Gardiner, *Impeachment,* pp. 244–279, particularly, pp. 275–279, and see also, SP 78/75, f. 211.

7. MS: *my.*

Mr. Matthew. We have not heard that Lord Admiral acquainted the Council Table with the return of the merchants because they were to be employed against Rochelle. Seeing the Duke had power enough to have prevailed with the King in this and did not, I think him guilty.

Sir Dudley Digges. That/
Committees of the whole House have often heard counsel. Moves that D/

Sir James Bagg. That he doubted not but to make it appear that he[8] was in no fault in that business, but if the House would be pleased to select 2 or 3 particular persons he would be ready to/
That he had no commission to tell this unto the House.

Secretary Coke. I had a great hand in that which was done by the Commissioners of the Navy and some particular employment beside. I drew the instructions, wherein if there was not a command to the merchants not to suffer the ships to be employed against Rochelle, let me suffer for it.[9] 2 articles that the merchants should take in no more men than the ships would carry victuals for, and suffer no strangers to come into the gunner room nor under hatches; with which articles the ambassador was much displeased, but the King allowed them. I never heard from the King nor the Admiral that the ships should be employed against Rochelle, but for the procuring of a peace for it and to go for Genoa.

[f. 149] Mr. Selden. That we should first censure the cause as it now stands before us, if the informations be true; and then give the Duke notice to answer, if it please him.

Chancellor Duchy. When this House sees what will be the end of this, I think they will be sorry that they have spent so long time about it. It was never otherwise till this parliament that the grand committee gave judgment until he were heard. Moves it may be so now.

Sir John Eliot. That Mr. Chancellor is mistaken in the orders of the House. Our judgment is not definitive nor condemnative, but a preparation to present.

Resolved upon question, that the Duke is the cause of the delivering of the ships to the hands of strangers which were employed against Rochelle.

The Speaker takes his chair.

MR. WANDESFORD report[s] this resolution of the committee to the House.

[*Committee of the Whole House*]

Mr. Wandesford in the chair.

Sir John Eliot reports from the subcommittee of causes of causes.[10] That with desire of a saving to add to this repute on further examination for the sale of places of judicature. The Duke of Buckingham has in 3 particulars been [*blank*]: Wardenship of the Cinque Ports, Mastership of the Wards, and Lord High Treasurership. Lord Zouche on a contract and composition between him and the Duke received money and pension which had continuance during his life, for leaving the place. [f. 149v] Duke of Buckingham confessed in the conference in the Painted Chamber that he did buy that place.[11] One said that he heard from Lord Zouche that he had received £500 per annum which co[mes][12] [*blank*] and £1,000 presently.

8. I.e., the Duke of Buckingham.

9. For the instructions, see *PP 1625*, pp. 741–743.

10. See Eliot's notes from the subcommittee, HofC, 21 March.

11. See HofL, 13 May, p. 413, n. 15.

12. *which comes from the King* is crossed out in the MS and *which co[mes]* is inserted. Eliot is referring here to the testimony of Sir John Backhouse; see HofL, 13 May, pp. 413–414.

Mr. Herman[13] said he heard Lord Middlesex say so. The committee was informed that £6,000 was paid by the Earl of Middlesex for the Mastership of the Wards.[14] That he paid the £6,000 to Sir Henry Mildmay by the appointment of the Duke.[15]

To the Treasurership sold to Lord Mandeville, Sir Thomas Fanshawe said that being at the court he found Lord [*blank*] unwilling of the place, wished himself at home again, but he saw him have the staff; and then Lord Mandeville said he was very willing to have delivered it up again.[16] Sir Charles Montagu said to Sir Thomas Fanshawe that it was the unhappiest thing that ever befell that family for that some of the money was owing yet which was paid for this place. Mr. Dixon[17] said that Lord President gave £20,000 for this place; and to Mr. Porter,[18] then the Duke's servant in Whitehall. The money was paid in the Duke's lodgings to the Duke's use by his hands and Sir Charles Montagu's.

Sir George Hastings and Mr. Fotherley affirm that the £500 per annum and the £1,000 paid to the Lord Zouche came out of the Lord Buckingham's revenues.

[f. 150] Resolved that this particular of buying of the Wardenship of the Cinque Ports shall be fixed to the head of buying of places of judicature by Lord Admiral.

Resolved that the particular of selling of the Treasurer's place to Lord Mandeville shall be fixed as a particular instance to the head of selling of offices of judicature by the Duke.

Sir John Eliot reports further concerning the intercepting, unnecessary exhausting, and misemploying of the King's revenues.[19] The subcommittee exceeded not past 3 or 4 years back, wherein they find by record publicly issued to him £71,522 within the space of 2 years last past, or little more. And through private doors what is issued to him, I dare not think; I fear can hardly be computed. Upon record 16 *Jac.* he gained a release of divers sums of money by him privately received, which he was to detain for support of his honor and dignity. 20 *Jac.*, another release of like quality. What the sums were, no man knows. 16 *Jac.*, he procured to himself a grant of all the subsidies and customs in Ireland for 10 years at [£]6,000 per annum rent. Of the crown lands in 17 *Jac.* he procured 14 manors formerly annexed to the crown to be granted to him. [f. 150v] This great man whom neither modesty nor law could bound procured this grant. 1 *Car.*, there are lands of £400 rents granted to Paul Peart and Henry Knollys for the use of the Earl of Anglesey, who for these lands received £4,960 in part of payment to the Earl of Anglesey.[20] 2 forests in Wiltshire, Blackmore and Pewsham,[21] as Mr. Pym affirmed, who was employed as a commissioner there,[22] was

13. MS: *Harman.* The reference is to Nicholas Herman, Secretary to the Master of the Wards. See Prestwich, *Cranfield,* pp. 485–488.

14. *Mr. Herman* is crossed out in the MS following *Wards.* Lionel Cranfield, Earl of Middlesex, obtained the office of Master of the Wards in 1619. See HofL, 15 May, p. 470, n. 86.

15. See Mildmay's testimony later this day, below; and see HofL, 15 May, p. 470.

16. See HofL, 15 May, p. 470, and n. 85.

17. Robert Dixon was a secretary to Henry Montagu, Viscount Mandeville. See Esther S. Cope, *The Life of a Public Man* (Philadelphia: American Philosophical Society, 1981), Index *sub* Dixon.

18. I.e., Endymion Porter.

19. See HofC, 25 March, n. 31 and see Christopher Wandesford's report from the committee of the whole, HofC, 22 April, OB.

20. See the warrant of 27 May 1625 concerning Peart and Knollys, *CSPD 1625–1626,* p. 539. See also, HofL, 15 May, p. 476, and n. 132.

21. See HofL, 15 May, p. 476, and n. 133.

22. John Pym had reported to the lords of the Treasury in September 1618 concerning raising money for the King out of Blackmore and Pewsham. SP 14/99:78.

granted. £2,500 in money remained of wood to the value of £5,000 and 2 parks. They are to the value of £900 per annum. These granted to the Earl of Anglesey, 4 *Junii*, 1 *Car.* 1 *Car.*,[23] at the request of the Earl of Anglesey, granted to Lord Mandeville the manor of Norton in Norfolk and the Forest of Dean in Gloucestershire, affirmed by a member of this House who called it the West Indies of England. Part of this forest was passed to Sir Edward Villiers, which was worth £20,000, but was stopped. There was passed to Sir Edward Villiers 500 acres of wood worth £12,000, part of that manor,[24] with condition to serve the King's iron mills with wood within these 2 years. Certain manors in fee farm granted in May last to 2 of Lord President's servants, Mr. Gualey and Mr. Dixon,[25] and lands worth £499 17s. 9d., the which were annexed to the crown; granted in consideration of £12,500, which should have been paid but was not. To Lord Mandeville's [f. 151] use the land was passed. The £400 land and his honor,[26] he received, and a table at the King's charge in regard that he so soon was put out of the Treasurer's place for which he paid so dearly, though never any table of diet in the court belonged before to that office.

21 [*Jac.*], a fine imposed on Middlesex in parliament of £50,000, afterward reduced to £20,000, which was by the King assigned for satisfaction of certain debts due to the Household and Wardrobe, February 1624.[27] A privy seal to the Lord Treasurer and Chancellor Exchequer that it should be paid and a warrant to Lord Middlesex to pay it. The officers sent by the Lord Steward came to the Lord Middlesex, who obtained 3 weeks time for getting the sum. Lord Middlesex wrote that he would be ready for the payment. When this money was expected by the officers, the old Countess of Buckingham by treaty intercepts the satisfaction. She threatened Lord Middlesex that the next parliament should take away his sugar patent. Lord Middlesex was drawn to give his house and lands at Chelsea, worth [£]8,000, and his sugar patent worth £16,000 and £5,000 in money for/

This by Mr. Fotherley[28] [who] was employed to take possession of the house and received the money, but/

The assurances passed in the King's name, but none of his servants used in it. [f. 151v] Lord Middlesex said that upon the last composition he was promised to be restored to his former favor[29] which the parliament took from him and to come to parliament.

Sir Walter Erle. That he has £1,000 out of the Court of Wards and £1,000 out of the Exchequer per annum.[30] The King gave lands to the value of £500 per annum for York House,[31] which house the Duke of Buckingham now has. £25,000 in 6 years appears to be given to the Duke. Sir Edward

23. On 4 June 1625 the Earl of Anglesey was granted an annual pension of £1,000. See C 66/2359, no. 7 (MS Cal. Pat. Rolls, 1 Car. I, pt. 12, f. 2).

24. See HofL, 15 May, p. 477.

25. For this grant of 24 May 1625, see C 66/2349, no. 4 (MS Cal. Pat. Rolls, 1 Car. I, pt. 2, f. 17). Concerning Dixon, see above, n. 17. The name given in the patent for the other servant is "William Wallye" rather than "Gualey" as here; we have not been able further to identify him.

26. Henry Montagu, Viscount Mandeville, was created Earl of Manchester on 5 February 1626.

27. See HofL, 15 May, p. 476, and n. 131.

28. *brought to conclusion* is crossed out in the MS following *Fotherley.* Concerning Fotherley, see HofL, 13 May, p. 413, n. 17.

29. *liberty* is crossed out in the MS and *favor* is inserted.

30. See HofL, 15 May, p. 475, and n. 125.

31. *The particulars amount to £15,000 wanting, £5,000 in 60 years* is crossed out in the MS following *annum.* See HofL, 15 May, p. 474, and n. 106; and 8 June, p. 581.

Villiers has now £100 per annum pension out of the Presidentship of Munster, drawn for the Lord of Thomond.[32]

Sir Robert Pye. That there were privy seals in the Duke's name for £80,000.

Sir Henry Mildmay brought in and asked, says that £6,000 was paid to his father-in-law, Alderman Hallyday,[33] to his use by Lord Middlesex. That the Duke of Buckingham had nothing to do with this business as he knows. That he has heard that it was given for the place of Mastership of the Wards.

The particular concerning the sale of the office of Master of the Wards is laid by and no question passed on it.

Mr. Fotherley. Never a penny of the £71,500[34] came to the Duke's purse, but was all or most of it paid for the provisions for the navy. The King receives now £9,000 per annum for the customs in Ireland from the Duke.[35] Lord Duke was a stranger to the grant of the forests and title of earl to Lord Anglesey, the Duke being then in Spain.[36] Lord Middlesex prayed the mediation of the Duke that he might give his house, [f. 152] his patent of sugar, and the £5,000 for his fine of £20,000. He received the £5,000 and paid it to the Household and Wardrobe.[37]

Resolved that the taking of Chelsea House, the patent of sugar, and £5,000 of the Earl of Middlesex shall be fixed to the head of misemploying the King's revenues, and the Duke's having of York House.[38]

Speaker takes his chair.

MR. GLANVILLE reports the desire of the committee of 12 that the question of common fame may tomorrow morning be determined, which will much further their proceedings.[39]

Ordered accordingly.

32. Villiers had been named President of Munster by James I in January 1625 and confirmed in that office by Charles I in May the same year. Donough O'Brien, Earl of Thomond, had been President of Munster until his death in September 1624 when he was succeeded by his son Henry, who served as commissioner for the Presidentship of Munster until Villiers's appointment.

33. Eliot reported earlier this day that £6,000 was paid to Mildmay by the Earl of Middlesex for the Mastership of the Wards. See above, n. 14. In April 1619, the same year that Middlesex obtained the office of Master of the Wards, Mildmay married Anne, daughter of William Hallyday, alderman of London. *DNB*.

34. See Eliot's report, above.

35. See HofL, 8 June, p. 583.

36. See HofL, 8 June, p. 577. Christopher Villiers had received the title of Earl of Angelsey in March 1623, during the period that his brother, the Duke, was in Spain with Prince Charles.

37. See HofL, 15 May, p. 476, and n. 131.

38. See above, n. 31.

39. See above, n. 4.

ORDER OF BUSINESS SATURDAY, 22 APRIL 1626

SATURDAY, 22 APRIL 1626

I. JOURNAL OF THE HOUSE OF COMMONS

[CJ 847; p. 27]
Sabbati, 22 Aprilis, 2 Caroli Regis

MR. MALET enters the debate whether common fame a ground for the Commons House of Parliament to proceed upon.[1] Is against it, though confesses he has seen few original precedents in the point. The point, whether an accusation upon common fame be to be entertained here; and thereupon transmitted to the Lords. Is against it: 1, because it will disadvantage the party accused, considering then he must answer the fame and also the accusation; 2, whosoever accused here and cleared is, by the justice of this House, to have remedy against the accuser; which by this course he shall want.

7 R. 2, an accusation of bribery by Cavendish, against the Chancellor; and the accusation being found false, he adjudged to pay 3,000 marks and be imprisoned, etc.[2]

17 R. 2, a complaint, by the Earl[3] of Arundel against the Duke of Lancaster. He acquit, and the Duke ordered in parliament to have satisfaction from Arundel.

That, if this had been an use in parliament, it would from thence been derived to other courts, where no temporal court has ever used it except in cases capital, as in the case of Michael de la Pole.[4] So, in the case of recusants thinks it may be lawful because the recusant, though indicted, yet conforming and taking the oaths, is freed from all penalties of the law. Not so in the case now in question.

If this were but to prevent a mischief, might be tolerated; *contra* here, where tends to a judgment.

This not like the inquiry of a grand jury; yet no grand jury (except in case of recusants) proceeds upon common fame without other proof. Likes the resemblance to a double judgment of account, where the 1st judgment must be grounded upon verdict or confession. Doubts this precedent may be dangerous to inferior temporal courts, by way of imitation.

The petitions to this House for a grievance are in writing; the petitioners present, and their hands unto it.

Remembers the case of the Bishop of Durham, 12 *Jac.*, which upon special reason, as concerning the honor of this House and for which they could have no other ground of proof, which yet rejected because it had no other ground.[5]

MR. WILDE, *contra.* Bracton: that all suspicion grounded upon fame.[6] Some presumptions admit proof to the contrary, others not. This fame must arise among the better sort. All our law books concur in this point. An act must 1st be done, and the fame rise in the county where that fact done. A good ground for arresting upon any felony, as murder, robbery, etc. 7 H. 4, 1, 2; 5 H. 7; 7 E. 4; 11 E. 4.[7]

1. On 21 April the House had resolved to debate the matter of common fame on this day. See HofC, 18 April, n. 20.

2. *Rot. Parl.,* 7 R. II, nos. 11–15. According to the Parliament Roll, John Cavendish was adjudged to pay 1,000 marks.

3. *D. of Lancaster* is crossed out in the MS preceding *Earl.* See *Rot. Parl.,* 17 R. II, no. 11.

4. Concerning the case of Michael de la Pole, see 11 R. II, Articles 1–25 (Howell, *ST,* I, 89–124; and see HofL, 13 May, pp. 416–417). Whitelocke cites 28 H. VI at this point, indicating that the reference might be to the case of William (which Malet cited on 22 March) rather than to Michael de la Pole. Concerning the case of William de la Pole, Duke of Suffolk, see HofL, 18 April, pp. 277–279; and HofC, 8 May, n. 12.

5. Concerning the case of Richard Neile (Bishop of Durham in 1626, formerly of Lincoln), in the parliament of 1614, see *PP 1614,* p. 339 n. 11, and pp. 340–347, 348, 354, 402–403; *LJ,* II, 709–713. The case was discussed earlier, see HofC, 16 March, n. 16.

6. Bracton, *Lib.* 3, treatise 2, chap. 22, f. 143. See HofC, 18 April, n. 20.

7. We are unable to find the first case, cf. *YB,* 7 H. IV, Hil., pl. 3. *YB,* 5 H. VII, Mich., pl. 10; *YB,* 7 E. IV, Mich., pl. 20; *YB,* 11 E. IV, Trin., pls. 8 and 11.

MR. LITTLETON, *accordant.* This not a House of definitive judgment, but of information, denunciation, or presentment, for which common fame sufficient.

[p. 28] A great difference between common fame and rumor. The general voice is common fame. *Vox populi vox Dei.* 11 E. 4, common fame more than the saying of any man,[8] for that the voice of many men. Common fame a good ground of imprisonment for treason, or felony, 7 Eliz., Dyer, but I may not say, he is a traitor or a felon.[9]

[CJ 848] In other states, ancient and modern, men have been not only accused but condemned by common fame.[10]

Precedents: 28 H. 6, Earl of Suffolk's case;[11] 29 H. 6, Duke of Somerset's case;[12] 12 *Jac.*, Bishop of Lincoln's case.[13]

That a man accused by common fame is to answer only the accusation, and not the fame.

MR. BROWNE, *accordant.* Accusation allowed, not calumniation. Calumniation is, in an unfit place, to lay an aspersion. Common fame called by civilians, *semi-plena probatio,* arising out of apparent signs. If a private man accuse, he liable to punishment if false, because has nothing to do in it; otherwise, where a member of the House does it. *Libere licet accusare,* where the place is proper for the accusation, otherwise not. Therefore the accusation in this House proper. No subject, how great soever, but questionable here if he be grievous to the commonwealth. So all former precedents; and this the only place wherein to question great men.

MR. WENTWORTH. If we could not present to the Lords upon common fame, yet we may inquire and accuse here upon common fame, as in Dr. Turner his case.[14] This the only safety for accusation of great men, where else no man dare accuse a great man for fear of danger. Men of ill fame not bailable, but to be bound to good behavior by act of parliament. If common fame sufficient for treason and felony, much more for lesser offense. *Scandalum magnatum* lies not where a man can bring forth but one author.

MR. SELDEN. The question now only whether this House may proceed to transmit to the Lords upon common fame; else no great man shall, for fear of danger, be accused by any particular man. The faults of the gods might not be told till the goddess fame born. *De eo male creditur,* upon a matter in indictments. This course of accusation held in all the courts in Christendom. That these cases are to be ruled by the law of parliament, and not either by the common or civil law. 28 H. 6, Duke of Suffolk: a general rumor and noise of great offenses against the state. The Commons, taking notice thereof, acquainted the Lords with that general rumor, praying them he might be committed to the Tower which the Lords, upon consultation with the judges, refused, because the charge only general. Thereupon the Commons instanced in a particular: that the French King ready to invade the kingdom through his default; thereupon he was presently committed to the Tower. 29 H. 6, in the Duke of Somerset's case, the like clamor upon common fame, and the parties complained of removed.[15]

MR. ROLLE, *accordant.* The Commons may present a Lord of the higher House to

8. *YB,* 11 E. IV, Trin., pl. 8.

9. 2 Dyer, *Reports,* Anonymous case, Hil., 7 Eliz. I, pl. 26, f. 236.

10. Littleton made reference here to Machiavelli. See below, n. 40.

11. See above, n. 4.

12. For the case against Edmund, Duke of Somerset, see *Rot. Parl.,* 29 H. VI, no. 16.

13. See above, n. 5.

14. See Dr. Samuel Turner's queries concerning the Duke of Buckingham, presented to the committee of the whole on 11 March.

15. See above, n. 12.

the Lords, for he not compellable to answer there and so, except we may present upon common fame, shall never be drawn to answer. [p. 29] If the offense tend to felony or treason, the Commons may pray he may be committed in respect of the quality of the fact, otherwise for smaller offenses.

5 H. 4, a complaint against the King's confessor; whereupon the Lords ordered they should be removed from the King.[16] Whereupon the King in parliament, though he knew no cause particularly, yet because the Lords and Commons had thought them unfitting, he there commanded them to come no more near unto him; and that, if there were any other against whom the Lords and Commons had indignation, he would remove them.

MR. SHERLAND. No damages awarded where *probabilis causa litigandi.* Where common fame, *semi-plena probatio.* The life and soul of the commonwealth of greater respect than felony. There is as well a real treason (and which is tantamount) as a legal treason; and therefore common fame a sufficient grounds there as well as for felony.

MR. NOY, *accordant.* Men bound by recognizance sometimes imprisoned upon common fame. Where we inquire only. No other way of inquiry here; no churchw[ardens], nor grand jury. No fault to go unpunished because no man dare accuse.

Upon question, common fame a good ground of proceeding of this House, either to inquire of here or transmit the complaint, if the House find cause, to the King or Lords.

Memorandum: MR. CHANCELLOR OF THE DUCHY delivered his opinion against this inquiry by common fame.

MR. NOY. That this a good ground to inquire 1, whether a common fame; 2ly, whether this fame true. We will not transmit without the 1st inquiry, but without the particular inquiry, we may; for peradventure we cannot come by the witnesses, as if the witnesses of the Lords House.

MR. GLANVILLE reports 2 particulars, and that the committee desires some members of this House, viz., Secretary Coke, Sir William Howard, Sir Robert Howard, Sir Robert Pye, Sir John Hippisley, Sir William Monson, Mr. Fotherley, and Mr. Okely, Sir William Russell, may be, by this House, enjoined to attend the committee in the Court of Wards, presently.[17] Ordered.

2ly, that the House will sit this afternoon to receive all reports from all committees concerning evils, causes, and remedies. Ordered.

Ordered, the select committee shall sit in the Court of Wards presently, upon the rising of the House. The committee to have power to send for[18] Sir William Monson, now at Chelsea, and to Sir William Howard.

The grand committee for evils, etc., to meet at 3 of the clock. Ordered. And then the House to sit when that committee ready.

My Lord Carey appointed also to attend the committee.[19]

16. *Rot. Parl*, 5 H. IV, no. 16. The King's confessor, L'Abbé de Dore, and three others were removed.

17. *at 1 of the clock this afternoon* is crossed out in the MS and *presently* is inserted. Glanville is reporting from the committee of twelve appointed on 21 April to consider the business concerning the Duke of Buckingham. The MPs listed were wanted to testify on aspects of the charges against the Duke. For Glanville's report on the testimony of the MPs, see HofC, 2 May, OB.

18. *any of the members* is crossed out in the MS following *for*.

19. For Glanville's report on Carey's testimony, see HofC, 2 May, OB.

[p. 30]

Sabbati, 22 Aprilis, 2 Caroli Regis
Post meridiem

Mr. Wandesford reports the head concerning the buying and selling of places of judicature, 3 particulars: 1, the Duke buying the wardenship of the 5 Ports of the Lord Zouche; 2, the mastership of the Wards; 3, the selling of the Lord Treasurership to the Lord Mandeville.[20] The 1st and last were, by several questions, fixed upon the Duke.

He further reports the intercepting, unnecessary exhausting, and misemploying of the King's treasure.[21]

A public issue proved by record, of £71,522. A release, 16 *Jac.*, for the support of the Duke's dignity, of divers sums by him received. The like, 20 *Jac.*

A grant to the Duke of all the customs and subsidies of Ireland, for £6,000 per annum, for 10 years.[22]

£4,960 to the Earl of Anglesey for lands sold, which were granted by the King to Peart and Knollys, in trust for him.[23]

£2,000 remaining due for woods unsold: £5,000 remaining in wood, and £900 per annum in the forests of Blackmore and Pewsham, in Wilts, passed to the Earl of Anglesey.[24]

The manor of Norton[25] in Norfolk, passed to Lord Mandeville at the suit of the Earl of Anglesey.

York House, for which the King's lands exchanged.[26]

Many acres of wood stored with excellent timber in the Forest of Dean, granted 1 *Caroli Regis,* to Sir Edward Villiers.[27]

The manor of Clerkenwell, and divers other manors in divers other counties, part of the annexed lands passed, *24 Maii* last, to Lord Mandeville, in consideration of £12,500 for which a tally struck, but no money paid;[28] but went in recompense of the money Lord Mandeville paid for his treasurership, and his honor, and a new table at court, besides.

Chelsea House and lands, which by the committee, upon question, fixed upon that head, which concerns the misemployment of the King's treasure.

Upon question, the Duke to have notice given from the House of these things charged upon him by the House.

[CJ 849] Monday next, 10 clock, shall be the time for the Duke to make defense, if he shall please to make any. The notice to be given by Sir John Hippisley and Mr. Gifford.

Nothing to be delivered in writing, but the messengers to inform themselves by perusal of the Clerk's book, but to take no copies, but to give notice of all, as well of that of the East India Company,[29] as other; but may take notes, for their own memory, of the heads, but those notes not to be delivered by them to the Lord Admiral.

II. DIARY OF BULSTRODE WHITELOCKE, ESQ., DD. 12.21, CAMBRIDGE UNIVERSITY LIBRARY

[f. 152]

April 22

Mr. Malet. Whether an accusation grounded upon common fame or report be

20. See Sir John Eliot's first report to the committee of the whole on 21 April for examining the causes of causes. See also, HofL, 13 May, pp. 413–414; 8 June, pp. 569, 576–577.

21. See HofC, 25 March, n. 31 and see Eliot's second report to the committee of the whole on 21 April. See also, HofL, 15 May, pp. 452–457.

22. See HofL, 8 June, p. 583.

23. See HofC, 21 April, n. 20; HofL, 8 June, p. 584.

24. See HofL, 8 June, p. 584.

25. Printed edition: *Horton.*

26. See HofL, 8 June, p. 581.

27. See HofL, 8 June, p. 585.

28. See HofC, 21 April, n. 25.

29. Concerning the East India Company, see Christopher Wandesford's report from the committee of the whole, HofC, 20 April; and see also, HofL, 8 June, pp. 573–575.

to be received into this House.[30] Whether an accusation on this ground may be transferred to the Lords. I think it cannot for it will drive the defendant to a double defense to answer to the fame and to the charge, and this may inveigle the court in their judgment. Whosoever is accused here of any crime, if he justify himself he is instructed. 7 R. 2, an accusation of bribery against the Chancellor de la Pole was not proved by Cavendish.[31] He accused. Wherefore Cavendish was fined. And 17 R. 2, a complaint by Earl of Arundel against the Duke of Lancaster [f. 152v] which, not being proved, the Earl was forced to submission.[32]

If this were good ground, I doubt not but it would have had some influe[nce]. I cannot find that any temporal court did ever receive indictment upon common fame only. But in cases where the crime and punishment for it is capital, both accusation and further proceeding have been on common fame, as in 28 H. 6.[33] In cases of recusants it may be lawful, but I think it is not used anywhere but in the north parts. The recusant, if he will be conformable, is discharged of all penalty of the law; but in this case no submission nor conformity prevents the judgment of the court, therefore the cases different. To inform this court how to prevent an abuse that is growing, I think this allowable; but when the proceeding tends to judgment, not. I do not like the resemblance of our proceeding to a grand jury of the kingdom. I like the resemblance of this House's proceedings to the common laws in an action of account where are 2 judgments. If we make this a leading case in this House, it will be brought into inferior courts, which may much prejudice the/

Processu punitivo not, but *processu* [f. 153] *informativo* this proceeding is used, against which proceeding in spiritual courts you have lately passed a bill.[34] A petition or information in case of a grievance from one that is no member of this House ought to be exhibited in writing, themselves being present. Bishop of Durham's case here in 12 *Jac.*,[35] there could be no other information. That complaint rejected because it was grounded upon common fame only. This House on a second message only desired the Lords to examine whether it were done or not.

MR. WILDE. Bracton prescribes the order of proceeding in all inquiries, shows *ex fama oritur suspicio ex suspicione praesumptio*,[36] which presumption will in some cases admit a proof to the contrary. Another kind of presumption will admit no proof to the contrary. Fame must arise from men of the better sort. No contrariety can be found in any book of law to the inquiry upon common fame. 7 H. 8, 1, 2; 5 H. 7; 7 E. 4; 11 E.4, case touching the confederates of Fauconberg.[37]

MR. LITTLETON. The question is whether there may be a proceeding in this House upon common fame. I conceive it is. This House is only a house of presentation, information, or denunciation. And common fame is sufficient for accusation but not for condemnation. [f. 153v] Suspicion is not transferable. I hold common fame the general voice. 11 E. 4, common fame is more than the saying of any man living,[38] and therefore if one man's information be su/

Upon general fame a man may be arrested and imprisoned, but not abused by

30. See above, n. 1.
31. See above, n. 2.
32. See above, n. 3.
33. See above, n. 4.
34. Malet is probably referring to the bill concerning citations issuing out of ecclesiastical courts passed by the House on 18 April.
35. See above, n. 5.
36. See above, n. 6.
37. See above, nn. 7 and 8.
38. See above, n. 8.

speeches: 7 Eliz., Dyer.[39] By our bill we have not taken away common fame. Machiavelli in his Florentine history says that men have been condemned upon common fame,[40] but I hope I shall never see it so here. 3 precedents: 28 H. 6, Duke of Suffolk's case; 29 H. 6, Duke of Somerset's case; 12 *Jac.*, Bishop of Durham's case,[41] wherein they proceeded upon common fame, and if the parliament had not broken up I know the Lords would have branded him with infamy to all posterity.

MR. BROWNE. The question is, as I conceive, whether accusation by a member of this House in this House against a subject upon common fame be a parliamentary way. Calumniation is an aspersion which is intolerable and not fit, but accusations must be admitted. *Semi-plena probatio, quae fit ex*/

Common fame is allowed by civil law, ecclesiastical law, and common law of this land. This out of the House had been a defamation.

MR. WENTWORTH. 4 H. 8, c. 8; 20 E. 3; 34 E. 3; 3 E. 3, [*sic*] Westminster 1; [f. 154] 23 Eliz., *et* 1/[42]

A man that has spoken seditious words is excused if he can show that he heard it from another.

MR. SELDEN. The question is whether a formal accusation in a parliamentary proceeding by common fame may likewise be exhibited to the Lords on common fame. By reason of conveniency it may, or else great men's faults would never come to light. The faults of the gods could not be known till fame was born, and then they came to light. 6 Eliz.[43] The ancient course was when a man was in indictments, such a man was *inventus mortuus* and such a one *inventus* [*blank*] *ideo.* 14 R. 2, there was an appeal from parliament and when they heard the opinions of the common and civil lawyers they said we are to be ruled by the law of parliament.[44] 28 and 29 H. 6.[45] The Commons in a conference with the Lords said that there was a general rumor that the Duke of Suffolk had done some things amiss against the kingdom, but alleged no particulars but desired he might be put in prison; but the Lords on advice taken did not commit him. After the Commons said that the rumor and noise [was] that the King of France was ready to invade this kingdom and that it was by the Duke's help, whereupon presently he was committed. [*Blank*] R. 2, there was an/

[f. 154v] MR. ROLLE. That we may present unto the Lords upon common fame the accusations against any Lord. In the case 28 H. 6, the Lords/

Because the charge was general and might as well include treason or felony as misprision of treason or trespasses, they did not commit him, but yet received the accusation upon common fame. 5 H. 4, a complaint by the Commons to the Lords against the King's confessor, the Abbot of Dore, and 2 other of his servants, whereupon the Lords removed them from being about the King and the King said that if there were any about him who were grievous to the commonwealth/[46]

I conclude that common fame is a good ground to introduce a thing here and to transfer it to the Lords.

MR. SHERLAND. If the plaintiff have but *probabilem causam litigandi,* no court allows

39. See above, n. 9.
40. Cf. *The Discourses,* Chap. 7.
41. See above, nn. 4, 12, and 5, respectively.
42. *SR,* 4 H. VIII, c. 8 (case of Richard Strode); *SR,* 20 E. III; *SR,* 34 E. III, c. 1; *SR,* 23 Eliz. I, c. 2.
43. It is not clear to what case Selden refers.
44. We have not found the case.
45. See above, nn. 4 and 12.
46. See above, n. 16.

damages to the defendant. If in cases that concern the life of a particular person common fame is allowed, shall it not likewise in a case that concerns the life and soul of the commonwealth, which though we cannot call legal treason yet we may call it real treason.

[f. 155] MR. NOY. In all courts temporal a man is bound over by recognizance upon common fame and imprisoned in some cases.

Resolved on question, upon long debate, that common fame is a good ground of proceeding in this House, either to inquire upon here or to transmit the complaint to the King or to the Lords if the House find cause.

MR. GLANVILLE reports from the select committee of 12. That they, finding it necessary they should have the testimony and knowledge of some members of this House delivered to them, desire that they may be enjoined by the House to do it at the committee this afternoon,[47] and that the House this afternoon take full report of all the committees concerning this business and thereupon appoint a time when the Duke may be heard.

The [House] requires the presence of those men at the committee and orders to have the reports.

[Committee of the Whole House]

Mr. Wandesford takes the chair.

Resolved that the particulars of the land passed and monies—mentioned by Sir John Eliot's reports yesterday[48]—to the Duke of Buckingham and Lord Anglesey shall be fixed to the head of intercepting, unnecessary exhausting, and misemploying of the King's revenues by Lord Duke of Buckingham.

Speaker takes his chair.

MR. WANDESFORD reports the resolutions of the committee concerning sale of places of judicature and exhausting, intercepting, and unnecessary employing of the King's revenues by the Lord Duke of Buckingham.

[f. 155v] Resolved that the Lord Admiral shall have knowledge given him from the House of those things which he is charged with at our H[ouse]. And Monday morning at 10 a clock appointed to be the time for him to answer if he please.

The messengers are Sir John Hippisley and Mr. Gifford. And they have liberty, for their better information, to see the Clerk's book and take notes for their memories.

Mr. Vice Chamberlain, SIR DUDLEY CARLETON, said that the Senate of Venice never delivers anything out in writing,[49] but if any desire to have it more perfectly than by speech only, the Secretary used to read it to him as often as he will and he takes what notes he will himself in writing for the help of his memory.

47. *Mr. Secr. Co.* is crossed out in the MS following *afternoon*. For the names of the members called to testify, see Glanville's report in the CJ, above, and n. 19.

48. See above, nn. 20 and 21.

49. *writing* is interlined above *paper* in the MS. Carleton had been English ambassador to Venice from 1610 to 1615. *DNB*.

Order of Business Monday, 24 April 1626

John Glanville: desires direction of the House how the committee of 12 for considering the business concerning the **Duke of Buckingham** shall proceed with regard to keeping their examinations private [*see below*]	53, 55, *21/4
Sir Clement Throckmorton	55
Sir Walter Erle	55
Orders concerning examinations by the committee of 12 for considering the business concerning the Duke of Buckingham	53, 54, 55
Sir Robert Pye	54
John Glanville	54
Resolved: MPs may not withdraw from the House during the forthcoming division	53
Upon a division: resolved that the committee of 12 for considering the business concerning the Duke of Buckingham may examine any newly propounded matter concerning the Duke	53, 54, 56
Ordered: no MP other than the committee members to be present at the above committee except during the examinations	53, 55, 56
Report of the Duke of Buckingham's answer to the message giving him notice of the charges against him (Emanuel Gifford)	53, 55, 56, 58, *22/4
Ordered: the Speaker to come to the House by 5 o'clock this afternoon	54
Resolutions in the House on the Duke of **Buckingham** as the **cause of the evils**	54, 55, 56, *24/2
[*Afternoon*]	
Committee of 12 for considering the business concerning the **Duke of Buckingham** [*see above*]: meets for examination of physicians concerning the **death of James I**	*25/4; 26/4; 27/4; 28/4
Dr. Alexander Ramsey testifies	57
Dr. Henry Atkins testifies	57
The Speaker resumes the chair	54
Report from the committee of 12 for considering the business concerning the Duke of Buckingham (Christopher Wandesford): that the committee will not be ready to report this day	54

MONDAY, 24 APRIL 1626

I. JOURNAL OF THE HOUSE OF COMMONS

[**CJ 849;** p. 31]
Lunae, 24 Aprilis, 2 Caroli Regis

MR. GLANVILLE moves from the select committee of 12, that they understand some exceptions taken by some members of this House against their keeping their examinations private without admitting some other members thereof.

That some great matters of weight more now propounded which,[1] if they shall be publicly now examined, may, by the notifying thereof, hinder the service and ends of the House. Desires the direction of the House in it.

Much dispute whether the members of the House not of a select committee may come to the select committee.

Upon question, the 12 already chosen to send for any witnesses they shall think [fit], without acquainting any therewith, to examine them; but that, at the examination, any member of the House may be present. And this committee has also power to send for any books or writings which they shall think fit. And that, if any of the witnesses shall be sick, or hindered by other impediment, that they cannot come to them, this select committee may appoint three of themselves or more which they will, to repair unto them to examine them; and then they to report those examinations to the select committee of 12, at which any other member of the House may be present. And those examinations to be set down in writing, with the witness's hand to it, or mark if he cannot write, if he will put his hand to it.

Much debate whether this select committee shall examine any new matter concerning the Duke not heretofore propounded in the House or at the grand committee.

Upon the question, this select committee to have power from the House to consider and examine of any new matter to be propounded to them concerning the Duke of Buckingham, though not heretofore propounded in the House or at the grand committee; with like power as aforesaid. The question being 2 put, the voice doubtful; [the] House divided. The yea went out.

Some, desiring they might go into the Committee Chamber as having given no voice, resolved by the House they might not; but that all present at the debate.[2]

Tellers for the yea:	Sir Francis Barrington
	Sir Thomas Hoby
Tellers for the no:	Sir William Strode
	Sir Robert Crane

With the yea: 228
With the no: 168
Difference: [60]

MR. GIFFORD reported the Duke's answer to the message sent by him and Sir John Hippisley, upon Saturday last.[3]

Ordered, that no member of the House shall be present at the debate, disposition, or penning of the business by the select committee; but only to be present at the examination, and that without interposition.

That they acquainting the Duke with the message, the Duke answered, he could not give answer before he had acquainted the Lords with it. That, having so done, he this forenoon asked leave of the Lords, who

1. See the afternoon meeting of this committee, below, where the examination of physicians took place regarding the application of a plaster to James I preceding his death.

2. Regarding members not withdrawing from the House during the putting of questions and divisions, see Hatsell, *Precedents,* II, 194–196.

3. The Clerk may have placed this entry incorrectly in the Journal. Whitelocke and Lowther, below, indicate that the following order concerning presence at the committee belongs before Gifford's report.

would by no means consent. And his answer being dictated, and put into writing, which he read.[4]

[p. 32] Mr. Speaker to come to the House by 5 clock this afternoon.

1. Upon question,[5] the Lord Admiral the cause that the Narrow Seas and our coasts have not been sufficiently guarded since the dissolution of the last treaties with Spain.

2. Resolved upon question, the plurality of the offices of Lord Admiral, Warden of the 5 Ports, and Master of the Horse, and other offices in the Duke's person, are to be affixed a cause of the diminution of the honor and strength of the kingdom.

3. Upon question, the particular concerning the Lord Robartes buying his honor to be an instance to be affixed upon the person of the Duke under the head of the sale of honor.

4. Upon question, the Lord of Buckingham the cause of conferring honors upon such for the maintenance of whom the King's revenue is exhausted.

5. Upon question, the Duke of Buckingham the cause of the delivery of our ships into the hands of the French, which were employed against Rochelle.

6. The extorting money from the East India Company, resolved upon question before, *Jovis, 20 Aprilis* last.

7. Upon question, the 2 particular instances of the Duke's buying of the Wardenship of the 5 Ports, and of the selling of the place of the Treasurership to the Lord of Manchester, are to be affixed to the person of the Duke, under the head of sale of great offices and places of judicature.

8. Upon question, the Duke of Buckingham a cause of the intercepting, unnecessary exhausting, and misemploying of the King's revenue.

Lunae, 24 Aprilis, 2 Caroli Regis
Post meridiem

Mr. Speaker being come and set, the select committee, by MR. WANDESFORD, informed that the select committee should not be ready to report anything unto them this night; and thereupon the House arose.

II. DIARY OF BULSTRODE WHITELOCKE, ESQ., DD 12.21, CAMBRIDGE UNIVERSITY LIBRARY

[f. 155v]

April 24

The select committee of 12 have power to send for any persons, books, etc., as shall be convenient for the business committed to them.

SIR ROBERT PYE. That the select committee of 12 examined what Sir James Whitelocke gave for his place of Chester to the Lord Duke.[6]

[f. 156] MR. GLANVILLE. That it is true such a thing was informed at the committee, but there was no color nor ground of proof for it.

By question and division, the ayes 228, the noes 168, the select committee have power from the House to consider and examine not only such matter as has been already propounded at the House or committees, but any new matter that may concern the Duke of Buckingham not here-

4. Copies of the Duke's answer, reported by Emanuel Gifford, circulated as "separates", see below, n. 26. The full answer from BL Add. 22, 474, is printed below, at the end of this day's proceedings. Concerning the Lords' refusal to give Buckingham leave to answer the charges, see HofL, 24 April, OB.

5. The following points had all been earlier considered and resolved in the committee of the whole on the evils, causes, and remedies: the first four on 24 March; the fifth, seventh, and eighth on 21 and 22 April; and the sixth on 18 April in the committee of the whole House and on 20 April in the House itself.

6. Sir James Whitelocke, father of Bulstrode, had been appointed to the chief justiceship of Chester in 1620.

tofore propounded, with like power as before ordered.

None shall be present nor interpose at that committee but only when they [are] in examination.

MR. GIFFORD. That he and Sir John Hipsisley, according to the order of the House,[7] told the Duke of the appointment of the House to them to give the Duke notice of the charge against him here and that if it pleased him he might this day answer. The Duke said it was but a very short time and prayed us to come to him this morning. That after he had moved the Lords he would give us his answer, which is/[8]

That Lords would by no means, as things now stand, give him leave to answer, but that it is not he that does refuse to answer.

[f. 156v] Resolved by the House,[9] that the Lord Admiral is the cause that the Narrow Seas and our coast have not been sufficiently guarded since the dissolution of the treaties with Spain.

Resolved by the House, that the plurality of offices of Lord Admiral, Warden of the Cinque Ports, and other offices [in the] Lord Duke's hand, is to be fixed upon his person as a cause of the diminution of the honor/

That the plurality of offices of Lord Ward/

That the particular of Lord Robartes's buying of his honor is an instance to be fixed upon the Duke under the head of sale of honor.

Resolved that the Duke is a cause of conferring of honor upon such for the maintenance of whom the King's revenues are exhausted.

Resolved that the Duke of Buckingham was the cause of the delivery of the ships into the hands of the French, which were employed against Rochelle.

Resolved that the buying of the place of Warden of the Cinque Ports by Lord Admiral and of the office of Treasurership by the Lord Manchester are to be fixed upon the person of the Duke of Buckingham under the head of the sale of offices of judicature.

Resolved, upon the particulars before alleged, that the Lord Admiral is a cause of the intercepting, exhausting, and unnecessary employing of the King's revenues.

III. DIARY OF JOHN LOWTHER, ESQ., D/LONS/L, CUMBERLAND AND WESTMORLAND RECORD OFFICE[10]

[f. 1]

24 Aprilis 1626

Select committee examining divers privately, and hearing the House or some disliked, GLANVILLE in the chair, desired the opinion of the House how to proceed; signifies also new matter not fit to be published to all, lest discovery of persons and matter might prejudice the cause.[11]

SIR CLEMENT THROCKMORTON showed the dislike of the proceeding privately; estranging the members unparallel[ed].

SIR WALTER ERLE does defend it by precedent of Merchant Adventurers, but it was by order.[12] Gave reason enforced against.

7. I.e., the order of 22 April, see OB. Concerning Gifford's report, see above, n. 4.

8. For the Duke's answer, see BL Add. 22,474, below.

9. See above, n. 5.

10. Several folios at the beginning of this diary are so frayed and torn on the outside margins that the folio numbers and some letters and words are missing or obliterated. See the description of the manuscript in the Introduction, volume I, p. 10. In cases where the missing letters are self-evident, we have included them within brackets in the text.

11. See above, n. 1.

12. Erle is apparently referring to the case of the select committee appointed on 8 April 1624 to view and search privately the books of accounts of the Merchant Adventurers. See *CJ*, I, 758; and see the records in the 1624 diaries [YCPH transcripts] of Pym (Finch-Hatton MS 50, f. 54v), Holles (Harl. 6383, f. 125–125v), and Nicholas (SP 14/166, ff. 123v–124).

Ordered, 3 of the select committees to take examination of an[y] if sick and to return it in writing, and any to be present at select committee. To reduce the old matter into form, but they have said it is new matter.

Upon the question whether select committee may bring in new matter propounded to them concerning the Duke though neither House directed heads, House divided. 60 odd that they may.[13] Yet many and most and better reasons to the contrary for the prejudice that may follow; for so may a select committee take what they will, refuse what they will, which only the House should do. And so shall we be guided by a few who, prepared, may blind our reason, we strangers. Which debated first and considered at committee could not be, but should be parliamentarily. A dangerous plot for a favorite parliament, now the contrary.

[f. 1v] Ordered, at select committee none to interpose in the ordering of the matter or penning, but all be present at examination at will.

MR. GIFFORD reports the leave given and notice to the Duke by notes, and said he might send for copies.[14] The Duke took it well; said after Lords sat he would give answer, which he did and gave all thanks for this favor since he desired nothing more than to satisfy us. That he gave thanks for the notice and though it might prevent perhaps our transmission to the Lords, which he considered how grievous it was the Lords would not give leave. But he pressed it not, though necessary, because the King's business and the occasions did so press him that it might spend time to his prejudice which he himself had rather endure. Knows his hazard to be reported to the Lords yet will not he, while he has any favor, forbear to do the best offices that he can for this House, nor he will not hinder the King's business. Shows his zeal to his country declared upon the dissolution of the treaties, and how hazarded King's favor in that for to [do] good to his country and to satisfy this House howsoever now thought.

[f. 2] 1. Duke no author of recusancy. As yet unresolv[ed].[15]

2. Resolved at committee he, Duke, cause of loss of [*illegible*] in not well guarding since treaty dissolved; and now in the House resolved.

3. Plurality of offices in one hand to be affixed on him. Resolved in him as before in the House.

4. That Duke is affixed to the sale of honors to Lord Robartes.

5. King's revenue to maintain honors instanced in his mother, two brothers, brother-in-law, and niece. Resolved, the Duke a cause of bestowing honors of those for whose maintenance King's revenue exhau[sted].

8. That Duke cause of ships delivered to French employed against Rochelle.

9. Resolved in the House, the £10 M of India Company an undue exaction by Duke.

7. Sale of judicature: Cinque Ports, Treasurership, affixed on him by the question.

6. Intercepting, exhausting, misemploying of King's revenue. Chelsea House agreed a cause, and all the other lands put upon Duke also.

13. I.e., the vote was carried by sixty; see the division figures in CJ and Whitelocke, above.

14. See above, nn. 4 and 7.

15. On 24 March following debate over whether the Duke was the cause of the increase and countenancing of popery, the committee of the whole resolved not to put the question. See HofC, 24 March, OB.

[*Afternoon*]

[f. 2v] Doctor Ramsey.[16]

There was neither eating, drinking, etc., but by consultation. This they knew not. Every consultation was set down under their hands. He knows not who made it,[17] but the general voice was it was made in the Duke's chamber. Divers physicians by when it was applied by Hay,[18] none contradicting but about an hour after he did. Laid on at 4 of clock to wrists; side, eight; continued till midnight; and after he declared his dislike to Gibb[19] and [*illegible*] it was taken off because King swooned. The next night he asked Chambers[20] and him what made him so evil last night. They gave natural causes as cold, as height of disease. But he said no, it was that he had from the Duke of B[uckingham]. But whether he meant the plaster or potion, he knew not. But the Duke brought him a potion twice and gave it at the beginning of his fit. But the third time King refused. [f. 3] An hour or half between the potions and so the third time, then he put it away with his hand.

Doctor Moore[21] showed a bill of the receipt. The symptoms that followed was panting, raving, swooning, uncertain beating of pulse. He says the ingredients of the bill were by them subscribed to be good upon question *loco et tempore*. Doctor Moore brought the bill after to be subscribed from the Duke, but whether they were in or not we know not. He thinks it was intended they should subscribe it was the same drink, but he knew nothing to induce his intendment. *All physicians did subscribe alike.*[22] The effects were all one of drink or plaster. Subscription required Sunday or Monday, but what the reason he was required to subscribe he knows not. Sir William Paddy[23] made the bill of it. He does not know that the Duke ever caused other physic to be minist[ered].

Doctor Atkins.[24] Few of them acquainted with it before, but they were told after. But they did not know what was in it, drink nor plaster, before applied. He was told it was treacle done by Duke's mother. They did nothing but by general conference entered and written. They directed a plaster, but to King's apothecary. If it was treacle, would do no hurt. His fever did grow upon him worse and worse until he died. But he was better before, and they conceived the disease to be declining until that this was offered in the prohibited time. They rather

16. A third of the folio has been left blank in the MS following *Ramsey*. Alexander Ramsey was a Scottish physician who was later physician to Charles I but who was said to have been "discourted" and imprisoned in his house as a result of some of his testimony before this committee. See the letter of 28 April to Joseph Mead, App., II, E; and see *CSPV 1625–1626*, p. 416, and Edward Kirton's remark in the House on 28 April, below.

17. I.e., the plaster applied to James I shortly before his death. On this matter, see the final charge in the articles of impeachment against the Duke of Buckingham, HofL, 15 May, pp. 472–473, and 8 June, pp. 578–579.

18. Archibald Hay, one of the King's surgeons. *APC 1625–1626*, p. 344. For Hay's testimony, see HofC, 25 April, and n. 23.

19. Henry Gibb, Gentleman of the Bedchamber. See HMC, *Marr and Kellie MSS, Supplementary Report*, p. 226.

20. I.e., James Chambers, physician to both James and Charles. See *CSPD 1625–1626*, p. 59. For Chambers's testimony, see HofC, 25 April, OB.

21. I.e., John Moore who, though not one of the King's sworn physicians, attended James during his final illness. Moore, well known to be a Catholic, was returned as such by the College of Physicians to parliamentary commissioners on 29 March 1626. Munk, *Roll of the Royal College of Physicians*, I, 174–175. He may have been Doctor to the Duke's wife, Katherine, Duchess of Buckingham. See SP 16/4:140.

22. The italicized words are underlined in the MS.

23. Paddy had been appointed physician to James I in 1603. *DNB*.

24. Henry Atkins, several times the president of the College of Physicians, was a physician-in-ordinary to James I and Charles I. Rymer, *Foedera*, VIII, pt. 2, p. 24; *CSPD 1603-1610*, p. 151; *DNB*.

disliked, but would say nothing lest might offend the Duke and the King.

[f. 3v] Does not know that Duke did know the prohibited hours. Chambers and Ramsey and Craig[25] there. The bill of the ingred[ients] was shown after by Doctor Moore from Duke and justified in due time and place to be successful, but whether made of those particulars he knows not. The subscription was only of the Duke. They think this drink not good in this time. Doctor Moore no sworn physician to his knowledge, nor told him that he made it. He knows not the effects. He was dry at his open; his humors in good temper.

IV. MR. GIFFORD'S ANSWER FROM THE DUKE OF BUCKINGHAM TO THE HOUSE OF COMMONS, ADD. 22,474, pp. 76-78, BRITISH LIBRARY[26]

This day his Grace gave us answer, after he had moved the Lords, that we should with great care make all due acknowledgment of your respect and favor in giving him this notice. Which though it do invite him to render unto you such satisfaction that he hopes might acquit and restore him to your good opinions and might prevent your proceedings, which otherwise by a parliamentary course are like to follow; yet according to his duty, having moved the Lords of the Upper House (upon your notice given him), they would by no means as things now stand give him leave to answer. Which he pressed, he said, with less earnestness in regard that he is not ignorant that you are presently to enter into consideration of his Majesty's late message[27] and that by any delay thereby your own purposes will be in some sort disappointed, and the affairs of Christendom much prejudiced. And for that upon a resolution you have deferred and respited that service until those things depending against him before you be determined,[28] he out of fear that his necessary defense would spin out a great deal of time, which is now precious, he is the willinger to obey their Lordships, that so you might hasten, without obstacle or interruption given by him, to keep day with his Majesty. And this he does, as he conceives, to his own infinite prejudice, knowing how heavy and grievous it is to be transmitted as a grievance by the votes of this House. But he does profess that he does rather choose to hazard the sacrifice of his fortune, reputation, and himself than to be the least occasion of anything that may work disaffection or misunderstanding between the King and his people. And it is his protestation that whatsoever interpretation is made of his actions, his endeavors shall be, as long as he has any favor with his gracious Master, to take all opportunity of doing good offices to this honorable House and of endeavoring all he can be able for the safety of the state and general good of the commonwealth. And this, he says, you may the easier believe, because the King can witness that he hazarded in his father's time the loss of the best affection of the best Master to obtain for them their desires. In this zeal he was desirous to have appeared unto you ever since the beginning of this parliament; in this zeal he does now present himself unto you. But to return to the main point, lest we should be mistaken, he gave us a caveat to remember you, in plain words, that it is not he that does refuse to answer, but their Lordships commanded

25. John Craig, Jr. (d. 1655), was first physician to James I and physician in ordinary to Charles I for life. *CSPD 1611–1618*, pp. 132, 205. *DNB*, *sub* John Craig (d. 1620). See also, HofC, 26 April, n. 18.

26. A copy of this report of Buckingham's answer, is also included, with occasional variations, in Lansd. 491 (ff. 175v–176). Copies of a different answer, possibly a proposed draft, are included in SP 16/25:30 and 60, erroneously calendared (*CSPD 1625–1626*, p. 318) as Gifford's report of this day.

27. I.e., the message of 20 April. See OB.

28. See the order, see 20 April, OB.

him not to answer, which he cheerfully obeyed in respect of his fidelity to prefer the universal weal before his own particular. And in the meantime he desires the charitable opinion of this honorable House until he be so convinced as he shall appear not to be worthy of it, which his own innocency makes him confident that he shall not.

Order of Business Tuesday, 25 April 1626

TUESDAY, 25 APRIL 1626

I. JOURNAL OF THE HOUSE OF COMMONS

[**CJ 849;** p. 32]
Martis, 25 Aprilis, 2 Caroli Regis

A motion made against leaving of gloves, etc., for keeping of places.

SIR BENJAMIN RUDYARD moves the consideration of supply, and therein the fall of subsidies.[1] Rents generally improving since 1 Eliz., only that to the King falls; only the nobility and clergy hold.[2] One cause, the multiplicity of commissioners who are the assessors of themselves. Certificates.[3] Moves the search of former schedules of subsidy. An increase of the rate of 4s. a pound for lands.[4] An increase of the number of subsidies. Erecting some forts, maintaining some ships for the defense of the kingdom, etc., at the country's charges.

SIR GEORGE MORE. To help the fall of subsidies: to give 1 subsidy and 1 15een more, payable after these 3 now agreed upon.[5]

MR. WANDESFORD moves for a grand committee to consider hereof.

Ordered, presently to consider of supply to his Majesty.

II. DIARY OF BULSTRODE WHITELOCKE, ESQ., DD. 12.21, CAMBRIDGE UNIVERSITY LIBRARY

[f. 157]

April 25

SIR BENJAMIN RUDYARD. Since Queen Elizabeth's reign the rents of every man's lands have risen and increased, but the subsidies have fallen.[6] The poorest minister pays more than the gentlemen ratably.[7] The number of commissioners which are commonly gentlemen who are their own assessors, and the abuse of certificates bring subsidies low. The gift we have given his Majesty, we ought to see that it shrink not. We are to consider how graciously the King has given us leaves to go on in our gr/

That we consider how by search and view of Exchequer rolls [*blank*]. We may advance the subsidy books by raising the 4s. in the pound according to precedents.[8] If we add by giving of more subsidies or other ways/

The giving his Majesty a real satisfaction will be for our good as much as his. Let us so carry ourselves that we may make[9] the parliament the King's favorite.

SIR GEORGE MORE. We may compare the kingdom to a pasture overlaid. Our rents are fallen. Almost a 4th or 3rd part is taken away by certificates. This that we have given is much too short.[10] If we give another subsidy and 15, or as you shall think fit, to be levied after the year, I think it would do well.

[f. 157v] MR. WANDESFORD. We have given already, and therefore there ought to be great reason showed to invite us to give any more so soon. Moves we may resolve ourselves into a grand committee for this business.

Ordered accordingly.

[*Committee for the Whole House*]

Mr. Littleton takes the chair.

1. Concerning the fall in the value of lay subsidies, see Dietz, *Public Finance,* pp. 382–393.

2. Regarding the value of clerical subsidies, see Dietz, *Public Finance,* pp. 394–396.

3. I.e., the misuse of certificates by the subsidy commissioners. See *SR,* 21 Jac. I, c. 33.

4. Rudyard is suggesting an increase in the rate assessed for land above 4s. in the pound that had been the standard rate in preceding subsidy acts.

5. I.e., the three subsidies resolved on 27 March to be granted to the King.

6. See above, n. 1.

7. See above, n. 2.

8. See above, n. 4.

9. MS: *may.*

10. See above, n. 5.

Mr. Vice Chamberlain. I hold it very necessary that none that speaks should say anything but what is to the point. That no man should in this business hold us with long harangues. The nature of a committee is to admit interlocutions, but instead of interlocutions not contentions. His Majesty rested very well satisfied with what we said. He rather expected we should think of his necessities. I could say much to make it appear that the 3 subsidies and 3 15[s] come very short of the present necessities. That we should think how to augment the supply by the proportion and by the number, by the number first.

Mr. Goodwin. That we should in a parliamentary way think of supplying and no otherwise.

Mr. Strode. That we are to consider of 3 things: 1, the King's necessities; 2, how he came into these necessities; 3, how we shall relieve him in his necessities. For the last, moves we may first set down the time when the supply shall be paid and then the proportion.

[f. 158] Mr. Clarke.[11] It is a true saying, the subjects are very poor. The writ *habeas corpus* runs sometimes too fast and sometimes too slow. Hearken to the cry of extortion and exaction as well in courts spiritual as temporal. The fees of the Pipe are advance[d] to a pound for a shilling in the ancient table.[12] The officers in all courts in Westminster are as bad. As there must be a present supply, so there must be a present redress of grievances. May not supply and grievances go hand in hand together as well as subsidies and privy seals? As the case stands with the subjects, we cannot now give any further supply now. That we should really engage ourselves to the King to give an ample supply in the next session and that we may meet for it long before the end of the payment of these already agreed on.

Sir Nicholas Saunders. There must be provided not only a present supply but a continuing support. This present supply is not to be levied by subsidies and 15[s], but some other course is to be thought on. I will propose that which shall be both honorable and profitable to his Majesty and pleasing and beneficial to the people: that we should desire the Lords to assist us in petitioning to the King for reviving the contract for the taking away the Court of Wards and for composition for the provisions.[13]

[f. 158v] Sir John Stradling. That we should divide the business and 1st consider whether we shall give more or not, 2nd what we shall give, and 3rd when.

Mr. Browne. It is not fit the number of subsidies should be augmented. That the proportion of the subsidies should be augmented I think may be well done; but that the poor men be exempted, that £5 men may pay as they now do, and that those above £5 may be doubled and pay 8s. in the pound.

Mr. Meautys. Nothing more hinders the success of great actions than when time for action is spent in consultation. The way of counterpoising the wants of the King is commonly by telling the wants of the kingdom. This counterplea is both displeasing to the King and to almighty God, from whose hand we now receive as much bless-

11. James or William Clarke or Henry Clerke; see the list of Members, App., I, A.

12. Concerning increased fees (and abuses) in the Pipe Office, see Aylmer, *King's Servants*, pp. 188, 191–194.

13. I.e., the Great Contract. Concerning the contract proposed in 1610 that included provision for the crown to surrender its rights of wardship and purveyance with compensation for the lost revenue, see Dietz, *Public Finance*, pp. 133–142, and *Proceedings in Parliament 1610*, I, Index, *sub* contract.

ing as ever this land did. Wishes we may go to the question for 2 subsidies and 2 15[s] more.

Mr. Crew. I think we are all resolved that we shall make an addition to the supply. That a select committee may consider of the propositions here made and of any other for the supplying of the King.

Sir James Perrot. That the unequal rating of subsidies is as great a grievance as the paying of them.

Sir Richard Grosvenor. 5 H. 4, the parliament gave so great a tax that they would let no record be of it nor any precedent to posterity.[14] Moves we may first resolve to give in an unparliamentary way.

Sir Dudley Digges. It is fit the court should know that the people is poor. And he that says otherwise, it is fit he should be cast out of [f. 159] the court. It is true the subsidies do fall. One of the true grounds thereof is multiplying of subsidies. That we should examine the bottom of this mischief.

Mr. Meautys desires that Sir Richard Grosvenor may explain himself for some which he said.

The House will admit no more reply.

Mr. Kirton. I think we have given enough now for the present occasions. For the navy, which has brought us nothing but dishonor and went out against our wills, I see no reason for us to give anything for the discharge thereof.

Chancellor Exchequer. His Majesty told us in his message that unless within 4 or 5 days, etc./[15]

Actions are in order after counsels but in effect before. If the time would permit it, the proposition of raising the subsidies were good. There cannot be a perfect and right understanding between the King and people unless we determine of something now to answer the King.

Mr. Coryton. I think we should give more.

Mr. Wandesford. That we may put it to the question that we will add to the supply already given.

Mr. Glanville. That we should not inform of the poverty of the people anywhere but within these walls.

Resolved upon question, to augment and enlarge the supply[16] already intended[17] to be made unto his Majesty in this session.[18]

[f. 159v]

Pomeridiem

At the committee select of 12 for preparing the business concerning the Duke of Buckingham, Mr. Glanville being in the chair and the committee in the House.

Doctor Beton,[19] brought in and examined, says that he was a sworn physician to King James and waited on him in the most part of the time of his last sickness. That some plasters and potions were applied unto him other than the [*blank*] directed, as

14. Concerning the subsidy grant and the order for burning all record of it by the parliament of 5 H. IV, see Cobbett, *Parl. Hist.*, I, 294; and Thomas Walsingham, *Historia Anglica* [*Chronica et Annales*], ed. by H. T. Riley (London, 1866), p. 381.

15. I.e., the King's message delivered to the House by the Chancellor of the Exchequer on 20 April.

16. *supply* is interlined above *gift* in the MS.

17. *resolved* is crossed out in the MS and *intended* is inserted. Concerning the earlier resolution on subsidies, see above, n. 5.

18. Following this corrected version the entire resolution is rewritten in the MS. Between the corrected version and the fair copy *Mr. Spencer* has been crossed out. The Lowther diary, below, suggests that Sir Edward Spencer spoke at this point.

19. I.e., David Beton had been appointed physician-in-ordinary to Charles I on 24 March 1626. See Rymer, *Foedera*, VIII, pt. 1, pp. 230–231; and Munk, *Roll of the Royal College of Physicians*, I, 197. Testimony regarding the plaster was continued from the previous day, see above, 24 April.

he heard by relation of the King himself and the other physicians, which were a julep and plaster for the stomach. The King said only that such a thing was applied. That he was not present. Those things which were appointed by the King's physicians were agreed upon by all the sworn physicians. That sundry times before he heard the Duke tell the King that he had used such a plaster which had done him much good. That they had a note after what were the ingredients of the plaster, but by sight of this plaster could not tell. That before that plaster applied the disease was somewhat declined and the fits lesser when he left him, which was some 6 days before he died. That they gave no directions for this plaster. That they knew not the ingredients of the plaster till after the King's death. That they set their censure to the note brought to them. Their subscription either Sir William Paddy or Doctor Moore has.[20] That precisely they could not know whether [f. 160] the ingredients of the plaster were the same which were mentioned in the bill. That Doctor Moore joined with them a little before the plaster applied, but thinks he was no sworn physician to the King. That he knows not who appointed him to join with them. That the King wished them to consult with Doctor Moore. He cannot tell whether Doctor Moore's hand were to the directions set down by them nor who made the plaster or julep. That when he came back to the King he found his fever more violent than before, but no symptoms other than before. That he heard not the King say that this plaster had done him hurt. The smell of it was like to some treacle composition. That he saw not the julep. That he would not have advised this plaster to have been applied, but thinks there was no great inconveniency in it.

Doctor Chambers,[21] brought in and examined, says that he was one of King James his sworn physicians. That there was a plaster, as he heard, laid to the King's side without their directions about the 5th fit of his disease, about a fortnight before his death. That the plaster was taken away and after that the King had better days. He heard that it was made of mithridate and had done good to my Lord Duke and others, and that it was applied by the King's surgeon. That on the Monday the King was pretty well, but on Tuesday very ill again. In the interim the plaster, as he heard, was applied again. That the King said to him that the warm drink which they made him to take and which he naturally abhorred did roast him [f. 160v] and was against his heart, but knows not who particularly was named. That to his memory he heard not the King speak of the plaster. That he set his hand to no paper.

Doctor Harvey.[22] That there was a plaster applied to the King's side twice. At the first application he was rather worse than better. 2nd application was about Monday before he died, in the afternoon about the beginning of his fit. The King himself was desirous to have it as commended by the Duke. That neither he nor some other of the physicians could give assent unto it, not knowing the ingredients; but the King calling for it they thought not necessary to oppose it, not thinking there could come any great hurt of it, being externally to be applied and to work while they stood by. And they pulled it off as soon as the King came to his hot fit. Mr. [*blank*],[23] the King's

20. Concerning Doctor John Moore and Sir William Paddy, see 24 April, nn. 21 and 23.

21. Regarding Dr. James Chambers, see HofC, 24 April, n. 20.

22. I.e., William Harvey, physician-in-ordinary to James I, later famous for his discoveries regarding the circulation of blood. *DNB*.

23. Archibald Hay was the King's surgeon who applied the plaster. See HofC, 24 April, n. 18.

surgeon, laid it on. Lord Duke prepared the julep, which the King drank of and commended. He knew not what it was, but the King called for it. And he knows of no advice of the physicians. That on Monday morning the King was as he used to be before his fit. That he much feared that that fit would be worse than any he had before, but told not this his conceit to the rest of the physicians.

III. DIARY OF JOHN LOWTHER, ESQ., D/LONS/L, CUMBERLAND AND WESTMORLAND RECORD OFFICE

[f. 4]

[25 April]

SIR BENJAMIN R[UDYARD] moves subsidies lessened in the gentry, not in nobility nor clergy, yet brought to half; whereas other men's lands are higher rented than of old. Therefore desires to improve the old ways. For a gentle[man] at £20 ennobled, £300. Therefore desires by Exchequer rolls to be augmented. And to maintain ports at country charge, and ships. Therefore desires we so proceed as to make the parliament his favorite. To exceed 4s. the pound.

SIR G. MORE agrees. Dislikes adding above 4s. Compares kingdom to a common pasture; care it be not overcharged. Sellers makes fall, buyers will not rise.

WANDESFORD desires a great committee as parliamentarily to proceed upon/

[*Committee of the Whole House*]

Littleton in the chair.

Vice Chamberlain. None to move unnecessaries nor long orations. Wherein interlocution, must avoid contention. Accounts his message. When we proposed supply all our debate truly reported. King satisfied; expected we think of necessities in time and proportion of aid. Now how to amend it; first in number, then in weight.

Strode, junior. The King's necessity though put on us, we did not agree to the 50 M£ a month abroad. Wherefore we did not bring it.

Clarke[24] speaks for dejected subjects. Grievances sound only in the ear, not redressed. *Habeas corpus* stops execution, precedency. Extortion in courts cry. Fees extraordinary in probate. Citation for fees. Exchequer fees advanced £1 in 1s., from 6s. 8d. to £8 6s. 8d.,[25] prescribe in 30 years so may these. [f. 4v] Offices in all courts [in] Westminster alike. Sheriffs sell their offices. Now applies as in a field too long for the day. These drones he would cast out the commonwealth, the home. He cites the hedgehog. May not subsidies and grievances go on as well as subsidies and privy seals? Now to give no more, but engage at next sessions and so from session to session while war continues.

Sir Nicholas Saunders. Would not have subsidy lest it be an annual revenue. Besides, cannot be maintained in this sort. Therefore proposes a help not new, honorable and profitable to King and pleasant to subject: Wards and purveyance to be taken at contract which King James gave way to.[26] This provides for future. Agreed to be £200,000 by year.

Browne. No more subsidies, but to augment them. Those under £5 to stand; above, doubled. Wards, etc., good if feasible; so resumption.

Meautys. Maturity of counsels and means good but both spend time which lost, they will not redeem. And though country's wants opposed to King's, he thinks now counterplea looks upon building, portions,

24. MS: *Cleark* or *Clerck*. See above, n. 11.
25. See above, n. 12.
26. See above, n. 13.

apparel, etc. Tells the tale of the goose roasted by sticks.[27] Proposes 2 s[ubsidies], 2 fifteens.

Crew. Agreed [to] supply more. A committee [of] 12.

Sir Richard Grosvenor. Give not [to] endanger commissioners as 12 H. 7 and H. 4 times when the gift so great.[28]

[f. 5] Digges. Country poor; who otherwise say, fit to be cast out of court. If add more subsidies they will spare themselves. Desires to advance the higher sort.

Kirton. Would not pay the dishonored navy. The rest to be considered of.

Chancellor Exchequer. If King not satisfied in 5 days, must go to new counsels.[29] Now time to resolve. Actions though after counsel, in power before. If time would suffer, to increase proportion of subsidies were good. Though no success, no cause to deny payment. He recites particular charge, fleet will take all this granted. Presses resolves of right understanding [between] King and people cannot be unless his holy [*illegible*] be taken hold of. Therefore desires first to resolve to give; next, how; and what, presently.

Wandesford. To resolve to give; tomorrow, what to give.

Glanville. Dare not blame counsels. Desires to know from us how to ground them. If burden be greater than that the kingdom can bear, will be amiss. Therefore would not have us talk of poverty to encourage enemies. Desires to resolve to give; after, consider what.

Sir E. Spencer has a motion but desires all to be brought in; to take the best.

Resolved to augment and enlarge the gift already intended to the King.

[*Afternoon*]

[f. 5v] Doctor Beton, a sworn physician.[30] Attended much. There was, as he heard, plasters and potions ministered without assent, as King told him. A julep given and a plaster to his stomach. Order given for their medicines by one consent for most part, not for this. He heard it acknowledged that Duke told King he had used such a plaster and it had done him good. He had a note given after of the ingredients, and he saw it but knows not what in it. Before the plaster given, the disease somewhat declined. He came to him 3 or four days ere he died. The note was sent to him after King's death, that day or next, to know whether the plaster or julep did hurt. It was set in a note Doctor Atkins had, but Sir William Paddy or Doctor Moore has it.[31] They conjectured by smell of plaster it was like the note. Doctor Moore joined in advice before the plaster, and was most part there. They saw the King talk with him and wished them to advise with him and approved their opinions to agree after. Wolfe has the note to which the hands are.[32] Who made them, he knows not. He found his fever more and yet no symptoms but before. A stopping of his breath by other causes. The fever increased. He smelled it. It was of treacle as the note showed. He saw no inconvenience in the plaster.

27. We have not identified the tale.

28. The subsidy granted in 12 H. VII (*SR*, 12 H. VIII, c. 13) precipitated a rebellion which began in Cornwall, spread north, and in Kent was led by James Touchet, Lord Audley, who was afterward executed for his part against the crown. See Cobbett, *Parl. Hist.*, I, 465, and Holinshed, *Chronicles*, III, 513–515. Concerning the subsidy in 5 H. IV, see above, n. 14.

29. See the King's message, 20 April, OB.

30. See above, n. 19.

31. Concerning Moore, Paddy, and Atkins, see HofC, 24 April, nn. 21, 23, and 24.

32. Apparently the apothecary Israel Wolfe who, in 1626, was renter warden of the Society of Apothecaries of London. H. Charles Cameron and E. Ashworth Underwood, *A History of the Worshipful Society of Apothecaries of London* (Oxford, 1963), I, 63.

Doctor Chambers,[33] a sworn physician, said there was a plaster when they were to purge, which they desired to be taken away when they purged about the fifth fit; it was above a fortnight ere he died. [f. 6] He heard no effect of it but murmured because they consented not. But he was little worse. We directed a plaster before. He heard this plaster given divers—Warwick, Carey, Duke—and had done good before. That Hay,[34] the King's surgeon, applied it as thinks, but he took it away. He was well the Saturday when he left, and on Monday ready to go abroad. To have fit that night; not well on Tuesday when he returned nor ever after. And Harvey that night with King told how the King was that night, and if had like could not [e]scape. The plaster he heard was applied in cold fit, taken away in hot. The night after Ramsey[35] and he watched. In the violence of it, King said he was far worse. He comforted him and said he abhorred that drink, yea a taste in it, though they prescribed it. They gave me warm drink that makes me burn and roast so; and would have given more, but he was cold. The drink prescribed was but a posset. But he said that whatever was said was written down and brought to the Council in the morning. The drink the Duke gave was a posset with gillyflowers he drank of. Resolved, a hot drink after cold, and to refrain, but not burned. He would say: will you murder me and slay me? What advised was under hand. Asked of the paper to certify, he was uncertain.

D[octor] Harvey.[36] A plaster applied to his side, thinks twice. First, his fit worse; secondly done in the afternoon at the beginning his fit. The King desired it; commended by Duke as good for him and Earl of Warwick. His opinion asked before done; he gave no opinion because ingredients not known. [f. 6v] He gave way to it, thinking it easy and could do no harm. He thought it not against his opinion nor consultation, and King desired it. It being external, to work while he by. And it was hot, and at his hot fit they took it off. Lister[37] present at the laying it on. The posset drink the Duke prepared. The King called for it, drank once or twice. Because it was commended, King desired it. Because the medicine Duke and Warwick had used it, King determined to take it. He knows no advice of doctors to take it. Sunday, King heavy; he got him to rise. Said better, but found heaviness at his heart. On Monday as in other fits, and he feared that fit would be worse because had less fit before, which he told physicians; his disease not mending. When that done, he first that spoke of King's danger before that fit twice and he was in fit before next consultation. Lister, Moore came, he thinks. Atkins, Lister opposed the posset, thinking King called for drink the night before. The ague in his opinion still increased. On Saturday at conference the physicians thought not the King was mending. The day the King died upon [*illegible*] Sir William Paddy brought the note and it was approved and might be used. Generally they disliked a plaster, but not this. [f. 7] They said the plaster was a secret of a man of Essex.[38] Hay laid it on. King liked it as appeared and experimented it; and King took divers things, whether they would not, undervaluing physicians. He commended the posset.

33. Regarding Chambers, see HofC, 24 April, n. 20.

34. Regarding Hay, see HofC, 24 April, n. 18.

25. Regarding Ramsey, see HofC, 24 April, n. 16.

36. William Harvey. See above, n. 22.

37. I.e., Matthew Lister, physician-in-ordinary to Charles I. Munk, *Roll of the Royal College of Physicians,* I, 123. For Lister's testimony, see below.

38. The man is identified as Dr. John Remington of Dunmow, Essex, by Thomas Fuller (*Church History,* V, 568) and William Sanderson (*A Complete History of the Lives and Reigns of Mary, Queen of Scotland, and her Son and Successor, James. . . .* [London, 1661] p. 591).

D[octor] Lister.[39] Heard and saw a plaster applied. Thinks it was of L. mithridate, as said; he smelled it and it seemed so. He was on Sunday with the King; contrary to Harvey he was not present when applied nor advised not in it. For the diet, they advised [*2 words illegible*]. King was loath to have plaster off. Though at hot they disliked it, at cold good. He present at posset giving. Who gave it he knows not. And he tasted of it after. Came with plaster. Resolution was but restraint if could do it well. But he wished him forbear, yet took it. And thought it could do no harm for he observed the gillyflower in the taste of another pot, part of it wherein it came. Harvey there. Moore joined in consultation, subscribed it, let blood in [*illegible*] vein and the fit more moderate but no declination. He did wait till he died. Subscribed Doctor Paddy's note; said he came from King or L. Duke or both. He never heard King dislike it.

Levingston heard of it but not present at plaster.[40] Never heard King speak of it nor the drink. One fit better after the plaster.

Hay, sworn surgeon. Plaster applied twice or thrice last Monday; he at doing of it. L. Duke's folks brought it in. [f. 7v] Second time he put it on by King's command to make the plaster out of the box. Baker[41] brought it up and tasted it when he gave it me. He put it on leather, one to stomach, twice. He told physicians of it. Some stood by, 4 the clock, afternoon, and one always there that night. He went to bed till almost day. But he thinks he was at taking of it off. He heard the Duke not persuade him but told it had done such good. No physician disliked it, was left to the room keepers to dispose of. He knew it laid on before. Some doctors not content with it, yet he did it by King's direction.

Commended, heard it called for and all present. Duke went to London, and [at] physician's direction he executed posset. He saw made in Duke's chamber. Baker one, as he thinks, perhaps he errs in that. Baker a barber. Many about it. Who brought it up, he knew not. He saw the King drink of it. He helped to mix it with gillyflower. He thinks not one in the chamber but did taste of it; he, a great deal after. Syrup came with the box. Whether in bowl or tankard the posset was, he knows not. Treacle or mithridate predominate in plaster. He neither said nor thought that [*illegible*] was in it.

Sir Edward Peyton. Of toad's flesh, he said of frogs.[42]

[f. 8] D[octor] Moore. No sworn physician. Came Thursday sevennight to King before he died. He was there every day. He was at all consultations after he came except save one. He set his hand to them, agreed or parted, apothecary Wolfe[43] has resolutions. No plaster directed by the physicians. A plaster applied, not spoke[n] of by the physicians that he knew. Warwick commended [*illegible*] Duke. He saw it taken off. Harvey saw it applied but not knowing the contents. He said he to blame. Craig[44] and Harvey all day there. Taken off about 8 a clock when cold fit left. [*Illegible*] with sweat fall off. Whether Warwick and [Duke] commended it or no, he knows not. A letter was written to the maker, who wrote it was London treacle and juice of citrons. All joined to have

39. See above, n. 37.

40. MS: *Levestone.* The reference is probably to John Levingston (Leveston), Jr., Groom of the Bedchamber. *CSPD 1603–1610,* p. 153.

41. In the Duke's answer to the charge against him concerning administering the plaster and posset (see HofL, 8 June, p. 578), he identifies Baker as John Baker, one of his servants.

42. Concerning the distilling of toads, see the testimony of Robert Ramsey, HofC, 26 April, OB.

43. See above, n. 32.

44. Regarding John Craig, Jr., see HofC, 24 April, n. 25.

the letter written. Hay said it was plain posset drink with hartshorn in it. Because Craig and Gibb[45] had spoke it did hurt, a note was made at Sir William Paddy's instance what [*sic*] it was not hurtful. Resolved, after bleeding, fit less, but no declination of disease. And ever after had a fever.

45. Concerning Henry Gibb, see HofC, 24 April, n. 19.

Order of Business Wednesday, 26 April 1626

WEDNESDAY, 26 APRIL 1626

I. JOURNAL OF THE HOUSE OF COMMONS

[CJ 849; p. 33]
Mercurii, 26 Aprilis, 2 Caroli Regis

Sir S. Weston, for sickness, has license to go into the country, with promise to return with all convenient speed.

Upon question, the contempt of the high sheriff of Leicestershire to be referred to

[col. 1]	[col. 2]
Sir H[enry] Poole	Sir Thomas Barrington
Sir B[enjamin] Rudyard	Sir William Bulstrode
Mr. John Drake	Sir G[ilbert] Hoghton
Mr. [Richard] Spencer	Sir Clement Throckmorton
Sir A[nthony] Forest	Sir John Jackson
Mr. [Thomas] Wentworth	Mr. Rolle

[col. 3]
Sir Richard Leveson
Sir G[ilbert] Gerard
Sir Roland Cotton
[Oliver] Lord St. John
Mr. [Edward] Littleton
Sir Edward Spencer
Mr. Jones

4 clock this afternoon, in the Court of Wards.

[CJ 850] Bill for attorneys, Friday[1] next, 2 clock, in the former place.

Apothecaries bill, Saturday,[2] 2 clock, in the Exchequer.

The bill against incontinency,[3] Friday next.

Concealments, tomorrow afternoon, with power to send for the officers of the Exchequer to attend the committee.

The debate of the business concerning Sir Robert Howard to be upon Friday morning next, and notice of that time to be given to the parties formerly appointed to attend.[4]

The committee for framing a bill of arms, tomorrow, 2 clock.[5]

Merton College bill, Friday, 2 clock.

Clerk of the market, Friday next, 2 clock.

A petition from the drawers of gold and silver, etc., read. Referred till the report made of the bill of apparel.[6]

The committee for the increase of mariners' wages, etc., to meet upon Monday next, in the afternoon, in the former place.

Bill of seacoals, Monday afternoon, 2 clock, Court of Wards.

The resolution of Mr. Montagu his business to be upon Saturday morning next.

Decrees in courts of equity, Friday afternoon.

Bill against buying[7] and selling offices, Monday, 2 clock, Exchequer Chamber.

1. *Thursday* is crossed out in the MS and *Friday* is inserted.

2. *tomorrow* is crossed out in the MS and *Saturday* is inserted.

3. I.e., the bill against adultery and fornication.

4. For the orders concerning parties to answer with regard to the proceedings against Sir Robert Howard, MP, see HofC, 21 March, OB.

5. The entry implies that it refers to the committee for framing a bill for finding of arms, appointed on 14 March, rather than to the committee appointed on 25 March to consider the bill sent down from the Lords for making the arms of the kingdom more serviceable. The two committees were joined together by order of the House on 27 April.

6. We have been unable to find the petition of the wiredrawers. For the debate of their petition in opposition to the bill concerning apparel, see the testimony of their counsel, HofC, 5 May.

7. *bribery* is crossed out in the MS preceding *buying*. This was the committee appointed on 3 March to consider the bill against the procuring judicial places for money.

Lord Morley's bill, Saturday, 2 clock, former place.

Bill for oath for public services, Monday, 2 clock.

Bill for muster masters, Wednesday, 2 clock, Court of Wards.

The committee for religion to proceed with the business for the Bishop of Bangor, tomorrow, 2 clock, in the Exchequer Chamber; and then to adjourn themselves, as they shall find cause, for that service.

Bill against transportation of ordnance, Tuesday in the afternoon.

Bill against simony, Tuesday afternoon.

Bill for King's revenue, Monday, 2 clock.

Bill of administrations, Wednesday, 2 clock.

II. DIARY OF BULSTRODE WHITELOCKE, ESQ., DD. 12.21, CAMBRIDGE UNIVERSITY LIBRARY

[f. 160v]

26 April

At the committee of 12.

Mr. Wandesford reports that he examined the King's serjeant surgeon,[8] who said, as before, that the King was much worse after the plaster had been applied to him. The King told him that he was the worse for that plaster. [f. 161] A little before the King died there came from him a great deal of black matter, very noisome, which was without purging.

Robert Ramsey,[9] brought in and examined, says that he heard Mr. Pierce[10] Butler say that so long as the King did entertain the Duke of Buckingham he would lose a great many of better friends. This about 6 weeks ago. And he said that the King and the parliament could do nothing to the Duke so long as he keeps one thing. Ramsey replied, if I were as he I would make much of that one thing. Whereupon Butler said that he knew who he might thank for it. And that Butler said he himself had some strange faculties, but it was at another time. That he saw Butler about a fortnight ago but since did forbear his company because he heard that he set one awork to distill toad[s],[11] by that Redman[12] told him that one Rennish[13] was set on work to distill the spirit of toads, which he made known to Mr. Kirk[14] of the Bedchamber.

Doctor Craig,[15] brought in and examined, says that there was plaster, as he thinks, twice applied to King James. That there was some complaint to the physicians of it, but it was quickly removed and they saw no effect of any hurt done then by it. That he and the rest [*blank*] did dislike the laying on of the plasters and it did heat him more. That the physicians sent him and

8. On 24 April the House had ordered that the committee of 12 could appoint three or more of themselves to take the examinations of any who could not come to the committee to testify; Wandesford is reporting his examination of the Serjeant Surgeon, probably Gilbert Primrose (*CSPD 1603–1610,* p. 219), whose testimony was cited by Sir Walter Erle on 27 April.

9. We have been unable to identify further Robert Ramsey.

10. MS: *Percival.* This is presumably the Pierce Butler who was sent for by warrant from the Privy Council on 28 April 1626. See *APC 1625–1626,* p. 450; *CSPI 1625–1632,* p. 135; *APC 1626,* p. 56 and *CSPV 1625–1626,* pp. 416–417, and see the reference cited in ibid., p. 605 note.

11. *poison* is crossed out in the MS preceding *toad.* At the committee meeting of 25 April, Sir Edward Peyton had mentioned toad's flesh in connection with the medications administered to James I before his death; see HofC, 25 April, OB.

12. We are unable to identify Redman.

13. The reference may be intended to be to Dr. John Remington of Essex, thought to be the person who created the recipe for the plaster. See HofC, 25 April, n. 38.

14. George Kirk was a groom of the King's Bedchamber. *CSPD 1623–1625,* p. 14.

15. Regarding John Craig, Jr., see HofC, 24 April, n. 25.

Doctor [*blank*] to this King[16] to desire him that he would advise the Lord [Duke] to remit all to the care of the physicians. That finding that fit was higher than his other, they might ascribe it to those applications. [f. 161v] Before this application they did think the fits were lesser and the disease to be declined. That Doctor Moore[17] and he being sent to the Duke, Doctor Moore undertook the business and left him. That he heard the posset was made in the Duke's chamber and that the King refused it once. He was dismissed because he said he was sorry the Duke should administer anything to the King.[18] This the Duke accused him of, and worse. He denied the worse word, but took these upon him, holding they might be spoken by one friend to another; but he was discharged before his accusation. That he heard in my Lord Duke's chamber that there was a rumor that he should say that which was given to the King by the Duke was as bad as poison, but he is assured that he spoke nothing of these applications[19] one way or other.

[*Committee of the Whole House*]

[f. 162] Mr. Littleton takes the chair.[20]

Mr. Wilde. H. 3 time the lands and goods of a great man were confiscated to the King.[21] H. 4 time/ 25 E. 1, a search into the places of magistrates and those that were faulty being mulcted there grew a great revenue to the King.[22] I do not think it a safe way to make any alteration by innovations, changing the ancient manner of paying subsidies. I had rather give way to another subsidy and 15.

Sir Robert Pye. That we should for the present make an addition of 2 subsidies more.

Sir John Savile. I desire no peace with Spain, and whensoever it comes I think it will [be] a means to be the bane of England. Neither can we maintain the war by parliamentary supplies, unless the King does really put to his hand. It's a dangerous precedent to give way to the proposition for paying 8s. in the pound.[23] Against giving of more subsidies now. If the proposition concerning the Court of Wards had not been neglected, the crown had by this received 2 millions of money.[24] Let him that has a title of honor given him be [as]sessed accordingly. I will give the King £15, half that which I am [as]sessed, and that within 3 months. And so wish other men will do too.

Sir William Bulstrode. I am an old man and I love old ways and my heart goes against new ones.[25] That the arrearages of all recusants' forfeitures may be reduced to

16. I.e., Charles I who was then prince. *the Duke* is crossed out in the MS and *this King* is inserted.

17. Regarding John Moore, see HofC, 24 April, n. 21.

18. See the letter of 22 March 1625 from Thomas, Earl of Kellie to John, Earl of Mar (HMC, *Mar and Kellie MSS, Supplementary Report*, pp. 225–226), that states that Craig "is now absented from court" as a result of the business concerning the plaster; and see Mead's letter to Stuteville, 9 April 1625, stating that Craig was "commanded out of the court" (Birch, *Court and Times of Chas. I*, I, 5).

19. *words* is crossed out in the MS preceding *applications*.

20. I.e., for the continuation of the debate on further supply begun the previous day (25 April).

21. In the parliament of 1258 the barons forced Henry III to agree to reforms that led to the banishment of Henry's half-brothers and other Poitevins and the resumption to the crown of lands that had been alienated. See Cobbett, *Parl. Hist.*, I, 28–30; Matthew Paris, *Chronica*, V, 695–704.

22. Wilde's date is incorrect. The great reform of the judiciary took place in 1289, 17 E. I. See Cobbett, *Parl. Hist.*, I, 37–38; Holinshed, *Chronicles*, II, 490–491.

23. On 25 April, Sir Benjamin Rudyard had first suggested increasing the rate assessed for land above 4s. in the pound, and Mr. Brown proposed doubling it to 8s. in the pound. For their speeches, see HofC, 25 April, OB.

24. Lowther, below, gives "3 millions". The reference is to the Great Contract, see HofC, 25 April, n. 13.

25. Bulstrode was born about 1561 and was knighted by the Earl of Essex in Ireland in 1599.

the King. [f. 162v] And give another subsidy to be paid some five months after the last payment of the subsidy already agreed on.[26]

Sir Thomas Hoby. That every one be held up in the subsidy book as they were in Queen Elizabeth's days. If the King's revenues may be handled as they were in Queen Elizabeth's days, the subjects will give as they did in Queen Elizabeth's days. For one subsidy more.

Mr. Carvill. That a present addition may be given out of the riches gotten by extortion of fees; 2, by selling of offices; 3, by selling of places of the Church; 4, by riches gotten by usury. E. 1.

Mr. Coryton. That it may be considered what the subsidies were in Queen Elizabeth's time and accordingly now be rated.

Sir Edwin Sandys. In all difficult cases I had rather hear than speak. 1, the improvement of the subsidies already given; 2, the addition of more subsidies; 3/

The[27] more we double the number of subsidies, the more the weight of them is diminished. The last subsidy in Queen Elizabeth was £130,000; the subsidy now £67,000.[28] I accept the proposition of reducing the subsidy to the ancient equality, but am against the raising of that which is paid in every pound. It is the £3 and £5 man that fill the King's purse. That no knight, baronet, nor viscount or peer of Ireland of the body of the commissions should [be] set at a lower rate than £20, [f. 163] no baronet less than [*blank*], no viscount less than £50 land.

Mr. Wandesford. That every shire's rates in the subsidy book as they are now may be looked into and presented to the House by the knights, citizens, and burgesses for every shire.

Mr. Noy. 1. No cause to raise the estimate. 2. To raise the rich and leave out the poor will breed a great indifferency and contention. 3. It is not safe to raise the rates which men pay, neither a good way nor a safe way to raise 4s. in a pound to 8s. in a pound. Before H. 5 time we find paid the 40th part and the 50th part and sometimes more, at last to the 15th part of their good[s][29]; since, it has so continued but will never go less again in any rates once raised.

Sir Peter Heyman. It could be carried with a great deal more equality if all the commissioners of every shire did come together to one place.

Mr. Noy. It is not possible to make a rate by viewing of the ancient rolls.

Vice Chamberlain. Every man that sits within these walls must be *pro rege, pro lege, et pro grege*. I have received a letter from the general of the horse to the King of Denmark,[30] who has now 44,000 foot and 11,000 horse in the field, and writes withal that if we embrace the present opportunity we shall make the war offensive and annoy the enemy; if not, he will subjugate us.

[f. 163v] Sir Thomas Fanshawe. About 7 King James, the commissioners for subsidy were commanded to raise the subsidy to the rate which was in 5 Elizabeth.[31]

26. I.e., the three subsidies resolved on 27 March to be granted to the King.

27. *against the improvement of subsidies* is crossed out in the MS preceding *The.*

28. Concerning the fall in the value of the subsidy grants, see Dietz, *Public Finance,* pp. 380–393.

29. Quinzimes or fifteens were levied as such at least as early as 1344 (*SR,* 18 E. III, st. 2, c. 1).

30. I.e., John Ernest, Duke of Saxe-Weimar. See 30 March, n. 14.

31. We have not found the directions to the commissioners in 1610. Regarding the subsidy, cf. *PP 1610,* II, 290, n. 3.

Resolved upon question, that we shall add a 4th subsidy to the supply already intended to be given to his Majesty in this session of parliament, to be rated and paid after the usual manner.

III. DIARY OF JOHN LOWTHER, ESQ., D/LONS/L, CUMBERLAND AND WESTMORLAND RECORD OFFICE

[f. 8]

[26 April]

Buying offices. Monday, Exchequer Chamber.

Lord Morley's bill. Saturday, first in turn.

To account upon oath, on Monday.

[*Committee of the Whole House*]

[f. 8v] Wednesday. How to augment supply.

Wilde cites the manor of [*illegible*] 8, 9th, 20th Hubert seized his land; E. 3. Marcher nobles.
Desires knight-service into socage.

Sir G. More. Multitude of commissioners hinders subsidy. Justice of peace, £20. Desires to add subsidy.

Sir John Savile. At breach of treaties engaged all to do it, and thinks breach with Spain best. Peace, bane to this kingdom. Other relief than subsidy. King must help if we go on, else we cannot undertake war. Set King's revenue. He will go on, else lack endanger us. A £3,000 man [has] no tenants to bear subsidy but a miller. From 4s. to 8, he dislikes. Remembers 2 subsidies first protested never to be precedented, yet precedented next parliament by him [who] said no.[32] If offer for Wards [had] been accepted, better to crown by 3 millions. Or this: baronets' arrears to pay to King to be £66 13s. 4d., has £100; knight, father dead, not in field, £30; justice, £20; he, being £30, offers £15 at first subsidy.

Sir William Bulstrode. Confident England send fleet to make Spain smoke. Dislike Spanish hearts in English bodies. Recusants forfeit King's own. And one subsidy more.

Hoby. Act of parliament of subsidy powerful enough in fining assessors and choosing them.[33] Would take away certificates. Landlord pay highest subsidy laid of any land since Queen Elizabeth's time. Compares to Fleet Street conduit; if stopped, to go to spring head and so come down, not make a new well. This done, adds a subsidy.

Carvill. To give out of usury—practiced by King E. 1—extorted fees, sale office, and Church livings if a part of lawful penalty.[34] Acquitting the payers and punishing receivers only to produce it.

Coryton rejects this as too long, indeed impossible.

[f. 9] Smith moves enhancement, double recusants.[35]

Sir Edwin Sandys. Necessary and difficult. King to others, we to him engaged. Moves order. We fly at all. First to amplify this; 2, addition; 3, all projects. Desires to set on first for order. Statute mentions "ut-

32. The parliament of 1589 was the first to grant more than one subsidy (*SR*, 31 Eliz. I, c. 15), and the next parliament (1593) granted three (*SR*, 35 Eliz. I, c. 13). See D'Ewes, *Journal . . . Elizabeth*, pp. 431, 433–434, 473–474, 477–478, 499–500, and 507. Francis Bacon wrote a note for the preamble to the 1589 bill to the effect that the extraordinary grant should not serve as a precedent to posterity, but he was one of the first to speak in favor of the grant of 1593 (ibid., pp. 433, 473).

33. The subsidy bills carried numerous provisions for penalizing and fining corrupt commissioners and assessors. See, for example, the subsidy act passed in 1625, *SR*, 1 Car. I, c. 6, pt. 10.

34. See Carvill's speech in Whitelocke, above.

35. I.e., recusants to pay double the rate paid by others.

most" value.[36] To increase it adds not to King, for we cannot exceed "utmost". Not to enhance it to Queen Elizabeth's time. Not now so able. Building, apparel, furniture, etc., signs of wealth, causes of poverty. Impositions add to poverty. We could do more for 5 than now for 7. By that means, when Queen Elizabeth's subsidies number increased, diminished in value. Fifteen and subsidy were 130,000; last, under 70,000.[37] He concurs with Sir John Savile, titles of honor to pay enlargement.

Whitson shows how Carleton, taken at Lancaster, had instruction to gather 70,000 for Douai expressed in a petition, and he cites Chancellor of Duchy to have it in his hands.[38]

Chancellor Duchy. Had an examination sent of a contribution by hearsay from a man to no purpose, so take heed of hearsay.

Wandesford approves Sir E. Sandys's, but not to idolize. Supposes the best way to increase. Desires every county to bring in their subsidies and present their opinions.

Sir Dudley Digges. The utmost value beyond charge and maintenance is intended in subsidy.

Sir P. Heyman. To make main commissioners and more to meet together to assess by voices.

Vice Chamberlain. No orator nor actor, no loss of time. Against Eliot. We must be *pro lege, pro grege, pro rege*. He heard how we [*illegible*] conquest. Not if we lose not [*sic*] opportunity. D. Weimar,[39] general of Denmark's force, he gone back in despair for our confusion here. Denmark has 55,000 men; embrace opportunity, shall have advantage. Eliot's distinction—likes not of Eliot—[40]likes not of augment and addition. Desires one subsidy.

[f. 9v] Chancellor Exchequer. The new proposition of difficulty; requires new parliament far beyond 5 days desired and the increase in those given. The conquering speech he does dislike.

Secretary Coke. This enlargement by us is but that which is given as before; for King by commissioners may expect advancement. We can do no more.

Resolved to add another subsidy to the 3 subsidies intended for supply.

IV. DIARY OF SIR NATHANIEL RICH, HIST. COLLECT. 143, HLRO

[f. 79v]

Wednesday, 26 April

[*Committee of the Whole House*]

At the committee for the King's supply. Mr. Littleton in the chair.

Mr. Wilde. The means: 1, by inquiry into great officers and their corruption; 2, to contract for the Court of Wards.[41]

Sir R. Pye. To add only 2 subsidies more without any xvths.

Sir G. More. Multitude of commissioners hinder greatly the quantity of the subsidy.

Sir John Savile. Peace with Spain the bane of England. The £4 man bear[s] three parts of 4 of the subsidy, so the poor carry the

36. Commissioners were to "inquire the best and most value of the substance of every person . . . without respect of any former taxation heretofore had . . . and the best and uttermost substance and value of every one of them, as well as lands, tenements . . . goods, chattels . . . without any concealment . . . ". *SR*, 1 Car. I, c. 6, pt. 8.

37. See above, n. 28.

38. We are unable to find additional information about Carleton.

39. MS: *Wymy*. See above, n. 30.

40. The reference may be to Eliot's speech, 27 March, the day the subsidy bill passed the Commons House.

41. See HofC, 25 April, n. 13.

burden. Not possible for the subject to bear the charge of the war except the King put his hand really to it. Fit the King's state therefore be rectified. There is a leak in the ship of the commonwealth which must be stopped. Men of £4,000 per annum have scarce 2 tenants able to bear subsidy. Subsidy is unproportionably laid. A man of 3 times his estate in some countries not pay so much as he. Likes not that 4s. subsidy should be made 8s. When 2 subsidies first granted to Queen Elizabeth, was promised before it should not be a precedent, yet the next parliament the same man/[42]

Likes not to give more subsidies at this time, this is to entail/

For the Court of Wards, the subject will buy it out willingly. Those that have not paid for their honors let them pay in and those that have titles of foreign honor to pay £100 also. Your baronets 100 marks. All knights to be assessed. Justices of the peace and commissioners for the subsidy be assessed[43] £20. He must go to the red ribbons.[44] He will not be a commissioner alone to rate; he will leave somewhat for other men. Yet all this will not serve the turn. All above £4 to give half that at which they are assessed; [f. 80] this money will come in quickly and easily. But will pay but for one subsidy and will pay no more till the great leak be stopped in the King's revenue.

Sir William Bulstrode.[45] He loves the old way, being an old man; wishes that we should not too much poverty England, confident of her own ability. Would have the books increased but left to the commissioners. Many that have money enough to support seminaries abroad. To call for arrearages of all the recusants. To add one subsidy.

Sir T. Hoby. For raising the subsidy book. The act is well enough already. The commissioners appoint the assessors of the best, and they may fine.[46] Many men live out of the country who have great estates and their tenants not able to pay subsidy who pay a racked rent. Some £3 men better able to pay their subsidy than the £5 men. Many commissioners fittest for the service so they be demanded and the commissioners to answer for their own division. Some buy land and have money in their purses at the old rent; and they let their term run out, then rack it and let it out to a shepherd and dogs. Thinks fit to take away certificates. What subsidy men have been found upon any land since 1 Queen Elizabeth let the landlord pay it. If the King's revenue were handled as in Queen Elizabeth's time the subject would give. The revenue like the conduit in Fleet Street, if they want water they go first to the head and if not there then look to the pipes and find quills that drive it away. These must be put out. Moves that the King's estate may be well looked to. Aids for war ought to be [f. 80v] but aids. Moves one subsidy more.

Mr. Carvill. Edward 1, aid given out [of] the 4 sort[s] of offenders: 1, by extorted fees; 2, by selling offices; 3, by selling of benefices; 4, money got by usury. To find these out by examination of such as have been compelled to pay them and acquits those that have paid and will confess it.

Mr. Coryton likes not giving before more subsidies, for this will put the country behindhand as the King now is. To only raise the former.

Mr. Smith[47] remembers the King said he would not have the burden lie on the

42. See above, n. 32.

43. *to pay* is crossed out in the MS and *subsidy* is inserted.

44. I.e., the Knights of the Bath, who wore crimson ribbons.

45. *Mr. Want.* is crossed out in the MS above *Sir William Bulstrode*.

46. See above, n. 33.

47. *Sir Edwin Sandys* is crossed out in the MS preceding *Mr. Smith*.

poorer sort.[48] That recusants shall pay as aliens, and to add a subsidy.

Sir E. Sandys. This business of importance and necessity and with all the difficulty. The King engaged to expedition and we engaged him in this. He had rather hear than speak. Difficulties must quicken industry, not dishearten. 1, to improve the subsidies already given; 2, to add more; 3, new projects.

That we resolve the first first, in which 3 propositions: 1, reducing it to better equality, and that implies an increase; 2, to enlarge it to the utmost extent of Queen Elizabeth's time; 3ly, the rating of men of quality at higher rates. But observe that all we can do in this kind is no performance of our order, for by the word of the law they are to be raised to the utmost.[49] The raising of men must be done by the commissioners. King James prayed us to give him aid so as it might not grieve the people, that were to bring a purse and a knife.[50] It will make [f. 81] great clamor to have 4 subsidies and to have them all raised, too. The kingdom is not of the ability we were in Queen Elizabeth's time. Observe sumptuous buildings, apparel, etc., these signs of wealth but causes of poverty. We must go to causes, not to signs. A great burden of impositions has lain long on the subject. He could do more for a thousand marks 1 *Jac.* than for a £, £1,000, now. Servants' wages increased; he could then pay [*sic*] a pair of shoes for 16d. which not now for 2s. 6d. Again, will you bring subsidies so thick and yet enhance them too? No men will look to be lightly assessed. When Queen Elizabeth, in her time, when subsidies increased, so they did diminish in their value. £67,400 was but a subsidy. When they granted 4 subsidies the value did diminish. So likes to reduce the subsidies to a better equality. 2, dislikes the general improvement of them. 3ly, Sir John Savile's proposition be taken into consideration. The gentlemen of the kingdom must maintain the war. A good honest motion but wants the foundation of experience. We see that gentlemen are doubled, trebled, when they are made noblemen. Likes that baronets, knights, barons, and viscounts of Ireland and Scotland, whose estates in England, to be highly raised. No knight to be under such a rate but not at an equal rate. So for a baronet, etc. The Marshal Court/

The knights of Rome did pay *censum equestrem.*

[f. 81v] Sir Edward Spencer. That propositions may be [*illegible*] all made and collected, then to choose which we like. He takes the proportion which we should aim at should be 2 subsidies at the old rate of £60,000, i.e., £120,000 in all. Moves that some men are grievous to the state, their fines will pay.

Mr. Whitson. For the recusants to pay deep.

Mr. Wandesford.[51] Every man has declared a good will to give the King the best satisfaction. Yesterday we resolved to augment this supply;[52] the question is how. He thinks it to stand with discretion and justice

48. See the last paragraph of the Duke of Buckingham's explanation on 30 March of the King's speech that was delivered on 29 March.

49. See above, n. 36.

50. See King James's speech to parliament, 21 March 1610, printed in McIlwain, *Political Works of James I*, p. 318: "But as upon the one side, I do not desire you should yield to that extreme, in giving me more than (as I said formerly) upon such occasions are fit for good and loving subjects to yield; for that were go give me a purse with a knife: so on the other side, I hope you will not make vain pretenses of wants . . . by alleging the poverty of the people".

51. MS: *Wantsworth.* Whitelocke and Lowther, above, confirm that the speaker was Christopher Wandesford rather than Thomas Wentworth.

52. See HofC, 25 April, OB.

to raise men of quality, but this not enough. 2 divisions: 1, whether a further addition; 2ly, whether an increase of these. He likes this last because it will give most content to the poor. The giving of many subsidies will lessen the value. First, to resolve how to increase these but not to deny to give more. Moves that every shire may survey the subsidy books and consider how to raise them.

Mr. Goodwin. To refer the consideration of all those propositions to a subcommittee.

Mr. Noy. 1, to raise men in estimation, as £10 to £20; 2, to raise the rate. For the first, the statute is already is [*sic*] of the value of every man's land and ground so much so the law cannot be altered. To raise upon thc rich only will make contention, every man will say he is poor; and he that looks on a man's face knows not what money in his purse. 2ly, to raise the rate, viz., from 4s. on the pound to 6 or 8s., this very unsafe. Every man pays [f. 82] more now than heretofore he did. Thinks not fit to alter the law; dangerous to press the raising of men to a value. Aids have multiplied and it began with 40th, 20th, and rested at 15d. since H. 5 time.[53] So tonnage and poundage from 3d. to 12d.,[54] it will never go to 10d.; so 4s. in land if raised will never come to/

Sir D. Digges likes the last motion. Not raise the rate but thinks it necessary that the subsidy be looked into. The utmost value mentioned in the statute is over and above debts and competent maintenance of his family according to his estate. Likes not increase of commissioners, for that increases favor.

53. See above, n. 28.

54. Concerning the rates charged for tonnage and poundage, see Coke *Fourth Inst.*, pp. 32–33.

Order of Business Thursday, 27 April 1626

Committee of **religion** given power to appoint members to examine witnesses concerning the **Bishop of Bangor**	83, *17/4
Committee on the bill for making void a decree in the Exchequer Chamber made in behalf of Sir Francis **Neale** against Sir Edward **Fisher** to meet on Monday [1 May]	83, *7/3
Mr. Rolle: moves for privilege for the factor of John Delbridge, MP	83, 84
Upon question, John Delbridge's factor to have privilege to stay a suit against him	83, 84, 86
Committee on the bill for the settling of certain **marshlands** by the name of the Isle of **Canvey** to meet Monday [1 May]	83, *21/3
Committee on the bills for the naturalizing of Samuel **Bave** and Thomas **Sotherne** to meet Saturday [29 April]	83, *27/2; 13/3
Committee on the bill for the better suppressing of **unlicensed alehouse keepers** to meet Tuesday [2 May]; all that come to have voice	83, *25/3
Committee on the bill to make void a decree in Chancery and assurances thereupon made by Sir Thomas **Jermy** to Sir Mark Steward to meet Friday [28 April]	83, *28/2
Committee of the whole for the **continuance and repeal** of divers **statutes** to meet Saturday [29 April]	83, 86, *23/3
Committee on the bill for the making of the **arms** of the kingdom more serviceable and the committee for framing a bill for **finding of arms** to be joined together and to meet tomorrow	83, *14/3; 20/3
Sir Nathaniel Rich: concerning the bill for a subsidy of **tonnage and poundage**	84, *23/3
Richard Spencer	83, 84, 86
Mr. Rolle	84
Mr. Mason	84
John Whistler	84
Sir Humphrey May (Chancellor Duchy)	84
Sir William Spencer	84
Sir John Eliot	84
Sir Benjamin Rudyard	84
Question for sending for the officers of the Custom House: declined	84, 86
Motion that the subcommittee for preparing a **Book of Rates** prepare heads for a remonstrance to the King concerning the taking of **tonnage and poundage** without grant in parliament	83, 85, 86, *27/3
Resolved: to stay further debate on a remonstrance concerning tonnage and poundage; the subcommittee for preparing a Book of Rates to meet this afternoon	83, 85
Report from the committee of 12 for considering the business concerning the **Duke of Buckingham** (John Glanville): on the examination of physicians concerning the **death of James I**	83, 85, 86, 87, *21/4; 24/4
Sir Walter Erle	86
Upon a division: resolved that the committee of the whole House sit presently to consider this business	84, 85

[*Committee of the Whole House:*

THURSDAY, 27 APRIL 1626

I. JOURNAL OF THE HOUSE OF COMMONS

[CJ 850; p. 34]
Jovis, 27 Aprilis, 2 Caroli Regis

Power given to the committee for religion to appoint 4 or more of themselves to go and examine any witnesses in or about the town concerning the Bishop of Bangor, and to bring the same to the committee and to send for books or writings concerning that business to inform them.

Sir Edward Fisher's bill, Monday next, 2 clock.

MR. ROLLE moves for Mr. Delbridge. That one Thomas Morrys, a factor to Mr. Delbridge, is sued in London concerning goods of Mr. Delbridge.

Upon question, privilege for stay of the suit.

Canvey Island, Monday, 2 clock.

Bave and Sotherne; Saturday morning, 7 clock.[1]

Alehouses, Tuesday, 2 clock; and every man that will come to have voice.

Lady Jermy's bill, Friday 7night, 2 clock.

Committee for continuance and repeal of statutes, Saturday, 2 clock.

The committees for the bill of arms and for framing a bill for finding of arms to be joined together,[2] and to be sat upon tomorrow, 2 clock, in the Star Chamber.

Memorandum: the petition for archery.[3]

Bill for tonnage and poundage.

MR. SPENCER moves a remonstrance to his Majesty concerning the taking of the tonnage[4] and poundage without grant in parliament.

Moved the subcommittee formerly appointed to take the Book of Rates into consideration,[5] with an addition thereunto now made, besides the power there given, to prepare heads for a remonstrance to his Majesty concerning the taking of tonnage and poundage without grant in parliament.

Resolved to let this stay to further debate, and to proceed with the bill for tonnage and poundage. But the said subcommittee to meet 2 clock this afternoon in the Star Chamber.[6]

MR. GLANVILLE reports from the select committee of 12, the examinations of a plaster and a posset given King James in his sickness.[7]

That divers of the King's sworn physicians examined.

That the sworn physicians agreed upon certain directions in general, and particularly that the King should have neither meat [n]or drink within certain hours before his fit.

[p. 35] That upon all this the committee of opinion that this should be annexed to

1. Regarding the committee, see 27 March, n. 2.

2. For the appointment of the two committees, see 25 March and 14 March, respectively.

3. We have not found the petition for archery, see HofC, 14 April, n. 2.

4. *custom of* is crossed out in the MS preceding *tonnage*.

5. I.e., the subcommittee for preparing a Book of Rates, appointed 27 March.

6. The following passage is crossed out in the MS following *Star Chamber:*

1. Upon question those farmers to be sent for to the committee for the bill for tonnage and poundage; to have power from this House to have power to send for the officers of the Custom House in the port of London which have received the tonnage and poundage without assent in parliament.

This question was declined by the House because it was considered prejudicial if the officers were sent for and not punished. See Lowther, below.

7. For the examinations taken by the committee, see HofC, 24, 25, and 26 April, OBs.

the Duke's charge as a transcendent presumption of dangerous consequence.

Upon the question whether the grand committee[8] of the whole House, Mr. Wandesford being in the chair, to sit presently, and take consideration of the business now reported, the question being 2 put, and the voice doubtful, the House divided. The yea went out:

Tellers for the yea:	Mr. Long
	Sir Ferdinando Fairfax
Tellers for the no:	Mr. Spencer
	Mr. Jermyn

With the yea: 191
With the no: 150
Difference: 41

II. DIARY OF BULSTRODE WHITELOCKE, ESQ., DD. 12.21, CAMBRIDGE UNIVERSITY LIBRARY

[f. 163v]

April 27

MR. ROLLE moves that an action of the case upon a promise is brought against a factor of a member of this House.[9]

The House allows privilege in this case and stays the suit.

SIR NATHANIEL RICH. It was never precedented that tonnage and poundage was taken by privy seal.

MR. SPENCER moves that we may make a remonstrance to the King concerning the taking of tonnage and poundage.

MR. ROLLE. That we proceed with the bill and send for the customers to know by what authority they take it before it be granted by the parliament.

MR. MASON. That the customers may be sent for. And after that we may make our remonstrance to the King, the bill being difficult to be framed and hard to be passed, it sticking with the Lords last parliament.[10]

MR. WHISTLER. That if we make a remonstrance we shall confess ourselves out of possession.

CHANCELLOR DUCHY. That tonnage and poundage was taken in King James's time and in Queen Elizabeth's time until the parliament granted it.[11]

[f. 164] SIR WILLIAM SPENCER. That it was never taken after a parliament.

SIR JOHN ELIOT. *Errores non sunt trahendi in exemplum.*

SIR BENJAMIN RUDYARD. I like remonstrances and messages both alike unless there be necessary cause.

The [House] declines the question for sending for the officers of the Custom House.[12]

8. *for evils, causes, and remedies shall* is crossed out in the MS following *committee.*

9. *by a charter-party* is crossed out in the MS following *House.* This was the case concerning Thomas Morrys, factor to John Delbridge, MP; see CJ, above.

10. The 1625 bill for the subsidy of tonnage and poundage was sent up from Commons and first read in the Lords House on 9 July; but the Lords proceeded no further with the bill, reportedly because the grant was limited to a single year rather than for life. See *PP 1625,* pp. 109, 110, 372.

11. I.e., taken by both Elizabeth and James between the times of their accessions and the grants of tonnage and poundage in their first parliaments (*SR,* 1 Eliz. I, c. 20; *SR,* 1 Jac. I, c. 33).

12. This sentence is interlined in the MS; crossed out below it is the following passage:

The House gives power to the committee for the subsidy of tonnage and poundage to send for the officers of the Custom House, etc. See above, n. 6.

The House appoints the subcommittee to prepare heads for a remonstrance to the King concerning this business.[13]

MR. GLANVILLE reports from the select committee of 12 the matter concerning some passages in King James's sickness about a plaster and potion.[14] Divers of the King's sworn physicians sworn. In the time of the sickness of King James he was attended by them, who set down under their hands what should be applied to him and nothing without their consent and approbation and made by the King's sworn apothecary, and no drink until his cold fit were over. By the examination of many of them in the affirmative it appears that a plaster was twice applied to him. Before the application thereof the disease was declining, and afterwards grew worse. 2[nd], it was applied by direction and recommendation of the Duke of Buckingham, after which he grew much worse and there were symptoms [of] found[er]ing, raving, and extreme heat. The ingredients of the plaster were of [f. 164v] a strong smell but could not be known expressly by the smell; that somewhat was in it which was invertive [*sic*]. A note was brought to the physicians of the ingredients of the plaster by Doctor Moore and Sir William Paddy[15] from the Duke of Buckingham, by occasion of some muttering. The Duke brought him posset drink; twice he drank of it, and refused it the 3rd time. The King replied: it is that which I have had from the Duke that makes me so ill. This affirmed by the man that saw the Duke give it to the King.[16] The opinion of the committee is that it should be annexed to the Duke's charge as a transcendent presumption of dangerous consequence.

Ordered, that a committee of the whole House shall take this matter presently into consideration.

[*Committee of the Whole House*]

Mr. Wandesford takes the chair.

Sir John Eliot. To be considered: the fact, the merits of the fact, and the proofs. He adds to the report that it appeared that some of the physicians said that as long as the plaster remained with the King they would not meddle with him. Though some of the physicians that were last examined, though they did not speak so fully as they that were examined first, yet they did not contradict one another.

[f. 165] Sir Nathaniel Rich. That first we are to consider the fact and state it; 2nd, the merits of the fact; 3rd, whether the Duke be the author.

Resolved that this is the fact, viz., that a drink was given to the King James in his last sickness and a plaster applied without advice of the King's sworn physicians, not made by his own sworn apothecary or surgeons but contrary to the general directions of the physicians and afterwards disliked by them.

Mr. Littleton. If a mad man kill the King it is High Treason.

Mr. Sherfield. A physician that is a recusant convict ought not to practice. Doctor Moore attended the King and was no sworn physician.[17]

13. There was a motion for the subcommittee on the Book of Rates to prepare a remonstrance concerning the taking of tonnage and poundage, but the House apparently resolved to stay the debate at this point; see CJ above. On 8 June the House resolved to proceed with the framing of a remonstrance. See OB.

14. See above, n. 7.

15. Regarding Moore and Paddy, see HofC, 24 April, nn. 21 and 23.

16. A reference to Dr. Alexander Ramsey. For Ramsey's testimony to the committee, see HofC, 24 April, and n. 16.

17. Concerning Dr. Moore, see HofC, 24 April, n. 21.

Resolved that this act is of a transcendent presumption and of dangerous consequence.

Chancellor Duchy, in[18] his speech being called to the point, breaks off and goes away.

Resolved that the Duke gave the King this drink, and the plaster applied by his direction.

Resolved that this matter is fit to be by the committee of 12 annexed to the charge against the Duke of Buckingham.

III. DIARY OF JOHN LOWTHER, ESQ., D/LONS/L, CUMBERLAND AND WESTMORLAND RECORD OFFICE

[f. 9v]

[27 April]

Mr. J. Delbridge's factor had privilege, being sued.[19]

Thursday, agreed, continuance of statutes to be on Saturday.

SPENCER. [*Illegible*] King, move for tonnage and poundage to be brought to a Book of Rates, and a remonstrance because of the last stay, and then the King's profit and our right to be remonstrated by a subcommittee.

[*Illegible*] moved, farmers who take customs by privy seal to be sent for.[20]

Ordered, a subcommittee, I one, to make rates; and a remonstrance desired. Avoided.[21] Meet two [o'clock], S[tar] Chamber.

Though customs taken before parliament at charge of King,[22] yet never after parliament as now. Therefore the customers that received it contrary may be questioned.

The question avoided lest send and not punish, prejudice.

GLANVILLE. Commanded by 12[23] to report the plaster and the posset drink to King James before his death. He reports substance of proof. Attended by sworn physicians. General direction, nothing [*blank*] but by advice; particular, no meat or drink before fits. 2 affirmatively, [f. 10] none contrarying: applied at prohibited times, plaster and posset, upon declination. It was done by direction of Duke. Continued most part of the night, then took off. Grew worse, the raving, etc., mentioned by one,[24] heat and draft. The note brought after to have subscription. Served to be good, *loco, tempore*. Some directly deny it. That Paddy and Moore came from Duke upon some muttering. The posset likewise drunk. One said King had it of Duke twice, 3rd refused another, Duke. Once plaster taken off because made him worse. He asked why worse; Ramsey, etc., answered, for cold. King said, it was that I had of the Duke.

They think it to be added to Duke's charge as a transcendent presumption of dangerous consequence.

Primrose[25] his testimony urged by SIR WALTER ERLE. In his confession he says he ate of it. That the Countess[26] said now was the time to lay it on.

18. *the middle* is crossed out following *in*. We have found no account of May's speech.

19. See above, n. 9.

20. Both Rolle and Mason moved that the customs farmers be sent for. See Whitelocke. Concerning the rejection of the order, see above, n. 6.

21. I.e., voided. See above, n. 13.

22. See above, n. 11.

23. I.e., the committee of 12 appointed on 21 April.

24. See above, n. 16.

25. Gilbert Primrose, the serjeant surgeon. See HofC, 26 April, n. 8.

26. I.e., Mary Villiers, Countess of Buckingham, mother of George.

IV. DIARY OF SIR NATHANIEL RICH, HIST. COLLECT. 143, HLRO

[f. 82]

27 April, Thursday

Tonnage and poundage bill. That in this may be contained a pardon for those that have taken it all this while with[out] act of parliament.[27]

MR. GLANVILLE's report from the committee of 12. One matter: a plaster and posset drink. Divers witnesses examined: Drs. Ramsey, Atkins, Lister, etc.[28] The substance of the fact upon these testimonies: King James attended by his sworn physicians and they directed that nothing should be applied but by general consent, and no drink for 2 hours before his fit nor till his cold fit over. Yet by 2 witnesses, the rest not contrary, yet a plaster applied to his stomach and wrists. The first application did no good so taken off; the King mended, the disease declined. The King dying, upon which some 6 days before these plasters [had been] again applied by one [*blank*] Hay[29] [f. 82v] by direction of the Duke. It continued on till the King complained of it, and so taken off. After the King's death a bill of particulars brought to the physicians to allow it; they could not tell of what it was made. Subscribed that these things were good, administered *loco et tempore*. Dr. Paddy and Dr. Moore[30] brought this bill for subscription. For the drink that was administered, viz., a posset not made by the King's apothecary, nor by the counsel of the physicians. The Duke gave it the King twice, brought it the 3rd time but refused. The plaster taken off because it bred him distemper. The King asked the reason. They said because he had taken cold. The King replied, no, it was that which I had from the Duke that did it.

The opinion of the committee that this to be annexed to the Duke's charge: a transcendent presumption of dangerous consequence.

27. Concerning the question of sending for the officers of the Customs House, see above, n. 6.

28. Regarding Ramsey and Atkins, see HofC, 24 April, nn. 16 and 24; concerning Lister, see HofC, 25 April, n. 37.

29. Regarding Hay, see HofC, 24 April, n. 18.

30. See above, n. 15.

ORDER OF BUSINESS FRIDAY, 28 APRIL 1626

FRIDAY, 28 APRIL 1626

I. JOURNAL OF THE HOUSE OF COMMONS

[CJ 850; p. 36]
Veneris, 28 Aprilis, 2 Caroli Regis

Sir J. Altham's bill, Monday, 2 clock.

L. 1a. An act for the increase of trade.[1]

MR. SAUNDERS informs,[2] that in a suit commenced by Sir Thomas Horwood concerning the inheritance of Mr. Unton Croke wherein the plaintiff has proceeded in examination of witnesses, notwithstanding it were known Mr. Croke was a member of this House/

MR. CROKE further informs, that Sir Thomas Horwood reviled him, saying he came to be a member of this House by bribery and corruption.

Upon question, resolved that Mr. Croke shall have privilege, and that Mr. Speaker shall write a letter to the Lord Keeper for suppressing of the depositions thus taken.

Resolved also, that Sir Thomas Horwood shall be sent for to answer his contempt to the House in his proceeding in Chancery, knowing Mr. Croke to be a parliament man; and also to answer the said words so spoken to Mr. Croke.

Resolved also, the commissioners[3] shall be sent for. The committee of privileges to examine them and report their opinions to the House. So also for Sir Thomas Horwood's offense aforesaid.

MR. NOY reports the bill of apparel: 1, that the committees held this a very necessary law; some amendments made, which 2 read.

The petition of the drawers, etc., of gold and silver thread read.[4]

Upon question, the petitioners to be heard before the bill about apparel pass.

2ly, upon question they shall be heard by their counsel, in the House, upon Monday morning.[5]

The bill,[6] upon question, recommitted, 2 clock, Monday.[7]

MR. WANDESFORD reports from the grand committee yesterday concerning the Duke of Buckingham.

A general resolution amongst all the King's sworn physicians that nothing should be ministered to the King without a joint consent of them all.

Reports the 4 things resolved by them upon question.[8]

[CJ 851] Killing of a c[ommon] person by a madman, no felony; his killing of a King, treason.[9] Otherwise, of offering to strike a King, whereby he may be killed.

That none of the questions so resolved were in any particular crossed by any testimony whatsoever.

1. This is the bill for the increase of trade that was brought down from the Lords on 18 March. An earlier bill for trade (the staples bill) had been rejected by the House on 14 March, see HofC, 14 March, n. 5.

2. *reports* is crossed out in the MS preceding *informs*.

3. I.e., the commissioners who took the examinations in the case. See Whitelocke, below.

4. This petition had been earlier read and deferred by the House, see HofC, 26 April, n. 6.

5. The wiredrawers' counsel was heard in the House on 5 May. See OB.

6. *Resolved to respite the recommitment* is crossed out in the MS preceding *The bill.*

7. *tomorrow* is crossed out in the MS and *Monday* is inserted.

8. For the four points resolved at the committee of the whole House, see HofC, 27 April, OB.

9. See *SR*, 33 H. VIII, c. 20, *An act for due process to be had in High Treason in cases of lunacy and madness;* see also Coke, *Fourth Inst.*, pp. 6–7.

1. Upon question, resolved that a plaster applied and a drink given to the late King in the time of his last sickness, without the advice of his sworn physicians, and not made by his sworn apothecaries or surgeons, contrary to the general directions of the physicians and after particularly disliked by them.

[p. 37] 2ly. Upon question, the application of the plaster and giving of the drink to the late King, agreed upon the last question, is an act of a transcendent presumption of a dangerous consequence.

3ly. Upon question, this drink was given to the late King by the Duke and the plaster applied to him by the Duke's direction.

4ly. Upon question, resolved that this shall be annexed to the rest of the Duke's charge.[10]

Resolved, the grand committee for grievances and all other the grand committees to proceed upon their several days appointed.[11]

Sir Robert Howard's business to be proceeded[12] in tomorrow, if conveniently may be; else, upon Monday next.

II. DIARY OF BULSTRODE WHITELOCKE, ESQ., DD. 12.21, CAMBRIDGE UNIVERSITY LIBRARY

[f. 165v]

April 28

MR. SAUNDERS. That between Sir Thomas Horwood and Mr. Unton Croke, a member of this House, a suit was begun in Chancery and answered by the member of this House before he had privilege. After, before the time of parliament, they joined in a commission which was not executed. But after, in time of parliament, the plaintiff renewed the commission and took divers depositions and examinations. The member of this House told them that he was a parliament man and required his privilege in the time of the examinations taken, but could not bring the Speaker's letter for staying the proceedings by reason of an order of the House that no motions should be heard. Mr. Horwood said that Mr. Croke came into the parliament by bribery and corruption.

Ordered by the House in this case, that the Speaker's letter shall be sent to the Lord Keeper for suppressing of the depositions taken, and the commissioners sent for, and Sir Thomas Horwood to answer the words spoken against the member of the House and his contempt against the privilege of the House.

MR. NOY reports the bill concerning apparel; which is recommitted.

Petition of the wiredrawers and weavers of gold and silver thread.[13] That there are 10,000 souls that live by this trade. Desires they may be heard by the counsel.

Resolved, that the petitioners shall be heard by counsel in the House on Monday morn next.[14]

MR. WANDESFORD reports from the committee of the whole House yesterday their resolutions concerning the matter reported from the committee of 12.[15]

[f. 166] CHANCELLOR EXCHEQUER. That the Duke cares not whether in this any man speaks for him or not, but relies wholly upon his own innocency. The word "presumption" does infer a crime following.

10. *to be prepared by the select committee* is crossed out in the MS following *charge*.

11. For the days assigned for the meetings of each of the grand committees, see HofC, 10 February, OB.

12. Printed edition: *proceeding*.

13. See above, n. 4.

14. See above, n. 5.

15. See above, n. 8.

SIR JOHN ELIOT. Variety of opinions have so good consequence that I must commend them, for by debate and reasoning pro and con truth comes to light. It is a weak argument for excuse of any future ill to allege former merits. Manlius Torquatus's example.[16]

MR. LITTLETON. The fact in this case is a presumption and that word not to be understood according to Chancellor Exchequer's sense.

MR. WHITAKER. *Res una testificatione probata nulli est momenti.* Doctor Ramsey's testimony is with me of little force,[17] I know him so well. Scipio example, and Hannibal's, being both questioned in their several countries about the same time, a senator of Rome said that the two great cities of the world are ungrateful/[18]

As the word "transcendent" is excluded out of the 10 predicaments,[19] and I think it fit to be left out of the 10 charges against the Duke.

MR. KIRTON. I would be glad to hear of the testimony of Doctor Ramsey; but this I hear, that he is imprisoned for the words which he spoke.[20]

CHANCELLOR DUCHY. The King desired this plaster and often called for it and the Duke denied it him and prayed him to have the advice of his physicians. This business will but add to the bulk of the [f. 166v] charge, but not the weight of it.

SIR THOMAS JERMYN. My opinion has ever been that this was a great indiscretion and rashness of the Duke of Buckingham. If wisemen were always wise, fools would beg their bread. The Duke was not wise in this.

MR. NEWBERY. That good intentions will not excuse in an act done against the King. The Lord Southampton's intention was only to remove some about the Queen, but yet it excused not his fault.[21] And Sir Walter Tirel, when he killed the King, shot at a stag and his intention was not bad.[22]

[SIR ROBERT MANSELL.][23] Foscarini, an ambassador here from Venice about 14 years ago. That ambassador wrote so against the Spaniards and the Pope, so that he was called the patriot of the Venice state. He had an unfaithful secretary, one Muscorno/[24]

Inquisitori di stato are such as upon public fame go to inquiries of particulars, which are changed every sixth month and new chosen. Mistake carried this man to a high court, where he was condemned and executed accordingly upon witness and testimony before them taken. After, the new

16. I.e., Titus Manlius Torquatus, who gained great honor by defeating a gigantic Gaul in single combat, but whose popularity was later tarnished by the severity he showed, as consul, in sentencing his own son to death for engaging the enemy against his orders. Livy, 7, 10 and 8, 7.

17. For Ramsey's testimony, see HofC, 24 April, and n. 16.

18. We have not found the reference.

19. The Schoolmen applied the term "transcendent" to predicates that could not be classed under any of Aristotle's ten categories or predicaments.

20. See HofC, 24 April, n. 16.

21. Henry Wriothesley, third Earl of Southampton, was found guilty of High Treason in the Essex conspiracy even though he had no intention to harm the Queen. *DNB*.

22. Tirel shot the arrow that killed William II. See Holinshed, *Chronicle*, II, 44–45. Regarding the matter of intent in cases of treason, see Coke, *Fourth Inst.*, p. 6.

23. There is a blank space in the MS; the identification of Mansell is from Lowther, below.

24. Concerning the dispute between Antonio Foscarini, Venetian ambassador in England (1611–1615) and Giulio Muscorno, his secretary, see *CSPV 1613–1615*, pp. 481–483, 493–494, 514, 556; ibid., *1615–1617*, pp. 592–606, Index *sub* Foscarini and Muscorno; ibid., *1617–1619*, Index *sub* Foscarini and Muscorno. See also, W. Carew Hazlitt, *The Venetian Republic* (London, reprint, 1966), II, 188–197.

inquisitors found the former testimonies to be false and they were condemned.[25] I do not think fit that this concerning the Duke should be transmitted to the Lords.

Resolved by the House according to the several resolutions of the grand committee yesterday.

III. DIARY OF JOHN LOWTHER, ESQ., D/LONS/L, CUMBERLAND AND WESTMORLAND RECORD OFFICE

[f. 10]

[28 April]

Unton Croke by privilege of parliament had examinations, taken against him in Chancery, by letter from Speaker suppressed. Yet commissioners sent for, though knew not but by his allegation that he was parliament man. The party plaintiff also sent for because he said Croke came in by bribery and corruption.

Bill of apparel reported by NOY.

We added proviso for women [*illegible*]. If Lords dislike, they offer conference, not we.[26]

[f. 10v] WANDESFORD reports the great committee's resolution of the select committee. If the fact merit. Consulted: no physic but by common assent. They sent after medicine given; two to Duke, 2 to King, to advise to give, to take no more.

Resolved that p[osset] drink given contrary to direction, without advice; disliked after.

If madmen excuse[d] against common person, excused not against King.[27]

Plaster given before, King worse after; declining before. He in King's [*illegible*] refused to lay it on; so King's physicians dissuaded second time, as he says.

Doctor Moore, recusant to [*illegible*].[28]

The application and drink transcendent presumption, dangerous consequence.

Reports potion's receipt from Duke by Baker,[29] his recovery; his joy to be experimented for King. Given [*2 words illegible*]. He contrary physician, being treacle only. Physicians say King compounded of inverting [*sic*] quality.

Hay.[30] King commanded to fetch Duke's plaster. How that he had from Duke made him sick.

Resolved, Duke gave drink; plaster applied by his direction.

Resolved, as select committee, this to be annexed to the Duke's charge.

[f. 11] They observed no contradiction but Duke's direction and contrary direction.

Maull[31] not called because upon hearsay desired direction for another business which be[ing] found foul. Never intended upon first two for [*illegible*], yet conceive somewhat material.

CHANCELLOR EXCHEQUER. These seem presumptions to us which to kings and their near ones are but liberty. The word "presumption" seems to induce a crime, therefore thinks this to be no cause for a charge.

SIR JOHN ELIOT. 1, without knowledge or consent applied; 2, they refused proceeding until taken off.

25. In April 1622 Foscarini was accused of having "secretly and frequently conferred with strangers by day and night", and was condemned and executed the following month. See *CSPV 1621–1623*, pp. 284, 317. In January 1623 the Council of Ten rehabilitated Foscarini, admitting that the trial testimony had been based on falsehoods, beginning with rumors spread by Muscorno. See ibid., p. 546.

26. I.e., if the Lords dislike a change made by the Commons to a bill originating in the Upper House, then they initiate the conference to rectify it.

27. See above, n. 9.

28. Regarding Moore, see HofC, 24 April, n. 21.

29. Regarding Baker, see HofC, 25 April, n. 41.

30. Regarding Hay, see HofC, 24 April, n. 18.

31. The reference is probably to Patrick Maull, Groom of the Bedchamber. *CSPD 1623–1625*, p. 314.

SIR F. STEWART. King could not endure hot drinks as Chambers said.[32] Therefore how King could desire it, judge.

SIR THOMAS JERMYN. Sorrow to speak here against opinion once more.[33] After that conference heard it at court first and since that great rashness and indiscretion. If wisemen always wise, fools might beg.

NEWBERY. Southampton had no evil intention when he would have surprised Queen Elizabeth for an hour or two to have removed some from the Queen, yet was it adjudged treason.[34] Sir Walter Tirel shot at stag, killed King; no treason, no evil intention.[35] Duke received it 30, killed him 60. The boldness.

Resolved, an act of transcendent presumption of dangerous consequence.

[f. 11v] VICE CHAMBERLAIN. Digges remembered so well of old that he cannot forget him late. This not fit to be added. If taken by most senses not to be added but if [*2 words illegible*] against this or higher matter.

MANSELL. Why rested so great a while? Was a parliament before.[36] Then if no evil intent, no danger to him. Why to be charged if this added silence the rest? Thinks the committee intended well to preserve blood royal rather than impeach him so dear to [*illegible*] and same [*blank*].

Cites Ambassador [Fos]carini from Venice. A letter written from him so opposite to Pope or Spain as he held a patriot of that commonwealth. Muscorno, his secretary, gathered matter of infamy to disgrace his master's merit. He therefore sent for, imprisoned 3 years. The master came home. After the inquisitors upon fame inquired, witnesses could not justify, cost lives. The knave brought such particulars as seemed to accuse and condemned to higher court where to death he hung out. His name razed out, a confiscation. They out of office as 6 months; now found first false, the second just. Witnesses executed. Restitution by Senate, all [f. 12] that could be, but could not give life.[37]

We concluded fair cause to inquire. We have proceeded to accuse. Concluded as before. We remit it to other courts. What they will do we know not. Who may not be accused by fame have a commission of inquiry. Therefore desires this charge not to be added.

LONG. Justifies his argument, fire and ashes. He spoke of the ashes. In *suo conscientia* he judge equal to and not injudicious. He had rather to have this set on Duke than this House having so far condemned the fact. We but inquisitors, they to jud[ge].

Resolved, [as by] that committee, this to be annexed to the Duke's charge.

IV. DIARY OF SIR NATHANIEL RICH, HIST. COLLECT. 143, HLRO

[f. 82v]

28 April, Friday

Privilege. Sir T. Horwood takes depositions in Chancery against Mr. Unton Croke. This agreed upon to be against privilege and the Speaker ordered to write to my Lord Keeper to suppress the deposition. The commissioners sent for to be questioned at the committee of privileges and Sir Thomas Horwood[38]self also to be sent

32. Regarding Chambers, see HofC, 24 April, n. 20. For his testimony at the committee, see HofC, 25 April, OB.

33. See Jermyn's speeches of 11 and 27 March (OBs).

34. See above, n. 21.

35. See above, n. 22.

36. I.e., the parliament of 1625 met between the death of James I and the current parliamentary investigation into the circumstances of his death.

37. See above, nn. 24 and 25.

38. MS: *Howard*.

for to the committee of privileges, who was accused of ill language given to Mr. Croke.

Report of the bill of apparel by MR. NOY in which observes that it concerns all strangers except ambassadors because all strangers being in England are for that time the King's subjects, are taken to take knowledge of the laws of England at their peril.

[f. 83] MR. WANDESFORD. Report of the plaster and posset given the King without advice, *in superis error crimen habere solet.* And if a madman kill a common person it is not felony, but if he kill the King it shall be treason as if it had been done by a man of reason.

MR. GRIFFITH. The witnesses differed in point of declination of the disease. Upon the testimony of Dr. Ramsey and Dr. Atkins,[39] he would if he had been of the Duke's jury, he would have condemned him to death.

39. For the testimony of Ramsey and Atkins, see HofC, 24 April, and nn. 16 and 24.

Order of Business Saturday, 29 April 1626

Committee on the bill for the abridging of the number of **unskillful attorneys** to meet on Monday [1 May]; all that come to have voice	97, *16/3
Committee on the bill for the preservation and increase of **salmon** to meet on Tuesday [2 May]	97, *14/2
Committee on the bill to enable James **Ward** to sell certain lands to meet on Tuesday [2 May]	97, *17/3
Committee of **religion** to proceed in the business concerning the **Bishop of Bangor** on Monday [1 May]	97, *17/4
Committee of **religion** given power to appoint subcommittees to go to examine those that are sick, etc., concerning saying **mass,** printing **popish books,** etc.	97
Committee on **Willes's** petition and the **Dover** business to meet on Wednesday [3 May]	97, *8/3
Petition from some **apothecaries:** read and referred to the committee on the bill for the avoiding of deceits in making of **medicines** and concerning **apothecaries**	97, *23/2
Petition from Mr. **Sewster:** read and referred to the committee on the bill to make void certain conveyances unconscionably gotten from Giles Sewster; nineteen members added to the committee; to meet on Thursday [4 May]	97, *20/2
Sir Dudley Carleton (Vice Chamberlain): moves for a committee for drawing a bill to prevent **contagion and plague**	97, 100, 102, *5/5
Committee for drawing a bill to prevent contagion and plague: appointed	97, 100
Sir James Perrot: concerning moving the Lords to join in a petition to the King for a **general fast**	100, *3/5; 6/6; 7/6; 9/6; 14/6
Sir Nathaniel Rich	100
Sir Dudley Carleton (Vice Chamberlain)	100
Committee for considering reasons to be used when the Commons pray a conference with the Lords about a general fast: appointed	98, 100
Message from the King regarding speedy presentation of the business concerning the **Duke of Buckingham** to him or to the Lords (Sir Richard Weston, Chancellor Exchequer)	98, 100, 102, *21/4; 3/5
John Glanville	100
Resolved: privy councillors of the House to give the King thanks for his message	98, 100
Resolutions concerning charges against Richard **Montagu**	98, 101, 102, 103, *20/2
Report from the committee of **religion** concerning way of transmitting charges against **Montagu** (John Pym)	98, 101
Sir Benjamin Rudyard	101
Sir Nathaniel Rich	99, 102, 103
Orders concerning transmitting the charges against Montagu to the Lords	99, 101, 102
Roger Matthew: concerning new stay of English	

SATURDAY, 29 APRIL 1626

I. JOURNAL OF THE HOUSE OF COMMONS

[CJ 851; p. 37]
Sabbati, 29 Aprilis, 2 Caroli Regis

Bill concerning attorneys, Monday, 2 clock, and all that will come to have voice.

Bill for preservation of salmon, etc., Tuesday next, 2 clock.

Ward's bill, Tuesday, 2 clock.

The committee for religion to proceed in the business for the Lord Bishop of Bangor upon Monday in the afternoon, and so to adjourn themselves as they shall find fittest for dispatch of the business.

The committee for religion to have power to make subcommittees to go and examine any that be sick, or in prison, or other lawful impediment, concerning saying of mass, or printing of popish books, or other thing of that nature.

Wednesday next, 2 clock, for Dover business.

A petition from some of the apothecaries, read.[1] This referred to the committee for the bill of apothecaries and they to hear counsel of both parts.

A petition from Mr. Sewster, read.[2]

Mr. [William] Coryton, Sir Thomas Grantham, Sir William Strode, Sir P[eter] Heyman, Mr. [Thomas] Smith, Mr. [Humphrey] Newbery, Sir Richard Buller, Mr. Browne, Sir Clement Throckmorton, Sir A[lexander] Temple, Sir A. St. John, Sir John Savile, Mr. [Edward] Bysshe, Mr. [Giles] Greene, Mr. [Paul] Speccott, Sir Charles Morrison, Sir John Gyll, Mr. [John] Pole, Mr. [Christopher] Erle, added to the committee.

Thursday next, 2 clock, in the former place.

MR. VICE CHAMBERLAIN moves a select committee for drawing a bill to prevent contagion.

[col. 1]
Mr. Vice Chamberlain
Mr. Chancellor Duchy
Knights and citizens of London and Westminster and Southwark
Sir Nathaniel Rich
Sir Thomas Grantham
Dr. [Samuel] Turner

[col. 2]
Sir H[enry] Poole
Sir George More
Sir Robert Harley
Sir John Finch
Sir H[umphrey] Lynde
Sir Nicholas Saunders

[col. 3]
Sir Francis Goodwin
Sir A[rthur] Ingram
Sir Thomas Dacres
Mr. [Edward] Littleton
Mr. Clarke
Mr. Rolle

[col. 4]
Mr. [William] Noy
Sir B[enjamin] Rudyard
Sir John Stradling
Sir William Slingsby
Sir John Savile
Mr. Lowther
Sir H[enry] Marten

[col. 5][3]
Sir Thomas Puckering
Mr. [Richard] Spencer
Sir Thomas Barrington
Mr. [John] Carvill
Sir William Owen
Mr. Francis Finch

1. We have not found the petition. Presumably it related to the apothecaries bill introduced on 23 February.

2. We have not found Sewster's petition. See the bill to void conveyances unconscionably gotten from Giles and Samuel Sewster, that had been committed on 13 March. The following names are being added to the original committee, although one included here, Sir Peter Heyman, had already been appointed.

3. The list set as column 5 was entered by the Clerk in the left-hand margin of the MS.

Monday next, 2 clock, Star Chamber; [with] power to send for physicians and apothecaries.

[p. 38][4] Much debate whether this question[5] should be 1st put; or a question for a select committee to consider of the reasons for which we move it.

Upon question, a select committee to be named to consider of and set down the reasons which shall be used by the committee when we pray a conference with the Lords about a general fast.

[col. 1]
Mr. Vice Chamberlain
Mr. Chancellor Exchequer
Mr. Chancellor Duchy
Sir Edwin Sandys
Sir Nathaniel Rich
Mr. [John] Pym

[col. 2]
Sir D[udley] Digges
Sir George More
Sir J[ames] Perrot
Sir John Stradling
Sir Robert Mansell
Sir Thomas Hoby
Sir Robert Pye

[col. 3]
Mr. [Humphrey] Newbery
Sir Thomas Barrington
Sir W[alter] Erle
Sir Robert Harley
Sir Eubule Thelwall
Mr. [William] Coryton
Sir H[enry] Poole

This afternoon, 2 clock, Exchequer Chamber.

MR. CHANCELLOR OF THE EXCHEQUER delivers a message from his Majesty: that he, having given way to the inquiry about the Duke of Buckingham, and hearing there is new matter intended to be brought in, in respect of the season of the year and the affairs of the state, desires the House therein will avoid all loss of time, and leaves them to their own way, either by presenting the [*blank*][6] to himself, or to the Lords.

Mr. Chancellor of the Exchequer, and Mr. Vice Chamberlain, and Chancellor Duchy, to return humble thanks to his Majesty for this gracious message.

Upon question, Mr. Montagu guilty in his books of publishing matter contrary to the doctrine of the Church of England.[7]

2ly, that many seditious passages in those books of Mr. Montagu apparently tending to the public disturbance of Church and state.

3ly, that many passages in those books tending to draw the subjects of this kingdom from the doctrine of the Church of England to the doctrine of the Church of Rome.

Upon question resolved, the 4 several heads of aggravations reported, to be added to his charge.[8]

All without 1 negative.

Upon question, these charges upon Mr. Montagu to be transmitted to the Lords for their judgment upon them.

MR. PYM reports that the committee thought fittest the way to be by a conference

4. The following entry is crossed out in the MS at the top of the page: *Upon question, resolved to desire a conference with the Lords to join in a petition to his Majesty for a public fast throughout the kingdom upon those important reasons which shall be proposed to their Lordships by those which shall be employed by this House in the conference.*

5. I.e., the question crossed out in the MS. See n. 4, above.

6. *complaint.* Cobbett, *Parl. Hist.*, II, 102. Although the speeches of the King and Lord Keeper to both Houses on 29 March had pressed the Commons to halt the inquisition concerning the Duke of Buckingham, following the Commons' remonstrance delivered to the King on 5 April the King refrained from direct attempts to restrain the Commons' inquiry. However, in his messages of 13, 18, and 20 April, Charles continued to urge the House to lay aside other business including the Buckingham inquiry, to provide for the King's supply.

7. The resolution on the three heads of the charge against Richard Montagu, reported from the committee of religion by John Pym on 17 April. See OB.

8. For the four "aggravations", see Pym's report in Whitelocke, 17 April.

with the Lords, and the charge to be distributed into 5 parts: 1, an introduction; 2ly, the [p. 39] charges concerning doctrine; 3, matter of sedition; 4, the seducing of the King's subjects; 5, the matter of aggravation and praying of judgment.

SIR NATHANIEL RICH. To have all this done by Mr. Pym, and to have it done not at a conference but by a message to be delivered at the bar in the Lords House, where it may be more public; which is the ancient way, and not fit for us to lose, and so was done 12 *Jac.*, by Sir Edward Hoby against the Bishop of Durham.[9]

Which ordered upon question.

This shall be delivered to the Lords by way of message; and this to be delivered by Mr. Pym at such time as Mr. Pym shall inform the House that he can be ready; and the exceptions to the books to be there left, in writing, for the better expedition of the business. The same writing to be first agreed upon by the former committee.[10]

MR. MATTHEW informs the House that a new stay is made of the merchants' goods in France, upon pretense of losses sustained here by unjust stay of the *St. Peter.*[11]

The further debate thereof referred to Monday next, 9 clock, upon question.

MR. SELDEN tenders interrogatories touching the proceedings against Sir Robert Howard.[12]

Moved Sir H. Marten should withdraw.[13]

SIR H. MARTEN heard to speak for himself. That he has neither vilified in word, nor act, the privileges of this House in the person of Sir Robert Howard. His answer 4 heads:

1. That he knew not privilege of parliament was due to Sir Robert Howard, *5* or *7 Martii* was 12month.[14]

[CJ 852] The parliament, *3 Martii,*[15] prorogued to 20 Apr. after.[16] He knew not he was a parliament man or ever had been, nor that *3 Martii,* any speech of a parliament. But *17 Martii* he claimed it, and it was then disputed. That he then knew not he was to have privilege of parliament, though he knew he was a parliament man.

2ly. That he was not bound to take notice that he ought to have that privilege. This knowledge out of his profession.[17] He never had been a parliament man.[18] He never had read anything about it nor knew what a prorogation meant, nor the difference between that and an adjournment. Thinks every man is to take notice of privilege of a parliament man in parliament time and *eundo* and *redeundo.*

3ly. He gave no opinion in it, nor ever was asked the question. It came never so low as Mr. Comptroller, there being no room for him to sit at the table.[19]

4ly. It had not been mannerly for him to have opposed, there being there so many

9. Concerning the case of Richard Neile, present Bishop of Durham, in 1614, see HofC, 22 April, n. 5.

10. I.e., the subcommittee for considering Montagu's books that, on 17 April, was made a select committee of the House for drawing interrogatories to be ministered unto Montagu. See HofC, 17 April, OB.

11. Concerning the seizure of English ships and goods in France, see HofC, 17 February, n. 20; and 22 February, nn. 3, 7, and 11. Concerning the stay of the *St. Peter,* see HofC, 22 February, nn. 4, 6, 8, 9, 10, and 15.

12. On 21 March the committee for Howard's case, appointed on 17 February, had been directed to consider questions to be asked of those who were to testify in the House concerning the case. See HofC, 21 March, OB.

13. I.e., because Marten, as a member of the High Commission, had been a party to the proceedings against Howard.

14. Concerning the dates related to the Howard case, see Selden's report, HofC, 21 March, OB.

15. Printed edition: *5.*

16. Concerning the prorogations of parliament, see HofC, 21 March, nn. 6 and 7.

17. I.e., as a civil lawyer.

18. Marten did not sit as a member of parliament until 1625.

19. I.e., at the High Commission. Sir John Suckling, Comptroller of the Household, signed the warrant committing Howard. See Selden's report, 21 March.

experienced parliament [*blank*] and he having had none.

Sir William Beecher. That Mr. Comptroller is sick.

Sir H. Marten, by direction of the House, after his speech, withdrew.[20]

1. That he knew nothing that Sir Robert was a parliament man *5 Martii,* 1624; but put his hand to the warrant, when brought him.

2ly. That they used not to sit but in full term. Upon occasions, upon the King's command or upon the Lord of Canterbury's special direction, sometime they do.

3ly. That they do sometime imprison close upon great occasions. That petty commissioners never do it, but great persons.

[p. 40] That he did nothing by any man's direction, or persuasion, about the commitment or excommunication of Sir Robert Howard.

Being demanded what he meant by the words, "That he came not to serve turns",[21] he said, [he] came not to serve any. And demanded who else did, says he knows not, but the assembly was extraordinary.

Being demanded whether the commission warrant close imprisonment he answers: it warrants imprisonment; but whether or not, remembers not.

Upon question, resolved to defer the further consideration hereof till Tuesday next, and against that time the rest to be warned, and then heard.

II. Diary of Bulstrode Whitelocke, Esq., DD. 12.21, Cambridge University Library

[f. 167]

April 29

Vice Chamberlain moves that a select committee may be appointed to consider of a law for the preventing of the increase of the plague hereafter and keeping out the infection.

Ordered accordingly.

Sir James Perrot. That we may move the Lords to join with us in a suit to the King for a public general fast throughout the Kingdom, for such important reasons as shall be set down in the conference with the Lords.

Sir Nathaniel Rich. In E. 3 time the King was petitioned for a general fast for the good success of the parliament and good correspondence between the King and the people.[22] Moves for a select committee to consider of the reasons for this fast before we desire the conference with the Lords.

Vice Chamberlain. In all places abroad they used first to set down the reasons whereupon they shall appoint a fast, and afterwards appoint it.

A committee is appointed to consider of those reasons which shall be used when we pray a conference with the Lords about a public fast.

[f. 167v] Chancellor Exchequer. I am commanded to deliver a short message from his Majesty: His Majesty, having given way to the proceedings of this House, desires this House to use all possible diligence and expedition in it and is indifferent whether you present it to him or to the Lords.

Upon Mr. Glanville's motion that some of the honorable person[s] may give the King thanks for this gracious message, all the Privy Council of the House are enjoined to do it.

20. After his withdrawal Marten was called back into the House where he responded to the following questions put to him by the Speaker.

21. Concerning these words, see Whitelocke and Rich, below.

22. We have not found the petition.

Resolved that Mr. Montagu is guilty of publishing doctrine contrary to the articles of religion established in our Church.[23]

Resolved, there are many seditious passages in those books of Mr. Montagu apparently tending to the public disturbance of Church and state.

Resolved that there are passages in those books tending to draw the subjects of this kingdom to/

Resolved that the 4 heads [of] aggravations reported by Mr. Pym, 17 April, shall be added to the charge of Mr. Montagu.[24]

Resolved that these charges against Mr. Montagu shall be transmitted to the Lords for their judgment.

[f. 168] MR. PYM. That the opinion of the committee of religion was that this should be transmitted to the Lords by a conference, which they divided into 5 parts: 1, introduction; 2, the charge; 3, sedition/

SIR BENJAMIN RUDYARD. That Mr. Pym may relate it to the Lords as he did here, and in their House.

Ordered that these charges against Mr. Montagu shall be delivered by way of message to the Lords.

Ordered that on Monday next at 9 a clock the business concerning the stay of the ship *St. Peter* of Newhaven shall be further considered of.[25]

Sir Robert Howard's business being called for, it is moved that Sir Henry Marten may withdraw, it concerning him.[26] But before he answer, the House will not cause him to withdraw.

SIR HENRY MARTEN. If I have either violated in words or vilified in deeds the privilege of this House in Sir Robert Howard's person, I/

Says that he was a Commissioner, but am not guilty of breach of the privilege of this House in his person—I utterly deny. There are 2 answers: *quoad hominem* and *quoad rem.* All that I am to say is *pro homine.*

I reduce my answer to 4 heads. [1.] I did not know that privilege of [f. 168v] parliament belonged to Sir Robert Howard, 17 *Martii,* nor that then he was or had been of a parliament.[27] 2. I was not bound by common intendment to have knowledge of it. 3. I did not overrule the court in this. 4. As I had not power to hinder the decision of that business, so it had not been manners nor discretion in me to have opposed it.

It is true that 17 *Martii* Sir Robert Howard did demand his privilege, and after argument it was resolved that he should not have his privilege. I was passively overruled. I gave no opinion against Sir Robert Howard, nor/

In the journal book 29 Eliz., Martin's case, said that the time was uncertain after or before sessions of parliament how long the privilege of parliament men should last.[28] Presently after 25 H. 8 this commission came forth, when it was acknowledged that the King was supreme head in spiritual matters.[29] And this High Commission does very much check popery and superstition,

23. See above, n. 7.
24. See above, n. 8.
25. See above, n. 11.
26. See above, n. 13.
27. See above, n. 14.
28. See D'Ewes, *Journal . . . Elizabeth,* p. 414; the case refers to either Nicholas Martin or Henry Martyn, both MPs in the parliament of 1586.

29. For the act establishing the King as the supreme head of the Church of England, see *SR,* 26 H. 8, c. 1; for the origins of the High Commission in a commission issued to Thomas Cromwell c. 1535, see Roland G. Usher, *The Rise and Fall of the High Commission* (Oxford, 1968), chap. 1; and see also, G. W. Prothero, *Select Statutes and other Constitutional Documents* (Oxford, 1898), pp. 404–407, 424–434.

and the popish party hold[s] it to be the greatest grievance in the kingdom.

SIR WILLIAM BEECHER. That Mr. Comptroller is sick.

Sir Henry Marten, being called upon to withdraw, goes out.[30]

That he knew not of any claim of Sir Robert Howard's privilege the first time, but did know of it the second time. That he did subscribe to the warrant and to the/

[f. 169] That they usually sit in full term, but upon the King's commandment or the Archbishop of Canterbury['s] special directions the High Commission Court does sit out of term. That it is unusual to commit to close imprisonment, but if the person or cause deserve it they do, but they never do it by the ordinary commission. That he is not so base a man as to follow any man's direction or contemplation when he sits in court, neither then did he. That he has not seen so great an appearance in the High Commission Court as was when Sir Robert Howard's business was handled, but cannot tell who of them came thither to serve turns, but thinks some of them were brought. That he knows not whether the Commissioners have power to commit close prisoners or not. That no man did solicit him to come to the court that day.

The consideration of this business concerning Sir Robert Howard is respited till Tuesday.

III. DIARY OF JOHN LOWTHER, ESQ., D/LONS/L, CUMBERLAND AND WESTMORLAND RECORD OFFICE

[f. 12]

[29 April]

VICE CHAMBERLAIN shows how the plague in Paris and Venice and other great cities through government does little hurt; in other places from excess.[31] Desires a bill, offers his knowledge to help. Care the King make no profit by the ordering.

CHANCELLOR EXCHEQUER. King having given way against Duke and hearing of new matter to be brought against Duke; wherein, desiring his honor should no[t] be in suspense, desires not hinder the business of commonwealth: it may be presented, cares not whether to King or Lords.

[f. 12v] Montagu resolved to be transmitted with the charge and aggravation: 1, publishing doctrine contrary [to] English Church established by the Articles and Homilies;[32] 2, seditious passage to disturbance of Church and state; 3, to draw English to Romish.

Disgrace of Protestant divines. Profaneness and scurrility at preaching and other divine exercises.

Required by SIR NATHANIEL RICH to be transmitted by message to be delivered at Lord's bar by Mr. Pym, as formerly done by Sir Edward Hoby against Bishop of Durham.[33]

Resolved accordingly; and the exceptions to be left in writing with the Lords, first to be approved by the committee.[34]

Monday 9 of clock French *Peter* stayed, to be put to question upon Duke.

MR. SELDEN. In Sir Robert Howard's case the High Commissioners under Lords to be questioned and questions prepared by committee.[35]

SIR H. MARTEN heard before proceeded to censure. Acknowledges if true the of-

30. See above, n. 20.

31. Sir Dudley Carleton succeeded Sir Henry Wotton as English ambassador in Venice in 1610-1615. He had spent time earlier in Paris, travelling with the Duke of Northumberland, and in 1625 accompanied the Earl of Holland on an embassy to Louis XIII. See HofC, 18 April, n. 4. *DNB*.

32. Concerning the Articles and Homilies, see HofC, 17 April, n. 10.

33. See above, n. 9.

34. See above, n. 10.

35. See above, n. 12.

fense great. Recites the resolution of the House of his claim that ought to be allowed, denied. He a Commissioner but denies breach of privilege. Mentions 2 answers, both good, one for the man, another for the matter. The matter is resolved and now must believe. For the man/

[f. 13] He makes 4 heads: 1, he knew not that he ought to have privilege; 2, not bound by reason to know it; 3, he overruled and passive as he; 4, it became not his degree.

To the first. Parliament began February, continued till May. Divers prorogations by proclamation last from 3 of March till 20 of April.[36] King died 27 *Martii.* His first vowing was 5 of March. If he did aver the first day he parliament man, motives honorable, etc.; then claimed no parliament. 17 [March] he argued it; showed how Keeper gave privilege for that. Keeper denied for that. All reasons avoided as no good challenge. So to have privilege he knew not.

2. Judge though must know things proper to his court, yet not things dehors, as physic. Parliament he not experienced,[37] not read, so not bound by law or reason to know it. He understood not difference between prorogation and adjournment, but if parliament had sat reason might prove it, but not now upon adjournment. Where he sits alone, he will allow it and *peccare tutior.*

3. He overruled. He gave no opinion. It came not so low as Comptroller, but overruled as he was.

4. When all Lords there he had no power, and discretion would not he should speak but when it is not in his element. [f. 13v] Should he say to Lord President, you have been judge of law, have no knowledge, and contradict? He a judge at his cost, attends not of his will nor of purpose, confesses an error in knowledge.

29 Eliz., Martin's case, time of privilege uncertain;[38] now students say 16 days allowed,[39] Clerk of Parliament says no. Therefore not to be intended to have so great knowledge as to know it.

Desires now upon occasion to think well of it, for 25 H. 8 it came in upon head of Church.[40] 1 Eliz., settled.[41] It checked popery until Gondomar took out recusants from it.[42] Prays, since they have no profit, to have good opinion.

Speaker to speak with his hat off that is a member,[43] so put off to Sir H. Marten when he questioned him upon interrogatories.

Ordinary Commissioners do not imprison closely nor excommunicate and imprison *simul et semel.*

IV. DIARY OF SIR NATHANIEL RICH, HIST. COLLECT. 143, HLRO

[f. 83]

29 April

Montagu—that the report should be made by Mr. P[ym] alone: 1, because the material well digested and already lodged in his memory, and approved by the House, and will be brief and yet substantial.[44]

Fit to be done in the House of Lords for 1, it will make a more lively and general impression; 2, be more entirely and fully delivered; 3, carried with secrecy; 4, it is more for the honor of our House and proper to transacting business in the place

36. See above, n. 16.

37. See above, n. 18.

38. See above, n. 28.

39. Concerning the sixteen-day period of privilege, see HofC, 9 February, n. 25.

40. See above, n. 29.

41. *SR,* 1 Eliz. I, c. 1, pt. 8.

42. Gondomar encouraged the practice of ambassadors from Catholic countries at the time of their departure from England requesting the release of recusants from prison. See SP 14/83:25. In June 1618, at Gondomar's request seventy-four priests were released to go abroad. SP 14/97:95.

43. I.e., Marten was to be recognized as a member, not simply as a witness. See Rich, below.

44. The following entries appear to be notes for Rich's own speech proposing that Pym deliver the charges against Montagu. See CJ, above.

where none but parliament are admitted than to move into a place free from [*2 symbols illegible*]; 5, it tends to the preservation of our privilege not to go always one way when we may both. This meeting at conference was first settled 2 R. 2, nos. 23, 24;[45] and Sir Edward Hoby, 12 *Jac.*, accused the now Bishop of Durham in the Lords' House too. It may disadvantage our accusation, the Lords appointing the number, time, and place.

SIR H. MARTEN. A double answer, both allowable: 1, *quoad rem;* 2ly, *quoad hominem.* For the first:

1. He did not know that privilege of parliament did belong to Sir Robert Howard. This privilege is sometimes apparent, sometimes not. The parliament began Feb. 21; 29 May then prorogued to November. Sir Robert Howard imprisoned the 5th of March. At that time he knew that Sir Robert Howard was a parliament man but the 17th of March Sir Robert Howard disputed it [*sic*]. [f. 83v] Lord Keeper told him he had not his *corpus cum causa,* not in contemplation of his privilege of parliament, but of the King's proclamation. 2ly, it was not proper to him to take knowledge of it, neither was he bound to know it, nor could do it, for he never had been of parliament, neither did he find it in books.

29 Eliz., the time of privilege of parliament uncertain. The High Commission began 35 H. 8[46] when ecclesiastical jurisdiction was first acknowledged to be in the person of the King, but this commission was first regulated by act of parliament, *a*[*nno*] 1 Eliz.[47] The papists taken out of the High Commission. Commissioners do not usually commit to close prison.

Rule for order. That Sir H. Marten having made his answer the House required him to withdraw, which he did; but then was called in again to his place and asked divers questions which were prepared by a committee. And after, divers members of the House prayed the Speaker to ask him other questions, as SIR JOHN STRANGWAYS (Sir H. Marten all this while sitting), whether whereas he had said he came not to serve turns, 1, whether he knew of any turn there to be served or any that came for that end. He answered no. Then MR. EVERSFIELD desired him to be asked whether they did not in the High Commission Court begin to give suffrage at the lower end. He answered they, at that time, gave no suffrage because no question asked, but when the question asked they begin at the lowest. Another question whether by their commission they may commit close prisoner. He answered he knew not, etc.

And note further of Mr. Speaker, when he questioned Sir H. Marten offering to sit with his hat on while he spoke, upon motion of SIR T. HOBY for the order of the House that he, speaking in his place of Speaker, should not question him but with his hat off, he standing up, which he did.

45. *Rot. Parl.*, 2 R. II, nos. 23–24.

46. The citation is incorrect. See above, n. 29.

47. See above, n. 41.

Order of Business Monday, 1 May 1626

Committee of the whole on the bill for the **continuance and repeal** of divers **statutes** to meet Wednesday [3 May]	107, 110, *23/3
Report from the committee on the bill for settling estates of tenants of Henry Lord **Morley**	107, *17/2
Ordered: the above bill to be engrossed	107, 110
L.1a. An act for sale of certain lands which were late Sir Henry **Clere's**	107, 110, *4/5; 23/5; 25/5
Resolved: report from the committee of **grievances** to be made on Thursday [4 May]	107, 110
Report from the committee on the bill against **secret offices** and inquisitions (Sir Thomas Malet)	107, 110, *13/2
Ordered: the above bill to be engrossed	107, 110
Report from the committee of **religion:** concerning Mr. **Cleydon** (John Pym)	107, 108, 110, *25/3
Sir Thomas Hoby	111
Resolved: Cleydon to bring a certificate of his taking the oaths and then to be dismissed	107, 108, 111
Report from the committee of religion: concerning **Morgan Lewis,** suspected of being a popish schoolmaster (John Pym)	107, *10/6
Ordered: Lewis to be sent for	107, 108
Edward Whitby: concerning the estate of Sir Richard **Grosvenor,** MP, and the actions of Dr. **Trevers**	107, 109
Resolved: to proceed no further in this business until the House is better informed	107, 109
L.2a. An act for restoring of certain monies to Dame Elizabeth **Dale,** widow, taken from Sir Thomas Dale	107, 111, *19/4
Robert Bateman	111
Sir John Eliot	111
Bill concerning Dale: committed	107, 111
Sir Peter Heyman: delivers in a petition of John **Brookes** against the **East India Company**	111
Brookes's petition is read and referred to the committee of **grievances**	108, 111
Report from the committee for preparing the business concerning **seizure** of the **wine merchants' goods in France** and the stay of the **St. Peter** (Sir John Eliot)	109, 111, *18/2
Sir John Finch	111
Sir Thomas Hoby	112
Sir Humphrey May (Chancellor Duchy)	112
Sir Dudley Carleton (Vice Chamberlain)	109, 112
Christopher Wandesford	113
Sir William Beecher	113
John Bankes	114
Mr. Rolle	109, 114
Sir Walter Erle	114
Mr. Browne	114
Mr. Long	114
William Strode	114
Sir Richard Weston (Chancellor Exchequer)	114
Sir Dudley Digges	114
Richard Spencer	114
Sir George More	114
Humphrey Newbery	115
John Pym	115
Sir William Strode	115
Sir George Goring	115
Sir Nathaniel Rich	115
Christopher Wandesford	115

MONDAY, 1 MAY 1626

I. JOURNAL OF THE HOUSE OF COMMONS

[CJ 852; p. 40]

Lunae, 1 Maii, 2 Caroli Regis

Continuance of statutes, upon Wednesday morning next, 8 clock.

Bill for Lord Morley's tenants reported without any amendments. *Engrossetur.*

L. 1a. An act for sale of certain lands which were late Sir H. Clere's, Knight and Baronet, deceased, for payment of his debts.

The report for the grievances unreported to be upon Thursday next.

The bill against secret offices (recommitted)[1] reported by MR. MALET. *Engrossetur.*

MR. PYM moves for Cleydon.[2] That he has promised to catechize his scholars hereafter and take the oaths of supremacy and allegiance; and that he would afterwards receive no scholars which should not come to church. That the committee thought fit to give him an admonition and, upon this promise of his, to dismiss him.

Resolved he shall be dismissed. And he to bring a certificate of his taking the oaths, and bring his license.

MR. PYM reports that the committee is informed by a member of this House that one Morgan Lewis, a schoolmaster in Abergavenny, gives overt suspicion, both by himself and his wife.[3]

Ordered, he shall be sent for to the committee for religion.

MR. WHITBY moves for Sir Richard Grosvenor. That one Dr. Trevers has entered (during Sir Richard Grosvenor his attendance) upon his ancient inheritance, ploughed up his grounds, and cut down his timber, etc.[4] Sir Richard his tenants for lives and years having, by confederacy, yielded up their estates to Dr. Trevers.

Resolved to proceed no further in this, till the House better informed of the state of the case.

L. 2a. Dale.[5]
Committed to

[col. 1]
[p. 41]
Sir Robert Poyntz
Sir James Perrot
Sir Peter Heyman
Sir John Savile
Sir Thomas Myddleton
Sir Thomas Barrington
Mr. [John] Alford
Sir John Eliot

[col. 2]
Sir Gilbert Gerard
Sir Thomas Grantham
Sir Clement Throckmorton
Sir A[lexander] Temple
Sir H[enry] Anderson
Sir Roland Cotton
Mr. Rolle
Mr. [Thomas] Malet

[col. 3]
Sir H[enry] Poole
Sir Robert Mansell
Mr. Herbert
Mr. Whitaker
Sir John Finch
Mr. [Edward] Whitby
Mr. [William] Cage
Sir Thomas Freak

1. Concerning the recommitment of the bill, see HofC, 21 February 1626.

2. Cleydon, a popish schooolmaster teaching in Suffolk, had been been sent for on 25 March to appear before the committee of religion. See HofC, 25 March, OB.

3. MS: *Aburgeny.* Lewis was the first known headmaster of Abergavenny grammar school and was married to Margaret Pritchard, niece to Fr. Augustine Baker and herself a practicing Catholic. See J. E. Lloyd and R. T. Jenkins, eds., *Dictionary of Welsh Biography* (London, 1959), *sub* Lewis, David, *alias* Baker, Charles; and Henry Foley, S. J., ed., *Records of the English Province of the Society of Jesus* (London, 1879), V, 912–913. For Pym's report on Lewis, see HofC, 10 June, OB.

4. We have been unable to identify Dr. Trevers.

5. Concerning the bill for Dame Elizabeth Dale, see HofC, 19 April, n. 3.

Wednesday, 2 clock, in the Court of Wards.

A petition by one Brookes, against the East India Company, read;[6] and referred to the committee for grievances.

The[7] debate concerning the second stay of the *Peter* of Newhaven, renewed.[8]

Upon question, [whether] the 2 stay of the *St. Peter* of Newhaven by the Duke of Buckingham after the decree in the Admiralty be a grievance or not; the question being 2 put, the voice doubtful. The yea went out.

Tellers for the yea:	Mr. Wandesford
	Mr. Long
Tellers for the no:	Sir George More
	Sir H. Poole

With the yea: 185
With the no: 148
Difference: 37

2ly, upon question, this to be added to the Duke of Buckingham's charge.

There being some question made about Mr. Speaker his breaking the orders of the House,[9] MR. SPEAKER (after the business then in hand finished) moved the House to proceed in the examination thereof; but the House, with one consent, cleared Mr. Speaker and stayed any further contestation about it.

A petition, with articles annexed, from the Lord Digby tendered to the House, and that and the articles read.[10]

The Lord Digby called in to avow the hand subscribed to be his own handwriting. Brought to the bar (it being down) with the mace.

Being demanded by MR. SPEAKER whether the name subscribed to the petition be his own handwriting, avows that, and the articles annexed; and that the name subscribed to the petition is of his own handwriting.

Resolved to defer the debate hereof till tomorrow morning, 8 clock.

Mr. Caple, of Gloucester, has liberty to depart home in respect of his sickness.

The counsel for the gold drawers, etc., to be heard upon Wednesday next.

II. DIARY OF BULSTRODE WHITELOCKE, ESQ., DD. 12.21, CAMBRIDGE UNIVERSITY LIBRARY

[f. 169v]

May 1

MR. PYM reports from the committee of religion that one Cleydon,[11] a schoolmaster, being before them for teaching children in popery, being found to [be] a good Protestant himself and promising to teach no more popish children but to take the oaths of supremacy and allegiance himself.

It is ordered that upon bringing of a certificate, that [if] he does this he shall be discharged.

And one Morgan Lewis,[12] another suspected popish schoolmaster, is ordered to be sent for to the committee of religion.

6. For the petition of John Brookes, former commander of the ship called the *Moon,* see *CSPC, East Indies,* IV, 192–193.

7. *Sir Robert Crane* is crossed out in the MS preceding *The.*

8. For the previous debate on the *St. Peter,* see HofC, 6 and 11 March, and see Eliot's speech in Grosvenor, below.

9. The point regarding the Speaker's procedure is unclear. See the discussion of the nature of the question in the speeches of Whitaker and Sandys in Grosvenor, below.

10. For the petition from George, Lord Digby, to the Commons concerning his father, John Digby, Earl of Bristol, see App. II, B. The annexed articles were the same as those presented this day (1 May) to the Upper House by the Earl of Bristol against the Duke of Buckingham. They are printed in full in HofL, 1 May, pp. 329–331.

11. See above, n. 2.

12. See above, n. 3.

MR. WHITBY moves that Sir Richard Grosvenor, a member of this House, seised in fee of a manor consisting of divers tenants, some of them for years and some for life, have surrendered to Doctor Trevers, he sitting here.[13]

The House allows no privilege in this case.[14]

SIR JOHN ELIOT, being called upon, repeats[15] the case concerning the ship *St. Peter* of Newhaven.

VICE CHAMBERLAIN.[16] The stay of the *Peter* of Newhaven is not the cause of the embargo in France, but the general stay of all the French ships here and the delay of the restoring of them is the pretended cause, but not the just cause, for there is no just cause. These ships stayed here were set out by the *almirantazgo* from Seville and were guarded by a Spanish convoy for Cadiz, thence the goods to be convoyed to Flanders.[17] And the solicitors of that business in the French court were the [f. 170] King of Spain's subjects. The agent[18] in this business here hated the Duke of Buckingham and when we wrote out of France of the commission for the release of the goods of our merchants,[19] this agent wrote into France for to stop the release, saying that the parliament here had taken notice of the stay of the *St. Peter* here, and that there were 2 parts to one against the Duke of Buckingham in it.

MR. ROLLE. Markham, Justice, told E. 4 that he could not arrest a man.[20]

MR. NOY.[21] Where goods are taken away by spoil, restitution must be made to the value that the owner will swear. If we determine that this stay was unjust, we shall condemn ourselves and be stopped to say the French did us injustice.

SIR JOHN ELIOT. If his Majesty did command this stay, yet the Duke used not the command, for Sir John Wolstenholme did not speak of the King's command when he arrested the *St. Peter*,[22] nor in the act of state no mention of the King's command.[23]

SIR JOHN SAVILE. That Mr. Attorney told him that that which he delivered here touching the King's command he had directions to deliver from the King.[24]

Resolved that the second stay of the *Peter* by Lord Buckingham is a grievance.

13. See above, n. 4.

14. The CJ, above, states that it was resolved to proceed no further in this business until the House was "better informed of the state of the case".

15. I.e., synthesizes the previous debate on the case. See Grosvenor, below.

16. Sir Dudley Carleton, Vice Chamberlain, had recently returned from an embassy to France that included instructions for a discussion of the embargo. See HofC, 18 April, nn. 4 and 7, and Carleton's report that day. See also, 22 February, nn. 6 and 7.

17. Concerning the *almirantazgo*, see HofL, 8 June, p. 572, n. 30. Regarding the embargo and the second stay of the *St. Peter*, see the Attorney General's opinion on 6 March.

18. I.e., Le Sieur de Blainville, the French ambassador to England. Concerning Blainville's involvement in this business, see *APC 1625–1626*, pp. 199, 209–210; SP 78/78, ff. 81–82 (below, App., II, F); and *CSPV 1625–1626*, pp. 316, 359–361, 397.

19. Regarding the commission for the release of the English goods in France, see Carleton's report on 18 April. For the arrêt concerning the seizure of the English goods see SP 78/78, f. 124 (6/16 March 1626) and SP 78/79, f. 31 (17/27 May 1626). It was reported by Holland and Carleton in February that the English ships were still stayed and the "monies and goods are here arrived at the fair of St. Germains and at Rouen". SP 78/77, ff. 252–255, and SP 78/78, ff. 15–16v.

20. Lovell's case, *YB*, 1 H. VII, Mich., pl. 5.

21. *After long debate* is crossed out in the MS preceding *Mr. Noy*.

22. I.e., at the second arrest of the *St. Peter*. See HofC, 22 February, n. 10.

23. I.e, in the proceedings at the Privy Council on 12 and 15 February. See *APC 1625–1626*, pp. 338–340.

24. I.e., in Attorney General Heath's answer to the Commons on 6 March regarding the stay of the *St. Peter*.

[f. 170v] Resolved that the second stay of the ship *St. Peter* of Newhaven by the Duke of Buckingham after the decree in Court Admiral is a grievance and shall be annexed to the charge against the Duke of Buckingham.

Petition of George, Lord Digby of Sherborne, that some course may be taken for the clearing of those aspersions/[25]

[1.] That the Duke did combine with Gondomar to carry the Prince into Spain.[26]

[2.] That Mr. Porter was made acquainted with it and sent into Spain and/

[f. 171] 3. That the Duke at his arrival nourished the Spanish ministers not only with belief that he was popish, but also/

Hope of the Prince's conversion/

4. That the Duke of Buckingham, having several times in the presence of the Earl of Bristol solicited the King to write to the Pope/

Not long after the Earl/

Sanctissime pater/

[5.] That the Pope sent to the Duke of Buckingham [a] particular bull for [*blank*] the Prince's conversion.

[f. 171v] 7. That after he intended to cross the marriage he [*blank*] diver[s] letters to his own use.

8. As he had formerly abused/

He abused both Houses of parliament.

9. As for the scandal given by his personal behavior/

Upon base and unworthy persons for the hire of his lust.

[f. 172] 10. That the Duke of Buckingham has in great part been/

11. That he has in his relations to both Houses of parliament wronged the Earl of Bristol.

12/

[f. 172v] Lord Digby, brought in by the Serjeant, the bar being down, and asked if he does avow the petition, says he does and that it is his hand which is to it.

III. DIARY OF SIR RICHARD GROSVENOR, MS 611, TRINITY COLLEGE, DUBLIN

[p. 3]

May 1, *2 Caroli Regis, 1626*

Wednesday morning appointed for the bill of continuance of statutes in the House.

The Lord Morley's bill passed to be engrossed.

An act for the selling of certain lands late of Sir Henry Clere, K[night] and Baronet, deceased, for the payment of his debts, etc.

Thursday appointed for Mr. Whitby to make report in the House of the grievances.

MR. MALET reported the bill against secret offices and inquisitions to be taken on his Majesty's behalf to the prejudice of the subjects.

Passed to be engrossed.

MR. PYM. One Mr. Cleydon, a schoolmaster convented before the committee of religion for keeping divers scholars, 6 or 4 which came not to church. This proved, as also that he did never catechize his scholars; had seldom prayers; never examined them of sermons; that he had no license under seal, but admitted 37 years ago; that he never took the oath of allegiance nor supremacy since he took his degrees in school. Yet, that he came to church himself, received 4 times a year. He humbled himself to the committee that he would never keep any scholars which would not conform; that he would catechize, use prayers, take the oaths, sue a license. The committee, some of them, thought it fit he should only re-

25. See above, n. 10.

26. The twelve articles summarized below (the diarist omitted number 6) were presented in the Upper House by the Earl of Bristol against the Duke of Buckingham. See HofL, 1 May, pp. 329–331.

ceive admonition there to do what he had offered; the rest, but the less part, thought him unfit to keep school hereafter.

SIR THOMAS HOBY moved that he might have a time to do these things and bring a certificate that he had done it, and then to be dismissed.

So ordered by the House.[27]

[p. 4] An act for restoring of certain monies to Dame Elizabeth Dale, widow, taken from Sir Thomas Dale in an adventure in the East Indies, to the value of £1,930.[28]

MR. BATEMAN.[29] That Sir Thomas Dale went as commander of the fleet to the East Indies and left the ship called the *Sun* and went for his pleasure into another ship. In the meantime the *Sun* perished, and all his goods, wherein were 200 men; 80 saved, the rest and all the goods perished. She petitioned to the late King, he referred it to the Commissioners of the Navy. There it was, she waives that, etc.

SIR JOHN ELIOT. That besides the personal estate in the ship when Sir Thomas Dale died there was a part in the adventure also. To have the bill committed and all parties to be heard.

SIR PETER HEYMAN delivered a petition whereby appeared the carriage of the governors of the East India Company.[30]

The bill committed, Wednesday, Court of Wards; and the petition to be preferred to the committee of grievances.

The debate of the business concerning the *Peter* of Newhaven.

SIR JOHN ELIOT. The *St. Peter* was about Michaelmas taken and brought to Plymouth;[31] taken out of her, and from those belonging to her, goods of great value. 8 bags of gold, 23 of silver, emeralds, jewels, 16 barrels of cochineal. The ship was sent about October or November into Thames, where she continued till February. 21 December and 28 the merchants petitioned the Council for a release in regard of their danger. 28 December, by his Majesty, an order made for the redelivery of that ship with all her goods. After this a letter from Secretary Coke to the King's advocate, that this ship might be restored. Accordingly, 26 January a decree in Admiralty for her release and a commission to restore the master to the possession. The ship and goods in her discharged but the rest taken forth, not redelivered. [p. 5] 6 February notwithstanding all this, this ship was, by the single direction of the Duke, stayed again. This act of 2d stay being irregular, without warrant from any judicial court, but contrary to all orders and decrees was altogether illegal. So the committee. The Lieutenant of Tower and Judge of Admiralty denied they gave any information for her stay. Concerning the goods taken out, these were not redelivered, nay, they had been put into the custody of Mr. Marsh,[32] who received them without account and knew not what he had.

SIR JOHN FINCH.[33] This was neither a grievance as the 2d stay nor can be ad-

27. Grosvenor omits reference here to the motion concerning his own estates made by Edward Whitby. See the other accounts.

28. See above, n. 5.

29. Bateman was a treasurer of the East India Company. See *CSPC, East Indies,* index *sub* Bateman.

30. I.e., the petition of John Brookes, see above, n. 6.

31. For the business concerning the *St. Peter,* see Eliot's report, HofC, 22 February; and also, HofL, 13 May, pp. 418–419; 15 May, pp. 466–467; and 8 June, pp. 571–573.

32. Regarding Gabriel Marsh, see HofL, 13 May, p. 419, n. 57.

33. *Sir William Beecher* is crossed out in the MS preceding *Sir John Finch.*

judged so by us that it perverts justice or is prejudicial to merchants.

1. It cannot be a grievance to bring a cause to examination in a legal course. If not so it must either have an act of council or decree in admiralty to hinder this. That the decree in admiralty was no hindrance since it was but an interlocutory decree with a *salvo jure* and might be stayed notwithstanding.

Objection: There must be proofs to stay it. Answer: To bring these to proof requires time and examination which could not be done if the ship were not stayed which would have been gone. That the information which was given did include the *Peter* as well as others. If there were no prosecution, lay the fault upon the prosecutors. The French have dealt worse with us and made us attend longer. No arguments to say there was no prosecution *ergo* the 2d stay is a grievance. The *Peter* was no more released by the King than all the rest, for the words of the order are, "the *Peter* and such ships as are not found to be falsely colored".[34]

[p. 6] 2. It can be no grievance in the Duke, for he received a command from the King to do it, so he did it as a servant not as admiral. The end of the stay was to bring it to justice, a necessity of the time. At the most it was but an error in the Duke, for there were days for hearing appointed and if they would have put in caution to answer colored goods they might have had their ship again. Time: if Great or privy seal come to stay justice it ought not to be obeyed, but this command was to bring it to a course of justice. This cannot be a grievance till it be proved whether the goods be colored goods or not. For if it shall appear that they were Spanish goods [and] we adjudge it [not] as a grievance to stay those goods, this can do our merchants no good.

Sir Thomas Hoby. That no new matter was given which caused the stay of the *Peter*. That when the King went into Scotland through Yorkshire he commanded the sheriff to do divers things against recusants, which he did, having only the King's word; yet, afterwards was questioned at the Council Table and because he had no legal authority he was sent to the Fleet.[35]

Sir H. May. If you carry this up the King avouches it to be his command. The Council had justified the Duke's proceeding in it. As for that of the sheriff, the King disavowed it.[36] Moved to decline this question. We might hurt ourselves; we can do no good.

Mr. Vice Chamberlain. The great evil is the interruption of commerce between 2 confederate kingdoms. And although this be renewed, yet I cannot blame those that complain; for who can suffer and not complain? Worth considering whether the stay of the *Peter* be any cause or not of that. [p. 7] The cause was the stay of the ships in general—[this] was the pretended cause but not the just cause. This cause was alleged to the E[arl] of Holland and himself in France.[37] And he there answered it and was sorry to hear so many advocates for France. Either this stay was an original or secondary cause but it is neither. For the *Peter* to be an original cause, notwithstanding ships should be taken [and] brought in, etc.; yet, by the 30th article there should be

34. See the order of the Privy Council, 28 December 1625, *APC 1625–1626*, p. 290.

35. Concerning the imprisonment of Sir Michael Warton, sheriff of Yorkshire, in 1617 for issuing a proclamation against recusants without written warrant, see *APC 1616–1617*, pp. 255–256, 264, 269, 273, 280–282, 301, 355.

36. Concerning King James's disavowal of the actions of Sir Michael Warton (see above, n. 35), see *APC 1616–1617*, p. 269.

37. See above, n. 16.

no embargo, no stay of ships, no reprisal.[38] Then whether the 2d stay was the cause, so much was it to the contrary that we having complained of it as contrary to confederation this was told us. Yet we told them that if there were ships of France here yet they might be stayed till we had our goods restored, since the breach of commerce began with them. These ships were sent out of Spain, the goods proper for the Low Countries. The King of Spain's subjects solicited the King of France for these goods, etc. If this had been a cause our goods had been restored, which is not yet. A commission was sent for restoring of our goods, but yet a stay.[39] The Chancellor replies and charges them with disobedience if they do not restore, yet this not done. The French are apt to seize our goods. We must complain of the officers at Rouen who will not obey the King. The remedy for this is not neglected; the King not negligent. The goods taken forth of the ships are satisfied, fourth of the goods due to the King. They are gone home satisfied. His Majesty has commanded the Judge of [the] Admiralty to search forth all order[s] that were in the time of Q[ueen] Elizabeth in the first rupture with Spain. When the King is able to revenge himself we shall have all right. [p. 8] The French think we should not touch a ship with the white cross, then would the Spaniards sail whither they will. In the Low Countries they seized many of our ships, 40 causes in hand at one time, all unduly taken. Yet they charged not the admiral as cause, the matter was righted and we [had] no cause to complain after. This reflecting upon Buckingham was some cause our goods were not restored to this day. The French ambassador,[40] he did mortally hate him; and when we had sent over that the King had ordered the restoring of our goods he reported it was not so, and that we should not have our goods. Nay, he wrote back to wish them held out for there were 2 parts of parliament against one, and if they could be persuaded that this was the cause of the embargo, his neck was broken.

Remedy: this arrest is unjust, we cannot make that man a cause who is none. Now they pretend to have damages, interest; what remedy then? But what one prince does against another that is [to] revenge himself, which our King is not in state to do nor to protect his friends, which if he shall be enabled to do then I can assure you neither those of our religion will be touched nor our goods stayed but will then join with us in our quarrel. Whereas if he want means he will have not friends. I wish that we might give that remedy to ourselves that we seek after, that the King might be valued in effect and that he might have credit to aid his friends. This grievance if any is but a light gray, and if you add this it will make it appear that the rest want weight.

Moved that this business should be let alone and we fall to our business.

[p. 9] MR. WANDESFORD. *Uno absurdo dato mille sequuntur.* The question is only whether the stay of this ship were legal; if the taking of the goods or ships were without law, fit we judge it so.

SIR W. BEECHER. Not fit for us to declare this a grievance till we have our goods restored. A remedy I propound is that it be fit to petition the King to show that our merchants traded more in France now than before, partly in regard of the wars with Spain, partly in regard of his personal union with France. That since our goods were not restored his Majesty would be

38. Presumably an article of the mutual defense treaty signed in 1610 between James I and Henry IV. Rymer, *Foedera,* VII, pt. 2, 171–175. The issue of renewing the treaty was part of the Holland and Carleton embassy, see HofC, 18 April, n. 4, and see SP 78/77, ff. 252–255.

39. See above, n. 19.

40. See above, n. 18.

pleased to give his subjects letters of marque that so we might recover that at sea that we have lost by injustice at land. That for the money taken forth of the *St. Peter,* better that the Duke should suffer and we think him to turn this to his own profit than be revealed at this time how this money was employed. Wished to decline the question.

MR. BANKES. If we judge this to be a grievance, we then justify the proceedings in France. The King is by the laws of this land trusted with confederation with princes and states. To judge this will tend to the dishonor of our state and disadvantage the merchant. For remedy, to petition his Majesty that he would take some speedy course to free this embargo in France.

MR. ROLLE. 2 parts: 1, whether the stay were legal; 2, whether the Lord Admiral may be excused upon his Majesty's command. 1. The stay was not legal in the manner, for it might have been only stayed upon new allegation and new proofs, both which wanted in this stay. 2. That the Duke ought not to have stayed it though the King commanded, for the King's command must be taken that he should only stay it so as by law he may do. His Majesty can do no wrong; it is his officers that must be punished for what is done amiss.

[p. 10] Judge Markham told E. 4 that he could arrest no man because if the arrest were false the party could bring no motion against him.[41] If this were unjustly stayed, it were reason they should have damages and that he should pay them that caused the stay.

SIR WALTER ERLE. That it was a grievance.

MR. BROWNE. A grievance is in the nature of a nuisance and that is a grievance which is not a particular man's but that which is *nocumentum* [*illegible*] *domini regis.* That this was no grievance.

MR. LONG. I no lawyer; if I were I would be a[n] English not a French advocate. Poison at the point, for no man will come at it. This is the grievance, that any one man should stay that which was legally discharged.

MR. STRODE. This cause not questioned here as it is national or by the event, but whether the stay was just or unjust. The reason why the King commanded the stay of the ship was by information from the Lord Duke which, being untrue, the stay was reversed.

SIR RICHARD WESTON. The Duke did not stay this of himself, though I think he might by virtue of his place. Is anything so usual among princes as either upon [*illegible*] or denial of justice to break peace? And this disagreement may give encouragement. If we have debated this so long and cannot tell how to judge it, my Lord of Buckingham might well be deceived, *ergo* once more put by the question.

SIR DUDLEY DIGGES. Had new matter appeared for the stay it had been legal, but none such. It was illegal and that the Duke did it. But for the name of the offense, when we come to that we may dispute it.

[p. 11] MR. SPENCER. That upon reprisal of goods before judgment that be not *bona peritura,* dangerous to have them sold, for then they may demand what they please for restitution; and to have them delivered without tale may prove very prejudicial to the King and state, but this stay no grievance.

SIR GEORGE MORE. Not safe for any man to do an act by command from the King except by warrant under the Great or privy

41. See above, n. 20.

seal, for kings speak not as other men, so the stay unlegal. For the Duke to do this is not such a grievance as should be presented. Moved that we should not offer this as a grievance.

MR. NEWBERY.[42] If we seek to do good to the merchants by this means, they can receive no good at home or abroad. If the Duke be found guilty it will be expected the Duke should make them recompense, which cannot be at home because the King does undertake it for letters of marque.

MR. PYM. [1.] Every interruption in a judge from doing justice is a grievance. 2. An unlawful act has been done under color of a great place, goods taken out at Plymouth without warrant and made away. By our doing justice we shall provoke the French to do us justice again. When Sir Edward Coke was L[ord] Chief Justice a Frenchman sued one in the King's Bench. They took bail but, that being not sufficient and proving so, Sir Edward Coke was adjudged to pay damages and paid £2,000.[43]

SIR WILLIAM STRODE. If a Lord Keeper make one illegal decree this shall not be a grievance.

SIR G. GORING. That the reason of the stay of the *Peter* was new proof, though it proved not current.

SIR NATHANIEL RICH. That the question should be whether the Duke has carried himself well by the duty of his place in this particular.

[p. 12] MR. WANDESFORD. Whether the Duke by staying the ship and taking these goods has done his duty.

SIR JOHN ELIOT. Question ought to be whether this be a grievance upon the whole matter.

SIR W. BEECHER. That this question cannot be put upon the whole matter because many things might so be answered, as the breaking of the bulk, which was done by certain captains without order, which is now in examination.

MR. NOY. The law is if a man will take away goods without an inventory, he is bound to restore as much as the party will swear to. Not good to go in haste to a question, for no man knows whether a war may follow of this or whether this were the whole cause of the stay. So if we determine this we conclude we gave them cause by injustice; for if they have taken our goods for injustice and it appear not how much, they may justly keep the goods.

SIR JOHN ELIOT. The ship is already released. So that the stay was wrong. The King did not command the stay, and that for these 3 reasons: 1, out of the King's speech, that however he wanted money yet he would never want justice;[44] [2,] again, in the stay, the King's name was never used by Sir John Wolstenholme;[45] 3, when the Duke, upon the 2d stay, came to Council Chamber there was no mention of the King's name, so the stay unjust.[46]

SIR WILLIAM RUSSELL. That the ship was only discharged upon caution. To restore the goods if they were colored.

SIR JOHN SAVILE. That he spoke with Mr. Attorney who told him that he spoke in a double person, both as the King's minister and by request from the Duke. That what he spoke of the King was by his express command.

[p. 13] MR. WHITAKER. That which has been debated should be put to the question, which had been: 1, whether the stay was

42. *Mr. Wentworth* is crossed out in the MS preceding *Mr. Newberry*.

43. We have not found the case.

44. See above, n. 31.

45. See above, n. 22.

46. See above, n. 23.

legal or illegal; 2ly, whether that stay was a grievance.

SIR EDWIN SANDYS. There is a question by order of a former day comes to be propounded.[47] The House may vary the question at their pleasure, for this is no standing order; but then you set the House at liberty and any man may speak again to that.

Question put whether the 2d stay of the *Peter* by the Duke was a grievance. The House divided: the yeas, 185; the noes, 147. So adjudged a grievance.

SIR LEWIS DYVE presented a petition from the Lord Digby, whereto was annexed the articles presented to the higher House by his father, the Earl of Bristol, against the Duke of Buckingham.

He was called into the House to the bar to justify that the hand to the petition was his own.

IV. DIARY OF JOHN LOWTHER, ESQ., D/LONS/L, CUMBERLAND AND WESTMORLAND RECORD OFFICE

[f. 13v]

[1 May]

The young L[ord] Digby, under 16 years,[48] petitions the Commons and desires to be inherited of his honor unspotted more than any other thing. And his petition says aspersions were cast upon his father by L. Duke both before the King and both Houses in parliament. And his father petitioned Lords in parliament showing how the Duke had abused in his relation both the King and both the Houses. And [he] desired that [f. 14] we to be pleased to hear him to void the aspersions, else to clear upon record his honor of those imputations laid upon him. And he annexed the copy of the articles his father did present in the Lords House against the Duke *ut sequitur:*[49]

1. That Duke conspired with Gondomar to carry the Prince, now King, into Spain to be perverted in religion and instructed in their religion.

[2.] Porter acquainted with it and messages delivered by Porter for a ground of that matter. And upon Porter his return leave gotten for the Prince to come, yet plotted and proposed by Duke before.

3. That Duke possessed Spain with his intention of their religion, yea so far concurred as to adore their sacrament, and came not to our prayers there, and caused Spanish to propose worse conditions than before for matter of religion.

4th. That Duke often moved King James to write to the Pope. And a letter drawn which he[50] so opposed that the Duke obtained it not while Bristol here. Duke after procured letter to Pope, writing therein "*Sanctissime Pater*".

[5.] Pop[e] sent a bull to him, Duke, to procure him to proceed to convert the Prince.

6. He discontented Spain so in his course that Spain broke off the match in dislike of him; for his aims not obtained was the cause of breach.

7. He made use of Prince's letters to his own ends and by concealment.

[f. 14v] 8. That King [*sic*] abused both Houses in every particular of his narration, which he will prove.

9. In procuring favors from Spain bestowed by Duke on base persons for his lust's satisfaction. He being solely sent ambassador did leave such scandal behind him.

47. On 11 March the House had resolved, upon a division, that the question of whether the second stay of the *St. Peter* was a grievance should not then be put. See HofC, 11 March, OB.

48. Born in Madrid in October 1612, George, Lord Digby, was only thirteen years old at that time. *Complete Peerage,* II, 321.

49. See above, n. 26.

50. I.e., Bristol.

10. He cause of Palatinate not restored.

11. He wronged Bristol in those aspersions.

12. That he, Earl Bristol, revealed all this to the King James who assured to hear him, and said he would hear him. He sent a little before his death when he, being perplexed by the Duke, died, being much pressed with the Duke his miscarriage towards him.

V. DIARY OF SIR NATHANIEL RICH, HIST. COLLECT. 143, HLRO

[f. 84]

1 May

The *almirantazgo* of Seville had only the shipping of all goods.[51]

51. See above, n. 17.

TUESDAY, 2 MAY 1626

I. JOURNAL OF THE HOUSE OF COMMONS

[CJ 852; p. 42]
Martis, 2 Maii, 2 Caroli Regis

Hobart's[1] bill, Saturday next, 2 clock.

L. 1a. An act for the naturalizing of Samuel Powell, the son of John Powell, of London, merchant, and Jane, his wife.

L. 1a. An act for the better discovery of church papists, and preventing their formal, but feigned, conformity.

SIR H. POOLE reports Sotherne's bill, without amendments. *Engrossetur.*

2 bills against cottages,[2] Thursday next, 2 clock.

L. 2a. An act for the mitigation of the sentence of greater excommunication and for the preservation of the ecclesiastical jurisdiction.

Committed to

[col. 1]
Mr. Jordan
[CJ 853]
Sir George More
Sir H[enry] Poole
Sir Eubule Thelwall
Sir William Strode
Sir Francis Barrington
Sir J[ames] Perrot
Mr. [William] Coryton
Sir John Pickering
Sir Thomas Barrington

[col. 2]
Mr. Dr. [Thomas] Eden
Sir A[lexander] Temple
Sir Roger Twysden
Sir Thomas Grantham
Mr. Lowther
Mr. [John] Wilde
Mr. Francis Drake
Mr. [Thomas] Bedingfield
Mr. Long
Sir John Stradling

[col. 3]
Mr. Attorney Wards
Sir A[rthur] Ingram
Sir Nicholas Saunders
Mr. Whitaker
Sir Nathaniel Rich
Sir Peter Heyman
Sir Robert Poyntz
Sir Richard Strode
Mr. John Drake
Sir Richard Grosvenor

Thursday, 2 clock, Court of Wards.

The patent about making salt to be further debated upon Friday morning next.

The petitioners[3] of the silkmen to be heard tomorrow by counsel, in the House, if they will, when the wiredrawers are heard.

L. 1a. An act for the ease of sheriffs and bailiffs of liberties for the passing of their accounts.[4]

L. 2a. An act for relief of the poor.[5]
Committed to

[col. 1]
Mr. [Henry] Sherfield
Mr. Jordan
Sir John Savile
Sir A[rthur] Ingram
Mr. John Drake

[col. 2]
Sir G[ilbert] Gerard
Mr. [Richard] Spencer

And all that will come to have voice; Star Chamber, Friday in the afternoon. And this committee to consider of all former laws

1. MS: *Hubbard's.*

2. I.e., the committee to meet that had been appointed on 4 March to consider the bill for avoiding the increase of cottages, and the bill for the restraint of new erections and inmates. See HofC, 4 March, OB.

3. Printed edition: *petition.* Mr. Herne, counsel for the silkmen, was heard on 5 May, see below.

4. *Resolved to sit every morning, 7 clock* is crossed out in the MS following *account.* This was a new bill prepared by the committee to replace the bill for the passing of the accounts of sheriffs that had received its first reading in the House on 10 March. See Wilde's report in Grosvenor, below.

5. Regarding this bill, see HofC, 11 March, n. 1.

concerning the poor; and to see how all may be reduced into one law.[6]

SIR D. DIGGES reports the 2 evils.[7] The causes, in number 10: 1, the not guarding the Narrow Seas sufficiently; 2, plurality of great offices in one hand; 3, sale of honors; 4, conferring of honors upon those whose estate maintaining [p. 43] by the King's revenue/

The 9th, the 2nd stay of the *St. Peter.* The 10th, the plaster and drink given by King James in his last sickness.

That the Duke of Buckingham found the cause of these causes.

The charge into 4 heads:

1. Offices: [1,] divers of them in his hand; 2, his buying 2 of these; 3,[8] ill execution of his office of admiralty; extorting money from the East India Company.

2. Honors: 1, the sale of them; 2, conferring them upon such of his kindred/

These drawn into articles legally and tendered to the House to be read; and read accordingly.

MR. VICE CHAMBERLAIN. That the charge about the 2nd stay of the *Peter* not fit to be transmitted to the Lords. It will not prejudice the Duke, for the King avows the act. This ship restored and in France; yet our goods and ships not restored, but more strictly restrained than heretofore. Doubts[9] the ambassador of France has practiced to incense this House to the Frenches' benefit and the loss of the English.

MR. GLANVILLE reports information given from the Lord Carey concerning the £6,000 paid for the Mastership of the Wards,[10] and other informations from Sir Robert Howard, Sir William Russell, Sir Robert Pye, Sir John Hippisley, Sir William Howard, and Sir William Monson.[11]

1, upon question, such of the charges passed by the vote of this House against the Duke of Buckingham which shall be thought fit by this House to be transmitted, shall be transmitted to the Lords.

2ly, upon question, the charge upon the Duke of Buckingham concerning the 2nd stay of the *Peter* of Newhaven to be transmitted to the Lords among the residue of the charges against him.

3ly, upon question, all other the several charges contained in the papers read, to be transmitted to the Lords.

The committee of 12 to consider of the papers and proofs, and of the distribution of them; and to report their opinions and proceedings therein to the House tomorrow morning.

MR. CHANCELLOR OF THE EXCHEQUER acquaints the House that the King accepts the subsidy in good part,[12] and desires that speed it may do him good.

6. A copy of the above committee list and order included among the papers of Henry Sherfield (44M69/xxxix/90), HRO, indicates that the committee was adjourned from Friday (5 May) to the following Thursday (11 May), when it was again appointed to meet on Tuesday (6 June), and then was adjourned to the following Thursday (8 June).

7. Digges is reporting from the committee of twelve appointed on 21 April to consider and reduce into form the business concerning the Duke of Buckingham. See the fuller accounts of Digges's report in the accounts below; and see the final articles of impeachment against the Duke, HofL, 15 May, pp. 463–477.

8. Printed edition: *2*.

9. I.e., fears. Concerning Blainville, the French ambassador in England, see HofC, 1 May, n. 18.

10. Concerning the purchase of the Mastership of the Wards by Lionel Cranfield, later Earl of Middlesex, see the tenth article against the Duke, HofL, 15 May, p. 470, and see Eliot's report from the subcommittee for examining the causes of causes, HofC, 21 April. Henry Lord Carey was married to Martha, Lionel Cranfield's oldest daughter. See Prestwich, *Cranfield,* pp. 485–488.

11. On 22 April these MPs had been appointed to testify to the committee of twelve.

12. I.e., the fourth subsidy that the committee of the whole had resolved on 26 April to add to the three already voted.

The grand committee to sit tomorrow morning, to agree upon the time of payment of the 4th subsidy, and like circumstances therein, and then to report the same to the House that so the bill may proceed; for that the King, upon the grant thereof thus far, the King can get no credit either at home or abroad.

[p. 44] SIR LEWIS DYVE. That the Earl of Bristol avows the charge delivered in yesterday by the Lord Digby; but that the Earl of Bristol has not delivered in as a charge here because that properly to be determined above; but that the Lord Digby has done it, being one of the Commons and desiring to have some course taken that he inherit not a tainted honor; and that the Earl of Bristol says that he has accused the Duke in the Lords House of High Treason.[13]

Sir Robert Howard's business to be tomorrow in the afternoon, and the House then to sit.

II. DIARY OF BULSTRODE WHITELOCKE, ESQ., DD. 12.21, CAMBRIDGE UNIVERSITY LIBRARY

[f. 172v]

May 2

SIR DUDLEY DIGGES [reports] from the committee of 12 the charges against the Duke.[14] The body of the charge will consist in 4 points: 1, concerning offices; 2, concerning honors; 3, concerning revenue of the crown; 4, concerning the King's person.

Offices in Lord Duke 3 ways to be considered: 1, that there are many in his hand; 2, that he bought some of them; 3, that he does not execute them well.

Consideration of honors: 1, the sale of them; 2, the conferring of them upon such whom to maintain the King's revenues are exhausted.

Exhausting the King's revenues. In a schedule appears these sums delivered to the Duke and his kindred:[15]

[col. 1]	[col. 2]
12,500£	1,000£
995£	1,000
8,000	2,000 per annum
60,000	7,000 per annum
30,000	1,000
20,000	

[col. 3]	[col. 4]
20,000£	400£ per annum
20,000	12,000 Sir Edward [Villiers]
120,000£	3,000£
400£ old rent to Lord Anglesey	500£
1,500	500£ per annum
	1,000£ per annum to Viscount Purbeck
£317,389	14-4-6

[f. 173] £20,563 6s. 8d. per annum old rent.

Sums paid to the Duke by privy seal/

VICE CHAMBERLAIN. That the business concerning the *Peter* of Newhaven, though it be enumerated amongst our grievances, yet is not fit to be transmitted to the King or to the Lords in this manner as it is, for it will be to no use for us and it will be to our irremediable damage beyond seas. The *Peter* of Newhaven is arrived in France, yet they are so far there from making restitution upon this release that there is a stricter command for the not delivery of our goods than was before, not till they have all damages delivered. The French are not to make an arrest of English goods there, although there be cause offered. And if there should be war between the 2 nations, *quod Deus avertat,* the merchants should have 3 months time to carry home their goods.[16]

13. For Bristol's charges against Buckingham, see HofL, 1 May, pp. 329–331.

14. See above, n. 7.

15. Cf. the schedule of gifts, beginning with that of 23 May 1625 to the Earl of Manchester, printed in HofL, 15 May, pp. 475–476.

16. See the Vice Chamberlain's speech, 1 May, Grosvenor diary.

Moves that we should lay open unto the King the case as it stands and show the wrong done.

SIR JOHN ELIOT. The question is fixed on our justice here.

MR. GLANVILLE reports from the committee of 12 the substance of that which was opened unto them by the members of the House.[17] Lord Carey said that the Countess of Middlesex told him that the Earl of Middlesex had disbursed £6,000 upon Lord Duke's word,[18] and so Mr. Herman told him.[19] Sir Robert Howard said that he had credibly heard and did believe that his brother[20] was to have [*blank*] for resigning his office of Master of the Horse. [f. 173v] Sir Robert Pye said that there was paid for the Admiral's place/[21]

Sir William Russell said that £5,000 was sent to him[22] by the Duke to be employed for the navy, and the money was again paid to the Duke out of the subsidy money.

Sir John Hippisley said that there was a commission to him and Sir Peter Heyman and others to sell the goods [that] came into Dover and to bring the money into the Exchequer.[23]

Sir William Howard said that he thought his brother/[24]

Sir William Monson said that he heard by the Countess of Nottingham that the Earl was willing to relinquish his office of Admiral and was promised to be made the chief earl of England and had money given him.[25]

SIR ROBERT PYE. That the Earl of Middlesex had the £6,000 paid again to him and £60,000 more.[26]

MR. LONG. That these charges may be presented to the Lords, because many proofs must be tendered and examined which the King should not be troubled withal.

SIR ROBERT PYE. That we should transmit it to the King.

17. I.e., the business concerning Cranfield and the purchase of the Mastership of the Wards.

18. See above, n. 10.

19. Concerning Herman, see HofC, 21 April, n. 13.

20. I.e., Thomas Howard, Earl of Berkshire. In 1614 Thomas Howard had become Master of the Horse to Prince Charles. Upon Charles's accession to the throne in 1625 there appears to have been some dispute over whether Howard (then Viscount Andover) or Buckingham, who had been Master of the Horse to King James since 1616, would hold the office. It was rumored at that time that Andover was to be given £20,000 in lieu of the Mastership, a figure that agrees with the total disclosed to Glanville's committee by Sir Robert Howard. See Grosvenor, below; see also Chamberlain, *Letters,* II, 615 and *CSPV 1625–1626,* p. 21.

21. Grosvenor and Lowther, below, give £3,000 as the sum paid to the Earl of Nottingham, then Lord Admiral. Concerning the purchase of the office, see the second article of impeachment against Buckingham, HofL, 15 May, pp. 464–465; and HofL, 13 May, p. 413, n. 15. Regarding Sir Robert Pye, see ibid., n. 17.

22. I.e., as Treasurer of the Navy. See Grosvenor and Lowther, below.

23. For the commission to Hippisley et al., dated 6 April 1626, see C 66/2390, no. 5 (MS Cal. Pat. Rolls, 2 Car. I, pt. 18d, f. 78). For an order of the Privy Council for drawing such a commission, see HofC, 8 March, n. 20.

24. None of the accounts for this day record the information given by Sir William Howard; he may have repeated what was said by Sir Robert Howard (see above) concerning their brother, Thomas, Earl of Berkshire (see above, n. 20).

25. Monson married Margaret (nee Stewart), widow of Charles, Earl of Nottingham. Concerning the purchase of the office of Admiral, see above, n. 21. In February 1619, Nottingham received a royal warrant granting him the precedency due to the Earldom of Nottingham created in 1377 and enjoyed by his progenitor John Mowbray under Richard II (SP 14/105:119; the warrant is partially printed in *Complete Peerage,* IX, 785n.).

26. Grosvenor and Lowther, below, give the figure as £120,000, which agrees with the amount on the schedule annexed to the articles of impeachment against Buckingham (see HofL, 15 May, p. 476; 8 June, p. 584).

SIR ROBERT HARLEY. Of the same mind.

SIR JOHN STRANGWAYS. That the old way is to transmit unto the Lords. Here first moved in H. 6 time, the Duke of Suffolk's case,[27] Lord Bacon's case in 18 *Jac.*, and Lord Middlesex's case.[28] By transmitting him to the Lords he shall have the most worthy and noble trial that may be.

[f. 174] SIR JOHN FINCH. I take it as a maxim of the pious sense of this House that they delight to reformation more than ruin. Though precedents have been alleged of going to the Lords, yet we may use the other way. And it be for the honor and privilege of the House to use variety of ways, and several.

Resolved that such of the charges against the Duke of Buckingham as the House thinks fit to be transmitted shall be transmitted to the Lords.

Resolved that the charge upon the Duke of Buckingham concerning the second stay of the *St. Peter* of Newhaven shall be transmitted to the Lords amongst the rest of the charges that the House shall transmit.

Resolved that all the several charges reported by Sir Dudley Digges shall be transmitted to the Lords.

The manner of the presenting referred to the consideration of the 12 to deliver their opinions in it.

CHANCELLOR EXCHEQUER. That the King gives us thanks for the gift we have ordered to give him this session and desires that we would as speedily as we can take a course to perfect it,[29] for it will not give him credit until it be passed.

Tomorrow morning ordered to consider of it.

SIR LEWIS DYVE. That Lord Bristol gave him authority to tell this House that he avows that the copy of the charge given in yesterday by his son is the true copy. And that he has charged the Duke of High Treason in the Lords House.[30]

[f. 174v]

Pomeridiem

At the committee for courts of justice.

Mr. Calthorpe,[31] being of counsel with Mr. Grimesdich,[32] cites the book of 23 H. 7, f. 96, in Keilway's reports for supplemental proofs,[33] and that they have been allowed in Chancery and by Lord Lincoln when he was Lord Keeper.

Mr. Churchill, a registrar in Chancery,[34] charged by Grimesdich for interlining an order of Chancery, and putting out some words, and not entering the order against his oath, and misleading Mr. Washington, the chief officer, to set his [*blank*] by writing under the order *examinatur*.[35]

27. Concerning the case of William de la Pole, Duke of Suffolk, see HofL, 18 April, pp. 277–278, and n. 27.

28. The House of Commons initiated impeachment proceedings for bribery and corruption against Sir Francis Bacon, Lord Chancellor, in 1621 (see Howell, *ST,* II, 1087–1120; *CD 1621,* I, Index, *sub* Bacon; and *LJ,* III, 84–86, 98–101, 105, 106), and in 1624 against Lionel Cranfield, Lord Treasurer, for high crimes and misdemeanors (see *LJ,* III, 344–383; Howell, *ST,* II, 1183–1254; and Cobbett, *Parl. Hist.,* I, 1411–1477).

29. See above, n. 12.

30. See above, n. 13.

31. Probably Henry Calthorpe, a lawyer whose services were much in demand. *DNB*.

32. John Grimesdich, deputy to Sir Roger Aston, Master of the Wardrobe until his death in 1612, had petitioned against John Williams, Bishop of Lincoln (former Lord Keeper), John Churchill, a registrar in Chancery, and a serjeant at arms for their actions concerning Grimesdich's cause against Aston's daughters regarding their legacy. See Sir Nathaniel Rich's report on Grimesdich's case, HofC, 11 May, OB; and see Sir Robert Phelips's report on a case concerning Grimesdich in 1624, *CJ,* I, 766.

33. See Keilway, *Reports,* 23 H. VII, Hil., no. 7.

34. Concerning John Churchill, see *CD1621,* VI, 274n. 8; Chamberlain, *Letters,* II, 355; SP 14/160:91; *CJ,* I, 766.

35. See *CJ,* I, 766. Concerning Lawrence Washington, registrar of the Court of Chancery, see *CSPD 1603–1610,* p. 96.

Mr. Herle,[36] of counsel with Mr. Churchill, says that there are 5 deputies under Mr. Washington, 3 attending at Westminster and 2 at the Rolls. And there are 2 other officers which enter all orders but draw none. The 5 deputies draw all orders but enter none. These are sworn to draw up and enter all orders without favor or corruption. It is usual for the registrar to interline orders according as his notes shall direct him and if he be mistaken before *examinatur* be written on it. Besides, if the clients will, they may have copies of the orders drawn of either side before they be entered. And this interlining was by Lord Chancellor's direction. And the putting out/

[f. 175] In the Lords House this parliament, in Pinckney's case, resolved that though the House wrote to Lord Keeper to rehear a case and he refused to do it because the complainant refused to stand to the orders of the Chancery, yet in that the Lord Keeper did his duty.[37]

Sir Eubule Thelwall.[38] There can be no bill of review but there must be new matter which was not known to the party before, or else there must be error in the body of the decree.

Or the decree must not be final in itself. Mr. Mason.

III. DIARY OF SIR RICHARD GROSVENOR, MS 611, TRINITY COLLEGE, DUBLIN

[p. 13]

May 2

1. An act for the naturalizing of Samuel Powell. The bill came from the Lords.[39]

1. An act for the better discovering of church papists and preventing their former [*sic*] but feigned conformity. SIR FRANCIS BARRINGTON presented the bill.

Thursday appointed for the 2 bills of cottages and inmates.[40]

SIR HENRY POOLE reported the bill for the naturalizing of Thomas Sotherne, born in Turkey. Passed to be engrossed.

2. An act for the mitigation of the sentence of the greater excommunication and for preservation of ecclesiastical jurisdiction.

Committed, Thursday, Court of Wards; self in.

Patent of salt of Mr. More, resolved to be put to the question Friday.

[p. 14] MR. WILDE reported the bill for the easy passage of sheriffs' accounts. That the bill was uncertain and the committee thought fit to draw another bill and to charge every shire according to the largeness thereof with a certain sum for the passing of their accounts.[41] The act entitled, *1.* An act for the ease of sheriffs and bailiffs of liberties for passing their accounts in the Exchequer and for taking away the abuse of sheriffs.

2. An act for relief of the poor.[42] That the church warden and 4 or 5 of the inhabitants to raise weekly sums for a stock for setting on work, etc.

MR. SHERWILL.[43] That this bill enacted what was before and no repeal of former laws. Moved a care at the committee lest we have double laws for one thing.

36. We have been unable to identify further Mr. Herle.

37. Concerning Pinckney's case, see HofL, 1, 2, 16, 17, 23, and 24 March, OBs.

38. Thelwall's name is interlined in the MS making it unclear which of the following words were spoken by Thelwall and which by Mason.

39. Powell's bill had been sent down on 15 April.

40. See above, n. 2.

41. See above, n. 4.

42. See HofC, 11 March, n. 1.

43. MS: *Shervile*. Possibly Henry Sherfield rather than Thomas Sherwill is intended. Sherfield was named to the committee (see CJ) and kept notes concerning the bill (see App., II, C).

MR. JORDAN. Moved that justices of the peace should be also punished if not careful to execute the law.

SIR GILBERT GERARD. That we might have put into this bill whatsoever concerned the poor; that we might have but one law.

Committed, Friday, Star Chamber, all that come to have voice.

SIR DUDLEY DIGGES reported from the committee of 12. First he remembered the 2 evils: 1, the diminution of the honor and strength, the stoppage of trade, there were causes of that:

1. That the seas were not guarded sufficiently snug [since] dissolution of the treaties.

2. An engrossing of offices into one hand.

3. That honors were sold.

4. Honors conferred upon persons not capable in regard of their estate, so chargeable to the crown.[44]

[p. 15] 6. Buying of places of judicature.

7. The sending of ships against those of our religion.

8. Injury done to the East India merchants.

9. The stay of the *Peter* of Newhaven.

10. That touching the person of the late King, the potion and plaster.

There was a cause of these causes, and my Lord of Buckingham a cause of them. The body of this charge of 4 parts: 1, concerning offices; 2, honors; 3, treasure of the crown; 4, the King's person.

That of offices: either as they are in the Duke himself or in others. As in him: 1, great many in him; 2ly, a buying of the Admiral's place and the Warden's. In these offices abuse in 5 particulars: 1, by color of the Admiral, there was money extorted from the East India merchants; 2, not guarding the sea; 3, the delivering over of a ship royal to the hands of the French; 4, a practice to have things against Rochelle.

Next, that of honors: 1, the sale; 2, conferrence [of] them upon his kindred.

3. The intercepting of the treasure in general.

Last, the King's sickness.

[p. 16] They have drawn all into heads and moved to have them read and as the heads were read he had a calendar to prove every head:

1 head: plurality of offices in one man's hands.

2 head: Admiralty bought of Earl of Nottingham, £3,000 and £1,000 a year annuity from the King to him.[45] 28 January, 16 *Jac.*, date of the Duke's patent.[46]

3. The Cinque Ports bought 22 *Jac.*, December, of the Lord Zouche £1,000, and an annuity of £500 per annum. Duke's patent bears date 6 December, 22 *Jac.*[47]

4. Lord Treasurer's office, and Master of the Wards sold.[48] December, 18 [*Jac.*], Viscount Mandeville's patent, for which the Duke received £20,000; and in January, 16 *Jac.*, Sir Lionel Cranfield, Master of Wards, the Duke had of him £6,000.[49]

5. East India Company, he extorted £10,000.[50]

6. Narrow Seas not guarded.

44. Grosvenor has omitted the fifth cause. See Lowther, below.

45. See above, n. 21.

46. MS Cal. Pat. Rolls, 16 Jac. I, pt. 17, f. 7. See HofL, p. 413, n. 15.

47. Concerning the purchase of the office of Lord Warden of the Cinque Ports, see HofL, 13 May, p. 413 n. 18; 15 May, p. 465; and 8 June, pp. 469–470. For Buckingham's patent, see C 66/2337, no. 4 (MS Cal. Pat. Rolls, 22 Jac. I, pt. 14, f. 143).

48. Concerning the purchases of the Lord Treasurer's office and the Mastership of the Wards, see HofL, 15 May, pp. 470, and 476–477.

49. For the patents to Henry Montagu, later Viscount Mandeville and Lionel Cranfield, see HofL, 15 May, p. 470, and nn. 85 and 86.

50. Concerning this and the following heads, see articles six, four, five, seven, eight, nine, eleven, and twelve, respectively, of charges against Buckingham, HofL, 15 May, pp. 465–472.

7. The *Peter* of Newhaven.

8. Delivery of the 7 ships to the French.

9. The ships against Rochelle.

10. Compulsion to buy honor, the Lord Robartes, £10,000.

11. Procuring honors for his kindred: Countess of Buckingham to his mother, Anglesey to Christopher Villiers, and his other brothers and brother-in-law.

12. Intercepting and exhausting the King's revenues. 14 *Jac.* divers manors of value, [£]747 13s. 4d., and others of £1,200 per annum. A schedule annexed:[51]

14 [*sic*] Jun., 14 *Jac.*, manor of Biddlesden £700. 23 Jun. [*sic*] 1623, Whaddon, £51 14s.; Hartington £747 14s.; manor of Combe £197; manor of Bisley £53 16s. 6d.; Timberwood and Ramshurst, Kent, £89 7s.; Westharmes, etc., £205; [Spalding,] 524 [*sic*] -7-0.

[p. 17] Grange [of] Bentley, 15-16-4; Over, Kent, 66[*sic*]-18-2; Leiston, 114-7-11; Brampton, 127-0-6; park of Rockingham, 10-16-8; £130 wood in a forest of Leighfield yield so much for 26-13, paid fee farm rent.

[*Illegible*] lands sold [by] his agents [*illegible*]:

£160 [*sic*]; £800; 1,636-13-4; £4,000; £1,860; £1,000; 1,906-6-8; 1,476-16-8; £3,284; £3,000; totals: 20,563-16-8. This sum for more and tallies stricken.

To Earl of Manchester for part of satisfaction for £20,000 paid for his office £12,500.

To Mr. Fotherley £995; to Sir Robert Pye £8,000 for Duke's use; [to Burlamachi] £60,000.

These free gifts: £30,000, £20,000. In 2 pensions £1,000 out of Court of Wards per annum. Out of the customs of Ireland £7,000 per annum; to the Admiral,[52] £1,000 per annum; £20,000, Middlesex's fine converted to his use. £1,500 to Worcester for Master of Horse's place per annum.

Grants to his kindred: Earl of Anglesey, £400 per annum, value £10,000; 2 forests worth £800 per annum, worth £20,000. £120,000 to Middlesex by marrying his kinswoman. To Sir Edward Villiers in Forest of Dean £12,000; more to him out of mint, £3,000; more to him, a pension out of the mint, £500; out of Court of Wards, £500. To Purbeck,[53] £1,000 yearly out of customs of strangers' goods. To Sir Anthony Ashley for marrying his kinswoman,[54] a blank. This last charge left out.

13. The King's physic without counsel of his physicians, etc.

MR. VICE CHAMBERLAIN. There is some precedent thing to be done before we resolve whether to send this. Moved that he might speak to that charge of the *Peter* of Newhaven.

The House gave him leave.

That not fit to be transmitted with the rest. Let not the speaker's imperfections put the House besides the gravity that becomes them. Circumstances must sometimes be [*illegible*].

I observe the recital of the grievance as it is said and it goes beyond the *Peter* to the other French ships.

1. It will be no use.

2. A[n] unremediable damage.

[p. 18] 1. It will be no charge to the Duke for he will say that he did that which he might do *jure belli*. The King avows it to be by his command. The ship is arrived in France and yet is a strict command laid

51. For the full schedule of grants and gifts, see HofL, 8 June, 579–585.

52. I.e., the pension to the Earl of Nottingham. See above, n. 21.

53. I.e., John Villiers, Viscount Purbeck, Buckingham's brother.

54. In 1622 Sir Anthony Ashley had married Philippa Sheldon, a cousin of the Duke of Buckingham and sister of Elizabeth Sheldon who married Christopher Villiers, Buckingham's younger brother. *DNB*.

upon the not restoring them there before. Our endeavors were according to our instructions and succeeded happily; for the King gave strict command to have our goods delivered and this House has rather hindered the business. The King will have cause to complain if we suffer ourselves to be carried away with the practice of foreign ambassadors. They will not restore our goods till all be restored, with damages and interest. What remedy? His Majesty thinks of the best that may be. The King is now sending an ambassador with instructions for this matter.[55] When he opens his mouth they will tell him that this House has adjudged that a grievance contrary to what we delivered there. But 2 remedies: one by way of negotiation. If that take not place must we go to war? There are many degrees to that one article. That though there happen war that the merchants shall have 3 months time for their goods.[56] Now, if war happen shall we make them a manifest that we have given the first cause of the war? I would go to the King, tell him how our treaties are violated and desire him to provide a speedy remedy and acquaint him with many arguments which I will be ready to furnish you with.

[p. 19] SIR JOHN ELIOT. I differ from the conclusion of that honorable person and though I ho[l]d it more proper to have spoken upon the whole, yet I will only address myself to give satisfaction in this particular. His reasons were 2: 1, if this should go to the Lords, in that respect it would be of no use to us; 2, a damage irrecoverable beyond the seas. For the 1 he argued thus: that by thus transmitting, if it should go with the rest we could not have the fruit of our desires. The ground is mistaken, for we have not this in consideration for the merchants but propose our endeavors for the safety of our justice as of our liberties and preservation of our laws. The question is [not] of our injustice here, but of goods unjustly stayed. May not the like be in you and me and all? Next, the irremediable damage beyond seas which may follow this course. Shall the acts of justice here prejudice abroad? Because we are thus just shall they do us injury? God forbid. The release of this ship; what has followed? A more strict stay. If this be done already it can not be the consequence of our act that shall follow. It pleased him to say that this House was stirred by the practice of a foreign ambassador.[57] It is not the practice of any foreign ambassador nor of any among us more powerful that is able to draw us from those causes that best fit for the honor of the House. We shall go to that which is our duty without [*illegible*], without obliquities.

[p. 20] MR. GLANVILLE reported what was conducing to the business in hand. The Lord Carey told us that the Countess of Middlesex said he [*illegible*] £6,000 disbursed. That Mr. Herman[58] told him that Middlesex laid out £6,000 on the Duke's word but could get no note.

Sir R. Howard informed them that the Earl of Berkshire was to have £5,000 in money and £15,000 in woods.[59]

Sir Robert Pye informed them that £3,000 was to be paid.[60]

Sir William Russell: that he, being Treasurer of the navy, had received £5,000 for the navy and was paid him again out of the subsidy money. That he had received 20 or 30,000£ out of privy seals as a free gift [*illeg-*

55. Sir Edward Barrett was being prepared for an embassy to France. For the instructions to him (two versions), drawn on 30 April, see SP 78/78, f. 247.
56. See above, n. 16.
57. See above, n. 9.
58. Concerning Herman, see HofC, 21 April, n. 13.
59. See above, n. 20.
60. I.e., for the office of Admiral; see above, n. 21.

ible] which he delivered to Sir Allen Apsley to victual the navy.[61] That he had a commission to issue all prizes by directions of the Duke, but a new co-commission ready to pass to issue all by the King's warrant.[62]

Sir John Hippisley: that he and Sir Peter Heyman had a commission to sell prize goods at Dover and return the money in;[63] that he had upon necessity sold £700 goods worth before.

Sir William Monson: that he had heard [from] the Countess of Nottingham that her husband was willing to resign his office of Admiralty and was offered to have the prize place of all the earls of England but that he had that of Mowbray his ancestor.[64]

[p. 21] SIR ROBERT PYE. That the Lord of Middlesex had received the £6,000 again with six score thousand pound more out of the King's estate,[65] *ergo* it was not the Duke that had it.

LORD CAREY.[66] That Sir Lionel Cranfield deposited £6,000 and was to be Master of Wards, but if the Lord Falkland were Master of the Wards then he to be Comptroller.[67] That Sir H. Mildmay had the £6,000 and Cranfield was to have security for repayment, which the Duke promised.[68]

SIR THOMAS HOBY. That the dispute of this day was to resolve which way to go, by the Lords or to the King.

MR. LONG. Because these things would require proof which would be too tedious for the King, *ergo* to go by the Lords.

MR. GRIFFITH. Moved that the grounds for the resolution of the committee should be made known to the House to guide their judgment also.

SIR G. GORING. I have a full and a sad heart, *ergo* of desire not to be misconstrued. We are upon a great rock. By this course we aim at one of these 2 ends, either to remove him or reform him. For the first, his Majesty's words may inform us of the issue; for the second, a heart so generous will reform itself by these cries. The surfeit of long peace will bring in abuses. If we look for amendment let us give some time. What fears and hopes, what enemies abroad. This should move us. Take heed what we do at this time. His Majesty's words that he will not make such a sacrifice.[69]

[p. 22] Moved that we take such a way as may give his Majesty sure ease in this extremity, for he is in a great strait.

SIR ROBERT[70] PYE. For pity and mercy.

MR. KIRTON. That those 2 gentlemen who had spoken had done it so feelingly that if it had been between man and man it would have moved him, but not being the interest of the commonwealth, to go by the Lords.

SIR WILLIAM BEECHER. We know the King has promised that he will reform those things we shall complain of.[71] Divers causes

61. See HofL, 15 May, p. 475, and nn. 123 and 124. Apsley was a Surveyor of the Victuals for the navy. *DNB*.

62. For the commissions to Russell to be receiver of money arising from the sale of prize goods, see HofL, 15 May, p. 456, n. 48.

63. See above, n. 23.

64. See above, n. 25.

65. See above, n. 26.

66. MS: *Sir Lord Carey.*

67. See above, n. 10. In November 1618 it had been rumored that Sir Henry Cary, later Viscount Falkland, who had been Comptroller of the Household since 1617, would obtain the office of Master of the Wards and that Sir Edward Villiers would receive the office of comptroller. See SP 14/103:99 and 110.

68. Regarding Mildmay's involvement in the business see his testimony at the committee of the whole, HofC, 21 April, OB.

69. See the King's message of 14 March.

70. *Walter* is crossed out in the MS and *Robert* is inserted.

71. See the King's letter to the Speaker on 20 March and the King's speech to both Houses on 29 March.

of our evils resolved of. Though the King gave us leave to proceed against the Duke, yet rather in the general to reform hereafter than upon his [*sic*] particular.[72] The Duke has petitioned this House for favor;[73] he may prove a faithful minister hereafter. If we spare him we engage the King the more. We have but 2 enemies: the Spaniard and the papistical faction within. And both hate the Duke next the King. Though we neither complain to the Lords nor King yet they cannot be ignorant what has passed here. The answer we shall receive in general will give content to us in this particular.

MR. CORYTON. To go by the Lords, for after their resolution it will be clear to the King.

SIR ROBERT HARLEY. When I consider the several natures of the accusations I look more upon the honor of the commonwealth than the person of the Duke. 2 charges will not take in that House: the *Peter* and that of the King's physic. Consider our honor in the reformation of this gentleman. To represent it to the King [p. 23] who, when he will cast his eye of love and justice upon us, and see his errors, we shall have the King engage himself to us for his reformation.

SIR JOHN STRANGWAYS. This business cannot now sleep here. To the Lords: 1, it is the ordinary way and warranted by ancient and modern precedents. In the case of Lord Admiral, E. 1;[74] Duke Suffolk, H. 6, moved here first; so of Bacon, Middlesex, and others here first.[75] If we decline the Lords, a show of distrust. 2, both Houses make but one body, not fit to divide the body. 3, if the Lords do not justice, we can demand a reason in a conference; and those who decline the Lords, decline the fairest and justest trial—all the peers, all the judges, are in that House.

SIR JOHN FINCH. A maxim: that this House intends to follow the example of God who delights in reformation not in ruin. We hear of articles exhibited against the Duke by Earl of Bristol.[76] If those be true we shall not need seek means to ruin him. If he free himself of those then any heart that inclines to his mendings will think to use those of a less nature to his amendment, and this would so work with him to be a servant and instrument to do all good offices to the commonwealth and this House. If we think fit to go by the King we may, and because we have used the other by the Lords this should move us for our privilege to run such a way that has formerly been used.

[p. 24] MR. GRIFFITH. I will never waive[77] the justice of the King or think that he will respect a private man more than the kingdom. The King is the worthier and to have the first place.

SIR ALEXANDER TEMPLE. To think day of the business and not presently to resolve, for he desired not the Duke's ruin.

MR. WHITAKER. When the Duke's head was demanded by Gondomar one said it warned him, another it was a transcendent demand.[78] I will not say his head but his ruin sought by another ambassador.[79] O tell it not in Gath;[80] retain some mercy. We

72. See HofC, 29 April, n. 6; and see Buckingham's speeches at the conference, HofC, 30 March, OB.

73. See Buckingham's speeches at the conference, 30 March.

74. See Coke, *Fourth Inst.*, pp. 142–143; and see Selden's speech, below, 8 May.

75. See above, nn. 27 and 28.

76. For Bristol's articles against the Duke, see HofL, 1 May, pp. 329–331.

77. Possibly *crave*.

78. Concerning Gondomar, see HofC, 30 March, n. 29.

79. I.e., Le Sieur de Blainville. See HofC, 1 May, n. 18.

80. 2 Sam. 1:20.

have enemies abroad seek his overthrow and I pray God we be not near a great blow. This Duke has been a means of the preserving this land; this integrity, we have it. Shall we be agents for a stranger who desires his ruin? Errors have been many, yet not so foul as I feared they would have proved. If God be extreme to mark what amiss who should be able to stand in His sight? I see great errors in the Duke, I wish they may tend *ad reparationem non ad ruinum.* That this be not quite declined, but to rest till we know what becomes of the charge above.[81]

SIR THOMAS JERMYN. Every man desires to reform what is amiss in the commonwealth; and so as we may retain the affection of the King to this cause we have now such an opportunity. All natures great and good, yea the divine nature takes delight in those that trust them. The King's nature such [p. 25] if we go to him we shall so engage his Majesty in a reformation that to say otherwise were improbable. If to the Lords, they will say we have dealt with our grievances as Solomon with his brass in the temple, without weight.[82] Moved to transmit these to the King.

By question resolved that the charges should be transmitted to the Lords.

By question resolved that the *St. Peter* should be transmitted with the other charges.

By another question, that all the rest of the charges should be transmitted.

The House referred it to the 12 to consider of the proofs and to distribute this into parts and to report their opinions tomorrow morning.

MR. CHANCELLOR moved that tomorrow morning the matter of subsidy might be handled, for till that be in a law his Majesty cannot be trusted. That his Majesty took the 4th subsidy in good part and thanked us for it.

IV. DIARY OF JOHN LOWTHER, ESQ., D/LONS/L, CUMBERLAND AND WESTMORLAND RECORD OFFICE

[f. 15]

[2 May]

SIR D. DIGGES reports the evils con[cerning] diminution of honor and strength, stoppage of trade.

Causes next resolved:

1. Seas not guarded since treaty.
2. Plurality of offices.
3. Honors sold.
4. Honors of men not deserving.
5. Exhausting and intercepting King's revenue.
6. Selling judicature places.
7. Ships to Rochelle sent [against] our religion.
8. East Indies merchant oppressed, 10,000£ extorted.
9. *St. Peter* of Newhaven stayed whereby a general embargo.
10. Consideration of the King's sickness; physic and plasters applied without physicians' assent.

Finds body 4 parts:

1. Offices. Consists of many parts in him and others; buying Admiral, Wardenry. Neglect, abuses [in]. 5 branches: first, extorting Indies; delivering ships; practicing against Rochelle.
2. Honors. Sale; 2 kings lose by it.
3. Intercepting *et* exhausting, with particulars.
4. The King's death.

Drawn into articles by the lawyers of the 12.[83] Offers proof or to take it by calendar, as every particular is suited with his proof.

[f.15v] 1 [Offices]:

81. I.e., the Earl of Bristol's charges against the Duke in the Upper House.

82. 1 Kgs. 7:47 and 2 Kgs. 25:16.

83. I.e., the committee of twelve from which Digges is reporting. See above, n. 7.

[1.] Duke's offices having been exercised by several persons, and every one requiring an able man. He young, ambitiously got them. Excluded deservers of hope.

[2.] Admiralty bought; against statutes for justice, castles, or fortresses. He [to be] adjudged disabled to hold it. Duke gave for the offices and surrender £3,000 to Admiral and an annuity of £1,000 per annum for his life. Whereupon Duke got them for life, 28 January, 16 Jac.[84] These do concern justice, and he uses them against the law.

[3.] Wardenry of Cinque Ports and Constable of Dover. Duke paid £1,000 to L[ord] Zouche and £500 per annum. He surrendered to King, and Duke obtained them 6 December, 22 Jac.[85] These concern justice and fortresses.

[4.] Treasurership, December, 18 *Jac.*, procured by him to L[ord] Mandeville for which he received £20,000. Master of Wards to Cranfield for which he, or some by him appointed, had £6,000.[86]

[5.] East India ships warlike to be nourished.[87] Duke, by color of parliament abusing the House, hearing of Hormuz good success, moved Lords whether he might stay; agreed he might. When petitioned, he denied stay by him but offered to move for them. Yet, gave leave. [f. 16] After, preserved in Admiralty to bring in 15,000£. After petitioned, Duke protest no release till he agreed. 23 of March they, considering their loss, agreed to give him the 10,000[£] for his false pretense of rights.

[6.] Narrow Seas not guarded. Duke ought to endeavor to supply wants from Lords and King. Duke for 2 years last has neglected his duty and broken trust, whereby the strength decayed, seas infested by pirate[s], and the dominion like to be lost.

[7.] *Peter* of Newhaven laden with 40,000£, in amity with [the] King, taken by his extraordinary commission upon pretense of Spain. And cochineal, gold, jewels worth 20,000£ taken out, delivered by Duke to Marsh. Though ship and goods ordered to be delivered and so decreed, except hides, ginger, etc., yet Duke did detain the things to his use and after unjustly caused the ship to be detained.

[8.] Ships as fortresses to be kept. No man to be dispossessed of his property in his goods. Duke, as Admiral, did procure the *Vanguard* with all furniture to be sent into France and with menaces caused 6 merchants with her to be delivered to the French King contrary to his office.

[9.] Against Rochelle. He, contrary to King's zeal, knowing them to be employed against Rochelle, our religion, and so used since, contrary to King's purpose; [f. 16v] yet intimated they were not nor should be so employed, at Oxford, contrary to King's purpose and abuse of both Houses.

2 [Honors]:

[10.] Compulsion to buy honor. Whereas honors due to virtue, he perverted it and enforced Robartes, Rich[ard],[88] to buy honor against his will.

[11.] Procuring honor to kindred, mother, brothers, and allies by him, whereby noble barons prejudiced and King disabled by their grants and pensions.

3 [Revenue]:

[12.] Interception and exhausting King's revenue. He, not content [with] what had got, 14 *Jac.*, procured £700 old rent; 16 *Jac.*, £120 [*sic*] old rent,[89] to have reprisal of bailiffs' fees, etc.—evil precedent. After, he surrendered £700 per annum and got other lands in lieu; and tallies struck for money paid never received but by him.

84. See HofL, p. 413, n. 15.
85. See above, n. 47.
86. See above, nn. 48 and 49.
87. See above, n. 50.
88. I.e., Richard, Lord Robartes.
89. See the twelfth article, HofL, 15 May, pp. 470–471.

Disbursed King's monies besides all his rewards. Got privy seals for allowance of payments and releases. Got like monies for navy contrary to Exchequer order. And his estate so mixed with King's as not discernible. Got releases of his receipts for his honor's maintenance.

[f. 17] 14 [*sic*] *Junii,* 14 *Jacobi,* Biddlesden, £700. And then the schedule was read reciting the particulars.[90] His endeavor to get the prizes to Marsh's hands.[91] To Sir Anthony Ashley for marrying his cousin, a blank.[92]

4 [King's Death]:

[13.] The King's physic. Where physicians to be sworn, kings' person so sacred as none to minister otherwise. His physicians upon consultation [resolved] nothing to be done but by general advice, and commanded a restraint before [each] fit. Duke, contrary [to] his duty and these, caused certain plasters to be prepared and drink to be ministered. Notwithstanding it had evil effects and that physicians refused until removed, he, when King in declination, made them be applied and given, whereupon great distempers and evil symptoms appeared, and physicians did after advise Duke to do so no more. Which is by us resolved a transcendent presumption of dangerous consequences.

[GLANVILLE.] Carey [told] of Countess of Middlesex and Herman, the officer of conference, said that the £6,000 was disbursed.

Sir Robert Howard heard and believed that Berkshire was to have £5,000 or 15,000£ out of Braydon for Master of the Horse.[93]

Sir Robert Pye said £3,000 of Duke's monies paid to L[ord] Admiral about the time.

[f. 17v] Sir William Russell. That £5,000 for navy was reimbursed by treasurers to Duke. Employed upon navy 30,000M[£] paid about *ultim*[*o*].[94]

He had a commission to take prizes adjudged to dispose by Duke's command; now a new commission in purpose at King's dispose.[95]

Sir John Hippisley. A commission to him [and] Sir P. Heyman to sell the prizes and bring to Exchequer. Before upon necessity [he] sold £800 to pay labor.

Sir William Howard/

Sir William Monson. That upon resignation of the Admiralty he[96] was offered prime earl, had Mowbray annexed, received the £3,000.

SIR ROBERT PYE. [Middlesex] had the £6,000 again and 120,000£[97] more when he made Treasurer.

L. CAREY said that Middlesex told him when he Master of Requests agreed this in effect by Falkland.[98]

CHANCELLOR EXCHEQUER moves, after orders of transmission, to have the subsidy proceed to passing, for until passed as law cannot have credit.

Ordered, tomorrow morning to be done.

V. DIARY OF SIR NATHANIEL RICH, HIST. COLLECT. 143, HLRO

[f. 84]

2 May, Tuesday

SIR D. DIGGES. Report. 2 [evils]: 1, diminution of honor and strength of the kingdom; 2ly/

90. See above, n. 51.
91. See HofL, 15 May, p. 476, n. 130.
92. See above, n. 54.
93. I.e., Braydon Forest, Wiltshire. Thomas Howard, Viscount Andover, later Earl of Berkshire, had been Lieutenant of Braydon Forest (*CSPD 1619–1623,* p. 512).
94. See above, n. 61.
95. See above, n. 62.
96. I.e., Charles, Earl of Nottingham. See above, n. 25.
97. See above, n. 26.
98. See above, n. 67. Cranfield had become a Master of Requests in November 1616.

1. Cause: that our seas not guarded.
2. Engrossing of great offices.
[3.] Honors bought and sold.
4. Conferred on parties incapable.
5. Exhausting of the King's treasure.
6. Buying and selling of places of judicature.
7. Ships against Rochelle.
8. East India.
9. The stay of the *St. Peter.*
10. The applying of plaster, etc., to the late King.

The cause of causes: the Duke.

The body of this charge in 4 parts: [1,] offices; [2,] honors; [3,] revenue; 4, the King's person.

[1.] Offices either in the Duke or in others. In him 3 ways: 1, a great many of them in his hand; 2ly, a buying of the Admiralty; 3ly, of the Cinque Ports. And then ill execution, which has 5 parts: 1, in color of his Admiral's money extorted from the E. India Company; 2ly, the neglect of the seas; 3, delivering of one of the King's ships and 6 other in the hand of strangers; and, 2ly, sending them against our religion.

2. Honors: 1, sold; 2, put upon persons near allied [to] the Duke.

[f. 84v] 3. Revenue anticipated, exhausted.

4. The King's person.

All these are drawn into articles which he offers to be read and has a calendar of proofs, they being the/

1. Plurality of offices—with exorbitant ambition are [in] his person engrossed to the prejudice of the King's service and discouragement of others.

2. Admiralty bought at the price of the Earl of Nottingham £3,000 and procured from King James to the said Earl £1,000 per annum annuity which Nottingham enjoyed.

3. The 5 Ports bought in December, 22 *Jac.*, of the Lord Zouche at the price of £1,000 and £500 per annum during the life of the said Lord Zouche; both bought, paid, and granted by the Duke.

4. Lord Treasurer's office and of the Master of the Wards sold. Sold to the Lord Mandeville for £20,000, paid to the Duke to his own use; and the Master of Wards sold to Sir Lionel Cranfield for £6,000 which was paid to the Duke or some other by his procurement.

5. East India ships stayed and released for money, and abuse of the parliament. This was oppression and extortion. He denied to the East India Company that he was the cause of the stay. The Duke protested that the ships should not go till they had compounded with him, which they were forced to do, and gave the Duke £10,000.

6. Narrow Seas not guarded according to the duty of his place and office.

7. The *Peter* of Newhaven.

8. Delivery of the ships to the French, July 1625, to the wrong of the honors. The ships: one of the King's called the *Vanguard* and six other merchant ships.

[f. 85] 9. These ships sent against Rochelle contrary to the purpose of his Majesty and abusing the parliament, violating its truth.

10. Compulsion to buy honor. By his importunate and subtle procurement of the Lord Robartes, Baron of Truro, compelled by the practice of the Duke and his agents to take the title of Baron of Truro for 10 thousand.

11. Procuring of honors for his kindred: to his mother, Countess [of Buckingham]; Earl of Anglesey to Christopher [Villiers]; Baron Viscount [Fielding]; and Earl of Denbigh, and Viscount Purbeck. To the dishonor of the barons and prejudice of the crown.

12. Intercepting and exhausting of the King's revenue. 14 *Jac.*, did obtain a boot of £747 13s. 4d. old rent, crown land and woods, that of the value of £30,000. And then 16 *Jac.*, £1,200 per annum old rent

with unusual clauses in after valuing the copyhold estates, which clauses have been followed by others; he then surrendered £700 and odd money paid. To this charge which annexed a schedule of grants to the Duke: 14 *Jac.*, £700 per annum; 1623, £51 14s. [*illegible*]; [£]747-13-4 1/2; [£]197-14-9, these passed 17 *Jac.* whereof part, viz., 723 surrendered. And many more/

Many of those lands sold as for the King but sold by the Duke's agents for his use and tallies struck as for the King. Total £20,566 made by sale of lands thus sold.

[f. 85v] 13.[99] Giving the King physic without advice of the physicians.

MR. VICE CHAMBERLAIN thinks fit not to transmit the business of the *St. Peter.* A new strict stay in France.

The merchants ought to have 3 months' warning to transport their goods in case war shall happen.

MR. GLANVILLE's report concerning part of the Duke's charge.

My Lord Carey gave information to the committee that the Countess of Middlesex told him that her husband paid £6,000 for the Wardship and had the office put upon him.

Sir Robert Howard informed that he had credibly heard that the Earl of Berkshire was to have £6,000, etc., to quit his claim of Mastership of the Horse.

Sir R. Pye paid of my Lord Duke's money £6,000 to the Earl of Nottingham.[100]

Sir William Russell received £5,000 of the Duke to be laid out for victual and was reimbursed out of the subsidy money; and that he had received 20 or 30,000£ as from the Duke as a free gift. And he has a commission to take all prize goods and to sell and issue the money by the Duke's direction.

Sir John Hippisley, a commission 7 April last, directed to him, Sir P. Heyman, etc., to sell prize good[s] taken at Dover for the King's use, but says he had paid 6 or 700£ before.

Sir W. Monson informs that he heard that the Lord Earl was desirous to yield up his place.[101]

99. MS: *15*.
100. See above, n. 21.
101. I.e., Charles, Earl of Nottingham. See above, n. 25.

Order of Business Wednesday, 3 May 1626

I.	Journal of the House of Commons,	139–142
II.	Whitelocke,	142–145
III.	Grosvenor,	145–151
IV.	Lowther,	151–152

L.1a. An act to enable all purchases of **copyhold lands** to dispose thereof: rejected	139, 145
Committee of **religion** may make a subcommittee to dispatch the business concerning the **Bishop of Bangor**	139, *17/4
Committee for considering reasons to be used when the Commons pray a conference with the Lords about a **general fast** to meet tomorrow	139, 145, *29/4
Committee on the bill to make the lands of **persons outlawed** for debt subject and liable to extents to meet tomorrow	139, *16/3
Committee on the bill for the better ordering of the office of the **clerk of the market** to meet Saturday [6 May]	139, 145, *7/3
L.2a. An act taking away **nichills accounts** of escheators in cities and towns corporate	139, 146, *7/3
Richard Spencer	146
Sir Walter Erle	146
Bill taking away nichills accounts of escheators: committed	139, 146
L.1a. An act for the draining of the **fens**	139, 146
Sir Edward Peyton	146
Sir Robert Payne	146
Resolved: the bill for draining the fens not to be read a second time unless it be called for in a full House after 9 o'clock	139, 142, 146
L.1a. An act establishing the **quarter sessions** of every county	139, 146
Report from the committee for framing a petition to the King for the **presentment** of **recusants** (John Pym)	139, 143, 146, *21/2
Upon question, the name of Sir William Herbert, MP, to be omitted from the presentment of recusants	140, 143
Rest of the business concerning presentment of recusants deferred until Saturday [6 May]	140, 146
Sir Dudley Digges: moves for appointment of MPs for delivering the charge against the **Duke of Buckingham** to the Lords [*see below*]	140, 143, 146, *21/4
Eight MPs appointed for delivering the charge against Buckingham; 16 assistants appointed	140, 143, 146, 151
The report from the committee of **grievances** to be deferred	140
[*Committee of the Whole House: Edward Littleton in the chair*] Sir Thomas Grantham: concerning **supply** and the time for payment of the fourth **subsidy**	147, *27/3
John Pym	147
Sir Thomas Hoby	147
Sir John Stradling	147
William Noy	147
Sir Peter Heyman	147
Sir William Bulstrode	147
Sir William Strode	147
Sir George More	147
Sir Robert Killigrew	147
Sir Anthony Forest	147
Sir John Savile	147
Sir Richard Weston (Chancellor Exchequer)	147
Mr. Jordan	147
Sir Gilbert Gerard	147
Sir John Strangways	147
Sir William Beecher	147
Mr. Coke	147
Sir William Constable	147

SIR HENEAGE FINCHE (Speaker): tells Hayward, Pope, and Mottershed the resolution of the House 142, 151
SIR WALTER ERLE: moves that John Glanville replace him in delivering the charge against the **Duke of Buckingham** [*see above*] 142
Ordered: as Erle moved 142

Report from the committee for considering the contempt of the **sheriff of Leicestershire** (EDWARD LITTLETON) [*see above*] 142, 145
Further debate on the contempt of the sheriff of Leicestershire respited till tomorrow 142, 145

WEDNESDAY, 3 MAY 1626

I. JOURNAL OF THE HOUSE OF COMMONS

[CJ 853; p. 44]

Mercurii, 3 Maii, 2 Caroli Regis

L. 1a. An act to enable all[1] purchasers of copyhold lands within the realm of England and dominion of Wales to dispose thereof before admittances to the same.

Upon question, rejected.

Ordered, the committee for religion may make a subcommittee of eight or more to dispatch the examination of the business against the Lord Bishop of Bangor.[2]

The committee for the reasons for the general fast to meet/

Committee for the bill for extents for outlawed persons, tomorrow in the afternoon. And all that will come to have voice.

Clerk of the market, Saturday, 2 clock.

Passing sheriffs' accounts, Friday, 2 clock.

L. 2a. An act for taking away escheators' accounts of nichills in cities and towns corporate.[3]

Committed to

[col. 1]
Mr. [Richard] Spencer
Sir W[alter] Erle
Mr. [John] Whitson
Sir Thomas Grantham
Sir H[enry] Poole

[col. 2]
Mr. Jordan
Mr. Lowther
Mr. [William] Cage
Mr. [George] Vernon
Sir B[aptist] Hicks
Mr. [Thomas] Bedingfield
Sir John Stradling
Sir Eubule Thelwall
Sir H[enry] Anderson
Sir Francis Barrington
Mr. [Richard] Taylor
Mr. [Thomas] Malet
Mr. [Christopher] Erle
Sir H[enry] Spiller
Sir John Savile
Mr. [Edward] Kirton
Mr. [John] Selden
Sir P[eter] Riddell
Sir Roger Twysden
Mr. [Anthony] Langston
Sir Thomas Fairfax
Sir William Strode

[col. 3]
Mr. John Drake
Sir William Alford

Friday, 2 clock, Exchequer Chamber. Clerk of the Parcels to attend.[4]

[p. 45] *L. 1a.* An act for the draining/[5]

Resolved, this bill shall not be 2ly read but after 9 clock, in a full House, and the House being 1st moved for the 2nd reading of it.

L. 1a. An act establishing the quarter sessions of every county within this realm to be held in the places accustomed.

MR. PYM reports from the committee about the petition for presenting the recusants.[6]

That the committee thought fit the Lord Mordaunt should be left out, in respect of divers testimonies of his inclination to conform himself to our religion; so John Preston, a bow-bearer; Sir Thomas Compton, dead since the 1st presentment;[7] so those which dwell in the country and resort to the City. These thought fit to be put out.

1. *copyhold tenants* is crossed out in the MS following *all*.

2. *at which examination no member of the House to be excluded* is crossed out in the MS following *Bangor*. Concerning Lewis Bayly, Bishop of Bangor, see HofC, 17 April, n. 3. For the earlier resolution empowering the committee of religion to appoint members to examine witnesses concerning Bangor, see HofC, 27 April, OB.

3. Concerning nichills, see HofC, 7 March, n. 6.

4. We are unable to identify the Clerk of the Parcels, who was an under officer in the Exchequer along with the Clerk of the Nichills.

5. Marginal note: "Fens". For a fuller title of the bill, see Grosvenor, below.

6. For the appointment of this committee, see HofC, 20 March, OB.

7. For the orders for the presentment of recusants, see 21 February; for the first presentments to the committee of religion, see 27 February, and n. 35. A letter of 10 April 1626 from Sir Benjamin Rudyard refers to the recent death of Sir Thomas Compton; see SP 16/24:59.

That the Earl of Arundel has 3 servants popishly affected.

Sir William Herbert[8] and Sir John Herbert, in Montgomeryshire.

Sir Richard Tichborne, made a deputy lieutenant.[9] Sir Walter Tichborne, having 3 daughters, one a convicted recusant, the 2nd popish, the 3rd sent over for a nun.

Mr. Warren, a minister and justice of peace of Suffolk, thought fit also to be presented.[10]

That within the Five Ports no commission or authority to inquire of recusants.

[CJ 854] That a Jesuit had lived divers years in Gray's Inn and Barnard's Inn; and that the committee desired a course might be taken for clearing the Inns of Court and Chancery from such dangerous persons.[11]

Upon question, Sir William Herbert's name to be omitted out of the presentment.

The residue of the business to be deferred until Saturday next.

SIR [DUDLEY DIGGES].[12] 1. An introduction, and a conclusion. These by two; the other parts will take up 6 more.

Moves 8 persons may be named, and they to divide the parts among themselves and every of them to choose two members to assist them in their preparation of the business.

Sir D. Digges	Sir Francis Barnham Mr. Littleton
Sir W. Erle[13]	Mr. Glanville Sir William Armine
Sir John Eliot	Mr. Noy Mr. Rolle
Mr. Herbert	Sir B. Rudyard Mr. Mason
Mr. Pym	Sir Nathaniel Rich Mr. Browne
Mr. Whitby	Mr. Sherland Mr. Wilde
Mr. Selden	Mr. Charles Jones Mr. Kirton
Mr. Wandesford[14]	Sir John Strangways Mr. Sherfield

[p. 46] These 8,[15] and 16 assistants, to agree upon the parts and divide the business among them. Agreed upon question.[16]

The report of the grievances to be deferred till this business past; and then the report to be made.[17]

The House turned into a grand committee about the time of the 4th subsidy.[18]

8. Sir William Herbert, MP for Montgomeryshire, was included in Pym's report from the committee of religion on 2 March as one to be left out of the presentment. See above. Concerning Herbert and his recusant wife, see *PP 1628*, IV, 319 n. 65.

9. The House had resolved that Sir Richard Tichborne, MP for Winchester, Hampshire, whose wife was a recusant, should be presented; see HofC, 20 March, n. 8. The previous July Sir Benjamin Tichborne had written to Lord Conway requesting that his son, Richard, join him in the commission, SP 16/521:103. See also, 23 May, below, where Sir Walter Tichborne is ordered to be left out of the presentment.

10. Concerning Robert Warren, see Pym's report from the committee of religion, HofC, 2 March, OB.

11. See below, 23 May. Edward Bysshe mentioned by name three popishly-affected lawyers who were living in the Inns of Court and Chancery. The House responded by adding lawyers to the committee with orders to consider how to prevent this practice.

12. The MS is blank; Digges's name is supplied from the accounts below. Digges is referring to the charge to be delivered to the Lords against the Duke of Buckingham.

13. *Thomas Lake* is crossed out in the MS and *W. Erle* is inserted. Later this afternoon Erle's part was assigned to John Glanville.

14. *Glanville* is crossed out in the MS and *Wandesford* is inserted.

15. All eight were members of the committee of 12 appointed on 21 April for considering the business concerning the Duke.

16. *Upon question, any of the 8 after distribution of the parts may* is crossed out in the MS following *question.*

17. On 1 May the House had resolved that the report from the committee of grievances would be made on Thursday, 4 May.

18. On 26 April the committee of the whole House had resolved to give a fourth subsidy; on 2 May the House ordered the committee of the whole to meet this day (3 May) to consider the time of payment.

MR. LITTLETON reports from the grand committee for the King's supply: that they have agreed to give a 4th subsidy to be rated and paid after the usual manner, to be paid the last day of July come 12month.

Upon question, to augment the supply formerly intended to be given this session by addition of a 4th subsidy. This to be paid the last day of July come 12month, and to be rated in the usual manner.

The conclusion of the transmission of the charges against the Duke read, and so the preamble.

All to be brought in tomorrow morning by the committee of 12, and then to be resolved on.

The sheriff of Leicestershire's business to be reported to the House this afternoon, if time, after Sir Robert Howard's business be dispatched; and he[19] then to attend.

MR. ERLE. That a grant to Burlamachi and Jacobson for carrying over iron ordnance.[20] That some are now ready to be transported. To have a message to the King for stay of them.

Upon question, Mr. Vice Chamberlain, Mr. Chancellor Exchequer, Mr. Chancellor Duchy to move his Majesty from this House that a stay may be made of transportation of any iron ordnance.

[*Afternoon*]

Mercurii, 3 Maii, 2 Caroli Regis

L. 1a. An act for free liberty to marry at any time of the year.

Sir John Hayward called in about Sir Robert Howard his business and interrogated by MR. SPEAKER, divers questions,[21] answers: He was not present when Sir Robert Howard was committed close prisoner. That he was present at the excommunication. He saw Sir Robert Howard tender a paper to the Lord Keeper but heard no word of privilege of parliament spoken of; and that the Lord Keeper gave it to the Lord President, and he heard them tell Sir Robert Howard it was not worth a straw. That he has not known those courts but very rarely kept out of term, and of late not at all. Comes very rarely thither, not at all in the winter season. That the commission warrants proceedings by imprisonment, fine, or otherwise by all or any of them.[22] That he was not spoken to by any to come to that court.

[p. 47] Dr. Pope[23] called in and interrogated, answers: 1st, he was present, 5 *Martii* and 17 *Martii.* That the 1st day he[24] claimed no privilege; the 2nd day he did. That 8 Lords there, parliament men. He ignorant of the privileges of parliament.[25] Gave credit to the opinion of those Lords and other which had been parliament men. That it never came to voices. That he set his hand to both sentences of imprisonment and excommunication; and the use is that all set their hands upon a consent by the major part, though a man, subscribing, have been against it. That these courts are kept rarely out of term, but by special mandate of the King or of the Lord of Canter-

19. I.e., Sir Thomas Hartoppe, sheriff of Leicestershire.

20. For the appointment of Philip Burlamachi and Philip Jacobson as sole agents for the exportation of ordnance, see *APC 1623–1625,* pp. 104–105, 136–137. See also, *PP 1628,* p. 82, n. 7.

21. Concerning the case of Sir Robert Howard, see HofC, 17 February and 21 March, OBs. The questions put to Hayward and Pope, the members of the High Commission examined this day, were the same as those put to Sir Henry Marten on 29 April, see OB. Regarding Sir John Hayward (not to be confused with the MP of the same name), see Levack, *Civil Lawyers,* pp. 237–238.

22. The commission of 21 January 1625 is printed in Rymer, *Foedera,* VII, pt. 4, pp. 171–181.

23. Edmund Pope. See Levack, *Civil Lawyers,* pp. 262–263.

24. I.e., Sir Robert Howard.

25. Dr. Edmund Pope had no parliamentary experience.

bury. That they may commit to close prison because the commission being to imprison, the other is *vicinum mandato*.[26]

Mr. Mottershed, the register,[27] called in and interrogated, confesses that he made the entry of the claim of Sir Robert Howard his privilege of parliament; and that Sir Robert Howard tendering a paper about it, the late Lord Keeper and the Lord President said it was of no worth, being no record. That one Porter of Ware was both committed close prisoner and excommunicated for refusing to take the oath.[28]

Upon question, all the proceedings in the High Commission Court against Sir Robert Howard from the 1st of February,[29] 22 *Jac.*, at which time he ought to have had his privilege of parliament, declared to be void and ought to be vacated and annihilated.

2ly, upon question, whether a letter to be written by Mr. Speaker to the Lord of Canterbury and the rest of the Lords and others of the high commissioners for annulling of the said proceedings, the House divided. The yea went out.

Tellers for the yea:	Sir H. Poole
	Sir Thomas Denton
Tellers for the no:	Sir Francis Foljambe
	Mr. Wandesford

With the yea: 105
With the no: 114
Difference: 9

Upon question,[30] Sir John Hayward, Dr. Pope, and the register called in, and the effect of the said order to be declared to them by Mr. Speaker; and that the House expects it be done, and to hear by Monday next that this be done and, in the meantime, the House will respite any resolution concerning themselves; and that they attend the House again upon Monday morning. And the like notice to be given to Mr. Comptroller and Sir H. Marten by the Serjeant. All which was done by MR. SPEAKER accordingly.

SIR W. ERLE moves that Mr. Glanville may, by the House, be ordered to deliver that part which was assigned to Sir W. Erle.

Ordered.

[p.48] MR. LITTLETON reports the complaint against the sheriff of Leicestershire:[31] that the sheriff/

That the committee of opinion that this a contempt against the privilege of free election.

That, in respect of the youth of the sheriff,[32] and that he protests he did it of ignorance, were of opinion that he should be only admonished by Mr. Speaker in the House, and bear Sir H. Hastings's charges of his witnesses.

The further debate hereof respited till tomorrow morning.

II. DIARY OF BULSTRODE WHITELOCKE, ESQ., DD. 12.21, CAMBRIDGE UNIVERSITY LIBRARY

[f. 175]

May 3

The sense of the House being to cast out a bill,[33] yet because it came from the King the House orders that it shall not be read 2nd

26. See above, n. 22.
27. Concerning Thomas Mottershed, see HofC, 21 March, n. 15.
28. We have been unable to identify Porter of Ware.
29. *since the 5th of March* is crossed out in the MS and *from the 1st of February* is inserted. In the insertion, *last* is crossed out preceding *1;* this change was made in accordance with an order of the House the following day. See HofC, 4 May, below.
30. *By direction of the House* is crossed out in the MS and *upon question* is inserted.
31. Concerning Sir Thomas Hartoppe, sheriff of Leicestershire, see HofC, 25 March, OB. Littleton is reporting from the committee appointed on 26 April.
32. Hartoppe must have been in his early or mid twenties, having matriculated at Cambridge University in 1616. *A. C.*
33. I.e., the bill for the draining of the fens.

time but sleep, unless it be called for in a full House after 9 a clock.

MR. PYM reports from the committee for that purpose the form of a petition.[34]

Ordered that Sir William Herbert shall be left out of the presentment of recusants in office.[35]

SIR DUDLEY DIGGES moves that there being required 8 members of the House to deliver the charge against the Duke of Buckingham (one the introduction, another the conclusion, and 6 the body of the charge by parts), that the House will appoint 8 for this business.

8 of the 12 are appointed accordingly,[36] and every man of the 8 chooses 2 assistants and nominates them in the House. Any of the 8 may, if there be occasion/

Ordered that the 8 and the 16 assistants shall agree amongst themselves for the distribution of the parts.

[*Committee of the Whole House*]

[f. 175v] Mr. Littleton takes the chair.

After debate whether the 4th subsidy agreed to be given in this session should be paid in July or September come twelvemonth,[37] ordered that it shall be paid in the last of July come twelvemonth.

Speaker takes his chair.

MR. LITTLETON reports the resolutions of the committee for the 4th subsidy and the time.

Resolved by the House accordingly.

CHANCELLOR EXCHEQUER explains the message of the King that we should make an end of this inquisition concerning the Duke of Buckingham and meddle with no more new matter, the time being so far spent and other businesses requiring speed.[38]

SIR JOHN ELIOT. That we may retain the liberty of inquiring or examining any further matter concerning the Duke of Buckingham according to the conclusion of his charge.[39]

Pomeridiem

Sir John Hayward, one of the High Commission Court, brought in concerning Sir Robert Howard, says that he was only once at the agitation of Sir Robert Howard's business, and that when the schedule of excommunication was read.[40] Whether he claimed privilege or not he knows not nor heard any word of privilege from Sir Robert Howard, but there [f. 176] was a paper presented at the upper end of the table, he sitting at the lower end. He did not set his hand to the imprisonment. He has not known courts kept of late out of term, and rarely heretofore. For denying the oath *ex officio*, the commission warrants that they may proceed by censures, by fines, imprisonment, or any or all of them.[41] But by reason of his seldom attendance there he knows not the precedents of proceedings there. That he was not spoken to by any man to go over.

Doctor Pope, for the same matter, says that he was a high commissioner and sat 5

34. I.e., the petition to the King for the presentment of recusants, drawn up by the committee appointed on 20 March.

35. See above, n. 8.

36. See above, n. 15. On folio 94 of his diary Whitelocke entered a few rough notes, including the names of the eight MPs and their assistants appointed at this time.

37. See above, n. 18.

38. Weston is apparently referring to the message delivered on 29 April.

39. Following Eliot's speech, Digges presented the conclusion of the charge against Buckingham. The conclusion was subsequently delivered to the Lords by Sir John Eliot at the conference of 10 May; see the report of that conference, HofL, 15 May, OB.

40. See above, n. 21.

41. See above, n. 22.

Martii when Sir Robert Howard was committed and 17 *Martii* when he was excommunicated. That he, sitting at the lower end of the table, could not well hear what he said and heard not that he claimed his privilege. The Lords overruled the matter. 8 of the commissioners were parliament men and 2 were of the body of this House. It[42] lay not in his power to cross it. That it was overswayed by them and never came to voices. He did set his hand to the commitment and excommunication. Imprisonments in the ecclesiastical courts/

The course is if the voices be against a thing yet all hands must be set to it. Unless in matters of high nature, the courts are not kept out of term. The matter of close imprisonment is sometimes used. A delegate must not exceed *fines mandati,* but they may do those things that are *vicinum* [f. 176v] *mandato.* He was not above a month before commissioner.[43]

Mr. Mottershed, deputy register in the High Commission Court,[44] says that nobody did direct him to enter that Sir Robert Howard showed no record nor other thing claiming his privilege. That Lord Keeper and Lord President said that the paper presented by Sir Robert was nothing, whereupon he made this entry. That one Porter of Ware was excommunicated and committed close prisoner by that court for/[45]

CHANCELLOR DUCHY. It is justly by the House overruled. That if a parliament be by prorogation to meet 16 *Martii* a member of the House is to have his privilege 1 *Martii,* 16 days before the sitting of the parliament,[46] and though there go out a proclamation before 1 *Martii* to diswarn the meeting.[47]

SIR EDWIN SANDYS. 1st consideration is to right the gentleman that is wronged; 2nd, to censure those that wronged him. I think all the proceedings during the time of his privilege/

That the register be charged not to make use of anything done against Sir Robert Howard and the like said to those of our House and cognizance and that a letter be written to the Archbishop of Canterbury that the proceedings in that case be all suppressed.

Resolved that all the proceedings in the High Commission Court against Sir Robert Howard from the 1st day of February 1624, when he ought to have had[48] his privilege, shall be declared to be vacated[49] and annulled.

[f. 177] MR. SELDEN. Against a letter writing to the Archbishop of Canterbury. That some of those that are within our jurisdiction are of the quorum[50] in the High Commission and any 3 of them may keep a court, whereof one to be of the quorum. Moves we may enjoin 3 of them within our cognizance to keep a court and suppress the proceedings. I conceive that those that are excommunicated by/

DOCTOR EDEN. Generally in absolutions an oath is required, and there was before the reformation a submission upon the

42. MS: *in.*

43. The commission was appointed on 21 January 1625 and Howard's case was heard in March 1625.

44. Concerning Mottershed, see HofC, 21 March, n. 15.

45. See above, n. 28.

46. Regarding the period of privilege before and after each session of parliament, see HofC, 9 February, n. 25.

47. On 16 February 1625, James I prorogued parliament to 15 March; on 3 March he issued a proclamation further proroguing the session from 15 March to 20 April 1625 (*Stuart Proclamations,* I, 617, 633).

48. *since the [5] of March, when he claimed* is crossed out in the MS and *from the 1st day of February 1624[/25], when he ought to have had* is inserted.

49. *void* is crossed out in the MS and replaced with *vacated.*

50. For the commission, see Rymer, *Foedera,* VII, pt. 4, p. 174.

knee used and required, but since left, and an absolution without the oath or submission is at this day good and effectual, and so was Sir Robert Howard's.[51]

MR. NOY cites Sir John Hall's case in the parliament.[52] And is for the general way of directions.

MR. SHERFIELD. If an act of the High Commission Court touch upon the privilege of this House, we may enjoin the Court to alter that act.

MR. TAYLOR. In Sir William Pope's and Sir George Marshall's case there was an order of this House to reverse a decree in Chancery, but the decree was not reversed.[53]

SIR NATHANIEL RICH. 43 Eliz., Belgrave's case,[54] a bill preferre[d] in Star Chamber against a member of this House by a member of the Upper House. The House resolved it to be a breach of the privilege of the House and there was a conference with the Lords.

Waived[55] upon question and division, the ayes 105, the noes 114, the writing of a letter to the Archbishop of Canterbury for the annihilating the proceedings against Sir Robert Howard.

[f. 177v] Resolved that Sir John Hayward and Doctor Pope shall be called in, and the register, and told the effect of the opinion of the House touching the vacating of the proceedings and annulling, and that the House expects this to be done and to hear by Monday next that it is performed, and in the meantime will respite any resolution[56] concerning them, and that they are to attend on Monday, and this notice is to be given to Mr. Comptroller and to Sir Henry Marten.

MR. LITTLETON reports Sir Henry Hastings's case.[57] That after he was cried up to be knight of the shire the sheriff did arrest him because he refused to disclaim his election. The opinion of the committee was that the sheriff should pay Sir Henry Hastings's charges and have an admonition from the House only, being himself a young gentleman[58] that knew not the privilege of this House.

The debate hereof deferred till tomorrow.

III. DIARY OF SIR RICHARD GROSVENOR, MS 611, TRINITY COLLEGE, DUBLIN

[p. 25]

May 3

1. An act to enable all purchasers of copyhold land in England and Wales to dispose thereof before admittance to the same.

Rejected upon the first reading.

Tomorrow, in Exchequer Chamber, for providing reasons for a fast.

Saturday for bill [for] clerk of the markets.

51. See Selden's report, above, 21 March. The High Commission had absolved Howard without his suit on 16 February 1626.

52. In the case of Sir John Hall and Thomas Fuller, heard by the House in 1621, the Commons questioned the jurisdiction of both the Court of Wards and the Court of Chancery and ordered that Hall and Fuller be freed from their imprisonment and that their cause be dismissed out of both courts. *CJ*, I, 535, 558–559; *CJ 1621*, Index, *sub* Hall, Sir John.

53. For the resolution of the House in 1621 concerning the case, see *CJ*, I, 599; and see also, Nicholas, *Proceedings and Debates in 1621*, I, 340–344, 366–367, and *CD 1621*, Index, *sub* Marshall, Sir George.

54. MS: *Bellingham's*. For the case involving George Belgrave, MP for Leicester, in the parliament of 1601, see D'Ewes, *Journal . . . Elizabeth*, pp. 612, 614, 666, 669–670, 672–673, 678–679, 688.

55. *Resolved* is crossed out in the MS and *Waived* is inserted.

56. *their censure* is crossed out in the MS and *any resolution* is inserted.

57. See above, n. 31.

58. See above, n. 32.

2. An act to take away nichills accounts of escheators in cities and towns corporate.

MR. SPENCER moved that the Clerk of the Parcels[59] might appear before them what he can say for himself that he gave £600 for himself. And that the bill might be committed.

SIR WALTER ERLE. That the charge in the Exchequer was £5 when the accounts came but to 5s.

Committed, Friday, Exchequer Chamber.

[p. 26] An act for the draining and inning of 360,000 acres of land lying in Huntingdon, Cambridge, with the Isle of Ely, Suffolk, Northampton, and unto the south side of the river of Glen.[60] 120,000 acres for the King, and he to drain it; 4,000 acres for the keeping the works in repair forever.

SIR EDWARD PEYTON. That this bill has a private end; that his country was against it; that it was rejected [in] 12 *Jac.*[61] Wished that either it should be rejected or else the country might have notice at the second reading to speak to it.

SIR ROBERT PAYNE against the bill.

The bill was to lie asleep, and ordered not to be read the second time till the House were made acquainted with it,

1. An act to establish the quarter sessions of every county to be held in the places accustomed. To be kept in the principal cities and towns, great part here used to be for 60 years past kept, except the justices of peace are under their hands, appoint otherwise by order.

MR. PYM reported that the committee had drawn a petition to the King about the recusants in place of authority. That the Lord Mordaunt[62] should be left out of the presentment because he showed himself willing to conform himself. John Preston, a bow-bearer, to be left out because he had no other, out. Sir Thomas Compton dead since the presentment.[63] Some then thought of putting in the Earl of Arundel who had 2 or 3 servants recusants. That Mr. Vaughan had commanded a formal presentment from Montgomeryshire against Sir William and Sir John Herbert. [p. 27] That Sir Richard Tichborne was since the presentment made a deputy lieutenant,[64] and Sir Walter Tichborne had 3 daughters papists, one gone over to be a nun. That Mr. Warren, a minister and justice in Suffolk, should be inserted.[65] That in the Cinque Ports they have no authority to indict recusants.

Saturday morning appointed to debate this business.

SIR DUDLEY DIGGES. 8 to be taken up in this business of the Duke's which was distributed into 6 parts together with the/

1. An introduction.
2. A conclusion.
3. Of the articles: neglect of seas; putting of the ships into the hands of the French and against Rochelle; stay of the *Peter;* sale of honor and office of judicature.

1. Sir Dudley Digges.	
Assistants:	Sir Francis Barnham
	Mr. Littleton
2. Sir Walter Erle.	
Assistants:	Mr. Glanville
	Sir William Armine

59. See above, n. 4.

60. MS: *Bleane.* The river of Glen, in Lincolnshire, served as a boundary of the north fenland.

61. Peyton sat for Cambridgeshire. The bill presented and read once in 1614 was for "salt marshes inned, gained, or lost by the sea". See *PP 1614,* pp. 348, 388.

62. MS: *Morley.* Regarding Mordaunt see the CJ, above, and the orders concerning the presentments on 11 May, below.

63. See above, n. 7.

64. See above, n. 9.

65. See above, n. 10.

3. Sir John Eliot.
[Assistants]: Mr. Noy
Mr. Rolle

4. Mr. Herbert.
[Assistants]: Mr. Mason
Sir Benjamin Rudyard

5. Mr. Pym.
[Assistants]: Sir Nathaniel Rich
Mr. Browne

6. Mr. Whitby.
[Assistants]: Mr. Sherland
Mr. Wilde

7. Mr. Selden.
[Assistants]: Mr. Jones[66]
Mr. Kirton

8. Mr. Wandesford.
[Assistants]: Mr. Sherfield
Sir John Strangways

These 8 to deliver the parts and distribute them among themselves, and to use the help of their assistants, if occasion, to speak for them.

[p. 28] Subsidy.

The Speaker went forth and Mr. Littleton came into the chair.

[*Committee of the Whole House*]

Sir Thomas Grantham. The time for payment is as much as the money. The purses of the poor are very short. Moved that the 4th subsidy should be paid at Michaelmas after the 3d paid.

Mr. Pym. As we have proportioned the sum to the great occasions, so the time to the same. Moved all should be paid within a year for these reasons: 1, that the bounty of the subjects may serve the King's occasion; 2, that we put not the King to extraordinary expenses for use. Moved Christmas.

Sir Thomas Hoby. 3 months after the 3d.

Sir John Stradling. At Christmas or midst of January.

Mr. Noy. For August or September after the 3d.

Sir Peter Heyman. In August twelvemonth.

Sir William Bulstrode. In September; the husbandman then has his corn and wool come in.

Sir William Strode. For September, because else the calling of the people together would be in the midst of harvest.

Sir G. More. 3 months after the last.

Sir Robert Killigrew. In June.

Sir Anthony Forest. July.

Sir John Savile. Would be glad the King should know the state of his subjects and that he should not presume of more from them than can be paid. For September.

Sir Richard Weston. The money given by the act gives the King credit from the first day. We have armies by land and our allies that we might pay it with the first.

Mr. Jordan. All in a year.

Sir Gilbert Gerard. For September.

Sir John Strangways. July.

Sir William Beecher. If war continue it will raise new occasions. To give it so far in the year will hinder that again.

[p. 29] Mr. Coke. A month will much forward the King's affairs. Put for July.

Sir William Constable. For September.

Sir H. May. That a million would be spent in wine between this and Michaelmas twelvemonth. This we give to set out a fleet to maintain a great army. For last of July.

By question, resolved to be paid the last of July come twelvemonth.

66. I.e., Charles Jones. See CJ, above.

The Speaker came into the chair and MR. LITTLETON reported it to the House.

By question, resolved to be paid the last of July.

SIR DUDLEY DIGGES, from the committee of 12, moved to know whether that committee should go on with examining of some things in their hands against the Duke or to discharge them.

MR. CHANCELLOR OF EXCHEQUER explained the message the King had sent;[67] that he desired and expected there should now be an end of the inquisition and entertain no new matter.

SIR JOHN ELIOT. If we desert our freedom we wrong ourselves. Have not we power to inquire of such things as are for the honor of the King, for the safety of the commonwealth? So not to be safe to lay by these inquiries; yet not to be inquisitive, but to accept of all informations that shall be of moment. To retain this still.

SIR DUDLEY DIGGES. Presented the conclusion and the preamble.[68]

SIR EDWIN SANDYS. If this be to be delivered by writing it is a new way and then there need no distribution of parts.[69]

The committee to think of this.

[*Afternoon*]

[p. 30] May 3, afternoon, the House sat.

Sir Robert Howard's business.[70]

1. An act for free liberty to marry any time of the year.

Sir John Hayward called to the bar when the SPEAKER demanded the questions former[l]y asked of Sir H. Marten:

To the first he answered that he was not there when he was committed prisoner, only once while that matter was agitated. That he knows not whether he challenged privilege or not. That he tendered a paper to the Lord Keeper; their answer was that it was naught, not worth a straw, that it was but a scroll.

2. His hand was not to his commitment.

3. 17 of March he was there. That they do not ordinarily keep their courts at such time, not of late out of term.

4. That he is sure that the commission does warrant to proceed by censure, fine, imprisonment, excommunication, either or all of them, but knows not whether they have used to proceed by both at any time for refusing the oath.

5. If I had been drawn over by any respect or persuasion, I should have gone oftener. That then I did not go by any motion of any, nor would I be so persuaded.

Dr. Pope called to the bar. The same questions:

To the 1, that he sat both those days as a commissioner. The 5 day was the 5 of March, when he was committed; 17 of March, excommunicated. The first day he carried himself modestly and too modestly, speaking to the Lord Keeper in his ear. The first day he claimed no privilege; the 2d day he did, but Lord Keeper told him he did not exhibit in lawful manner, it was no record. 12 were of the higher House when they had delivered their opinions; it had been to little purpose to oppose them, neither did it come to voices, and I followed their judgments.

[p. 31] 2. The use of the High Commission, though they differ in opinion yet they all set to their hands. So did I to both im-

67. See above, n. 38.

68. I.e., of the charge against the Duke of Buckingham; see above, n. 39.

69. See Sandys's speech in Lowther, below.

70. This heading belongs to the business following the reading of the bill for free liberty to marry. Concerning the case of Sir Robert Howard, see above, n. 21.

prisonment and excommunication. That they have power to join all together: fine, imprisonment, excommunication. That none but such as Legate ever refused to answer,[71] and if he had taken the oath there were of his friends would have showed him all favor.

3. That they used not to sit out of term unless the King send some Jesuit or schismatical man to them, then they sit out of term.

4. For close imprisonment sometimes it is used and according to law, for the commission gives warrant to imprison *ergo* close, this is *vicinum mandato*. They may commit *ad tempus* or *in perpetuum* as they did in the case of Legate, but they could not exceed *fines mandati*, not drawn by respect or command.

The register of the Commission courts called in, Mottershed:

1. Who commanded him to enter into his book. That he entered into the register that Sir Robert Howard claimed his privilege but showed no record, which he did because the Lord Keeper and Lord President had said it was no record. That he did this of himself.

2. He knew it was decreed that an excommunication should go out. That Innocent Lanier[72] called for it. He paid the fees and had it out, put hands.

3. It is not usual to keep courts so long after term.

4. That it is not the use to proceed by imprisonment and excommunication at once and has not known any but one Porter for refusing to take the oath.

MR. BROOKE moved to have a question asked of the register whether there was any examination or other act done after Sir Robert Howard claimed his privilege, because it would be fit to undo what was so done.

[p. 32] SIR HUMPHREY May. That whatsoever was done before as well as after within the days of privilege ought to be undone.

16 days[73] before sitting of parliament are due for privilege, although by proclamation the time be further adjourned.[74] For that we should meet is of record, the proclamation every man cannot take notice of.

MR. LONG. That what was done against Sir Robert Howard in the Commission Court might be taken off the file and he set in the same estate he was before.

SIR G. MORE. That the privilege was broken. What to be done? Sir H. Marten said they did not go to votes.[75] Something fit to be done that we maintain the privileges of the House.

MR. CORYTON. Moved that first we put to question whether all done against Sir Robert Howard should be made void. Then what to do to our members.

SIR EDWIN SANDYS. 2 parts: [1,] for the righting of this wronged and oppressed gentleman; 2, for the punishing of those that wronged him. It is clear that all proceedings within the compass of 16 days or so long after ought to be suppressed. The question, how they shall be suppressed. For we have to do with a high court and with men without our jurisdiction: their *dominum*

71. Probably a reference to the case of Bartholomew Legate who was burned at Smithfield in 1612, although he was tried in the consistory court of London. See Fuller, *Church History*, V, 419–423; *DNB*.

72. Innocent Lanier had been recommended by the Duke of Buckingham to supply Chief Justice Crew with particulars concerning the case of Sir Robert Howard and Lady Purbeck. See SP 14/183:41, 66, and 184:7.

73. *Dr. Eden* is crossed out in the MS preceding *16*. Concerning the period of privilege for MPs, see HofC, 9 February, n. 25.

74. Concerning the proclamation, see above, n. 47.

75. See Marten's response to the question posed by Nicholas Eversfield in the House on 29 April.

decreverunt. The great men did it without the vote of the rest. My opinion: first, the register charged that he make no use of what has been done to the prejudice of Sir Robert Howard, and the like declared to them; and that if any such thing be, it shall be taken as a wrong to the privileges of the Commons of England. [p. 33] And then a message sent to the Archbishop to tell him that we have decried this and to desire him that nothing be done to the prejudice of the gentleman upon those proceedings within the 16 days before and 16 days after.

By question, resolved that all the proceedings that have been in that court against Sir Robert Howard from the first of February 1624, at which time he ought to have had his privilege, should be declared to be void.[76]

SIR WILLIAM SPENCER moved that the register should bring in his book hither, and we to see all the proceedings torn out.

MR. SELDEN. Against writing to the Archbishop. That 3, whereof one of the quorum, may hold a court.[77] That some of these gentlemen of our House are of the quorum and they may keep a court. That we enjoin them to keep a court and make void all these acts. If they refuse, they are subject to a second censure. That Sir Robert Howard is not yet absolved and so we all in danger. Whosoever is excommunicate by them cannot be absolved without a submission. That order made by them is to make us believe he is absolved.[78]

DR. EDEN. That Sir Robert Howard was absolved as he was excommunicated by a decree. In absolutions there was wont to be a submission upon the knee and an oath taken as a thing of convenience, not of substance. That his absolution is good without an oath.

SIR DUDLEY DIGGES. That the absolution was very solemn and without any submission or reservation.

MR. NOY. Though 3 may keep a court, yet others may come thither which are not of our cognizance. Moved that a command shall be given that it be done, and no question but they will do it.

[p. 34] SIR PETER HEYMAN. That the 2 members of this House should be employed to procure the taking of this of the Archbishop, and not to come into the House till that were done.

MR. SHERFIELD Not to go by way of entreaty.

SIR THOMAS HOBY. That we respect the judgment upon the offenders. To let them know the opinion of this House that this be done by a day; if not, let us punish them and pass a bill that it may be done.

MR. WILDE. By command to the court.

MR. TAYLOR. That in the matter between Sir William Pope and Sir George Marshall for buying honor there was an order of this House to take the decree and all things off the file.[79] This was brought to the Chancery by the now Earl of Dorset, but the truth was that was not done, the parliament ending. Moved for a letter.

SIR NATHANIEL RICH. For a letter expressing the injury done to the House and expecting to be righted, etc.

SIR JOHN ELIOT. First to command these men to keep a court and to set Sir Robert free. If they cannot, then to proceed with a letter.

76. *last* is crossed out in the MS preceding *first*. See above, n. 29.

77. See above, n. 50.

78. See above, n. 51.

79. See above, n. 53.

SIR JOHN DANVERS. Not a letter, but by intimation to the Archbishop of our resolutions by so noble persons.

SIR FRANCIS FOLJAMBE moved to commit these commissioners presently till they had done Sir R. Howard right, and they would then presently petition the Lords to right him.

MR. PYM. 1, I would not bring or venture the authority into an uncertainty. If our mandate be disobeyed we cannot punish. 2, I would not begin with extremes, but reserve something to a second. *Ergo* no mandate letter. [p. 35] 3, I would not run such a way[80] as should imply that we cannot redress ourselves against such as shall offend against our privileges. For a letter, wherein I would set down the justice of our cause and our expectation that they shall right us.

MR. LITTLETON. That we command these commissioners to disannul the proceedings. If they do not then we may commit them and take this course after.

By question, resolved that a letter should not be sent to the Archbishop intimating the injury done to our privileges and requiring to have the acts annihilated. The House divided: the yeas were 114, the noes 105.[81]

Sir John Hayward and Dr. Pope and the register called in. The SPEAKER acquainted them that the House does expect a[n] annihilating of all proceedings against Sir R. Howard and look for the performance of this by Monday next, and then to have account from them. In the meantime the House does respite any judgment against them. And ordered that Mr. Comptroller and Sir H. Marten should have notice hereof also.

IV. DIARY OF JOHN LOWTHER, ESQ., D/LONS/L, CUMBERLAND AND WESTMORLAND RECORD OFFICE

[f. 17v]

[3 May]

8 of the 12, each assisted with two, to deliver the Duke's charge; 2 to prologue and epilogue, six to the parts. [f. 18] The eight: Digges, Eliot, Erle, Pym, Selden, Whitby, Wandesford, Herbert. Each one two assistants. The assistants to enable them with reasons [and] precedents to speak, but not to speak. The 24 to agree how to distribute the business amongst them.

LITTLETON reports. Resolves the increase by a subsidy to be paid the last of July 1627.

So resolved *nullo contradicente* in House.

SIR [DUDLEY] DIGGES desires from committee [of] 12 to know whether they shall proceed with more, to inquire of new, and proceed with what [they] have some proof of.

SPEAKER accords.

CHANCELLOR EXCHEQUER from King. Expects an end of inquisition and that commonwealth be no more hindered nor his honor in suspense but to be presented.

ELIOT. To preserve our liberty. Not lay them by, but to have liberty still to present more.

DIGGES presents preamble and conclusion. Last read: We by protestation saving liberty to add and reply and to offer proof. Pray Duke to be put to answer, and such proceeding [and] examination may be had of every of them as to law and justice/

[f. 19v][82] The preamble shows how the Commons by their bill declares against

80. MS: *was*.

81. Grosvenor has reversed the numbers for the yeas and noes; see CJ and Whitelocke, above.

82. Folios 18v and 19 are blank in the MS.

Duke of B[uckingham], with all his titles, misdemeanors, misprisions, offenses, and crimes hereafter following and him do thereof accuse.

SIR EDWIN SANDYS thinks not necessary both to plead it verbally and deliver it in articles too, for so was done in Middlesex's case.[83]

DIGGES. Intended both, and to enforce them with proofs and precedents.

[*Afternoon*]

In Sir Robert Howard's case, resolved that the proceedings in the High Commission against him within the sixteen days of the day of prorogation, notwithstanding the proclamation for further prorogation, shall be all annihilated and all that ensued thereupon void.

But, after long debate, resolved not to write to the high commissioners (because most Lords) to annihilate them, both because it is against our dignity to entreat and not prevail, so likewise not to command because we cannot enforce.

And though moved that there being a sufficient number of commoners commissioners to keep a court and to annihilate the proceedings,[84] yet they being opposed by the Lords the greater; therefore that way also shunned.

But the commoners commissioners being brought in and reprehended were admonished to see it done as[85] expected; if not, then to join the Lords, since but one body and the wrong to our privilege equal.

[f. 20] In this case was cited the case of two knights, Sir William Pope and Sir [George] Marshall, in Chancery, where a decree, being given for money promised upon sale of honors, was by order of this House sent to L[ord] Keeper by Sir Edward Sackville, now L[ord] of Dorset, to be taken off that file;[86] but our order neglected and nothing done upon it. For if any court of Westminster break our privilege because they are members of the Lords House it seems we have no remedy but to complain to the Lords.

83. Concerning the case of Lionel Cranfield, Earl of Middlesex, see HofC, 2 May, n. 28.

84. See John Selden's speech in Whitelocke and Grosvenor, above.

85. MS: *at*.

86. See above, n. 53.

Order of Business Thursday, 4 May 1626

Committee for considering **defects in victuals,** etc., in Count **Mansfeld's** voyage to meet this afternoon.	155, *22/3
Committee of the whole on the bill for the **continuance and repeal** of divers **statutes** to meet on Saturday [6 May]	155, *23/3
L.1a. An act for confirmation of certain articles of agreement by the consent of the lords and tenants of manors in **Feltwell**	155, 158, *6/5; 23/5
L.2a. An act for sale of certain lands which were late Sir Henry Clere's: committed	155, 158, *1/5
Report from the committee on the bill for the abridging of the number of **unskillful attorneys** (Edward Bysshe)	155, 158, *16/3
Amendments to the bill on unskillful attorneys: read twice; bill is engrossed	155, 158
Francis Drake: moves for a committee to consider the **King's estate** [**revenue**] [*see below*]	155, 156, 158, *24/2; 8/5
Ordered: Drake's motion to be further considered when the House is fuller	158
Committee on the bill against the procuring **judicial places** for money and against **bribes** to meet tomorrow afternoon	155, *16/2
John Selden: moves for altering the time in yesterday's order concerning Sir Robert **Howard** from last to first of February	155, 158, *17/2
Ordered: as Selden moved	155, 158
Sir Thomas Hartoppe, **sheriff of Leicestershire,** brought to the bar	155, 156, 163, *25/3
Sir Heneage Finch (Speaker): declares Hartoppe's offense	155, 156, 158
Sir Thomas Hartoppe makes his submission	155, 156, 158, 163
Sir Heneage Finch (Speaker): pronounces the judgment against Hartoppe	155, 156, 158, 163
Sir James Perrot: renews Drake's motion for a committee to consider the **King's estate** [**revenue**] [*see above*]	156, 159, 163
Sir George More	159, 163
Edward Bysshe	155, 157, 159, 163
William Coryton	159
Sir Henry Poole	159
Sir Peter Heyman	157, 159
Sir Robert Pye	159
Sir Dudley Digges	159
Sir John Savile	159
Richard Spencer	159
Sir John Eliot	157, 159
Sir Thomas Hoby	159
Anonymous Speech	155
Resolved upon question: a committee to be chosen to frame a petition to the King	156, 159
Committee for preparing petition to King concerning rectifying his revenue: appointed	156, 157, 159, 163
Report from the committee on the bill to enable James **Ward** to sell certain lands (Henry Pelham)	156, 157, 160, *17/3
Amendments to Ward's bill: read twice; bill is engrossed	156, 160
Sir John Hotham: moves to debate whether the **Duke of Buckingham** is the cause of	

THURSDAY, 4 MAY 1626

I. JOURNAL OF THE HOUSE OF COMMONS

[CJ 854; p. 48]

Jovis, 4 Maii, 2 Caroli Regis

Committee for the voyage of Count Mansfeld, 2 clock this afternoon.

Committee for repeal of statutes, Saturday in the afternoon.

[CJ 855] *L. 1a.* An act for confirmation of certain articles of agreement, and a decree thereupon made in the Court of Chancery, by the consent of the lords, tenants, and inhabitants of several manors in Feltwell, in the county of Norfolk.

L. 2a. Clere.
Committed to

[col. 1]	[col. 2]
Sir A[lexander] Temple	Mr. Mason
Sir Thomas Denton	Sir G[ilbert] Gerard
Knights and burgesses of Norfolk and Suffolk	Mr. A[rthur] Goodwin
Sir A[lexander] Denton	Sir Robert Pye
Sir H[enry] Poole	Sir George More
Mr. Lowther	Mr. John Drake

[col. 3]
Mr. [Hugh] Cholmley
Sir Eubule Thelwall
Sir John Stradling
Sir Thomas Grantham
Sir Edward Peyton
Sir Clement Throckmorton
Sir John Hare

Monday, 2 clock, Court of Wards.

MR. BYSSHE reports the bill of attorneys, with amendments; which 2 read. *Engrossetur.*

MR. FRANCIS DRAKE moves a committee to consider of further means for defense of King and kingdom as by looking into the King's estate, forfeitures of recusants' lands, remote forests and parks, exorbitant pensions extremely increased, viz., from £15,000 per annum to £120,000.[1]

Bill of bribery, tomorrow afternoon, Exchequer Court.

[p. 49] MR. SELDEN moves that the day of the last of February may be altered because by the prorogations he had privilege 1 February.

The last of February, by order, made the first of February, 1622 [*sic*].[2]

The debate concerning the high sheriff of Leicestershire renewed.

The sheriff called in and, upon his knees at the bar, his offense declared him by MR. SPEAKER of his great contempt against the election. He submits himself, acknowledging his error and craving the pardon of the House. The House thereupon, by MR. SPEAKER, pronounced his discharge, paying Sir H. Hastings's charges, and the officers' fees of this House.

MR. BYSSHE to the motion of Mr. Drake (now renewed)[3] adds the consideration of the Court of Wards. Moves a message to his Majesty for his consent to treat about this.

Moved, a select committee to consider of the propositions which have been made, and of a fit address to his Majesty to desire his consent to treat of those things they shall

1. Similar proposals for increasing crown revenues and decreasing expenditures had been made by Sir Edward Coke on 5 August 1625. See *PP 1625*, pp. 391–392, 402–405, 407–408, 544–546, 658–660. See also, n. 18, below.

2. I.e., 22 Jac. 1624. Concerning the change in the order in Sir Robert Howard's case, see HofC, 3 May, n. 29.

3. I.e., Sir James Perrot; see other accounts, below.

think fit for the good of King and kingdom; and to prepare a petition.

Upon question, a select committee to be named to consider of the way of a petition to be presented to his Majesty wherein the desire of the House may be intimated to his Majesty for the rectifying and augmenting his revenue.

[col. 1]	[col. 2]
Mr. Chancellor Exchequer	Sir John Eliot
Mr. Vice Chamberlain	Sir John Strangways
Sir J[ames] Fullerton	Sir Nathaniel Rich
Sir Robert Pye	Sir P[eter] Heyman
Sir D[udley] Digges	Sir J[ames] Perrot
Chancellor Duchy	Sir Edward Peyton
Sir A[rthur] Ingram	Mr. [Richard] Spencer
Sir Roger North	Mr. [Edward] Bysshe
Sir Robert Crane	Sir Edward Spencer
Sir B[enjamin] Rudyard	
Sir William Spencer	

[col. 3]
Sir John Savile
Sir H[enry] Poole
Mr. [John] Pym
Sir Thomas Fanshawe
Sir Thomas Hoby
Mr. Francis Drake
Sir A[nthony] Forest
Lord St. John
Sir George More
Mr. [William] Coryton

This afternoon, 2 clock, in the Exchequer Chamber.

MR. PELHAM reports Ward's bill, with amendments;[4] which 2 read. *Engrossetur.*

Motion made to debate the business left undecided, viz., whether the Duke a cause of the increase and countenancing of papists;[5] and that thereupon every man may deliver what he knows or has heard to prove this against the Duke.

[p. 51][6] Hereupon SIR LEWIS DYVE proposed that he had heard by one Mr. Everard[7] that the Duke, in Spain, did adore the host; and that he was ready without, to prove it.

Upon question, Mr. Speaker to leave the chair that the grand committee for evils, etc., may sit.

Mr. Speaker took his chair.

MR. WANDESFORD reports that Mr. Everard produced [as] a witness before them.

SIR JOHN STRANGWAYS. That he shall be here again tomorrow.

Counsel for the wiredrawers, etc., to be heard tomorrow, 8 clock.

II. DIARY OF BULSTRODE WHITELOCKE, ESQ., DD. 12.21, CAMBRIDGE UNIVERSITY LIBRARY

[f. 177v]

May 4

Sir Thomas Hartoppe, sheriff of Leicestershire, brought in and kneeling is told his fault by the SPEAKER. And then he confesses his errors and submits himself to the pleasure of the House, whereupon the SPEAKER tells him the judgment of the House according to the opinion of the committee yesterday.

SIR JAMES PERROT seconds a motion of Mr. Drake's for a committee to consider of

4. See HofC, 18 April, n. 2.

5. The motion was made by Sir John Hotham, see below. On 24 March the committee of the whole resolved not to put the question to vote regarding the Duke as the cause of the increase and countenancing of papists. See HofC, 24 March, OB.

6. The MS was incorrectly paginated, p. 51 follows directly after p. 49.

7. We have not discovered Everard's Christian name. For his testimony in the committee of the whole later this day, see Whitelocke and Grosvenor, below.

the King's estate and of parks and remote forests whereof the King has no benefit but is put to charge by them, and of pensions going out, they being in Queen Elizabeth's time but £15,000 per annum and are now £130,000 per annum, and of arrearages of recusants due to the King, and of whatsoever else may conduce to the rectifying of the King's revenues.[8]

MR. BYSSHE adds the consideration of the Court of Wards. If it shall please the [f. 178] King to give us leave for this, the pensions, and the forests, chases, and parks, for without his leave we cannot meddle with them.

SIR PETER HEYMAN. That a committee may be appointed to consider of a parliamentary way and a mannerly fashion whereby we may know the King's pleasure.

SIR JOHN ELIOT. That we may observe the same way now which was thought on in the beginning of this session.[9]

A select committee nominated to consider of the way of a petition to the King in which the desire of the House may be expressed for the rectifying and augmenting of the King's revenues.

MR. PELHAM reports a private bill.[10]

SIR JOHN HOTHAM moves that the question [be] whether the Duke be the cause of the increase of popery and the countenancing thereof.[11]

SIR LEWIS DYVE. That he heard one below in the hall say that he saw the Duke adore the sacrament in Spain. And if please the House he may be sent for. It is one Mr. Everard.[12]

MR. VICE CHAMBERLAIN. I have myself put off my hat when the sacrament came by, and the Earl of Nottingham prayed us to do it.[13] Count of Olivares hated the Duke of Buckingham because the young Prince, as he said, would have easily been won to their religion if it had not been for the Duke of Buckingham.[14]

MR. KIRTON. That the Duke of Buckingham has behaved himself so that he may be hated both by papists and Protestants for his religion. That we may presently go to the Lords and show what we have heard and what is with us,[15] and desire that the Duke may be sequestered both from the House and the court until he be cleared of the accusations against him.

[f. 178v] Many crying to call in Mr. Everard.

SIR DUDLEY DIGGES. That we should not send for this gentleman, but let the Lords know that such proof is tendered to us and that we refused it, being in their House.

SIR JOHN ELIOT. That hearing that the Duke is accused of High Treason in the Lords House, hears it likewise with wonder that he should be at liberty contrary to the

8. See above, n. 1.

9. Following consideration of the King's estate and revenue on 24 February, the House resolved that the Chancellor of the Exchequer should have leave to acquaint the King with that debate.

10. I.e., for James Ward's lands; see HofC, 17 March, n. 2.

11. See above, n. 5.

12. See above, n. 7.

13. Dudley Carleton (present Vice Chamberlain, ktd. 1610) had accompanied Francis, Lord Norris, to Spain as an attendant to Charles Howard, Earl of Nottingham, during his ambassadorial mission in 1605. See *Memorials of Affairs of State . . . Collected chiefly from the Original Papers of the Right Honourable Sir Ralph Winwood*, ed. by Edmund Sawyer (London, 1725), II, 50–77.

14. Concerning the strained relations between Buckingham and Olivares, see HofL, 1 May, p. 330, n. 17.

15. I.e., the Earl of Bristol's articles against the Duke that had been annexed to the petition of George, Lord Digby, when it was presented to the Commons on 1 May.

law of the kingdom. That if the Lords have not already done it, that we may by a message move that he may be committed.

MR. DYOTT. That this motion is not just, not regular. When the Commons accuse a man of treason, they use to pray that he may be committed if he a peer. But if a peer accuse another, it is not precedented that the Commons interpose for his commitment.

[*Committee of the Whole House*]

Mr. Wandesford takes the chair for the committee of evils, causes, and remedies.

Sir Nathaniel Rich. That Mr. Everard may be called in.

Chancellor Duchy. That he may be first asked when he last received the communion.

Sir Thomas Fanshawe. That he himself and other members of this House have been sent out to administer the oath of allegiance to some that were to be examined.

Sir George More. That nothing is more usual.

Resolved that Mr. Everard shall be called in and examined about the adoring of the host by the Duke of Buckingham.

[f. 179] Mr. Everard, brought in, says that he was in Spain when the Duke was there and that he saw the Duke kneel to the sacrament as it passed by in public procession, the King of Spain being in procession. The Duke kneeled in a window, a balcony.

The committee adjourned till [to]morrow.

III. DIARY OF SIR RICHARD GROSVENOR, MS 611, TRINITY COLLEGE, DUBLIN

[p. 36]

4 May

1. An act for confirmation of certain articles of agreement [and] a decree made in Chancery by consent between the lords and tenants of the manor[s] of [Feltwell in] Norfolk, for dividing of north fen.

2. An act for the sale of Sir Henry Clere's land, Kt., Baronet, for pay[ment] of his debts and maintenance of his lady, etc.

Committed Monday afternoon.

MR. BYSSHE reported the bill for abridging of the number of unskillful attorneys, etc.

Passed by question to be engrossed.

MR. DRAKE moved for a committee to look into the King's estate, what his comings in, what going out. To look into the forfeitures of recusants' lands, into forests and parks remote, that they may be disforested. To look to annuities which are increased from £14,000 to £130,000. And by this means we may enable the King, according to our former engagements, to make him feared abroad and honored at home.

Ordered to be moved when the House was fuller.

MR. SELDEN moved that in the matter of time the order in Sir Robert Howard's case should be altered. That because the parliament had been adjourned from November to the 16 of February, so that his privilege was from the first of February.

So that it was ordered to mend the last order by changing the last of February to the first.[16]

The sheriff of Leicestershire's business argued in the House. Sir Thomas Hartoppe.

Ordered he should acknowledge his fault to the House on his knees and was dismissed, paying the charges of Sir Henry Hastings's witnesses.

Which he did on his knees.

16. See above, n. 2.

SIR JAMES PERROT re-moved the motion of Mr. Drake. And that if there were such a committee, the penalties of recusants in arrear should be collected and bestowed upon the defense of the kingdom, being £80,000.

[p. 37] SIR G. MORE. About 7 years ago a commission directed to consider of all matters to be thought of for abating of his Majesty's expenses and the regulating of his revenue.[17] What was done upon that would give a great light to this business.

MR. BYSSHE added a 4th to the other 3 for the increasing of the King's revenue. That was the Court of Wards, which were [*sic*] a flower of the Crown. And all chases, pensions, were and ought to be tenderly dealt in, and by the King's consent. For the present, the revenue of that Court not much to the King, about £43,000 in all; but the cry of the people: nay. No great sum of this comes to the King, for when a wardship is compounded for, some or other begs it, so that it never comes to the King's coffers. This revenue, upon a composition, would be much more than now. Moved that we should send to the King for leave to deal in this business.

MR. CORYTON. Mention a resumption of crown lands and that his Majesty be moved, and a committee named.

SIR H. POOLE. Not to have a committee, but a business of this moment to be argued in the House.

SIR P. HEYMAN moved for a petition wherein to insert these 4 things: pensions, Court of Wards, parks, recusants, but not resumption of crown lands, and this in a parliamentary course. To declare that we mean to enable his Majesty in his estate, and present this to his Majesty by the Speaker, and to argue it in the House, and then to a committee to draw the form.

SIR ROBERT PYE. That we look upon proceedings at Oxford, how far the King was pleased to give way there;[18] and upon that to proceed for the increase of his revenue and cutting of unnecessary expenses, etc.

[p. 38] SIR DUDLEY DIGGES. That we let his Majesty know our intentions and give us leave. But how to do this. By a committee; for though his Majesty will rather suffer wants than send to us, yet moving from hence he will graciously relieve us and harken to us.

SIR JOHN SAVILE. To save time, to know his Majesty's pleasure; to consider of a parliamentary way how to move his Majesty.

MR. SPENCER. For a remonstrance to the King to show the necessity of this course, for his good; a committee to draw this.

SIR JOHN ELIOT. This proposition formerly named and Mr. Chancellor had intimation from the House to know his Majesty's pleasure to tell him how for the honor of him and the kingdom we intend to proceed.[19]

SIR THOMAS HOBY. Not to send a message by way of intimation.

By question, resolved that a select committee should be chosen to frame a petition to be presented to the King in which their desires may be expressed for the rectifying and augmenting the King's revenue. This afternoon, in Exchequer Chamber.

17. It is not clear to what commission More refers. See, for example, the commission of 2 November 1619 appointing Sir Lionel Cranfield and others to examine the King's debts and the fees, pensions, and annuities due to the crown and "to treat for compositions thereof". *CSPD 1619–1623*, p. 89.

18. The speeches to both Houses by the King and Sir John Coke (at the King's direction) at the Oxford session, 4 August 1625, led to the debate in the Commons on 5 August concerning the King's estate. See *PP 1625*, pp. 386–408.

19. See above, n. 9.

MR. PELHAM reported the bill for enabling James Ward, alias Farmer,[20] the selling of certain lands in the parish of Ibstock, in Leicestershire, for the payment of his debts.

Passed to be engrossed.

SIR JOHN HOTHAM moved that it might be disputed in the House whether the Duke were a countenancer of popery or not, that he might either be freed or condemned.

MR. CORYTON. That if it were true that the Duke adored in Spain, likely he a countenancer and cause of the connivancy in England.

SIR LEWIS DYVE said that Mr. Everard told him that he saw it with his own eyes in Spain.

SIR ROBERT PYE. That if we send to Spain, Brussels, France, they will say the Duke a suspected recusant. Perhaps these are sent of purpose to do the business; let not us do it for them. [p. 39] To enter into this when he is questioned in the higher House *in capita* is but a supplemental proof. Hoped we would not enter into it.

MR. VICE CHAMBERLAIN. I am glad to see such a heat in this House upon any motion made about religion, but this heat many times turns into a fire, and this motion into a commotion. That the Duke should adore the sacrament, he could not believe it; but if, coming by, he put off his hat because he would not give offense, it is no more than I and others have done. In France they are offended with the Duke because he employs not his power with the King for Catholics. In Spain Olivares hates him because the young Prince could not have gained him.[21] From Brussels a libel written by a Scottishman against him.[22] When the Duke was at Hague, against Arminian[s].[23] He subscribed that the rising of them was the fall of Protestants, as the rising of the Guelphs was the death of the Ghibellines and *e contra*. Moved we should not fall upon him for matter of religion.

MR. KIRTON. That the Duke might be of any religion—half Protestant, half papist. Moved that we go to the Lords, deliver to them how we received a petition against the Duke,[24] desire them to examine it; that in the meantime the Duke may be sequestered from the King and court till he had cleared himself.

MR. WANDESFORD. That if the Duke, while he [re]presented the person of the Defender of the Faith, should adore the sacrament, which was different from a compliment, we cannot sit here and hear this but we must do something. Moved that the man who would affirm he saw him should be sent for up.

MR. GRIFFITH. That it stand not with the correspondency between the Lords House and ours to enter into examination of anything agitated in that House.

[p. 40] SIR JOHN HIPPISLEY. That he was

20. MS: *Farrer*. See HofC, 17 March, n. 2.

21. See above, n. 14.

22. I.e., George Eglisham, a Scottish physician who had retired to Brussels. *DNB*. Eglisham wrote a Latin tract, *Prodromus Vindictae*, accusing Buckingham of poisoning James I, the Marquis of Hamilton, and others. The tract was translated into English and printed in Frankfort in 1626 under the title, *The Forerunner of Revenge* (*STC*, no. 7548). For reports on Eglisham's libel, see the letter from Nicholas Herman to Lionel Cranfield, Earl of Middlesex, 2 May 1626, App., II, E; and see Birch, *Court and Times Chas. I*, I, 98–99; *CSPV 1625–1626*, p. 416; and SP 16/31:93.

23. Dudley Carleton, then English ambassador to the Hague, knew of Buckingham's activities at the Congress of the Hague in November-December 1625, and had written the speech delivered by the Duke at his public audience. *DNB*. Carleton returned to England with Buckingham to assume the office of Vice Chamberlain. *CSPV 1625–1626*, pp. 235, 269.

24. I.e., the petition of George, Lord Digby, presented to the Commons on 1 May.

in Spain with the King.[25] That the King of Spain put a trick upon our King: that having him with him in the garden the Ave Mary bell rang, the King fell down upon his knees to urge the Prince to do so but he did not, but many others did. Among others he himself. That the Duke was on horseback with his lance and hit him on the head with it, saying: Arise thou great ass, must thou be so mad to kneel with others?

SIR ANTHONY FOREST. Would not have him sent for. A man might be a rogue, a renegade.

SIR JOHN STRANGWAYS said that he that informed this was a gentleman of credit, no rogue or renegade, a Norfolk gentleman.

SIR EDWARD SPENCER. That if the man were called in, he might first be examined whether he would take the oath of allegiance.

SIR G. GORING. That a committee might also examine what the Duke has done against this course and whether he have done more than others in his place have done.

MR. SPENCER. That we should not examine any one part of this information without we examine all; that it would not correspond with the Lords to examine any part of them, having agitation there.

SIR JOHN SAVILE. That this man be examined in the proper place with the Lords; that we inform the Lords that there is such a man that so they may examine him.

SIR ROBERT HARLEY. Not to call him in.

SIR DUDLEY DIGGES. This particular is in the higher House; not to call for this man in, but to let the Lords know upon what reasons we do decline this cause.

[p. 41] SIR JOHN ELIOT. If this charge arise upon any motion formerly made concerning the Duke, then within our power; but if out of the copy of the charge in the higher House, then not to examine it. That fear, terror, a danger of our prince and state. That Bristol has charged the Duke with treason. I no lawyer, but I know how far the charge of treason stretches. I[f] a man be charged with felony, not to be at liberty; and if not in that, then in case of treason it should not be. I hear, and that with wonder, that there is no presention [*sic*] of that part. We know the trust and power this man has in Ireland, Scotland, at home, in the shipping, navy, ports; the locks and keys of this land rest in his hands. It is a terror to think that this man thus charged is at liberty. For the safety of his Majesty and kingdom, that if the Lords have not done their duty in this particular we intimate to them our sense of it and move them to do it.

MR. DYOTT. The motion last made not just, not regular. If the Commons charge a man with treason, then they have moved the Lords to commit him; but not if another private man do charge him, there is no cause we should then interpose. There is a due to the devil; shall we execute before judgment? Shall we be jealous of the Lords' discretion? It will break the good correspondency between them and us.

SIR THOMAS HOBY. That we let the Lords know what complaints are made here and what witnesses produced that they may make use of them.

SIR WILLIAM STRODE. This business sent hither by E. of Bristol; brought in by his son, followed by a son-in-law, Sir Lewis Dyve.[26] Wished we should not tell the Lords they have not done their duties.

25. Hippisley, one of Buckingham's favorites, had accompanied the Duke and Prince to Spain in 1623. Keeler, *LP*.

26. Dyve had been the first MP to propose bringing Everard in as a witness (see above). His mother, Beatrix, was the Countess of Bristol, having married Sir John Digby following the death of her first husband, Sir John Dyve. *DNB*.

[p. 42] SIR JOHN HOTHAM. That he might be called in.

SIR GEORGE MORE. If we make slight matter of religion we should show ourselves not to be religious at all. First to let Lords know of this information; and in due time to examine him, but not yet.

MR. MALET concurred with the last. That we command this witness to attend *de die in diem.* That if the Lords examine him not, then we may.

MR. LONG. If this debate result out of any former debate about religion, then he to be called in; but if out of anything else, then not.

SIR CLEMENT THROCKMORTON. That this debate and motion has risen from that formerly: whether the Duke was cause of the increase of popery by countenancing those who were in authority.

SIR ALEXANDER TEMPLE moved the man should be called in upon that reason but not upon anything delivered by the Lord Digby. And after, he would deliver some probable reasons why the Duke should be hated both of papists and Protestants.

The House turned to the great committee, Mr. Wandesford came in.

[*Committee of the Whole House*]

The evils, causes, and remedies.

Mr. Spencer. The question is whether the Duke be cause of the increase of popery by countenancing men in authority. Moved to have the question stated.

Sir William Strode. That he heard Mr. Everard had been brought up in Spain, was a kinsman of Bristol's.

Sir John Strangways. That he was brought up there by the Earl of Bristol, that he received the sacrament, had sermons, came to church.

Sir Nathaniel Rich. Fit to be called in, for this conduces mainly to the question. If the Duke profess one religion and do the ceremonies of another, he but counterfeiter.

[p. 43] Sir H. May moved that he should be asked whether he would take the oath of allegiance and when he received the sacrament. That when the Prince was in Spain, Archie was with him.[27] He, being urged by the King of Spain to adore the sacrament, though the Prince would not, he told him he would kneel. Being asked whether he believed that Christ was really in the sacrament, said he could not. The King said he would have him into the inquisition house if he would not; he said he could not believe it. The King said he would have him into the inquisition house if he would not tell him a reason. He then answered that Christ was so ill used when he was on earth that he thought he had no mind to come among them again.

Sir Thomas Hoby and Mr. Selden said it was not the use of this House to examine a witness produced, at first, whether he was a papist or had taken the oath of religion.

Sir Thomas Fanshawe affirmed that he had been sent with other ministers by the House forth to give the oath to witnesses before they were brought in.

Mr. Drake. To call him in because this testimony would produce to the question even though he were a papist.

Mr. Dyott. That first we understand the

27. Archibald Armstrong, known as Archie, King James's jester, had accompanied the Prince to Spain. *DNB*. Although we are unable to substantiate May's story, Sir Edward Zouche wrote to Lord Zouche on 17 November 1623 that regarding the marriage Archie the fool spoke what "I dare not write". SP 14/154:38. Archie was given Spanish apparel by Olivares. SP 14/154:28, 29.

credit of this witness before we examine him, for it may be he has changed his religion.

Sir John Strangways. That one or other time the E. of Bristol had 4 or 500 at times in his family.[28] Never had papist but one. That an Irish footman, which, when he knew, he turned him away. And he was sound in his religion and had excellent divines to his chaplains.

[p. 44] Resolved by question to call him in.

Mr. Everard called in. First, he answered that he was in Spain when the Duke was there; that he saw him kneel to the sacrament as it passed by in public procession, he being then in a window in a house near as it passed by. He was in a balcony, and the King of Spain went that time in a procession.

Sir James Bagg moved that the Serjeant should attend this gentleman; that no man should speak with him till he were called in again.

Mr. Long moved that he should be asked whether he kneeled to the sacrament or to the King as he passed by.

Sir John Strangways said that ambassadors used not to kneel to foreign kings.

Sir James Bagg. To ask him in what room this gentleman was when he saw the Duke kneel, and how long he kneeled, and who were present; for, making a low congé might be taken for a kneeling.

Sir Robert Harley. That he might be asked what honorable persons of England were by, whether the King were there.

The House cried no.

Mr. Vice Chamberlain. This from a small beginning will prove important in the ending. I am sorry that we talk in this House in sides. Two noblemen questioned, both sound in religion. This name of religion is a color of somewhat else. Be not transported with the name of religion. Moved that he should be asked what company was by, because they might also be examined of the truth.

Sir Dudley Digges. That he might be asked whether the Earl of Bristol were by and what other Lords or servants of the King's.

[p. 44a] Sir Robert Payne told the House that Mr. Everard was gone, so the committee adjourned till tomorrow morning.

IV. DIARY OF JOHN LOWTHER, ESQ., D/LONS/L, CUMBERLAND AND WESTMORLAND RECORD OFFICE

[f. 20]

[4 May]

Sir Thomas Hartoppe, sheriff of Leicestershire, for offering an arrest upon a commission of rebellion to Sir H. Hastings, being in election for knight of shire, though he elected, yet brought to bar on his knees and upon submission ordered to pay charges and discharged.

Moved by DRAKE [and] SIR JAMES PERROT to retract pensions, disafforest, to take recusants' lands to supply King.

SIR G. MORE. A commission was 7 years since for this where these and many more are inquired of; it was a summer's work.[29]

BYSSHE moves the Wards in, and a message to King to ask.

Ordered, a committee to draw a remonstrance to King for rectifying his revenue upon these grounds. Tomorrow, Exchequer Chamber.

28. I.e., as attendants during his foreign employments. Concerning the religion of his attendants and chaplains, see Bristol's answer to the seventh article of the charge against him, HofL, 19 May, p. 520.

29. See above, n. 17.

SIR JOHN HOTHAM moves to consider, since in suspense, whether Duke cause of evils in religion.

CORYTON. To note it if he adored in Spain as in articles alleged.[30] To hear witnesses.

[f. 20v] SIR L. DYVE names Everard as a witness.

SIR ROBERT PYE notes how he hated by papists; infers that this a practice of papists. He observes the current of those that 18 *Jac.* went one way, now go another way. Dislikes this supplemental proof; is with Lords, let them there try it for their lives.

VICE CHAMBERLAIN notes this heat turns into fire, motion turns sometimes into commotion. He does desire preventive care. Who may not put off his hat when sacrament came by, as he did? L. Admiral of old did.[31] He hated because that this match affects not papacy. So Spain hates because he served not them. Olivares hates because he suffered not Prince to be converted. He joined in article against Arminian[s] most freely under his hand.[32]

KIRTON thinks he has so carried that he may be hated of both Protestant and papist. Desires the notice taken of young Digby's petition in it. Never heard one so charged stand before King and to come in parliament. Desires to go to Lords to have him removed.

WANDESFORD infuses, if it be but compliment, lost matter. Yet he ambassador representing King, to adore mass in such [is] matter of treason; to be sent for.

SIR JOHN HIPPISLEY shows how King of Spain played tricks and kneeled never before [f. 21] to draw in our King. He did not, nor Duke, but Sir John did.[33] Duke knocked him on head to rise and did call him great ass.

SPENCER enforces it as a charge directly in the petition, not upon fame, but direct, and desires direction.

ELIOT mentions the treason charged on Duke by Bristol in Lords House. Fit to be committed, as in felony not allowed. Hears this not prosecuted, wonders at. His power [in] England, Ireland, Scotland, elsewhere; this affrights, he to stand uncommitted. Moves if Lords have not done their duties, we to desire it of the Lords.

30. See above, n. 15.

31. I.e., Charles Howard, Earl of Nottingham. See above, n. 13.

32. I.e., at the Hague. See above, n. 23.

33. See above, n. 25.

Order of Business Friday, 5 May 1626

Friday, 5 May 1626

I. JOURNAL OF THE HOUSE OF COMMONS

[CJ 855; p. 51]
Veneris, 5 Maii, 2 Caroli Regis

L. 1a. An act to enable the sale of the manors and lands late of Richard Fust, deceased, and for the assignments of 2 several manors of £6,000 to give satisfaction to the kindred of William Hill, deceased, of the money raised by the said Richard Fust out of the estate of the said William Hill.[1]

Simony of selling of livings and drunkenness to be added to Lord of Bangor's charge.[2]

L. 1a. An act for explanation of 2 several provisos contained in one deed indented, made 9 *Jac.*, by Thomas, late Earl of Exeter.

L. 1a. An act to enable Sir Timothy Hutton, Knight, and Matthew Hutton, Esquire, his son and heir apparent, to sell certain lands for the payment of their debts and raising of portions for their younger children, and for establishing other lands in lieu thereof of as good value.

Mr. Coryton moves against the sheriff of Flint.[3] Divers misdemeanors about the last election of the knight of the shire there; that all these abuses proved by 4 witnesses of great worth in the affirmative. Moves, where the committee gave a month's time for him to come up, that this time may be shortened.

Upon question, the sheriff to be sent for to appear upon Tuesday fortnight before the committee of privileges.

The committee for prevention of contagion, Monday, 2 clock, Exchequer Court.

Mr. Browne reports the bill against unlicensed alehouse keepers, with amendments; which 2 read. "One witness," made, "2 witnesses," at the Board. *Engrossetur.*

Mr. Vice Chamberlain reports from the select committee of a petition to be presented to his Majesty about rectifying and augmenting of his revenue, and tenders a draft of it; which 2 read and, with amendment of 2 words, ordered to be engrossed.

Mr. Davis, of counsel with the wiredrawers, etc., came to the bar. Of counsel with the old wiredrawers who opposed Fowle's patent.[4]

This manufacture profitable to the King. The bullion imported for this £40,000 per annum, so the King's custom £1,000 per annum. The working of the coin of this kingdom no gain for them, the weight of our coin being abated. They pay to the merchant for Spanish silver, 5s. 2d. and upwards, where ours worth not above 4s. 10d.; so as if this be not bought by them, it will be bought up and exported by strangers. [p. 52] 20,000 people maintained by this manufacture. Gold wiredrawers, etc., 9 in number.[5] The loss by the use, little. 29s. in bullion will make again 26s. More of this silver

1. For background on this bill, see the accounts of the case concerning the administration of Hill's estate. Nicholas, *Proceedings and Debates in 1621,* I, 233–249; *CD 1621,* Index, *sub,* Fust.

2. I.e., to the complaints against Lewis Bayly, Bishop of Bangor. See HofC, 17 April, n. 3.

3. Thomas Evans was appointed sheriff of Flintshire in 1624 and apparently continued in office until the appointment of Thomas Mostyn in 1627. *List of Sheriffs for England and Wales,* Lists and Indexes, IX (London, 1898).

4. I.e., the patent to Matthias Fowle, et al., 14 June 1623, C 66/2296 (MS Cal. Pat. Rolls, 21 Jac. I, pt. 2, f. 105; printed in Carr, *Select Charters,* pp. 122–136). Concerning the wiredrawers and Fowle's patent, see also *CD 1621,* VII, 364–370; *CJ,* I, 705, 726–727, 753, 765, 777, and 795; *Stuart Proclamations,* I, 578–581, 593–594. A copy of the patent can also be found in HLRO, Parchment Collection, Box 1F. Another bill concerning apparel was introduced in 1628, see *CD 1628,* IV, 86, 98.

5. I.e., nine trades live upon the manufacture of gold lace. See Grosvenor, below.

comes to the mint by this than any other ways. £18,000 in a month[6] to the mint of bullion of gold and silver ends. Other countries desire this manufacture, as France, Denmark, etc. The merchants of our kingdom will sustain prejudice by the banishing this commodity. That a 3[r]d part of gold and silver lace is good when worn. And therefore, since men and women will be brave, no bravery can be with less charge.

That divers, not apprentices to the trade, have taken up the use of it; and wish that may be reformed.

They pray some longer time ere this be banished.

The committee for apparel to take consideration of that now delivered and report their opinions to the House. To meet Monday, 2 clock, in the former place.

Mr. Herne,[7] of counsel for the silkmen, called in and heard. **[CJ 856]** That he is not only for the silkmen but for their work folks, being in and about London at least 10,000 families. That for our coarse cloths, vented in Italy, gold and silver thread is returned. In Germany bills of exchange. That all gold and silver thread brought in yields, when worn, a 3[r]d in bullion. That it vents our own cloth here. That the excess in silk will far exceed the others in gold and silver lace.

Mr. Serjeant Hitcham tenders the bill of subsidies.

Mr. Chancellor of the Exchequer. That the King has commanded him to tell the House that, if the House shall not now give way to go on with the subsidy, which he has given order to send in, he shall hold it not only a neglect of his affairs but also of his person.[8]

Resolved upon question to name a select committee to consider of, and prepare, a fit preamble for this act of subsidy.

[col. 1]	[col. 2]
Mr. Vice Chamberlain	Chancellor Duchy
Chancellor Exchequer	Sir Edwin Sandys
Sir D[udley] Digges	Sir George More
Mr. [William] Noy	Mr. [Edward] Kirton
Sir Thomas Hoby	Mr. [Christopher] Brooke
Sir B[enjamin] Rudyard	Mr. Serjeant Hitcham
Sir Nathaniel Rich	Mr. Rolle
Mr. [Christopher] Wandesford	

[col. 3]	[col. 4]
Mr. Lowther	Mr. Herbert
Sir John Eliot	Sir H[enry] Wallop
Mr. [Edward] Littleton	Sir John Strangways
Mr. [John] Pym	Mr. [John] Glanville
Mr. [William] Coryton	

Tuesday next, 2 clock, in the Exchequer Chamber.

The debate concerning the patent for salt renewed.

Mr. More heard to speak for himself and then, by direction, withdrew.[9]

1. Upon question, this patent a grievance both in creation and execution; without 1 negative.

2ly, Mr. More to be called in and admonished by Mr. Speaker. Which he did, taking his place, he standing up uncovered, and Mr. Speaker in like manner.

6. £18,000 in 6 months according to Grosvenor, below.

7. A London lawyer, we have been unable to identify further Mr. Herne. He also represented the brewers, see HofC, 2 June, below.

8. The House had resolved on 27 March that the bill would not be brought in until after they had received the King's answer to their grievances. See the debate in Whitelocke and Grosvenor, below.

9. Concerning the salt patent held by John More (MP for Lymington, Hampshire), et al., see HofC, 7 March, n. 7. Whitby's report on the patent and More's response are printed on 28 March, above.

He gives now his own voice for damning this patent.

The petition,[10] engrossed, read and allowed; and to be presented by the 3 privy councillors (Mr. Vice Chamberlain, Chancellor Exchequer, Chancellor Duchy) and Sir J. Fullerton.

II. DIARY OF BULSTRODE WHITELOCKE, ESQ., DD. 12.21, CAMBRIDGE UNIVERSITY LIBRARY

[f. 179]

May 5

Against the bill concerning apparel.

Wiredrawers' counsel heard in the House.[11] Speak not against the cloth of gold and tissue nor against the gilding. Bullion brought into this kingdom for this manufacture amounts to £40,000 per annum. Sometimes it is brought from beyond sea in gold and silver thread, sometimes in bullion. At the mint 5s. ob[olus] to the goldsmith; 5s. 1d. to the wiredrawers; 5s. 2d. in own bullion will yield to the merchant and that he may not sell it to the wiredrawers. No merchant will bring bullion into this kingdom but carry it into Holland where it will yield/

20,000 people are maintained by this trade. Gold lace yields 26s. at the melting pot the gold bullion to make, which cost but 29s. H. 4 of France gave £60,000 for the bringing in this manufacture into his kingdom,[12] and most other kings have been diligent to introduce this trade into their realms. 3 and 22 E. 4.[13] 1 H. 8; 22 H. 8.[14] An ordinance 12 E. 3 to take away the wearing of gold and silver and all foreign commodities, but was found so inconvenient that it was never published nor put in execution.[15] Desires further time in the bill.

[f. 179v] The consideration of this business referred to the committee.

SERJEANT HITCHAM prefers the bill of subsidy.

But the silkmen's counsel are to be heard.

Silkmen's counsel brought in, say[s] against the bill concerning apparel:[16] about 10,000 people set on work in this trade. That which goes out a pound in cloth for gold and silver thread, after wearing that thread yields a noble.

The consideration hereof likewise referred to the committee concerning apparel.

MR. KIRTON. That we should remember the order of the House.[17] Wonder Serjeant Hitcham would break it.

SIR GEORGE MORE. That a committee may be appointed to consider of a preamble for the bill of subsidy.

SERJEANT HITCHAM. That what he did was by command. The King's Attorney signified to him that he should bring in the bill.

SIR BENJAMIN RUDYARD. I do not like the dark ways of jealousy and suspicion. I cannot believe the King will do so dishonorably as to take our money and refuse our justice.

10. I.e., the petition to the King concerning rectifying his revenue. For a draft, see Grosvenor, below.

11. See above, n. 4.

12. We have not found the source of the story.

13. See *SR*, 3 E. IV, c. 5 and *SR*, 22 E. IV, c. 1. Both acts regulate apparel.

14. *SR*, 1 H. VIII, c. 14. In 1531 (22 H. VIII) the King had given instructions that a bill of apparel be prepared for the beginning of the next parliament (*State Papers Published Under the Authority of his Majesty's Commission*, I [King Henry the Eighth], [London, 1830], p. 382), but the act was not passed until 1533, see *SR*, 24 H. VIII, c. 13.

15. We have not identified the unpublished ordinance of 12 E. III. See, however, the articles of 11 E. III against the purchase and import of foreign cloth and against the wearing of furs, *SR*, 11 E. III, cc. 2–4. Holinshed states that this act "was not long observed". Holinshed, *Chronicles*, II, 605–606.

16. See above, n. 7.

17. See above, n. 8.

A frank and free commerce of grace and supply between King and people is the best way to preserve correspondence between King and people. That we may do our parts clearly, freely, and seasonably. And appoint a committee.

CHANCELLOR EXCHEQUER. I would be very glad to hear a sound reason why the bill should not now be brought in. We have for our own safeties already/

[f. 180] His Majesty commanded me to tell you that if through any jealousy or fear that according to his royal word that he would not give you just redress to your grievances you should now delay the subsidy, he should take it as a neglect not only to his affairs but to his person.

MR. WILDE. As the gift is our own, so the time ought to be ours for the perfecting of it. That till the grievances are brought in the bill may not be taken into consideration.

CHANCELLOR DUCHY. I have seen many requests made unto him, and I should be sorry any request from him to us, much so small a one as this, be denied. Moves for a committee.

VICE CHAMBERLAIN. Nothing is hitherto done by way of fact but by way of intention. Grievances must proceed from the King by way of justice and grace to be redressed. But he will neither sell the one nor the other. Those that are so sick of the grievances here at home do not think of the grief and danger that hangs over them from abroad: *quibus animi aegrotant illi dolores corporis non sentiunt.*

SIR JOHN ELIOT. We have not been faulty. *Anima sequitur temperaturam corporis.* Is the demand of that which is just a buying of it or a commercing for justice? Of opinion for a committee to consider of the preamble for the bill of subsidy, but that the time may be for Tuesday next.

The committee named to consider of a preamble for the bill of subsidy on Tuesday next.

[f. 180v] To Mr. More's patent for salt, he withdraws.[18]

MR. MALET. I conceive this patent is void, being granted upon a false suggestion, and a grievance in that it is against the liberty of the subject by Magna Carta.[19] 50 E. 3, Pecchee's case in parliament for a patent for 4s. for every tun of wine.[20]

Resolved that the patent of Mr. More for salt is a grievance both in the creation and execution thereof.

MR. GLANVILLE. In Sir Robert Flood's case those men that were found projectors of monopolies were put out of the House if they were members, in 18 *Jac.*[21]

SIR GEORGE MORE. I never knew any restitution made by order of this House.

SIR WILLIAM SPENCER remembers Sir Henry Britain upon such a case was cast out and Sir Robert Flood, their elections being questioned.

CHANCELLOR DUCHY. Patents of privilege are favored and justified by the common law. Mr. More's patent has borne the proof of a *quo warranto.*[22]

Mr. More admitted in again and, taking his place, is admonished by the House not to put in execution any such thing hereafter

18. See above, n. 9.

19. See Sir Edward Coke's gloss on Magna Carta, c. 29, wherein he states that: "Generally all monopolies are against this great charter, because they are against the liberty and freedom of the subject, and against the law of the land". Coke, *Second Inst.,* p. 47.

20. *Rot. Parl.,* 50 E. III, no. 33.

21. Concerning the expulsions of Sir Robert Flood, Sir Giles Mompesson, and Sir Henry Britain from the Lower House, see *CJ,* I, 512, 536, 566–567, and *CD 1621,* VI, 83, 359–360.

22. See John More's speech, 28 March.

nor by his money to procure the invention of any such thing.

MR. SALISBURY moves/

Resolved that the sheriff of Flintshire complained of, Mr. Evans, shall be sent for to be here by Tuesday fortnight.[23]

Petition to the King concerning our desire to consider of the state of his revenues sent to the King by the privy councillors and Sir James Fullerton.

III. DIARY OF SIR RICHARD GROSVENOR, MS 611, TRINITY COLLEGE, DUBLIN

[p. 44a]

May 5

1. An act for the sale of lands of Richard Fust and for the assignment of 2 bonds, etc.[24]

May 5.

1. An act for the explanation of 2 several provisos contained in one deed indented, made 9 *Jac.*, by Thomas, late Earl of Exeter.

1. An act to enable Sir Timothy Hutton, Knight, and Matthew Hutton, Esquire, for the sale of certain lands in Yorkshire for the payment of their debts, and the estating of other lands in lieu thereof to as good value.

MR. CORYTON. That the sheriff of Flintshire had miscarried himself ill before the election saying: Here are a great many come; but know my power—that how many soever here, yet is the election in my power. I may choose whom I will.

That some of Mr. Salisbury's men spoke these words: That their master would have it by the sword if he could not otherwise have it.

That the sheriff asked curious questions. That they knew not what to answer. Shall he put by 40s. men? Put some by upon *quaeres*. They gave a month's time to send for the sheriff.

Moved that Mr. Hanmer, having proved this in the information, that a short[er] time might be assigned for the sheriff's coming up than a month.

Resolved that the sheriff should be sent for to be here upon Tuesday fortnight, before the committee of privileges.

Monday, Exchequer Chamber, to draw a bill about prevention of infectious diseases.

MR. BROWNE reported the bill for the better suppressing of unlicensed alehouse keepers.

MR. SPENCER. One thing may be prejudicial to this and other laws: that a man should not be convicted upon one witness. Moved to be recommitted.

SIR JOHN SAVILE. For 2 witnesses.

SIR ROBERT PYE. That no alehouse should be allowed but in open sessions.

[p. 44b] The bill passed to be engrossed.

MR. VICE CHAMBERLAIN made a report of the way of a petition to his Majesty about the augmenting and rectifying of his revenue. This grew upon several notions, as: arrearages of recusants, unnecessary pensions, forests, chases, Court of Wards.

Offered the draft of the petition on revenues:

To the most gracious Sovereign, your Majesty's most humble and dutiful subjects, the Commons in this present parliament assembled, taking into consideration your Majesty's great occasions and extraordinary charges not unlikely to continue, which we have for the present agreed to assist with a larger supply than was ever given to king in parliament, the shortness of time of payment considered, and desiring they may be always supported with as much ease to your Majesty's subjects as may be, do conceive nothing to conduce better thereto than that

23. See above, n. 3.

24. See above, n. 1.

some certain and speedy order may be taken for the rectifying of your own revenue. Then/

Wherein because your Majesty may require the help of your parliament, with presentation to your Majesty of our ready service; which, if your Majesty will please to use, we make no doubt so to employ our endeavors as may turn to your Majesty's great advantage both for honor and profit.

The counsel for the gold wiredrawers called in. These came against the bill of gold lace.[25]

[p. 45] Their lawyer, Mr. Davis. The law, a necessary if it trench not too much against the commonwealth. They spoke not against that part of the act for wearing of gold cloth, nor gilding, but that of wearing gold lace. It is beneficial for the King, commonwealth, and subjects to continue the wearing of gold lace. 1. For the King: the bringing in of bullion for this manufacture amounts to £40,000 per annum. They buy this foreign bullion in gold thread made; sometimes in Spanish silver and make it here. This they buy for 5s. 2d. per ounce. This profit encourages the merchant to bring it in, for at the mint it will afford but 5s. ob[olus], or to the goldsmith who will give 5s. 1d.; these men give 5s. 3d. So if there should not be this use of it, then the merchants should not have his [*sic*] price and so would carry it into Holland. The benefit to the kingdom: they employ in their trade £40,000 per annum, they employ 20,000 persons in this trade, about 8 or 9 other trades live upon this trade.

29s. a pound in lace will yield 26s. in the melting. It is true that when it comes from the weaver it loses in 3 [*illegible*] a pound, when this comes again to the melting pot. There is much of this comes to the mint, for £18,000 in 6 months.[26] And they bring it thither because it would cost them much to make it fit for their trade again. H[enry] the 4, it cost him [*blank*] to bring this manufacture into the kingdom,[27] and the King of Denmark has labored to bring it into his country. If former laws were put in use, 3 E. 4, 22 E. 4, then moved underbarons should wear gold.[28] And 1 H. 8 an exception of women; 22 H. 8 only to restrain degrees, not wholly.[29] But 12 E. 3 a general ordinance to take away the wearing of gold and foreign commodities.[30]

[p. 46] Concluded that the House would give a further time that so many be not overthrown on a sudden.

Ordered that the committee of the bill for gold lace should take what had been delivered into consideration and report the bill Monday afternoon.

Counsel for the silkmen brought in to the bar.

Mr. Herne of counsel. For the poor 10,000 people. In point of state. Our cloths of the coarser sort vented in Italy where the exchange is gold and silver thread; in Germany, by bills of exchange into Italy. This gold thread leaves behind it a 3[r]d part when it is worn. For the poor, they are such as have been long at the trade and have bred many under them. There are 10,000 families. Hard to unlearn a trade and learn a new.

SIR ROBERT PYE desired they might be asked whether they had not been heard by their counsel in the Upper House in those very points.[31]

25. I.e., the bill concerning apparel. See above, n. 4.
26. £18,000 in a month according to the CJ, above.
27. See above, n. 12.
28. See above, n. 13.
29. See above, n. 14.
30. See above, n. 15.
31. A bill concerning apparel was first read in the Lords House on 28 March. On 3 April a committee reported that the body of the bill was imperfect and Serjeant Crew was directed to draw up a new bill. The new bill was read a third time and assented to on 15 April. We have found no record of testimony by counsel concerning this bill in the Upper House.

SERJEANT HITCHAM tendered the bill of subsidy.

MR. SPENCER. That it was usual to agree of a preamble in the House before the body was presented.

SIR G. MORE. That ever there had been care to draw a preamble since subsidies so many that they should not be drawn into precedent.

SIR THOMAS HOBY. That this should rest till we had transmitted the Duke to the Lords, according to his Majesty's gracious pleasure.[32]

SIR BENJAMIN RUDYARD. To perfect our gift speedily. We lay a good foundation for his Majesty to give way to our just desires. The King so good, so gracious, can never take our money and refuse us justice. I like not jealousies. Some think the King cannot govern the humors of his people while he needs our purses, [p. 47] but I hold a frank and free commerce between the King and his people to be the best and safest, etc. Moved to go to a committee speedily and seasonably.

The order read for the granting of the 3 first subsidies: *ultimo* July, *ultimo* October, *ultimo* April, and the bill to come in so soon as we had presented our grievances; 4, *ultimo* July.[33]

CHANCELLOR OF EXCHEQUER. I would be glad to know a sound reason why the bill of subsidy should not now be brought in, which were given not only to his Majesty but our ends. We have done it in the manner cheerfully without precedent; so his Majesty takes it. I was sent for to his Majesty this morning and think that we know something more, that are near him, than others; and we spoke with affection. Think it not good to put off the bill till another time. That if through any jealousy we should think he would not give us remedy to our grievances or if out of any end we shall delay it, he will take it an effect of a neglect to his affairs and his person. That his Majesty's message was ever that after they had given him content in passing the subsidy he would give them all reasonable content.

MR. WILDE. As the gift is our own, so fit the time should be our own also. It might trench upon our liberty if we be moved in point of time. Moved that some of the Council would let his Majesty k[now] that we would not be slack in expediting this business. That the grievances should be reported before this bill, and this is no disrespect either of his Majesty's person or affairs.

SIR H. MAY. A request from the King strengthens our liberty. I persuade the House to make a committee for the framing of a preamble. Take your own time and read the bill when you please.

[p. 48] MR. CARVILL. Mentioned how the people thought now that the parliaments were called for nothing but to give subsidies. Remembered 18 *Jacobi* the parliament ended without doing anything, and the last parliament how ended at Oxford contrary to promises and expectation.

Moved to have our grievances first redressed.

MR. LONG. For a committee presently.

SIR ROBERT PYE. For a present committee. If we prepare not, all our money to no purpose. Since this parliament, the want of money at this instant has cost the King every day above £1,000 a day in pay, for such which may well be put off. For the

32. I.e., according to the message from the King delivered to the House on 29 April and further explained by Weston in his speech of 3 May.

33. See the resolutions for granting subsidies, HofC, 27 March and 3 May.

sweetening of the King and furtherance of our grievances, that a committee be presently named.

Mr. Wandesford. His Majesty's message is no command. Let us do that which may be without disrespect to his Majesty. To content him in the manner as we have done in the matter. This naming of a committee crosses not that order, but not to sit till we have transmitted Buckingham to the Lords.

Mr. Vice Chamberlain. It is fit to weigh what time is past since this business came into this House, which was in March; now May. The question now, when we shall set pen to paper to make an act for this gift. I remember [*illegible*] we are so sensible of our grievances as we see *quibus animi aegrotant illi dolores corporis non sentiunt:* not the swords hanging over our heads nor the wounds given our estate. Our soldiers at home ready to come up to cry for money, our mariners ready to go for want of pay, our allies ready to despair of us, our ships shortly not be sent out. The hindrance of this proceeds of a fear that unless grievances precede this act, it will be fruitless. I sorry to hear of such distrust. Grievances are matters of justice and of grace. His Majesty has a good heart to do us justice and grace, but withal he has a great [p. 49] and stout heart like a king. He will sell neither one nor other; he will not be conditioned with.

To make a committee, but to meet when they please. His Majesty will think it an abuse, for when we name a committee we take the first occasion. That we go about it presently.

Sir John Eliot. The many diversions and innumerable directions have been the occasion this business has been so long, not out of sense or dullness that we did not consider the dangers we are in. Whereas he said that *quibus,* etc.; I answer this: that *anima sequitur temperiam corporis.* Whereas he said that his Majesty would not sell his justice, far be it that we should have that mind to contract with others, much less with his Majesty, for justice. It is our complaint. Is the demanding of justice to buy it? We give freely, and I hope we shall receive his grace as nobly. That a committee be presently named and Tuesday appointed for the day.

Resolved by question to name a committee for to consider of a preamble for the bill of subsidy, Tuesday, Exchequer Chamber.

Debate of Mr. More's patent of salt called for.

Mr. Spencer moved that Mr. More might, if he had anything to say in defense, he might; and then to withdraw while the matter was debating.

Mr. More. That his patent had been adjudged legal by the judges. In 21 *Jacobi* this patent was suffered to pass as legal.[34] He desired that whatsoever was done against him might not prejudice the Earl of Warwick who had the greatest part of this patent.[35]

Sir Nathaniel Rich said that he knew the Earl of Warwick so desirous to keep his credit with this House that he would never enter into a business of this kind and *ergo* he dared in the name of the Earl throw the first stone at it.

[p. 50] Mr. Malet. That Mr. Packer[36] had to do in it, after the grant he laid out £80, has had nothing but infamy; that it is a void patent and a patent of grievance because against Magna Carta, runs against liberty; void because upon an untrue sugges-

34. See More's speech following Whitby's report from the committee of grievances, HofC, 28 March.

35. The Earl of Warwick had bought shares in the project. See Whitby's report in MS P552, printed at the end of the day's proceedings, 28 March.

36. See HofC, 28 March, n. 22.

tion pretending a new model, but that has been invisible. A clause that none make salt in this way upon pain of forfeiture and imprisonment, and forfeiture of penal laws given the patentee. 50 E. 3, John Pecchee had a license for sole selling of all sweet wines in London by virtue whereof he took 4s. 6d. per tun.[37] It was adjudged void, the party who executed it was imprisoned and fined, and to [make] restitution. For Mr. More, he urged only that he should restore to the poor men of the town the damages he had done them, and a committee to be named to consider the manner and quantity.

MR. BYSSHE remembered the arguments that Mr. More had used in his defense,[38] as that he had been careful to make his patent a parliament patent and that he was as careful to preserve the beauty of it as ever virgin was to preserve her beauty, and retorted them upon himself.

MR. EVERSFIELD. That Mr. More has abused this House by going about to confirm his patent by an act.[39] *Ergo* moved that both he and his patent should be thrown out as unsavory salt from off the House.

By question, resolved to be a grievance both in the creation and execution.

MR. GLANVILLE moved that Mr. More might be heard to show whether he were not a projector of this patent. If he were, to be thrown out as Sir Robert Flood was in 18 *Jac.*, being projector of the patent for sole engrossing of wills.[40]

[p. 51] SIR H. POOLE. That we should not forget the abuse to the House of bringing in a public bill hither to justify his patent under that pretense.

SIR HUMPHREY MAY. This was a patent of privilege which is maintainable by the common law and has borne examination of a *quo warranto*.[41] To make a difference between this patent and others of worse nature and not to proceed against him.

MR. PYM. That we should not condemn a member of our House before we hear his defense. Moved that he be called in, a day appointed for him to make his defense, and then to proceed against him.

SIR DUDLEY DIGGES. That he might only have some reprehension from the Speaker without further proceeding against him.

MR. BROWNE. That as judgment begins at the house of God, so[42] justice should begin at this House. For punishment.

Mr. More called in to his place and the SPEAKER standing up told him (he also standing barehead) that the House had condemned his patent as a grievance both in creation and execution. As concerning himself, the House had chosen to tread in the paths of mercy, commanding him hereafter not to put it in execution. And that since all sit here to reform abuses of the commonwealth, that hereafter he never have hand in any such like projection hereafter.

MR. SALISBURY.

IV. DIARY OF JOHN LOWTHER, ESQ., D/LONS/L, CUMBERLAND AND WESTMORLAND RECORD OFFICE

[f. 21]

[5 May]

Petition to King. Considering his charge, our greatest supply; conceive best to maintain it to strengthen his revenue to the ease

37. *Rot. Parl.*, 50 E. III, no. 33.

38. I.e., in his speech of 28 March.

39. A bill for the increase of the manufacture of salt had been read and rejected in the House on 7 March, see above.

40. See above, n. 21.

41. See above, n. 22.

42. MS: *and*.

of the commons as he desires. Wherein offers our service which we hope to show to his honor and profit.

The wiredrawers' counsel heard in the House. Urged against bill of apparel that it was profitable to King [and] commonwealth to have the trade, for they give [5s.] 3d. the ounce for bullion where the teller for mint gives but [5s.] obolus, which occasions much custom and bullion to come in. They also show how of £1 they make £3, how our money is now unprofitable to convert; that all that is worn leaves still a third part after the wearing.

[f. 21v] A committee to be to pen a preamble to subsidy because increased from 32 Eliz. first two unto 4 and 8 fifteens 43 Eliz.,[43] more King James's time, now in more haste than ever.

HOBY urged out of King's message[44] nothing to be done until Duke transmitted.

SIR BENJAMIN RUDYARD. Not to suspect King to take money and refuse justice. Some think King cannot govern humor when needs purse. He thinks freeness better; the other humor for Italy.

Salt, greed, for the patent.[45]

The order read: not to come in until grievance be answered; 27 *Martii*. Then the other order read for the last subsidy.[46]

CHANCELLOR EXCHEQUER desires good reason why bill [of] subsidy not to be brought in. None so near as we to King. Speaks with passion before he speak what King commanded, and until find them faulty desires to think the[y] speak with equal affection.

King desired if out of jealousy we delay the subsidy, he take it neglect of his affairs and his person. His former message mistaken; bill of subsidy to come in last.

WILDE moves after grievances, by Whitby to be presented, after Duke. Thinks touches on liberty.

[f. 22] CHANCELLOR DUCHY. Privileges gained by King's request. CHANCELLOR desires committee for preamble as suiting King's ends. Have not we our own ends in it?

CARVILL. We come only to give subsidies. Wishes his treasure may be as Queen Elizabeth: not to be on suddens, but out of providence before need. So [*illegible*] 18 *Jac.*, subsidies granted, hope to sit, but all dissolved. So shows all failure of promises on state's part. Therefore first purge corruptions, then give. Therefore prays no bill in till order be performed and grievance [*illegible*].

WANDESFORD. To hold our power; agree to committee, but not to cross any way [the] first order. No jealousies to be talked of when we delay but proceed parliamentarily. Hopes all so cleared [that] no putting off again. Give King a committee, ourselves the time.

VICE CHAMBERLAIN. This motion began in March, now May. Questions not whether give, but to set pen. *Quibus aegrotant animi illi dolores non sentiunt.* Grievances, sick of. See not the sword upon us. Prejudice to report; soldiers' mutinies, time passed, friends despair because intend only. The fear of counsel, hindrance. Grievances redressed by justice and grace from King's good heart,

43. The motion was made by Sir George More, see Grosvenor, above. Concerning the passage of the first double subsidy in 1589 (32 Eliz. I) and the bill for four subsidies and eight fifteens in 1601 (43 Eliz. I), see D'Ewes, *Journal . . . Elizabeth*, pp. 444, 668; and see *SR*, 31 Eliz. I, c. 15, and *SR*, 43 Eliz. I, c. 18.

44. See above, n. 32.

45. It is unclear why this entry occurs at this point; the consideration of John More's patent for salt was not undertaken until after a committee was appointed to prepare a preamble to the bill of subsidy. See OB.

46. See above, n. 33.

but great heart. Will give both, sell neither. If we proceed thus, committee may do what will; but when this published is it not abuse? [f. 22v] Desires to accommodate and proceed to both. Glad upon petition of estate will be sufficient. Shall we be talking of grievances until enemy come upon us? Desires committee presently to consider our first occasion.

ELIOT. Interruption cause of delay, not want of sense. We sick in mind, feel not body. He said: *anima sequitur corporem;* the body grieved. He answers: King great heart, we contract not the other great heart they intend. Desires King know we confident on him; desires him so of us. Moves Tuesday committee.

Committee, Exchequer Chamber, Tuesday. I there.[47]

[GLANVILLE.] 18 *Jac.,* Sir Robert Flood [and] Sir H. Britain cast out as a projector. So moved for Mr. More for his monopoly of the salt patent.[48]

47. Lowther was appointed to the committee for preparing a preamble for the bill of subsidy. See CJ, above.

48. See above, n. 21.

Order of Business Saturday, 6 May 1626

Committee on **Willes's** petition and the **Dover** business to meet on Tuesday [9 May]	180, *8/3
L.1a. An act touching the makers and **weavers** of baize: rejected	180, 183
L.2a. An act for confirmation of certain articles of agreement by the consent of the lords and tenants of manors in **Feltwell:** committed	180, 183, *4/5
L.2a. An act for **subscription:** committed	180, 183, *15/2
L.2a. An act for free liberty to **marry** at any time of the year: committed	180, 183, *3/5
Resolved: Sir Dudley Digges to inquire of the Archbishop of Canterbury by what warrant proceedings in High Commission Court against the **Bishop of Bangor** were taken off the file and burned	181, 184, *17/4
L.2a. An act for relief of **clothworkers** and dyers: upon question, not to be committed; rejected	181, 183, *18/4
Framlingham Gawdy granted license to depart	181
Report from the committee of 12 for considering the business concerning the **Duke of Buckingham** (Sir Dudley Digges)	181, 182, 183, 184, *21/4
Sir Heneage Finch (Speaker)	184
Preamble of the charge against the Duke of Buckingham: read	181, 183, 184
Sir Humphrey May (Chancellor Duchy)	182, 183, 184
John Selden	182, 183, 184
The preamble: allowed	181, 183, 184
The part of the charge to be delivered by Herbert: read and allowed	181, 183(2), 184
The part of the charge concerning not guarding the Narrow Seas: read	181, 83, 184
Sir Robert Mansell	184
Part of charge concerning not guarding Narrow Seas: allowed	181, 183(2)
Part of charge concerning staying the **St. Peter:** read	181, 183, 184
Sir Dudley Carleton (Vice Chamberlain)	182, 183, 185
Sir John Eliot	182, 185
Sir Humphrey May (Chancellor Duchy) or Sir Richard Weston (Chancellor Exchequer)	182, 185
John Pym	182, 185
Sir Dudley Carleton (Vice Chamberlain)	182
Part of charge concerning staying the **St. Peter:** recommitted	181, 185
Part of charge concerning East India Company business: read	181, 184, 185
John Glanville	185
Part of charge concerning East India Company business: recommitted	181, 184, 185
Parts of charge concerning delivery of ships to the French and their use against Rochelle: read and allowed	181, 183, 184, 185
Part of charge concerning compulsion to buy honor: read	181, 184, 185
John Glanville	182, 185
Sir Robert Pye	182, 185
Sir William Strode	182, 185
William Coryton	182
Part of charge concerning compulsion to buy honor: allowed	181, 183, 184
Part of charge concerning sale of offices of Treasurer and Master of the Wards: read	

Saturday, 6 May 1626

I. JOURNAL OF THE HOUSE OF COMMONS

[CJ 856; p. 53]
Sabbati, 6 Maii, 2 Caroli Regis

Dover business, Tuesday next, 2 clock.

L. 1a. Weavers.
Upon question, rejected.

L. 2a. An act for confirmation of certain articles of agreement, and a decree thereupon made in the Court of Chancery by the consent of the lords and tenants of Feltwell.

Committed to

Sir Edward Peyton
Sir Eubule Thelwall
Sir John Corbet
Sir Thomas Grantham
Knights and burgesses of Norfolk and Suffolk
Sir Richard Grosvenor
Sir John Stradling
Sir Thomas Fairfax
Mr. [Thomas] Paramore
Sir John Hare
Sir Thomas Denton
Sir Robert Quarles

Mr. Lowther
Mr. Carvill
Mr. [Benjamin] Tichborne
Sir Thomas Puckering
Sir John Pickering
Mr. John Drake
Sir Roger Twysden
Sir Francis Barrington
Mr. [John] Saunders
Sir Edward Scott
Sir Thomas Barrington

Tuesday,[1] 2 clock, Exchequer Court.

L. 1a. [*sic*][2] An act for subscription.

Committed to

[col. 1]
Sir Francis Barrington
Sir W[alter] Erle
Sir Nicholas Saunders
Sir George More
Mr. [William] Coryton
Mr. [Francis] Rous
Sir William Spencer

[col. 2]
Mr. John Drake
Mr. [William] Trumbull
Sir H[enry] Poole
Sir Clement Throckmorton
Sir A[lexander] Temple
Sir H[umphrey] Lynde
Sir J[ames] Perrot
Sir John Corbet
Sir Edward Hales
Mr. Lowther
Mr. [Roger] Matthew
Mr. [John] Carvill

[col. 3]
Sir Richard Grosvenor
Mr. Francis Drake
Mr. [John] Whitson
Sir Thomas Barrington
Sir William Strode
Sir G[ilbert] Gerard
Sir W[alter] Covert
Sir Edward Scott
Mr. [John] Saunders
Mr. [Christopher] Herris

Wednesday next, afternoon, Court of Wards.

L. 2a. An act for free liberty to marry at any time of the year.

Committed to

[col. 1]
Mr. [Richard] Spencer
Sir John Stradling
Sir W[alter] Erle
Mr. [Anthony] Langston
Mr. [Christopher] Sherland
Sir Francis Barrington

[col. 2]
Mr. Lowther
Mr. [Robert] Caesar
Sir H[enry] Poole
Mr. Jordan
Mr. [James] Lewis
Sir G[ilbert] Gerard

[col. 3]
Sir Francis Goodwin
Sir John Jackson
Sir H[enry] Anderson
Mr. [John] Delbridge
Sir Richard Buller
Mr. [Francis] Rous
Sir J[ames] Perrot

[col. 4]
Sir George More
Mr. Francis Drake
Sir J[ames] Fullerton
Sir Thomas Grantham
Sir Thomas Fairfax

Wednesday, 2 clock, Court of Wards.

1. *Monday* is crossed out in the MS and *Tuesday* is inserted.

2. I.e., *L.2a.* The bill was first read on 15 February.

[p. 54] Sir D. Digges to entreat the Lord of Canterbury to know by what warrant the proceedings in the High Commission Court against the Bishop of Bangor were taken off and burnt.[3]

L. 2a. Clothworkers.

Upon question of committing, the House, upon uncertainty of the voice, the question being 2 put, the voice doubtful, the House being to be divided, the Yea yielded rather than they would go out.

Upon a 2 question of engrossing, the bill rejected.

Mr. Gawdy, for sickness, licensed to go into the country.

SIR D. DIGGES reports he is to make the introduction.

2. Mr. Herbert, the plurality of offices; Admiralty bought, and 5 Ports bought.

3. Narrow Seas not guarded, and the *Peter* of Newhaven, to Mr. Selden.

4. East India Company business; delivery of the ships to the French; the ships against Rochelle/[4]

1. The preamble read, and *una voce* agreed.[5]

2. That for the plurality of offices, read and allowed.

3. Buying of the Admiralty, so also.

4. 5 Ports bought, so also.

5. Narrow Seas not guarded, so also.

6. The *Peter* of Newhaven, recommitted.

7. East India Company, recommitted.

8. Delivery of our ships to the French, so this also.

9. Ships against Rochelle, so this also.

10. Compulsion to buy honors, so this also.

11. Lord Treasurer's office, and of the Master of the Wards, sold, so this also.

12. Procuring of honors for his kindred, so this also.

13. Intercepting and exhausting the King's revenue, so this also.

The schedule to be annexed to the last charge, read and recommitted.

14. The late King's sickness, so this also.

15. The conclusion, so this also.

Mr. Vice Chamberlain to be present[6] at the committee upon recommitment for the *Peter.*

This committee to meet again at 2 of the clock, in the Treasury Chamber.

The House to sit at 5 of the clock.

[p. 55]

Sabbati, 6 Maii, 2 Caroli Regis
Post Meridiem

SIR D. DIGGES reports the articles recommitted, for the *Peter* of Newhaven, and East India Company, with some amendments; which read and allowed.

So the schedule; and that, with the amendments, allowed.

Upon question, all to be engrossed, with the addition of the words "and Duchy of Lancaster", in the article of intercepting of the King's revenue, upon question.

The committee for continuance and repeal of statutes, Wednesday next, 8 clock.[7]

3. MS CJ and printed edition: *brent.* Digges brought a letter of explanation into the House on 24 May (see OB).

4. For the complete list of speakers assigned for the conference with the Lords on 8 May, see Grosvenor, below.

5. Listed here are the articles against Buckingham that were reread this day and put to question whether they were to stand as they were written or to be recommitted for redrafting. They vary somewhat from the final order of the articles, see HofL, 15 May, pp. 463–477 and 8 June, pp. 566–585. For the reports of the joint conference of 8 May, see HofL, 13 May, pp. 408–442, and 15 May, pp. 445–460.

6. *added* is crossed out in the MS and *to be present* is inserted. See, however, Whitelocke, below.

7. *in the forenoon* is crossed out in the MS and *8 clock* is inserted.

II. DIARY OF BULSTRODE WHITELOCKE, ESQ., DD. 12.21, CAMBRIDGE UNIVERSITY LIBRARY

[f. 181]

May 6

SIR DUDLEY DIGGES reports from the committee for the Duke's business that to 4 of the short robe and 4 of the long robe the charge is committed: introduction to himself; concerning plurality of offices, buying of the Admiralty and Cinque Ports, to Mr. Herbert; not guarding of the seas and his unjust stay of the *St. Peter* after sentence, to Mr. Selden; [*illegible*] the East India, extorting £10,000 of the Company and abuse of the parliament, and delivery of our ships to the French and sending them against Rochelle, to Mr. Glanville; compulsion to buy honor, Lord Treasurer's place and Master of Wards, to Mr. Whitby; the procuring of honors to his poor kindred and intercepting and exhausting the King's revenues, to Mr. Whitby [*sic*]. Transcendent presumption in giving physic to King James by the Duke, to Mr. Wandesford. Conclusion of the charge committed to Sir John Eliot.

CHANCELLOR DUCHY. That this preamble is not according to the later ways. We call it a bill. I have not seen the like in parliament. But desire that the gentlemen that we trusted with it will satisfy us.[8]

MR. SELDEN. 50 E. 3;[9] 28 H. 6,[10] some excused by clamor of the Commons, some by mouth of the Commons. 50 E. 3, [Adam de Bury][11] accused by long bill. 28 H. 6, the same way as is[12] now used.

MR. VICE CHAMBERLAIN. That the recital concerning the *St. Peter* goes far beyond the intention of the House. The ships sent into France are safely returned. Moves that proceeding with the rest of the charges we should recommit this and he will attend and make it appear where it is fit to be altered.

SIR JOHN ELIOT. Takes exception to the words of Mr. Vice Chamberlain that he said, "the recital was not according to the sense of the House", thereby taxing the committee.

CHANCELLOR DUCHY. If we employ our great memories and our great wisdoms to sharp contentions, we shall discourage men from doing [f. 181v] service; and [it] breaks the orders of parliament. Desires this may be left.

MR. PYM. Pretense argues an aberration of the will.

MR. VICE CHAMBERLAIN. I will not reply any one word to Sir John Eliot, but refer it to the consideration of the House which of us was most out of compass. But I do not except against the matter of this charge, only desire some of the words may be altered.

MR. GLANVILLE desires that Lord Robartes may be cleared by this House from any imputation of buying his honor.[13]

SIR ROBERT PYE. That Lord Robartes offered £20,000 for his honor, as Sir William Strode knows.[14]

SIR WILLIAM STRODE justifies it.

MR. CORYTON. That Lord Robartes refused to pay any money.

8. For the preamble and introduction to the charges, see HofL, 13 May, pp. 408–409.

9. The case of Adam de Bury, citizen of London, wherein the charges against him were detailed in "*une grant bill baille en parlement de darrain jour de cest parlement a Eltham*". *Rot. Parl.*, 50 E. III, no. 47.

10. *Rot. Parl.*, 28 H. VI, no. 18, the preamble to the case of William de la Pole, Duke of Suffolk.

11. The MS is blank.

12. MS: *in*.

13. Regarding Lord Robartes, see HofL, 15 May, p. 469, n. 84.

14. See the Duke's response to the ninth charge, HofL, 8 June, p. 576.

All the several papers of the charges against the Duke of Buckingham allowed of by the House, only that concerning the *St. Peter,* and that concerning the East India ships and the schedule recommitted, and Vice Chamberlain added to the committee.

Pomeridiem

SIR DUDLEY DIGGES reports from the recommitment some few alterations.

And the papers are allowed by the House and ordered to be engrossed.

III. DIARY OF SIR RICHARD GROSVENOR, MS 611, TRINITY COLLEGE, DUBLIN

[p. 52]

May 6

1. An act touching the makers and weavers of baize and says.

Rejected upon the first reading by question; it had a private end.

2. An act for the confirmation of certain articles of agreement and a decree made in Chancery thereupon between the lords of the several manors in Feltwell, in the county of Norfolk.

Committed, Tuesday afternoon, Exchequer Court. I one of them.

2. An act concerning subscription. That none be forced to subscribe but to the Book of Articles, that none subscribe otherwise, that all canons made different from that act be made void.

Committed, Wednesday, Court of Wards. I one.

2. An act that all men may marry any time of the year.

Committed, Wednesday, Court of Wards.

2. An act for relief of clothworkers and dyers.

Rejected by question.

SIR DUDLEY DIGGES reported the business of the Duke's, how prepared to go up to the Lord[s].

Introduction to Sir Dudley Digges.

Mr. Herbert: Plurality of offices, buying of Admiral's place, and Lord Warden's.

Mr. Selden: Narrow Seas, Newhaven.

Mr. Glanville: Ships against Rochelle.

Mr. Whitby: Sale of honor.

Mr. Pym: Conferring honor upon such as the Kings/

Mr. Wandesford: Physic.

Sir John Eliot: Conclusion.

[p. 53] That which was to be delivered the Lords, and to be engrossed, was delivered in to be read.

The preamble.

SIR HUMPHREY MAY desired to know the reasons why we go in a new way, calling this a bill, different from the late way.

MR. SELDEN. Of late times, true, we used to make the accusation of those persons accused by word of mouth, and that a good course. But as true that when accusations are of many parts this course was also used, as 50 E. 3;[15] 28 H. 6.[16] Adam de Bury accused by a long bill, and 28 H. 6 there a large accusation is called a bill and runs this way with a preamble and a conclusion.

Sir Dudley Digges: The preamble, by question allowed of.[17]

Mr. Herbert: Plurality of offices, allowed; Admiralty bought, allowed; Cinque Ports bought, allowed.

Mr. Selden: Narrow Seas not guarded, allowed; The *Peter* of Newhaven stayed after sentence, allowed.

MR. VICE CHAMBERLAIN. He had received a letter: it is much wondered that the parliament of England take up their time in private quarrels without respect to the public danger. That in Brussels 4 ambassadors sit

15. See above, n. 9.
16. See above, n. 10.
17. See above, n. 5.

in judgment upon England; that they could want no agents in England who either is a Jesuit or friend of Gondomar.

East India Company, allowed.[18]

Mr. Glanville: Delivery of the ships to the French, allowed; the ships against Rochelle, allowed.

Mr. Whitby: Compulsion to buy honor, allowed; Lord Treasurer's office and Master of the Wards sold, allowed.

Mr. Pym: Procuring honors for his kindred, allowed; intercepting and exhausting of the King's revenue, allowed; the schedule, [recommitted].

Mr. Wandesford: The [*illegible*] King's sickness, allowed.

Sir John Eliot: The conclusion, allowed.

MR. KIRTON moved that Sir Edward Villiers being President of Munster an unfit man for such a place, being a province where the Spaniard used to land; should be put into the charge.

IV. DIARY OF JOHN LOWTHER, ESQ., D/LONS/L, CUMBERLAND AND WESTMORLAND RECORD OFFICE

[f. 22v]

[6 May]

Order from King James to take off the file proceedings in High Commission against Bishop of Bangor.[19]

D. Digges: Introduction and preamble.

Herbert: Plurality; buying of offices.

Selden: Narrow Seas; *Peter* stayed.

Glanville: Rochelle ships; East Indies extortion.

Honor; Judicature: Whitby.

Honors maintained by King's revenue: Pym's.

And presumption for physic: Wandesford's.

Conclusion; recapitulating: Eliot.

[f. 23] SPEAKER. None to except but [*illegible*].

[1.] Commons declare and accuse Duke of misdemeanors, misprisions, offenses, and crimes.

CHANCELLOR DUCHY asks upon what ground we go by bill in this form; unprecedented of late.

SELDEN. Of late we accused by word St. Albans and Middlesex.[20] Ancient words and writing: 50 E. 3;[21] 28 H. 6;[22] 10 R. 2,[23] examples of both. 50 E. 3, Adam de Bury accused by long bill hereunto annexed; so 28 H. 6.

Allowed by question, the bill of preamble to go.

2. Plurality of offices procured by him by exorbitant ambition to discouragement of others. Allowed.

3. Who buy office, direct or indirect, etc., he disabled. The Duke bought Admiralty and surrender of it to intent to obtain it, and got annuity of King, and he occupied them ever since, contrary statutes. Allowed.

4. Cinque Ports in like sort allowed.

5. Where Duke ought to have kept seas and endeavored to get supply from King and lords he neglected trust, whereby trade decayed, infested with pirates.

SIR ROBERT MANSELL says Narrow Seas is from Calais to Beachy Head and therein no haven. Meant of sea coasts.

6. *Peter* of Newhaven, Mailleu master. Duke retained gold, pearl[s] to his use and stayed ship to public violation of justice.

18. The article regarding the East India Company was recommitted. See CJ, above.

19. See above, n. 3.

20. Concerning the proceedings against Sir Francis Bacon and Lionel Cranfield, see 2 May, n. 28.

21. See above, n. 9.

22. See above, n. 10.

23. *Rot. Parl.*, 10 R. II, no. 5, the case of Michael de la Pole, Earl of Suffolk, wherein "*touz les Communes . . . lui accuserent par demonstrance de bouche* . . . ".

VICE CHAMBERLAIN. Letter sent into the House that the[y] wonder we so follow private quarrels. That in Brussels/

[f. 23v] Recital in *St. Peter* transcends the House his sense, for meant only the illegal stay.

1. Makes *Peter* seized first by pretense of Spanish.

2. We give scandal to governor of Newhaven. *Scandalum datum et acceptum.*

Desires to proceed. This to be recommitted.

ELIOT wonders that any private man should say that it is against sense of the House, which is the act formally. Thinks the exception unnecessary and recommitment necessary.

CHANCELLOR EXCHEQUER desires forbearance humbly of sharp reprehension.

PYM affirms they objected parliamentarily and desires his motion may be affected.

7. East India Company. Duke abused Lords in parliament; extorted £10,000 which he by his ministers from February agitated. In March twelvemonth moved Lords. 5 *Martii* said he no occasion of stay, desired their reasons yet gave leave to fall down to Tilbury. He procured suit for £15,000. Not released until he satisfied in his false pretense.

GLANVILLE conceives we abused in our desire of stay by answer Duke had stayed it before.

Recommitted, as *St. Peter* was.

8. Rochelle ships delivered; and law of property of the merchants' ships taken. Allowed.

9. The employment of them against religion contrary to King's intention, and abused both Houses by intimation and violating the truth.

[f. 24] 10. Perverted old way. Made Robartes purchase his Lordship of Truro by threatening.

GLANVILLE moves that L. Robartes may have a clause not to be dishonored because compulsion.

SIR ROBERT PYE and SIR WILLIAM STRODE. That he did offer £20,000 for it before and was denied by Duke.[24]

11. L. Treasurer and Master of Wards sold, Duke procured.

12. Honoring his kindred who our King's revenues maintain, to prejudice barons by their viscountcies. Allowed.

13. Intercepting and exhausting King's revenue. Not satisfied with what King gave; procured a grant of *mandamus* £32,000; got monies for victualing navy, whereof King can expect no account, bei[ng] out of Exchequer way. Adds a schedule of other particulars.[25]

14 [*sic*] June, 14 *Jacobi*, [Biddlesden,] £700 rent.

1623—	Whaddon	£5	3s.
	Hartington	£700	
14 *Jac.*,	Combe, etc.	£114	
	Bisley, Gloucester	53	
	Timberwood	89	
	Stoke	500	
	Over, Kent	56	
	Leiston	114	
	[Total:]	[£]1,198	4

Exchange with York House	£140
[Lands sold by his agents:]	
1622—	£160
	£800
	£1,636

24. See above, n. 14.

25. The schedule was later corrected, see HofL, 15 May, pp. 473–477 and 8 June, pp. 579–585.

	£4,000	
	£1,860	
	£1,000	
	£1,906	
	1,476	
	3,284	
	£3,000	
[total:]	£2,500	
Earl Manchester	£1,200	[*sic*]
[Fotherley]	£995	
	£9,850	to R[obert] P[ye]
[Burlamachi]	£600,000	[*sic*]
For navy	£20,000	
Pensions	£2,000	
Ireland	£7,000	per annum

Pensions paid by King, £2,000 for him; his endeavor for prizes, 60,000; Middlesex's fine, 20,000.

[f. 24v] Middlesex got by kindred marriage £120,000

To Sir E. Villiers, £3,000.

Purbeck a pension of £1,000 by year.

14. King James his physic ministered presumptuously, and the particular supposition of the 2 witnesses recited.

Epilogue: Duke to be put to answer, and according to law and justice to proceed.

To meet afternoon at the committee and to vote all, as well committed as these allowed.

Order of Business Monday, 8 May 1626

MONDAY, 8 MAY 1626

I. JOURNAL OF THE HOUSE OF COMMONS

[CJ 856; p. 55]
Lunae, 8 Maii, 2 Caroli Regis

Sir William Spencer, Sir William Masham, Sir Thomas Puckering, Sir A[lexander] Temple, Sir H[umphrey] Lynde, Sir Thomas Grantham, added to the Lady Dale's bill.

L. 1a. An act for naturalization of Sir D. Deligne, [of] Harlaxton, in the county of Lincoln, Knight.

L. 1a. An act for the better allowance from nonresidents to their preaching ministers.

[CJ 857]
L. 2a. Snell.[1]
Committed to

[col. 1]	[col. 2]	[col. 3]
Sir H[enry] Poole	Knights and burgesses of Wilts	Mr. [Richard] Spencer
Mr. Long	Sir Thomas Denton	Mr. [Humphrey] Newbery
Sir Robert Poyntz	Sir Thomas Thynne	Mr. Lowther
Mr. [Edward] Kirton	Sir [James] Perrot	Mr. Rolle
Mr. [Robert] Caesar	Sir William Strode	Sir J[ohn] Stradling
		Mr. [Richard] Dyott

Wednesday afternoon, Exchequer Court.

MR. WILDE moves from the committee concerning the bill of excommunication, an addition: Sir H. Marten and Dr. Eden, added; and Mr. Whitaker, Sir George More, Sir D. Digges.

This afternoon, Court of Wards.

MR. VICE CHAMBERLAIN reports:[2] 1, that his Majesty does thank the House for the care of his estate, and gives leave to enter into it. Desires the committee for it may not be great, but select persons, such as may not discover the weakness of it. That his officers shall attend the committee. That he desires the committee may 1st agree upon the heads, and that he may be acquainted with them.

[p. 56] That, for the transportation of ordnance, the lords of the Council being absolutely against it that, upon debate thereof, they were all turned in their opinion. That the committees may, before the bill brought in,[3] be acquainted with those reasons; that they may either be satisfied, or else what other course they shall think fit. That none have been carried over since November last,[4] nor any shall be while this business is in agitation.

Ordered, the committee for the bill shall hear the reasons;[5] and Mr. Vice Chamberlain, Mr. Chancellor of the Exchequer, and Mr. Chancellor of the Duchy, added to that committee.

For the other committee,[6] there to be a committee of the whole House to agree upon the heads. This to be upon Wednesday morning next, and they to name a select subcommittee.

1. I.e., the bill to enable Sir Charles Snell to make a jointure to any wife he shall marry, etc., first read on 27 March.

2. On 5 May a petition was submitted to the King regarding the rectifying and augmenting of crown revenue, see above. Sir Dudley Carleton is reporting Charles's response to that petition; for another copy of the King's response, see SP 16/523:122.

3. The bill was read a second time on 14 February but did not receive a third reading in this session.

4. See HofC, 14 February, n. 65.

5. I.e., the bill regarding ordnance. The committee was appointed on 14 February, see above. See below, n. 15.

6. I.e., the committee concerning the rectifying and augmenting of the King's revenue.

The engrossed articles and schedule read,[7] and in some small things amended by the Clerk at the board, and a title and marginal notes delivered in and, upon question, allowed, and ordered to be inserted.

Doubt/

Ordered, a message to be sent up to the Lords to desire a conference by a committee of both Houses, if so their Lordships shall think fit, as soon [as] their Lordships' occasions will give leave after this forenoon.

The message to be delivered by Mr. Vice Chamberlain.

The sum of the message shall be to desire a conference with the Lords and by a committee of both Houses if it may stand with their Lordships' liking, concerning the impeachment and accusation of a great peer of that House, with as much convenient speed as their Lordships' occasions will permit after this morning.

SIR JOHN FINCH reports from the committee for privileges concerning the case for Warwick.

Friday next appointed for the report of it.

L. 2a. An act to direct the true and real conformity of popish recusants.

Committed to

[col. 1]	[col. 2]
Sir M[iles] Fleetwood	Sir Humphrey Lynde
Sir Thomas Hoby	Sir Edwin Sandys
Mr. John Drake	Sir George More
Sir Thomas Fanshawe	Mr. [Thomas] Malet
Mr. Serjeant Hitcham	Sir A[lexander] Temple
Mr. Herbert	Sir H[arbottle] Grimston
Sir B[aptist] Hicks	Mr. [Humphrey] Newbery
Mr. [Richard] Spencer	Sir Thomas Barrington
Mr. [Thomas] Wentworth	Mr. Lowther
	Sir Thomas Hoby
	Mr. Rolle

[col. 3]	[col. 4]
Sir Robert Harley	Sir Eubule Thelwall
Sir Edward Scott	Sir B[enjamin] Rudyard
Sir Edward Hales	Mr. Whitaker
Mr. Attorney Wards	Sir Francis Vincent
Sir William Masham	Sir H[enry] Marten
Sir A[rthur] Ingram	Sir H[enry] Poole
Mr. [Francis] Rous	Sir John Corbet
Sir Nicholas Saunders	
Mr. [Christopher] Sherland	

Thursday, 2 clock, Court of Wards.

L. 2a. An act for the better discovery of church papists.

Committed to the former committee, at the same time and place.

[p. 57] MR. VICE CHAMBERLAIN[8] brings answer from the Lords that they accepted not a conference, but a meeting at 2 of the clock in the afternoon,[9] in the Painted Chamber, by a committee of both Houses.

The manner of amplifying or aggravating of the charges.

Sir D. Digges, in his part 1, thanks to the Lords for their ready yielding; 2ly, to intimate that nothing reflects upon the late or now King. Resolved.

The committees to have liberty to leave the proofs with the Lords, which they have digested in calendars. Resolved.

That the parts of the articles may be read according to the direction of the charges, by one of the assistants, and then every man to amplify and aggravate that part. Resolved.

7. I.e., the engrossed charge against the Duke.

8. *Whistler* is crossed out in the MS and *Vice Chamberlain* is inserted.

9. A meeting as opposed to a conference provided the Lords the opportunity to listen to the arguments of the Lower House and receive the list of proofs without disputing the issues. See Grosvenor, below. Regarding procedures at meetings and conferences, see Foster, *The House of Lords*, pp. 126–133.

Ordered, that fit places shall be left for these 8, and their 16 assistants, for their better ease and honor of the House, and silence of all the House without expression of any liking and disliking.

The titles and marginal additions read, allowed, and to be left with the Lords this afternoon.

Moved[10] we should move the Lords, upon this, to sequester the Duke.

Moved again to move a commitment, not upon these articles, but upon the Lord Digby his petition, whereunto articles are annexed, containing High Treason.[11] That the Earl of Bristol (as opened in the House) does charge him with High Treason. That in the Duke of Suffolk's case, 38 H. 6,[12] no particular charge expressed of any crime; that upon this affirmation from the Earl of Bristol, we may pray he may be committed. That the pressing of the Lords from this House is no tax of their not doing their duty. Mortimer's case, in 2 H. 6.[13]

Upon question, to debate this question further tomorrow morning, at 9 of the clock.

II. DIARY OF BULSTRODE WHITELOCKE, ESQ., DD. 12.21, CAMBRIDGE UNIVERSITY LIBRARY

[f. 182]

May 8

VICE CHAMBERLAIN reports that having delivered to his Majesty the petition concerning the rectifying and augmenting his revenues, his Majesty does very much commend your care and thanks you for it and continues in the same mind that he was at your former [*blank*]. That you may, if you please, enter into it, but desires that the committee may not be great but choice and select men. That he may be acquainted with your heads, and he will concur with your desires.[14]

Concerning the license for transportation of ordnance, it was granted in his father's time and the lords of the Council with a general consent without one negative voice yielded to it.[15] And would have those reasons that were rendered to the lords of the Council showed to the committee. Since November last no ordnance have been transported.[16]

Ordered that the committee for the bill of ordnance shall hear the reasons alleged to the lords of the Council for the license to transport ordnance.

The title of the charges against the Duke is "The Commons' declaration and impeachment against the Duke of Buckingham", which is read after engrossing.

And MR. VICE CHAMBERLAIN, sent to pray a conference with the Lords concerning the impeachment of a great peer of their House, reports that the Lords admit a meeting but not a conference, because they will only lend us their ears, and this meeting to be this afternoon at 2 a clock.[17]

[f. 182v] The manner of aggravating or amplifying the charges left to the 8, each in his several part, and the proofs and the bill the committee may leave with the Lords at the meeting.

10. I.e., by Mr. Kirton. See Whitelocke, below.

11. See HofC, 1 May, n. 10.

12. *Rot. Parl.*, 28 H. VI, nos. 14–52, articles against William de la Pole, Duke of Suffolk (Howell, *ST*, I, 271–276; Hatsell, *Precedents*, IV, 66–69). See also, HofL, 18 April, pp. 277–279.

13. *Rot. Parl.*, 2 H. VI, no. 18, the case of Sir John Mortimer. After conviction and imprisonment he escaped, was caught, and subsequently indicted by parliament. See Howell, *ST*, I, 267; Cobbett, *Parl. Hist.*, I, 350–351.

14. See above, n. 2.

15. The license for exporting iron ordnance had been granted to Philip Burlamachi and Philip Jacobson in October 1625 (*APC 1623–1625*, pp. 101–105, 136–137).

16. See HofC, 14 February, n. 65.

17. See above, n. 9.

MR. KIRTON. That the gentleman that speaks the conclusion may desire that the Duke be sequestered according to the precedent of the Duke of Suffolk in H. 6 time.[18]

MR. NOY. It is not for us to give the Lords directions what to do in that which is before them. 28 H. 6.[19]

MR. SELDEN. I do not understand the word sequestration, neither in law/

It is the first time that ever I heard that a man suspected, much more accused, of treason should stand at liberty. 2 H. 6, Sir John Mortimer indicted of High Treason.[20] The indictment laid still in the Upper House, whereupon the Commons prayed that the indictment might go on and he attainted and committed, which was done. Croyland's story in 17 E. 4, accusations against the Duke of Clarence in the parliament roll.[21] The Commons put the Lords in mind and prayed that he might be committed, which was done.

SIR WALTER PYE shows the precedent of 2 H. 6 in a book,[22] and that Sir John Mortimer was attainted of High Treason.

SIR EDWIN SANDYS. In Lord Middlesex's case and Lord St. Alban's case no desire from the Commons of sequestration.[23]

This question resolved to be debated in the House tomorrow morn at 9 a clock.

[f. 96]

Maii 8

At a conference with the Lords in the Painted Chamber.

Sir Dudley Digges, after a short preamble of his own, reads the introduction to the charges against the Duke of Buckingham, and after/[24]

Mr. Herbert reads the charge against the Duke of Buckingham concerning his plurality of offices.[25] To find the ships, the fortresses of the kingdom, in an unexperienced hand, and so in [*illegible*] insufficient hand. Too much power to betray the state if he were false and too little ability to do service if he used his best industry. Great Admiral has co/

Every ship is a fort by his/

As this is too great a power, so it is an ill-gotten power, as appears by the next charge. [f. 96v] That the Duke is incapable of the places of Admiral and Warden of the 5 Ports. 5 E. 6.[26] A speedy redress, a sharp and quick judgment will do more in this case than any enforcements of [*illegible*]. As all offenses are so because they are against the law, so this/

It was the duty of Admirals heretofore/

Mr. Selden reads the charge of not guarding of the seas and makes 4 observations: 1, the fact; 2, that it was the Duke's duty to have guarded the seas; 3, that it was the duty of Admirals heretofore; 4, the na-

18. See above, n. 12.
19. See above, n. 12.
20. See above, n. 13.
21. See *Ingulph's Chronicle of the Abbey of Croyland with the Continuations by Peter of Blois and Anonymous Writers*, trans. and ed. by Henry T. Riley (London, 1893), pp. 458–480; and *Rot. Parl.*, 17 E. IV, the attainder of George, Duke of Clarence. See also, Howell, *ST*, I, 275–276; Cobbett, *Parl. Hist.*, I, 434–437.
22. See above, n. 13.
23. Regarding Lionel Cranfield, Earl of Middlesex and Francis Bacon, Viscount St. Albans, see HofC, 2 May, n. 28.
24. For Sir Dudley Digges's preamble and introduction, see HofL, 13 May, pp. 408–409.
25. For the reports of the delivery of the charge against Buckingham and the speeches by members of the Commons at the meeting or conference this day (8 May), see HofL, 13 May, pp. 413–442.
26. Whitelocke's account is so abbreviated it is difficult to know what case he is citing. Cf. HofL, 13 May, p. 419, n. 59.

ture of his offense in not guarding of them. [*Illegible*] *generalis praefectus marium et classium,* by his patent.[27] The kings of England possess the seas no otherwise than as the demesne of their crown. In records the King called *rex maris* and lord of the seas. E. 1 time, record in the Tower and a concurrence of/

Reymer Grimbald, Admiral of France, called [f. 97] some/[28]

All merchants strangers made a declaration that the kings of England have been and are the possessors and owners of the sovereignty of the seas, *metae Britannis Litora sunt aliis.*[29] Before we had the word "admiral" among us, that officer was called *custos maris.*[30] 48 H. 3, parliament roll [*sic*], Thomas of Moleton, [and] 19 H. 3, Hamo C[revequoer] made *custos maris.* Lord High Admiral was bound at least once a year to certify to the King or the Council the state of every ship of the kingdom, as by a book that has the name and hand of Lord Clinton and Lord Howard there appears, and by divers records in the Paper Chamber.[31] 7 H. 4, certain Admirals made in parliament, one then was made Admiral that was a knight of the Lower House, namely Richard Clytherowe, and by act of parliament his voice given to the other knight.[32] No ship of war was to go forth without making the Admiral acquainted with it. Cherishing of virtue and chivalry and 2nd, the cherishing of merchants and trading. I do not think so great a trust has been so committed and so broken. 10 R. 2, a complaint against Michael de la Pole, Chancellor.[33] And in 28 H. 6 time against the Duke of Suffolk.[34] E. 3 time cited in a parliament of R. 2, num. 38, Lord Greystoke's case, [f. 97v] 1 R. 2, William de Weston's case.[35] 11 R. 2, Lords appellants' case.[36]

Reads the charge of the Duke's unjust stay of the ship *St. Peter* of Newhaven and detaining of them. This a great offense against the marine laws and the laws of this kingdom and against the law of nations. 2 E. 3, c. 8; 20 E. 3, c. 1.[37] 28 H. 6, Duke of Suffolk's case. 2 and 3 E. 6, Lord Seymour's case.[38]

Mr. Glanville reads the article of extorting £10,000 from the East Indian Company and abuse of the parliament. Declares the state of the case at large. 10 R. 2, Michael[39] de la Pole's case. There does not belong to the Admiral of England the 10th of all reprises. 2 *et* 3 E. 6, Lord Seymour's case.[40] Earl of Middlesex's case;[41] part of it, he pretended to have a right of a 32th part of [*blank*] and released his right for money. [f. 98] Reads the articles concerning the delivery of our ships to the French and sending them against Rochelle. Declares the state of the case fully at large. Westminster 1, c. 30. 2 *et* 3 E. 6.[42]

III. DIARY OF SIR RICHARD GROSVENOR, MS 611, TRINITY COLLEGE, DUBLIN

[p. 54]

May 8

1. An act for the naturalizing of Sir Daniel Deligne, born in Frankfurt.

27. I.e., by Buckingham's patent for Lord High Admiral. C 66/2181 (MS Cal. Pat. Rolls, 16 Jac. I, pt. 17, f. 7; printed in Rymer, *Foedera,* VII, pt. 3, 86–89).

28. Reymer Grimbald was master of the French navy in 18 E. I. See Coke, *Fourth Inst.,* p. 143.

29. See HofL, 13 May, p. 415, and n. 29.

30. See HofL, 13 May, p. 415, and nn. 31 and 32.

31. See HofL, 13 May, p. 415, and n. 34.

32. See HofL, 13 May, p. 415, and nn. 35 and 36.

33. See HofL, 13 May, pp. 416–417, and nn. 41–43.

34. See above, n. 12.

35. See HofL, 13 May, p. 417, n. 48.

36. See HofL, 13 May, p. 418, n. 50.

37. See HofL, 13 May, p. 418, nn. 54 and 55.

38. Regarding the Duke of Suffolk, see above, n. 12, and for the case against Seymour, see *SR,* 2 & 3 E. VI, c. 18.

39. MS: *William.* See HofL, 13 May, pp. 416–417.

40. See HofL, 13 May, p. 419, and n. 59.

41. See HofC, 2 May, n. 28.

42. *SR,* 3 E. I, c. 30; and HofL, 13 May, p. 419, n. 59.

1. An act for better allowance from nonresidents to their under-curates. That every bishop and other nonresident provide a sufficient preaching minister and pay £40 yearly, to be paid quarterly, and the usual house for to live in, 20s. [*2 or 3 words illegible*] for every quarter day[43] withal; not to displace him except for not preaching, or catechizing, or other scandalous offenses.

2. An act to enable Sir Charles Snell to make a jointure to any wife that he shall marry, and to make sale of land for payment of debts, and his sisters' portions.

Committed, Wednesday, Exchequer Court. Court.

MR. VICE CHAMBERLAIN gave account of the petition concerning the rectifying and augmenting his Majesty's revenue, the other concerning the license of transporting of ordnance. The one you desired to have had granted, the other restored. For the first, his Majesty thanks you for your care and commends you for your zeal and that you may, if you please, enter into it, but desires that the committee be not too great but choice persons such as may be secret and not discover the weakness of his estate, in that his servants who can give any notice to them shall attend them. That you first agree of the heads, that he be acquainted with them first.

Concerning the license, it was granted in his father's time upon information that such a thing might be granted without prejudice to the commonwealth, opposed by the Council but found to be a popular error and that it might be granted to his profit without hurt to the state.[44] That the committee for the bill would hear those reasons then alleged and as they find cause to proceed. [p. 55] Moved that Burlamachi and some others, and some of the Council, might be sent for to attend the committee and to give those reasons that have been given to the lords to see if it will satisfy them.

And for the other, that the House would first agree of a small number.

MR. WANDESFORD moved that a committee of the whole House should propound the heads in the House and they to name a subcommittee.

Wednesday morning appointed for a committee.

The Duke's charge being engrossed was read in the House.

Resolved to send a message presently to the Lords to desire a conference in a committee of both Houses, if so their Lordships like, touching some matters of impeachment and accusation against a great peer of their House. This at such time as their Lordships shall be pleased, after this morning. Mr. Vice Chamberlain sent on the message.

2. An act/

2. An act for the better discovering of church papists and discovery of their former [*sic*] but feigned conformity.

SIR THOMAS FANSHAWE. That the penalty is too heavy, that if he relapse the 2d time he can never be restored.

MR. SPENCER. That an exception might be not to tie the Lords to the oath more than now they are.

Thursday, Court of Wards.

MR. VICE CHAMBERLAIN returned and reported that the Lords admit a meeting but not a conference; for they would only lend us ears but not confer with us.[45]

This at 2 of the clock in the afternoon.

43. MS: *4 days withal.*

44. See above, n. 15.

45. See above, n. 9.

IV. DIARY OF JOHN LOWTHER, ESQ., D/LONS/L, CUMBERLAND AND WESTMORLAND RECORD OFFICE

[f. 24v]

Monday, 7 [*sic*] *Maii*

VICE CHAMBERLAIN reports King's answer. That King content that we consider his revenue. Desires committee not great lest his weakness be discovered. His officers shall attend. Desires we to set down heads and acquaint him with, and King will assent both to rectify and to augment King's revenue as we desire.

For license of ordnance transporting, King his father granted it. That lords of Council did think it no error to transport by license, thinking it a popular error. King desires us to hear reasons that moved lords. To do then what we will.

Desires committee to send for persons to give information.

Desires committee for estate to be limited.

[f. 25] For the speedy redress of the evils the kingdom suffers and for the King's honor, the Commons prefer this bill of titles and accuse the Duke.

By protest saving reply, further proof, new accusation; desires law and justice.

[SELDEN.] 2 H. 6, Sir John Mortimer.

17 E. 4, accusation before Lords against Duke of Clarence. Lords did not commit, but Commons came up and requested it and he was committed to Tower.

VICE CHAMBERLAIN. They have used precipitation and we shall spend more time about it. Then we have to go to conference. Where we want example, must care what we leave to posterity; his saying after learned in precedents.

He speaks lest *respublica,* consisting of King, peers, Commons, be disturbed. King gave liberty with regret; we to proceed but on what before us. Shall we oppose him [for] whom King has thus declared his affection? If not forbear at King's request, yet go not too far. If Lords will not, how can we mend it? Consider, lest offends Lords.

[*Afternoon*]

[f. 25v] [Selden.] *Temps* E. 3, Baron Greystoke, Captain of Berwick, left it to lieutenant. He adjudged to death because taken, though lieutenant, in R. 2 [*illegible*]. Weston, not dying in the castle, hanged and drawn.[46] *St. Peter* stayed against common law and the marine law.

Digges, in his preamble,[47] compared Commons to earth, the center; judges to air, that counsel them in their labors; Lords to planets; King to sun; Duke to a prodigious comet drawn out of the dross of the earth even above the planets as one said to be into the Chair of Cassiopeia, which prognosticates the ruin of commonwealth. Said the many evils we suffered in the large circumference by many lines drawn from one point, the Duke.

46. See HofL, 13 May, p. 417, n. 48.

47. See above, n. 24.

Order of Business Tuesday, 9 May 1626

Sir Daniel **Deligne** takes the oaths of supremacy and allegiance [*see below*]	199, 205, *8/5
L.1a. An act for naturalizing sons of Sir Jacob **Astley**	199, 205, *11/5; 5/6; 6/6
L.2a. An act for the naturalizing of Sir Daniel **Deligne:** committed [*see above*]	199, 205
Committee on the bill for the naturalizing of Samuel **Bave** to meet tomorrow	199, *27/2
Report from the committee on the bill for the relief of the **poor:** bringing in a bill for **apprentices** (William Noy)	199, 205, *9/3
L.1a. An act touching the taking of **apprentices**	199, 205
Committee on the bill concerning **apparel** [new] to meet tomorrow	199, *15/4
Committee for considering **Heaman's** complaint and such other **defects in shipping,** victuals, munitions, etc., to meet tomorrow	199, *22/3
Committee on bill against all pretenses of **concealments** to meet tomorrow	199, *13/2
Committee for considering a course for a **war at sea** to meet Thursday [11 May]	199, 205, *14/3
Committee on conformity of **popish recusants** to meet Friday [12 May]	199, 205, *8/5
Committee on **Willes's** petition and the **Dover** business to meet tomorrow	199, 205, *8/3
Committee on the bill for the better ordering of the office of the **clerk of the market** to meet Saturday [13 May]	199, 205, *7/3
Committee on the bill for the making of the **arms** of the kingdom more serviceable to meet Saturday [13 May]	199, *20/3
L.2a. An act for better allowance from **nonresidents** to their **preaching curates**	199, 205, *8/5
Mr. Whitaker	205
The above bill: committed	199, 205
L.2a. An act concerning **appropriations and vicarages:** committed	200, 205, *18/4
John Pole: tenders a bill to avoid suspicion of **injustice** in any **MP**	200, *1/6; 10/6
L.1a. An act to avoid suspicion of injustice in any MP	200, 205
Sir Dudley Carleton (Vice Chamberlain)	206
Sir George More	206
L.2a. An act to avoid suspicion of injustice in any MP	200, 206
William Coryton	206
Sir Humphrey May (Chancellor Duchy)	206
Sir Henry Marten	206
Sir Peter Heyman	206
Sir Thomas Hoby	206
Sir Nathaniel Rich	206
The above bill committed	200, 206
John Wilde: informs the House that Mr. Whitby is sick, moves that Mr. Sherland be chosen to deliver his part of the **charge** against the Duke of **Buckingham**	200, 202, *21/4
Resolved: Christopher Sherland to deliver Whitby's part of the charge against Buckingham; he is given leave to go out of the House to prepare himself	200, 202, 206
Message from the Lords desiring continuance of the **conference** concerning the **charge** against **Buckingham** (Sir Thomas Trevor and Sir Charles Caesar)	200, 202, 206

Tuesday, 9 May 1626

I. JOURNAL OF THE HOUSE OF COMMONS

[CJ 857; p. 58]
Martis, 9 Maii, 2 Caroli Regis

Sir D.[1] Deligne took his oath in court.

L. 1a. An act for the naturalizing of Isaac, Henry, Thomas, and Bernard Astley.[2]

L. 2a. Deligne.
Committed to

[col. 1]
Sir W[alter] Erle
Sir George More
Mr. [Thomas] Smith
Sir Edward Peyton
Sir Richard Buller
Sir William Owen

[col. 2]
Sir H[enry] Poole
Sir J[ames] Perrot
Sir A[lexander] Temple
Sir John Stradling
Mr. John Drake
Sir Nicholas Saunders
Sir Richard Grosvenor

[col. 3]
Sir Robert Quarles
Mr. [Humphrey] Newbery
Mr. [William] Noy
Mr. [William] Coryton
Mr. [Christopher] Sherland
Sir H[enry] Anderson
Sir Thomas Myddleton

Tomorrow, 7 clock, Court of Wards.

Bave his bill, tomorrow, 7 clock.

Mr. Noy reports from the committee for the bill of the poor a desire of an addition for taking apprentices, and of taking no money with them; and tenders a bill for it.

L. 1a. Apprentices.[3]

Bill[s] of apparel, shipping,[4] and concealments: tomorrow in the former place.

Sea war, Thursday afternoon, in the House.

Practicing papists, Friday afternoon, Star Chamber.

Dover business, tomorrow afternoon, Star Chamber.

Bill, clerk of the market, Saturday, 2 clock.

Bill of arms, Saturday, 2 clock.

L. 2a. An act for better allowance from nonresidents to preaching curates.
Committed to
Sir A[lexander] Temple
Mr. Whitaker
Sir W[alter] Erle
Mr. [Humphrey] Newbery
Sir Francis Barrington
Mr. John Drake
Sir H[enry] Poole
Sir John Pickering

All that will come to have voice, Thursday afternoon, Court of Wards.

1. MS: *S.* By act of 7 Jac. I, c. 2, it was necessary to receive communion within one month of exhibiting a bill for naturalization and to take the oaths of allegiance and supremacy.

2. I.e., the sons of Sir Jacob Astley, himself one of the younger sons of Isaac Astley, late of Melton Constable in the county of Norfolk. Regarding Sir Jacob, see *DNB*. The bill received a second reading on 11 May and was reported on 6 June but never received a third reading. It was reintroduced and passed in the parliament of 1628.

3. An act touching the taking of apprentices and money with them. See Whitelocke and Grosvenor, below. The bill was introduced by William Noy.

4. Presumably the committee for the preparation of a bill for the increase of mariners' wages and pay for ships. See Sir Robert Pye's motion on 22 March. The bill on trade initiated in the Lower House on 1 March had already been reported on 14 March and the bill from the Upper House, read first on 28 April, was not committed in this session.

L. 2a. An act concerning appropriations and vicarages.

Committed to the former committee.[5]

[p. 59] MR. POLE tenders a bill about an oath to be administered to the members of the Commons House of Parliament; which read.

L. 1a. An act for to avoid suspicion of injustice in any member of the Commons House of Parliament.

Upon question, to be presently read again.

[CJ 858] *L. 2a.* An act for to avoid suspicion of injustice in any member of the Commons House of Parliament.

Committed to

Mr. Vice Chamberlain
Mr. Chancellor Exchequer
Mr. Chancellor Duchy
Mr. [John] Pole
Sir Thomas Hoby
Sir Francis Popham
Mr. [Edward] Kirton
Sir H[enry] Poole

And all that will come to have voice, Friday, 2 clock, in the Star Chamber.

MR. WILDE informs that Mr. Whitby is sick, and moves Mr. Sherland may perform his part.[6]

Resolved.

And leave given him to go out now to prepare himself, and Mr. Noy to assist him.

Mr. Baron Trevor and Sir Charles Caesar bring a message from the Lords: That touching the great meeting yesterday, the Lords desire it may proceed presently, in the former place, if it may stand with our conveniency.

Answer returned by those messengers: That we will forthwith return answer by messengers of our own.

Answer returned: That, in respect of Mr. Whitby his sickness, another being newly put in, we cannot, with any conveniency, do it until the afternoon.

The High Commissioners in Sir Robert Howard's case to attend again upon Friday next, 9 clock.

MR. BYSSHE reports the bill concerning the measuring of seacoals, with some amendments; which 2 read. *Engrossetur.*

Escheators, Saturday next.

L. 2a. An act for reformation of abuses in pressing and taking of soldiers.

Committed to

Sir P[eter] Heyman
Mr. [Edward] Bysshe
Sir H[enry] Poole
Mr. Charles Price
Sir John Stradling
Mr. [William] Coryton
Sir Edward Hales
Sir Roger North
Sir G[eorge] More
Sir William Spencer
Sir Clement Throckmorton
Sir A[nthony] Forest
Sir Richard Buller

And all that will come to have voice, Monday, 2 clock, Court of Wards.

L. 2a. Attainted persons.

Committed to

Mr. Chancellor Exchequer
Mr. Chancellor Duchy
Sir Thomas Fanshawe
Sir P[eter] Heyman
Sir George More
Sir H[enry] Poole
Sir William Spencer
Sir Nicholas Saunders

And all that will come to have voice. Monday, 2 clock, Exchequer [Court].

[p. 60] Answer returned from the Lords that they have appointed 8 clock, tomorrow morning, to proceed with the conference; which they do out of respect to this House, that Mr. Whitby may be then able to perform the service, or the other have the more time to prepare himself.

5. I.e., the committee previously named for preaching curates.

6. I.e., in the continuation of the meeting with the Lords begun on 8 May. The second half of that meeting was this day (9 May) postponed until the following day (10 May).

A motion being made[7] about the extraordinary gilding of the cross in Cheapside, and the images thereupon;[8] referred to the committee for religion, and they to consider thereof and report their opinions therein to the House.

The debate of the matter disputed yesterday, renewed, concerning the message for committing of the Duke of Buckingham.

MR. NOY, having yesterday spoken in it, demanded whether he might this day again speak to the same matter;[9] and resolved he might.

Upon some words spoken by Mr. Dyott,[10] the House took offense and, upon a general acclamation, "To the bar", he was heard to speak for himself, and was then withdrawn.

1. Upon question, Mr. Dyott, by words lately spoken here, has given just offense to the House.

2ly, upon question, Mr. Dyott to be sequestered, for this offense, from the House during the pleasure of the House.

Upon question, whether this House to move the Lords that the Duke of Buckingham may be committed to prison. The House divided. The yea went out.

The no yielded; but the yea would not accept it, desiring to be numbered.[11]

Tellers for the yea:	Mr. Long
	Mr. Wandesford
[Tellers] for the no:	Sir Robert Pye[12]
	Sir George Dalston

With the yea: 225
With the no: 106
Difference: 119

A committee of 20 to be nominated to consider of the manner how the commitment shall be prayed.

[col. 1]	[col. 2]
Sir Nathaniel Rich	Mr. [Edward] Littleton
Sir D[udley] Digges	Sir P[eter] Heyman
Sir H[enry] Marten	Mr. [Peter] Ball
Mr. [Edward] Kirton	Mr. [John] Selden
Sir Clement Throckmorton	Sir Thomas Lake
Mr. [William] Coryton	Sir John Strangways
Sir Francis Stewart	Sir H[enry] Anderson

[col. 3]
Sir W[alter] Erle
Mr. Rolle
Sir Francis Popham
Mr. Browne
Sir Robert Mansell
Mr. [Henry] Sherfield

To meet at 4 of the clock, in the Treasury Chamber.

The House to sit this afternoon as soon as Mr. Speaker shall have knowledge, by the Serjeant, that this committee is ready.

[p. 61]

Martis, 9 Maii, 2 Caroli Regis
Post Meridiem

SIR NATHANIEL RICH reports from the committee to consider of the manner of moving the Lords for the Duke's commitment. That this motion be made at the bar

7. I.e., by Ignatius Jordan. See Whitelocke and Grosvenor, below.

8. The cross in Cheapside was erected in 1290 and rebuilt in 1441. In 1547 it was altered and redecorated for the coronation procession of Edward VI and was apparently regilded sometime in 1625 or 1626, perhaps in anticipation of Charles's coronation. See Whitelocke and Grosvenor, below. See also, C. S. Cooper, *The Outdoor Monuments of London* (London, 1928), p. 124. The subject did not come up again in this session.

9. The stricture was that "no man may speak twice to one bill the same day". BL Add. 36,856, f. 53 (ed. by Elizabeth R. Foster, "Speaking in the House of Commons", *BIHR,* XLIII, no. 107, May 1970, p. 52).

10. For Dyott's speech, see Whitelocke and Grosvenor, below. He was readmitted to the House on 23 May.

11. *whereupon the noes went out* is crossed out in the MS following *numbered.*

12. *H. Poole* is crossed out in the MS and *Robert Pye* is inserted.

in the Lords House upon Thursday morning. This to be done by Mr. Speaker.

The frame set down in writing, which he read, and was twice afterwards read by the Clerk.[13]

Upon question, this contained in this paper to be delivered to the Lords at the bar in their House. This to be done by Sir Nathaniel Rich, upon Thursday morning next.

II. DIARY OF BULSTRODE WHITELOCKE, ESQ., DD. 12.21, CAMBRIDGE UNIVERSITY LIBRARY

[f. 183]

Maii 9

MR. WILDE moves that Mr. Whitby being sick and so not able to do the service appointed at the conference with the Lords concerning the Duke of Buckingham, that Mr. Sherland may supply his place.

Mr. Sherland is appointed in Mr. Whitby's room.

Baron Trevor and Sir Charles Caesar bring a message from the Lords: That touching the committee of both Houses that met yesterday, the Lords desire that it may go on presently in the same place if it may stand with our conveniency.

Sir Dudley Digges is sent to the Lords to let them understand the cause why we cannot meet this morning.

MR. JORDAN. That a great abuse is committed in the City concerning the painting of images. The cross in Cheapside has cost almost £3,000. There is not the like cross in Rome; and if it stand, some will come on pilgrimage from Spain hither and from other places. Moves that the Lord Mayor of London[14] may be sent to know who were the doers of this, and that they that procured it may be fined £200,000.

SIR DUDLEY DIGGES reports that the Lords, having taken consideration of his message, return an answer that they will meet tomorrow morning at 8 a clock.

Mr. Jordan's motion referred to the committee of religion.

To the business for this day.

MR. KIRTON.[15]

MR. NOY. The question is whether in that which is depending before the Lords, whereof we have notice, that we should desire a commitment. 2 H. 6, Sir John Mortimer was committed to the Tower upon suspicion of treason against H. 5. He broke prison and went at large.[16] After, he was indicted and the indictment brought into the parliament by the Lord Chancellor. He brought it to the bar, and the indictment [f. 183v] read before the Lords and Commons. The Commons averred it to be a true indictment and prayed judgment against him, which the Lords gave accordingly. Moves that we may first inform ourselves fully and clearly whether the charges against the Duke of Buckingham by the Earl of Bristol be treason or not before we pray any commitment.

MR. WANDESFORD. That the Duke sat yesterday hearing his charge with more confidence than I could deliver it.[17] Though we had no precedent in this case, it were fitting to make one now and pray that the Duke may be committed.

13. For the form of the matter to be delivered to the Lords, see Whitelocke and Grosvenor, below.

14. I.e., Sir Allen Cotton, Lord Mayor of London, 1626.

15. For Kirton's speech, see Grosvenor, below.

16. See HofC, 8 May, n. 13.

17. Sir Simonds D'Ewes reported to Sir Martin Stuteville that at the meeting (8 May) Buckingham was "sitting there outfacing his accusers, outbraving his accusations, to the high indignation of the Commons who, incensed thereby, are resolute for his commitment". Birch, *Court and Times Chas. I*, I, 101. See also, ibid., p. 102, where the Duke was said to "jeer openly" in parliament.

CHANCELLOR DUCHY. Take heed of new precedents, for if we make new precedents the King will make new precedents and the Lords will make new precedents. I reverence antiquity but do not dote upon it. If a petition should be brought against 12 of our House charging them with treason and the Lords desire of us that they may be committed, how many members might they take from us?

SIR GEORGE MORE. I am not of opinion that we should be[18] afraid to make new precedents.

MR. DYOTT. I may term it an insolence in any man to charge the Lords with any such poorness or pusillanimity.

For words to this effect Mr. Dyott is called to the bar and after explaining himself is caused to withdraw.

Resolved that Mr. Dyott has given just offense to the House by the words which he spoke and that he shall be sequestered the House during the pleasure of the House.[19]

[f. 184] MR. BALL. Upon mere complaints of misdemeanors the Commons have desired the commitment of a peer and it has [been] granted by the Lords. 5 R. 2, parliament roll, a complaint of the Commons not amounting to treason, the King referred it to the consideration of the Lords and bishops; the Lords, according to the desire [of] the Commons, did sequester the King's confessor.[20] 10 R. 2, Michael de la Pole procured divers grants from the crown; the Commons complained against him; he answered and the Commons replied; and before the proofs taken he was upon the demand of the Commons imprisoned by the Lords.[21] 21 R. 2, Archbishop of Canterbury, Chancellor of England, accused of High Treason; the Commons desired that he might be committed.[22] 4 R. 2, Sir Rauf[23] de Ferriers's case; he cleared of treason by the parliament, was notwithstanding committed for the suspicion. Moves that we may set down the reason to the Lords why we think it fitting that he should be committed.

MR. LITTLETON. That there is nothing in all our charges that is sufficient to induce to a present resolution to pray a commitment of the Duke. Upon the accusation of the Duke of High Treason in the Lords House we may pray a commitment.

SIR THOMAS FANSHAWE. 1 H. 4/[24]

MR. SELDEN. In 29 H. 6 the Commons complained in general that there were divers Lords in court that by their begging from the King, subverting the laws [*blank*] had almost brought the kingdom to ruin, and they desired that the Duke of Somerset, one of the accused, [*illegible*] [f. 186][25] might be suspended from court and not come within 12 miles of it for many years, which the Lords did. The 23 Eliz., if any man persuade another for his allegiance, it is treason.[26] 3 *Ass.*, E. 1 time, taken for treason for a man to bring a bull from the

18. MS: *we*.
19. See above, n. 10.
20. *Rot. Parl.*, 5 R. II, no. 18.
21. Regarding Michael de la Pole. See HofL, 15 May, pp. 416–417.
22. For the case against Thomas Arundel, Archbishop of Canterbury, in 1397, see Holinshed, *Chronicles*, II, 839–840; Cobbett, *Parl. Hist.*, I, 224–225.
23. MS: *John*. The case of Sir Rauf de Ferriers, *Rot. Parl.*, 4 R. II, nos. 17–26.
24. *SR*, 1 H. IV, c. 10. The repeal of all treasons not enacted by the statute 25 E. III, st. 5, c. 2.
25. Whitelocke's account of the proceedings on 9 May skip from f. 184v to 186 (see Introduction, *PP 1626*, I, 122). For the citation, see *Rot. Parl.*, 29 H. VI, no. 16.
26. *SR*, 23 Eliz. I, c. 1, pt. 1, whereby persons pretending to any power of absolving subjects from their obedience to the Queen . . . are declared guilty of High Treason. Referred to in HofL, see 1 May, p. 340, n. 61.

Pope.[27] 11 R. 2, in parliament declared treason that a man procured a bull from Rome according to the King's desire.[28] 7 H. 4, there were accusations in parliament upon treasons and judgment upon it.[29]

MR. VICE CHAMBERLAIN. That in the Upper House now is a recrimination rather than an accusation. A French writer says that when God was angry with the English and left to bless them he gave them over to quarrels amongst themselves.[30] I would gladly see where any dishonor lies upon this person.

SIR DUDLEY DIGGES. That the Duke in the Painted Chamber confessed buying of the Warden's place of the Cinque Ports and strangely said: Who can cast the first stone at me? Middlesex nor St. Albans nor Bishop of Norwich were not present at our accusation.[31] It is necessary and just we should pray a commitment of the Duke of Buckingham. That it is not a recrimination in the Upper House. That the honorable person that spoke against precedents has in time past defended the making of new precedents.[32]

MR. BANKES. For matters coming before us extrajudicially and whereof we have [f. 186v] had not consideration and that is not depending before us, I think it not safe we should move for a commitment.

MR. MASON. If a man be but accused of treason, it is enough to commit him. And better that one man should suffer, if he were not justly accused, than that the commonwealth should be in danger. Moves we may desire of the Lords that the Duke of Buckingham may be committed.

Resolved that this House shall desire the Lords to commit the Duke of Buckingham.

The resolution by question, the no being 106, the aye 225.

The manner how this shall be desired of the Lords is referred to a committee and the Speaker is to be here to take the report when the committee is ready this afternoon.

Pomeridiem

SIR NATHANIEL RICH reports that the committee for consideration of the manner for us to desire of the Lords that commitment of the Duke of Buckingham, that they have framed the matter to be delivered in the Lords House at the bar on Thursday morning next by the Speaker, which is their opinion, and the matter is to this effect:

The Commons, taking into their serious consideration the manifold and apparent mischiefs and inconveniences under which this renowned kingdom does now suffer, threatening manifold danger to the state and commonwealth, have, by search and disquisition of the causes thereof, found they do principally flow from the exorbitant power and abusive carriage of the Duke of Buckingham, whereof he has this present parliament been impeached before your Lordships by the Commons, besides an accusation by a peer of

27. 30 *Ass.*, pl. 19. See also Coke, *Third Inst.*, pp. 100–101.

28. *Rot. Parl.*, 11 R. II, art. 11, the case against Alexander Neville, Archbishop of York; Robert de Vere, Duke of Ireland; and Michael de la Pole, Earl of Suffolk. See also, Howell, *ST*, I, 89–124.

29. *Rot. Parl.*, 7 & 8 H. IV, nos. 2–15, petitions concerning the perpetrators of rebellion in York.

30. Comines, *History*, III, 42. "For when God meant to withdraw his goodness from the English men . . . . all was turned topsie turvie in England. For civil wars arose among them which have endured almost till this present by reason that the House of York usurped the crown . . . ". See the fuller version of the Vice Chamberlain's speech in Grosvenor, below.

31. Concerning Lionel Cranfield, Earl of Middlesex and Sir Francis Bacon, Viscount St. Albans, see HofC, 2 May, n. 28. For the proceedings against Samuel Harsnet, Bishop of Norwich, in 1624, see *CJ*, I, 784, 786, 789, 797, 798; *LJ*, III, 362, 384, 387, 388, 390. See also, Howell, *ST*, II, 1253–1258.

32. I.e., Sir Humphrey May, Chancellor of the Duchy of Lancaster.

your own House, as they are [f. 187] informed, has charged him with High Treason. They therefore with one voice make this entire declaration: they hold it a dangerous thing both for the present and future that a man of so great eminency, power, and authority, being thus impeached and accused, should yet enjoy his liberty, hold so great a part of the strength of this kingdom in his hand, sit as a peer in parliament, and be acquainted with the counsels thereof, whereby inevitable mischief may suddenly fall upon King and kingdom. Wherefore they have thought it their duties to recommend this their unanimous desire to your Lordships as agreeable to law and reason: that you should forthwith commit the person of the Duke to safe custody.

Resolved that this matter shall be spoken to the Lords by Sir Nathaniel Rich on Thursday morning next.

III. DIARY OF SIR RICHARD GROSVENOR, MS 611, TRINITY COLLEGE, DUBLIN

[p. 56]

May 9

Sir Daniel Deligne came into the House and took the oath before his bill for naturalizing read 2[n]d time.[33]

1. An act for the naturalizing of Isaac Astley, Thomas Astley, and 2 other children of Sir Jacob Astley.[34]

2. An act for the naturalizing of Sir Daniel Deligne.

Tomorrow, at 7 of the clock morning, Court of Wards. Self one.

MR. NOY brought in a bill for apprentices.[35]

1. An act touching the taking of apprentices and money with them.

That every householder using a plow land shall be required by the churchwardens, etc., by assizes of 2 justices of the peace, take one prentice to serve in husbandry till he be 21 years old. This by indenture between churchwarden and party. If any refuse, he to forfeit £40. After six months after this parliament none shall take with a prentice in money or other consideration but 2 suits of convenient apparel.

Thursday in the House, for sea preparations and war.

Friday, Star Chamber for practicing papists.

Wednesday in Star Chamber, Dover business.

Saturday, bill for clerk of the market.

2. An act for better allowance from nonresidents to their curates.

MR. WHITAKER desired an addition that such as were not nonresidents, but curates, might be forced to have under them a preaching minister, under the same penalty, that if they will not preach themselves they may have one to speak for them.

Committed, Thursday, Court of Wards.

[p. 57] *2.* An act concerning appropriations and vicarages. To ordain a vicar and endow him with [*blank*] if a 3d part of the impropriation will reach, or else with a 3d part.

Committed to the former committee.

1. An act to avoid suspicion of injustice in any member of the Commons House of Parliament. That every member shall take an oath before his admission before the Lord Steward: That I will truly and indifferently give my voice and opinion without any affection or respect of persons, freely, and indifferently. £100 to be forfeited to the King for not taking the oath. If any give a bribe given to a member to speak in this cause, 100 times so much forfeiture. If any

33. See above, n. 1.
34. See above, n. 2.
35. See above, n. 3.

member take a bribe, to be adjudged a felon.

MR. VICE CHAMBERLAIN. This bill is so good for avoiding of partiality that he wished a second reading. That at the committee they might put in promises of preferment.

SIR G. MORE. That the bill should not be so hastily committed.

It was read the 2[n]d time.

MR. CORYTON. For commitment.

SIR HUMPHREY MAY. That the Lords also might take an oath as well as we, for they are made of the same clay, and more dangerous there than here.

SIR H. MARTEN. A man knows how to be honest but not how to protect himself from villains. One witness not sufficient.

SIR PETER HEYMAN. Not to put in the Lords, reason: because they take no oath already. Thought it would overthrow the bill to put them in.

SIR THOMAS HOBY. That no advantage should be taken of forfeitures after the rising of this House lest revenge after they trouble us.

[p. 58] SIR NATHANIEL RICH. That many times the Commons have desired the Lords might be sworn, and so have been. That the Lords might be put in, and if they liked not of it they might put out themselves.

The bill committed. All that come to have voice, Star Chamber, Friday.

Mr. Sherland was chosen to deliver Mr. Whitby's charge against this Duke because Mr. Whitby was fallen sick.

A message from the Lords brought by Baron Trevor and Sir Charles Caesar. The message: That the Lords desired to proceed in the business of the great committee of both Houses presently this morning, if it might stand with our conveniency.

In regard of Mr. Whitby's sickness, resolved that by messengers of our own an answer should be forthwith returned.

Sir Dudley Digges sent on the message, who to acquaint the Lords with the reason why we could not meet presently but after dinner as soon as they please.

An act to prevent the abuses used in the measure of seacoals reported by MR. BYSSHE; passed to be engrossed.

2. An act for preventing the abuses in pressing and taking of soldiers.

MR. BYSSHE desired to know whether the bill did reach into Wales, for there all were gentlemen. Moved that gentlemen of blood, if they would live idle, might be pressed.

Committed, Monday, Court of Wards, all that come to have voice.

[p. 59] *2.* An act for making the estates of attainted persons liable for payment of their debts.

SIR THOMAS FANSHAWE moved that the Duchy might also be inserted.

Committed, all that come to have voice, Monday, Exchequer Court.

MR. JORDAN moved against the gilding of the cross in Cheapside. That the projector[s] of it might be sent for, which were Captain Williams and one [*blank*], that they should be fined £200,000 and the City pay £100,000 a year for 7 years. That he knew no punishment too little [*sic*] for them.[36]

SIR DUDLEY DIGGES returned from the Lords, who appointed tomorrow morning

36. See above, n. 8.

at 8 of the clock in hope that then Mr. Whitby might be well, or else the other to have more time. That they did this out of their respect to this House.

SIR ROBERT HARLEY seconded Mr. Jordan. That we should not countenance idolatry. A precedent in Queen Elizabeth's time that the cross[37] was put into one color and no show of the words, etc.

Ordered that the committee of grievances [*sic*][38] should take this into their consideration.

Whether the Duke should be moved to be committed or not, argued according to the order of the last day.

MR. KIRTON. That little had been said against it yesterday. Moved to put it to the question.

MR. NOY. Question whether we move for a commitment upon those things before the Lords. 2 H. 6, Sir John Mortimer committed to the Tower upon suspicion of treason supposed against H. the 5. He broke prison, that was High Treason.[39] During the parliament a commission to the mayor and others. He was indicted in the Guildhall, certified to the Chancery, delivered by the Chancellor to the parliament. Sir John Mortimer was brought [p. 60] to the bar by Scot,[40] Lieutenant of the Tower. The indictment was read before the Lords and Commons. They affirmed it a true indictment and desired judgment, which they did that he should be sent to the Tower, then to Tyburn, his head cut off, he divided, set upon 4 gates. So that he was in prison before the Commons complained.

Articles exhibited by the E. of Bristol containing divers particulars.[41] How come we to the knowledge of these things? A young gentleman brought us a petition and articles annexed,[42] told us this was a true copy of such articles as were before the Lords. This gives us only notice of such things. If we desire a commitment upon this we shall judge 2 things: 1, that they contain probable matter at least; 2, that the matter therein contains treason. So that we take upon us to do half of that which they should do. So no fit time to move for a commitment, but we may take notice that there are such things before the Lords and to desire to know of them whether there be or not. That then we may examine the matters and present them to the Lords and then we may take that course that is moved.

MR. BROWNE. The question whether we ought to desire a commitment from the Lords: 1, that we cannot take notice upon this slight ground of this matter; it is not judicially before us but from that which depends before us. In that regard we may desire that a peer may be committed. We know the power of this great man; we know not how his countenance may terrify us. His carriage was [p. 61] yesterday such as gave us ill content,[43] a slighting what was said which is of a high nature. I commend the courage of those gentlemen that delivered his charge, that they would not be put out of countenance. Moved to proceed to give him the rest of his charge and then to consider of this.

MR. WANDESFORD. We came from our counties with a certified conscience not to condemn the Duke beforehand, yet with a

37. I.e., the cross in Cheapside. See Jordan's motion, above.

38. The matter of the gilding was referred to the committee of religion, see CJ.

39. Sir John Mortimer's case, see HofC, 8 May, n. 13.

40. Sir Robert Scot, Keeper of the Tower of London. Howell, *ST*, I, 267.

41. For the Earl of Bristol's articles against Buckingham, see HofL, 1 May, pp. 329–331.

42. I.e., the Earl's son, George, Lord Digby. See HofC, 1 May, n. 10.

43. See above, n. 17.

jealousy that things would prove as they do. At Oxford parliament never House more willing to satisfy the King than we; yea, we resolved that if the King would give us leave to go on we would give, but Buckingham coming in question all was rent. The parliament dissolved. All our grievances meet in him like a center. I was sorry and ashamed to see yesterday, to see him sit there with a greater confidence to hear his charge than I should be to deliver it. Shall we suffer him to sit there to out-countenance us? If there wanted a precedent we should make this a precedent. Not fit for us to see him thus outface us. We may justify this in our judgments; it stands with our duty to desire this. We touch not upon the Lords. Let us do it and leave the success to God.

SIR HUMPHREY MAY. I sorry to hear a prudent gentleman to make a new precedent. If we, the Lords, and King make new precedents, we shall breed a confusion. *Ergo,* beware of new things. I never saw where [*illegible*] prosecution did good in a court of justice. This cause is before the Lords; if we petition them to commit him, it is a second task upon their discretions, so should I think. If such a petition against 10 or 12 of this House, the Lords might send to us to sequester them in the like cause.

[p. 62] SIR FRANCIS FOLJAMBE. We sit here to make laws. His carriage yesterday were ground enough to have him committed.

MR. CORYTON. That upon the whole matter, not upon the Lord Digby's information of that before the Lords, and upon that we saw yesterday in his strange carriage so to outface those things brought against him by the commonwealth. To the question to be committed.

SIR G. MORE. We ought not to be afraid to make new precedents, for what was the precedent of the first. But in this case neither old precedents, nor his behavior, nor creating of precedents should be occasion to deal unjustly. Shall we commit a man before we examine him? Let us first attend the success with the Lords and stay the further prosecution at this time.

MR. DYOTT. For the Duke's presence there yesterday, I wonder why offensive? How shall a man defend himself if not present? I saw a cheerful countenance but no affront to any man there, no disparagement to us if he contend that charge against him or be quit because he is only by us presented; we have not examined upon oath.

It is an indignity to the Lords to think them thus poor and pusillanimous, nay, it is a base thought, I speak it confidently; it is an insolency [to] any of this House, so to them.

SIR DUDLEY DIGGES. It was time for this House to look to this great man, since a member of their House dared give this affront to the House. He feared that he might be hired to do it.

He[44] was commanded to withdraw, the House being highly offended with him.

[p. 63] SIR JOHN ELIOT. That the words might be first stated.

MR. WANDESFORD. His words: one was that no man would be so "base" to think the Lords would, and matter of "insolency" for any to charge the Duke so.

SIR DUDLEY DIGGES. That the Speaker might give him an admonition.

MR. PYM. We see there is an influence from the great man upon some men when they shall dare to speak in his defense in so high a strain. Moved that he should be called in and be admonished and suspended this House for a day.

44. I.e., Richard Dyott. See above, n. 10.

MR. GLANVILLE. Moved to sequester him during the pleasure of the House.

SIR JOHN ELIOT. As I affect justice, so I love mercy; for sequestration during the pleasure of the House.

SIR G. GORING. In part the offense may be qualified because in part he was put out by the word which I will not name. Take into consideration what a sharp reproof he had from Sir Dudley Digges, and what to think of his salve and gentle reproof which he gave. That bar is as hideous a place as can be to me, think of the sharp censure that he may be suspected to be heard.

By question, resolved that Mr. Dyott should be sequestered during the pleasure of the House. He to take notice at his peril.

Then they came whence they left.

SIR JOHN STRANGWAYS. 2 objections made against the motion of commitment: 1, no just cause. Answer: when there is [no] law to ground precedents on, it is just to make one. The Duke has delivered a ship royal into strangers' hands and administered physic to the King, he died, which is felony. In these respects we should move a commitment.

[p. 64] SIR ROBERT PYE. We have presented the Duke's charge in as high a nature as they will bear. Concerning the Duke's carriage, I have known a man laugh with a sore heart. That neither upon the matters with the Lords nor in our own House we move for a commitment, but leave him to make his own defense. If he do it not well, it will be too heavy for him to bear.

MR. WHITAKER. Among the Romans nothing conduced to make their justice level as when the greatest man in their estate might be questioned. In Magna Carta: *Nullus liber homo imprisonetur nisi per judicium parium aut per legem terrae.*[45] The Duke yet a free man, ought to be free till he have passed the judgment of his peers and law is now against him. Precedents that have been alleged: Mortimer, Suffolk, Clarence,[46] etc., all these were for High Treason in a high degree because a competition with the crown. Mowbray and Duke of Hereford were both by R. 2 committed because they accused one another of treason.[47] If this business should sleep with the Lords, then just for us to awaken them. 3 precedents in our times: St. Albans, Middlesex, B. of Norwich.[48] His charge as great as the Duke's, but no imprisonment of him; that no motion for commitment be made.

MR. BALL. The offenses of the Duke are thus stated: some against the King's dignity, some against the crown, some against the liberties of the subjects, and kingdom. Our presentment in nature of an indictment, but we in parliament not tied to ordinary form of common law. The House of Commons have, sometimes with presentment sometimes without, petitioned a commitment and [it] has been done. [p. 65] 5 R. 2, the King's confessor was sequestered from the court except the 4 great feasts; he was not accused but in a generality.[49] 10 R. 2, Suffolk, the complaint that he had procured grants of divers crown lands without good consideration.[50] He pleaded, but before the Lords proceeded to proof he was committed to the great Constable of England. But because the matter was not capital he was bailed by divers of the Lords. 21 R. 2, the Archbishop of Canterbury accused of High Treason, in which case/[51]

45. A paraphrase from 9 H. III, Magna Carta, c. 29. "No free man shall be imprisoned but by lawful judgment of peers or by the law of the land".

46. See HofC, 8 May, nn. 13, 12, and 21, respectively.

47. See above, n. 29.

48. See above, n. 31.

49. See above, n. 20.

50. See above, n. 21.

51. See above, n. 22.

4 R. 2, Sir Rauf[52] de Ferriers accused for treason for delivering a castle into the enemies' hand; he was committed before examination. In point of misdemeanor, if they be of transcendent natures, it is in the power of this House to move the Lords for a commitment, and then leave it to them what they will do.

SIR JOHN FINCH. In this case I should be loath to give my judgment upon the precedents cited till I weigh them well. But it is the honor of our House to go the same way that our predecessors have done. The end of imprisonment is for fear the party will start away or flee. No man thinks he will flee. When a cause is just and equal, potency cannot stand against justice. To commit him now were to step between the King and his justice.

SIR R. WESTON. [1,] consider what we are about to do; 2, what is proper for us. This is a prejudice which is a sentence before a judgment. It may be just upon due circumstance, when there is a certain knowledge of the fact, when an orderly proceeding in force of law. I profess the consideration of this makes me speak for the honor of this House.

[p. 66] If we do this the first punishment is to believe that a man accused is guilty. We cannot lay this punishment upon him yet. He has a right to the fame he was possessed of; and except we assured that all those proofs were made good against him, it behooves not the gravity of this House to lay a certain infamy upon him for an uncertain crime. For precedents, in our time we have had none such. To make our proceedings perfect inquire whether we have authority either upon the cause or person, but upon those things depending here. I move you would not put one grain into the balance one way or other but leave all to the courage and justice of the House.

MR. LONG. A difference between restraint before punishment and after punishment. That it is a felony in the law for a common person to give physic and the person die upon it;[53] it is felony. The Duke is no physician; he has applied potions to the King. If then it be felony in a private person, then what is this? To go to the Lords.

MR. LITTLETON. 1, nothing in our accusations whereby we should pray a commitment. There are errors, not crimes; 2, it is a parliamentary course to go to the Lords upon matters depending before them. Upon an accusation of treason every man ought to be committed, as Duke of Suffolk was upon fame. Indeed there was an imminent danger, but no difference in treason. Fit to go to the Lords. Now this sticks with me, how we shall take notice that this accusation of treason is in the Lords House. If we go to them we must go thus: say we understood that there is an accusation and if there be such, that they would commit him.

SIR THOMAS FANSHAWE. Upon the statute 1 H. 4, a question.[54] The Duke is not accused by common fame by this House, nor by indictment. Now, appeals for treason cannot be brought in parliament by virtue of that statute.

MR. SELDEN. 1, it is a parliamentary way to move the Lords; 2, we ought to do it. 29 H. 6, there the Commons complained that divers Lords that had, by their importunate begging of the King the revenues of the crown, brought the kingdom almost to subversion. Upon these general heads they desired that these persons should not come near the King for 12 miles for 10 or 12 years, which was yielded to by the Lords; so

52. MS: *John*. See above, n. 23.

53. Regarding the giving of a posset to King James, see HofL, 15 May, pp. 457–460, and n. 60.

54. See above, n. 24.

it is proper for us to do it.[55] We ought to do it upon the articles in the Higher House: 1, the nature of them; 2, how we should have notice of that; 3, how we shall secure ourselves that we fall not upon the privileges of the Lords.

1, for the nature of them. He that is suspected of treason ought by the law to be committed. There he stands accused for conspiring with Gondomar to carry the Prince into Spain and there to have him converted. This is a heavy charge: 1, generally of persuading a subject from his allegiance and to reconcile to Rome.[56] This falls near treason, the carrying of the Prince to that purpose, putting him into the hands of those must needs be his enemies. It was treason to bring a bull from Rome.[57] 12 R. 2, treason that some had procured a bull from Rome at the King's request to make Ireland a kingdom,[58] because this lessened the King's power. [p. 68] How we should come to have notice of this? No matter how, so we hear of it. We may take notice of it being of record in their House as well as if it were in the King's Bench. Whether we shall not fall upon the Lords' liberties? To send to them in this case is far from that; the objection is we desire them to do this that they should do. To the statute of 1 H. 4, that he knew not what those appeals in parliament were in that time. But since that time, 6 years after, there have been accusations in parliament, in treason, judgments of them, as in the Duke of Clarence's case as the proceeding was by accusation;[59] so that we ought to proceed and move the Lords for a commitment.

MR. VICE CHAMBERLAIN.[60] If every gentleman in this House that delivered his opinion yesterday would have refrained there to give their judgments this day, I should have sat still. I am wedded to no opinion, nothing leads me to this more than the matter does bear. And when I see the matter meet with a person of honor, I know no reason to make me change my mind in that respect of the matter. I observe precedents alleged on both sides, *ergo, quod hodie exemplis non tenetur instar exempli erit.* Appeal is a recrimination, no accusation. Bristol is accused, by way of recrimination he accuses the Duke. If a recrimination be an accusation of treason, if upon a simple accusation or recrimination a man might presently be committed, then L. Conway must be committed. I have had from him many dispatches of confidence. If I accuse him, he must be committed; and 20 rebels in this House as arrant traitors as myself. [p. 69] Somewhat has been spoken here that has made the Duke more odious than he was, *vulta saepe laeditur pietas.* If the Duke would set a good face upon an ill game, let not that carry us into passion. If we move the Lords to commit him, we think him fit in our judgments to commit him, and this for nothing in our House. 1 *Jac.*, corruptions were crept into the realm. Sir H. Neville made a motion.[61] He stood in the midst of the House—there was not then the commodity of a gallery, yet then as much modesty, respect to this House as ever since. He said the point of treason is so tender and ought to be regulated, for no man sits sure upon his question, no man safe in his house, no rich man but may be questioned. He would have treason no larger. 2 kinds of commitment: *ad prosequendam ad custodiam. Ad prosequendam,* we must not. He has not yet answered *ad custodiam,* he need not; he will not run his

55. See above, n. 25.
56. See above, n. 26.
57. See above, n. 27.
58. See above, n. 28.
59. For the case of the Duke of Clarence, see HofL, 8 May, n. 21.
60. *Sir William Strode* is crossed out in the MS and *Mr. Vice Chamberlain* is inserted.
61. See *CJ*, I, 153–154. Neville's motion (26 March 1604) was for a declaration of all kinds of treasons; his speech regarding the motion is not included in the *Commons Journal* or Cobbett, *Parl. Hist.*

ways. Let us keep good correspondency with the Lords. 1 *Jac.* a return of a knight of the shire, Sir Francis Goodwin, Sir J. Fortescue, the House was divided and as much heat as now. The King called us to Whitehall. There he concluded: Goodwin and Fortescue, lay them both aside and fall to your business.[62] I say Buckingham and Bristol are in the Upper House, let us lay them aside and fall to our business, and not do such an act that may prejudice our posterity and the honor of this House.

[p. 70] SIR DUDLEY DIGGES. An appeal is when one will say you are a traitor and will fight with him, so the other. This is an appeal. We have made an accusation ourselves, and upon that ground we may proceed. This great man confessed before us all that he had bought his offices, saying: Who can cast a stone at me for this? So he has confessed himself guilty; this struck near to the heart. It was too much favor that he should be suffered to come to affront us who came to accuse him for the service of the commonwealth. It is both just and necessary to commit him. There is such a precedent of power in the Duke as cannot be precedented in parliament; let us take this course that we be not affronted when we shall do so worthy as to charge so great an offender.

MR. BANKES. No reason for us one day to charge the Duke and the next day to desire he should be committed before he make his answer.

MR. MASON. To commit a man before he answer is not to take away his justification. Reasons why we should move the Lords: not for his carriage yesterday, but out of the accusations both in that House and this, which I would join both together.

By question, resolved that this House shall desire the Lords to commit the Duke of Buckingham to prison. The House divided: the noes 106, the yeas 225.

A committee named to consider of the manner how to move the Lords and they to return it to the House at 5 of the clock. The Speaker to be here.

[p. 71] May 9, Afternoon, held late.

SIR NATHANIEL RICH reported what the committee had done about sending to the Lords concerning the Duke's imprisonment, viz., that they conceive it fit that this motion be made to them at the bar, not in the committee but in the House, and this according to precedents by the Speaker himself; and this they had set down in writing:

The Commons, taking unto their serious consideration the manifold and apparent mischiefs and inconveniences under which this renowned kingdom does now suffer, and threatens manifold danger to the state and commonwealth, have, by search and disquisition of the causes thereof, found that they do princip[ally] flow from the exorbitant power and abusive carriage of the Duke of B[uckingham], whereof he has this present parliament been impeached before your Lordships by the Commons, besides an accusation by a peer of your own House against the said Duke who, as they are informed, have charged him with High Treason. They *ergo* with one voice make this their entire declaration: that they hold it a thing of most dangerous consequence for the present and future that a man of so great eminency, [*illegible*] and power, being thus accused, should enjoy his liberty and sit as a peer in parliament and be acquainted with the counsels thereof,

62. The House met with James I on 28 March 1604 and the meeting was reported the following day. See *CJ*, I, 158. The report does not concur with the Vice Chamberlain's memory. The same year the House met with the King at Whitehall on 30 May (ibid., 229) but the report of that meeting is not extant.

whereby inevitable mischiefs may suddenly fall upon King and kingdom. Wherefore they have thought it their duties to commend this their unanimous desire to your Lordships as agreeable to law and reason: that you would forthwith be pleased to commit the person of the said Duke to safe custody.

By question resolved, this to be delivered.

SIR DUDLEY DIGGES. That Sir Nathaniel Rich should deliver it to the Lords,[63] for that the Speaker was usually sent to the King.

SIR NATHANIEL RICH. That it was used in the House for the Speaker to go to the Lords, and this was the ancient usage of the House for the Speaker to go up.

[p. 72] SIR ROBERT PYE. This was no part of judgment, *ergo* moved that a member of the House might bring it up.

SIR JOHN ELIOT. That this was but a circumstance which was less than the matter. *Ergo,* that the Speaker should not go, but Sir Nathaniel Rich.

MR. CORYTON. For the Speaker.

SIR THOMAS HOBY. Not for the Speaker to go up because he was not employed but to ask judgment, then judgment must be first given. He was sent to the King; there is a difference between the King and the Lords, moved for Sir Nathaniel Rich.

MR. SHERWILL. Precedents are that complaints have been brought up by the Speaker, but then none else was to speak but he. This is no dishonor to the House, for this is a message of great importance for the state which brings the other to the end. *Ergo,* this concerning the state so much that this motion should be made; the Speaker fit to deliver it.

MR. WANDESFORD. In the consequence not so much material whether the Speaker or a member in the name of the House deliver it. Now in doubtful ways take the most usual; that Sir Nathaniel Rich be sent up.

MR. LONG. That the gentlemen who vouched precedents would satisfy the House in those.

MR. SPENCER. To go the safest way as was resolved the other day to present Montagu;[64] by a member of the House.

SIR NATHANIEL RICH excused himself, not able to stand so long in a crowd.

[p. 73] By question, resolved that Sir Nathaniel Rich should deliver this at the bar in the Lords House upon Thursday morning.

IV. DIARY OF JOHN LOWTHER, ESQ., D/LONS/L, CUMBERLAND AND WESTMORLAND RECORD OFFICE

[f. 25v]

[9 May]

Resolved, Wednesday, 8 a clock, to proceed with the other half of Duke's charge to committee of Lords.

MR. NOY. To the question of Duke's commitment to be desired at Lords upon notice of the complaint with the Lords [*illegible*] charging him but as misdemeanors.

2 H. 6, Sir John Mortimer, committed for treason to H. 5; broke prison, made it High Treason; by commission indicted at Guildhall; sent into Chancery; delivered into parliament by Chancellor by King's command; brought to Lords' bar by Scot, Lieutenant of Tower; [f. 26] indictment

63. I.e., as chairman of the committee appointed to consider the matter. See CJ, above.

64. On 17 April the Lower House had appointed a day wherein Richard Montagu would respond to interrogatories prepared by a committee of the Lower House and administered by the Speaker.

read before all Lords and Commons; he confessed; Commons prayed judgment; he hanged, drawn and quartered, set up. Not committed at Commons' request, for there before.

Hear Digby as we hear articles.

Now whether Commons thrust in or called in [*illegible*]. Infant Digby gives articles; another says it is treason. This is no ground for us. Upon once reading, we not fit to pray commitment for treason, for we forejudge Lords. If we pray Lords to be acquainted with it, then if they give leave we may examine and proceed as the cause requires.

BROWNE thinks as his carriage slighting, therefore *dicere causam in vinculis*, but not until his charge be given.

WANDESFORD. We came with jealousy that things would prove as now. Gathered at Oxford where parliament was rent in pieces, he being named, though we offered to supply.

All causes meet like a center upon him. He wonders at his confidence, not his innocence, therefore we to require commitment. Slight Noy's precedent. Thinks the things we charged fit be in other names. King committed Somerset for felony. If want a precedent, to make this a precedent. [f. 26v] Treason alleged, one part proved. Thinks we may justify it to the Lords, and then to leave it to God.

CHANCELLOR DUCHY. Fears new precedents lest end not in ourselves. If we do new, King new, Lords new. A sharp spirit hurts his cause. Desires moderation. We cannot require it but by taxing Lords. God [grant] our posterity curse not us, as ancestors did passionately. Suppose treason put against 12 of us, should we presently commit our members?

FOLJAMBE. We sit here to make precedents. His yesterday carriage fit for commitment.

CORYTON. Takes hold of 12 of us. This the cry of the whole land. Thinks words to be added to the charge to require.

SIR G. MORE. Fears not new precedents, for reason did guide the first. Thinks justice will not allow us to commit before we examine the cause as in all cases. Therefore moves stay.

[BALL.] 5 R. 2, complaint not treason, confessor sequestered from court but at 4 feasts. 11 R. 2, M. de la Pole got crown land without consid[eration]. He answered, Commons replied. Committed before judgment to Constable; after, bailed. 21 R. 2, Canterbury accused of treason for executing [f. 27] articles. Commitment desired, Lords advised. 4 R. 2, Sir Rauf[65] de Ferriers for giving ports and forts to French, though committed, cleared, yet recommitted.

To propose reasons to Lords whether commit or no.

CHANCELLOR EXCHEQUER. This request of commitment is a prejudice which ought not to be but upon certain knowledge with full authority. Doubts if do. We cannot believe him guilty yet, which is the first judgment, for he has yet a right to his fame. Therefore no certain punishment upon uncertain crime. Late no such precedents. Last, if authority either of the cause or person. Digby's copy is but a relation. If we proceed, offend the cause. Therefore to leave it to Lords.

LONG. Heard speaker say it was felony if one give physic and the other die, being no physician.[66]

LITTLETON. Nothing with us to commit, for but misdemeanors; so all judges' opinion, 28 H. 6, Duke Suffolk. For things de-

65. MS: *John*. See above, n. 23.

66. See above, n. 53.

pending before Lords, we may move the Lords parliamentarily. Upon accusation of treason we may pray commitment howsoever it be; so here. This sticks with him, here is no [*illegible*], therefore cannot but go conditionally.

[f. 27v]˙FANSHAWE. 1 H. 4, no appeal for treason shall be preferred in parliament in time to King.

SELDEN. For our own accusations we may; for the other charge we ought. 29 H. 6, in like presentment as we. Duke accused for conspiring with Gondomar to carry Duke [*sic*] to Spain to be converted in religion. This a persuading King's subject to treason; this is treason by 23 Eliz. 30 *Ass.*, to bring from Rome excommunication. So, 11 R. 2, adjudged in parliament because one procured King to write to Pope to make Ireland a kingdom, as derogatory from King. Notice sufficient if hear but of it, but now it is a record there we may take notice of it. They perhaps have reason not to do it on proof, we none. 2 H. 6, 17 E. 4, we desired judgment upon their record because we affirmed indictment true; supposed then we may and did then examine it. We have sent to call for their Lordships' assent. 11 R. 2, 17 E. 4, whole House prayed judgment upon Duke of Clarence. For 1 H. 4, whether accusation there properly by appeal in parliament, [f. 28] how appeals expanded, knows not; but 7 H. 4, many rolls of accusation there; so 17 E. 4, but that an act of parliament, all present.

VICE CHAMBERLAIN sees neither precedent nor reason to guide him. Precedents on both sides. To do what just and equity. No accusation in Lords House. This against Duke but a recrimination. Be it either, if he committed, evil consequence; Lord Conway desired to be committed by Bristol, refused by Lords. The times noted, precedents full of faction and destruction. P. Commines said when God left English and [they] fell upon themselves, lost all in France.[67]

Duke's carriage aggravates instead of compassion. Let us not be carried into an evil cause. 1 *Jac.*, Sir H. Neville—no gallery then but as good reverency—presented 10 points.[68] 1 of treason, for as it stood no man knew when he was safe. Desired it to be no longer. Commitment *ad poenam*. We cannot do unheard, and custodian needs not; he will not fly.

Remembers a thing, 1 *Jac.*, Sir Francis Goodwin, Fortescue, returned knight[s]. A competition. All business stayed till that King desired to let them both alone, Goodwin, For[tescue], For[tescue], G[oodwin], and so done.[69]

[f. 28v] DIGGES. If those might not trouble us, he wished he in the upper world. He thinks commitment necessary. Appeals of [*2 words illegible*] for parting, not so in accusation. We not so, but on our own grounds we may go on.

DUDLEY DIGGES thinks him dishonored by his confession of Cinque Ports, and casting first stone. He wondered. Therefore cause. Thought men would make him see his fault. He was struck at his presence. Too much countenancing to see and hear his accusation, but Middlesex, St. Albans, Norwich all not like him, though he not discouraged. He thinks it fit to be done. It is upon record not answered. Therefore desire to decline. This no recrimination. Attorney accuses Bristol. No precedent prejudicial. He remembers Chancellor Duchy neglect precedent. Now to use precedent of power when never like precedent of power. Then not to fear confronting.

[f. 29] Resolved on Tuesday, we sitting until three of clock, that we go with a re-

67. See above, n. 30.
68. See above, n. 61.
69. See above, n. 62.

quest to Lords for Duke his commitment, and a committee to prepare the manner.

The House divided upon the question: 226 for commitment, 125 no. When ayes gone out, noes would yield. They, to have honor in it, would not take it. The House within would also go out. The greater number opposed and did make a terrible contestation offering, etc., and fearful to see what a great number opposed will not do. The lesser number glad to yield to what desired, though Privy Council there said the greater number might fine and imprison lesser.

V. DIARY OF SIR NATHANIEL RICH, HIST. COLLECT. 143, HLRO[70]

[f.86]

[9 May]

38 H. 6, num. 38, in the petition of the Commons, the Commons accuse the Lord Stanley of sundry particulars of confederacy with the Duke of York and pray that he may be committed to prison. Response: The King will be advised.[71]

33 H. 6. The Commons require the Lords to move the King for an able protector of the realm and renew this suit the third time at bar. The Duke of York is appointed.[72]

2 H. 6, num. 28. John Mortimer, Knight, adjudged to be hanged, drawn, and quartered, for that being committed to prison for suspicion of treason against H. 5 he broke out of the Tower, 1 H. 6, and was thereupon indicted of treason.[73] *Vide* also the case of William Talbots, 28 H. 6, num. 56.[74]

4 H. 6. The Commons misliking the dissension between the nobles, the Lords make a decree that they would, without affection, hear and end the dissension between the Duke of Gloucester and the Bishop of Winchester so as neither of them should be encouraged to break the peace. To which order, after every of the said Lords were sworn, they sent the copy thereof to the Commons.[75]

24 H. 6, num. 44. It is an article of the Commons petition that John Bolton, who had murdered another man's wife and was pardoned of felonies, might, notwithstanding, be executed. No answer made thereto.[76]

28 H. 6, num. 16. The Commons require that the Duke of Suffolk might be committed to ward, 16 January. But this the Lords think not fit unless some special matter were objected against him. The 23 of January the Speaker declares how the Duke of Sussex, as was said, had sold the realm. Part of his charge was for procuring himself to be Earl of Pembroke, num. 41.[77]

29 H. 6, num. 16. The Commons pray the King that the Duke of Suffolk, the Bishop of Chester, the Lord Dudley, and above 20 knights and squires might be abandoned the King's presence during their lives and not come within 12 miles of the court, for that the people spoke ill of them. The King is content that all shall depart unless they be Lords and a few other necessary persons and that they should so continue for a year to see if any one duly improve them[selves].[78]

[f.86v] 29 H. 6. An act that the abbot of Bury should not have benefit by the general

70. The precedents below are included on an undated page in Rich's diary directly following his entries for 2 May and immediately preceding those for 9 May. The editors have placed them on 9 May because they all address the issue of the commitment of a peer, the issue at hand regarding Buckingham.

71. *Rot. Parl.*, 38 H. VI, no. 38, Lord Stanley's case.

72. *Rot. Parl.*, 33 H. VI, nos. 31–35, 38, request for the Duke of York to assume the title and duties of Protector.

73. See HofC, 8 May, n. 13.

74. See HofL, 13 May, p. 419, n. 58.

75. *Rot. Parl.*, 4 H. VI, nos. 12 and 13.

76. *Rot. Parl.*, 23 H. VI, no. 42.

77. See HofL, 18 April, pp. 277–278, and n. 27.

78. *Rot. Parl.*, 29 H. VI, n. 16.

pardon for matter of access, for that it was no meaning of the King to pardon the same. *Vide* 27 H. 6.[79]

31 H. 6, num. 30. The Commons require the Lords to remember the hazard of Calais, the safekeeping of the seas, etc., Ibid., tonnage and poundage appointed to certain Lords to keep the seas.[80]

My own thought: We have just cause by this sad accident, just cause to fear that we are fallen into the King's high displeasure it appears.

[f.87] MR. NOY. The question is whether/ 2 H. 6. The indictment read before the Lords and Commons. The Commons justified the indictment and prayed execution, which was done.

[WANDESFORD.] The Lord Somerset sequestered upon suspicion of felony six weeks before his trial.

DYOTT. I do wonder that any man should have so poor and base an opinion of their Lordships as to think that they would do not their duty, and so speak it freely; it were an insolency for any man so to think.

79. *Rot. Parl.*, 29 H. VI, no. 22; ibid., 27 H. VI, no. 25.

80. *Rot. Parl.*, 32 H. VI, no. 30.

Order of Business Wednesday, 10 May 1626

WEDNESDAY, 10 MAY 1626

I. JOURNAL OF THE HOUSE OF COMMONS

[CJ 858; p. 61]
Mercurii, 10 Maii, 2 Caroli Regis

The Serjeant sent with his mace to fetch all the members of our House, now at the Painted Chamber door; and to give Mr. Maxwell charge that no other be admitted into that room.[1]

The committee for courts of justice to sit tomorrow in the afternoon.

II. DIARY OF BULSTRODE WHITELOCKE, ESQ., DD. 12.21, CAMBRIDGE UNIVERSITY LIBRARY

[f. 98]
Maii 10

Mr. Sherland reads the charge of compulsion to buy honor. Buying of honor takes [*2 words illegible*] fair and frugal way of rewarding virtue. This not to be paralleled by any precedent but it is time to make a precedent of this great man. 5 H. 5, roll 10, Martyn and Babington and others', serjeants, case.[2]

Reads the article of Treasurer's place bought and Mastership of the Wards, sale of places of judicature.

Magna Carta: *Nulli vendemus.*

Aristotle, 5, 1 *Politics,* c. 8; Aristotle, 3, 1 *Politics,* [c. 3]. A law of the Thebans.[3]

Papal constitutions, rot. 2, a bull of Pius Quintus against buying of offices. Gregory 13, in his title *De datis et acceptis.*[4]

2 and 3 E. 6, Duke of Somerset's case.[5]

I leave myself to the judgment of your favor and charity, etc., this great man the Duke to the just censure.

[f. 98v] Mr. Pym read the charge [of] procuring honor for his poor kindred. In respect of the/

28 H. 6, in 31 article against William de la Pole. 17 E. 4, Duke of Bedford's case, John Neville.[6]

Reads the charge [of] exhausting, interrupting, and misemploying of the King's revenues. *Summa totalis recepta in 10 annis* £162,995, [*blank*] 120,000.[7]

10 R. 2, 3 articles against Michael de la Pole. 11 R. 2, 5 and 7 articles against the Earl of Oxford and others. 28 H. 6, 29 article against William de la Pole.[8]

Reads the schedule.

Mr. Wandesford reads the charge of applying of physic to King James. 32 H. 6.[9] We find not recorded to any posterity the precedent of any such thing as this. Duke of Somerset's case for carrying the young king.[10] [f. 99] Bracton says that if a man that is no physician take upon him the knowledge and practice physic/[11]

As in this he has made this a precedent not known to former ages, so I hope your Lordships will make him an example to all posterity.

Sir John Eliot. A canker in the King's treasures, a moth to goodness. Sejanus's description by Tacitus applied to the Duke. Sejanus's neglect of counsels; veneries, venefices, I will not mention. By him came all our evils; in him we find all the causes; and on him must be effected the remedies. In R.

1. On 9 May the Lords had appointed 8 o'clock this morning (10 May) for the continuation of the meeting regarding the charges against the Duke.
2. *Rot. Parl.,* 5 H. V, no. 10, the case of John Martyn, William Babington, etc., serjeants at law. See also, HofL, 15 May, p. 448.
3. For the references to Aristotle, see HofL, 15 May, p. 450, and nn. 24 and 25.
4. Regarding the papal bulls, see HofL, 15 May, p. 450, and nn. 26 and 27.
5. See HofL, 15 May, p. 450, n. 29.
6. See HofL, 15 May, p. 452, nn. 32 and 33.
7. See HofL, 15 May, p. 454.
8. See HofL, 15 May, p. 457, nn. 49–51.
9. See HofL, 15 May, p. 458, and n. 55.
10. See HofL, 15 May, p. 459, and n. 59.
11. See HofL, 15 May, p. 460, n. 60.

1 time the Bishop of Ely's case.[12] *Pereat qui*/

Reads the conclusion and apologies for himself.

III. DIARY OF SIR RICHARD GROSVENOR, MS 611, TRINITY COLLEGE, DUBLIN

[p. 73]

May 10

The House sat not, the whole committee meeting with the Lords in the Painted Chamber where they delivered the remaining charges against the Duke.

IV. SIR JOHN ELIOT'S CONCLUDING SPEECH AT THE JOINT CONFERENCE, 10 MAY 1626, PORT ELIOT, VOL. II, ff. 81–85[13]

My Lords;

I have heard in the labors of these two days spent in this service, a representation from the knights, citizens, and burgesses of the Commons House of parliament of their apprehensions of the present evils and sufferings of this kingdom; of the causes of those evils; and, of those causes, the application made to the person of the Duke of Buckingham, so clear and fully as I presume your Lordships now expect rather I should conclude than anything more or further should be added to the charge.

You have heard how his ambition is expressed in getting, in procuring the great offices of power and strength in the kingdom and, in effect, the government of the whole into his own hands. You have heard with what practices and means he has attained them and how money has stood for merit. How these have been executed, how performed, it needs no argument but the common sense. To the many miseries, misfortunes, which we suffer adding but one: the right, the title of the seas, the ancient inheritance of our princes, the honor of this land, lost or impeached makes it too apparent, too much known, I need not further press it. But from here my observations must descend upon his other virtues or this come extracted from those parts which you have had delivered and that, by way of perspective, I will give so near and shortly as, I hope, your Lordships shall conceive it rather an ease and help to excitate your memories than to oppress your patience.

And first, I must take the inward characters, the patterns of his mind as you have heard them opened, full of collusion and deceit, crimes in themselves so odious and uncertain as the ancients knew not by what name to term them and therefore [f. 81v] they expressed them in a metaphor, calling them *stellionatus* from a discolored beast so doubtful in appearance as they knew not what to make it.[14] And thus, we find it here in this man's practices, first on the merchants by his arts and fair persuasions drawn with their ships to Dieppe, there to be entrapped. Then, to the King and state with shadows and pretences coloring that foul design which secretly he had plotted against Rochell and religion. Then, to the parliament after his work was finished or in motion and the ships given up into the French men's hands, not only in disguising but denying the truth of that he knew, a practice both in the precedency and act as dangerous, and dishonorable to us or in the effect and consequence it proved disadvantageable, prejudicial to our friends.

The next presented was his high oppression, and that of a strange latitude and extent not unto men alone but to the laws, nay, to the state. The pleasures of his Majesty,

12. For Eliot's speech of conclusion at the conference, see the holograph account printed at the end of this day's proceedings. For the report of that speech to the Upper House, see HofL, 15 May, pp. 460–463, and App., II, C.

13. The speech printed below is in Eliot's hand and was endorsed: "Sir J. E. upon the charge of the D. of Buckingham. The conclusion, Parl. 2 Car.". Underneath is written: "Keep this safe where it may not be lost".

14. See HofL, 15 May, p. 461, n. 63.

his known directives, his public acts, his acts of counsel, the decrees of courts, all must be made inferior to his will. No right, no interest may withstand him, but through the power of state and justice he dares strike at his own ends. And this your Lordships had sufficiently expressed in point of the *St. Peter* and for the ships at Dieppe, wherein I shall desire your Lordships to observe one particular more than formerly was pressed concerning the duty of his place. That though he were not faulty in sending the ships away (especially the King's), though in that he had not injured the merchants, misinformed the King, nor abused the parliament, nay, if by a fourth, more ill than those, he did not now seek to excuse himself therein by entitling it to his Majesty. Or if [f. 82] in that his Majesty were pleased to have consented, or to have commanded, which I cannot believe, yet they could no way satisfy for him, nor make any extermination of his fault. For he should have proposed it by his prayers, by his intercessions to his Majesty, making known the dangers, the inconveniences that might follow; and if that prevailed not, must he have rested there? No, but have addressed himself to your Lordships sitting in council, and there have made it known, there have desired your aids, nay, if in this he [*illegible*] not, he should have entered there a protestation for himself that he was not consenting. This was the duty of his place; this has been the practice of his elders, and this being now neglected leaves him without excuse and because I have heard it spoken that the ships are now come home (though I confess I know it not)[15], give me leave I beseech your Lordships, in prevention, to object to that, that it lessens not the fault. It may commend the French but cannot excuse him. His error was in sending them away, and when the French once had them (for ought I know) they might have kept them still, notwithstanding all his greatness, as well we know they did to the perfection of their work against Rochell and religion.

The next your Lordships had was his extortion, the unjust exacting of £10,000 from the Eastland merchants without right or color which, as you had it exquisitely expressed by the gentleman that had that part in charge, who mathematically observed the reason upon which it was enforced, a secret of the seas in taking of the wind which at the cape they have at known certain times; so may your Lordships now observe in him that skill was lately gotten in the late voyage to which you [f. 82v] know who sent him.[16]

(And here one of the Lords, interposing a criticism and censure that it was the King, being overheard, there was occasion taken for the protestation following.

Because I heard a mention of the King, his sacred name in this, I must crave your Lordships leave thus far to digress as here to make this protestation which I had in charge from my masters the knights, citizens, and burgesses of the Commons House of parliament: That in nothing we intend to reflect the least ill odor on his Majesty or his most blessed father of happy memory, but with all honor of their names we do admire them and only strive to vindicate their fames from such as would eclipse them.)[17]

After this, my Lords, followed his corruption, his sordid bribery in sale of honors, in sale of offices. That which was the ancient crown of virtue now made mer-

15. See HofL, 15 May, p. 461, n. 64.

16. See HofL, 15 May, p. 461, n. 65.

17. The two paragraphs enclosed by the editors in parentheses are omitted from the record in the Lords Journal. We are not able to identify the Lord who interposed the criticism. The inclusion of this interruption in Eliot's account suggests that he made the fair copy of the speech after having delivered it.

chantable, and justice itself a prey to the great man. All which particulars, as you have heard them opened and enforced with their several circumstances, reasons, and proofs, to show what in themselves they are, what in their consequences, what they may now merit, I presume I need not to debate, your Lordships knowing so well, but leave them to your judgments.

And from here I am raised to observe a wonder, a wonder both in policy and nature, how this man so notorious in ill, so dangerous in the state, so disproportionable both to the time and government can of himself subsist or keep a being. And this, I confess, as it has wonder so it must have art to help and underprop it or it could not have been so long. To that end, therefore, your Lordships may now note him to have made a party, a party in the court, a party in the country [f. 83] a party almost in all the parts of government both foreign and at home, raising, preserving to honors and commands those of his own alliance, those of his kindred, and affections how mean soever, crossing, opposing others thought most deserving that are not within this compass.

And having thus drawn to himself a power of justice, a power of honor, a power of offices and, in effect, the powers of the whole kingdom either for peace or war and, to strengthen himself in that, made an alliance. He then sets upon the revenues of the crown, intercepts, exhausts, consumes that fountain of supply, breaks those nerves and sinews of the land, the stores, and treasures of the King which are the blood and spirit of the kingdom and that not only to satisfy himself, his own desires, and avarice, but to satiate others with pride and luxury he empties those veins in which that blood should run, and by division of its proper course casts the whole body of the land unto a deep consumption. This your Lordships saw in the opening of that point concerning the revenues. What vast treasures he has gotten, what infinite sums of money, and what mass of land, which, if your Lordships please to calculate, you will find amounting to little less that all those subsidies which the King has had within that time. A lamentable example of the subjects' bounties so to be employed. But is this all? No. Your Lordships may not think it. Those are collections of a short vein, used only as an epitome for the rest, and so for that there needs no search, tis too, too visible. His profuse expenses, [f. 83v] his superfluous feasts, his magnificent buildings, his riots, his excesses, what are these but a chronicle of his immense exhausts out of the crown revenues? No wonder then the King is now in want, this man abounding so, and while he abounds the King must still be wanting.

But having thus prevailed in wealth and honors he rests not there. Ambition had no bounds, but like a violent flame breaks further, catches at all, assumes new boldness, gives itself more scope; not satisfied with the injuring of justice, the wrong of honor, the prejudice of religion, the abuse of state, or that of the revenues. But his attempts go higher to the person of his sovereign, making in that his practice in such a manner and with such effects as I fear to speak it, nay, I doubt to think it, in which respect I'll leave. Cicero did the like, *Ne gravioribus utar verbis quam [rei] natura fert aut levioribus quam causae postulat.*[18] The examination with your Lordships will show you what it is. I need not name it.

In all these now your Lordships have the idea of the man, what in himself he is, what in his affections. You have seen his power and some, I fear, have felt it. You have known his practice, you have heard the effects. It rests then to be considered what, being such, he is in relation to the King, in relation to the state, how compatible or in-

18. See HofL, 15 May, p. 462, n. 67.

compatible with either. What he is to the King you have heard—a canker in his treasures, one that restlessly consumes and will devour them. What to the state you have seen, a moth to goodness, not only by his precedence of ill ways but in preventing better. His affections are apparent not to be the best, his actions prove it. What hopes or expectations then he gives, I leave it to your Lordships.

[f. 84] I will not only see by comparison with others where I may find him likened and so consider what may now become him and from thence render your Lordships to a short conclusion. Of all the precedents I can find none so near resembles him as does Sejanus, and him Tacitus describes thus: That he was *[animus] audax, sui obtegens in alios criminator juxta adulator et superbia.*[19] And if your Lordships please to measure him by this, pray see in what they vary. He is bold. We had the experience lately and such a boldness, I dare boldly say, as is seldom heard of. He is secret in his purposes and more, that we have showed already. Is he a slanderer? Is he an accuser? I wish this parliament had not felt it nor that that was before. And for his pride and flattery, what man can judge the greater? So as I think thus far the parallel holds. And now I beseech your Lordships look a little further, tis likewise noted of the other amongst his policies, amongst his arts, that to support himself he did *clientes suos honoribus aut provinciis adornare*—he preferred his friends, he preferred his clients to second, to assist him.[20] And does not this man do the like? Is it not a special cause in our complaint now in the same terms? Does not this kingdom, does not Scotland, does not Ireland speak it?

I will observe but one thing more and end. And that's a note upon Sejanus's pride, his high ambition (as it is there set down), for of his salaciousness, his neglect of counsels, (his veneries, his venefices, those I will not mention, only this particular of his pride which thus I find: that in his public passages and relations he would mix his business with the prince's, seeming to confound their actions),[21] and was after styled *laborum imperatores socios,*[22] his fellow, his companion [f. 84v] in his travails. And does not this man do the like in his whole practice? How often, how lately have we heard it? Did he not in the same place, in this same parliament under color of an explanation for the King, before the committees of both Houses too freely do the same? (Beside that mixture and confusion which you have heard he uses upon the King's estate not leaving a destination in that ? Tis too, too manifest.

I have done. Your Lordships know the man, what have been his actions, whom he is like. I leave him to your judgments.

This only is conceived by us the knights, citizens, and burgesses of the Commons House of parliament: that by him came all our evils. In him we find the causes, on him must be the remedies, and to this end we are now addressed to your Lordships in confidence of the justice to which some late examples and your wisdoms do invite us. We cannot doubt your Lordships the greatness, the power. The practice of the whole world we know to be all inferior to your greater judgments, and from thence we take assurance. To that, therefore, we do refer him. There to be examined, there to be tried, and in due time from thence we shall expect such judgment as his cause merits.

And now, my Lords, I will conclude with a

19. See HofL, 15 May, p. 462, n. 69.

20. See HofL, 15 May, p. 462, n. 70.

21. The section enclosed by the editors in parentheses is omitted from the Lords Journal and garbled or omitted in the printed texts of Eliot's speech (Howell, *ST,* II, 1367–1370; Rushworth, *Hist. Collections,* I, 354–355). Apparently the Bishop of Norwich did not have a copy in hand of Eliot's speech from which to make his report but relied on his own notes.

22. See HofL, 15 May, p. 462, n. 71.

particular censure given on the Bishop of Ely in the time of R. I which I find thus (after a recapitulation of his faults):[23] that having the King's treasures at his command, he had luxuriously abused them, that his obscure kindred were married to earls, barons, and others of great rank and place, that no man's business could be done without his help, that he would not suffer the King's counsel to advise in the affairs of state, that he gave the custody of castles and great trusts *ignotis personis et obscuris*, that he went on in such a [f. 85] height of insolence and pride as he was not fit for mercy. Therefore, says the original, *per totam insulam publice proclamatur pereat qui perdere cuncta festinat opprimatur ne omnes opprimat.*[24]

And now, my Lords, I am to read unto your Lordships the conclusion of this charge and so to present it to your Lordships which thus I find. And the said Commons, by protestation saving to themselves the liberty of exhibiting at any time hereafter any other accusation or impeachment against the said Duke, and also of replying to the answer that the said Duke shall make unto the said articles or to any of them, and of offering further proofs also of the premises or any of them as the case shall require according to the course of parliament, do pray that the said Duke may be put to answer to all and every of the premises and that such proceeding, examination, trial and judgment may be [*illegible*] and used as is agreeable to law and justice.

And now, my Lords, having discharged this trust imposed upon me (unworthy of that honor) and therein made myself too open to your Lordships in the imperfectness which naturally I suffer, I must now crave your Lordships' pardons and become a petitioner for myself that those weaknesses which have appeared in my delivery may, through your noble favors, find excuse for which, as that gentleman, my colleague who first began, made his apology by color of command and mine, my Lords, is likewise spoken in my obedience. I was commanded and I have obeyed. Wherein let me desire your Lordships that, notwithstanding the errors of which I may be guilty, nothing may reflect upon my masters or be from them admitted unto your Lordships' judgments to diminish or impeach the reputation of their wisdoms, which I hope shall give your Lordships and the world such ample testimonies as may approve them in the ancient merits of their fathers, still to be deserving. This for them I crave, and for myself I humbly now submit in confidence of your favors.

23. Marginal note: "*Ex libro de Norwich, apud R. Cott. mil.*". See also, HofL, 15 May, p. 463, n. 72.

24. See HofL, 15 May, p. 463, n. 72.

Order of Business Thursday, 11 May 1626

Thursday, 11 May 1626

I. JOURNAL OF THE HOUSE OF COMMONS

[CJ 858; p. 61]
Jovis, 11 Maii, 2 Caroli Regis

Bill of salmon, this afternoon.

Committee of religion to meet this afternoon, 2 clock.

L. 1a. An act for relief of John Porter, guardian of John Levett, an infant, against a decree made in the Court of Chancery, the 27th day of June in the 20th year of the reign of the late King, of famous memory, between Sir Gerard Sammes, Knight, and John Argoll, Esquire, plaintiffs, and John Porter, defendant.

L. 2a. [Wagstaffe.]

[col. 1]
Knights and burgesses of Warwickshire and Worcestershire
Sir George More
Sir John Stradling
Mr. John Drake
Sir Eubule Thelwall

[col. 2]
Mr. Lowther
Sir Richard Grosvenor
Sir Nicholas Saunders
Mr. [Richard] Spencer
Sir M[aurice] Abbot
Mr. Francis Drake

[col. 3]
Sir George Rivers
Sir Thomas Myddleton
Mr. Whitaker
Sir Thomas Hoby
Sir Francis Barrington
Mr. [William] Cage
Sir J[ames] Perrot

Monday, 2 clock, Exchequer Court.

Committed to

[col. 1]
Mr. [Richard] Spencer
Mr. John Drake
Mr. [John] Thompson
Mr. Whitaker
Sir Robert Quarles
Mr. [Robert] Bateman
Sir Nicholas Saunders
Mr. [Edward] Bysshe

[col. 2]
Sir Richard Grosvenor
Captain [Thomas] Brett
Mr. Francis Drake
Sir Francis Barrington
Sir George More
Sir M[aurice] Abbot
Sir Clement Throckmorton
Sir Richard Buller

[col. 3]
Mr. Owen
Mr. [Christopher] Erle
Mr. Lowther
Sir Thomas Myddleton
Sir William Owen
Sir William Strode
Mr. [Thomas] Wentworth
Mr. [Robert] Bateman

[col. 4]
Sir John Stradling

Tomorrow morning, 7 clock, Court of Wards.

Bave his bill, at the same time.

[CJ 859] *L. 2a.* Hutton.

Committed to

Mr. [Christopher] Wandesford
Sir H[enry] Poole
Sir H[enry] Anderson
Knights and burgesses of Yorkshire[2]
Sir Francis Barrington
Sir John Stradling
Sir A. St. John
Sir John Delavale
Sir Richard Strode
Sir John Fenwick
Mr. [John] Lowther
Mr. [Edward] Littleton

This afternoon, in the Court of Wards.

The committee for the King's revenue, this day, 9 clock.

Mr. Lowther reports Sir Brian Cave's bill; that the committee cast it by one voice to be rejected.

1. Concerning the Astley bill, see HofC, 9 May, n. 2.

2. *and Durham* is crossed out in the MS following *Yorkshire*.

Upon question, not to be recommitted.
Upon question, not to be engrossed.

A petition against one [Gyles][3] with articles read; and a book annexed. Referred to the committee for religion; and the party to be sent for to attend the committee.

SIR NATHANIEL RICH reports from the committee for courts of justice, Grimesdich his petition against the Bishop of Lincoln, Churchill, and the Serjeant at Arms who arrested him. Nothing resolved against the Serjeant, nor against Churchill.[4]

The question, between the coheirs of Sir Roger Aston and Grimesdich £1,140. This claimed by the coheirs of Sir Roger Aston as the proper money of Sir Roger, upon their bill exhibited. Grimesdich, upon his oath, affirmed it was the King's money. At the hearing, Grimesdich proved this: 1, by a note under Sir Roger's hand; 2ly, by another note, wherein, and in his will, all Sir Roger Aston's estate set down under his hand, yet that omitted; 3ly, by a book of account proving payment of it to all the parties.

For the 1st, they said this might be a blank which he used to make to Grimesdich. For the 2nd, that this was not the note delivered Sir Thomas Ireland. For the 3rd, that the hands subscribed to the receipts were not their own. Hereupon, in favor of the plaintiffs, Grimesdich ordered to prove all these.

[p. 63] A commission hereupon awarded;[5] witnesses examined on both parts. The plaintiffs hereupon petitioned the last Lord Keeper who, upon the not entering of the order, suppressed the depositions and decreed £600 against Grimesdich; whereas, if so much due as the committee conceived, the whole £1,140 due.

The letter of the House, 21 *Jac.*, to the Lord Keeper, for rehearing the cause. No rehearing. Fetched up by a serjeant at arms and forced to enter a/[6]

1. The suppression of this proof held irregular, and the proof in this case lawful.

2. This done by a private order in a chamber; Grimesdich not called to it, that being contrary to the King's proclamation.

3. The ground of refusing it, which was the not entering of the order, for which he ought rather to have punished the register whose fault it was not to enter it, rather than prejudice an innocent party.

4ly. That upon the hearing he held the note produced to be false because, upon his own knowledge, £100 therein set down to be lent Grimesdich was given him by Sir Roger Aston, out of his pocket; where this plainly appears to be otherwise.

5. Having thus stripped him of his proof, he commits him close prisoner—no writ, *de executione decreti,* being served.

That[7] the committee waived all matters against the Lord Keeper, he being not in town and therefore could not answer.

The committee of opinion this House should write a letter to the now Lord Keeper, to rehear the cause again, *super totam materiam,* upon all the proofs taken in the cause.[8]

3. I.e., William Gyles, vicar of Elm, a "whorer" and a "drunkard". See Grosvenor, below.

4. John Grimesdich's petition against the Bishop of Lincoln was introduced on 21 February. See HofC, 2 May, n. 32. Regarding Humfrey Leigh, the Serjeant at Arms of the House of Lords who arrested Grimesdich, see 28 February, n. 22.

5. See *CJ,* I, 766.

6. The order of the House on 14 April 1624 was, "That Mr. Churchill shall attend the House *de die in diem,* during the pleasure of the House, and a letter written by Mr. Speaker to the Lord Keeper to have this cause heard again, *super totam materiam,* as he shall think fittest". *CJ,* I, 766.

7. Marginal note: "To the masters in Chancery".

8. *And that the cognizance of £1,000 entered unto by Grimesdich may be suspended till the hearing and yet be then continued for security for Grimesdich's performance what the court upon the hearing shall order, and for nothing else, no other purpose. This, upon question, ordered, this also to be contained in the letter* is crossed out in the MS following *cause.*

Ordered upon question, without 1 negative.

To be desired also in the letter that the recognizance taken may be withdrawn and like new security to be given by Grimesdich.

Ordered, before Grimesdich shall have this letter he shall consent to let Sir G. Hoghton and the rest to have, at their charge, the copies of all such books as he has.

SIR THOMAS HOBY moves the petition for presenting recusants may be now determined.[9]

Bill for quiet of ecclesiastical persons, Saturday, 2 clock.

Bill of excommunication, Monday afternoon.

Sir Nathaniel Rich sent up with the message concerning the committing of the Duke;[10] and Mr. Vice Chamberlain and Chancellor Duchy directed, among others, to accompany him.

Canvey Island bill, tomorrow in the afternoon.[11]

L. 1a. An act for the further punishment of adultery and fornication.

[p. 64] Upon question, the Lord Mordaunt to be spared.[12]

Sir Thomas Compton, being dead, to be stricken out.[13]

SIR NATHANIEL RICH reports from the Lords that they will take the message into their consideration, and in due time send answer by messengers of their[14] own.

Upon question, whether John Preston, a bow-bearer, to be left out; the question 2 put. Question, whether the No or Yea should go out; much debate about it.[15]

A rule that whosoever will have a thing must go out and so get it.

At length the No yielded, and so the division of the House spared.

Upon question, Sir William Yelverton to be left out.

Upon question, the presentment [of] confined persons resorting to London, to be left out.

That of Morgan Voyle, in Flint, to be left out.

Upon question, Mr. Warren, a minister and justice of peace of Suffolk, to be put into the presentment.

II. DIARY OF BULSTRODE WHITELOCKE, ESQ., DD. 12.21, CAMBRIDGE UNIVERSITY LIBRARY

[f. 7]

Maii 11

SIR NATHANIEL RICH reports from the committee for courts of justice, Mr. John Grimesdich his complaints against the Bishop of Lincoln, Mr. Churchill, and Mr. Leigh, Serjeant at Arms.[16] The complaint against Mr. Leigh—and he himself—dismissed by the committee. In regard Churchill's fault, in he committed any, might be sheltered under the last general pardon, the committee likewise dismissed

9. The names had been presented on 27 February by order of the House made on 21 February. Regarding the presentment, see HofC, 27 February, n. 35.

10. I.e., the message drafted on 9 May, see above. The Lords responded that they would send answer by messengers of their own. See HofL, 11 May, OB. And see Buckingham's speech, HofL, 11 May, OB.

11. Preceding the reading of the bill against adultery *Mr. Smith reports Sir D. Deligne's bill* is crossed out in the MS. Regarding the bill for adultery, see Grosvenor, below, and n. 27.

12. I.e., from the presentment of recusants. See the explanation regarding Lord Mordaunt, 3 May, CJ.

13. Regarding Compton, see 3 May, CJ.

14. Printed edition: *our*.

15. Regarding Preston, see above, 3 May, CJ. In the midst of the reading of the recusant list Sir Dudley Digges and Sir John Eliot were summoned to the Tower on a warrant from the King for their parts in the meeting of 8 and 10 May. See Lowther, below.

16. See above, n. 4.

the complaint against him. Bishop of Lincoln's case was this: Sir Roger Aston, Master of the Wardrobe to the King, and Mr. Grimesdich, his deputy. Sir Roger Aston died, 1612, and left his estate to his 4 daughters, some few legacies excepted. After this, question grew between those that married the daughters and Mr. Grimesdich about £1,100. Grimesdich said that this was the King's money. This case heard, 18 *Jac.* Mr. Grimesdich, to show it the King's money, showed 2 notes under Sir Roger [Aston's] hand, and the book of accounts which he kept for the King's money. The counsel for Sir Roger alleged that there should be proofs that those were the same notes and that the accounts should be proved by the parties whose hands were in the book, which was ordered accordingly but the order not entered. After, in the Bishop of Lincoln's time, this petition of those that married the daughters, because the order was not entered. The proofs that were made by Grimesdich were suppressed by a private order, the defendant not called to it, and decreed against the defendant for £600. One of the proofs for one of the notes the Lord Keeper said he knew to be otherwise, but as appeared afterwards was mistaken. The defendant was arrested for not obeying the decree and, being in prison, entered into a recognizance for performing the decree. [f. 7v] The committee concerning the person of the Lord Bishop of Lincoln gave no opinion, he being not heard, but think fit that a letter be written to the Lord Keeper that now is for the rehearing of the cause upon all the proofs in the court.

Ordered, according to the opinion of the committee, to rehear the cause upon the proofs taken by the commission as well as others, and that it be reheard also upon the proofs that will be afforded upon the notes and books examined by 2 masters of the Chancery, and the recognizance to be discharged and a new taken in the same sum for Grimesdich to stand to the decree.

SIR THOMAS HOBY. That the petition concerning popish recusants may have a resolution in the House.[17]

MR. PYM reports from the committee of religion the names of some recusants added to be inserted in the petition to the King, and some to be spared and left out.

Resolved that Lord Mordaunt shall be spared.[18]

SIR NATHANIEL RICH reports that he having delivered the message to the Lords for commitment of the Duke,[19] that the Lords answer that they will take the message into consideration and in due time return answer by messengers of their own.

Resolved that John Preston shall be spared, being but a bow-bearer to the King.[20]

In all cases upon a division, those that are for the introducing of a new thing and would have it done, they must go out; those that would have things stand as they are, they must go out [*sic*].[21]

Resolved, that Sir William Yelverton shall not be presented.

III. DIARY OF SIR RICHARD GROSVENOR, MS 611, TRINITY COLLEGE, DUBLIN

[p. 73]

May 11

1. An act to relieve John Porter, guardian of John Levett, an infant, against a decree

17. I.e., the presentment list. See HofC, 27 February, n. 35.

18. See above, n. 12.

19. See above, n. 10.

20. See above, n. 15.

21. Marginal note: Mr. Brooke. The meaning of the name is unclear, perhaps it is simply the name of the speaker, Christopher Brooke. Customarily in a division those for change go out; those for leaving things as they stand remain in the House.

in Chancery made between Sir Gerard Sammes and John Argoll, plaintiff, and John Porter, defendant.

2. An act for the sale of certain manors, lands, etc., Timothy Wagstaffe, Esq., for the payment of his debts and raising portions for his younger children.

Committed, Monday, Exchequer Court.

2. An act for the naturalizing of Isaac Astley, and Henry Astley, and Bernard Astley, sons of Sir Jacob Astley.[22]

Committed, Court [of] Wards, tomorrow morning. Self one.

2. An act to enable Sir Timothy Hutton and Matthew Hutton for the sale of lands for payment of their debts and estating other lands in lieu thereof.

Committed, Court of Wards, this afternoon.

MR. LOWTHER reported the bill for the sale of Sir Brian Cave's lands for relief of his creditors. That the committee had rejected it by one odd voice.

Rejected.

SIR EDWARD PEYTON delivered a petition against William Gyles, vicar of Elm, in Cambridge and Norfolk; a whorer, a drunkard. Churchwardens chosen by him to waste the parish money; a reviler of his members, calling them knaves, etc. His doctrine: real presence. That Perkins's books will be offered as ballast, slanders Luther, Beza.[23]

Referred to the committee of religion. This afternoon for committee of religion.

[p. 74] Ordered that the vicar should be sent for to attend the committee of religion.

SIR NATHANIEL RICH moved that he might report a business from the committee of courts of justice. They have met only 3 days: the first spent in reading petitions and prescribing rules for their after proceedings.[24] The first petition exhibited by John Grimesdich complaining against the B. of Lincoln, Churchill, [a] register, Serjeant Leigh, and that was for an unlawful arrest, for an unlawful fee taken from him, and for his horse taken from him. For the first: the committee freed him because he was but an officer, and for his fee he showed that he took no more than others had done, and so for his horse; so they dismissed him. For Churchill, the complaint that he had not entered an order made in Chancery according to his oath; his answer was that he had taken the oath and had drawn up the order, but it belonged to another to enter the orders. Another complaint that Churchill had rased and interlined the order after he had written *examinatur*. His excuse: that the Lord Keeper commanded him to alter it thus. This excuse was not allowed for a sworn officer, though by command in a chamber to alter an order made in public court, the committee thought that this fault was within the pardon; *ergo*, dismissed it.

Concerning the B. of Lincoln: 1, the whole cause; 2, the irregularity of justice in this proceeding; 3, the opinion of the committee. The case: Sir Roger Aston, Master of the Wardrobe; Mr. Grimesdich, his deputy, died 1612. He left his estate to 4 daughters and heirs. There grew a question between them and Grimesdich [p. 75] about £1,140 which Sir R. Aston had lent to divers persons and had taken bonds in his own name, so the heirs had a good color. Grimesdich said this was the King's money, not Sir Roger Aston's; so answered in the Chancery when the cause came to a hearing, 18 *Jac.*, before Bacon, L. Keeper. He, to prove it the King's money, showed a note

22. See HofC, 9 May, n. 2.

23. William Perkins, Martin Luther, and Theodore de Beza. Richard Montagu, the Arminian, spoke of Perkins and Beza as "your own dictators". See *PP 1625*, p. 332, n. 15.

24. I.e., 21, 28 February and 2 May.

under Sir R. Aston's hand that these parcels lent was of the King's money. [2.] The next was a note under his hand of all his personal estate, as a preparative to his will. In this, no mention of this sum as his own money. 3. A book of accounts wherein were acquittances subscribed by every man who had received money from the King.

The counsel of the other side said that first note might be a blank, for, he used in that office to give out blanks. For 2, that the same note must be proved to be the same which was delivered to Sir Thomas Ireland. 3, to prove the several hands to the several acquittances.

All this Grimesdich proved in Chancery by commission. Before return of this commission that L. Chancellor was removed and Lincoln succeeded, who must hear this business. These gentlemen, finding that all their allegations were taken away by proof, they petition Lord Keeper that all these proofs might be suppressed because the order was not entered. The proofs were suppressed, and being stripped of his proofs the cause was decreed against him, that he should pay £600, which the committee saw no cause for at all, for if that were due, the £1,140 was also due.

The last parliament wrote to the L. Keeper to hear the cause.[25] He delayed him. Grimesdich went into the country; the L. Keeper sent a serjeant for him, [p. 76] put him in prison, then would not release him till he had entered into a bond of £1,000 to stand to his order.

The irregularity: 1, the suppressing of the proofs; 2, the manner of suppressing, by a private order in his chamber and the defendant not called to it; 3, the ground upon which this was suspended because the order was not entered, for he being a judge of equity should rather have [*illegible*] for this have been punished, than the party have lost his cause for this neglect; 4, the note of Sir R. Aston's own hand: took notice himself that this note might be false because he knew one sum of £100 mentioned to be lent to Dr. Field was not lent. And this was hard that a judge upon his own knowledge should decree against proofs. Last, he decreed this against him: commits him close prisoner and bound him to obey the order, which is against the rules of that court because he should first be served with a writ *de ordine exequenda,* which was not done.

The opinion of the committee to suspend all opinion concerning the person of the Bishop because he was not heard; but thought of the easiest way was to give Mr. Grimesdich relief, that a letter might be written to this L. Keeper that he would be pleased to hear the cause *super totam materiam,* upon the proofs now in court, and that the former recognizance may be suspended till the cause heard and yet remain as a security for him to stand to the order that shall be made if it be made against him.

[p. 77] By question, resolved that such a letter should be written to the Lord Keeper; that the first recognizance should be discharged and another entered into by Mr. Grimesdich to pay such monies as shall be ordered.

Sir Nathaniel Rich sent up with the message about the Duke's commitment. The answer was that they would take the message into consideration and would in due time return an answer by messengers of their own.

MR. SMITH reported the bill for naturalizing Sir Daniel Deligne of Lincolnshire.[26]

1. An act for further punishing of adultery and fornication. Adultery: 1st offense £50, 2d offense £100, and so every time £100. Fornication: 1st offense £30,

25. See above, n. 6.

26. Notice of Smith's report was deleted in the CJ, see above, n. 11.

2d offense £50, and so for each offense. The forfeitures to be employed: 1st, 3d part to the King, another 3d part to the poor, one other 3d part to the informer. If not paid within a month, then double forfeiture. Under a gentlewoman or gentleman of blood to be whipped. If a man and a woman be found in bed together by 2 witnesses, shall be a conviction. To be questioned within 12 months after the offense committed.[27]

This day were Sir Dudley Digges and Sir John Eliot sent for out of the House and by a warrant from his Majesty carried to the Tower; which the House understanding, in a general discontent, broke off in the midst of a report—the Speaker repeating the same concerning those[28] in commission who were recusants or suspected—and refused to proceed but abruptly broke off. No committees meeting in the afternoon, crying "Rise, rise".

IV. DIARY OF JOHN LOWTHER, ESQ., D/LONS/L, CUMBERLAND AND WESTMORLAND RECORD OFFICE

[f. 29]

Thursday [11 May]

Gyles, the person sent for at Balan's suit[29] for his scandalous life and his doctrine and notes in the margin of the book of the Synod of Dort scorning our writers, esteeming most fables and lies.

The[30] Commons, taking into their serious consideration the manifold and apparent mischiefs and inconveniences under which this renowned kingdom suffers, threatening danger to it, have by search of causes found that they do principally flow by the abusive carriage of the Duke of Buckingham, whereof he has been now impeached by us before you, besides an accusation by a peer before you of treason, as we hear. Therefore they with one voice declare, holding it dangerous for present and [f. 29v] future that a man of his eminence so accused should hold such strength and sit as peer to know the counsels. Wherefore thought it duty as by law and reason to commend their unanimous consent as to desire that they will commit the Duke his person to safe keeping.

Lords returned answer by [SIR] NATHANIEL RICH, who carried up the message, that they would return answer by their own messengers and consider of it in due time.

Then were Sir Dudley Digges, who made the prologue or preamble, and Sir John Eliot, who made the epilogue, sent for by two messengers. The Serjeant told them privately that two messengers were come for them, and they did go out and were carried to the Tower. Supposed for their presumptuous carriage or for aggravation and amplification of things and, etc.

All at silence till restored, save they cleared by protestation.

27. This was a new bill for punishment of adultery and fornication drafted after the second reading and commitment of the first bill on 4 March.

28. *offices* is crossed out in the MS following *those*.

29. We are unable to determine what is meant here, perhaps a reference to Balaam.

30. This was the message drafted on 9 May and carried by Sir Nathaniel Rich to the Upper House this day.

Order of Business Friday, 12 May 1626

FRIDAY, 12 MAY 1626

I. JOURNAL OF THE HOUSE OF COMMONS

[CJ 859; p. 64]
Veneris, 12 Maii, 2 Caroli Regis

MR. VICE CHAMBERLAIN. Will speak to the silence of the House, which he desires may continue till he have spoken. Commends Mr. Pym's speech and advice yesterday to do things wisely and temperately, and not tumultuarily.[1] Relates a passage of his at sea where, touching 1st upon one sand then upon another, at last they stuck fast. At length freed, by advice, to look how we came on; and so by the same compass going off whereby they came in, they happily got off. Our compass lies upon this table. To look to that. Have touched before upon the sand, never stuck fast till now. Thus come on by missing our course. Will lay no imputations upon the House; would not have particular man's errors affixed upon the House.

"This man", in the epilogue, without other addition contrary by the 6 who used fair words.[2]

The cause of this: a high offense taken by the King at certain words spoken, as affirmed. That speaking of the plaster he said he would therein spare the honor of the King. This depends upon the point of true, or false, information.

In the epilogue, never heard the like in parliament. Has heard the like when a criminal indicted or accused at a bar. He spoke much against the sense of the House. Speaking of the redelivery of our ships, he said: "They say they are redelivered, but I know it not".[3] Which he spoke, as in the person of the House, where he was informed in the House, and privately told, they were come home.

That in his speech about the plaster he intimated that *aliquid latet quod non patet,* contrary to Sir D. Digges his affirmation in the House.

These the 2 points whereat his Majesty takes offense. Speaks not this by commandment, but as getting knowledge of it by his attendance upon his Majesty.

The remedy: to sink or swim with these, if these have not exceeded their charge; else cut them off, and let us go on.

[CJ 860] Our ship like to be beaten with a terrible tempest from abroad.

That the King will never take new counsels while we do that here which is *dignum nobis.* The like parliaments as ours in other countries, yet all abandoned but here. And the difference between their commons and our exceeding great.

[p. 65] Moves a grand committee to consider of the best remedy for this strait wherein we now are.

1. Upon question, this House not to proceed in any other business until we are righted in our liberties.

2ly. Upon question, a grand committee of

1. Sir Dudley Digges and Sir John Eliot were summoned to the Tower by royal warrant during the course of Pym's report from the committee of religion on the presentment of recusants the previous day (11 May). We find no record of Pym's remarks regarding the imprisonment. Sir S. D'Ewes wrote to Sir M. Stuteville on 11 May and added, "this private news, which I desire you to keep to yourself as your own, by separating this half-sheet and burning it. . . .The King was, this morning, in the Upper House and there complained of Sir John Eliot for comparing the Duke to Sejanus, in which, he said, implicitly he must intend himself Tiberius. Shortly after, about eleven of the clock, he sent both him and Sir Dudley Digges to the Tower". Birch, *Court and Times Charles I,* I, 101. Digges was released on 15 May (see *APC 1625–1626,* pp. 478–479) Eliot, on 19 May (see below).

2. For the report of Eliot's epilogue to the meeting on 10 May, see HofL, 15 May, pp. 460–463. A holograph version of the epilogue is printed at the end of the day's proceedings for 10 May, above. See also, SP 16/26:71.

3. Regarding the return of the ships, see HofL, 13 May, p. 437, n. 125.

the whole House presently to sit to consider of the best way and means for effecting this.

3ly. Ordered, that at this committee none shall go out without first asking leave.[4]

MR. SPEAKER, taking his chair, ordered the Clerk shall attend the subcommittee now appointed to sit this afternoon about the remonstrance.

II. DIARY OF BULSTRODE WHITELOCKE, ESQ., DD. 12.21, CAMBRIDGE UNIVERSITY LIBRARY

[f. 8]

May 12

MR. SPEAKER puts the House in mind where they left yesterday.

The House cry, "No".

MR. WILDE. *Curae leves loquuntur ingentes stupent.* I see a veil of sadness covering the face of this House. Causes of grief in private men are loss of friends and loss of liberty, in a public body this sorrow the greater. And we sitting here have cause to reflect upon this loss. Bewail the want of 2 whose excellent abilities, whose indefatigable labors for preserving these liberties have been fresh in our memories. The cause of their absence I cannot but be bold to desire to know. We cannot think the King will stop his ears to the just complaints of his subjects. Our ancestors said; *Nolumus leges Angliae mutare.*[5] Moves we may consider of some way of remonstrance or declaration to the King concerning this, and desire we may have our members again and that we may punish them if they have done any offense within our cognizance. That we appoint a committee for this.

After long silence, MR. SPEAKER rose and said, "I am sorry to see so general sadness and silence".

The House cry, "Sit down".

But the SPEAKER goes on and repeats the motion.

VICE CHAMBERLAIN. I will speak to the silence of the House, which I pray you continue while I have done. It was well moved yesterday that what we do we should do it gravely and not tumultuously.[6] [f. 8v] In my youth going beyond sea in a ship, in the night we lost our course and the ship first touched upon one sand and then on another and at last stuck fast. At last a wise experienced seaman told us the way to get off the sand is to know how we came on; by that means we came off safe and saved both ship and passengers. I make/

Once or twice this parliament we have touched upon the sand, but never stuck fast till now. We came to stick fast in somewhat missing our course. Mistake me not, I mean not to lay any imputation to the House; no man in this House but may commit errors, and yet the House commit none. I have often observed in parliament that the silent part of the House is the wisest part, but not silence. By an order which was given here to the gentlemen to enforce such matter as they had there to handle, we came upon this sand. The inconvenience of that order I think will force us hereafter not to make the like. For the whole matter, for aught I could perceive, they went no further than as they had in charge, only there might be some slips. In the preface it went very high against a man that stands yet *rectus in curia.*[7]

Hereat the House cries, "No".

4. *but the key to be brought up* is crossed out in the MS following *leave.*

5. "We do not want to change the laws of England". *SR,* 20 H. III, *Provisions of Merton,* c. 9.

6. See above, n. 1.

7. For Digges's introduction, see HofL, 13 May, pp. 408–410; also see copies in SP 16/26:65 and 66. Sir S. D'Ewes wrote to Sir M. Stuteville that, "Sir Dudley Digges [spoke] in the afternoon comparing the Duke to a comet, exhaled out of base and putrid matter". Birch, *Court and Times of Charles I,* I, 100–101.

MR. VICE CHAMBERLAIN. That if he does not, yet he is no condemned man. [f. 9] The epilogue still styled him "this man". For the entrance, it was no new thing. I have seen the like in parliament. Sir Francis Bacon would use many pretty inventions whereby to introduce his matters. And since it has been done, it might be done again. And though he did liken that great peer to a meteor, yet he said there was a sun shining in our firmament. And I think every member is bound to make this House acquainted with what we think to be mischiefs. Our evils are the losses of some members of our House. The causes, a high offense the King takes at certain scandal[ou]s words that passed in that speech, some words in the prologue "that he would therein spare the honor, of the King that is now living",[8] speaking of the plaster applied to King James. I cannot say these were the words, but some strangers in our court could say it, and this depends upon the point of true or false information. In the epilogue, for that I never heard the like in this House. When a criminal has been at the bar I have heard the like, but never at a conference. It did much grieve me that that gentleman did employ his good parts to ill, to his own hurt and to the disadvantage of the cause. In particular points he went directly against the sense of the House. The point of the *Peter* of Newhaven and rendering the ships, but upon this he said: "They say they are restored, but I know it not".[9] He needed not have used so voluntary an ignorance. [f. 9v] In his speech concerning the plaster he left somewhat that seemed *aliquid latet quod non patet*. The sense of this House was that there was no ill intent in the applying of this plaster. I omit many other points. At these two his Majesty takes offense. But I speak not this by commandment. Our remedies must be getting off of this sand whereon we are now stuck. This House is the ship whereon all our fortunes are embarked. If any man commit anything to endanger this ship, cut him off if it be out of the charge and order of the House; but if they do nothing but by our commands, let us sink or swim with them. This ship has many leaks within and without and storms coming from abroad. I have heard a word here of new counsels. The extent of this word has troubled me, but/

This manner of parliament has been almost in every state in Christendom but has been altered by new counsels. To preserve this liberty, the medium between height of prerogative and tumultuary liberty must be observed. Moves that the Speaker may leave the chair and we resolve ourselves into a committee for consideration of this [*sic*] remedies.

[f. 10] SIR BENJAMIN RUDYARD. I heard one thing here spoken of with horror and I beseech that there may be no more spoken of.[10]

MR. KIRTON. That honorable person's speech is subject to as much misunderstanding as that which was said by our members that are now imprisoned. Till we hear what it is why they are imprisoned, we are imprisoned with them and our liberties. I think by the charge laid open by the honorable person they have done nothing but what we commanded them.

MR. CORYTON. For the matter and speeches of coming home of the ships, for my part I know not to this day that they are come home.

SIR NATHANIEL RICH. Our liberties now suffer in a higher manner than ever they did in the memory of man. Moves that we

8. See HofL, 13 May, p. 410.
9. See above, n. 3.
10. Perhaps a reference to the analogy of members as pinnaces in a cockboat to be cut off in a tempest in order to save the ship. See Grosvenor, below.

may resolve first to meddle with no other matter but this.

SIR WILLIAM[11] SPENCER. That Mr. Vice Chamberlain said: that if the King had not been sensible of those things, he had not been worthy to have worn his crown. Desires he may explain these words.

VICE CHAMBERLAIN. *Optimus ille qui minimus urgetur.* Every man is subject to errors and so am I. Those words, "I were not worthy to have the crown on my head if I were not sensible of this", were the King's own words.[12]

Resolved that we shall lay aside all other businesses till we are righted in our liberties.

And the House shall presently resolve into a committee to consider of the ways and means how to effect it.

[f. 10v] Resolved that none shall go forth of this committee without first asking leave.

[*Committee of the Whole House*]

Mr. Rolle takes the chair.

Mr. Wandesford. I think this evil has sprung from the same root which all the rest have done: misinformation. Moves that we may make a humble remonstrance to the King concerning this and tell the cause why we think this is, and for whose benefit. And after declaring the heads, appoint a committee to prepare it.

Sir John Savile. I was committed out of this House, sitting parliament and being a member of this House. And after 3 weeks imprisonment I was at the Council Board and they asked me why I sued not for my liberty. I said I knew not why I was committed. And they told me that if I would know I must ask the Queen, and so sent me back again to prison. But after in the parliament they only petitioned or made a remonstrance to the Queen and I was released. But they would not determine whether the privilege of parliament was broken hereby, nor the cause of my commitment was not known to them.[13]

Sir Thomas Hoby. That Sir John Savile was committed before the parliament sat by the Council Table.[14] I never knew any two sent for out of the House to be committed, and think it a great wound to our privilege.[15] Our remonstrance must be that this is unprecedented, that we are grieved much at it and desire that if the commitment be for anything done at the conference that we may examine [f. 11] it and determine their punishment if their fault be within our cognizance.

Mr. Long. 2 H. 4,[16] upon like occasion to this, the Commons said to the King that no member of this House ought to be committed for anything but felony or treason. This privilege allowed of. Not only these gentlemen are imprisoned but, as I have heard,

11. *Sir Edward Spencer* in Grosvenor and Lowther, see below.

12. See the explanation made by the Vice Chamberlain, in Grosvenor, below. And see the Lord Keeper's reply to the Speaker, HofL, 8 February, p. 35, where he speakes of "his Majesty's piety in attending the hearse of his father".

13. Sir John Savile was brought before the Privy Council in February 1598, presumably for encouraging the clothiers in Hull not to support the levy for a ship for the Cadiz expedition. Hasler, *House of Commons 1558–1603*, III, 351–352. See below, n. 31.

14. The parliamentary session began on 24 October 1597 and ended on 9 February 1598. Savile was committed to the Fleet on 23 October 1597 (*APC 1597–1598*, p. 46). The commitment was within the sixteen-day period of protection by customary privilege of parliament (see HofC, 9 February, n. 25). He was returned from Yorkshire for that session.

15. In 1614 MPs had been imprisoned after the close of the session. See *PP 1614*, index, *sub* imprisonments. In 1621 Sir Edwin Sandys was committed during the adjournment. See *CD 1621*, II, 483–486.

16. *Rot. Parl.*, 2 H. IV, no. 10. See also, *Rot. Parl.*, 5 H. IV, nos. 71 and 78; *Rot. Parl.*, 31 and 32 H. VI, nos. 26–29.

their papers and their studies ransacked, they having been in the chair and taken up most of the proofs.[17] That we should show in our remonstrance that these infringements have been, as we conceive, by occasion of the [Duke] of Buckingham.

Vice Chamberlain. This that I said to be the points that moved the King, I heard him say he heard by 4 or 5. That work was thought to have *aculeum in cauda.* My Lord Duke was not there the last day.[18]

Sir John Savile. That he was committed 14 days after the parliament sat and taken as he was coming into the House.[19]

Sir William Strode. That we should first go to the King and know the cause of their commitment.

Mr. Noy. If they be committed for anything done amongst us, we should know the cause and have the examination thereof, and the parties to be among us.

Resolved that we shall present a remonstrance to the King touching the imprisonment of these 2 members.

[f. 11v] Sir Edwin Sandys. The 1st part of wisdom is to propound a good end. The 2nd part, the means to attain unto that end. Our ends are two in this: to give the King satisfaction, and to get satisfaction to ourselves for the breach of our liberties. In matters where objections are plain, I think it wisdom to anticipate the answer.

Resolved that a subcommittee shall be named for the framing of this remonstrance *super totam materiam* debated here this morning.[20]

The committee named of 20.

III. DIARY OF SIR RICHARD GROSVENOR, MS 611, TRINITY COLLEGE, DUBLIN

[p. 78]

12 May

The House sat long silent, no man offering to speak till MR. WILDE spoke to this purpose. *Parvae curae [leves] loquuntur ingentes stupent.* A sad face has possessed this House: the loss of friends, the loss of members. Can the bowels be taken away and the heart not grieve? For ourselves sitting here as a representative body have cause to reflect upon the like loss. The broad charter of our great inheritance, gained with so great cost, so often confirmed, we ought with all care to convey the same to our posterity as our ancestors have done to us. The consideration of this gives new cause with sense to bewail the want of 2 whose excellent parts and indefatigable labors are fresh in our memories for the service of this House and of the commonwealth. What their offense should be I would with humility desire to understand. If a man be called in question for an offense, though criminal or of what nature soever, if it be followed in a legal course (though it tend to the scandal of the party) yet he can have no remedy. No man but has so much assurance of his own integrity that he would perform all dutiful service to the King, which he can do with respect to the duty he bears the commonwealth. The pain we have taken to inquire into the miseries of the kingdom, etc., are like to perish in a moment. Let us in an humble manner, as becomes subjects, lay open our grief unto the King. He will, as a loving father to his people, apply a remedy to our griefs. In a case of legitimation the answer of the Lords and Commons were:

17. See SP 16/26:72, a contemporary copy of the charges against the Duke endorsed "found in Sir John Eliot's chamber".

18. See the account Dr. Meddus wrote to Rev. J. Mead, 12 May, describing "the second part of the charge against the Duke at what time the Duke himself was absent, as well became him". Harl. 390, ff. 55–56v, printed below, App., II, E.

19. See above, n. 14.

20. The subcommittee membership is not recorded.

Nolumus leges Angliae mutare.[21] Let us go to him with prayers and tears and let him know that we will never part with our liberties, [p. 79] and that we think of some way of remonstrance and to petition his Majesty that we may have our members restored us out of that fatal place, the mortar whereof was made of blood, and that we may be restored to our privileges.

The House sat silent till/

MR. VICE CHAMBERLAIN. I will not speak to the motion because I heard it not, but to the silence of the House which I desire may continue till I have done. It was yesterday very discreetly moved by a gentleman,[22] who merits much, that what we did should be done wisely and gravely, not tumultuously. That was said to still a voice which I have heard now of, "Rise, rise"; and I rise to speak to this stillness, this sad and melancholy silence. But it were a high point of wisdom to find a means to get off that rock on which we are cast almost in the end of our affairs. This puts me in mind of an accident that happened in my youth. It was in one of those many passages I have had by sea when, missing by night of our course, with many other passengers, we touched first upon one sand then upon another, and at last stuck fast; we were all in confusion, we knew not what to do, till an experienced man told us that the way to get off was to find how we came on, and by viewing the compass find in what point we came on. So by casting out of anchors and other diligence by time, bless[ing] of G[od], we came off again and saved both ship and passengers. I make myself one of the passengers in the ship of this House and have a part in our safe sailing to a safe port. But we must choose the means to serve ourselves and to look upon our compass, which lies upon this table; by that we may see how we came upon this sand, and by that means we may see also how to come off. We have now twice touched on this sand but never stuck fast till now. [p. 80] How came we on? Even in somewhat missing our course. I mean to cast no imputation on the House; for I have in former parliaments know[n] the House one or 2 days miss their course and the 3rd day have rectified themselves. And if I light on any particular person and touch upon them I would not have the House entitled to it; for no particular man but may commit errors, yet still the House maintain the reputation of not committing errors. I have oft observed that the silent part of the House is the wisest, so it be not as this is a silence opinionated. But let us inquire why and how came we upon this sand whereon we now stick. It was by an order which was given here to those gentlemen who were to deliver the matter of charge for the Lords to enforce those matters. Yet, however the order was well done, I think it not fit for us to go so uncertain a course as to give liberty at large. The gentlemen performed the matter very well, but there was a preface and there was a conclusion. For the whole matter we went not out of the compass of the charge unless it were some slip, which, *ergo,* I will let it sleep. But for the preface and conclusion—that went beyond the matter, very high against the man who yet stands *rectus in curia,* yet upright. If he were not so, I am sure he was no condemned man; yet was he named in a contemptible and [*blank*], "this man" and "the man".[23] The rest did it materially, mannerly, effectually. I cannot say the other did so: who really touched upon the matter but fell more angrily upon "the man", still styling him "a man" and "the man". For the entrance, it was no new thing. I have seen the like in parliament before; I have known Sir F. Bacon would use many pretty inventions,

21. See above, n. 5.

22. I.e., John Pym. See above, n. 1.

23. See above, n. 2.

poetical and historical, to introduce his matter [p. 81] somewhat. I say in condemnation in his speech, for though he likened that great peer to a meteor, or comet, for yet that presupposed that there was a sun still in our firmament much to the honor of the King. And though we have no complaint here against him, yet everyone ought to acquaint us, the House, with what he knows.

The evil we suffer is we lack some of our necessary members; they are taken from us in this service. The cause is a high offense the King takes at certain scandals and words passed in that speech touching the end of the last King which was inferred as hastened by a drink and plaster. Therein he said particularly that he would therein spare the King's honor now living. *Ergo,* marvels not though the King be sensible of it; nay, it is the belief of strangers in our court that such words were uttered. If he were not sensible of it he were not worthy to wear the crown, *ut* this depends of true or false information. In the epilogue—what should I say? For the latter an epilogue I never heard the like in this House. I have heard the like when a criminal has been indicted at the bar, but at a conference with the Lords in a parliamentary proceeding I never saw it. I should speak sparely in this if private respects could take away my public service. He that has patience in his own affairs has some in another man's. As I respect the good opinion of this House, it grieve my heart that that gentleman did misapply those good parts to his own disgrace and disadvantage of the cause. It was an invective of such a kind as in many particulars against the sense of this House, [p. 82] a sense he had studied much and would defend it as his own child. Somewhat in the *Peter,* of Newhaven; thence, he flew to the putting the ships into the French King's hand. When he came to the restoring of the ships he said: "They say they are restored, but I know it not"; which, speaking from the House, it must be understood the House knows it not.[24] He was in this House when it was spoken that they were come into our ports. What need he then to have used some voluntary ignorance.

In the other point of applying the plaster, he applied his speech as though something were in that head which was not discovered; whereas the House thought there was no ill intention. And shall the contrary then be said to the House? Many other things I observed. I will not make myself an advocate to plead against him; I wish he had not been an advocate to have reflected upon himself. So I have related the evils and the cause, now to the remedy. I must return to the similitude, to look upon our compass and to know how to get off. Pardon me if I be studious to think of a fit remedy, it is the saving of the ship wherein our lives, means, and honors are embarked; and let us make any particular member, myself also, but as a pinnace in a cockboat, and in a tempest let us cut off the boat to save the ship. And if any man in this House do anything against the order of the House to endanger the ship, cut him off; else, if he has said nothing but by your command, you must maintain him. [p. 83] But if they have exceeded their commission and provoked the King's displeasure so that our ship is in danger to be beaten with a terrible tempest abroad, we have then great cause to save the ship if possible and bring it to a safe port, though it be by cutting them off, and I would save it as it is, except such faults as you shall acknowledge. I have heard in this House a word of new counsels. His Majesty's love to us is such that so long as we carry ourselves as fitting dutiful subjects toward so good a prince, he will not take new counsels. This kind of parliament has been formerly in most kingdoms, but in most monarchy is changed by

24. See above, n. 3.

new counsels, for when they changed their parliamentary liberty into tumultuary endeavors, it was changed by the sovereign to another form of government. We are the happiest of nations. In this kingdom I see men look like men; they have flesh on their backs and clothes to cover that flesh. In other places the men look like ghosts, their bodies clothed with canvas suits and wooden shoes. I dare not name the nation, for what I have spoken has been delivered out of this House, translated into French, put into the ambassadors' hands to my disgrace. Somebody is much to blame for it. I say somebody, not the House. My zeal to save this ship transports me for, unless the dangers will be corrected, the ship will sink of itself. Brings me back to come off the same way we came on. We began in a great committee to help ourselves in our grievances. We are now in a great extremity worthy of the consideration of the House. Then to come out of the extremity, this will not be [by] the silence I found you in, nor by length of speech, but by replying one to another and so to think of a fitting course.

[p. 84] SIR BENJAMIN RUDYARD. This House is conscious to itself, and we have carried ourselves dutifully to the House. I heard the word with some horror; I pray we may not hear any more of it.

MR. KIRTON. What the 2 gentlemen did was by command of the House. Till we know what they were committed for, we were all committed with them. That gentleman (Mr. Vice Chamberlain) has given them a charge. Moved that he might set it down in writing, then a committee to examine whether they spoke such words or not.

MR. CORYTON. We are on a rock. We must look from heaven for assistance and integrity to secure us. If these gentlemen have exceeded their limits, I shall be ready to condemn them. They were commanded from this House to expose the truth of the facts as they were able. I think they did it faithfully with a great deal of sufficiency. For the stay of the ship, however it might be a child of his, it was the opinion of the House. For the royal ship, it was amplified no further than the matter would bear. For his saying he knew not that they were come home; no more do I. I hear it and I believe it, but I know it not. I am glad to hear they have done no greater crimes. Moved for a committee to examine the same.

SIR NATHANIEL RICH. We are now a little out of the way, for it is an improper question to debate whether these things laid to these gentlemen's charges are so or not, and I am glad no greater matters against them. [p. 85] If we show any opinion now we shall prejudice ourselves more than we are prejudiced by the act. If these gentlemen had been here and been accused, the wisdom of this House would have examined it to the bottom and given his Majesty satisfaction. Every man's heart here is grieved within him, when he sees the liberties of the kingdom do suffer and in so high a nature as ever was in the memory of man. What shall we do? First, put to the question that we, conceiving our liberties are touched, we apply ourselves to that and not to intermix with other business. And I hope that God that has brought us off will also now, though we seem to be dashed all to pieces. Then to a committee to consider what is fit for us to do.

SIR EDWARD[25] SPENCER. Some of Mr. Vice Chamberlain's words stuck with me, viz.: that if the King had not been sensible of some things said, he had not been worthy of his crown. No man but will think him worthy whatever he speaks or does.

MR. VICE CHAMBERLAIN explained him-

25. *Sir William Spencer* in Whitelocke, see above.

self. What I said in that kind was said by the King, viz., that if he were not tender of this point of the death of his father, he was not worthy to wear the crown.[26]

MR. ROUS. This gentleman has interpreted himself. I wish the same favor may be allowed other members of the House, and then I hope all will be well.

[p. 86] SIR G. MORE. We are all free born and I hope we stay free men. We are called hither freely to advise the King and one another. Let us lay down our sense and feeling we have for the loss of our members and how we have labored from the beginning to do that which may be for the honor of the King and kingdom.

Moved that the question should be this before, our addition of these words: "wherein we conceive our liberties to be infringed".[27]

MR. BROWNE would not have the word "righted", but, "till it be determined".

SIR ROBERT HARLEY. If we "right" not our liberties we do nothing; not to waive that word.

SIR JOHN SAVILE. That the word "righted" was not fit, because that showed that we were wronged. Let us not judge till we have examined it.

By question, resolved that the House should not proceed in any other business till we be righted in our privileges.

Resolved by question that the House should presently be resolved into a committee.

By question, ordered that none shall go forth of the committee without leave.

The Speaker went forth and Mr. Rolle called in.

[*Committee of the Whole House*]

Mr. Wandesford. What it is to lose a member every man knows, but to lose 2 members in this case concerns us more than ordinary. To search into it and to right ourselves. I have heard there has [been] a member taken out in parliament but never heard that 2 members should be taken out,[28] we never knew when nor for what before the House acquainted with it. [p. 87] I think this information has sprung from the same root that all the rest have done. If we look upon the many diversions we have had and consider the times, nay, may see from whence all this is. Moved for a remonstrance to his Majesty and therein to deliver plainly whom we think to be the cause of this, and to let his Majesty know that he is the cause of all our grief and that we expect justice from him; he is the man that interposes between the King and his people. Let us go to a remonstrance, then to a subcommittee to prepare the heads. Wished that they might be heard to explain themselves, as Mr. Vice Chamberlain was, and he doubted not but they would clear themselves. And that as we do dutifully to the King, so resolutely that we go to our countries with the same liberties we brought up.

Sir John Savile. That he had served in this House 3 princes' time.[29] That he himself was committed out of this House sitting the parliament. I continued prisoner 3 weeks, then called to the Council Table and demanded by Lord Burghley why he sued not to be released. He answered, because he knew not wherefore he was committed. The answer was that if he would know that, he must go to the Queen, so was sent back again. Sir Edmund Knyvet moved in this House the same, in effect: that he being committed it might be declared a breach of

26. See above, n. 12.
27. See the questions, CJ, above.
28. It is unclear to whom he refers. See above, n. 15.
29. I.e., under three sovereigns, Elizabeth, James, and Charles.

privilege.[30] Moved for a remonstrance that it might be demanded to be set down what he had offended in. The House then agreed to let her Majesty only know that a member was committed and desired to know the reason of. He was presently released. He thought it fit to make a remonstrance and therein not to ground anything upon what was delivered by Mr. Vice Chamberlain [p. 88] but to touch therein that 2 of our members are imprisoned, which may concern the privileges of this House.

Sir Thomas Hoby said he was of the parliament when Sir John Savile was committed, but he was committed by the Council before the House sat. That Sir Edmund Knyvet never made such a motion, neither did the House ever desire his liberty.[31] Where we find ourselves wounded in our privileges, there we are wronged. I never knew 2 sent for out of the House to be committed. The very commitment is a great wounding of our privileges, for if any of us offend before the Lords they must either accuse them or we. If they, they must send down their charge and we should have allowed them their answer and explanation. Our remonstrance must be this: that it is without precedent, and a grievance against a privilege; and to move the King that if there have been offenses done in the Lords House or this, they may come hither to make their answers.

Mr. Long. The imprisonment of these gentlemen grieved me as much as any. I have endeavored to know whether ever precedent. I hear of none, only one in Q[ueen] Elizabeth's time that spoke in the House what the House upheld him not in.[32] I have heard of a precedent 2 H. 4, when upon such an occasion the Commons showed the King that no member should be committed but for felony or treason, and that spoken in his hearing.[33] That Buckingham is cause of all this, for all our interruptions have happened when his business has been in handling. [p. 89] These gentlemen were employed in the examining of these offenses of the Duke. Their papers are taken and seized on, we know not whether all the proofs are gone.[34] We ought to make such a remonstrance there in this infringement of our liberty, that we have our members and their papers; to preserve our honor, and maintain what we have done.

Mr. Vice Chamberlain. That we should not ground this remonstrance upon the Duke as cause. First, to fasten upon him as a misinformer we cannot, for the King said he heard it of 3 or 4. For the first day, being there, he might inform as well as any other, but the other day when the conclusion had *aculeum in cauda,* a sting in the tail; for, he not being there, could not inform.[35]

Sir John Savile. That the parliament had sat 10 if not 14 days before he was committed. He was taken at the bar, coming into the House, and was brought to the Council Chamber, and therein committed.[36]

Sir William Strode. That we take notice that 2 members are taken forth of our House by the King's command. Let us move the King to know the cause, and then we shall apply ourselves to that which shall be

30. See below, n. 31.

31. See above, n. 14. Henry Knyvet spoke on 2 March 1593 regarding the privileges of the House. See Hasler, *House of Commons,* II, p. 423.

32. Perhaps the case of Peter Wentworth, imprisoned with others in 1593 for holding a meeting or conference before the session. No member came to their defense. See Neale, *Elizabeth I and her Parliaments,* II, 255–260; Hasler, *House of Commons 1558–1603.* See also, above, nn. 13 and 14; Thomas Wentworth's speech, below, and HofC, 17 May, n. 9.

33. See above, n. 16.

34. See above, n. 17.

35. See above, n. 18.

36. See above, n. 14.

best. I would meddle neither with the Duke nor with precedents as yet.

Mr. Noy. Let us not prejudice ourselves; to be righted signifies to be rectified, supposes no wrong. It will be necessary for us to make a declaration to the King and let that contain certain things. That we miss 2 members; we understand they are imprisoned by his command. Be suitors that he will impart the occasion. If it be foreign, nothing concerning us; then we may proceed. If concerning ourselves, if they were things done by our command, then we as faulty as they. If they have exceeded their commission, then that we will be ready to punish them [p. 90] and that the parties may be sent among us, otherwise we cannot charge them, nor they answer. And in the meantime that precedents may be forborne; and when we know the reason, precedents may be best employed.

Sir Robert Harley. By way of remonstrance that we beseech the King that he would be pleased to declare the cause of the imprisonment of our 2 members. When we have an answer we may proceed as we find cause, and to petition him if for anything done before us to restore them to our judicature; and this to be by the Speaker and the whole House.

Mr. Coryton.

Sir Richard Hutton. The House inclines to a remonstrance, but him to go to his Majesty by petition. To acknowledge his grace and power to dissolve us.[37] That we may have our members. If they have done anything in this House, that we will examine.

Mr. Newbery. That in every monarchy there is a government by law and by prerogative. If these clash, a certain token of ruin. These 2 are taken away by his prerogative; if we ask him the cause, he is not bound to tell it. That we move him to have them sent us to answer their offenses here, or else that we may go all to lie with them there.

By question, resolved that this House should present unto his Majesty a remonstrance touching the imprisonment of our two members.

Sir Nathaniel Rich. That he could not be persuaded that all his Majesty's displeasure was only for words spoken at the conference. But that there has been some ill information to his Majesty of all our proceedings. Wished that we declare all our proceedings and crave a release, that we may proceed with alacrity; otherwise the kingdom would be in great danger.

[p. 91] Mr. Browne. Touching the manner and frame of this remonstrance: 1, to declare with what a ready mind we came hither to serve him, how cheerfully we have proceeded; next, to declare what interruptions we have had so that we cannot go on so cheerfully as we should have done; then, that by taking our members out of our House we conceive our privileges violated. I have heard of Mr. Wentworth committed, but this was for speaking of a successor, which was treason.[38] He had no charge to speak it and the House disavowed him. These gentlemen in a miserable case. If they had refused the service, you would have sent them to the Tower. Now they have done our command, they are sent thither. This is a great breach of privilege to take them away before they be heard to answer for themselves.

Mr. Wentworth. That his father was committed before the parliament about the

37. The power to summon and dissolve parliament rested with the crown. See Coke, *Fourth Inst.*, pp. 4, 26–27.

38. See above, n. 32 and see the speech of Thomas Wentworth, Peter Wentworth's son, below.

matter of succession because he and others had secret conference to move it in parliament.

Mr. Sherwill. For the heads: 1, a declaration of the matter of fact—2 of our members imprisoned; 2, our apprehension that our liberties is by that broken; 3, a declaration from the beginning of the parliament of our hearty desires to do good service and our hopes that we shall bring happiness to the state; 4, the miseries that must ensue upon the commonwealth if we still have such interruptions; 5, that to the end we may perfect what we have begun, that he would restore us our members without whom we cannot proceed.

Sir G. More. 1, the care we have had for the good of the kingdom; 2, the impediments that have hindered us in that cause; 3, how we are disheartened by taking away our members; 4, by a petition of right for the restoring of these members that so we might freely go on in that course wherein we begun.

[p. 92] Sir Thomas Hoby. For a subcommittee to think of the manner of the remonstrance.

Mr. Sherland. We are not ripe for a subcommittee, for first you must provide for them the general materials that they may have a ground to work on.

Sir Edwin Sandys. In a matter of this high nature wherein we have to deal with the King, not fit to put it upon a subcommittee. They only to frame the manner. For the matter of the remonstrance: not to make a declaration of all our proceedings, for this is already done in our remonstrance which he has accepted of and gave us leave to go on. The first part of wisdom is to propound a good end; 2, to find the means. We must go about to satisfy his Majesty. He has proceeded with us sweetly this parliament; he has requested, not commanded. In Dr. Turner's speech and Mr. Coke's, he referred their words to our trial.[39] He put us in mind of it. To let him know that we were going about that business that we should.

That after, we had dispatched the great matter against the Duke and testified what we went about to supply him. And now we were going on to the perfecting of the rest of the business in hand, which hitherto we could not do by reason of the many interruptions. And for these 2 imprisoned gentlemen, draw our right; and that whereas we understand that his Majesty has committed them for doing the command of the House, that he would be pleased to refer the deciding of the cause to the Houses before whom the words were spoken.

[p. 93][40] By question, resolved that a subcommittee should be named to draw a remonstrance to the King upon the whole business debated this day.

20 named of the subcommittee, Court of Wards this day, 2 of clock.[41]

Sir Dudley Digges's charge: That in speaking of the plaster and potion he said he could speak more but he would not for sparing the King's honor; hence, an inference that something was done which might not be related for questioning the King's honor.

IV. DIARY OF JOHN LOWTHER, ESQ., D/LONS/L, CUMBERLAND AND WESTMORLAND RECORD OFFICE

[f. 29a]

[12 May]

VICE CHAMBERLAIN. Where we in silence, desires to continue it till done. Notes Pym to have moved well to proceed wisely to stay

39. See the King's message, HofC, 14 March, OB.

40. Preceding the question the names *Mr. Pym* and *Sir H. May* are crossed out in the MS.

41. See above, n. 20.

the cry of rising. He rises to speak to waken the silence. He thinks it time to get off the rock we fallen upon.

Tells his story. He at sea out of way, fall on divers sands. At length stuck. At a maze. One stood up to see which way we came on. By the compass, went same way back.

He now a passenger, not the pilot. Desires to look how we came on, and so to go off. We had like touches before, never stuck until now. Desires time to think how we came on: in missing our course. Former parliaments have done it and rectified themselves. If he fall on particulars, desires the House not to apply it to the House. Found in former parliaments the silencer part, the wisest. So it be not in opinionality as now. We came onto the rock by an order to give them leave to enforce their matter at the conference. Proved a meeting, but what did enforce matter we bound to maintain by six. The matter went within compass except a slip, but for preface and conclusion against a man, [f. 29av] he saying he yet *rectus in curia*.

Cried, "No", by many.

Offered to stay if we weary. If not *rectus*, not condemned. They called him still, "this man, this man". Prologue and epilogue still touched on him, "this man, this man". Sir F. Bacon used to introduce his matter by poetry and history, a man most elegant. Though likened to a meteor, yet was [*illegible*] our King. Everyone bound to find causes of evils and remedies. Evil: they taken away; he hears, for scandal in words taken by King touching the point of King's death as though it were hastened. Prologue: said because said he would therein forbear to speak further in regard of the King's honor that is now living. King [has] reason to be sensible, for strangers in court believe it was said. This depends of true or false information. Epilogue: he heard never the like in parliament but when a criminal at bar for treason. Speaks not out of offense given him by his sharp speech, for he had patience.

He grieved to hear him dishonor himself; dishonor himself and the cause as he protested. This not in his charge, but he went against the sense of the House. A point he studied much, [f. 30] made it his child, as the ship *St. Peter*. Went to Rochelle: "They say restored, but I know it not"; he said it by obedience. He was informed in House and private; what needed he such voluntary ignorance to enforce? In the plaster, as though *aliquid latet quod non patet*. Left evil. Believe this not directed; but the House declared that there was no evil intent. Observes many other points but will not be an advocate against him. His own pleading too much does reflect upon him.

The evil and the cause, now to remedy. All lives, fortunes, and honors here embarked. If any do to endanger ship, though a cockboat, cut him off. We danger of tempest from abroad. Need therefore to care to save it. Without alteration. He has heard new counsels (meaning from King) brought hither. Knows not whither it may reach, but while we do worthily, will not. All other monarchies changed by new counsels the medium between prerogative and tumultuary license. This way to preserve it. We here in happiness look like men, in other nations like ghosts in canvas and wooden shoes. What he said here sent out in their language, given to ambassador. This speech exceedingly disliked though I see not the cause. [f. 30v] Somebody much to blame for it.

We began in this business in a great committee, now in great extremity. Therefore desires a great committee to consider and to reason pro and con.

SIR BENJAMIN RUDYARD. Conscious we dutiful [to] King. He heard one word spoken, would no more.

KIRTON thinks Vice Chamberlain's word subject to as great interpretation. They imprisoned; with them, we. Desires he may set down their charge, then we at committee to consider whether the House did authorize them.

CORYTON commends their learning and knowledge and believes/

N. RICH thinks we should show no opinion. Glad to hear it is no worse from him. Far from us to justify what not in charge. No man here but grieves to see our liberty suffer as now in high measure as ever in man's memory.

First therefore to desire solely to proceed for our liberty, then to have a grand committee to do it.

EDWARD SPENCER. Such words and no plots. If those words were said by Vice Chamberlain—[f. 31] that the King if he should not be sensible of something, he were not worthy of his crown—he desired to explain.

[VICE CHAMBERLAIN.] He explains he delivered nothing by command. He told what he conceived cause. Because he did none no more. The King said if he should not be sensible of his father's death he were not worthy of his crown, for so the King said.

ROUS approves the interp[retation].

Resolved by question to proceed in no other business until righted in our liberties.

Resolved by question to have great committee to consider how to do it.

Moved to have key up at committee.

CHANCELLOR EXCHEQUER moves against that as a fundamental law of House, though once done at this parliament.

Ordered to have the key because when it is disliked many great persons draw with them near.

[*Committee of the Whole House*]

Wandesford. Glad to see how advisedly we proceed. Has heard a member taken out of parliament; two, for they know not what, never heard. Root of all: misinformation. If we look back, easy to see cause. Desires remonstrance. [f. 31v] Desires to move King to right that Duke the misinformer, and to have our liberties home.

Sir John Savile. Served in 3 princes' times. He committed out of the House 3 weeks, heard nothing. He asked of lords why sued not for the deliver[y]. He asked the cause, sent back to go to Queen. L. Knyvet moved for him as now to have a petition to Queen to know cause.[42] House answered, would not conclude privilege broken. House petitioned to know the cause. Delivered, no cause assigned. Wishes a mannerly remonstrance. To ground nothing of Vice Chamberlain.

Sir Thomas Hoby. Hear that said he was committed by Council before parliament sat, but he will in modesty conceal the cause.

Finds the whole sense of the House grieved. If for offense at conference, we or Lords should have taken it, and called answer. But sent for without cause known unprecedented but to find no cause.

Long. 2 H. 4, Commons showed no person committed but for treason and felony and [*illegible*] and that in King's presence. He thinks Duke always cause. [f. 32] Hears they, their papers, and lodgings ransacked. He in his opinion condemned. Hopes none so impudent as to testify otherwise than here. Desires all to be restored.

[Sir] John Savile. Was taken upon the door of the House 10 days after parliament began.

42. See above, n. 31.

Noy. If committed for things foreign, we satisfied; if by our command, to justify; if exceed, to condemn. If we charge Duke, if untrue, dishonor to us. Likes no precedents until cause known. Reason the best precedent.

Sir Richard Hutton.

Newbery. King to give account to God, not to us; and cause: if prerogative and laws clash, ruin of kingdom. Laws here violated. Desires to have restitution and we punish them, else we all to go lie there since they by our command.

Remonstrance ordered to be made by question for the imprisonment of 2 members. And to show how good purposes and proceeding we had and how interrupted and how we intend to proceed to his honor.

V. DIARY OF SIR NATHANIEL RICH, HIST. COLLECT. 143, HLRO

[f.87v]

[12 May]

May 12, Friday, the day after Sir D. Digges and Sir John Eliot committed.

MR. WILDE. 2 causes of grief to private men: loss of friends, liberty. These both light upon this body. Desires to know the cause the law is that if a man be called in question for any cause a grief excessive to lose *tot tantos exanclatos labores*.

What to do. The King *parens patriae*. Then to lay open our griefs and smarts unto him, let us not doubt. In the case of legitimation when they were, etc.: *Nolumus leges Angliae mutare*. To prostrate ourselves before the King with prayers and tears, to pray that those liberties and privileges left us by our ancestors may be preserved, and that we may have our members.

MR. VICE CHAMBERLAIN. I will not speak to the last motion but to the silence which I [desire] to continue till I have done. It was yesterday discreetly moved by a gentleman of much merit that what is done in this case should be done gravely and not tumultuously. I speak to this still sad and melancholy silence. It is a high point of wisdom to get off that rock on which we are now cast. It puts me in mind of an accident in my youth in a passage by sea. We touched first on one sand and then on another and then stuck fast; we knowing not what to do, one told us the way to get off was to examine how we came on. So we did, and got off. I am a passenger in this ship and engaged in the voyage. We have touched on sands this parliament but never [stuck] fast till now, and now so fast that no man offers to speak to get off. I think that we have been out of our course. I pray entitle not the House to the faults of any particular man who may fail and be told of them. The silent part of the House is the wisest part of the House, so as it be not as this a silence of opiniastrety.

We came upon this sand by reason of an order given to those six gentlemen to enforce the parts of that charge. We are bound, whatever was within the body of the charge we are to maintain. The matter was delivered by six persons and in this we went not out of the compass of the charge, except it were a slip and so shall sleep. But the preface and conclusion were from the matter and fell upon the man who stands *rectus in curia*.

"No, no".

The style of the epilogue was "this man, this man".

For the entrance, it was no new thing. Sir Francis Bacon would use many pretty inventions, poetical and historical, to introduce the matter. The question is the more or less. I commend that speech, but though he compared this great peer to a comet, yet he spoke honorable of the King that shined in our firmament. The evil is that we want our members. But the King took offense at certain words in that speech concerning the poisoning of the last King. He said in that he would spare [f. 88] the King's honor in that business. Marvel not that the King is troubled at this; if he were not, he were unworthy to wear the crown which is upon his head.

For the epilogue, he never heard the like unless to a criminal at the bar for felony or treason, but not at a conference with the Lords. Fears lest it may be thought he did meditate revenge for he had sufficient satisfaction that he heard a sharp speech not applauded by the House. It grieved him that that gentleman did employ those good parts to great dishonor himself and disadvantage of this House. And yet not to be condemned if allowed by the House, but he spoke against the sense of the House as in this. For the ships of Newhaven and lending the ships to the French, this was well aggravated, but he said "they say they were restored, but I know it not", which must be understood of this House. And he was told it in the House. And in the point of the physic given to the King, his speech tended to this: *aliquid latet quod non patet;* this was contrary to the sense of the House who held no suspicion. Of his knowledge, these are 2 things that his Majesty took offense at: the evil, their suffering; the cause is related. Now for the remedy. The way to get off is to cut these men off if they have gone beyond the bounds of their command. This kingdom in danger to be beaten with a terrible tempest from abroad, it behooves us to save the ship if we can. The word[s] new counsels often spoke in these walls; he knows not what to do. *Dum quod te dignum est facis,* he will never entertain new counsels. This kind of parliaments have been in all monarchies but changed by new counsels while the height of prerogative and parliamentary liberty in a tumultuary license did strive. But in this House and kingdom we look like men; in other places they look rather like ghosts than men. While he says somebody, he says not the House which will not allow such courses.

Moves for a general committee to debate this business.

SIR BENJAMIN RUDYARD. This House conscious how warily and dutifully spoken of the King. He has heard something with horror, desires it may not be spoken.

MR. KIRTON. We all imprisoned in our liberties with these gentlemen.

[f. 88v] MR. CORYTON. The best way to come off is honesty and integrity.

Note D. D[igges's] exception: he would spare the King's honor in that business.

Sir J. Eliot, for saying, "that man, that man"; 2ly, that he knew not whether the ships were delivered; 3ly, that in that matter of the physic given the King, *aliquid latet quod non patet.*

SIR G. MORE. To express our grief for loss of our liberty to justify our proceedings.

Ordered that no business shall be proceeded in until we be righted in our liberties, and the way how to effect this referred presently to a committee of the whole House.

[*Committee of the Whole House*]

Mr. Wandesford. This a new thing and proceeds from misinformation. But one way to right ourselves, by a remonstrance. To set down the cause of this misinformation—a great peer who he thinks not clear because impeached. And now he se[e]s this one way left: to tell his Majesty that we hold the Duke the cause of all our griefs and that we hope the power of the prince will never be interposed.

The heads. That our liberties wounded, sensible of that and of the cause of it; of the Duke of Buckingham, and for his own defense because this cause no question.

Sir John Savile. A wrong is a wrong whether by misinformation or otherwise.

He was committed out of this House sitting parliament, continued prisoner and heard nothing; after 3 weeks called to the Council Board and asked why he did not petition. He answered, because he knew not the cause. His answer was short: that he must ask that of the Queen. There was a remonstrance from the House. Would have this remonstrance now made and wishes it had [been] made many years ago, then had he not lain by the heels 7 weeks.

Sir Thomas Hoby. He served when Sir John Savile was committed; but this was before the parliament, by the Council. It was moved in parliament they did not desire his liberty. We are hurt in our privileges; [f. 89] he never knew two sent for out of the House. He stands not upon the cause, the very commitment a wound to our privileges. If any exceptions had been taken, it should have been either by the Lords or by this House. If by this/

Our remonstrance must be that this is unprecedented.

Mr. Long. He has but a short memory and therefore desires to speak till it be in his memory. This commitment not by information of the Lords, for they were not possessed of it nor by/

2 H. 4. No[ne] of the Common[s] House ought to be imprisoned but for felony or treason. This liberty broken by the means of the Duke. All the disturbances of this parliament have been when his business has been in agitation. We cannot proceed in the examination of the business concerning the Duke till those men be present to prove their parts.

Vice Chamberlain. We find that the King is highly offended. The King said he heard this by 4 or 5. The Duke could not inform the King of the last day's work because he was not present.

Sir William Strode. To take notice of the commitment of 2 members; to go to the King and know the cause.

Mr. Noy. This word "righted" imports "rectified"; it does not imply wrong. In our declaration to mention things true and certain, not doubtful; as that our members are imprisoned. To pray him to impart us the cause. If it concerns things concerning ourselves, then we are interested. Not to mention/

Mr. Kirton. That the Duke has hindered the good proceedings of the commonwealth and desire him to put no man in balance with the commonwealth.

Sir Robert Harley. To know the cause of it.

Coryton. Whoever stands between the King and his subjects, he the worst of subjects.

Mr. Newbery. Not to call to the King for a cause, who is only bound to give account to God of his doings. Our members taken away against law.

[f. 89v] Mr. Browne. 1, to declare with what a willing mind we came to serve him and how we have applied ourselves to that; 2, what interruptions we have had that we could not proceed as we would; 3, concerning our own liberties violated by taking away those 2 men, but this without all precedent. Mr. Wentworth meddled with that which was almost accounted High Treason, to talk of a successor. This a high point, had no authority to speak of it. Those gentlemen, if they had refused the service, they would have been sent to the Tower; hard now to send them that they have done their service. It is strange to cut them off unheard. To declare our right of free speech. 4, to pray the King to restore them back to us and that we may judge them according.

Mr. Wentworth. His father was committed before the parliament sat because he had consulted with others.

Mr. Sherfield.[43] Declaration of the fact; 2ly, how sensible we of it that our birthright, our liberty, taken from us; 3ly, declaration of our intention and proceedings this parliament and of our hopes to bring happiness to the state; and of the great extremities and mischiefs if we be hindered; lastly, that we may go on with the great work we have.

Sir G. More. 1, to lay down the proceedings of this parliament; 2ly, the impediments that have taken us from doing that we intended; 3ly, to allege the taking away of our members; 4, a petition of right, for that our liberties infringed. To desire their restitution, that we may go on cheerfully [with] what we have begun.

43. *Sherwill* in Grosvenor, see above.

Order of Business Saturday, 13 May 1626

SATURDAY, 13 MAY 1626

I. JOURNAL OF THE HOUSE OF COMMONS

[CJ 860; p. 65]
Sabatti, 13 Maii, 2 Caroli [*Regis*]

Prayers being said, the committee about the privileges of the House, sat.[1]

MR. ROLLE reports from this committee the words delivered whereat his Majesty had taken offense at Sir D. Digges,[2] viz., that he should say, by the command of the House, upon the particular of the plaster applied to the body of the late King, that he did forbear to speak any further in regard of the King's honor; or words to that effect.

That the committee has resolved 1, that a solemn protestation shall be made by every member of this House: 1. Whether he did consent/

Upon question, this protestation shall be taken by all the members of this House.[3]

2ly. The names to be called by the book.

3ly. All that are absent to make the like protestation, when they come.

Upon question, this to be done presently.

Upon question, all that have now made default, as soon as they come to the House, before they give their voice, to take the like protestation.

II. DIARY OF BULSTRODE WHITELOCKE, ESQ., DD. 12.22, CAMBRIDGE UNIVERSITY LIBRARY

[f. 11v]

Maii 13

Mr. Rolle takes the chair.

[*Committee of the Whole House*]

Mr. Littleton reports from the subcommittee for preparing the remonstrance.[4] That they found that the words whereupon Sir Dudley Digges was committed/

The matter whereupon the King took offense at Sir Dudley Digges was that he should say by the commandment of the House,[5] upon the particular of the plaster applied to his late Majesty, that he forbore to speak any further in regard of the King's honor, or words to that effect. The committee found this a matter of too great weight for their consideration and caused the report of it for the consideration of the grand committee.

Sir Benjamin Rudyard. That man had a venomous nature that either suffered or hatched this point. And it concerns highly the honor [f. 12] of this House to find out the author or inventor of this mischief.

Vice Chamberlain. Let us engage ourselves with judgment and discretion. It was not one man but 4 or 5 that informed the King of this, as I heard the King himself say. I think they were as far mistaken as it is possible for men to be. I will undertake that all good offices are done by those that are members of this House near the King.

His Majesty, upon my request and desire of him to know what were the words that his Majesty took [offense] at of Sir Dudley Digges, said the very same words that Mr. Littleton had reported. And I telling his Majesty that the committee stopped at

1. I.e., the grand committee to discuss the infringements of the privileges of the House by the imprisonment of Digges and Eliot. Mr. Rolle was in the chair, see below.

2. For Digges's introduction at the meeting with the Upper House (8 May), see HofL, 13 May, pp. 408–410. The passage in question was with regard to the last charge, see HofL, p. 410. Digges was reported to have said: "The last of the charges that are prepared will be an injury offered to the person of the late King. . . . But upon this occasion I am commanded by the Commons to take care of the honor of the King our sovereign that lives, and long may he live". For the speeches in the committee of the whole, see the accounts below. See also, the Millington letter of [8 May], SP 16/26:67, App., II, E.

3. For the words of the protestation, see Grosvenor, below. Members took the protestation over the next several days, see below.

4. I.e., the subcommittee appointed yesterday (12 May).

5. See above, n. 2.

those words and said that if he spoke them he was not worthy to live; his Majesty was extremely tender of the tenderness of the committee of his honor in this point, and said which I inform you of by leave: They take it as they should do, but I was far from imagining it was the sense of that House. And therefore, taking dislike at some particular persons, I took the same course which my predecessors have done in matters of like nature. And said that Sir Dudley Digges might in the abundance of his speech paraphrase upon the text, and yet from the point and matter.

Mr. Kirton. That we may make a remonstrance to the King upon this particular and desire we may know these informers and they may be punished that are in fault.

Sir Nathaniel Rich. I cannot [think] these words of such prodigious nature could be spoken and all we so stupid as not to [f. 12v] take notice of them and apprehend the speaker of them.

Mr. Littleton. Upon my life, Sir Dudley Digges said no such thing as these words. But as far as I remember, he spoke to this effect: My Lords, the Commons have commanded me to let your Lordships know that in all their inquisitions concerning the Duke of Buckingham they have not found anything that tends to the dishonor of the late King or the King that now is.

Sir Francis Stewart. Whosoever informed these words, he is a traitor in his heart.

Mr. Coryton moves that we may have a conference with the Lords about this matter and let them know the words, and both of us together go to the King about it.

Mr. Pym. That every member of this House that was present at that conference should make a solemn protestation that he never heard these words, and that such a protestation be entered in the book, and that we go to the Lords and acquaint them that we are both Houses charged with the silent hearing of the greatest treason that can be against the King, and both go to the King and desire that the traitors may be known to be punished.

Mr. Littleton. That everyone may say: I protest before God and the body of the Commons, by the faith of a Christian, that I heard [f. 13] not these words nor any to this effect.

Sir Nathaniel Rich. That every man should protest first whether he gave any consent to the speaking of those words, 2nd whether he heard any such words spoken, 3rd whether he does believe that they were spoken or not.

Sir Thomas Lake. That it be added: nor did not report them to the King nor to any other body with intent to have them reported to the King.

Mr. Sherfield. That they may say: nor did to any person affirm them to be spoken.

Sir Nathaniel Rich. That he may say likewise whether he knows of any man that did inform the King of it, but that the King's sworn counsel may be spared from this last words.

Mr. Glanville. That every man should protest: Whether did you consent that those words or any words to such effect should be spoken by Sir Dudley Digges, or did hear any such words spoken, or believe that any such were spoken by him, or did report them to the King or know or hear who did report them to the King.

Resolved that there shall be a solemn protestation. And shall be contained in the protestation: that every man shall say whether he did consent that those words or any words to such effect should be spoken by Sir Dudley Digges, or did hear any such words spoken by him, or believe that any such words were spoken by him, or whether he did ever affirm that Sir Dudley Digges spoke these words or words to this effect, and that the [f. 13v] Clerk shall call them by the book and those that are absent shall afterwards make the like protestation.

Speaker takes his chair.

MR. ROLLE reports the resolutions of the grand committee.[6]

Ordered accordingly by the House.

The Clerk calling them in order, every particular member in the House as he was called made his protestation before God, and the House, and by the faith of a Christian, that he did not give his consent that Sir Dudley Digges should speak those words wherewith he is charged, nor words to the like effect; that he did not hear them, he did not believe that he did speak them, nor affirm to anybody that he did speak those words or words to the like effect.

III. DIARY OF SIR RICHARD GROSVENOR, MS 611, TRINITY COLLEGE, DUBLIN

[p. 93]

May 13

The Speaker came in, said prayers, and then went forth. Mr. Rolle came in.

[*Committee of the Whole House*]

Mr. Littleton reported what the subcommittee had done about the remonstrance. That they had caused him to take in writing the words that Mr. Vice Chamberlain said [of] Sir Dudley D[igges].[7]

The words these: The matter whereupon the King took offense at Sir D[udley] D[igges] was that he should say by command of the House, in the particular of the plaster applied to his late Majesty, that he forbore to speak any further in regard of the King's honor, or words to that effect.

Sir Benjamin Rudyard. Nothing more precious to the people than the honor of their sovereign, which has made this parliament so careful, so tender, as not to put any scandal upon the King's government, much more not upon his sacred person, which, when I heard a sound of, I could not hear it with patience. Fame will fly abroad and such a report will go of his Majesty and this parliament that my heart abhors it, and what tongue dares speak it! That man has a venomous tongue that ever hatched this point. I hope his Majesty will be sensible of that odor which stinks in the nose of God and man. It [is] fit [for] us to bring to punishment the author of this villainy, whether he that spoke it or he that poisoned[8] it.

[p. 94] Sir Dudley Carleton. I do much approve the sense Sir B[enjamin] R[udyard] has of this matter amongst us and likewise of his private engagement which is a public engagement, for we are all interested in it. But let us engage ourselves with judgment and discretion and take things rightly as they are and then we shall have no shame of our proceedings.

Quis quod recipitur/

A man's word so taken and received that they are carried to a contrary construction. Not that I would bring anything new to be discussed of, that not fit. *Ad modum recipientis:* it was not one or 2 that informed the King of this but 4 or 5, for so his Majesty said.[9] Had there been but one I would have been so discreet to let it fall, let the man be buried rather than such a word be spoken. But if so many came to the King there might be many more who were mistaken, as I think they were as far as men might be.

6. See the CJ, above.

7. See the Vice Chamberlain's speech, 12 May; and see above, n. 2.

8. *Poisoned* is crossed out in the MS and *or him that poisoned it* is added. See also Rudyard's speech in Lowther, below.

9. I.e., privately to Sir Dudley Carleton. See Whitelocke, above, and Lowther, below.

I like his motion that would have us light on that point of misinformation, for the inference when it was a number to no purpose. We are on a tender point, and as in consideration of the many great affairs now in parliament, and in regard of the loss of time, as yesterday, I broke a still and sad silence, whereby we might go on in our affairs. So I was loath we should wander in a mist, and that made me freely desire the cause of the evil which caused our silence, and that was the words which I related to you. I was not of the subcommittee, but finding it [*illegible*] by some, though disliked by others, I studied to conform myself to the [p. 95] sense of the whole House, to be there and not to be there. And think well of us that are near the King concerning carriage of things abroad, good offices. As I was there present, and did freely satisfy them touching the words, I was demanded what authority I had. I answered, the authority of truth, but that made me think necessary to require more. And now more I have, for attending his Majesty at supper time I beseeched his Majesty to know what were the words he took so highly offensive at Sir Dudley Digges. He repeated the same words. I desired to have them in writing. He said no, for he had many and all to that purpose. I told him the committee was so tender of that that they held the speaker of them unworthy of life. He made this his answer: The House takes it as they should do, but I was far from imagining there was any such sense in that House; for if I had, I should not have stayed thus long from sending them a sharp message. And *ergo*, having taken offense against [*blank*] I took the like course as my predecessors have done against parties that they have taken offense at for matter of high nature. I did think when I first heard it that Sir D. Digges might use a paraphrase upon the text but far from the text.

Mr. Kirton. That we might make a remonstrance of this particular to the King. That if we were guilty, we might suffer; if not, the party that goes about to set dissension between the King and people.[10]

[p. 96] Sir Nathaniel Rich. He has no English heart but of a traitor that can hear and consider of what latitude this charge is that does not apply himself to vindicate the honor of King and kingdom which, if highly touched in this, it implies that which my soul abhors to think. I dare not speak of it; if I must, this prodigious monster, whoever, has gone about to lay the greatest dishonor upon the King that can be. Shall such words be spoken before both Houses of parliament and neither be sensible of them? But this must be carried by a private information.

1. For the clearing of the honor of this House: I wish every man in particular show his zeal, his affection, and protest that he never thought such a thing nor never heard such a thing. We had all ears, we harkened and observed his words; such words to be spoken and we not hear were impossible. *Ergo,* we may say in this case they were not spoken, nay, he declared himself otherwise. First, that we may clear ourselves that we abhorred such words and that we never heard them, nay, I should have hardly held violent hands off him.

Mr. Littleton. I stood near him and observed him and I dare say on my life that he spoke no such words, nay, I say more, that he said as much as might be for the honor of both the King/

These words he spoke: The Commons have commanded me to declare that in all their inquisitions against the Duke of Buckingham they have not found anything at all that might reflect or touch upon his late Majesty nor the present King.

10. Kirton was cleared of casting an aspersion on the Vice Chamberlain, see below.

[p. 97] Sir Francis Stewart. The House was wary and commanded that nothing should be sent that might trench upon anything against the King's.

There is a water that will turn all things to stone. Such are they that convey these things into the ears of that just King. They that do it are traitors in their hearts; I will justify it in any place of the world. Fame flies fast, loses nothing in the journey. Let us move his Majesty that we may know who these are, that we may know the foul hearts of traitors from the loyal hearts of his best subjects.

Sir G. More. I conceive I never heard anything better delivered with more duty to the King and to the House, or better to the sense of the House.

Mr. Coryton. This concerns the whole kingdom. That we desire a conference with the Lords that we may join together to petition the King to know the men that have done us this injury.

Mr. Pym. Fit that it should be solemnly done by every particular member to protest before God and his allegiance that he heard no such words. Then a solemn protestation that there was no such direction given by the House. Then to go to the Lords and tell them that we are both accused to hear the greatest treason that ever was spoken, to desire the King that the party might be produced and receive the reward of the greatest traitor.

Sir H. May. As false reports do harm, so false suspicions do a great deal of harm; for Mr. Kirton doubted Mr. Vice Chamberlain to be the informer, but he has made an honorable satisfaction by saying he rests satisfied. I like the way propounded; I heard no Lord or other but cleared Sir D. Digges.

[p. 98] Mr. Kirton excused himself and said that if he had named no man he might have thought him the author.

Mr. Vice Chamberlain said openly: Thank you for nothing.

Then Mr. Kirton required the justice of the House that parliament men should not thus be baffled.

The House cried: To the chair.

Sir Robert Mansell. Say the gentlemen had mistaken one another. Wished that we might proceed in unity, for now the time was unseasonable.

Sir D. Carleton. That every man might say these words: I heard no such words, nor words to that effect.

Mr. Littleton. That everyone should speak these words: I protest before God on the faith of a Christian and before this representative body of the Commons that I heard no such words; neither did I tell it to the King nor to any other man.

Sir Nathaniel Rich. These words protested:

1. That he gave no consent to the speaking of such words.

2. That he heard no such words spoken.

3. That he does believe they were not spoken.

Sir T. Lake. [To be added:] nor did report them to the King nor any other with intent they should be carried to the King.

Mr. Sherfield.[11] Be added: neither have I affirmed to the King or any other person that those words were spoken.

4. Whether he affirmed to any that he ever heard them.

5. Whether he ever heard who informed the King with them.

Mr. Glanville. These words:

1. That he consented not that those

11. *Mr. Pym* is crossed out in the MS and *Mr. Sherfield* is inserted.

words or any others to that effect should be spoken by Sir D. D[igges].

2. Nor did hear or believe that such words were spoken by him.

3. Or reported them to the King or did know or hear who reported them to the King.

[p. 99] By question, resolved that every member should make a solemn protestation. That it should be contained in this protestation:

1. Whether he did give consent that Sir D. D[igges] should speak the words mentioned or words to that effect.

2. Whether he did hear those or any such words spoken by Sir D. D[igges].

3. Whether he do believe that Sir D. D[igges] did speak those or any such words.

4. Whether he have affirmed that Sir D. D[igges] did speak those words or any other to that effect.

The Speaker went into the chair and MR. ROLLE reported what was resolved at the committee, which was by question resolved in the House and confirmed.

The House was called by the book and every man made his protestation accordingly.

My protestation: I protest by the faith I owe to God as a Christian and by the duty I owe this House as a member that I never gave consent that Sir Dudley Digges should speak the words mentioned, or any words to that effect. That I did never hear, or believe, or ever affirmed that he spoke those or any other words to that effect. [*Blank*]

[p. 100] Sir R. Grosvenor[12]

We have dealt discreetly and answerable to the reputation of this House in the carriage of the last business concerning Sir Dudley Digges wherein we proceeded with as much respect to the honor of our sovereign as ever subjects did. Yet not altogether without regard to ourselves, to our own privileges. We were not rash in our proceedings but dealt deliberately, well knowing that of Livy to be true. *Temeritas praeterquam quod stulta, est etiam infaelix:* rashness, besides that, is foolish, [*illegible*], for the most part unfortunate.[13] And that also of Thucydides. *Celeritas et ira duo sunt adversissima [illegible] menti:* haste and anger are great enemies to settled and calm dispositions.[14]

We have found, Sir, that some (ill affected to the prosperous and good success of this House) have, by the engine of a crafty wit, labored to sow the seeds of dissension between the King and his people. These have gone about by their false surmises to supplant our hopes, to undermine our desires (which have aimed at nothing beyond the honor of his Majesty, the prosperity of his kingdoms) and I hope before they have found a means (whoever they be) to plant their own assurance.

We have done discreetly in proceeding so deliberately for, as wildfire is put out by milk, so I hope his Majesty's favor will be restored us in a full measure by rendering to us all our rights; when he shall see and find that we oppose only the shield of reason and truth against those venomous shafts of falsehood and untruth which have been shot against the truest hearts which ever king was possessed of.

For favor comes by forbearing, not by force.

[p. 101] We ever find it true by experience that the traps and treasons of this world are most commonly bent against those who are best inclined. We have had our parts of such practices, but by this time (I hope) by hear-

12. What follows is a speech drafted by Grosvenor but apparently not delivered in the House. The image of a wildfire put out by milk was used in his draft speech of 23 April 1628, see *PP 1628,* III, 52.

13. Livy, *History of Rome,* XXII, 38, 12.

14. Thucydides, *Peloponnesian War,* III, 42, 1.

ing what we censure such to be, they are sensible of their own villainy and understand the truth of that in Tacitus: *Perfecto demum scelere magnitudine euis intelligatur.*[15]

And though they should think themselves to be as yet but in their full career, yet assuredly they have hitherto followed the chase of their violent and virulent desires to blemish and obscure our labors and honors, even to their own destruction, which fortune I shall ever wish to those who shall attempt to wrest in pieces that chain, to break asunder that cord which links and ties, and unites the hearts and affections of the Prince and people together.

And I hope his Majesty will now at last discover the wicked intentions of these firebrands and imitate God himself who, as St. Bernard tells us, is *Sapiens nummularius, qui nummum fractum non recipit,*[16] is so perfect a money teller that he cannot be cozened with false and counterfeit coin.

Sir, as we have begun in this mild and moderate way to examine the business of one of our members (which has thus happily succeeded),[17] so my motion is that we proceed and go on in the same method to inquire of the other; and I hope we shall find him as guiltless and as free from error and just exception. And therein, if that noble gentleman who first informed us of the exception taken against the former, would be pleased also to do us the like favor in the latter; he should add to his merit from this House so much to forward our business, wherein we cannot proceed till we shall by one means or other be acquainted with his charge.

[p. 102] And when we shall understand the nature of his supposed offense, we may address ourselves to such a way of disquisition as may sort with the matter, and with the honor and justice of this House.

So shall we best discover the truth of his errors, if he have committed any, and be enabled either to censure or acquit him.

Truth will in time prevail, and *mendacia diu non fallunt.* Lies cannot long deceive the judgment of a just prince, so willing to embrace truth.

IV. DIARY OF JOHN LOWTHER, ESQ., D/LONS/L, CUMBERLAND AND WESTMORLAND RECORD OFFICE

[f. 32v]

Saturday [13 May]

Sir B. Rudyard. King's honor to be most dear to us. We therefore shunned aspersion of King's government much less his honor. Fame will by growing spread such reports all over. *Quod recipitur est secundum modum recipientis.* We to bring to punishment him that spoke it or him that poisoned it. Now we all engaged in it.

Vice Chamberlain desires to engage ourselves with judgment and discretion. He finds *modum recipientis* spoken here, carried with contrary instruction. Not one man informed King of this, but four or five, which King yesterday informed him of again. If they were mistaken, he thinks more might be. He does think they were mistaken. Desires to fall on the information because a ticklish point. Let's know for loss of time now spent that as yesterday broke silence, and yesterday satisfied what was spoken. Asked his authority for speech; had but truth. At supper he asked King cause of offense at D. Digges in particular. He desired to put it in writing. King said no, it was the sense of divers. He said to King how tender we; that he not worthy to live that spoke them or commanded. King said House did take it right, thinks House commanded not. He took like cou[r]se there-

15. Tacitus, *Annals,* XIV, 10, 1.

16. St. Bernard. Grosvenor included a note of this citation from St. Bernard on p. 1 of his diary. See the Introduction, *PP 1626,* I, 9.

17. I.e., Sir Dudley Digges.

fore as his predecessors did in like case. Thought D. D[igges] used it [f. 33] as a paraphrase of the text, far from the text. And so this he said by explanation.

Kirton. He has well acquitted[18] himself before we take him for the author. If they did it by our command, we guilty. To desire King to have agents punished, for thinks it treason in highest degree to set this division between King and people.

Sir Nathaniel Rich thinks him as a traitor that does not endeavor to vindicate honor of King and kingdom which this prodigious traitor has raised. Shall neither Commons nor Lords take notice? And yet it came to King. Therefore to declare he spoke not to say this, nor to this effect, nor so commanded by us, nor we heard it not.

Littleton. Stood by and on his life said no such thing, and spoke to King's honor. Said: My Lords, the Commons commanded that in all they have not found anything that reflected on King's honor that dead is, or is now.

Sir F. Stewart. Whoever informed are traitors in heart, which he will prove.

Resolved by question that everyone shall protest before God that he never counseled [*sic*] that D. Digges should/

2. That he heard him not speak those words.

3. That he believed not that he spoke them.

4. That he did not affirm he spoke the words or to that effect.

This was done, and who sick gone unto.[19]

18. Possibly *acquainted*.

19. For the list of those members who were sick and took the protestation from a visiting committee, see below, 15 May.

ORDER OF BUSINESS MONDAY, 15 MAY 1626

Committee for going to MPs who are sick to receive their **protestations** concerning the words spoken by **Digges** at the conference of 8 and 10 May: appointed	263, *13/5; 16/5
Resolved: other MPs in town are to make their protestation in the House tomorrow morning	263
SIR HENEAGE FINCH (Speaker): makes his protestation	263(2)
SIR NATHANIEL RICH: moves for a **conference** with the Lords	263
Resolved: to desire a conference with the Lords by committee of both Houses	263
Resolved: the former **subcommittee** for drawing a **remonstrance** to the King is made a committee for considering **heads** for this **conference**	263(2), *17/5; 19/5; 20/5; 22/5; 3/6; 5/6; 6/6; 10/6; 12/6; 13/6

Monday, 15 May 1626

I. JOURNAL OF THE HOUSE OF COMMONS

[**CJ 860;** p. 66]

Lunae, 15 Maii, 2 Caroli Regis

Sir Edwin Sandys, Sir John Rous,[1] Sir Clement Throckmorton,[2] Mr. Whitby, Mr. Thomas Gurlyn, Sir John Skeffington.

Sir Francis Barrington, Sir Thomas Hoby, Sir George Fane, Sir Francis Barnham, Sir Thomas Barrington, [and] Mr. Long to repair to these several persons, being sick in town, and to receive their protestations in like manner as others of this House have here made. This to be set down in writing under the hands of the protestants and of these which take them. 3 to go to 3, and the other 3 to the 3 residue.

Those members of the House which are in town, peremptorily, to make their protestation tomorrow morning.[3]

Mr. Speaker makes his protestation in like manner.

Sir Nathaniel Rich moves to have this our proceeding in this manner to be solemnly entered here, and a conference to be prayed with the Lords by a general committee of both Houses concerning matters much importing both their House and this.

Upon question, to pray[4] a conference with the Lords by a committee of both Houses upon some matters of importance concerning the honor of both Houses.

The former subcommittee of [*blank*] to set down the heads of this conference. Mr. Glanville to be enjoined to attend this service. They to meet in the Star Chamber, at 2 clock in the afternoon.

II. DIARY OF BULSTRODE WHITELOCKE, ESQ., DD. 12.22, CAMBRIDGE UNIVERSITY LIBRARY

[f. 14]

Maii 15

Some that protested not before, protest to the like effect as the rest.

Resolved to pray a conference with the Lords by a committee of both Houses upon some matters of importance concerning the honor of both Houses, and the subcommittee appointed for the remonstrance to consider of the heads by way of preparation for this conference.

III. DIARY OF SIR RICHARD GROSVENOR, MS 611, TRINITY COLLEGE, DUBLIN

[p. 102]

[15 May]

Upon Monday, the 15th day, the bird called a kingfisher flew in at the window of the House and fled up and down till a gentleman took it alive in his hand and turned it forth at another window. Some saying it came to complain of the Lord Admiral because the Narrow Seas were lost and she was disturbed by the Dunkirk[ers].[5]

1. Either Sir John Rous of Dunwich, Suffolk or Sir John Rowse of Worcestershire.

2. *Mr. Gewen* is crossed out in the MS and *Sir Cl. Throckmorton* is inserted.

3. For the protestation regarding the speeches of Digges and Eliot at the meeting of both Houses, 8 and 10 May, see above, 13 May. Members of the Upper House took a similar protestation this day, see HofL, 15 May, p. 482, and n. 168.

4. *demand* is crossed out in the MS and *pray* is inserted.

5. The entrance of the kingfisher was also reported in a letter to Spain, see SP 16/27:36.

Order of Business Tuesday, 16 May 1626

Members make **protestation** concerning the words spoken by **Digges** at the conference of 8 and 10 May [*see below*]	266, *13/5
Thomas Jermyn: makes his protestation	265, 266
Jermyn is questioned about part of his protestation and is given time until tomorrow to answer	265, 266, *17/5
Sir Dudley Digges: makes his protestation and thanks the House for their care of him	265, 266, 267
Resolved: Thomas Lawley to make his protestation in the House tomorrow	265
Report from the committee for going to MPs who are sick in town to receive their protestations: bring in and read those protestations	265, 266, *15/5
Mr. Clarke: moves that John **Colley,** servant to Francis Smalman, MP, be given privilege from arrest	265, 266, *23/5
Resolved: Colley to have privilege	265, 266
Sir Dudley Digges	266
Message from the King regarding the **commitment** of **Digges** and **Eliot** (Sir Richard Weston, Chancellor Exchequer) [*see above and below*]	265, 266, 267, *11/5
Sir Nathaniel Rich	266
Edward Kirton	266
Sir John Strangways: moves that the word "extrajudicial" be explained	265, 266, 267
Sir Richard Weston (Chancellor Exchequer)	265
Sir Thomas Grantham	266
Resolved: to consider the King's message further tomorrow morning	265, 266
Sir John Hotham: moves that the other MPs who delivered the charge against the Duke of Buckingham at the conference (meeting) of 8 and 10 May be cleared	267
Resolved: the MPs who delivered the body of the charge at the conference (meeting) 8 and 10 May did not exceed their commission from the House	265, 267
Edward Kirton: moves that Sir John Eliot also be cleared by vote of the House	267
House defers Kirton's motion until after further consideration of the King's message [*see above*]	267

TUESDAY, 16 MAY 1626

I. JOURNAL OF THE HOUSE OF COMMONS

[CJ 860; p. 66]
Martis, 16 Maii, 2 Caroli Regis

MR. THOMAS JERMYN, making his protestation concerning Sir D. Digges his words, protests his not consenting, his not hearing, his not affirming those words, or words of any such effect; but, for the believing, says he heard them spoken in such presence as he cannot but believe he spoke them.

Time given him till tomorrow morning to make his full answer in the House.[1]

SIR D. DIGGES makes his protestation fully and that, as these were far from his words, so they never came into his thoughts. Gives great thanks to the House for their respect of him, and that he has received a most gracious testimony from his Majesty of his satisfaction. Desires his occasion may not longer hinder the service of the House.

Mr. Lawley peremptorily to be here tomorrow morning to make his protestation.

The protestations of Sir Edwin Sandys, Sir John Rous,[2] Mr. Whitby, Sir Clement Throckmorton, Sir John Skeffington, and Mr. Thomas Gurlyn under their hands, and subscribed by the committee appointed to take them, brought into the House and read.

MR. CLARKE moves that John Colley, servant to Mr. Smalman, was yesterday arrested and taken in execution, and there detained.

John Colley to have privilege. A warrant for a *habeas corpus* to bring him hither.[3]

[p. 67] MR. CHANCELLOR OF THE EXCHEQUER. That the King very careful not to enter upon our privileges; whereof has given good testimony by his proceedings with Sir D. Digges. That the King informed by the sight of many notes there taken, that words, to the effect of the words charged, were spoken by Sir D. Digges; but having heard/

That Sir John Eliot's business of another nature. Although his Majesty, by the information given him, dislikes the whole manner of his delivery of that which he had commandment from this House to speak, that the King charges Sir John Eliot with things extrajudicial to this House and therefore wishes we should proceed on cheerfully with the business of the House, resting upon his Majesty that he will by no means violate any of our privileges.

It being desired that the word "extrajudicial" might be explained,[4] MR. CHANCELLOR said it was his Majesty's word and therefore cannot do it without his Majesty's leave; but will move the King for his leave, and then willingly satisfy the House.

Upon question, to take this message into consideration tomorrow morning.

Upon question, Mr. Herbert not exceeded his commission given to him by this House in anything which passed from him in the conference with the Lords.

The like for Mr. Selden, Mr. Glanville, Mr. Sherland, Mr. Pym, Mr. Wandesford.[5]

1. For Jermyn's explanation, see below, 17 May, OB.

2. See HofC, 15 May, CJ, and n. 1; and HofC, 13 May, n. 19. These were the members too ill to come into the House.

3. Colley was brought in on 23 May and discharged. See below.

4. I.e., desired by Sir John Strangways; see Whitelocke, below. As late as 18 May the House believed Eliot to have been imprisoned "for some words spoken in parliament". Bevil Grenville to his wife, 18 May 1626. Roger Granville, *History of the Granville Family* (Exeter, 1895), p. 161. See also, 19 May, n. 1. When examined on 18 May Eliot was questioned about being around Gray's Inn the previous Sunday (14 May) and about his meeting with foreign ambassadors, all of which he denied.

5. I.e., the assistants at the meeting of 8 and 10 May.

II. DIARY OF BULSTRODE WHITELOCKE, ESQ., DD. 12.22, CAMBRIDGE UNIVERSITY LIBRARY

[f. 14]

Maii 16

Sir Dudley Digges being at liberty and sitting in the House.

Some that protested not before protest to the like effect as before.

Only MR. THOMAS JERMYN protests that he did not consent, nor hear, nor affirm that those words were spoken by Sir Dudley Digges with which he is charged; but to the point of belief, he said that he heard it from such that he cannot but believe that he spoke them.

Being called upon to name them, he desires that he may know the King's pleasure first, because he heard it in the King's presence.

Mr. Thomas Jermyn has time till tomorrow to make his answer.

SIR DUDLEY DIGGES gives thanks to the House for their care of him, a poor member, and makes his protestation that those words were never in his thoughts. Says that he has received a great deal of grace [f. 14v] from the King and desires the House, if it shall so please them, that nothing concerning him may divert the business of the commonwealth.

The committee brings in protestations from several members that are sick.

MR. CLARKE[6] moves to know whether the House will take consideration of an obstinate and willful breach of the liberties of the House notwithstanding the last order made:[7] the arrest of Mr. Smalman's man in execution yesterday.

Resolved that he shall have his privilege.

SIR DUDLEY DIGGES moves that a course may be taken as speedily as may be for the/

CHANCELLOR EXCHEQUER. I am commanded by his Majesty to tell this House that would not/

The ground of his commitment was that his Majesty hearing that he spoke some words in the latter end of his speech which has been formerly told you, but since finding not so, his Majesty has graciously released him and sent him hither.

In the case of Sir John Eliot, his business is something of another nature. His Majesty believes that he exceeded his commission of this House; charges him with some things that are extrajudicial to this House, and if he detain him somewhat longer he hopes you will not take this as a breach of the privilege of this House. And desires that you would proceed with the business of this House.

[f. 15] SIR NATHANIEL RICH. That this gracious message is of great importance and I not so well prepared as to speak to it on the sudden. Moves that tomorrow morning we may take this message into consideration, and in the meantime the order of the House to stand unreversed.

MR. KIRTON. That we may now clear Sir John Eliot.

SIR JOHN STRANGWAYS moves that the word "extrajudicial" might be understood and explained.

SIR THOMAS GRANTHAM moves that Sir John Eliot's charge may be laid down, whereby we may the better judge.

Resolved, to take the King's message into consideration tomorrow morning.

6. MS: *Clearke.*

7. On 12 May the House had resolved "not to proceed in any other business until we are righted in our liberties". Clarke's motion was in regard to the arrest of John Colley. See above, n. 3.

SIR JOHN HOTHAM moves that the 6 men that delivered the body of the charge against the Duke may be cleared, or punished if any man can object against them.

Resolved that Mr. Herbert has not exceeded his commission that he had from the House in anything that passed from him in the conference which we prayed with the Lords, nor Mr. Selden, nor Mr. Glanville, nor Mr. Sherland, nor Mr. Pym, nor Mr. Wandesford.

MR. KIRTON moves that Sir John Eliot may now also be cleared by the vote of the House as the rest have been. That he has not exceeded his commission.

The House puts it off until they have had consideration of the King's message this day sent.

III. DIARY OF JOHN LOWTHER, ESQ., D/LONS/L, CUMBERLAND AND WESTMORLAND RECORD OFFICE

[f. 33]

[16 May]

And so, the House having cleared itself and the members of those [f. 33v] speeches by Sir D. Digges, notice was taken of it at court by the King and Council. Sir D. Digges sent out of the Tower without any petition and came into the House the next day being Tuesday.

[SIR DUDLEY DIGGES.] There gave thanks to the House, showed the King's grace to him and his content. Desired to proceed and petition for Eliot which he thought would do.

And then the CHANCELLOR OF EXCHEQUER delivered a message from King how King satisfied, was cleared. Loath to infringe privileges, yet Eliot detained for matters extrajudicial also.

That word after desired to be explained, but nothing done nor agreed to be done until privileges righted.

Order of Business Wednesday, 17 May 1626

WEDNESDAY, 17 MAY 1626

I. JOURNAL OF THE HOUSE OF COMMONS

[**CJ 860;** p. 67]
Mercurii, 17 Maii, 2 Caroli Regis

MR. THOMAS JERMYN. That the King has given him leave to let the House know that his Majesty himself told him Sir D. Digges spoke the words wherewith he is charged; and that he did it out of divers men's notes[1] taken at the conference. And that now his Majesty being satisfied, he himself does constantly believe Sir D. Digges did not speak those words, or words to any such effect.

The Serjeant sent down with his mace to fetch Mr. Glanville and all the lawyers to attend the service of the House.

MR. GLANVILLE reports from the committee to prepare heads for the conference with the Lords,[2] and tenders the heads in writing, which were 2 read by the Clerk.

[**CJ 861**] Upon question, recommitted, 2 clock in the afternoon, in the Star Chamber.

The House turned into a grand committee upon the business concerning Sir John Eliot.

Upon question, the House to be adjourned till Friday morning saving the subcommittee now appointed.

The House adjourns itself accordingly. This pronounced by MR. SPEAKER.

II. DIARY OF BULSTRODE WHITELOCKE, ESQ., DD. 12.22, CAMBRIDGE UNIVERSITY LIBRARY

[f. 15v]

May 17

Some make their protestation that protested not before and/

MR. THOMAS JERMYN says (the King having given him leave) that the words he heard from the King himself, who since has found that he was misinformed.[3] And Mr. Jermyn does protest that he does not believe that Sir Dudley Digges did speak those words or words to the like effect.

MR. GLANVILLE reports from the committee to consider of heads for a conference with the Lords. The heads drawn by them:

1. To declare how at the meeting several speeches were delivered, as they remember.
2. That Sir Dudley Digges that then spoke was upon Thursday next following[4] committed by his Majesty's command for some words supposed to be spoken by him at that meeting.
3. We are informed by Sir Dudley Carleton, as well as from himself as by leave from his Majesty, etc., that the matter whereupon the King took offense was *ut antea*.[5]
4. That he further declared that the King having taken notice by the report of sundry persons that Sir Dudley Digges used such words or the like, his Majesty called for 4 or 5 table books and found in them such words.
5. The Commons conceive this a most willful and malicious misinformation, for that Sir Dudley Digges had express order to the contrary to express the true intent of our order. And if such words had been spoken, they had/
6. This misinformation tends to raise a hateful aspersion upon his Majesty which the Commons abhor to think. It trenches upon the loyalties of both Houses of parliament and the liberties of parliament. If the authors hereof pass unpunished, it will encourage the like in others and leave a color for truth of the present misinformation.

1. Printed edition: Noes.
2. I.e., the subcommittee of twenty appointed to draft a remonstrance to the King and on 15 May ordered to prepare heads for a conference with the Lords.
3. See Jermyn's speech in the CJ, above.
4. I.e., 11 May.
5. See the Vice Chamberlain's speech, 12 May.

To show the [f. 16] protestation made by our members. To entreat their Lordships to remember the laws touching this matter, specially the statutes of Westminster 1, 3 E. 1, c. 33; 2 R. 2, c. [5]; 12 R. 2, 9, 16; 1 and 2 P. *et* M., c. 3,[6] to punish such as/

To desire their Lordships to take into their speedy consideration how some course may be taken by both Houses for the finding out of these misinformers and for the punishing of them agreeable to justice and their demerits.

MR. PYM. I think these heads must be now altered, being things stand not as they did when these were drawn. Moves that they may be recommitted.

This recommitted to the same committee.

MR. WANDESFORD moves that we resolve ourselves into a grand committee for consideration of the King's message yesterday sent concerning Sir John Eliot.

Ordered accordingly.

[*Committee of the Whole House*]

Mr. Rolle in the chair.

Chancellor Exchequer. I have leave of his Majesty to explain the word "extrajudicial" to you, which is that the offenses are high crimes done to his Majesty out of this House, for which Sir John Eliot is committed.[7]

Mr. Coryton. That we may go on to clear Sir John Eliot for as much as we know, or punish him if he has been faulty.

Sir Peter Heyman. That we may know first whether those crimes be treason or felony or breach of the peace without giving surety.

Sir William Spencer. General words may carry away all the members of this House, such as these are.

[f. 16v] Sir Nathaniel Rich. No man can say that one has done such a thing until it be proved and he heard.

Vice Chamberlain. Had I not been bitterly offended by Sir John Eliot, by a declamation made by him against me, I should have said much more than I did.[8] Neither the time nor occasions do give us leave to lay aside all other businesses until this be ended. I know no state in the world at this day standing in more danger than this of a sudden mutation and change from a long felicity to almost the contrary. If we can comply with his Majesty and preserve our liberties, it will be the wisest way. Some say let us leave our liberties to our posterities. I say let us see that we leave our lands to our posterities. In Queen Elizabeth's time some members of this House imprisoned *sedente curia,* and yet the business of the House went on: Sir Anthony Cope, Sir Henry Bromley, and Sir Henry Savile.[9] 25 Eliz., an Attorney of the Court of Wards, by name [*blank*] Morice, and Sir Edward Hoby and Mr. Beale, Clerk of the Signet, sent to

6. *SR,* 3 E. I, *Statutum Westm. Prim.,* c. 34; *SR,* 2 R. II, Stat. 1, c. 5; *SR,* 12 R. II, c. 9; *SR,* 1 & 2 P. & M., c. 3.

7. See HofC, 16 May, n. 4.

8. Sir Dudley Carleton was offended by Eliot's remarks made on 6 May directly following his own speech that day, see OB.

9. Sir Anthony Cope met with Peter Wentworth and others before the parliament of 1586–1587. He subsequently offered a bill for reformation of the Church along Presbyterian lines, for which he was imprisoned. See D'Ewes, *Journal . . . Elizabeth,* pp. 412–415; Neale, *Elizabeth I and her Parliaments,* II, 148–165; Hasler, ed., *House of Commons 1558–1603.* See also, below, n. 34. Sir Henry Bromley was part of the group organized by Peter Wentworth that met preceding the session in 1593 to consider the issue of succession. See D'Ewes, *Journal . . . Elizabeth,* p. 470; Neale, *Elizabeth I and her Parliaments,* II, 255–260, and Hasler, ed., *House of Commons 1558–1603.* Regarding Savile, see his speech and Sir Thomas Hoby's clarification of it, 12 May (OB), and nn. 13, 14, and 31.

the Tower sitting the Court, and yet the parliament business went on and our liberties remain.[10] Moves it be so now.

Mr. Wilde. The prerogative of the King and the liberty of the people must have a reciprocal relation and respect. [f. 17] A proclamation does not make a law, but declare[s] a law; and the coronation does declare the right of succession. So our Speaker does not pray our liberty of speech from the King, but declares it.

4 H. 8, c. 8, Richard Strode's case.[11] The precedents remembered may put us in mind the rather to take some course for the righting of ourselves in this and prevent that there be no more made in this kind.

Moves we may pass a bill for the declaration of our privileges.

1 *Jac.*, Pigott's case,[12] the House have been suffered to punish offenders, members of this House. Generals are not admitted for any accusations.

Sir Thomas Hoby. I remember all the precedents by Vice Chamberlain alleged, but it will not be found that they were committed for anything done by them in the House. I think it is the wisdom of the House not to petition for that which conceive will not be granted. No man has ever been taken away from us for faults but the faults have been made known. Doctor Parry was taken out of this House,[13] sitting the House, and hanged, drawn, and quartered, but the reason known why.

Sir George More. Sir Anthony Cope was imprisoned for preferring a bill here for the alteration of religion when the Queen had sent a message that she would not have the House meddle with that matter. For a speech to that purpose, Mr. Morice was also committed.[14]

Chancellor Duchy. In some great cases the telling of the particulars overthrows the business, and we do not believe that the King has told us an untruth. Moves we may go on with the business of the House to give the King satisfaction.

[f. 17v] Mr. Browne. A king can do no wrong because we think he will do no wrong, and if wrong be done it is through misinformation. We must not say because the King has done it therefore it is no wrong, but we must examine it. 34 Eliz. [*blank*] by the judges resolved that if the Queen committed anyone and the judges sent a *habeas corpus* for him, the cause of the commitment must be shown.[15] And the King cannot detain anyone in prison above 24 hours without the showing the cause of his imprisonment if it be demanded. Magna Carta.[16]

Mr. Mason. We sit not here as private men but as public vessel[s] for the commonwealth's service, and therefore ought not to be questioned for anything but wherein the commonwealth has an interest and for offenses done against the commonwealth. There may be offenses against the King

10. Sir James Morice, Sir Edward Hoby, and Robert Beale, Clerk of the Privy Council, were imprisoned in 1593. See Neale, *Elizabeth I and her Parliaments*, II, 267–276, 277–278; Hasler, ed., *House of Commons 1558–1603*. And see below, nn. 17 and 35.

11. *SR*, 4 H. VIII, c. 8.

12. On 13 February 1607 Sir Christopher Pigott made an invective speech against the Scots (*CJ*, I, 333). An argument ensued over how to punish him and on 16 February Pigott was heard at the bar, committed to the Tower, and expelled from the House. Ibid., 335–336; *Ambassades*, II, 87–90, 120–121.

13. Dr. William Parry spoke against the bill for the Queen's safety in 1584–1585 and was implicated in a plot against Queen Elizabeth. He was subsequently hanged, drawn, and quartered. See Neale, *Elizabeth I and her Parliaments*, II, 39–41, 48–51, 54. See also, Howell, *ST*, I, 1095–1112.

14. See above, nn. 9 and 10.

15. Regarding the maxim that the King can do no wrong, cf. Bracton, *Lib.* 1, f. 5b. Anderson, *Reports*, I, Resolution of the Judges, 34 Eliz. I (The Resolution is printed in *PP 1628*, I, Legal Citations, p. 106).

16. 9 H. III, Magna Carta, c. 29.

and high crimes which may not tend to the destruction of the commonwealth, as contempts, encroaching upon the liberties of the crown, etc. It is fit before we proceed in other matters we should be an entire body or else know matter that may make us utterly relinquish this member.

Sir Dudley Digges. Never man was commanded particularly all his words by this House, but they might speak the best of their knowledge and their learning for the furtherance of the business of the House. Moves that those that think Sir John Eliot exceeded his commission may tell us wherein that we may proceed upon it.

[f. 18] Vice Chamberlain. Sir John Eliot has no accuser in this House. Partly that which he said at the conference and partly that which is discovered moved the King for Sir John Eliot's commitment. Mr. Beale was committed for producing a record.[17]

Sir Walter Erle. That the particulars charged upon Sir John Eliot by Vice Chamberlain may be taken into consideration and cleared or otherwise.

Mr. Wandesford alters his opinion and moves that we should make our remonstrance before we go to clear Sir John Eliot.

Mr. Pym. It is a privilege of every member of this House not to have determined anything against him or for him until he do answer here for himself.

This referred to the committee for the heads for the conference to [take] consideration of the whole debate and a remonstrance thereupon to be framed.

Speaker takes his chair.

SPEAKER. The House has not sat upon Ascension Day since 12 *Jac.*[18]

Resolved by question to adjourn the House till Friday morning.

Adjourned accordingly.

III. DIARY OF SIR RICHARD GROSVENOR, MS 611, TRINITY COLLEGE DUBLIN

[p. 103]

May 17

The Serjeant was sent with the mace for Mr. Glanville and the rest of the House forth of the Hall.

MR. GLANVILLE reported that a committee of 20 were appointed to set down the heads of a conference with the Lords concerning matters of great importance touching both Houses. The heads for the subject of the conference were agreed on and drawn into form by him.[19] It was read in the House on 15 May 1626, at the select committee.

1. To declare to their Lordships how at the meeting of both Houses, 8 May, several speeches delivered by some members of the Commons House.

2. That Sir Dudley Digges, one of the members who made the preamble, was the Thursday following[20] committed to the Tower by command of the King for words supposed to be spoken at that meeting.

3. That Sir D. Carleton informed us the Friday following,[21] as taking it from relation of his Majesty.

4. That the matter of offense, that he should say by command of the House that he forbore to speak any further in regard of the King's honor.

5. That Sir D. Carleton did inform us that

17. Robert Beale had written a book regarding the oaths ministered in the Court of High Commission that was printed abroad and brought into England shortly before the parliament of 1593. Neale, *Elizabeth I and her Parliaments,* II, 277.

18. The House did not sit on Ascension Day in 1614. See *PP 1614,* pp. 405, 409, 411.

19. See above, n. 2.

20. I.e., 11 May.

21. I.e., 12 May.

the King had been told by 4 or 5 persons that he spoke such words.

6. That this is a most willful misinformation to his Majesty and to express our reasons here, viz.:

1. For that Sir D. D[igges] had direction by order of the House to the contrary and to express the substance and true intent of that order.

2. For that in pursuit of our order the words related were contrary thereto.

3. If the words had been spoken, it was impossible but both their Lordships and the Commons should have observed them.

And this misinformation does tend to raise a most hateful aspers[ion] upon his Majesty and the Commons, and they hate to think on, as the Commons hate to think.

[p. 104] It trenches deeply upon the privileges of parliaments. That these informations are of most dangerous consequence as breeding disturbance between the King, nobles, and Commons. That if the authors escape unpunished it may encourage others to offend in the like kind and give color of some truth to have been in the information.

To express what we have done by protestation. To show how clear we are that no such words were spoken. To put them in mind [*blank*]; 2 R. 2, cap. 5; 1 & 2 Phil. [and Mary], cap. 4.[22] To desire them take course in to find out the authors, and for punishment to be inflicted on them agreeable to their demerits.

SIR DUDLEY DIGGES. Moved those words concerning his disgrace to be left out, for he had received some full satisfaction and as he would never have expected to have deserved; for it was now the greatest honor that could come to him or his posterity.

MR. GOODWIN. That nothing should be left out but we to complain to the King and desire justice against those who went about to undermine the commonwealth.

MR. PYM. That they might be recommitted because they were provided as matters stood formerly.

By question, recommitted, Star Chamber, afternoon.

Yesterday's order read that his Majesty's message should be taken into consideration.

[*Committee of the Whole House*]

Mr. Rolle[23] came into the chair. The grand committee to consider of Sir John Eliot's commitment and his Majesty's message.

Sir Walter Erle. Moved to know what the order was.[24]

Sir Richard Weston says the message was to desire us to go forward in the business of this House,[25] notwithstanding his restraint of Sir John Eliot seeing he had dealt so graciously in that which concerned Sir Dudley Digges. [p. 105] He was committed for causes "extrajudicial"; now he had command from his Majesty to tell us that the offenses are high crimes done to his Majesty out of this House.

Mr. Kirton.

Sir Robert Harley. Whether we may proceed as a free body, our liberties standing thus. We have freedom of speech. The question is whether we may now proceed, this member taken from us, without breach of liberty.

Mr. Coryton. 2 things: whether we may

22. *SR*, 2 R. II, Stat. 1, c. 5; *SR*, 1 & 2 P. & M., c. 3.

23. *Mr. Wandesford* is crossed out in the MS and *Mr. Rolle* is inserted.

24. The order of 16 May was that the Commons take the King's message into consideration this day (17 May).

25. See the message delivered by Sir Richard Weston, Chancellor of the Exchequer, 16 May, OB.

proceed and whether fit to proceed. To examine as much as we know. Let us clear him or condemn him so far that that befalls him may befall any of us. Let us go on with our conference to the Lords.

Mr. Glanville. To go on to clear him is not the right way. Sir D. Digges was accused for words said at the conference, the other for acts done out of the House. He knew not the way.

Mr. Long. Desired to know whether out of this House might not be said to be done what was said at committees.

Sir P. Heyman. 1. To know whether matter of treason, felony, or things not bailable are to be discussed by us. If of any other nature, we are competent judges as any other.

Sir John Strangways. If he be committed for any offense done out of the House, then let us clear him for anything done in this House.

Sir William Spencer. Whether to say that this was for words out of this House. Might not upon the same generals take from us any of our members. Would have it explained.

[p. 106] Sir William Armine. 2 things laid to Sir John Eliot's charge: 1, words delivered at their conference; 2, for things extrajudicial. Moved, 1, to proceed with those words, then to the other and/

Sir Nathaniel Rich. That if proceed to clear him before anything laid to his charge, and he not here to answer, we shall more wound our privileges. It had been more agreeable to the privilege of this House to have acquainted the House with it before. To entreat his Majesty to know the crimes, what they are, that if they be true we will crave to have him more punished; but to detain a member upon general terms may be all our cases.

Mr. Wandesford. That it stands with justice that we should clear Sir John Eliot of what he did by command of the House. Why should we be tender to clear him in that since his speech there is exclusive. And do this not rashly but take the particulars into consideration. That who in the House can charge him, let him charge now.

Mr. Spencer. Let us clear him in due time. 1, to go on in a remonstrance. If he had offended against this House, he ought to be tried here, not taken forth of this House. 2, that this is of a dangerous consequence and may happen hereafter, that for supposed high crimes 300 may be taken forth and the rest left to the business of the House.

[p. 107] Mr. Vice Chamberlain. I must confess that ill construction of somewhat I have said and misreporting of it abroad. That I spoke to break a silence has made me silent ever since,[26] and so I should do still had I not found myself oft called on. For I had rather use the liberty of my judgment than expose myself to the sharpness of censure where I have been subject. Anything that deserves debate in this House I shall be ready to give satisfaction; if any other desire it, I shall do it at any time as a friend or neighbor.

2 gentlemen that spoke lately, I concur with both. The first, that we clear Sir John Eliot for all things he did by command of this House, but everything must be in his proper time, and then if he did *mandati fines praeterire* that is a fault he must answer for, not we. Memory is prefixed upon meditation; yet, I then named 1 or 2 points which I conceived to be against the sense of the House, but this not proper at this time because he is absent and cannot make his in-

26. See the Vice Chamberlain's speech, 12 May, OB.

terpretation. Till then he spoke many things for which he had no good order. But then had not I been offended deeply against a declamation made against me in this House, I should have spoken more.[27] I heard his Majesty take deep displeasure at many passages in his speech there. [p. 108] That we do petition his Majesty to have him here.

Such a time it is and such are the occasions that a man may be forced to say that [that] may offend tender and delicate ears. The times now are such as should make us lay aside all other occasions; that we proceed with the business of the House. I make this petition one of the mean business; but that not all, for no kingdom in the world that stands in greater danger to change the happiness into the contrary.

The dangers from abroad still increase and a few days misspent will make them remediless. Let us comply with his Majesty's message, yet lose nothing of our privileges. We speak of leaving our liberties to posterity, I speak of preserving our liberties and lands to posterity. Take the example of our ancestors. I look into Queen Elizabeth's days and I remember certain examples of members of this House taken forth *sedente curia,* yet the privileges last to this day. I name 3: one, Sir Anthony Cope; 2, Sir H. Bromley; 3d, Sir John Savile, who neither know[s] how he got in or out.[28] 3 other cases in 25 Eliz.: one, an Attorney of the Court of Wards, one Morice; 2, Sir Edward Hoby; 3, Clerk of the Signet, Mr. Beale.[29] Notwithstanding all this the parliaments went on happily. Our predecessors proceeded with much respect to the Queen, [p. 109] not so much as petition her. Let us go on with the petition and whether to go on with other business within and without doors I leave to your better judgment.

Mr. Wilde. I will not touch upon his Majesty's prerogative, it is a point too high for me. But the King's prerogative and the subjects' liberty must have a reciprocal abiding. There is a certain duty owing as well from the imperial crown to the laws, as a loyalty from the subject to the prince. In this prerogative something for imprisoning subjects, I will not dispute it; but we have some resolutions in our books that the King may in some cases commit a man without showing the cause, but this is in cases out of parliament. But in parliament I find no case or precedent that there is any warrant for it. Here is a commitment of our members; wherein we must know there is a liberty of freedom of speech belonging to every member of this House to declare himself, and this is so ancient, and without this the freedom use[d] of parliament is gone. This is declared at beginning of parliaments by L[ord] Keeper, which is no other but a declaration of our rights.[30]

A case in print: Richard Strode, in H. 8. He was a burgess for Plymouth; preferred a bill.[31] He was fined at the Stannary in £60 as doing this as against the right of the Stannaries. This beggar of the King cast into prison during parliament. This being done for following a bill in this House. It was taken as a wrong to the privilege of this House. He was by bill in this House released and discharged from all fines and whatever was done against him.

[p. 110] In that precedents are remembered against us, it must move us the rather

27. See above, n. 8.
28. See above, n. 9.
29. See above, n. 10.
30. A reference to the petitions customarily addressed to the King by the Speaker at the opening of parliament: (1) for access to his Majesty, (2) for freedom of speech and, (3) for freedom from arrest. See Elsynge, *Parliaments,* 175–192; Hatsell, *Precedents,* I, 75–76; II, 226. See also, the Speaker's speech, 8 February 1626, HofL, pp. 28–29.
31. See above, n. 11.

to look to ourselves, for, unless there be course taken against them, they will be still argued against us, and the circumstances omitted.

Moved to draw an act, and though it should miscarry yet would it appear to all posterity as an act of this House. Except in treason, felony, or breach of peace, the members of this House cannot be restrained. Unless this be an offense out of the power of the House, to take notice of; for in generals we cannot accuse any man.

Sir Thomas Hoby. Not to go about to clear Sir John Eliot till we have his particular charge. But to clear the precedents mentioned:

1. It will never be found that any of them[32] were imprisoned[33] for matters said or done in the House, nor so done as that the House ever made means to have them released. This is no breach of privileges when the House thinks it not fit to petition. For a remonstrance, therein to petition that we may have him restored or else to know for what cause we have him not, that so we may proceed and not to go thus on in generalities.

Sir G. More. The great happiness of the subject and honor of the King: that he rules over free men not bondmen. *Ergo* this House has been ever careful to preserve their liberties. I differ from Sir Thomas Hoby. I think it fit for us to clear him for what we know; for when we find him committed immediately after those speeches; and that words were offensive to the King, to make it appear that he had no commission [p. 111] from this House to speak anything that might give just offense.

For precedents alleged: I was here when they were all taken, and no breach of liberties. Sir Anthony Cope's case: a motion made in this House to alter the government of the Church. She sent by Sir Christopher Hatton that she would not have the government changed; yet, after, Sir A. Cope delivered a short bill into the House to alter the whole government. Sir Walter Mildmay said it was a strange bill, at once to cut off all the heads of Church government, at once of all laws.[34]

Mr. Morice was taken away for making a long speech to make the same alterations, but first the Queen sent a command not to meddle with it.[35]

Sir H. Bromley was committed for meddling with the matter of succession; so was Mr. Beale, too. And the House did not then think it fit to meddle but to pass it over.[36]

But if these precedents be still urged against us, and our members taken away, may touch us deeply. Moved that for so much as concerned Sir John Eliot concerning the conclusion, we may examine whether he has exceeded his commission. If not, let us leave ourselves and him. By remonstrance or petition to know the cause why taken away.

Sir William Constable. 2 questions: 1, whether, Sir John Eliot being committed, it be safe for us to proceed in business; 2, whether fit to clear him.

[p. 112] Sir H. May. The King can do no wrong, so the law, nor will do no injustice,

32. *Sir Anthony Cope* is crossed out in the MS and *any of them were* is inserted.

33. MS: *imprisonment.*

34. See above, n. 9. Sir Walter Mildmay's speech of 4 March 1587 is not included in D'Ewes; see Neale, *Elizabeth I and her Parliaments,* II, 161. In reference to the second enacting clause in Cope's proposed bill Mildmay said that, "To cancel and cut off at one blow so many laws, made so many years past, even from the statute of Magna Carta, is a thing that has never been offered in this House".

35. For Sir James Morice's speech, 27 February 1593, see D'Ewes, *Journal . . . Elizabeth,* p. 474 and Neale, *Elizabeth I and her Parliaments,* II, 268–269.

36. See above, n. 10.

nor say an untruth. He has sent to let us know that for high things done against his Majesty, extrajudicial, he is committed. Now to say that this may be dangerous to us all, the King must answer to God for injustice. We must believe in his justice that he has done no wrong. Our privileges stand firm when it may appear in the Clerk's book that Sir John Eliot was committed for high crimes out of this House. Think them not broken; the King will not break them. Go on in business.

Mr. Browne. The prerogative of the King and privileges of the subject are equal—both great. A reciprocal relation between the King and us. He is sworn to govern us according to the law. Examples may be dangerous; we are governed by laws not by examples. What is law in this case, and how far *regia manu* a man may be imprisoned. The King can do no wrong; yet, in many cases, we must appeal from Philip sleeping to Philip waking. For the King does many things upon false information, an example fresh that Sir D. D[igges] committed without cause. When he was rightly informed, he satisfied. To inquire of the matter is not to lay the fault upon the King. Magna Carta doubly broken, no free man to be committed but for a lawful cause, and judicially.[37] [p. 113] It has been in 34 Eliz. a resolution that neither she nor her Council could commit any man but a certain time, but must upon a *habeas corpus* must let the cause be known.[38] Let us make a humble remonstrance that these are our liberties which we must preserve as our lives, this is according to the laws and Magna Carta. And when he is rightly informed I hope we shall have that justice we have had.

Mr. Mason. 1, what our privileges are; 2, whether this be a breach. The reason of our privileges: we serve for counties, boroughs, and so as public persons for the service of the commonwealth. Our liberties such not to be questioned but for felony, treason, etc. The reason, that we being public persons should enjoy our privileges against any private cause. But if the commonwealth has an interest, then we be but private men. Such are treason, felony, and not finding sureties of the peace, are offenses against the commonwealth. This gentleman committed for high crimes, extrajudicial. There may be high offenses against the King that do not trench upon the commonwealth. Any disobedience as encroaching upon the privileges of the crown or against process, if such high crimes be committed, touch not the commonwealth. Now till we have Sir John Eliot here we cannot tell how to quit him. For precedents alleged, that the Commons never petitioned for them; it appears they were committed for just causes. [p. 114] It is a wrong to him and to us; for by a voice many times things are carried. Moved not to proceed without we be an entire body. To desire his Majesty to declare the reason of his commitment.

Mr. Wandesford. First to declare whether he transgressed the command of the House. The King will do no injustice as the law says he can do none.

Sir Dudley Digges. There may be discovered since this time matter that happened before by the search of their papers. A man may speak to the best of his understanding to forward the service and business of this House. I know not that he offended that day in any word against the sense of this House.

Mr. Vice Chamberlain. This not a fit time to examine this; for Sir John Eliot has no accuser in this House. The accusation proceeds from his Majesty. This is a mixed cause, partly that which was spoken at the conference, partly that which might be dis-

37. 9 H. III, Magna Carta, c. 29.

38. See above, n. 15.

covered since. A spark gives fire to combustible matter.

Foreign danger knocks at our doors. Let not distrust and diffidence open them. Let us beseech his Majesty concerning our privileges and go on with our business lest he condemn us of neglect.

Sir William Beecher.[39] To go to acquit him if nobody spoke against. That those who were not present could neither give yea or no.

[p. 115] Sir Robert Harley. A remonstrance.

Sir Walter Erle would have the particulars wherein he was charged first debated. That Mr. Vice Chamberlain:[40] that this gentleman was committed for a mixed cause; partly at the conference, partly discovered since. That could not be, for he was committed for words spoken; and if anything discovered since, he could not be committed for that.

Mr. Vice Chamberlain. If we shall say that all was well done and by commission at the conference before we know that he is charged with, not fit or sensible. Moved for present remonstrance.

Mr. Wandesford. That he had altered his opinion because he heard now that he was committed for a mixed offense, partly for words spoken in the House. To go on with a remonstrance or a petition.

Mr. Pym. Neither just towards him nor the privilege of this House to go about now to clear him, for we must hear him first speak. Again we have a cognizance of that part of the cause that was done at the conference. Let us have him here before we judge him. This is a dangerous precedent that the King should say I will commit him and then you shall examine whether I have done it justly or not. For a remonstrance, and if we hear of such a particular as is not within our cognizance, we shall do what shall be fitting.

Sir Thomas Hoby. That the Speaker might go into the chair and resolve of the remonstrance, and whether to sit tomorrow or not.[41]

IV. DIARY OF JOHN LOWTHER, ESQ., D/LONS/L, CUMBERLAND AND WESTMORLAND RECORD OFFICE

[f. 33v]

[17 May]

[GLANVILLE.] 15 May. Heads for conference.

[1.] How head of impeachment of Duke; speeches delivered.

2. Ho[w] D. Digges committed for words supposed spoke there by command.

3. How informed by D. Carleton by leave from the King that the words were put.

4. That King informed by 4 or 5.

Conceived a malicious and willful misinformation.

Reasons:

1. For that he had contrary order.

2. For that the words were contrary.

3. If spoken, should be observed by Lords and us. If it should [be] so, this misinformation reflected on King as aspers[ion], the which we grieve to hear, abhor to think.

To show how breaks privilege by commitment, discouragement, makes division between King, nobles, and Commons. If this not discovered, occasions [f. 34] the like; color of truth also. Show how we cleared. That if the Lordships would have apprehended and [*illegible*] to remember Westminster 1, 3 E. 3; 2 R. 2; 12 R. 2; 1 *et* 2 Ph. [and] Mary,[42] of those that raise sedi-

39. *Mr. Coryton* is crossed out in the MS and *Sir William Beecher* is inserted.

40. See his speech, above.

41. I.e., on Ascension Day, see Whitelocke, above.

42. See above, n. 6.

tion between Lords and Commons, and the punishment. To have punishment inflicted according to justice and their demerits. How course may be taken by both Houses for the discovery and punishment.

D. DIGGES. Dare not speak against where goes further than him. Imprisoned was disgrace, now grace more. Desires all to be left out concerning him.

Recommitted to comprehend Eliot.

[*Committee of the Whole House*]

Vice Chancellor [*sic*][43] expounds the "extrajudicial" to be high crimes committed against the King out of this House. So commanded to declare. Desires to proceed with the business of the House, which was the King's message.

Kirton. If we not satisfied in what, who can speak safe?

Sir Robert Harley. Question whether we may proceed, a member thus taken.

Coryton. Question also whether fit.

Sir Peter Heyman. To be informed if felony, treason, or peace; else we judges and to hear it.

[f. 34v] Sir William Spencer. To take liberties in consideration else by such a color may every man be taken and this made no House.

Strangways moves we to clear him of things done in the House and for the House.

Nathaniel Rich. Not to clear him until accused, for he is not charged as Digges. For he may [be] committed in parliament time, but such cause should be made known, else may concern all. To desire to know the cause.

Wandesford. Just to be cleared of what he did by the command of the House. Then petition for cause.

Vice Chamberlain. The evil construction abroad of what he said to break silence, made him silent since. Rather judge than subject him to reprehension. Concurs to clear him in all he did by command, but if he did exceed. The last day he did say somewhat not with sense but against it, and so he thinks he did and when desired he will do it. There were points. He present when King took exception. And fit to remonstrate to crave cause. Wherein King denies him not absolutely. Times such now as a man may offend tender ears. Thinks this business fit but not all the business, else we may be irremediable. Desires to leave land, as liberty, to posterity. *Tempore* Queen Elizabeth [f. 35] members taken, yet privileges continue: Sir Anthony Cope, Sir H. Bromley, Sir John Savile, yet House proceeded. 25 Eliz., Attorney Wards Morice, Sir Edward Hoby, [and] Beale, Clerk of Parliament [*sic*], all committed, yet proceeded; and all ended happily, not petitioned. He desires to petition and also to proceed.

[Wilde.] 4 H. 8, Richard Strode, occasion of law against all proceeding against parliament men.

Therefore to prevent precedents now and avoid the past.

Sir [Thomas] Hoby. Not time to clear before accused. Answers precedents: not for public speech in House, so as House would not petition for them. Not so now. Parry was hanged, drawn, and q[uartered] sitting House.[44] So desires remonstrance.

Sir G. More. Happy for subjects to be free in England. Honor King so preserved. Differs from last. Thinks we should clear him

43. I.e., the Chancellor of the Exchequer, see other accounts.

44. See above, n. 13.

before charged. Notwithstand[ing] this *nescio quid vult ista purgatio mali.* Yet [*illegible*] speech offensively taken. To precedents, he present when all committed; cause known; no breach of liberty. Motion made for change in Church government. Queen prohibited by message. Cope delivered a bill after to make alteration. Mildmay said strange by a short bill to cut off the heads of all the laws past, for which he taken.[45] [f. 35v] Morice did like after command. So the rest, but Bromley charged for meddling in succession, so Beale, all which slipped away without notice.

C. Duchy. King can do no wrong, say no wrong. He says high crimes, not to be supposed but it is so. To answer to God if do wrong. Perhaps when go to him will tell no reason for state, which if we suppose, then lose we our labor of conference. Therefore he indifferent if rest upon this or go with remonstrance; for this entered so is no breach of privilege. Therefore desires to go on with business. King might have said so an[d] D. Digges would nothing, but truth so not so said.

Browne. 34 Eliz., resolved by all judges, King nor Council cannot commit above 24 hours but must assign cause if *habeas corpus* come.

Mason. Not to commit but for f[elony] or tr[eason].

Sir D. D[igges]. That he used words perhaps beyond command. But if matter considerable, the papers.

[f. 36] Vice Chamberlain. This not time to clear him; he has no accuser. He aimed but knew not. Hit off Sir D. Digges's cause, so is cleared. His a mixed cause; partly that at conference, partly else. Perhaps by his papers as Sir D. Digges, perhaps by other matter before. Precedents he cited as accidents, not justified. Beale committed only for bringing subsidy roll that belonged to us, not Lords, to confer[ence].

Desires to go on with religion, war, sickness, etc., now depending before us; to go on.

V. DIARY OF SIR NATHANIEL RICH, HIST. COLLECT. 143, HLRO

[f. 89v]

Tuesday, 17 May

MR. GLANVILLE'S report of the heads of the conference with the Lords which he presents in writing.

This a malicious information for:

1. Sir D. Digges had order [*illegible*] upon his own motion to the contrary.

2. The words charged are direct contrary.

3. Such words must needs have been understood, being opposite.

4. Those words raise a hateful aspersion on his Majesty.

5. Reflects disloyalty on both Houses, and dishonor.

6. Breaks the privileges of parliament as having drawn on the commitment of Sir D. [Digges].

7. These informations of dangerous consequence to interrupt the proceedings of parliament and sow discord between King and subject.[46]

[*Committee of the Whole House*]

[f. 90] Sir T. Hoby answers the precedents of 27 Eliz., that of Sir Anthony Cope, then committed. The cause was such that the House would not petition for them and therefore no privilege broken. Moves to go on with our remonstrance and desire that he may be restored or else the matter assigned that we may judge.

Sir G. More. A happiness to the King that he rules over free not over bondmen, and it is a happiness also to the subject. The case:

45. See above, n. 34.

46. MS possibly *parliament.*

Sir Anthony Cope was about alteration of government of the Church. The Queen, hearing hereof, sent word to the House that she would not have that government altered, yet Sir Anthony Cope put in a bill to alter that government. And the Attorney of the Court of Wards, Morice, seconded him with a powerful speech.[47] So did Sir H. Bromley, who also meddled with the matter of succession, and Mr. Beale for the like. And the House of Parliament did connive. Now, if those precedents shall be alleged and members of the House taken away under color/

Sir H. May. The King will tell no untruth.

Mr. Browne. The prerogative of the King great, so is liberty of the subject, and the King tied by his oath to govern according to law. This an honor to the King. The question how the King may by law imprison. The King can do no wrong, but he does by [mis]information. We may appeal from Philip sleeping to Philip waking; the King did no wrong in committing Sir D. Digges, but misinformed. The rule of the law is not because the King did it therefore well done, but we must inquire into the cause. Magna Carta: no man committed but *per legale judicium,* and this the ground of the writ *habeas corpus.* 34 Eliz., a resolution of all the judges of England that the Queen nor Council can commit above 24 hours but the cause must be rendered, and this was reported to the Queen.

Mr. Mason. 1, what our privileges are; 2ly, whether there be a breach. The reason of our privilege: we serve for counties and boroughs, not as private men; therefore we are to be free from arrests except in case of treason, felony, or surety of the peace. We ought not to be questioned except in something against the commonwealth, as in those 3 cases which are against the commonwealth. Now, high crimes are charged on Sir John Eliot committed against the King. There may be high crimes against the King which trench not against the commonwealth, as standing out to a committee of rebellion, encroachings upon liberties of the crown. Now what nature these crimes are, we know not; the King may be misinformed. The King needs not declare the truth in [f. 90v] particular. For the precedents, they are all answered with his own words that the Commons did not petition, which showed that they thought or knew the case of his commitment to be just. Our war we undergo is for the honor of King and kingdom and to preserve our privileges.

47. See above, nn. 9 and 34. Rich has conflated the argument.

ORDER OF BUSINESS FRIDAY, 19 MAY 1626

I.	Journal of the House of Commons,	283
II.	Whitelocke,	283–284
III.	Grosvenor,	284–286
IV.	Lowther,	286

Message from the Lords bringing the bill for estates of tenants of **Bromfield and Yale** (Sir Thomas Trevor and Sir Peter Marten)	283(2), 284, *25/5
SIR DUDLEY CARLETON (Vice Chamberlain): concerning a warrant for Sir John Eliot's release	283(2), 284, 286, *11/5
Report from the committee for considering **heads** for a **conference** with the Lords (JOHN GLANVILLE)	283(2), 284, 286, *15/5
The heads for a conference: read twice by the Clerk	283, 286
SIR NATHANIEL RICH	285
SIR DUDLEY CARLETON (Vice Chamberlain)	283(2), 285, 286
EDWARD BYSSHE	285, 286
SIR RICHARD WESTON (Chancellor Exchequer)	283, 284, 285, 286
SIR DUDLEY DIGGES	283, 284, 285, 286
SIR WALTER ERLE	285
RICHARD SPENCER	285
By question: heads for a conference are recommitted; three members added to the committee; committee went presently to the Committee Chamber	283, 285
Report from the committee for considering heads for a conference (JOHN GLANVILLE)	283, 286
Upon question: the heads for a conference allowed to pass	283, 284, 286
JOHN GLANVILLE	286
Resolved: Glanville to deliver the message to the Lords	283, 284, 286

FRIDAY, 19 MAY 1626

I. JOURNAL OF THE HOUSE OF COMMONS

[CJ 861; p. 68]
Veneris, 19 Maii, 2 Caroli Regis

Mr. Baron Trevor and Sir P. Mutton bring from the Lords a bill entitled, An act for the establishing of the estates of the tenants of Bromfield and Yale in the county of Denbigh and of the tenures, rents, and services thereupon reserved.

MR. VICE CHAMBERLAIN moves we should now proceed on with the business of the House, he having seen a warrant signed with the King's hand for his[1] release; and makes no doubt but he is by this time at liberty, for this warrant is sent to the Tower by a pursuivant.

MR. GLANVILLE reports from the committee to whom the heads for the intended conference with the Lords was recommitted that they have agreed upon a form in writing;[2] which read 2 by the Clerk.

MR. VICE CHAMBERLAIN avows the 3d article in every part;[3] but, for the 4th, whereas said there that the King told by 4 or 5 that those words were spoken by Sir D. Digges, the truth is that the King, hearing by common report that such words were spoken, whereat the King highly offended, sent for 4, 5, or 6 notebooks, and therein found those words, or such in effect.

MR. CHANCELLOR EXCHEQUER *concordat.* And that it was the mistaking of some that took notes.

SIR D. DIGGES moves to stay any further proceeding herein, and will take it a great favor from the House to him so to do. Howsoever, moves a recommitment for something therein concerning himself.

Upon question, recommitted, presently, in the Committee Chamber. Mr. Vice Chamberlain, Mr. Chancellor Exchequer,[4] and Mr. Chancellor Duchy [added].

MR. GLANVILLE reports again from the committee with some alterations which, being read, were upon question allowed to pass as the heads of the conference.

He that shall deliver this message, agreed upon by those heads to be amplified and applied according to the judgment of the party.

Upon question, this to be delivered by Mr. Glanville.

II. DIARY OF BULSTRODE WHITELOCKE, ESQ., DD. 12.22, CAMBRIDGE UNIVERSITY LIBRARY

[f. 18v]

May 19

Baron Trevor and Sir Peter Mutton bring a bill from the Lords.

VICE CHAMBERLAIN. I saw a warrant under the King's hand for the release of Sir John Eliot this morning before I came hither,[5] but for that I know not whether he will come hither presently or not. I desire you would go on with the business of the House.

MR. GLANVILLE reports from the recommitment the heads for the conference to be desired with the Lords.[6]

VICE CHAMBERLAIN. That if he said the King was told by 4 or 5 that Sir Dudley Digges spoke those words, he did not well

1. I.e., Sir John Eliot's. We have not found the writ. On 18 May, prior to his release, questions drafted by the Lord Keeper were put to Eliot by Lord Chief Justice Crew and Attorney General Heath. See SP 16/27:17 and 18, printed below, App., II, F.

2. For the heads, see Glanville's report, 17 May.

3. For the altered heads for the conference, see Grosvenor, below.

4. *Sir Dudley Digges* is crossed out in the MS following *Chancellor Exchequer.*

5. See above, n. 1.

6. For the altered heads, see Grosvenor, below.

express himself. But he meant, and so said, that the King hearing a rumor of some such words took 4 or 5 notebooks, and examining them, found words to such effect in them. And therefore moves we may set by the remonstrance to the King and the conference.

CHANCELLOR EXCHEQUER. That he was present with the King with Mr. Vice Chamberlain and did not hear the King say those words that he was "told by 4 or 5".

SIR DUDLEY DIGGES. I have had every way as fair usage and as good satisfaction as possible could be, and full contentment. Moves that, if it be possible, we may lay this aside and, if not, yet recommitted.

The heads for the conference, after twice recommitment, are allowed of by the House, and Mr. Glanville resolved to be the person to deliver from the House the matter of the conference.

III. DIARY OF SIR RICHARD GROSVENOR, MS 611, TRINITY COLLEGE, DUBLIN

[p. 116]

May 19

The House sat, but for above an hour's space they sat doing nothing.

A message from the Lords by Baron Trevor and Sir Peter Mutton, brought in a bill for the settling of the estates of the tenants of Bromfield and Yale in Denbigh.

MR. VICE CHAMBERLAIN. I saw a warrant under his Majesty's hand for Sir John Eliot's release. This is sent by a messenger in haste to the Tower to fetch him thence. Moved that we might go on with our business, for he knew not whether Sir John would come directly hither or go visit his friends in the town; if so, we may still look one upon another.

MR. GLANVILLE reported the heads for a conference with the Lords and delivered it in writing upon the recommitments. Heads:

1. To declare how at their meeting by committees of both Houses several speeches were delivered by certain members upon the cause of their impeachment against the Duke of B[uckingham].

2. That Sir D. D[igges], one of those who then spoke and made introduction, was committed to the Tower by his Majesty's command for words supposed to be spoken there by command of the House.

3. That Mr. Vice Chamberlain informed us that the matter of offense taken against Sir D. D[igges] were the words, etc.

4. That he declared to us that the King had taken notice here by the reports of several persons that Sir D. D[igges] had used those speeches; that he called for 4 or 5 table books wherein he found those or the like words.

5. That we conceive this to be a most malicious information: 1, because Sir D. D[igges] was ordered otherwise; 2, that the words were expressly against these words reported to the King.

6. If these words had been spoken they had and this information, they must have been observed by their Lords and the Commons.

7. It reflects upon both Houses in point of loyalty, whereof they are tender; and their Lords like affected.

[p. 117] 8. This trenches deeply upon the privileges of parliament as having drawn on the commitment of Sir D. D[igges] to his disgrace.

9. To show that this and like informations are of dangerous consequence by interrupting the great affairs, and to breed dissension between the Exchequer, King, Lords, and Commons.

10. To represent how, if the authors escape unpunished, it may raise a causeless jealousy; expressing the course we took in clearing the same and the success thereof.

11. To show how clear and well assured

we are that no such words were spoken by Sir D. D[igges] as were related to the King.

12. To put them in mind of the laws touching this matter: West. 1, 3 E. 1, cap. 33; 2 R. 2, cap. 5; 12 R. 1 [*sic*], cap. 9, against those that raise discords by rumors and lies.[7]

13. To desire them to take into their consideration how some course may be taken by both Houses for discovery of the authors [of] those informations, and so punishment according to their demerits.

SIR NATHANIEL RICH. Wished that we should take notice of the noble dealing of the Lords in clearing him as we had done.[8] That also that we should acquaint them what we had done for discovering of the offenses; not to prescribe them a way, but out [of] that free expression used between both Houses to let them know what we had done and then leave it to themselves.

[p. 118] MR. VICE CHAMBERLAIN. If this conference should follow, then I like those propositions. It is necessary that some points in this should be cleared by me before we proceed because I find myself in the 3 and 4th articles: the 3d, I avow every word; for the 4th, there is some mistaking. If I did say the King had been so told, I did not well express myself. I say that the King conceived that those were the words out of certain notes he had seen out of certain men's hands. That his Majesty, hearing of the words at which he was offended, sent for 4 or 5 notebooks and papers and found in them words which I delivered, or to that effect. This caused the misfortune of that gentleman, but I will not call it so because it is turned to his honor.

We have 2 businesses in hand, one is a petition or remonstrance, the other is a conference. For the first, we have reason to cease it absolutely; for the other, I move it be recommitted that this which is the foundation may be certain.

An objection which may receive an answer, that needs no reply; not fit to make.

MR. BYSSHE. The duty of every man to discharge his own cause freely. When Mr. Vice Chamberlain first spoke he said that he was in presence when the King he was told by 5 or 6 that those words were spoken.

MR. CHANCELLOR OF EXCHEQUER. On my knowledge, I have been in presence of the King since this business was in hand and this gentleman never said that the King said he was told by 5 or 6; but he said that the King was informed and understood it by 4 or 5, in which words great difference.

[p. 119] SIR D. DIGGES. I have had as fair usage from the [*illegible*] ministers, as good satisfaction and as much grace from a gracious sovereign as ever poor subject had. Moved us to go [on] in our business.

SIR WALTER ERLE. That this business had relation not merely to him but to the privilege of the House.[9] Moved it might go on.

MR. SPENCER. 2 reasons why we should not thank the Lords: 1, because we could take no notice of what they had done; 2, because it concerned the Lords in honor as much as us. Where it was said that the King sent for notebooks, that was done upon information so that first there must be an informer.

By question, recommitted; and Sir Dudley Carleton, Sir Richard Weston, and Sir H. May added to the committee. They went into the Committee Chamber.

7. *SR*, 3 E. I, *Statutum Westm. Prim.*, c. 34; *SR*, 2 R. II, Stat. 1, c. 5; *SR*, 12 R. II, c. 9.

8. On 15 May many of the Lords protested that Digges said nothing treasonous. See HofL, pp. 482–484, and n. 168.

9. As far back as 1401 the Commons petitioned the King not to give hearing to reports of business in the Lower House until they were official (*Rot. Parl.*, 2 H. IV, no. 11).

After a while the committee returned with the heads of the conference.

By question, agreed that those heads should be allowed for the heads of the conference.

Mr. Glanville was named to deliver this at the conference to the Lords; he made his apology.

By question, resolved that Mr. Glanville should deliver the message.

IV. DIARY OF JOHN LOWTHER, ESQ., D/LONS/L, CUMBERLAND AND WESTMORLAND RECORD OFFICE

[f. 36]

[19 May]

Friday after Ascension.

VICE CHAMBERLAIN signifies after long silence how the King sent a warrant to deliver Sir John Eliot; and he is coming.

Yet no business proceeded in until heads of conference read, reciting as before the heads.

Further shows our protestation to contrary, but all as before.

VICE CHAMBERLAIN says he expressed not himself well when he said he had heard it of 4 or five, for he said it arose out of notes which King sent for, four or 5. Now, common report coming to King, he sent for notes.

For business, it seems none but remonstrance and conference. He at liberty, takes away the remonstrance. If proceed, desires recommitment.

[f. 36v] Objection that upon answer can have no reply, best to be spared.

BYSSHE charged him that he said King told by 4 or 5, as Chancellor Exchequer.

CHANCELLOR EXCHEQUER. Said King was so informed, not told by 4 or 5, which makes difference. King called for notes upon evil sound, which taken with no evil sense. Might be mistaken. Desires to proceed.

DIGGES. Thought unfortunate committed, now more if prosecution has had such fair carriage. Desires to proceed or recommitted.[10]

10. The heads were altered and allowed to pass. See CJ, above.

Order of Business Saturday, 20 May 1626

SATURDAY, 20 MAY 1626

I. JOURNAL OF THE HOUSE OF COMMONS

[CJ 861; p. 68]
Sabbati, 20 Maii, 2 Caroli Regis

MR. PYM moves for Mr. More that he was arrested 23 Feb., 22 *Jac.*, during the privilege of parliament, and a trial upon it at the assizes at [*blank*] sitting the parliament at Oxford, while a special order to restrain absence.[1] This upon a *nihil dicit* because he, nor his counsel, appeared there.

Upon question, a letter to be written to the judges of the King's Bench to desire them to stay the judgment there until the business be examined here concerning Mr. More his privilege.[2]

The case referred to the committee formerly appointed to consider of Sir Robert Howard's privilege, to meet this afternoon, in the Exchequer Chamber;[3] and Mr. More to give notice to the other part.

Motion made concerning Sir John Eliot; whether he be to come and sit here, having been accused of high crimes extrajudicial to this House.

[p. 69] Sir John Eliot sent for to come into the House. And coming, and taking his place:

MR. VICE CHAMBERLAIN. Not to charge him, but to give him occasion to discharge himself of whatsoever might be objected against him for anything passed from him at the conference.

That all the other 7 used respective words against[4] the Duke. That for the manner of his speech, it was conceived it was too tart and harsh to the person of the Duke.

In the matter: 1, representing a character of the Duke of Buckingham's mind comparatively with a strange beast called *stellionatus*.[5] This not in his charge.

Something contrary to the mind of the House, as his not knowing of the return of the ships out of France. "They say they are come, but I know it not", which might be conceived to be a doubt of the House, he saying in obedience to the House he spoke it.[6]

"That man": in all languages this phrase accounted base, and a great indignity to be used to persons of honor.

The offense sounding very ill abroad were historical comparisons: 1, of Sejanus; 2ly, of the Bishop of Ely. *Audax superbus adulator.* Speaking of Sejanus, said he would not touch his venefices and veneries.[7]

1. It is unclear whether it was John or Poynings More who was arrested in February 1625 and tried in August the same year in a suit involving one Mr. Hodges. On 11 July 1625 an order was passed for the calling of the House on the third day of the August session and that those absent were to be censured. *PP 1625*, pp. 369–370. On 22 May 1626, below, the committee appointed to examine the matter was augmented.

2. The committee to examine Howard's privilege was appointed on 17 February, see CJ.

3. *Court of W.* is crossed out in the MS and *Exchequer Chamber* is inserted.

4. MS: *used respective words used.*

5. See HofL, 15 May, p. 461, and n. 63. For the report of Eliot's speech in the Upper House, see HofL, 15 May, pp. 460–463. Eliot's account of the speech is printed at the end of the day's proceedings for 10 May, above.

6. Regarding the return of the ships, see HofL, 13 May, p. 437, n. 125.

7. In the fuller version of the speech in Eliot's handwriting Sejanus's pride and ambition are noted but, "his neglect of counsels, his veneries, his venefices, those", said Eliot, "I will not mention". See the holograph speech printed at the end of the day's proceedings on 10 May, above. Eliot said that he used those words as a reference to Sejanus's preferring of his friends and his lechery with Livia. See Grosvenor, below.

Wherein he was conceived to aim at the Duke.

The main, that he cut off the words of the last charge with some words out of Cicero,[8] as if something were in the charge covered, which might be discovered. All this spoken to the end *supra.*

SIR JOHN ELIOT. That it was yesterday, half an hour past eleven, before he heard of the warrant for his enlargement. Gives thanks to Mr. Vice Chamberlain for his plain dealing with him, and ministering him occasion to clear himself. Desires the particulars against him may be particularly charged, and so he may answer them one by one.

Moved, that if any in the House will charge him further, they may now charge him that he may answer them severally.

1. For the *stellionatus.* That, for his honors, offices, etc., he sailed with his ambition. For his deceit and fraud, because no word could decipher it, he used the word *stellionatus,* which is a beast of so many colors as one beholding it cannot tell of what color it is. The instances herein was his fraud in drawing money from the merchants; 2ly, his getting the merchants to transport their ships into France,[9] there to entrap them; [3ly,] to abuse the King herein; [4ly,] to abuse therein the parliament. All these under this word *stellionatus.*

2. For his saying he knew not the ships were come, and this in obedience to the House, confesses he said he did not know, though he did hear, they were returned. For it is [true],[10] he heard it in this House, but neither then nor yet knows [it].

[p.70] 3. For the words, "the man". Speaks not by the book, but suddenly. Did often use his titles but, for brevity, used the words, "the man"; which used in all languages. *Ipse ille.* Thinks it not fit at all times to reiterate his titles; and yet thinks him not to be a god.

4. For Sejanus and the Bishop of Ely. 1, for the last: 1, the exhausting and luxurious employing of the King's revenue; 2, conferring honors upon obscure and unknown persons; 3, boldness; 4, *pereat ne omnes pereant.*

For Sejanus. He paralleled him in 4 particulars, viz./

For veneries and venefices, he spoke it only exclusively. He intended it not. If applied by him to himself, prays his misapplication may not make that, which he never intended to be, his fault. He protests he, in none of these examples, to parallel times or any other person but the Duke.

For the cutting off the last with the words of Cicero, that this fell not from him in the conclusion. And relates the particulars of his words and, as he remembers, the very syllables.

For the manner of his speech: too much vigor and strength. Will not excuse his defects in nature, but then did, and ever in this House, desire to avoid passion; only desired to discharge his duty to this House with the best life he could.

[**CJ 862**] For exceeding his commission he desires to understand particulars wherein, and then he will give an answer.

Sir John Eliot of himself withdrew, the House refusing to order his withdrawing.

Upon question, Sir John Eliot has not exceeded the commission given him by the House in anything passed from him in the late conference with the Lords.

8. See HofL, 15 May, p. 462. The passage from Cicero: "Nor do I use harsher words than nature has made, nor lighter ones than the case demands".

9. *to Rochell* is crossed out in the MS and *into France* is inserted.

10. The MS is frayed at the bottom of the page; the words in brackets, here and below, are taken from the printed Journal. Regarding the return of the ships, see HofL, 13 May, p. 437, n. 125.

The like for Sir D. Digges; both, without one negative.[11]

The committee for the remonstrance to meet at 2 clock this afternoon, in the former place.

II. DIARY OF BULSTRODE WHITELOCKE, ESQ., DD. 12.21, CAMBRIDGE UNIVERSITY LIBRARY

[f. 19]

May 20

Resolved that a letter shall be written to the judges of the King's Bench for stay of a judgment this day to be entered against Mr. More, a member of this House, in a case wherein he ought to have had his privilege.[12]

MR. CORYTON moves that we may examine Sir John Eliot's business now; and if he have done or spoken amiss, to punish him; and if not, to clear him.

SIR WALTER ERLE. That we may resolve ourselves into a grand committee for this.

MR. PYM. That Sir John Eliot may be sent for.

SIR THOMAS HOBY. That wc may first know how he stand in the King's eyes.

CHANCELLOR EXCHEQUER. Sir John Eliot has been examined by the King's commandment and has given his negative answer,[13] which the King has taken, and thereupon his Majesty has remitted him to his liberty for those matters which were charged upon him extrajudicial to this House.

Sir John Eliot sent for. Comes in and takes his place.

SIR PETER HEYMAN moves that Sir John Eliot's charge may be made known to us.

VICE CHAMBERLAIN. Do not take this that I say as a charge against Sir John Eliot, but as an occasion for him to clear himself. I meddle not with that which was said [f. 19v] to be extrajudicial to the House. You enjoined me to pray a conference with the Lords concerning the impeachment of a great peer of their House. Those that delivered the body of the charge deserved no condemnation but commendation. Every respective word to the person was a wound to the person, every disrespective word a wound to the cause. It pleased Sir John Eliot to desire their Lordships if any errors were committed to impute it to his weakness, not to the House. But I rather think he erred in his too great vigor and vehemency. His commission was to "amplify" and "aggravate" his part,[14] and his part was likewise to recapitulate the body of the charge and refresh their memories, but not to bring in any new things therein. He represented a character of the Duke of Buckingham's mind comparatively to a strange beast called *stellionatus*, of such strange colors that none knew what to make out.[15] This I do not find to be within the compass of his charge; and none know men's minds but only *scrutor cordis*, God. A doubt he cast in a thing of great importance, the rendering back of the ships sent from Rochelle, which was most sure. He said, "They say they are come, but I know it not".[16] This might be taken as a doubt of the House, because he said I do this in obedience to the House. In all languages if you come to that word "that man", it is a word of the greatest [f. 20] baseness and indignity that can be. Still [*illegible*] his own particular reason and sense.

11. *Informed that the Bp. of Bangor has labored to seduce witnesses telling them if they answer in the negative they commit/* is crossed out in the MS following *negative*.

12. See above, n. 1.

13. See HofC, 19 May, n. 1.

14. For the instructions to the speakers for the meeting or conference with the Lords, see HofC, 8 May, OB.

15. See above, n. 5.

16. See above, n. 6.

The offense that sounded ill abroad was certain comparisons historical that were used by him, which were carried further than he made application. In Sejanus his comparison he used the word "*adulator*". I do not think that it was in the charge. And the words "veneries" and "venefices" he said he would not mention.[17] And he compared him to the Bishop of Ely. He said he could not speak and did doubt to think it, speaking of the last charge, the particular of the plaster, and concluded with words of Cicero. He spoke as if that somewhat was yet covered which might be uncovered.

This I speak as a subject whereupon Sir John Eliot may clear himself, and that I desire he may do.

SIR JOHN ELIOT. It was yesterday half an hour after 11 a clock before I heard of the warrant for my delivery, and it was no visitation of friends that kept me from the service of the House. Desires that the particulars in doubt or question may be singled out and his single answer be made to every particular, that he may give the more clear satisfaction to them all.

MR. SPEAKER repeats the first particular: that he compared the Duke in his mind to the beast *stellionatus*.

[f. 20v] SIR JOHN ELIOT. To avoid tautologies and the same languages, I used other words; as for his many offices, I called it his ambition. *Stellionatus* is a metaphorical word and used for faults of collusion. The particulars of his abusing the parliament at Oxford and abusing the King and deceiving the merchants to get them to Dieppe, etc., speaking one thing and knowing another, the character of his mind in this I compared to the beast *stellionatus*.

MR. SPEAKER repeats the 2nd particular: that he said he knew not that the ships were come back from Rochelle, and in obedience to the House.

SIR JOHN ELIOT. I used the words there and I heard them here, but I hope you will pardon me. I must justly say still the same: I do not know that the ships are come back.

MR. SPEAKER repeats the 3rd particular: in that Sir John Eliot styled him, "that man".[18]

SIR JOHN ELIOT. I did affect the service of this House as much as I could, and to avoid tediousness and contract myself.

The Latins use this.

That there should be offense taken that I should call him, "that man", truly [f. 21] I do yet believe he is no god. I gave him all his respects and titles, but sometimes/

MR. SPEAKER repeats the 4th particular: in his comparison to Sejanus he said he was *audax superbus adulator* and "I will not mention his veneries, his venefices", which might be taken/[19]

SIR JOHN ELIOT. I shall speak also of the 2nd comparison. 4 R. 1, a particular censure of the Bishop of Ely:[20] the exhausting or luxuriously misemploying the King's revenue, and preferring uncertain persons and obscure men to places of trust and honor, and his boldness [and] confidentness were laid to his charge, and *per totam insulam publice proclamatur, pereat qui/*

I conceive these were within my charge and that it was boldness in him to stay a ship after an order of the King and state.

In my compari[son] of Sejanus I mentioned that he was *sui obtegens, audax superbus adulator, clientes suos honoribus et provinciis, laborum imperatores socios.*

The words "veneries" and "venefices" I

17. See above, n. 7, and see HofL, 15 May, p. 462.

18. In Eliot's holograph (10 May, above) the phrase is "the man".

19. See above, n. 7.

20. Regarding the censure of William Longchamp, Bishop of Ely, see HofL, 15 May, p. 463, and n. 72.

included, but they lay so necessarily in the way of the story, and I meant them not to the King but know not how they may apply them.

MR. SPEAKER repeats the 5th particular: that Sir John Eliot spoke upon the particular of the plaster as if *aliquid latet quod non patet,* and he wanted words to express the heinousness of the fact.

[f. 21v] MR. WANDESFORD moves that Sir John Eliot may explain himself, that in his comparison he went no further than the person of the Duke in his intent.

SIR JOHN ELIOT. I gave no words that could admit an interpretation that any person greater than the Duke. If they mean my Sovereign, I make this protestation: that I carry a heart as loyal and as faithful to his service as any man that is about him and had not manner of such intention as to touch him in those comparisons. And that the House should tie me to every syllable, I know it was not their meaning.

I used these words: that he not contented with the injury of justice, wrong of honor, and contempt of the state. He went higher making his practices upon the King, which I said I could not speak and did doubt to think, and ended *ne gravioribus utor verbis quam natura fecit, nec levioribus quam causa postulat.* For that it is said that my expression was too violent, what I have received from God or nature in this kind I hope shall not at [all] prejudice me. And what I spoke then I spoke not in passion, but to do this House service.

Sir John Eliot being called to withdraw.

SIR JOHN JACKSON. That he is not to withdraw unless a charge be delivered against him.

Sir John Eliot of himself, not being [f. 22] required by the House, does withdraw after short debate.

Resolved by question, that Sir John Eliot has not exceeded his commission which he had from this House in anything that he spoke at the conference with the Lords concerning the impeachment of the Duke of Buckingham, *nullo* negative.

Resolved that Sir Dudley Digges has not exceeded his commission which he had from this House in anything that passed from him in the late conference with the Lords, *nullo* negative.

SIR ROBERT HARLEY moves that it may be entered that no aggravation be ever admitted hereafter in such case but that first they shall give in the heads of their aggravation.

Non allocatur.

III. DIARY OF SIR RICHARD GROSVENOR, MS 611, TRINITY COLLEGE, DUBLIN

[p. 120]

May 20

MR. CORYTON moved the House to consider of the accusations laid to the charge of Sir John Eliot. That if he were faulty we might punish him; if he proved guiltless he might come into the House.

SIR WALTER ERLE. That the House might be turned into a committee to examine the matter.

MR. PYM. That Sir John Eliot should be here to hear his charge.

SIR THOMAS HOBY. That we might know how he stands in his Majesty's eyes before we send for him hither, because so much.

MR. CHANCELLOR OF EXCHEQUER. That for all matters which were extrajudicial to this House Sir John Eliot had been examined and denied all things. Wherewith his Majesty has been satisfied and has taken his denial and gave him free liberty for anything done out of the House; to come hither.

The Serjeant was sent for Sir John Eliot.

SIR NATHANIEL RICH. That it was declared by all the judges in Queen Elizabeth's time that neither the Queen nor counsel could commit any man above 24 hours without expressing the cause of their imprisonment, for that was against Magna Carta.[21] Now Sir John Eliot had been divers days imprisoned and no cause shown why, but in general terms for high offenses. Moved there should be no entry made of it lest it might be urged hereafter that the cause was just for his imprisonment, to our prejudice.

Sir John Eliot came into the House and took his place.

SIR P. HEYMAN. I have heard in this House that what this gentleman spoke was so false in his speech from top to toe; moved that some of those near the chair would let us know what that was.

MR. VICE CHAMBERLAIN. It is expected that somewhat be said concerning the clearing of this worthy gentleman or his condemning. That I say is to minister subject to him to clear himself, and if therein he will acknowledge obligation to him. *Ergo,* take this not as a charge but as an occasion for him to discharge himself.

[p. 121] I will discharge the duty of a member, that what he did by order of this House I will approve; if otherwise, though never so well done, I allow it not.

The conference demanded by me from the House to hear the impeachment against a great peer of this realm.

The entrance into the speech gave more distaste abroad than to the hearers, which yet, by his Majesty's benignity, was turned into sweetness. The whole other six, in place of condemnation, deserved commendation. Every respective word given by them to the person was a wound to the person; every disrespective word, a wound to the cause.

His too much vigor, strength, and vehemency I condemn. For the matter, I must go punctually and first look into the commission, which was that every man might "amplify" and "aggravate" his part.[22] This was very large but, being his commission, he is to be justified in everything that was his part, which was to have the conclusion read and to contain himself within the compass of that conclusion. Yet, I allow him further by way of recollection and recapitulation to represent it to their Lordships' memories of things past if anything [come] forth of this that was not in his charge.

I will touch some particulars which relished ill with some strangers. He represented a character of the Duke of Buckingham's mind: no such thing in the charge, only God is *scrutator cordium.* His mind was likened to a strange beast, *stellio,* of such strange color and lines that no man could tell what to make of it.

Other things I formerly touched here when I represented some narrative reasons why these gentlemen were committed, and that gave us a handle how to draw them out again. Some things said against the mind of the House, viz., they doubt of a certain thing, the rendering of the ships, which was a[s] certain as could be except we had seen them in [the] Thames.

[p. 122] He said, "They say they are come, but I know it not". This doubt might be taken as a doubt of the House because he said whatever he had said was in obedience.

The whole style, using the word of "this man". "The man" was offensive to my ears and the word "that man" is a word of the greatest baseness and indignity that can be

21. Concerning the Resolution of the Judges, see HofC, 17 May, n. 15.

22. See above, n. 14.

in the world in all languages. Those that spoke in this style did much disadvantage the cause.

In the conclusion, where we reserved the liberty to charge him further, there he named the Duke; but in his particular reasons he went another way.

To let you know the offense of a mixed nature, was comparisons historical which were further carried than his application. They were 2: one of Sejanus; 2, of the Bishop of Ely.

Audax superbus adulator: these are good words but out of the charge. As for veneries and venefices, he said he would not touch upon them, but it was taken as meant that the Lords should look into it.

This historical part was applied further to those who were in the top of our government. But the point of the greatest sharpness, coming to the last, repeating that all the wrongs had some more matter in them; and in the last charge he cut that off with certain words of Cicero as if Cicero, an excellent orator, had not words to explain so much. This was delivered as though something more in that not yet discovered. Now I have discovered all which has rested in my cogitations in this business and must desire a favorable exposition, for I should have been contented rather to have spent my breath in clearing of him, which I desire he will now do himself.

[p. 123] SIR JOHN ELIOT. I shall not use the art of apology for myself, only this excuse of my late coming: no neglect of my duty but want of intelligence and ignorance of the favor done me. Yesterday after 11 before I heard of any warrant.

I take it a noble favor done me to give me this occasion to discharge myself. But because the particulars are many and may concern me near, because the question will now be whether I be worthy to sit here to be your servant, this contains many particulars. I shall not be able in a continued discourse to give satisfaction to all. Moved that they might be singled out into particulars and he would labor to give present satisfaction to them all.

The SPEAKER named the first charge, of the character of the Duke's mind.

SIR JOHN ELIOT. For this particular, that you may better to understand me in this and the rest, I will state my method shortly, for the coherence and connection will best show it. After a short mention of the first stating of the business of the evils and cause, I descended into the particular things of the charge and therein observed as well as I could my duty not to exceed your commission.[23] To avoid tautologies of those offenses, I changed the names, not the substance; for getting his honors and great offices, I termed that his ambition.

Collusion: *dolus malus.* I thought these words not apt enough to express it, but consulted with my memory how such things had been formerly expressed and I found them thus: those which were of fraud or collusion, and *ergo* they called it by this word, *stellionatus*—a dispotted beast.

[p. 124] The particulars upon what this was insisted on were 3:

1. The art used to persuade the merchants to go with their ships to Dieppe, there to entrap them.

2. That of the King, that he did with shadows and pretenses color their going to serve at Rochelle.

3. The abuse of the p[arliament] after the ships were delivered up, when, at Oxford, he shadowed and disguised the intent as though no such thing.

These of that head I expressed by

23. See above, n. 14.

stellionatus and called it the character of his mind. And if in this I have offended I crave pardon.

The next, that he said he knew not the ships were come.

SIR J. ELIOT. I will neither come short nor exceed. This House neither if, and, of; we tie men to that. I used the words that I did not know, though I heard that the ships were come home. It is true, I heard it said in this House. I believe not all I hear to be true, nay, I have heard many things I dare not tell. I say again: I do not know it.

"This man", "the man".

SIR JOHN ELIOT. I am not so fortunate as others that can speak by book; but yet with as much caution as I can, not to err. In this what I intended, I know my own conscience, I labored to contract myself to avoid tediousness. I did not neglect the titles of that Duke, but when of his faults I called him "the man", no such ill speech in the language. You know how used in the Latin: *Ille ipse ad [illegible] ipse dixit.* I know it not to be a fault.

Comparisons historical carried further than his application went, that of Sejanus.

[p. 125] SIR JOHN ELIOT. True, I used such comparison. That of the B[ishop] of Ely I need not answer. I hear nothing against it, because I heard it only mentioned. Yet, I will tell you clearly what that was. 4 R. 1, he was censured.[24] It came onwards in these parts and took out only the particulars that came home to this charge: 1, the luxurious misemployment [of] the King's revenue; 2, the preferring to honors, to places of trust and command to obscure and unknown persons; 3, of his boldness, confidence, and that I might parallel with some parts of our charge when the King's warrants were contradicted; *supra totam insulam publicae proclamatur pereat qui.*

That of Sejanus had more parts: *audax sui obtegens clientes suos honoribus,* styled *laborum imperatores socios.* Between these did I use the words of veneries and venefices, for in the story between that of preferring his friends come[s] in his lechery with Livia and his poisoning of Drusus. Yet these I spoke exclusively and had no relation to this man except he so apply them. I meant it not; let not their misinterpretation be my fault. This you may see in the history which has been more sold by the stationer more since this charge than in a year before.

Upon MR. WANDESFORD's motion, he explained himself that those things spoken in the examples of Sejanus and Ely he intended not in the application, nor had no thoughts or words to carry it that it should reflect upon any other but the Duke himself.

For that concerning the words of Cicero, these were my words: that, having from the former parts of the charge of collusion, ambition, etc., then by way of wonder, as a transition to the rest, I marveled how this man could stand or subsist of himself, [p. 126] being a man dangerous to the state, disproportionable in regard of his greatness. This could not be done without much art. Then to his conferring honors upon his kindred—this he used as an art to uphold himself. Then that he set upon the King's revenue—this later I urged as a boldness more as a fire that catches at all things and, not contented with the injuries of justice, wrong of honor, prejudice of the estate and honor, but then went further to the person of a king. I feared to say I would leave it as Cicero did the like, hoping their Lordships would discover the rest, and *ergo* to them I left it.

2 things more are objected: the one, the manner of my speech; the other, the mat-

24. See above, n. 20.

ter. In the manner, that I used too much vigor and strength, as if his expression were too violent. What my nature is and what I have received from God in that particular, I am not master of it. If a tone or sound might prejudice, it might do so now. Seldom here have I felt passion, and there I spoke not passion but so far to give life to that I was commanded. So this I hope pardonable—a fault of nature, not of me.

That I was to read the conclusion of the long bill and to have contained myself within that and have gone no further. Till the particulars show my exceeding the charge, I can say nothing. If any please to charge me, I shall give the best answer I can.

[p. 127] SIR ROBERT PYE. That he was not at the charge but heard that it was very bitter, so he thought it was. That in that business of the transcendent presumption, this House intended it only as a crime. By that application of Sejanus he expressed that which was against the sense of the House. The committee were satisfied that there was no ill intention in it.

SIR WALTER ERLE. That the intention of 1 or 2 should not be taken to be the vote of the whole House.

MR. CORYTON. To clear him whether he has done well or not; then to consider the weight of the charge, which has been heavy.

MR. LONG. But one thing excepted against this gentleman, but that a heavy one.

MR. GOODWIN. It was objected that Sir J[ohn] E[liot] was somewhat bitter. It was in errors touching the commonwealth. No tongue, no mouth wide enough to utter these crimes. To the question to clear him.

MR. CREW. This gentleman undertook this service by command of the House imposed on [him] out of their good opinions of his worth and ability, as *in multiloquio non deest peccatus.* So many time[s] words are mistaken by the hearers.[25]

By question, resolved that Sir John Eliot has not exceeded the commission given him by the House in anything that passed from him at the conference with the Lords.

And both without one negative voice.

MR. WANDESFORD moved for the like justice to be done to Sir D. Digges; to be cleared by question.

By question, Sir D. Digges was also cleared.

SIR ROBERT HARLEY moved that in regard of these troubles to those gentlemen by aggravating, moved that it should be entered that hereafter never any should be allowed to aggravate any matter without first delivering in the heads of what they would speak to the House.

IV. DIARY OF JOHN LOWTHER, ESQ., D/LONS/L, CUMBERLAND AND WESTMORLAND RECORD OFFICE

[f. 36v]

Saturday [20 May]

A letter agreed to be sent by Speaker to stay judgment against Mr. More until privilege examined, notwithstanding supposition of his consent.[26]

CHANCELLOR EXCHEQUER showed how Sir John Eliot made a negative answer to things done without the House and extrajudicial, and the King has accepted it.

Nota: not satisfied, so he was sent for to his chamber, and King gave liberty to come hither, and he came in.

25. *Mr. Spencer* is crossed out in the MS preceding *By question.*

26. See above, n. 1.

Then [SIR PETER HEYMAN] moved some to charge him because said all [false] from top to toe.

VICE CHAMBERLAIN. Charges not. Expects thanks to give occasion. Commends what House directed; what more, disliked. Conference first demanded concerning an impeachment of a great man of the realm. The words they used of respect wounded the person; disrespect, the cause. Commission was to amplify and to aggravate his part, his was to contain him [f. 37] within the compass of his chapter and recapitulate. But if anything new, without his charge.

1. Began with a character of Duke his mind.

Only God [is *scrutator cordium*]. Compared to a beast, *stellio stellionatus,* so changeable as none could tell what to make of it.

2. Contrary to sense of the House in doubting the restitution of ships went to Rochelle, which he was certained of by letters. A needless unacknowledgment. Proceeding out of obedience, as he conceived he related.

3. This word of "this man". "This man" offended many as a great indignity to any man in all countries.

4. Historical comparisons as parallels, 2: the one of Sejanus, the other Bishop of Ely. *Audax superbus adulator.* Of veneries, venefices would not speak. That of Sejanus was further applied to top of government perhaps than he meant.

5. The greatest sharpness, that above all injuries, further meaning King's physic, and would not speak, doubted to think. Cut it off with words of Cicero, as though had not words enough to express it. Speaking of the last charge as though somewhat were therein covered that were not discovered.

So desires he may clear himself for he accuses not.

[f. 37v] SIR JOHN ELIOT excuses his not coming by ignorance of the favor bestowed on [him] till near eleven, or heard of discharge yesterday. He confesses the obligat[ion] to Vice Chamberlain to give him occasion to discharge himself. The charge many particulars; concerns his fitness or unfitness to serve here, dearer than life. Asks time to answer them particularly.

SPEAKER proposes them particularly.

He answers and showed his method. That he did not exceed. To avoid tautology he changed the names, as "ambition" for "offices". This part was in English. Collusion, *dolus malus,* and he found this short, but expressed it by a metaphor of *stellionatus* from a beast of divers colors. Thereby he did express [1,] the art to merchants' entrapping at Dieppe; 2, his coloring to the King the ships to go another way; 3, the abuse of parliament by disguise, possessing us after he knew ships were delivered otherwise.

2. His profession of obedience. He will therein be neither short nor over. Desires no favor not to of, etc. There he said he did not know the ships delivered, though he heard it; for so he said in the House, and so yet.

3. "This man, this man". He speaks not as some by book; he confesses, by contraction. If of Alexander, *ille ipse.* To call him a "man", thinks no offense. Thinks him no god-man.

4. For Sejanus and the intimation that there was something for the Lords to go further. [f. 38] Tells what he meant by Ely who was only named. 4 Richard, where are many charges he took what fit: luxurious misemploying of King's revenue; conferring honors of obscure men; boldness, paralleling it now to this time when King's orders contradicted *per totam insulam publice proclamatur pereat quod omnes [perimere conatur] opprimatur quem [sic] omnes opprimat.*

Sejanus in effect *stellionatus* that he did *clientes honoribus et provinciis adornare.* How he was *laborum imperatorum socius.* There used "veneries" and "venefices" for there cares in his lust to Livilla, his poisoning of Drusus. These he excluded as impertinent if he apply it not. He meant it not. Let not their interpretation be his fault. Now more of these books bought since, more than within a twelvemonth before.

5. Last, for intimation of *aliquid latet.*

Interrupted by WANDESFORD and required to show how he meant these examples nothing further than this person; not to any greater.

[SIR JOHN ELIOT.] Which he did accordingly, and said for he [would] sacrifice himself for King so soon as any.

Gives words of 5th charge so near as can. Upon having used corruption, extortion, oppression, etc.; after, wonder how could subsist being so proved being dangerous in state, so many fault[s]. Not without art. Honors of kindred to support him and alliance. Then set on King's revenue. Then this latter as a boldness more, comparing it to fire. And not content with injuries of justice, honor, state, but attempts person of King in such a sort [f. 38v] as fears to speak, doubts to think, lest as Cicero use *graviora quam res exigit vel et leviora quam causa postulat* and left it to the Lords' consideration.

2 things more he observed unanswered: his manner and matter. 1. Too much vigor. What his nature, not his fault. Seldom felt passion though his love may covet it. 2. Though he was to be contained in his read epilogue; if any particulars be without, he will answer, but he knows none but passages, as his exclusion.

Resolved by question, he exceeded not his commission given by the House at conference.

So for Sir D. Digges for all, being before but one point.[27]

SIR ROBERT HARLEY desires hereafter no aggravation to be admitted hereafter, but first to give in heads in the House.

This denied lest might seem to disallow what was done.

27. I.e., on 13 May.

Order of Business Monday, 22 May 1626

MONDAY, 22 MAY 1626

I. JOURNAL OF THE HOUSE OF COMMONS

[CJ 862; p. 71]
Lunae, 22 Maii, 2 Caroli Regis

[col. 1]	[col. 2]
Mr. [Edward] Bysshe	Mr. [Humphrey] Newbery
Sir George More	Mr. Rolle
Sir John Savile	Sir William Strode
Sir Thomas Puckering	Sir Thomas Grantham
Sir Thomas Freake	
Mr. [Anthony] Langston	

[col. 3]	[col. 4]
Mr. Whitaker	Sir Nicholas Saunders
Sir John Stradling	Sir Richard Buller
Sir B[aptist] Hicks	Sir Robert Crane
Sir H[enry] Anderson	Sir Thomas Myddleton

Tomorrow, 2 clock, in the Exchequer Chamber. These committees added to the committee appointed to examine the matter of privilege between Mr. More and Hodges.[1]

The House turned into a grand committee to receive the remonstrance from the subcommittee.[2]

Resolved now to proceed on with other business.

The copy of a letter, pretended to be written by Sir John Savile, delivered in by SIR FRANCIS FOLJAMBE and, by a general acclamation, 2 read by the Clerk.[3]

SIR JOHN SAVILE denies this to be a copy of any letter which he wrote. And being pressed whether he did write any letter wherein any such clause is which concerns the privilege of this House, he answers he did write no letter nor subscribe any letter written to any such purpose.

SIR FRANCIS FOLJAMBE desires Thursday fortnight to prove the copy now produced and written to have been a copy of a letter written by Sir John Savile.

And Sir John Savile, at his own charge, to bring up any[4] witnesses in his own defense. A warrant for the witnesses, etc.

SIR JOHN SAVILE, letting fall some speeches trenching upon Sir William Armine and Sir John Eliot, who had last before spoke in this business,[5] the House ordered he should withdraw while this was debated.

Much debate whether he should acknowledge his error and give satisfaction to the 2 gentlemen at the bar or in his place.

Resolved upon question, he should do it in his place; which he accordingly fully did.

Ordered, Mr. Whitby shall, tomorrow morning, begin to report the grievances and so proceed till his report be finished. But the business concerning presenting popish recusants to be 1st proceeded with and ended.

Liberty given to the committee for religion to examine the indirect and undue solicitation of witnesses to be produced against the Bishop of Bangor, by himself or his agents.[6]

2ly, to examine his keeping of 21 churches or chapels, which he keeps in his hands, and ill serving them.

1. Regarding the arrest of John or Poynings More, see HofC, 20 May, n. 1.

2. I.e., the proposed remonstrance regarding the imprisonment of Digges and Eliot; see the debate in the accounts below.

3. For the letter, see Whitelocke, below.

4. *to produce witnesses, and the same time given to Sir John Savile to prove any conspiracy or combination in this accusation against him* is crossed out in the MS following *any*.

5. For the speech trenching on Armine and Eliot, see Whitelocke, below.

6. See HofC, 20 May, n. 11. Regarding Lewis Bayly, Bishop of Bangor, see HofC, 17 April, n. 3.

Resolved that charges may be allowed to such poor witnesses as are to be produced in this case.

The committee for religion to sit this afternoon.

The committee for the King's revenue to sit upon Wednesday morning.

The committee for the preamble for the subsidy to sit tomorrow in the afternoon.

All grand committees for grievances and courts of justice from henceforth to hold their former days.

The committee for the naval war to sit upon Thursday next, and all that will come to have voice, Court of Wards.

[p. 72] All bills to be brought in by the committees to the Clerk, that so new fit days may be appointed for them.

The subcommittee for the Book of Rates to sit upon Wednesday next, in the afternoon, in the former place.

II. DIARY OF BULSTRODE WHITELOCKE, ESQ., DD. 12.22, CAMBRIDGE UNIVERSITY LIBRARY

[f. 22]

May 22

[*Committee of the Whole House*]

Mr. Rolle in the chair.

Mr. Littleton reports the remonstrance framed by the committee for that purpose concerning the imprisonment of Sir Dudley Digges and Sir John Eliot.

To the King's most excellent Majesty:

Most gracious Sovereign, we your Majesty's/

[f. 24] Mr. Pym. That this remonstrance may be laid aside and that we may proceed by a bill to confirm our privileges.

Sir Nathaniel Rich. I do not find that this House suffered so much in their liberties in any king's time as in the last King's. Freedom of speech, freedom of person, and freedom from misinformation are those among the rest that we desire now.[7]

Mr. Wandesford. That this remonstrance may be recommitted and the committee be appointed to frame a bill for the preservation of our liberties.

Mr. Glanville. In 18 *Jac.* in the House was framed a remonstrance to the King of their privileges for the present and a bill prepared for the future, but by reason of a message from the King they were both laid aside.[8]

Mr. Whistler. I am absolutely against a bill for confirming those privileges which are our own undoubtedly already, and by a

7. For the customary privileges petitioned for by the House of Commons, see HofC, 17 May, n. 30.

8. On 12 February 1621 following Sir Edward Coke's report on free speech from the committee of privileges (appointed 5 February) the same committee was ordered "to draw a bill for the future". *CJ,* I, 518. A petition and remonstrance were drawn in early December of the same parliament regarding matters of state that broached on privilege, but it was withdrawn from presentation to the King following James's letter to the Speaker of the House on 4 December 1621. (Ibid., 657–658, and see *CD 1621,* II, 499–500; VI, 224; VII, 721). On 6 December a new declaration to the King was drafted (*CJ,* I, 660; printed in Nicholas, *Proceedings and Debates in 1621,* II, 289–293). On 12 December a message from the King encouraged the House to continue with the bills, but the debate on privileges continued. James refused to hear the declaration and, after engaging in further debate, on 15 December a committee of the whole was again ordered to consider "things incident or concerning the privileges of the House". Their response was to draft another protestation concerning the matter of "sundry liberties, franchises, and privileges of parliament", that was presented to the House on 18 December (ibid., 668; printed in Rushworth, *Hist. Collections,* I, 53) the day preceding the adjournment. On 30 December, while the House was in recess, King James tore that protestation from the Journal book. See also, Gardiner, *History of England,* IV, 249–265.

bill we must have the Lords' consent and the King's.

Mr. Sherland. That the bill may be declarative, not enacting, and sure it will not stay with [f. 24v] the Lords nor, I hope, with the King.

Mr. Wilde. That the remonstrance may be made *viva voce* and not by writing.

Mr. Selden. That a remonstrance now is necessary for that it may appear we were careful and sensible in the commitment of our members and breach of our liberties, and thereby inform the King of those things which by bill we cannot. And yet that we may use a bill which will be long. And move that this remonstrance may be recommitted.

Sir Dudley Digges. If this case be well entered and registered, it will be more effectual than a bill or a remonstrance.

The remonstrance recommitted.

The subcommittee ordered to take consideration of a bill, or remonstrance, or protestation to be framed, or all of them, and to frame them accordingly.

Speaker takes his chair.

SIR FRANCIS FOLJAMBE moves that the copy of a letter may be read, which he presents to the House, being a copy of a letter of Sir John Savile.

The letter was to this effect:

My Masters: I thought it necessary to give you an account upon what terms things now stand in parliament which most and especially concern the places where I live,[9] that is the clothiers generally of our country. I have divers times moved and offered unto the consideration of this House the inconvenience and mischief that must of necessity follow if the merchant be debarred from free trade,[10] whereby the clothier must be enforced to discharge his servants, who having no other means must of necessity seek [f. 25] some other means to live by, which in respect of their numbers would be a thing of a dangerous consequence, more than I fear is well conceived of. But they are so resolutely bent and with such eagerness upon the pursuit of a great man as rather than they will fail or surcease they are resolved to hazard the whole estate of the commonwealth, as I fear. I would advise you to appeal unto his Majesty and unto his Council of state and to lay down unto them plainly and clearly the estate of the clothiers, how it now stands, if present remedy be not provided and some order taken, which we fear under favor is not in the power of any justice of peace or other subordinate officer in the country. The things must be plainly and fully delivered, the number especially of those that now live and maintain themselves by clothing, which I have estimated to the number of 30,000 one and another. My meaning was not to speak short, and yet in my conscience I am persuaded I have spoken within compass. As you desire to maintain my credit whereby I may be enabled to do you service in this or any other thing, that you will use care and all possible expedition in this business, whereof I hope you will not fail. And so in haste I rest,

Your loving friend,
John Savile

London, February 27, 1625

To my good friends Mr. John Harrison, Mr. Daniel Foxcrofte, Mr. Thomas Metcalfe, and the rest to whom it may appertain, deliver with speed.[11]

[f. 25v] SIR JOHN SAVILE moves that he that preferred this letter may make proof that it is a true copy of his letter. If this be proved to be a copy of my letter, I will have

9. I.e., Yorkshire.

10. See Savile's speeches on 27 February (and n. 30), 16 March, and 3 May.

11. John Harrison was a collector of the privy seals in the West Riding. (*APC 1625–1626*, p. 424) and had served as deputy mayor of Leeds under Sir John Savile in 1621 (R. V. Taylor, *The Biographia Leodiensis*, [Leeds, 1865], p. 92). Daniel Foxcrofte and Thomas Metcalfe were townsmen from Leeds. *Wentworth Papers 1597–1628*, Camden Fourth Series, no. 12 (London, 1973), pp. 250–251.

my hand struck off at the bar and my head too, which I deserve if it were so. I never wrote/

Desires he may have day to bring up his witnesses to prove the conspiracy, and [desires] the warrant of the House.

Sir William Armine. That before he name those that he conceives are in the conspiracy and that there is a conspiracy, he may not have a warrant from the House.

Sir John Eliot. To the same purpose.

Sir John Savile. That he may suspect that those that speak against this may be in the conspiracy.

For this aspersion laid upon Sir John Eliot and Sir William Armine, Sir John Savile is caused to withdraw. And, upon the motion of Sir John and Sir William, called in again and makes an acknowledgment of his fault, not at the bar but in his place of his fault, and says he is sorry for it if anything that fell from him might lay an aspersion upon Sir John Eliot or Sir William Armine.

Day given to Sir Francis Foljambe till Tuesday fortnight to prove the copy of this letter.[12] And Sir John Savile has liberty to bring up what witnesses he will for his own defense.

[f. 26] Upon Sir Eubule Thelwall's motion, ordered that the committee for the Bishop of Bangor's business shall examine of the Bishop's soliciting the witnesses brought up against him to give false testimony, and of his keeping 25 churches or chapels in his own hands.[13]

III. Diary of Sir Richard Grosvenor, MS 611, Trinity College, Dublin

[p. 128]

22 May

Sir William Strode, Sir Dudley Digges, Sir G. More, Sir Thomas Hoby moved to go on in our business and to lose no longer time.

Mr. Rolle came into the chair; the House turned into a committee.

[*Committee of the Whole House*]

Mr. Littleton reported what the committee had done in the remonstrance to the King concerning the committing of our 2 members.

It was delivered in in writing and read by the Clerk.

Mr. Pym. No reason why we should send a remonstrance at this time. We have our members again; we may receive such an answer as may make us worse, not better. That we may proceed more by way of a bill in this House than by this remonstrance, that will more maintain our privileges.

Sir Nathaniel Rich. A great comfort to see every man so sensible of their liberties which is the liberty of the whole kingdom. He agreed fully with Mr. Pym that a bill was the best way; not fit now to make this remonstrance. That which this House suffers is under the precedents of the last King and Queen Elizabeth, never so much in former times. We made a remonstrance in the first year of King James,[14] 2 or 3 in 18 *Jac.*[15] We know how we were entangled; such answers drew on declarations and letters one after

12. A petition from Thomas Metcalf was read in the House the following day. See below, 24 May, OB. On 8 June Mr. Farrer, Anthony Foxcrofte, his father, Daniel Foxcrofte, and John Harrison testified regarding the letter, see below.

13. See above, n. 6.

14. I.e., in the first parliament of James I. For the petition expressing the "ancient, general and undoubted right of parliament to debate freely all matter which do properly concern the subject", see *CJ*, I, 431–432; *PP 1610,* II, 110–113.

15. See above, n. 8.

another. Then we fell to protestations, after to a dissolution. Freedom of speech, freedom of person, freedom from misinformation: we have formerly taken course for.

Mr. Kirton. To go on with a remonstrance.

Mr. Long.[16] Both for the remonstrance and a bill; and to have the remonstrance enlarged and therein to desire this Majesty to punish those who have made him break his royal word, which was that we should have full liberty of speech.

[p. 129] Mr. Wandesford. A bill will advantage as much as a bill [*sic*]. Moved to have this remonstrance not cast away but recommitted, and the same committee to draw a bill; and if by a bill we may more surely maintain our privileges, then to waive this remonstrance.

Sir W. Strode. To lay this remonstrance by and choose a committee for a bill.

Mr. Coryton. To go on in the remonstrance. He thought the King did not know all that has been done, for it may be it was not his pleasure these gentlemen should be taken forth of the House. This might have bred much trouble.

Mr. Glanville. In 18 *Jac.* the House fell upon 2 courses in their privileges: to have a remonstrance of their privileges for the present and a bill for the future.[17] Then resolved that all faults committed here, if they deserved no greater punishment than this House could inflict, they ought not to be punished but by the House.[18]

Mr. Pym. This remonstrance a pretty cross play to a game in government called[19] a "Keeping in Ignorance". If this shall procure another remonstrance, that will only be (if we be in danger) to lose the parliament. To let the King know that as we should have gone on well and cheerfully into our countries if we proceed happily, so sorrowfully if we be broken off.

Mr. Newbery. No remonstrance. We have our members again. There have been remonstrances in King James's time. If we do this still and be foiled in it, it will do us harm.

Mr. Whistler.[20] Against any bill, for before it passes we must have the Lords' consent and the King's; if it stop there, it is a show we had no such privilege.

Mr. Sherland. To let this remonstrance rest awhile, but not to waive it. Arguments from terror or fear of success move me not. But we have lost much time; the business[es] of the commonwealth are pressing. If we pass a bill I would make it declarative which, I hope, would neither stick with the Lords nor the King.

[p. 130] Mr. Wilde. That we might claim our privileges by Mr. Speaker *viva voce* [*illegible*] of the whole House.

Mr. Selden. Both for a bill and a remonstrance. A bill would be long and no man knows whether it could pass. That this remonstrance proceed because thereby we give him that [*illegible*] information which otherwise he cannot know or we came by these interpretations. It were fit to inform him how much time we have spent by reason of these interpretations.

Sir Dudley Digges. For a recommitment to make a declaration of circumstances. It is a [*illegible*] thing when our own speakers are

16. *Wentworth* is crossed out in the MS and *Long* is inserted.

17. See above, n. 8.

18. A reference to the privileges claimed in the protestation submitted to James on 18 December 1621 and by him torn from the record. *CJ*, I, 668 (printed in Rushworth, *Hist. Collections*, I, 53).

19. MS: *calling*.

20. *Smith* is crossed out in the MS and *Whistler* is inserted.

arrested by other men. And if we shall be too cautious in the account of circumstances done by men employed [*illegible*] may fall upon that error. If we see it entered well into the Clerk's book that we have our members this parliament, then above a remonstrance or a bill. And we should not have such a precedent [*illegible*] them back again.

By question, the remonstrance recommitted.

By another: that they should consider whether it were fit for this House to use a remonstrance, a bill, or any other way.

Committee adjourned until Wednesday at 9 of the clock.

Mr. Speaker came into the chair.

SIR H. POOLE moved to go on in other business of the House.

SIR FRANCIS FOLJAMBE moved to have a letter read which was sent by a member of this House, which touched the honor of this House. It was a letter from Sir John Savile to Mr. John Harrison, Mr. Daniel Foxcrofte, Mr. Thomas Metcalfe, etc., Feb. 27, 1625.[21]

My Masters: An account how things stand in parliament. Have divers times moved and offered the consideration what mischief must follow if the merchants have naught for trade. A pursuit of a great man, but they are so resolutely bent with such eager[ness] in the pursuit that they would hazard the whole estate of that commonwealth before [p. 131] they would surcease, as I fear.

SIR JOHN SAVILE entreated this favor: that he that preferred this might be called in to justify that this was a true copy of his letter, which he denied. That if this were his letter he would have his head and hand stricken off.

SIR F. FOLJAMBE moved that he might have a warrant to send for some witnesses.

MR. PYM wished that Sir John Savile should express himself whether he ever wrote that or any such clause as that which concerned the privileges of the House.

SIR JOHN SAVILE answered that he never either wrote or subscribed any such letter.

Thursday come fortnight given to bring up his witnesses, as also Sir John Savile to bring up any witnesses he pleased to prove a conspiracy against him.[22]

SIR JOHN ELIOT and SIR W. ARMINE moved that he should not have a warrant for witnesses till he accused some particular.

SIR JOHN SAVILE said that he held the 2 to have a hand in this combination. Whereupon he was much spoken against. He explained himself and made it worse, saying he knew nothing by them but had most reason to suspect them because they spoke against him. He was commanded to withdraw, which he did. Some would have him to the bar, others in his seat to acknowledge the wrong he had done to the House and those gentlemen.

Resolved he should, in his place, acknowledge the wrong he had done to the 2 gentlemen, and that he knew nothing by them, that he had gone too far, and was sorry for it.

He came into his seat, the SPEAKER told him the vote of the House.

SIR JOHN SAVILE did so.

[p. 132] Ordered upon SIR WILLIAM SPENCER's motion that Mr. Whitby should begin tomorrow morning with the report of the grievances, and so to go on.

SIR EUBULE THELWALL moved that the witnesses against the Bishop of Bangor

21. For the letter, see Whitelocke, above, and see also, n. 11.

22. See above, n. 12.

might be examined by the committee of any practice of his which [solicits] them not to bear true witness.

Ordered that they should examine this, and about his keeping of 21 livings in his own hands.

MR. GRIFFITH moved that it should be lawful for him who served for that country, without tax of conspiracy, might relieve the witnesses which were come up against the B[ishop] of Bangor, and that the committee might sit this afternoon.

So ordered.

MR. PYM moved for the committee of religion to sit.

MR. CORYTON. That we should proceed in the business for the rectifying of the King's revenue Wednesday morning.

MR. CHANCELLOR OF EXCHEQUER. For the preamble to the act of subsidy. To appoint a time to report it to the committee.

Tomorrow afternoon.

SIR THOMAS HOBY. To go first on with the petition for putting out of popish commissioners.

All set standing committees to keep their days.

SIR NATHANIEL RICH. For the naval war upon Thursday.

Ordered that all bills should be brought in and the Speaker to order them so that they may go on with them.

IV. DIARY OF JOHN LOWTHER, ESQ., D/LONS/L, CUMBERLAND AND WESTMORLAND RECORD OFFICE

[f. 39]

[22 May]

[*Committee of the Whole House*]

Mr. Pym moved for a bill, not remonstrance; but the committee both, he [thinks] this will do no good for that liberty of speech we have. And the example of deliverance better than that of imprisonment.

But the sufferance was in King James's time, said Rich, and Queen Elizabeth's time, when we made remonstrance, and answer, and reply, letters, protestation, and dissolution. Freedom of speech, person, information. Therefore to avoid dispute desires a bill. Temps H. 8 produced act of parliament lest not got by debate.[23]

Wandesford. For bill, and to proceed to business.

Glanville. Resolved, 18 *Jac.*, we no power but to fine and imprison; Lords to judge. Then was a bill proposed and agreed upon.

Ordered, a committee to consider whether a remonstrance, or bill, protestation, or all, and to prepare it. Afternoon, Star Chamber.

SIR F. FOLJAMBE brings in a letter out of Yorkshire.

Read, because brought by member of House, before the Speaker read it.

Sir John Savile's letter, copied, to John Harrison, D. Foxcrofte, Sir Thomas Metcalfe, etc.:

He gives account of parliament concerning their clothiers. He often moved the inconvenience in setting down the trade, being many, and the mischief if merchants debarred of free trade. They so resolutely bent and eager in pursuit of a great man that they will [*illegible*] hazard the state of commonwealth as he fears rather than s/

[f. 39v] He spoke of 30,000 men. Meant not short. Desires to use care and expedition to maintain his credit.

SIR JOHN desires who offers copy to prove it. If this be a true copy, desires to have his

23. Perhaps a reference to *SR*, 4 H. VIII, c. 8, the act for Richard Strode.

hand and head struck off, for he deserves no less.

FOLJAMBE. Has order for witnesses to prove it.

PYM moved that he should clear if he spoke to that effect.

SIR JOHN denies that any can be shown, and he denies his writing, he subscribing, or directing any such clause.

He in the end denied to answer by order of House, and it was allowed.

GLANVILLE. His judgment of himself is like to be true by his consent if it be true.

Ordered to withdraw; and to come in upon suit of the wronged gentlemen[24] and to acknowledge an error in his place, which he did.

Mr. Whitby tomorrow to report the grievances.

WANDESFORD reports the honor that Sir W. S./[25]

CHANCELLOR EXCHEQUER moves to proceed on King's revenue and to bring in preamble of subsidy.

Wednesday morn for revenue.

Thursday, the naval war.

All general committees to proceed.

Tonnage and poundage Wednesday afternoon.

24. I.e., Sir William Armine and Sir John Eliot. See Whitelocke and Grosvenor, above.

25. Sir William Spencer. See Grosvenor, above.

Order of Business Tuesday, 23 May 1626

Committee on the bill for avoiding of deceits in making of **medicines** and concerning **apothecaries**	311, *23/2
Committee on the bill for confirmation of certain articles of agreement by the consent of the Lords and tenants of manors in **Feltwell** to meet this afternoon	311, *4/5
Committee on the bill for sale of certain lands which were late Sir Henry **Clere's** to meet tomorrow; four members added	311, *1/5
Committee on the bill against all pretenses of **concealments** to meet tomorrow	311, *13/2
Committee on the bill for a better allowance from **non residents** to their **preaching curates** to meet Thursday [25 May]	311, *8/5
Committee on the bill for the better ordering of the office of the **clerk of the market** to meet Thursday [25 May]	311, *7/3
Committee on the bill for free liberty to **marry** at any time of the year to meet Thursday [25 May]	311, *3/5
Committee on the bill against the transportation of **ordnance** to meet tomorrow	311, *13/2
Committee on the bill for making void a decree in the Exchequer Chamber made in behalf of Sir Francis **Neale** against Sir Edward **Fisher** to meet Thursday [25 May]	311, *7/3
Committee on the bill to make void certain conveyances unconscionably gotten from Giles **Sewster** to meet Friday [26 May]	311, *20/2
Committee on the bill for the mitigation of the sentence of the greater **excommunication** to meet this afternoon	311, *10/3
Committee on the bill to enable Sir Charles **Snell** to make a jointure to meet tomorrow	311, *27/3
Ordered: a new writ to be issued for **Huntingdonshire** to fill the place of Edward Montagu, Lord Mandeville, called to the Upper House	311
Committee on the bills for **arms** to meet Thursday [25 May]	311, *14/3; 20/3
Committee on the bill to make the lands of **persons outlawed** for debt subject and liable to extents to meet Friday [26 May]	311, *16/3
Committee on bill for making the estate of **attainted persons** liable for their **debts** to meet Friday [26 May]	311, *14/3
Sir John Hare granted license to depart	311
Report from the committee on the bill for avoiding of the increase of **cottages** in cities (John Whistler)	311, 313, *17/2
Amendments to the bill on cottages: read twice; bill is recommitted	311, 313
Report from the committee on the bill for the naturalizing of Sir Daniel **Deligne** (Thomas Smith)	311, 313, *8/5
Amendments to Deligne's bill: read twice; bill is engrossed	311, 313
John Wilde: moves that Richard **Dyott,** MP, be restored to his place; delivers in a petition from Dyott	312, 313, *9/5
Dyott's petition is read	311
Richard Dyott called in to his place	311, 312, 313

TUESDAY, 23 MAY 1626

I. JOURNAL OF THE HOUSE OF COMMONS

[**CJ 862;** p. 72]
Martis, 23 Maii, 2 Caroli Regis

Apothecaries bill, tomorrow, 2 clock.[1]

Feltwell bill,[2] this afternoon, 2 clock.

Clere's bill, tomorrow, 2 clock. Mr. [Humphrey] Newbery, Mr. [Christopher] Erle, Mr. [Edward] Kirton, Mr. [Richard] Taylor, added to the committee.

Bill of concealments, tomorrow in the afternoon.

Allowance from nonresidents, and impropriations, upon Thursday, 2 clock.

Clerk of the market, Thursday, 2 clock.

Bill for marriage, Thursday, 2 clock.

Ordnance bill, tomorrow afternoon.

Sir Edward Fisher's bill, Thursday afternoon.

Mr. Sewster's bill, Friday afternoon.

Excommunication, this afternoon.

Sir H. Snell, his bill, tomorrow in the afternoon.

A warrant for a new writ for a knight for Huntingdonshire in place of Lord Mandeville, called by writ to the higher House.[3]

The committee for arms, Thursday afternoon.

Bill for outlawed persons to have their lands extended, upon Friday in the afternoon.

Bill to make estates of persons attainted subject to payment of their debts, upon Friday afternoon next.

Sir John Hare licensed to go down and return at the end of the next week.

MR. WHISTLER reports the general bill of cottages,[4] with amendments; which 2 read.

Upon question, recommitted. Every man that will come to have voice; 2 clock this afternoon, in the Exchequer Court.

Sir D. Deligne's bill reported, with amendments; which 2 read. *Engrossetur.*

A petition from Mr. Dyott, sequestered from the House, read.[5]

This gave the House good satisfaction. And thereupon he called to his place, and MR. SPEAKER, standing up bare, told him the House rested satisfied with his submission; for which he gave thanks to the House.

Bill for Sir James Altham's lands, Thursday next, afternoon.

Upon question resolved, upon Thursday next, at the rising of the House, to adjourn it until Thursday in Whitsun week.

Upon question, the House to be called upon Friday next.

Upon question, those which shall then make default without a just excuse to be allowed by the House shall pay £10 at the least, besides further punishment as the House shall inflict.

[p. 73] Mr. Smalman's man brought in by *habeas corpus* which, and the return, read by the Clerk.

1. By order of the previous day new times were to be appointed for hearing bills, see 22 May, OB.

2. *tomorrow* is crossed out in the MS and *this afternoon* is inserted.

3. Edward Montagu, Viscount Mandeville by courtesy, was summoned to the Upper House as Lord Kimbolton, by writ of 19 May. See HofL, 22 May, pp. 540, 541 and 543. He was the son and heir apparent of Henry, Earl of Manchester.

4. I.e., An act for the avoiding of the increase of cottages in cities. The bill did not receive a third reading in this parliament.

5. On 9 May Dyott had been sequestered for offensive words spoken in the House. We have not found his petition.

The servant discharged, and the officer[6] which brought him so much informed by MR. SPEAKER.

Garland and Harrison, the serjeants which arrested this man, to be sent for to be here.

The man, called in again, affirms that when he was arrested he told the serjeants he was Mr. Smalman's man, a member of this House, and that he [*sic*] said he would, notwithstanding, carry him to the Counter.

Complaint made that the serjeant which now brought him/

The business concerning the presenting of recusants, renewed.[7]

MR. BYSSHE mentions Mr. Hill, dwelling in Holborn, and one Mr. Minshull, which are popishly affected and live out of the Inns of Court, and yet practice.

[**CJ 863**] All the lawyers of the House to be added to the committee appointed to consider of the presenting of recusants; and by them consideration to be taken of the best means to discover popishly affected persons living in Inns of Court and Chancery, or that are lawyers and practice the law but live abroad, and to prevent all hurt which can grow by them.

Upon question, Sir Walter Tichborne to be left out of the presentment.[8]

Upon question, the Earl of Arundel to be spared.[9]

Upon question, the petition preceding the names, allowed by the House.

The particular names and the conclusion read and allowed and ordered to be engrossed, saving only a reservation for putting in Mr. Warren, a minister of Suffolk; which to be perfected against tomorrow morning.[10]

The grievances to be reported tomorrow morning.

Mr. Hutton's bill, tomorrow in the afternoon.

A warrant for a writ for Hastings, in the room of Sir D. Carleton, called in by writ to the Upper House.[11]

II. DIARY OF BULSTRODE WHITELOCKE, ESQ., DD. 12.22, CAMBRIDGE UNIVERSITY LIBRARY

[f. 26]

Maii 23

MR. WILDE prefers to the House the petition of Mr. Dyott for his admission into the House, being before sequestered.[12]

Mr. Dyott is called in and comes not to the bar, his submission deserving favor, but in his place.

The SPEAKER tells him the favor of the House.

And he gives his thanks to the House.

Resolved to adjourn upon Thursday next till Thursday sennight. And the House to be called on Friday in Whitsun week; and those that shall then make default shall pay £10 at the least for a penalty besides such punishment as the House shall further think fit to inflict, if there be no lawful excuse allowed by the House.

John Colley, the servant of Mr. Smalman, a member of the House, brought to the bar

6. MS: *officers*.

7. Concerning the recusant lists and presentments, see HofC, 27 February, n. 35.

8. Concerning the Tichbornes, see HofC, 20 March, n. 8; and 3 May, n. 9.

9. I.e., Thomas Howard, Earl of Arundel and Surrey, Earl Marshal.

10. Regarding Mr. Warren, see 2 March, CJ; and see HofC, 24 May, n. 4.

11. Sir Dudley Carleton was summoned to the Upper House on 22 May as Lord Carleton of Imbercourt. See HofL, 22 May, pp. 540, 541, and 543. C 66/2389, no. 2 (MS Cal. Pat. Rolls, 2 Car. I, f. 77; printed in Rymer, *Foedera*, VIII, pt. 2, p. 62).

12. See above, n. 5.

by *habeas corpus* and delivered. The fees which the serjeant took for bringing him hither are ordered to be paid back. And they that arrested him sent for.

[f. 26v] On the business concerning the presentment of those that are in office popishly affected.

MR. TICHBORNE speaks in excuse of his father.[13]

Sir Walter Tichborne ordered to be spared.

Earl of Arundel ordered to be spared out of the petition to the King concerning those that are in office being recusants convict or justly suspected or presented.[14]

III. DIARY OF SIR RICHARD GROSVENOR, MS 611, TRINITY COLLEGE, DUBLIN

[p. 133]

May 23

MR. WHISTLER reported the bill to avoid the increase of cottages and inmates.[15] Recommitted. All that come to have voice, this afternoon, Exchequer Court.

MR. SMITH reported the bill of the naturalizing of Sir Daniel Deligne. Passed to be engrossed.

MR. WILDE moved for the restoring of Mr. Dyott to the House and delivered in his petition, which was very submiss[ive].

After some debate he was sent for into the House and took his place, where the SPEAKER acquainted him with the mercy of the House.

MR. DYOTT said he was infinitely obliged to the favor of this House. He could offer no more for himself but to make this error of mine an instruction to me of more temperate and inoffensive carriage hereafter.

Ordered by question to adjourn the House upon Thursday noon till Thursday morning after; and that the House shall be called upon Friday. £10 forfeiture for absence, besides other punishment as the House please.

Mr. Smalman's man (John Colley, tailor) a member of the House, having been arrested, was by a *habeas corpus* brought by the sheriff's man to the bar. The SPEAKER told the officer who brought him that the House discharged the prisoner.

No man can protect any man; but the law protects a member's servants of this House: menial servants, bailiffs, receivers of rents, etc., not servants at large.

The serjeants who arrested him were sent for, and the man who brought him and had taken 4s. was commanded to restore it.

The SPEAKER went on with the business concerning the presentment of recusants in authority and any commission of trust, which had been interrupted by the commitment of our two gentlemen.

MR. BYSSHE moved that course might be taken to move the judges to put lawyers suspected for religion forth of their practice, such as: Mr. Hill, Mr. Minshull, Mr. Browne.

The petition to the King for putting all suspected forth of any commissions was read, so was the book, also made perfect and passed to be engrossed.

IV. DIARY OF SIR NATHANIEL RICH, HIST. COLLECT. 143, HLRO

[f. 90v]

[23 May 1626]

On Tuesday before Whitsuntide the House agreed the adjournment should be

13. See above, n. 8.

14. See above, n. 9.

15. See above, n. 4.

on Thursday (noon) until Thursday in Whitsun week; and that the next day, being Friday, the House shall be called, and every man that is away to pay ten pounds besides such further punishment as the House shall think fit. This penalty unless a sufficient excuse such as the House shall allow of be alleged.

ORDER OF BUSINESS WEDNESDAY, 24 MAY 1626

Wednesday, 24 May 1626

I. JOURNAL OF THE HOUSE OF COMMONS

[CJ 863; p. 73]
Mercurii, 24 Maii, 2 Caroli Regis

Sir[1] Robert Crane licensed to depart and to be here again[2] with all convenient speed.

A petition from Metcalfe read, desiring to be presently examined in the business of the letter concerning Sir John Savile.[3]

The petitioner to attend Sir Francis Foljambe at the rising of the House and, if Sir Francis will use him and signify so much tomorrow morning, then/

That concerning Mr. Warren, the minister, read.[4]

Mr. [John] Pym, Sir Nathaniel Rich, Sir W[alter] Erle, Sir Thomas Hoby, Sir Edward Peyton, Sir Francis Barrington, Sir G[ilbert] Gerard, presently to go into the Committee Chamber and perfect it.

Upon Sir Nathaniel Rich's report from the committee for courts of justice, ordered John Bryers shall be sent for to testify and to have privilege for coming, staying, and returning.

[p. 74] *L. 2a.* An act for explanation of two several provisos contained in a deed indented.

Committed to

[col. 1]
Mr. [William] Noy
Sir H[enry] Vane

[col. 2]
Sir Francis Stewart
Sir A[nthony] Forest
Sir M[iles] Fleetwood
Mr. [Christopher] Sherland
Mr. Whitaker
Mr. [Richard] Spencer
Sir H[enry] Poole
Sir William Spencer
Sir Roland Cotton
Sir A[rthur] Ingram
Sir G[ilbert] Gerard
Mr. Coke
Sir William Crofts
Mr. Long
Sir Thomas Grantham
Mr. [Bryan] Palmes
Mr. [Edward] Littleton
Sir D[udley] Digges
Sir Robert Pye
Captain [Thomas] Brett
Sir Thomas Cheeke
Mr. [Robert] Caesar
Sir George More

[col. 3]
Mr. Rolle
Sir William Herbert
Sir[5] John Monson
Sir H[enry] Anderson
Sir Nicholas Saunders
Mr. [John] Selden
Mr. [Edward] Kirton
Sir William Uvedale
Sir William Armine
Sir Robert Quarles
Sir Thomas Hoby
Sir P[eter] Heyman

Friday 7night, Exchequer Chamber; notice and counsel.

A letter read from King James to Archbishop of Canterbury concerning the proceedings against the Bishop of Bangor.

A copy of this letter to be taken and then to be delivered to Sir D. Digges, who brought it from the Archbishop.[6]

The committee for religion to examine

1. *Ordered the committee for religion* is crossed out in the MS preceding *Sir.*

2. *upon Thursday by Friday in Whitsun week* is crossed out in the MS and *with all convenient speed* is inserted.

3. Savile's letter is printed in Whitelocke, 22 May, see above.

4. By order of the House the previous day the inclusion of Mr. Warren in the presentment of recusants was to be "perfected". See above, 23 May, and regarding Warren, see also, 2 March, CJ.

5. MS: *Mr.*

6. We have not found the letter. On 6 May Digges had been ordered to inquire of the Archbishop under what circumstances the proceedings against the Bishop of Bangor in the Court of High Commission had been burned. On 28 July 1621, Chamberlain had reported to Carleton that Lewis Bayly, Bishop of Bangor, had made "a very insufficient answer, and that the High Commission had given him time till Thursday next to mend it . . . they pursue and have picked him out for simony". SP 14/122:46 (printed in Chamberlain, *Letters,* II, 392–394). See also, HofC, 17 April, n. 3.

the matters against the Bishop of Bangor this vacation.

Mr. [Edward] Littleton, Mr. [Christopher] Sherland, Mr. Rolle, Mr. [William] Noy, Mr. [John] Selden, Sir Thomas Hoby, Sir Nathaniel Rich, Mr. [John] Pym, and Sir D[udley] Digges to draw a bill against stopping any proceedings in the High Commission Court, Star Chamber, etc.

That concerning Warren brought in, read, and allowed upon question; and ordered to be engrossed.[7]

The preamble for the subsidy read and, upon question, recommitted; this afternoon, in the Court of Wards.[8]

MR. WHITBY reports the grievances:[9] 1, by impositions, without common assent in parliament. The opinion of all the committee that this should be again presented to his Majesty as a great grievance under which the subject suffers.

2ly. The license to dispense with retailing of wines, the late King's answer and promise it should continue but during late Lord Admiral's pleasure.[10] The committee of opinion that a general dispensation with a penal law/[11]

Upon question, the dispensation with retailing of wines to be in like manner presented.

3ly. That the subject may have liberty of free fishing in the parts of America, with the incidents of timber, etc., which, being restrained in the King's answer, to desire it may be enlarged; and the restraint to be presented as a grievance.[12]

[p. 75] 4ly. That in our[13] petition against briefs the King's answer was: No more such be granted but by certificate from the justices at assizes or sessions. Yet used still otherwise; and an instance for a bridge at the mill dam in Westminster.[14]

Upon question, the King to be petitioned that no briefs may be hereafter granted contrary to his Majesty's answer.

5ly. Concerning the lighthouse, called Wintertonness, the patent whereof held by Sir John Meldrum. Resolved by the committee to be very grievous to the subject; in which the King's answer gives no satisfaction.[15]

This patent to be presented to the King again as a general grievance.

6ly. The office of survey of seacoals.[16] Above 100 bonds returned into the Exchequer against such as carried coals from

7. See above, n. 4.

8. *former place* is crossed out in the MS and *Court of Wards* is inserted.

9. For Edward Whitby's notes from the meeting of the committee of grievances, see App., II, C. A similar petition had been prepared in 1624, and was reintroduced in the parliament of 1625 when King Charles responded article by article to those grievances, see *PP 1625*, pp. 301–305 and 307–309.

10. For discussion of impositions and the wine trade, see HofC, 20 February, particularly, nn. 40 and 41; and Sandys's report, 25 May 1624 (*CJ*, I, 711). Regarding the complaint in 1610 against the monopoly of license to sell wines and the reference to the case of penal statutes, see *PP 1610*, II, 270–271 and James's response that a law be passed for restraint of such licenses (*LJ*, II, 639).

11. *not good* is crossed out in the MS following *law*.

12. The complaint was directed at the patent for the New England corporation, under which Sir Ferdinando Gorges stood to benefit by a virtual monopoly over the fishing industry in that area. C 66/2231, no. 1 (MS Cal. Pat. Rolls, 18 Jac. I, pt. 16, f. 190v). See *PP 1625*, p. 302, n. 47.

13. Printed edition: *any*.

14. Regarding briefs and the King's response to that grievance, see *PP 1625*, p. 302, n. 50.

15. Regarding the patent for the lighthouse at Wintertonness held by Sir William Erskine and Sir John Meldrum (C 66/2151, no. 7; MS Cal. Pat. Rolls, 15 Jac. I, pt. 22, f. 134v), see *PP 1625*, p. 303, n. 52. Regarding the history of the patent, see *CD 1621*, VII, 397–402.

16. The complaint was directed specifically against Sir Robert Sharpeigh and Alexander Hartley who held the patent for the office of surveyorship of Newcastle coals. See *PP 1625*, p. 303, n. 56; below, n. 17; and HofC, 27 March, n. 3.

Newcastle, who could get no cockets there by reason of the refusal to pay the 4d. a chaldron upon that office.

Petition to be made to his Majesty from the House, for stay of these suits and cancelling of these bonds.

Sir A. Boyd (if he be able) or else some instructed for him, and [*blank*] Cotham, to attend the committee for grievances upon Friday in Whitsun week; and Sir Robert Sharpeigh then also to attend, and bring in his new patent.[17]

7ly. The impositions by the Merchant Adventurers amongst themselves. Though these abated, yet the committee of opinion that the imprest money should be forthwith laid down, and the King to be petitioned for this accordingly.[18]

The King to be petitioned for the present laying down hereof accordingly.

8ly. That the Merchant Adventurers wronged by the United Provinces by consumption money, and by taring.[19] That his Majesty's answer was: Order should herein be taken by his ambassadors. But the grievance still remains: The King to be petitioned in this.

The King to be petitioned in this.

9ly. Undue exactions of fees by officers of the Custom House. The answer: A course should be taken for regulating these fees. That, by the course which has been taken to reform these, they are made worse; their demands being before without all color, but now armed with authority.[20]

This to be recommended again by petition to his Majesty.

10ly. Suit to his Majesty to increase the license for transportation of white cloths, from 30,000 to 50,000 cloths per annum.[21] To this no answer given.

This to be recommended from this House to his Majesty.

[p. 76] 11ly. The pretermitted customs. The opinion of the committee to help this, upon the penning of the act of tonnage and poundage.

This concerning the pretermitted customs to be contained in the petition of grievances to his Majesty.[22]

17. The patent was issued to Sharpeigh on 20 September 1623, C 66/2310, no. 11 (MS Cal. Pat. Rolls, 21 Jac. I, f. 125). For an abstract of the patent, see SP 14/152:58. Sir Andrew Boyd was a surveyor of Newcastle coals, SP 14/131:34; 132:106; and see *CD 1621*, VII, 429–430. William Cotham had been sent from Newcastle to London at the instigation of Andrew Boyd, "to view and survey that no fraudulent mixture be made of pan coals or other base coals of low price". *APC 1621–1623*, pp. 318–319.

18. Several articles regarding the Merchant Adventurers and the cloth trade were discussed in 1624 and 1625. See *PP 1625*, pp. 303–304, nn. 62–70. For the Company's patent, see C 66/2148, nos. 1 and 2 (MS Cal. Pat. Rolls, 15 Jac. I, pt. 19, ff. 160v, 161). See also, *CD 1621*, VII, 412.

19. See *PP 1625*, p. 304, n. 63.

20. Regarding fees exacted by the Customs House, see *PP 1625*, p. 304, n. 64. The response in 1625 was that the fees should be "regulated" and that tables should be "appointed". Concerning the collection of tonnage and poundage and the pretermitted customs by Charles I, see *PP 1625*, pp. 313–314, 317, 318 (5 July); and HofC, above, 6 March, n. 27; and below, n. 22. A bill against Edmund Nicholson, projector of the "pretended" pretermitted customs had passed the Commons on 20 March 1626 (see above), was sent to the Lords on 22 March, and was rejected by the Upper House on 22 April. See HofL, pp. 300 and 303. See also, below, n. 47.

21. George Clifford, Earl of Cumberland, had been granted on 16 May 1605 a special license for transporting cloth, C 66/1663, no. 7 (MS Cal. Pat. Rolls, 3 Jac. I, pt. 1, f. 168). And see below, n. 54.

22. *This to be coupled with the grievance of taking of tonnage and poundage without grant in parliament, we having last parliament passed a bill for it in this House and that parliament being passed/* is crossed out in the MS preceding *Upon question.* The bill for tonnage and poundage passed the Lower House on 28 July 1625 (*PP 1625*, p. 349), was sent to the Upper House on 9 July when it was first read (ibid., pp. 110, 112) and rejected (ibid., p. 526).

Upon question, the taking of tonnage and poundage without assent in parliament to be presented to his Majesty as a grievance.

To finish this report tomorrow morning.

[CJ 864] The committee for apparel to sit again this afternoon in the Star Chamber.

II. DIARY OF BULSTRODE WHITELOCKE, ESQ., DD. 12.22, CAMBRIDGE UNIVERSITY LIBRARY

[f. 26v]

May 24

SIR EUBULE THELWALL moves that the subcommittee concerning the Bishop of Bangor may proceed in that business during the recess of the House.

Hereupon SIR DUDLEY DIGGES presents to the House a letter of King James to the Archbishop of Canterbury for taking away all the proceedings against the Bishop of Bangor, which the House enjoined Sir Dudley to desire.[23]

A committee appointed to frame a bill against the stopping of proceedings in the High Commission Court and Star Chamber, etc.

CHANCELLOR EXCHEQUER reports the preamble for the bill of subsidy.

Which is read twice and recommitted to this afternoon.

MR. WHITBY reports the grievances. Of the old grievances, the committee found some yet continuing and some in part redressed and to some [f. 27] no answer. 7 King James the grievance of impositions presented, but no answer given to it, and the impositions are increased.[24] The committee's opinion is that this grievance should now be presented to the King.

Resolved by the House accordingly.

MR. WHITBY. The grant granted to the late Lord Admiral for the imposition of wines was presented in 3 *Jac.* and desired in 7 *Jac.* to be taken [a]way.[25] The opinion of the committee is that this be presented to the King, and that the law of 7 E. 6/[26]

Resolved accordingly by the House.

MR. WHITBY reports Sir Ferdinando Gorges's patent restraining free fishing, which was presented to the King before but no full answer[27] given to it. The opinion of the committee is that a more full answer be desired for it now.

Ordered accordingly by the House.

MR. WHITBY reports the grievance of begging briefs grown to an excessive number. The House petitioned they might be restrained. The King answered before that they should be restrained, but they are not. The opinion of the committee [is] that this may be again commended to the King.[28]

Ordered accordingly by the House.

[f. 27v] MR. WHITBY reports the grievance of the patent of Sir John Meldrum for erecting a lighthouse in [Wintertonness]. Before, the payment was but 6d. a chaldron of coals; he now makes them pay 3s. 4d. for every chaldron passing by. The committee's opinion that this be presented again to the

23. See above, n. 6.

24. The question of impositions was debated in 1610 and included in the petition of grievances drafted in that session. See *PP 1610*, II, 253–254 and 266–268 and see below, n. 36.

25. The patent for the license on wines granted to Charles Howard, Earl of Nottingham, was complained about in 1606 (9 April, *CJ*, I, 295) and again in 1610 (*PP 1610*, II, 270–271, 275). That year King James responded that he was content "a law be passed for the restraining such license to be made in time to come". *LJ*, II, 639.

26. *SR*, 7 E. VI, c. 5, *An act to avoid the great price and excess of wines.*

27. *that all may have free fishing* is crossed out in the MS following *answer*. See above, n. 12.

28. See above, n. 14.

King and desired that the patent be vacated.[29]

Resolved accordingly by the House.

Mr. Whitby reports the grievance of the patent of surveyorship of Newcastle coals procured by Sir Andrew Boyd.[30] Some bonds were put in suit against some men about this. The committee's opinion to petition the King for the cancelling of those bonds.

Resolved accordingly by the House, and that Sir Andrew Boyd or some for him attend the committee about this.

Mr. Whitby proceeds to the grievance of the patent of the Merchant Adventurers, which was presented before and redressed.[31] Only the charge of imprest money remains, which was imposed by the merchants, themselves consenting. The committee's opinion that the King be desired that this imprest money be presently laid down.

Resolved accordingly by the House.

Mr. Whitby proceeds to the grievance of consumption money and taring of cloth. The committee's opinion to petition to the King to take some course for redress.

Resolved accordingly by the House.

[f. 28] Mr. Whitby proceeds to the grievance of exacting of fees by the Custom House officers. The committee's opinion that this be recommended to the King.[32]

Ordered accordingly by the House.

The grievance of the shortness of the number of cloths allowed by the statute to be transported, viz., 30,000 cloths, and the merchants desire to be allowed to transport 2,000 [*sic*] more.[33] The committee allow their desire and that the King be petitioned for it.

Resolved accordingly by the House.

The grievance concerning the pretermitted custom. The opinion of the committee that the King be no further petitioned concerning this, but that it be referred to the bill of tonnage and poundage to be considered of.[34]

Sir John Savile. The custom of cloth in Yorkshire comes to above £8,000 per annum.

Resolved upon debate, that this grievance shall be contained in the petition of grievances to the King; and the taking of the tonnage and poundage by the King without assent of parliament be presented to the King as a grievance.

III. DIARY OF SIR RICHARD GROSVENOR, MS 611, TRINITY COLLEGE, DUBLIN

[p. 134]

May 24

Sir Eubule Thelwall moved that the committee of religion might proceed to sit during the recess.

Ordered that they should sit.

Sir Robert Crane had license to depart home, his wife being very sick.

2.[35] An act for explanation of 2 several provisos contained in one deed indented made 9 *Jac.* by Thomas, late Earl of Exeter.
Committed, Friday sevennight, Exchequer Chamber.

29. See above, n. 15.
30. *which was made void* is crossed out in the MS following *Boyd.* See above, n. 17. The complaint was directed particularly against Sir Robert Sharpeigh and Alexander Hartley.
31. See above, n. 18.
32. See above, n. 20.
33. See above, n. 21.
34. See above, n. 20.
35. I.e., the second reading of.

The King's warrant to the Archbishop of Canterbury for the taking off the file the articles in the Commission Court against him.

SIR RICHARD WESTON presented the preamble agreed upon by the committee for the bill of subsidy.

It was read and recommitted, this afternoon, Court of Wards.

MR. WHITBY reported the grievances: 1, the former grievances, with the answers, in the late King's time.

1. The grievance of impositions which was presented in 7 *Jac.*: That by the common law and right the subject has that right in his goods that no impost can be imposed on them without their consent, or by act of parliament. They then prepared a bill against the same, which passed this House.[36] This pressure continues with additions on the subjects' goods. The committee thought it fit to prefer this as a grievance continuing on us still.

By question, resolved to present this grievance to the King.

2. A patent granted to the late Lord Admiral for imposition upon retailing of wines presented as a grievance 7 *Jacobi.*[37] The King's answer was that, after the experience of that patent, there should never be more granted; yet, it is still used. The committee thought it fit to petition the King that the penal law might be abrogated.

Resolved to be presented.

[p. 135] 3. Sir Ferdinando Gorges's patent for fishing in Newfoundland presented in 21 *Jac.*[38] His Majesty's answer was that the subjects should have free liberty of fishing, giving content for the wood they should have to the owners of the land. This the committee thought inconvenient because then they would set what rate they pleased upon them.

Resolved to be presented.

4. The licenses for begging briefs from pretended losses by fires, etc., presented 21 *Jac.*, whose answer was that none should be granted but upon certificates made in open sessions.[39] Yet, still, these continue to be granted. The committee thought it fit to present this, as also that a bill should be drawn to declare the King's pleasure that none such should be granted but upon certificates at quarter sessions.

Resolved that this also should be presented.

5. Sir John Meldrum's patent for the erecting of a lighthouse in Wintertonness, this was in 21 *Jac.*[40]

Resolved to present this as a grievance.

6. The new office of surveyorship of coals at Newcastle, to cancel 1,200 bonds returned into the Exchequer sued by Sir Andrew Boyd.[41]

Resolved to petition the King for the stay of these suits and cancelling of the bonds.

MR. PYM moved to send for Sir Andrew Boyd because he presented this upon an unjust project.

Ordered, that Sir Andrew Boyd or, being sick, some factor from him, should come to the committee of grievances to answer this, and Cotham, and the patent to be brought

36. Regarding the debate on impositions in 1610, see above, n. 24. On 14 July 1610 a committee was appointed to prepare a bill concerning impositions (*CJ*, I, 449–450). The bill was reported and engrossed on 16 July (ibid., p. 450). The session was prorogued on 23 July (ibid., p. 454).

37. See above, n. 25.

38. See above, n. 12.

39. See above, n. 14.

40. See above, n. 15.

41. See above, nn. 16 and 17.

in, and Sir Robert Sharpeigh to come also before the committee of grievances upon Friday in Whitsun week.[42]

7. Concerning decay of trade: 1, impositions laid by the merchants themselves, called imprest money; 5s. upon a broad cloth, 7s. 6d. upon a long cloth. That this imprest should be laid down presently.

SIR WILLIAM SPENCER said that £25,000 was divided between the lords of the Council.

Resolved, to be petitioned to lay it down presently.

[p. 136] 8. The States had imposed upon all long cloths, English, 32s. consumption money; nothing upon their own. So it hinders our trade, puts off their own cloth.[43] To petition his Majesty to take a course for redress from the impositions and the trouble they are put to for taring their cloths, for faults in the cloth.

Resolved.

9. Exactions of fees by the officers of the customs in port towns.[44]

Resolved.

10. That whereas the Merchant Adventurers had a license to transport but 30,000 cloths, they desired they might have allowance to transport 20,000 more.[45]

Resolved to petition the King for this.

11. Pretermitted customs: That this should be accommodated upon the bill of tonnage and poundage and not presented to the King.[46]

MR. PYM and MR. WHISTLER. That this should not go as a grievance.

SIR JOHN SAVILE. The sum of pretermitted customs upon cloth in Yorkshire comes to above 8,000 pound by year. The projector, Nicholson, receives £1,000 by year.[47] If we may not be relieved by parliament, let us think of some course by composition. That it be preferred to the King.

Resolved to be presented.

[*Afternoon*]

May 24, afternoon, at the committee of grievances.

Greg's business.[48]

Serjeant Thynne of counsel with him; Mr. Greg brought in what orders he had here. For the patent, exceptions:

1, that it is new because there are words of creation in both patents.

[Answer:] But this does not imply a new thing, but transferred to a new person; for the Chamberlain of Chester, from 9 Queen Elizabeth, had the grant till the time of Prince Henry, who granted it, nor King James before/[49]

[p. 137] The office of examiner in court is no new office, yet that is granted by words of new creation.

42. See above, n. 17.

43. See above, n. 18.

44. See above, n. 20.

45. See above, nn. 18 and 21.

46. See above, n. 20, and below, n. 47.

47. Edmund Nicholson (with Thomas Morgan), projector of the pretermitted customs by patent granted in 1618 (C 66/2197, MS Cal. Pat. Rolls, 16 Jac. I, f. 57) had argued that the statute of tonnage and poundage of 1 Jac. I (*SR,* 1 Jac. I, c. 33) allowed for the collection of customs on cloth made of wool as well as on wool itself. In 1624 the House had determined that such customs on cloth were excepted from the statute of tonnage and poundage and therefore had no legal basis. See *CJ,* I, 693, 764–765, 768–769, 778, and see above, n. 20. See also, *CD 1621,* VII, 423–425.

48. Edward and Robert Greg had been sent for by order of the House. See 28 February, OB, and n. 4.

49. Edward Greg's patent was for the examination of witnesses within the County Palatine of Chester, in all commissions of that court. Until 1547 the Chamberlain of Chester was the leading administrative official in the Palatinate. In 1610 Prince Henry was created Earl of Chester and assumed a limited role in the administration of the county. See, VCH, *Chester,* II, 18, 36.

Objection: That it grants him liberty to take such fees as have been taken however.

Answer: 1 *in facto,* but 12d. for every witness in court, 2s. when he rides. This must be reasonably construed in law to take lawful and reasonable fees.

Objection: That he is a commissioner of the quorum.

[Answer:] No such words in the patent, but that he should be named a commissioner in all commissions, and by that has no more authority than the rest. Others may sit without him.

Objection: This to the prejudice of the gentlemen, that so mean a man should be joined with them and say for him.

Yet, this no more than they did for the escheater; but this not so, they may proceed without him.

Much good to the country. He is a sworn officer, and though I presume [*illegible*] they will be honest, yet I have known them otherwise. They come too much affected to the cause. In Peacock's case a commissioner would not suffer him to explain himself; this punished.[50]

Objection: But the like patent was procured for Lancashire, but in that excessive fees allowed.

[Answer:] No clerk will take so little; he must set down the depositions, engross them, take pains to ride, and pay his own charges. The gentleman's certificate, that they like it well, and so the officers of the court.

Objection: That this trenches to the liberty of the subject.

Answer: This has no relation to that, for where the subject has a lawful liberty; but this arises nearly out of favor, for every man ought to examine in court.

IV. DIARY OF JOHN LOWTHER, ESQ., D/LONS/L, CUMBERLAND AND WESTMORLAND RECORD OFFICE

[f. 40]

Wednesday, [24 May]

WHITBY reports grievances formerly not answered, or not well, and new ones.

1. Impositions. Presented 7 *Jac.:* that by law none can be imposed but by parliament. Show impositions and desired to lay all down. Not answered, but new added.

Resolved by question to be presented as great grievance.

[2.] 3 *Jac.*, the license of wines enhancing price by dispensation of antiquated laws by subject.[51] King did answer: after that patent ended, no more granted. Patent now ended, yet the license kept on foot by this general dispensation. Desires to have the law repealed.

Resolved to be presented as grievance.

[3.] Ferdinando Gorges's patent, 21 *Jac.*, to restrain the free fishing in America. His answer short because they were to give satisfaction for wood. Desire liberty for wood at pleasure; not within a quarter of a mile of the planters' habitation or fishing.

4. That for begging briefs, 21 *Jac.*, presented, to be totally prohibited. Answered: none to be but upon certificate in sessions and that county one. This is not observed. As by precedent for a bridge at Westminster.

Resolved to be re-presented.

5. Sir John Meldrum's patent at Wintertonness exacting above proportion fit for a lighthouse at Wintertonness; from 6d. to

50. Richard Peacock's case, 9 Coke, *Reports,* Trin., 9 Jac. I, pp. 128–129.

51. Wine prices were to be regulated by statute, *SR,* 7 E. VI, c. 5. See above, n. 26.

3s. 4d. extorted and enforced. Answered: to refer it to committee of both Houses to proportion it. First thought to pray a conference. Yet, resolved to re-present it because it is judged by us properly.

[f. 40v] 6. New surveyorship of coals erected. 7s. 6d. a chaldron paid for transport, 12d. for import within kingdom, and to bring cockets to discharge bonds entered for so doing; yet cockets denied to discharge their bonds until 4d. a chaldron paid to surveyor. Prays to have the bonds discharged which were extended for the projectors' benefit, being 1,200 bonds.

Resolved to petition to have the 1,200 bonds discharged.

Sir Andrew Boyd and Cotham, the projectors and prosecutor sent for to the House.

7. Merchant Adventurers' patent. Answered: they satisfied, and dyed and dressed at liberty. Yet the impost of 7s. 6d. a cloth continues abated to half and to cease in August 1627.

To petition to lay down the imposition totally.

8. Where States imposed 32s. of English cloth as consumption money to our hindrance, and the taring to be brought to one place, drawn now to 28.

To desire King to now move for help while they need.

9. Fees of customers, exacting in some case[s] equal to custom. Desires now to be reformed, for worse than before by allowance to take fees.

10. Merchants having dispensation for 30,000 cloths, desired to have 20,000 more. This not answered. Cumberland has patent; expires this May. Now to re-petition.

11. Pretermitted customs misgrounded upon statute of tonnage and poundage by Nicholson's projection by color of equity upon wool to be laid down. Answered: at next meeting to do what is fit for a good king. [f. 41] Desires now to provide for it in the new bill of tonnage and poundage upon which grounded. And now not to re-petition upon it not singly les[t] we admit others, but to mention tonnage and poundage exacted illegally, so the rest.

12. Tonnage and poundage taken without act, to be presented as a grievance. And to consider under whether this or impositions pretermitted customs to be.

V. DIARY OF SIR NATHANIEL RICH, HIST. COLLECT. 143, HLRO

[f. 90v]

[24 May]

Wednesday, report of grievances.

[MR. EDWARD WHITBY.] 1. Grievance of 7 *Jac.* of impositions. That the subject[s] of England have such propriety in their goods that cannot be taken from them.[52] Petition that all impositions laid on without common assent may be taken off. To this no answer given in 7 [*Jac.*]. This the first grievance. The bill which then passed in this House slept in the Lords House.

Upon question, resolved this to be presented to the King as a great grievance.

2ly. The patent for licensing of retailing of wines, this presented 7 *Jac.* His Majesty's answer to this in 3 [*illegible*]. The committee thought fit to petition the King to repeal this law upon which this patent is grounded.

3. A petition exhibited 21 *Jac.* against Sir Ferdinando Gorges his patent for New England.

4. Another, 21 *Jac.*, against briefs.

52. For Sir Nathaniel Rich's collection of precedent material regarding impositions, see App., II, C.

5. The patent to Sir John Meldrum for a light at Wintertonness contrary to the law 8 Eliz. that gives this power to the Trinity House.[53]

6. The surveyorship of coals at Newcastle to Sir Andrew Boyd.

7. A clause of the patent of Merchant Adventurers of laying impositions upon themselves: 5s. on a short cloth and 7s. 6d. on a broad cloth, called "imprest money". But this is abated, viz., 2s. 4d. for the short, and 3s. 6d. for the broad for a time to continue to the first of August 1627; and this allowed [f. 91] by the commissioners of trade and consent of the lords, yet the committee think fit the whole should be laid down.

MR. BATEMAN. 12d. on the short and 1s. 6d. on the broad cloth is laid on for bearing of the common charge of the merchant, very profitable for the commonwealth.

8th. A petition for the Merchant Adventurers against 32s. on a long cloth [*illegible*] and so ratable which the States had imposed upon the English cloth. This 32s. on a long, short, and ratably is called "consumption money".

9. A petition 21 *Jac.* against fees and exactions in the Custom House. His Majesty's answer was there should be a course taken in it. Some course taken but in some things worse, as 2s. 6d. for dispatch, insomuch that they cannot transport goods from one port to another without fees.

10. A petition exhibited 21 *Jac.* for the Merchant Adventurers that notwithstanding 23 H. 8 they may venture 50,000 white cloths whereas by that statute they can transport only 30,000. And my Lord Cumberland has a license to dispense and takes 2s. 8d. for each cloth.[54]

11. Against the pretermitted custom 21 *Jac.*, 14d. on a cloth and 6s. 8d. for a sack of wool.

Resolved upon the question after long debate whether the pretermitted subsidies [*sic*] should be presented as a grievance, that only mention should be made of it. But whereas tonnage and poundage was now taken without act of parliament, and that the committee had taken no consideration of that, it was now resolved by the House that the taking of tonnage and poundage without act of parliament should be presented as a grievance and that of the pretermitted custom to be mentioned by way of aggravation or else among the impositions as the committee should think fittest that should be appointed to draw up these grievances.

The day being spent, the reporter is enjoined to leave here and to report the rest tomorrow. And each of these grievances were reported singly to be so put to the question; and still as one was reported the reporter sat down.

53. *SR*, 8 Eliz. I, c. 13, *An act touching sea marks and mariners*.

54. Cf. 33 H. VIII, c. 19, *An act expounding a certain statute concerning shipping of cloths*. See also, above, n. 21.

Committee on the bill to make void certain conveyances unconscionably gotten from Giles **Sewster** to meet Saturday sevennight [3 June]	329, *20/2
Committee on the bill for sale of certain lands that were late Sir Henry **Clere's** to meet Saturday sevennight [3 June]	329, *1/5
Committee on the bill for the sale of certain lands, tenements, and hereditaments of Timothy **Wagstaffe,** Esq., deceased to meet Saturday sevennight [3 June]	329, *25/3
Committee on the bill for making the estate of **attainted persons** liable for their **debts** to meet Monday sevennight [5 June]	329, *14/3
Committee on the presentment of **recusants** to meet Monday sevennight [5 June]	329, *21/2
Committee on the bill for the mitigation of the sentence of the greater **excommunication** to meet tomorrow sevennight [2 June]	329, *10/3
Committee on the bill for the settling of certain **marshlands** by the name of the Isle of **Canvey** to meet Monday sevennight [5 June]	329, *21/3
L.1a. An act for explanation of one clause of the act concerning monopolies which concerns Sir Robert **Mansell's** patent for making **glass**	329, 334
L.1a and L.2a. An act concerning **hearing of preaching:** committed	329, 334, *14/6
Six MPs granted license to depart	329
Committee on **Willes's** petition and the **Dover** business to meet Friday sevennight [2 June]	329, *8/3
L.1a. An act for estates of tenants of **Bromfield and Yale**	329, 334, *19/5; 1/6; 2/6
SIR RICHARD WESTON (Chancellor Exchequer): moves for a meeting of the committee for preparing a **preamble** for the bill of **subsidy**	329, 334, *27/3; 5/5
Committee for preparing a preamble for the bill of subsidy to meet Thursday [1 June]; seventeen members added	329, 334
JOHN PYM: moves from the committee of **religion** for money to be given to John **Tendring** from that collected at the communion	329, 334
House refuses to use money from the communion for Tendring; he to be helped some other way	329, 334
Report from the committee on the bill concerning **apparel** (WILLIAM NOY)	329, 332, 334, *15/4
Amendments and a proviso to the bill concerning apparel: read twice and allowed	330, 334
WILLIAM NOY: moves that a bill be read for the shortening of **Michaelmas term**	334, *7/6
L.1a. An act for the shortening of Michaelmas term	330, 334
Report from the committee of **grievances** continued from 24 May (EDWARD WHITBY):	

THURSDAY, 25 MAY 1626

I. JOURNAL OF THE HOUSE OF COMMONS

[CJ 864; p. 76]
Jovis, 25 Maii, 2 Caroli Regis

Sewster's bill, Saturday 7night, in the afternoon.

Lady Clere's bill, the same time, Court of Wards.

Wagstaffe's bill, the same time.

Attainted persons, Monday 7night.

Recusants, Monday 7night.

Excommunications, tomorrow 7night.

Canvey Island, Monday 7night.

L. 1a. Glass.[1]

L. 1a. An act concerning hearing of preaching.

L. 2a. An act concerning hearing of preaching.
Committed to

[col. 1]	[col. 2]
Mr. Jordan	Mr. Serjeant Towse
Sir Thomas Hoby	Sir H[enry] Poole
Sir Eubule Thelwall	Mr. Rolle
Sir Francis Barrington	Sir Nicholas Saunders
Sir John Stradling	Sir William Strode
Sir James Perrot	Sir George More
Mr. [John] Pym	
Sir Clement Throckmorton	

And all that will come to have voice; Saturday 7night, Court of Wards.

Sir G. Hoghton has license, in respect of the sickness of his wife, to go down and return as soon as he can.

Mr. Keeling licensed to go down and to return again upon Saturday in Whitsun week.

Mr. Cage has leave to go down and return again upon Wednesday after Whitsun week.

Mr. Upton has liberty to stay 3 or 4 days after Friday in Whitsun week.

[p. 77] Sir John Offley, leave until Thursday after Whitsun week.

Sir Robert Oxenbridge has leave, for sickness.

Committee for Dover business,[2] Friday 7night; with power to send for witnesses.

L. 1a. Bromfield.

MR. CHANCELLOR moves Thursday afternoon in Whitsun week may be for the preamble, in the Court of Wards.

Ordered.

Sir H[enry] Poole, Mr. [Richard] Spencer, Sir John Stradling, Sir Clement Throckmorton, Sir Thomas Grantham, Sir W[alter] Erle, Mr. Long, Sir William Strode, Sir Thomas Fairfax, Sir Francis Barnham, Sir Thomas Puckering, Sir Nicholas Saunders, Sir H[enry] Vane,[3] Sir P[eter] Heyman, Mr. Goodwin, Mr. John Drake, Mr. [John] Selden added to the committee for the preamble.

MR. PYM moves from the committee for religion that Tendring,[4] one that has taken great pains in discovery of papists, might have £10 out of the money given at the communion.

But this the House refused, being before given to the poor, but left to be helped some other way.

MR. NOY reports the bill of apparel. That

1. I.e., the bill concerning Sir Robert Mansell's patent for glass making. See below, n. 30.
2. I.e., regarding the selling of goods stayed at Dover. See HofC, 8 March, and n. 20.
3. *Mr. Noy* is crossed out following *Sir H. Vane.*
4. John Tendring, Provost Marshal of Middlesex, presented information to the House of Commons regarding Catholics in the New Prison. See SP 16/22:111 and 112.

the gold wire drawers, etc., have a further time given them, viz., till March come 12month; and liberty given to strangers born out of the King's dominion to wear them.

The amendments 2 read and a proviso in paper.

The amendments allowed and the proviso to be engrossed.

L. 1a. An act for the shortening of Michaelmas term and for speedy/

MR. WHITBY further reports:[5]

The particular imposition upon currants, 12ly.

MR. NOY. Not to petition for remove of this, as directed by the committee: not because the cause for it not good, for that will imply that if the cause be good it may be set without common consent in parliament; nor because it is of too high a proportion, because that implies a lesser proportion may be taken without assent in parliament.

Upon question, this imposition upon currants to be particularly presented to his Majesty as a grievance.[6]

13ly. The abuses of the deputy alnager: 1, extending it to stockings, waistcoats, etc.; 2ly, selling the seals by bushels: taking 1d. where should have but[7] ob[olus]; makes but a fee farm yearly rent thereof in cities and boroughs; never looking to the abuse for which the office appointed. No reformation hereof, notwithstanding the King's answer. The committee thought a bill fittest to regulate this.

Upon question, the abuses in the alnager to be presented as a grievance to his Majesty.

[p. 78] And Mr. Rolle, Mr. [William] Noy, Mr. Herbert, Mr. [Thomas] Malet, Mr. [William] Coxe, Mr. [Robert] Bateman, Sir M[aurice] Abbot,[8] Mr. [Benjamin] Tichborne,[9] Mr. [Edward] Whitby, Sir Nathaniel Rich, Mr. Browne, Mr. Richard Spencer to draw a bill to regulate this. And the same committee to consider of all the laws concerning this, and how they may be reduced into one law. To meet and perfect this, this vacation,[10] and present it at the next access.[11] And any of this House that will may be present and inform them.

Motion being made whether a message should be sent to the Lords to let them know we intend now to adjourn, resolved, after much debate, not to do it.

14. The grievance of purveyance:[12] sending 40 or 50 miles for provisions. In poultry great abuses. Purveyance for hawks, new; Andrew Pitcairn's patent dated *1 Caroli.* Pigeons, 6d. a dozen; hens, 2d. apiece. Dangerous in point of precedent, for a set price under the Great Seal. Sir Thomas Monson

5. I.e., the second part of his report on the grievances begun the previous day (24 May). See HofC, 24 May, n. 9.

6. The matter of the imposition on currants was also tied to the grievances of the Levant Company. See *PP 1625*, pp. 305 and 309, nn. 73 and 110. The impost on currants reimposed in 1619 was farmed to Thomas Howard, Earl of Arundel in a patent dated 27 May 1620 to run for thirty-one years (C 66/2233, MS Cal. Pat. Rolls, 18 Jac. I, pt. 18, f. 139).

7. Printed edition: *have been but.* Concerning abuses in the Alnager's office, see *PP 1625*, p. 304, n. 67.

8. *Mr. Sher/* is crossed out in the MS following *Mr. Abbot.*

9. *to draw a bill* is crossed out in the MS following *Mr. Tichborne.*

10. *afternoon* is crossed out in the MS and *vacation* is inserted.

11. *beginning of that session* is crossed out and *next access* is inserted.

12. For discussion of Andrew Pitcairn's patent, see HofC, 3 March and n. 16. We have not found Sir Thomas Monson's commission. Sir Anthony Pell, Master Falconer (SP 14/169:17), had been granted a commission in July 1620 to sell hawks' meat. See *Cal. SP Dom. 1619–1623,* p. 166.

the 1st ever had such a commission, but never executed it. Sir A. Pell the 1st that ever put it in execution.[13]

Upon question, this patent a grievance both in the creation and execution.

[col. 1]	[col. 2]
Sir William Spencer	Sir Francis Barrington
Mr. Richard Spencer	Sir H[enry] Poole
Sir John Boteler	Sir George More
Sir Charles Morrison	Sir William Walter
	Sir Thomas Denton

[col. 3]	[col. 4]
Sir O[liver] Luke	Mr. [Thomas] Bowyer
Sir Francis Barrington	Sir Thomas Grantham
Serjeant [William] Towse	Sir Edward Peyton
Sir John Strangways	Sir Nicholas Saunders
Mr. [John] Glanville	
Mr. William Clarke	

And all that will come to have voice. This committee to consider of the other abuses of purveyors and to present them, together with the last grievance, to his Majesty. To meet tomorrow 7night,[14] in the Court of Wards.

15. Proclamations for Lent for butchers, etc., to be bound by recognizances against killing and dressing of flesh; with 2s. 6d. fee to the clerk of the peace for every one. The being bound to observe any law, very mischievous. That the proclamation may extend as well to bind men in recognizances from eating as well as from dressing flesh. This held by the committee a great grievance.[15]

Upon question, this a great grievance and so to be presented to his Majesty.

16. Greg's patent for examination of all witnesses within the County Palatine of Chester, as well by commission as otherwise; both for examination, writing, and copying of them. This thus granted to Edward Greg, for his life, and after to Robert Greg his son, for life.[16]

Upon question, this patent a grievance both in the creation and execution, in the parts of it now reported a grievance; and so to be presented to his Majesty.

[p. 79] 17. Abuses of Dr. Anyan in causing Dr. Allen to be arrested, with charge to arrest him on the Sabbath day, and so [*blank*] which done accordingly. And a warrant to deduct out of Dr. Barcroft and [*blank*] exhibition, his own charges expended at his attendance in parliament.[17]

That the committee thought this to trench much to the contempt and breach of the privileges of this House.

A warrant to bring him and Benjamin Eliott[18] to attend the committee of grievances Friday 7night.

Motion being made to present the patent for making salt. MR. MORE, for his part; SIR NATHANIEL RICH, for the Earl of Warwick's part; MR. MALET for Mr. Packer; MR.

13. Printed edition: *put in execution.*

14. *this afternoon* is crossed out in the MS and *tomorrow 7night* is inserted.

15. See the proclamation for the restraint of killing, dressing, and eating flesh in Lent, or on fish days, etc., 14 November 1619. *Stuart Proclamations,* I, 450–454.

16. Regarding Edward and Robert Greg, see HofC, 24 May, nn. 48 and 49. The two were sent for by order of the House, see 28 February.

17. Concerning the charges of misconduct against Dr. Anyan, see *PP 1625,* p. 260, n. 19. Anyan had Dr. Richard Allen arrested in 1624 when it became apparent that Allen had petitioned the King for a royal commission to investigate Anyan's immorality and administrative corruption. Subsequently, Dr. Barcroft joined Allen in a complaint against Anyan in the parliament of 1624 (*CJ,* I, 692, 707, 777, 791). See also, *APC 1623–1625,* pp. 235, 237 and Thomas Fowler, *The History of Corpus Christi College* (Oxford, 1893), pp. 178–180.

18. Benjamin Eliott was the dean of Corpus Christi College, see Grosvenor, below.

TRUMBULL, for himself, are willing this patent shall be annihilated.[19]

Agreed by MR. MORE that, in the beginning of the term, a disclaimer shall be entered upon the *quo warranto* depending in the King's Bench.

[CJ 865] Upon question, a select committee to pen and order and marshal the grievances now reported and ordered to be presented to his Majesty; and to make subcommittees, as they shall think fit.

[col. 1]	[col. 2]
Sir Nathaniel Rich	Mr. [William] Noy
Mr. [John] Pym	Mr. [Edward] Littleton
Mr. [Edward] Whitby	Mr. [John] Glanville
Sir H[enry] Poole	Mr. Rolle
Sir M[aurice] Abbot	Mr. Browne
Mr. [Richard] Dyott	Sir Thomas Barrington
Sir Robert Cotton	Mr. [John] Selden
Sir Edward Spencer	Sir G[ilbert] Gerard
	Sir Thomas Lake

[col. 3]	[col. 4]
Sir John Stradling	Sir William Armine
Mr. [John] Bankes	Mr. [William] Coryton
Mr. Richard Spencer	Sir Richard Grosvenor
Sir Thomas Fanshawe	Sir J[ames] Perrot
Sir John Eliot	Mr. [Robert] Bateman
Sir William Spencer	Mr. [Peter] Ball
Sir John Strangways	Serjeant [William] Towse
Sir Edward Peyton	Mr. [John] Lister
Sir William Owen	Mr. [Thomas] Sherwill
Sir Robert Payne	

To meet tomorrow morning, at 9 of the clock, in the House.

Mr. Arnold, leave to depart and stay 2 days longer than Friday.

So, Sir A. Forest has the same leave.
So, Sir John Evelyn.

John Cadwallader served with a warrant for a witness against the Bishop of Bangor and kept in the Bishop's house so that he cannot be examined. Resolved to defer this till our meeting.[20]

Sir A. Denton has license till Tuesday after Whitsun week.

Lady Jermy's bill, Saturday 7night.

Sir Charles Howard and Sir Thomas Bludder, leave; and to be here upon Saturday in Whitsun week.

The House adjourns itself until Thursday next, 8 clock; with a saving of all committees specially ordered to meet or proceed in any businesses.[21]

II. DIARY OF BULSTRODE WHITELOCKE, ESQ., DD. 12.22, CAMBRIDGE UNIVERSITY LIBRARY

[f. 28v]

May 25

MR. NOY reports the bill concerning apparel. In 1 Queen Eliz., upon the alteration of religion,[22] many artisans, as bead makers, holy water stoup makers, etc., petitioned that they should lose their trade and be undone; but yet, God be thanked, our religion is changed and those tradesmen lived well after. In gold and silver stuffs there is as much as a million comes to that is now in England.

MR. WHITBY proceeds in his report of the grievances. The impositions upon currants in King James's time. The committee thinks fit to be presented as a grievance, it not being imposed upon just cause.

19. Regarding the patent issued to Charles Thynn, Thomas Mosely, and John More for making salt (C 66/2018, no. 3; MS Cal. Pat. Rolls, 12 Jac. I, pt. 2, f. 92), see HofC, 28 March, OB, and 5 May, n. 35.

20. See HofC, 20 May, n. 11.

21. On 23 May the House had resolved to adjourn from this day (25 May) until Thursday in Whitsun week (1 June).

22. I.e., with the act for the uniformity of common prayer and divine service in the Church and the administration of sacraments, *SR,* 1 Eliz. I, c. 2.

MR. MALET. This imposition has been countenanced with a judgment.[23]

Resolved that this shall be particularly mentioned in the petition of grievances to the King.

MR. WHITBY proceeds to the grievance of the deputy alnager, who sells his seals by the bushel, and the clothier may put them on what cloth he will. And the alnager's trade is made a fee farm. The committee think the best way for redress herein will be by bill.

Resolved that the abuse of the alnager's office shall be presented to the King in the petition of grievances, and a committee named to draw a bill for reformation herein and to consider how all the laws concerning this may be reduced to one head.[24]

[f. 29] MR. WANDESFORD moves that according to the ancient custom we should send to the Lords of our adjournment this day.

Non allocatur.

MR. WHITBY proceeds to the grievance of purveyance and names Mr. Pitcairn's patent for purveyance for hawks' meat. The committee think fit the King be petitioned for the putting down of this patent.[25]

SIR ROBERT PYE. That this patent has been anciently heretofore granted.

SIR THOMAS FANSHAWE. We never heard of this patent till within this 3 or 4 years. Now by virtue of this patent they have sent for many dozens of poultry, and the falconers themselves eat most of them themselves.

Resolved that this patent for purveyance for hawks' meat is a grievance in the creation and execution thereof, and a committee named to consider of the other abuses in purveyance and of presenting them to the King, and to meet tomorrow sennight.

MR. WHITBY proceeds to the grievance of entering into recognizances for observing of fish days.[26]

Resolved that this shall be presented to the King as a grievance.

MR. WHITBY reports the grievance of a patent of one Mr. Greg for examination of witnesses for the court of exchequer in the County Palatine of Chester. [f. 29v] The opinion of the committee that this patent is void in the creation and against law, and that it should be presented as a grievance to the King.[27]

Resolved by the House that this patent, forasmuch as Greg must be of the quorum and examiner, etc., is a grievance in the creation and against law, and shall be presented to the King as a grievance.

MR. WHITBY proceeds to the complaint of Doctor Allen and others against Doctor Anyan, president of Corpus Christi College in Oxford, who caused Doctor Allen to be arrested, who had complained before in parliament against him with others.[28] Doctor Anyan also made a warrant for taking out of the exhibitions of some scholars of the College that had complained against him in parliament, all his charges that he was put to in attending the parliament. The committee think this trenches far into our liberties and was done in great contempt to the House.

23. A reference to the upholding of the crown's right to impose in the case of John Bates, Mich. 4 Jac. I, f. 22, Lane, *Exchequer Reports*. See also, Howell, *ST,* II, 371–394, and above, n. 6.

24. Regarding the alnager, see above, n. 7. For the committee named to draw a bill for reformation of that office, see CJ, above.

25. See above, n. 12.

26. See above, n. 15.

27. See above, n. 16.

28. I.e., in 1624. See above, n. 17.

Ordered that Mr. Doctor Anyan shall be sent for and Mr. Benjamin Eliott to attend the committee tomorrow sennight.

Mr. More's patent for salt being in question,[29] all the patentees or those that have interest in it offer to disclaim their rights in the patent.

And SIR THOMAS [f. 30] FANSHAWE offers, if Mr. More will consent, to enter a disclaimer of the patent in his office without fees.

MR. MORE consents to it and disclaims his patent.

A committee named to digest and order the several grievances to be presented to the King, with power to appoint subcommittees for the penning of them.

The House adjourns till Thursday in Whitsun week.

III. DIARY OF SIR RICHARD GROSVENOR, MS 611, TRINITY COLLEGE, DUBLIN

[p. 138]

25 May

1. An act for explanation of one clause of the act concerning monopolies and dispensation concerning penal laws in that which concerns Sir Robert Mansell;[30] to repeal the proviso.

1. An act concerning hearing of preaching; none to be punished for going to sermons in other parishes.

2. It was liked well and read the 2d time. Committed, all that come to have voice, Saturday, sevennight, Exchequer.

1. An act for the establishing the estates of the tenants of Bromfield and Yale in the county of Denbigh and of the tenures, rents, and services thereupon reserved.

MR. CHANCELLOR OF THE EXCHEQUER. That he attended yesterday 3 hours and could get no committee for the preamble of the subsidy. Wished that Thursday should be appointed for the committee, and those who excepted against it should be added.

So ordered and the committee augmented, myself one.

MR. PYM moved for one Tendring, who had done good service to this House in discovering priests and Jesuits; that he was become poor by the charges in this service. Moved that he should have £10 out of that money collected at the communion.[31]

But this was disliked because that money was given to the poor; they would not change that but reserved it to another opportunity.

MR. NOY reported the bill for apparel: that they had given time till March come twelvemonth. They excepted strangers.

The amendments allowed and the proviso by 2 several questions, so passed.

MR. NOY. We have had complaints of excesses by poor people. The law of the leet is one of the best reformations, which falls after Michaelmas, which cannot be well attended because of the term.

Moved to have a bill read for the abbreviation of Michaelmas term.

[p. 139] *1.* An act for the shortening of

29. See above, n. 19.

30. I.e., regarding Sir Robert Mansell's patent for glass purchased from Sir Edward Zouch. The patent (C 66/1993, no. 4; MS Cal. Pat. Rolls, 11 Jac. I, pt. 16, f. 265) had been complained about in 1614 (*PP 1614*, p. 110, n. 12) and again in 1621 (*CD 1621*, VII, 539–549). Mansell had proposed a new means for manufacturing glass, see his tract, "Manufacture of glass with fuel, not being timber or wood", (22 May 1623), printed in A. Hartshorne, *Old English Glasses* (London, 1897), pp. 416–423, and the reasons for and against the patent, SP 14/152:63 and 64 (also printed in Hartshorne, pp. 423–431). See also a proclamation touching the manufacture of glasses, *Stuart Proclamations*, I, 342–343.

31. See above, n. 4.

Michaelmas term and for the speedier passing of common recoveries.

MR. WHITBY proceeded in his reports:

12. The Turkey merchants' complaint of the great imposition upon currants: 18d. custom, 3s. 4d. upon old currants more (18 *Jac.*, 2s. 6d. in all), 7s. upon the hundred, which is the 4th part of the commodity.[32]

MR. NOY. That this was not fit to be presented as now is delivered to us because it is said to be cessed upon a wrong cause. H. 7 time the state of Venice had Candia,[33] thither we went for malmsey. They imposed 18s. upon every tun. This was complained in parliament. An order made that they should pay 18[s.] for every tun brought into the kingdom. Moved that we should only in the general complain that these impositions were put upon us, and this in particular.

MR. MALET would have this particularly mentioned for these reasons:

1. It has been countenanced by a judgment.[34]
2. It encourages the Venetians to put an imposition upon our goods.
3. The profit goes to a subject.
4. It was never in the Book of Rates.

MR. WHITBY proceeded: 13. The deputy alnager 1 cause of grievance—now extends it to caps, waistcoats, and all things of wool. He sells his marks by bushels; he doubles his fee. They make a fee farm of this in most parts of the kingdom. The committee thought it fit to draw a bill for relief of this.[35]

Resolved by question to be presented, and a committee named to draw a bill.

MR. WHITBY proceeds: 14. Purveyors. A grievance by purveyors as by sending for their proviso 40 miles. Hens, etc. If he wanted what was commanded, they would make the rate 18d. apiece and would pay but 6d.

[p. 140] The patent for purveyance of hawks' meat, Mr. Pitcairn the patentee, to take hens at 2d. apiece, pigeons at 6[d.] per dozen, and 3 sheep hearts for 1d.[36]

Condemned for a grievance.

A committee named to consider of all the abuses of purveyance, Friday sevennight, Court of Wards, all that come to have voice.

15. Proclamations enforcing alehousekeepers and butchers to enter into recognizance against dressing of flesh in Lent and other days prohibited. The butcher must pay 2s. 6d.; the alehousekeeper, 12d.[37]

Resolved by question, a grievance.

16. Greg's patent. Condemned as a grievance in that part of the patent which give[s] him power to be clerk and of the [quorum] in all commissions, and is a grievance in the execution in taking of those fees.[38]

17. Dr. Anyan's contempt against this House in refusing to pay Dr. Allen's allowance, because he had complained in parliament, till he had been paid, out of the fellows' exhibition who complained against him, all his charges he had been at in following that business.

Dr. Barcroft and Mr. Howard were fellows, a warrant from Dr. Anyan to the bursars to pay them nothing.[39]

Resolved that Dr. Anyan, president of Corpus Christi College, and Mr. Eliott, dean, should be sent for to be here before

32. See above, n. 6.

33. MS: *Candy*. See *SR*, 7 H. VII, c. 7, and see also, A.L. Simon, *The History of the Wine Trade*, (London, 1907), II, 222–228.

34. See above, n. 23.

35. See above, n. 7.

36. See above, n. 12.

37. See above, n. 15.

38. See above, n. 16.

39. See above, n. 17.

the committee of grievances tomorrow sevennight.

A committee named to digest and order and pen these grievances to be presented to the King and to make subcommittees; self one. Friday, tomorrow morning, in the House.

The House adjourned.

IV. DIARY OF JOHN LOWTHER, ESQ., D/LONS/L, CUMBERLAND AND WESTMORLAND RECORD OFFICE

[f. 41]

[25 May]

[MR. WHITBY.] 13. [*sic*][40] The impositions of currants to be presented.

14. [*sic*] The deputy alnager exacting 1d. for ob[olus], and upon shopkeepers. King answered: Should [be] mended. To desire a bill to regulate it.

[f. 41v] Thursday before Whitsuntide we adjourned, without any intimation from the Lords or King, until that day sevennight, as we may upon such festivals, but upon other occasions some thought we might not, and the Lords did not adjourn until Friday and then until Friday after us.

V. DIARY OF SIR NATHANIEL RICH, HIST. COLLECT. 143, HLRO

[f. 91v]

[25 May 1626]

[MR. WHITBY.] 13. [*sic*][41] The Turkey merchants' complaint of impositions grievous upon currants to which the King, 21 *Jac.*, answered that it was no more than was laid in Queen Elizabeth's time. But his was mere misinformation.

14. The deputy alnager extended to caps, etc., as was complained 21 *Jac.* No amendment. Wishes that one law made to comprise all laws.

15. A patent for hawks' meat. This never heard of until within 3 or 4 years. Moved to provide against purveyance in general as now it is used. The complaint of this 18 *Jac.*

16. A new grievance concerning a proclamation touching Lent and recognizances to be taken thereon. A great grievance for the subject to enter into bond for performance of a law 5, 27, 25 Eliz. *et Jac.*[42] By the same reason a man may be bound to observe a penal law.

17. The inhabitants of the county of Chester complain of a patent granted to [Greg], that no commission shall issue out of that court but he to be a countyman. Commissions are not of the mere grace of the King, for many ought to be relieved in equity.

18. A great contempt against the House done by Dr. Anyan, James, etc.

Thursday noon, 19 [*sic*] May, the House adjourned itself till Thursday following, 8 a clock.

40. Both Lowther and Rich, below, follow a different numbering scheme from the other diarists.

41. See above, n. 40.

42. See *SR*, 5 Eliz. I, c. 5; 27 Eliz. I, c. 11 (act of continuance); and *Tudor Proclamations*, II, 503 and 535. See also, n. 15, above.

Order of Business Thursday, 1 June 1626

I.	Journal of the House of Commons,	339–341
II.	Whitelocke,	341
III.	Grosvenor,	341–342
IV.	Lowther,	342

Committee on the bill for **reversing** erroneous decrees in **courts of equity** to meet tomorrow	339, *17/2
Committee on the bill for the avoiding of a lease of the manor of **Malden,** parcel of the possessions of **Merton College,** to meet Monday [5 June]	339, *11/2
L.1a. An act for settling of a jointure upon the wife of Sir Thomas **Littleton**	339, 341, *9/6
Resolved: letter to be written to barons of the Exchequer for discharge of process against Sir John **Strangways,** MP	339
Committee for considering **Heaman's** complaint and such other **defects in shipping,** victuals, munition, etc., to meet tomorrow	339, *22/3
Committee on the presentment of **recusants** to meet Monday [5 June]	339, *21/2
Committee on the bill concerning the granting of **administrations** to meet Saturday [3 June]; members added	339, *24/2
Committee on the bill for the better ordering of the office of the **clerk of the market** to meet tomorrow	339, *7/3
Committee on the bill to avoid suspicion of **injustice** in any **MP** to meet Monday [5 June]	339, *9/5
Committee on the bill for the mitigation of the sentence of the greater **excommunication** to meet Monday [5 June]	339, *10/3
Sir John Eliot: moves that Thomas Meautys and other MPs be appointed to witness the opening of **Eliot's papers** that had been taken from his chamber	339, *2/6
Committee for Eliot's papers: appointed	339
L.2a. An act for estates of tenants of **Bromfield and Yale:** committed	339, 341, *25/5
L.2a. An act for the **punishment of adultery** and fornication: committed	339, 341, *11/5
Sir Henry Poole: presents a bill for the better venting of **white cloths**	339, 341, *5/6; 10/6; 12/6
L.1a. An act for the better vent and sale of white cloths	339, 341
L.2a. An act to enable the sale of manors and lands late of Richard **Fust:** committed	340, 341, *5/5
Petition of the **merchants** trading in **France** concerning the **embargo** there: read twice	340, 341(2), *18/2
Richard Spencer	342
Edward Kirton	342
Cristopher Wandesford	342
William Coryton	342
Resolved: further consideration of this petition deferred until Monday [5 June]	340, 341, 342
L.2a. An act for the naturalizing of Samuel **Powell:** committed	340, 342, *2/5
L.2a. An act to punish Sir Robert **Sharpeigh** for reviving the imposition upon Newcastle **coals**	340, 342, *27/3
Sir Peter Riddell	342
Committee on bill to punish Sharpeigh: appointed; Sharpeigh to attend with his counsel	340, 342
Cristopher Wandesford: moves to renew the	

THURSDAY, 1 JUNE 1626

I. JOURNAL OF THE HOUSE OF COMMONS

[CJ 865; p. 80]
Jovis, 1 Junii, 2 Caroli Regis

Bill for reversing decrees in equity, tomorrow, 2 clock, Star Chamber.

Merton College bill, Monday, 2 clock.

L. 1a. An act for the more convenient settling of a jointure upon the wife of Sir Thomas Littleton, Knight and Baronet.

A letter to be written from Mr. Speaker to the barons of the Exchequer[1] for discharge of the process of *distringas* against Sir John Strangways, awarded against the commissioners for the subsidy in *com. Dorset,* for not returning the subsidy.

The committee for ships and shipping, tomorrow in the afternoon.

Bill for declaration of recusants, Monday, 2 clock.

Bill of administrations, Saturday afternoon; and all the lawyers, common and civil, added to the committee.

Clerk of the market, tomorrow in the afternoon.

Bill for oath of the members of this House, Monday afternoon.

Excommunication, Monday afternoon.

SIR JOHN ELIOT. That Mr. Meautys, and some others, may be appointed to see the opening of his papers, which were taken by Mr. Meautys and were by him sent sealed up, to see whether they be all there.

Ordered, Mr. Meautys to attend and Sir William Spencer, Sir Thomas Hoby, Sir William Armine, this afternoon, 5 clock, at Sir John Eliot's chamber.[2]

L. 2a. Bromfield. Committed to

Mr. Attorney Wards	Sir George More
Sir Richard Grosvenor	Mr. [Robert] Caesar
Sir Eubule Thelwall	Mr. [Edward] Bysshe
Sir John Stradling	Sir J[ames] Perrot
Sir Thomas Morgan	
Mr. [William] Ravenscroft	
Knights and burgesses of Wales and Cheshire	
Mr. Rolle	
Sir Robert Pye	
Mr. [Edward] Littleton	

Tomorrow morning, 7 clock, Court of Wards.

L. 2a. An act for further punishment of adultery and fornication.

Committed to

[col. 1]	[col. 2]
Mr. Jordan	Sir George More
Mr. [Edward] Bysshe	Mr. Attorney Wards
Sir Edward Peyton	Mr. Herbert
Sir H[enry] Poole	Sir Gerrard Fleetwood
Sir William Bowyer	Sir William Walter
Sir Anthony St. John	Sir Francis Barrington
Mr. [Robert] Caesar	

And all that will come to have voice; Wednesday afternoon, Exchequer Chamber.

[p. 81] SIR H. POOLE tenders a bill for the better venting of white cloths.

L. 1a. An act for the better vent and sale of white cloths made of the wool of this kingdom.

1. *King's remembrancer* is crossed out in the MS and *barons of the Exchequer* is inserted. Dorset was not singled out as delinquent in the subsidy treasurers' account given in 1625 for the 1624 collection, Harl. 161, ff. 55–56v (printed in *PP 1625,* pp. 289–292). For the subsidy returns in Dorset, 1624, see PRO, E 179/105,30b.

2. Eliot's papers were confiscated when he was sent to the Tower on 11 May. See HofC, 11 May, n. 15; 12 May, nn. 1 and 17; 16 May, n. 4; and 19 May, n. 1. Regarding Thomas Meautys, see HofC, 6 June, n. 7.

L. 2a. An act to enable the sale of the manors and lands late of Richard Fust, deceased, and for the assignment of 2 several bonds of six thousand pounds to give satisfaction to the kindred of William Hill, deceased, of the money raised by the said Richard Fust out of the estate of the said William Hill.

Committed to

[col. 1]
Mr. [John] Pym
Mr. [Thomas] Malet
Mr. Rolle
Sir H[enry] Poole
Sir William Strode
Dr. [Thomas] Eden

[col. 2]
Sir B[aptist] Hicks
Sir H[enry] Spiller
Mr. [Francis] Rous
Sir Francis Barrington
Sir John Strangways
Mr. Lowther

[col. 3]
Mr. [George] Vernon
Mr. Nicholas Jordan
Sir Thomas Barrington
Sir Thomas Canon
Mr. [Edward] Whitby
Mr. [John] Wilde
Mr. [Robert] Caesar

[col. 4]
Knights and burgesses of Gloucestershire
Sir Thomas Hirne
Mr. [Anthony] Langston
Mr. [William] Coryton
Mr. [Robert] Bateman

This day 7night, Exchequer Chamber.

A petition from the English merchants trading France, about the continuance of the embargo, 2 read.[3]

The further consideration hereof to be taken upon Monday next.

L. 2a. An act for the naturalizing of Samuel Powell, the son of John Powell, of London, merchant, and Jane, his wife.

Committed to

[col. 1]
Sir M[aurice] Abbot
Sir John Stradling
Mr. [Robert] Bateman
Sir Roland Cotton
Mr. [Edward] Bysshe
Sir A[rthur] Ingram
Sir H[enry] Poole

[col. 2]
Mr. [William] Coryton
Sir Richard Grosvenor
Mr. [John] Wolstenholme
Sir Edward Hales
Mr. Herbert
Sir Francis Barrington
Mr. [Thomas] Sherwill
Mr. [William] Strode

[col. 3]
Mr. [Robert] Caesar
Sir John Gyll
Mr. [Edward] Roberts
Sir H[umphrey] Lynde
Mr. Lowther
Mr. Goodwin
Sir A[lexander] Temple

Tomorrow, 7 clock, Court of Wards.

L. 2a. Sharpeigh.

Committed to

[col. 1]
Sir George More
Sir H[enry] Anderson
Sir P[eter] Riddell
Sir John Stradling
Sir John Savile
Sir Thomas Grantham
Mr. Rolle
Mr. [Edward] Kirton
Sir Francis Barrington

[col. 2]
Sir Thomas Hoby
Sir A[rthur] Mainwaring
Mr. [John] Bankes
Sir Ferdinando Fairfax
Sir H[enry] Poole
Sir Edward Hales
Sir William Spencer
Sir Edwin Sandys
Sir A[rthur] Ingram
Burgesses of London

[col. 3]
Mr. Whitaker
Sir Francis Vincent
Mr. Attorney Wards
Mr. [Christopher] Herris
Sir William Constable

3. A draft petition regarding the embargo was read in the House on 16 March, committed for consideration, read again on 17 March (where it is printed at the end of that day's proceedings), and was recommitted. See 17 March, nn. 10, 12, and 23. Regarding the seizure of English ships and goods in France, see also, HofC, 29 April, n. 11; 1 May, nn. 16 and 19.

Mr. [William] Coryton[4]
Mr. Richard Spencer
Sir William Spencer
Mr. [Christopher] Wandesford
Mr. Goodwin

Tuesday afternoon, Exchequer Chamber. He to have notice, and to be heard by counsel, if he will.

The committee about naming committees to give account upon Thursday next what they have done in that business.

[p. 82] MR. LOWTHER reports Sir Timothy Hutton's bill, without any[5] amendments, save some words stricken out. *Engrossetur.*

Engrossed bills to be read upon Saturday next, 9 clock.

Bill against lapses, Wednesday next, former place.

Sir Charles Snell's bill, Saturday next.

Bill against simony, Saturday next.

Bill against buying and selling of offices, Monday afternoon; and Sir Edwin Sandys added to the committee.

Bill against weirs, Monday afternoon, former place.

Sir James Altham's bill, Monday, former place.

II. DIARY OF BULSTRODE WHITELOCKE, ESQ., DD. 12.22, CAMBRIDGE UNIVERSITY LIBRARY

[f. 30]

[1 June]

June 1, Thursday in Whitsun week.[6]

Me, B.W., absent.

Some private bills read and another petition of our merchants trading into France concerning the embargo of their goods there, which is not yet fully released. The debate thereof deferred till Monday next.[7]

III. DIARY OF SIR RICHARD GROSVENOR, MS 611, TRINITY COLLEGE, DUBLIN

[p. 141]

1 June 1626

1.[8] An act for the more convenient settling of a jointure upon the wife of Sir Thomas Littleton.

2.[9] The act for Bromfield and Yale. Committed, Court of Wards, at 7 of the clock.

2. An act for the further punishment of adultery and fornication. Committed, Wednesday, Exchequer Chamber.

1.[10] An act for the better sale of white cloths made of the wool of this kingdom, presented by SIR H. POOLE.

2. An act for the sale of the lands of Richard Fust, deceased, and for the assessment of certain bonds made for the putting in of a perfect account and putting in a true inventory. Committed, Thursday, Exchequer Chamber.

A petition of the merchants trading into France: That an embargo had been made in France upon the arrest of the *St. Peter* of Newhaven. That order had been taken to release such of their goods as were bought in France, and their debts due the last month are paid but those not then due yet detained. 4 months since the arrest, whereby many thousands utterly impoverished.

Moved that the House would petition the

4. *and all that will come to have voice* is crossed out in the MS following *Mr. Coryton.*

5. Printed edition: *without amendments.*

6. The House adjourned on 23 May with an order to reconvene on Thursday in Whitsun week.

7. See above, n. 3.

8. I.e., read for the first time.

9. I.e., read for the second time.

10. *Mr. Bysshe* is crossed out in the MS and *1* is inserted.

King that some speedy course might be taken to free their goods and the better settling of future trade.

MR. SPENCER moved for a committee to draw a petition and therein to represent unto the King the wrong the French do us who were not to embargo our goods, etc.

MR. KIRTON. That we had petitioned the King already.[11] Our merchants cannot get off *St. Peter* 's rock.[12] Moved we might go to the Lords and show them the cause of all which is, they say, of the goods of the *St. Peter,* and that we add this to the rest of our complaint.

[p. 142] MR. WANDESFORD. That because the House was thin we might put it off till Monday or Tuesday.

MR. CORYTON. To go to the Lords. The Duke cause of this. This would aggravate that one cause, etc.

Ordered that this petition should be referred—the debate—till Monday next.

2. An act for naturalizing of Samuel Powell, the son of John Powell of London, merchant. Committed, self one, tomorrow morning in Court of Wards.

2. An act for the punishment of Sir Robert Sharpeigh for reviving the imposition of 4d. upon a chaldron of Newcastle coals and for the preventing of the like in time to come.[13]

SIR P. RIDDELL. That it might be committed and a day appointed for the party to be heard by his counsel.

Committed,[14] Tuesday, Exchequer Chamber, and he to have notice to attend with his counsel if he please.

MR. WANDESFORD moved to renew the committee for settling of committees, Thursday next.

MR. LOWTHER reported an act to enable Sir Timothy Hutton and his son for the sale of lands to pay his debts, etc.

Passed to be engrossed.

Saturday, at 9 of the clock, appointed to read engrossed bills.

Wednesday, Exchequer Chamber, for the bill to prevent lapses in spiritual livings.

Monday, the bill against buying and selling of offices.

IV. DIARY OF JOHN LOWTHER, ESQ., D/LONS/L, CUMBERLAND AND WESTMORLAND RECORD OFFICE

[f. 41v]

[1 June]

Thursday we met, read some bills.

I reported Matthew Hutton's bill.

Committees ordered, and no more.

11. For the House's petition to the King regarding the rectifying of his revenue, see HofC, 5 May, OB. The Vice Chamberlain delivered the King's answer on 8 May, see OB.

12. A reference to Sir Dudley Carleton's speech, 12 May.

13. Regarding Sharpeigh's patent, see HofC, 24 May, nn. 16 and 17.

14. *all that come to have voice* is crossed out in the MS following *committed.*

Order of Business Friday, 2 June 1626

Committee on the bill against all pretenses of **concealments** to meet Monday [5 June]	344, 345, *13/2
Report from the committee on the bill for estates of tenants of **Bromfield and Yale** (Sir Walter Pye, Attorney of the Court of Wards)	344, 346, *25/5
Committee on the bill for relief of the **poor** to meet Tuesday [6 June]	344, 346, *9/3
Committee on the bills for **arms** to meet tomorrow	344, 346, *14/3; 20/3
Report from the committee on the bill for the naturalizing of Samuel **Powell** (Edward Bysshe)	344, 346, *2/5
Committee for **Eliot's papers** to meet this afternoon	344, *1/6
Committee on the bill for better allowance from **nonresidents** to their **preaching curates** to meet tomorrow	344, 346, *8/5
Committee on the bill for the better ordering of the office of the **clerk of the market** to meet this afternoon	346, *7/3
Anthony Langston: prefers a complaint concerning a warrant of the clerk of the market	344, 346
Sir Robert Pye	346
Sir Thomas Fanshawe	346
Committee on the bill for the clerk of the market: member added	344
Matter of the warrant of the clerk of the market is referred to the committee of **grievances;** they to make a subcommittee; clerk of the market and his deputies to attend	344(2), 346
Committee on the bill for the better preserving of his **Majesty's revenue** to meet Monday [5 June]	344, 346, *20/2
Order of 23 May for the House to be **called:** read	346, *23/5
Sir Nathaniel Rich	346
Orders concerning those that are absent at the calling of the House	344(2), 346
The House is called; twenty-five MPs make default	346, 347
[*Afternoon*]	
Committee of **grievances**	
Mr. Herne, counsel for the **Brewers:** prefers a complaint against the imposition on malt	344
Sir Robert Heath (Attorney General)	345
Mr. Stone	345
Mr. Herne	345
Sir Robert Heath (Attorney General)	345
Counsel withdraw	345
Richard Taylor	345
John Wilde	345
Resolved: to consider this matter further on Wednesday [7 June]	345

FRIDAY, 2 JUNE 1626

I. JOURNAL OF THE HOUSE OF COMMONS

[CJ 865; p. 82]
Veneris, 2 Junii, 2 Caroli Regis

Bill of concealments, Monday afternoon, in the former place.

MR. ATTORNEY OF THE WARDS reports the bill for Bromfield and Yale (which came from the Lords) without any amendments.

Bill for the poor, Tuesday afternoon, in the former place.

Arms and armor, tomorrow afternoon, in the former place.

[CJ 866] MR. BYSSHE reports Powell's bill, without any amendments; which came from the Lords.

The committee for Sir John Eliot's papers to meet at Sir John's chamber, at 5 clock.[1]

Vicars' maintenance and allowance from nonresidents, tomorrow in the afternoon.

Mr. Langston added to the committee of the bill for the clerk of the market; and a warrant read. This matter referred to the committee for grievances, and Mr. May and his deputies to attend; and they to make a subcommittee, if they think fit.

Committee for the King's revenue, Monday morning, in the House.

The House to be called and no excuse to be made till the House be fully called over, and then the excuses to be heard. The forfeitures to be disposed and distributed in such sort as the House shall think fit; and if any failing, and their excuse not allowed, shall not pay the money forfeited within a week, then a serjeant at arms to be sent for him to come to the House to answer it. And, after the House called over, the defaulters to be presently called.[2]

II. DIARY OF BULSTRODE WHITELOCKE, ESQ., DD. 12.22, CAMBRIDGE UNIVERSITY LIBRARY

[f. 30v]

June 2

MR. LANGSTON prefers a complaint against the clerk of the market and shows a printed warrant of the clerk of the market for the general summoning of all that use any weights or measures to come to show them.[3]

This referred to the committee of grievances.

Ordered that the House shall be called presently, and after the House is wholly called the excuses of those that make default to be made. The forfeiture to be distributed as the House shall think fit. If any fail in their appearance and pay not within a week their forfeiture, they shall be sent for by the Serjeant.[4]

Pomeridiem

At the committee of grievances.

Mr. Herne,[5] of counsel with the Brewers,

1. I.e., those appointed on 1 June to witness the returning of the papers taken from Eliot's rooms when he was imprisoned on 11 May.

2. At the time of the adjournment on 23 May it was resolved that the House would be called this day, i.e., Friday after Thursday in Whitsun week. For a list of the defaulters, see Grosvenor, below.

3. Simon Chamber was the clerk of the market (SP 16/20:56). We have not found the warrant.

4. See above, n. 2.

5. Regarding Mr. Herne, see HofC, 5 May, n. 7. The complaint was preferred again on 30 April 1628 (*PP 1628,* III, 173–174, 176, 180); on 21 May of the same year it was resolved in committee that the imposition was a grievance both in creation and execution (ibid., III, 52); on 4 June it was reported to the House (ibid., IV, 82, 85, 89, 97); and on 19 June it was voted a grievance by the House (ibid., 373, 376, 378, 381, 382).

prefers a complaint of the Brewers of the City of London and within 4 miles thereof against an imposition of 4d. on every quarter of malt. Heavier than 40 subsidies upon each particular man per annum. 1614 it began.[6]

Mr. Attorney. Against this complaint. Purveyance is an ancient right of the crown and purveyance for beer and ale as ancient as other purveyance. This 4d. upon a quarter of malt was a voluntary composition made by the [f. 31] Company of Brewers with the King for purveyance of beer and ale. And if after any particular man refused to pay that composition, suits must necessarily arise. But if there have been any undue carriage in those suits, it is the court's fault; I come not to defend it, nor any personal faults if a purveyor have committed faults in the execution of his office.

Mr. Stone. No purveyance at all ought to be taken of beer, it being a thing compounded and the King has only purveyance of things simple, else he should have purveyance of the same thing twice. The brewers were promised by [*blank*] that they should have a toleration and a *non obstante* for those penal laws whereunto they were b/

The composition was void and ought not to endure. It was illegally made, not having the seal of the corporation to it.

Mr. Herne remembers the statute of 1 E. 3.[7]

Attorney. Purveyance has been taken in progress and standing house ever, and purveyance of things compounded is taken. Purvey[ance] of malt is allowed per statute 36 E. 3.[8]

Mr. Attorney. It will appear by divers commissions and by records out of [the] Green Cloth that purveyance of beer has [f. 31v] been usually taken for hundreds of years.

They withdraw.

Mr. Taylor. I conceive that the King cannot take purveyance for beer in his set household, but upon necessity in his progress. *Pandoxator hospitii* is an officer of the King's household.[9] Anciently the King paid as much for those commodities which he took of the subject as any other man did. No compositions before 12 *Jac.*

Mr. Wilde. All the charters and customs of the City of London are confirmed by act of parliament.[10]

The committee appoint Wednesday next for Mr. Attorney to speak to the right of purveyance for beer and to show the commissions mentioned by him and make proofs of the execution of them, and to speak to the composition. And a caution given to the brewers that they make no agreement for this while it is depending in the House.

III. DIARY OF SIR RICHARD GROSVENOR, MS 611, TRINITY COLLEGE, DUBLIN

[p. 143]

June 2

Monday for the bill of concealments.

6. See *APC 1613–1614,* pp. 647–649, and ibid., *1615–1616,* p. 9. See also, *PP 1628,* III, pp. 173–174, nn. 20–27.

7. I.e., the charter of 1327 (1 E. III), given in answer to a parliamentary petition, prohibited the King's taking of goods without the subjects' consent. Purveyance was regulated by statute, *SR,* 5 E. III, c. 2.

8. *SR,* 36 E. III, c. 2.

9. See Jacob's *Law Dict.*

10. Cf. Coke, *Second Inst.,* f. 249. London "may make constitutions and laws . . . for the good government of the City. So as these constitutions and laws be not contrary to the laws and statutes of the land".

SIR WALTER PYE reported the bill of Bromfield and Yale and brought it in without amendments.

Tuesday for the bill of relief of the poor.

Saturday, the bill for armor.

MR. BYSSHE reported the act for the naturalizing of Samuel Powell without amendments.

Saturday, Court of Wards, the bill for increase of poor ministers' maintenance.

This afternoon the bill concerning the clerk of the market.

MR. LANGSTON delivered in a printed warrant from the clerk of the market to the constable of Eldersfield in Worcestershire:[11] to warn 2 or 3 sufficient persons to appear by 8 to do according as on their oaths should be; to warn all kind of artificers and tradesters that have weights sealed or not sealed. He said that in that county the King's fines came not to above 40s. a year; now the clerk has farmed it; the fines are worth above £60 per annum.

SIR ROBERT PYE. That the clerk should pay the King £400 rent but had for many years paid nothing.

SIR THOMAS FANSHAWE. That in his country[12] the clerk of the market did not only fine but collect it themselves; break open men's doors.

Ordered that it should be referred to the committee of grievances, and they to make subcommittee and to send for the clerk and his deputies.

Monday morning appointed for the committee for the ordering of the King's revenue.

The order of 23 May upon the recess was read for the calling of the House and the paying of £10 by the absents.

[p. 144] SIR NATHANIEL RICH moved that those who were absent should be committed to the Serjeant till they had paid their fine.

Ordered that the fine should be disposed of by the appointment of the House.

Ordered that he that is absent and his excuse not allowed and pays not his forfeiture within a week,[13] then the Serjeant to be sent for him to come up and answer. That the House be wholly called and no excuse to be made till after all be called, and then the defaults to be called and they to make their excuses.

The House was called.

These absent without excuses, which not allowed: 25.[14]

[col. 1]	[col. 2]
ex. Sir John Backhouse	Sir George Fane, cleared
Sir Robert Knollys	Sir Robert Monson
Mr. Arthur Champernowne	Sir Henry Hastings
ex. Mr. [John] Delbridge	ex. Mr. Thomas Standish
Sir Christopher Hildyard	Mr. [Christopher] Sherland
ex. Mr. John Browne	Mr. [John] Crew
Mr. [John] Whitson	Sir Edward Baynton
Mr. [William] Marlott	Sir Henry Compton
Mr. [James] Lewis	

11. See above, n. 3.

12. I.e., in Lincolnshire.

13. *day* is crossed out in the MS and *week* is inserted.

14. The figure is inaccurate. Grosvenor apparently corrected his list after Berkeley and Fane were cleared the following day. See below, 3 June.

[col. 3]
Mr. Owen[15]
Mr. [Francis] Smalman
Mr. Mason
Sir Nathaniel Barnardiston
Sir Roger North
Sir Edward Rodney
Sir Walter Covert
Sir Maurice Berkeley, cleared
Mr. [John] Sackville
Mr. [John] Haselock

IV. DIARY OF JOHN LOWTHER, ESQ., D/LONS/L, CUMBERLAND AND WESTMORLAND RECORD OFFICE

[f. 41v]

[2 June]

On Friday we called the House according to our order at recess and 25 only made default on whom, by former order, £10 apiece was set for a fine, and further as the House should think fit. But no order for levying it, and reasonable excuses were admitted after to divers.

15. *Mr. Gurley* is crossed out in the MS preceding *Mr. Owen,* i.e., Thomas Gurlyn.

Order of Business Saturday, 3 June 1626

Saturday, 3 June 1626

I. JOURNAL OF THE HOUSE OF COMMONS

[**CJ 866;** p. 83]

Sabbati, 3 Junii, 2 Caroli Regis

Sir M. Berkeley, absent yesterday, now present; upon question, spared. So Sir George Fane.[1]

L. 1a. Lady Lambart.

The grand committee for evils, causes, and remedies to sit upon Tuesday next, in the House.

The preamble to the subsidy tendered by Mr. Chancellor of the Exchequer , and read; and then the bill of subsidy tendered by Sir John Finch.

The committee for penning the grievances to meet upon Tuesday next, in the Court of Wards. And the committee has power to send for the commissioners, or collectors, about the licensing of the selling of wines.

Resolved, the House presently to be turned into a grand committee to consider whether fit to desire a conference with the Lords; and, if that shall be resolved, then upon what heads that conference shall be.[2]

The committee to prepare the business to be left with the Lords about Mr. Montagu to meet upon Monday next, in the afternoon; Mr. Noy, Mr. Glanville, Mr. Littleton, Mr. Selden, Mr. Wilde, added to the committee.[3]

Sir Montague Bertie desiring leave to go to his company in the Low Countries, it was not yielded.[4]

Mr. Herbert reports from the grand committee some words used by Mr. More,[5] or words to that sense and effect: That we were born free, and must continue free, if the King would keep his kingdom. And his discourse upon supposition, what a tyrant may do or not do within this kingdom, adding these words: As, thanks be to God, we have no occasion, we having a just and pious King.

Mr. More heard to explain himself, and then withdrew.

Mr. More by all which spoke (which were many) cleared from any ill intention in speaking his words.

Upon question, Mr. More to be sent to the Tower during the pleasure of the House for his offense in speaking the words now reported; which judgment Mr. Speaker accordingly pronounced to him, kneeling at the bar.[6]

Resolved for the present to proceed no further in punishing him.

Tuesday,[7] for reading the petition against recusants in authority.

Wednesday, for reading engrossed bills.

II. DIARY OF BULSTRODE WHITELOCKE, ESQ., DD. 12.22, CAMBRIDGE UNIVERSITY LIBRARY

[f. 32]

June 3

Chancellor Exchequer reports the preamble for the bill of subsidies.

1. For the list of those absent at the calling of the House, see Grosvenor, 2 June.
2. For the debate in committee, see the accounts below.
3. For the orders regarding transmitting the charges against Richard Montagu to the Lords, see 29 April.
4. On 1 June the Council of War, taking into consideration a petition to the King regarding the preparedness of the Spanish, ordered all colonels and other officers and troops in the service of the United States of the Low Countries to return there. SP 16/28, f. 2; see also, SP 16/29:29.
5. For More's speech and his explanation of the speech, see the accounts below.
6. More was restored to his place in the House on 7 June, see below.
7. I.e., 6 June.

Which is read.

SIR JOHN FINCH presents the bill.

MR. KIRTON calls for the order made at the agreement of the subsidies.[8]

Which is read.

MR. CORYTON moves that we may resolve ourselves into a committee to consider of some heads for a conference with the Lords considering the time and stay of businesses, or give power to the former committee for the conference.[9]

Ordered that the House shall presently be turned into a grand committee to consider whether it be fit to have a conference with the Lords. And if they resolve it be, then to consider and frame the heads for it.

MR. SPENCER moves that Sir Montague Bertie may have leave of the House to go over into the Low Countries.

Non allocatur.

[*Committee of the Whole House*]

Mr. Herbert in the chair.

Resolved that there shall be a conference with the Lords touching the privilege of parliament and the retardation of our businesses hitherto and such other heads as we shall debate of.

[f. 32v] Sir John Strangways. That by common fame it is come to our ears that the University of Cambridge has chosen the Duke their Chancellor,[10] which is in contempt of the justice of this House. This is fit to be considered of.

Mr. Kirton. We hear too that the Duke has gotten the title of president of the Council of War.[11] And there is one called out of this House to the Lords who we all know had not a place to be made Lord of.[12] And others are taken up, I will not say to make a party above but we may suspect. And I think it done in affront to this House and fit that we acquaint the Lords about this.

Mr. Coryton. If, as common fame is, the Duke was the cause of the coming together of the parliament at Oxford and the dissolution of it, making of sheriffs[13] and sending away to sea, meaning Mr. Glanville,[14] and other things, I think it were fit to be known; and the way to know: to go to the Lords.

Mr. Long. What we may expect when judges are called up who are of alliance with the Duke, and some whose fortunes depended upon his favor, and some kept away from the Lords, as the Bishop of Lincoln, who for ought I know is kept [f. 33] away for nothing but because they think he will give his voice against the Duke; and the Lord

8. I.e., on 27 March.

9. I.e., a conference regarding complaints against the Duke of Buckingham, see the debate in committee, below. The former committee may refer to that appointed on 15 May.

10. George Monteigne (Montaigne), Bishop of London, apparently solicited the Chancellorship for the Duke after the death of the Earl of Suffolk. See Sir Benjamin Rudyard to Sir Francis Nethersole, 2 June, App., II, C (SP 16/29:9). The election brought congratulations from the King, see SP 16/29:28. See also, John to Gilbert Millington, 6 June, App., II, C (SP 16/29:31) and Birch, *Court and Times Chas. I,* I, 107–108.

11. The Duke's presidency of the Council of War may have been a rumor. See App., II, E(8).

12. I.e., Sir Dudley Carleton, Vice Chamberlain of the Household, summoned to the Upper House on 22 May as Lord Carleton of Imbercourt. See HofC, 23 May, n. 11.

13. I.e., the pricking of sheriffs before the elections to the present parliament, see App., II, D.

14. I.e., the appointment to foreign employment as a means of punishment, see HofL, 15 May, p. 461, n. 65. For Glanville's arguments against such employments abroad, see SP 16/6:132.

Arundel is kept away.[15] He is made president of the Council of War, who sent away our forces against the Protestants. I cannot think this kingdom can stand as long as this man does thus affront the highest court of England. I desire some use may be made of this in our conference with the Lords.

Mr. Wentworth. These words are in the statute of 25 E. 3: the King ought and is bound and it is a right of the crown to redress grievances.[16] 38 E. 3, the Lords and Commons are bound to counsel and advise together for the good of the country.[17]

Mr. Pym. It is not unknown that a member of the Lords House went to solicit the business of Chancellorship for the Duke to Cambridge,[18] and some that are inclined to Mr. Montagu's opinions,[19] as Doctor Cosin and Mr. Mason.[20] I desire these two may be sent for.

Mr. Goodwin. The manor of Imbercourt belongs to the crown, but I'll not meddle with how. Those words which Sir Dudley Carleton spoke here were of a dangerous consequence, and I desire that it may be branded as an inconsiderate speech.[21]

Sir Dudley Digges. I hope it is a mistake that such words should be mentioned by so discreet a gentleman. He that shall go about to counsel the King for those alterations which the gentleman spoke of,[22] as they say, if he were my father I should count him a greater traitor to the King than those [that] have been accused of treason lately.

[f. 33v] Chancellor Exchequer. In excuse and commendation of Sir Dudley Carleton. He never flattered this House nor the King when he came to advise on businesses concerning this House. He spoke here only what he had seen in other places fall out upon ruptures between King and people, and at a time when there was a fear of such a thing here. He has served the King abroad these 16 years and is returned with great reputation.[23] And for reward of his virtue the King has bestowed on him a title of honor, and let no man think it done for other ends.

Mr. Coryton. Let us consider the time of the honor given him and his favor expressed here towards the Duke. His speeches here were very unfit for this place.

Mr. Spencer. I think it not fit that this speech should be a head for this conference, because he sat in the House many days after businesses were open here.

Mr. Kirton. We see the kingdom cannot

15. John Williams, Bishop of Lincoln and Lord Keeper, was relieved of the latter position in October 1625, and remained out of favor with Charles, being sequestered from the coronation (see HofL, 6 February, p. 24, n. 18) and from parliament (see SP 16/20:43). Regarding Arundel, see HofL, 14 March, p. 149, n. 2.

16. It is unclear to what statute he refers.

17. Cf. *Rot. Parl.,* 38 E. III, no. 2, Wentworth's citation is incomplete.

18. I.e., George Monteigne (Montaigne), the Bishop of London. See above, n. 10.

19. I.e., the Arminian Richard Montagu's opinions. See below, n. 30.

20. John Cosin, prebendary of Durham, was an Arminian whose works would come under examination in the parliament of 1628 and who, shortly thereafter, would be pardoned by the King. See *CD 1628,* IV, 237, n. 7. Robert Mason, fellow of St. John's College, Cambridge, was secretary to the Duke of Buckingham. See *PP 1628,* VI, 126.

21. See above, n. 12. Carleton's speech in question is that of 12 May regarding the words of Digges and Eliot at the joint conference of 8 and 10 May.

22. The reference is to the suggestion in Carleton's speech of 12 May of "new counsels". See Coryton's speech in Grosvenor, below.

23. Sir Dudley Carleton had recently returned from a mission to France. See HofC, 18 April, n. 4. He had been ambassador to Venice, 1610–1615, and ambassador to the Hague, 1616–1625. G. M. Bell, *A Handlist of British Diplomatic Representatives 1509–1688* (London, R. H. S., 1990).

subsist with the infinite pride and superfluities of some men.

[f. 34] Mr. Long. Let us confer with the Lords to know if there are any such new counsels. And if there be, to make a protestation that those that do forward or execute them shall be traitors.

Mr. More. It is an impossible thing for this kingdom to be brought to that which new counsels have brought other kingdoms to if God should send us a tyrant, as, God be thanked, we have a pious and a good king now.

Chancellor Exchequer interrupts him and say[s] it is far from the point and not fit to talk of tyrants and such discourse here.

Mr. Wandesford moves that Mr. More's words may be reported to the House.[24]

Chancellor Exchequer. I took the words to be that the King could not keep his kingdom if he would do this. These words offended me.

Mr. More explains himself and denies those words. As they were not in his heart, so he hopes not in his tongue.

Mr. Littleton. I think we cannot pass over these words with our loyalties.

Sir John Eliot. That it is fitting this should be reported to the House presently.

Sir John Finch. I think his words were: we were born free and must be free if the King will keep his kingdom. This he said speaking of the yeomanry of England and peasantry of France.[25]

[f. 34v] Sir John Eliot. Mark but the words spoken by him—"if the King will keep his kingdom"—which are contrary to our tenets in religion and in any sense cannot but be ill taken.

We cannot sit here loyally to hear the words here of supposition that there is a possibility of the King losing his kingdom or of a supposition of tyranny in this realm.

Resolved that Mr. Herbert shall report to the House that Mr. More spoke these words, viz., "We were born free and must be free if the King will keep his kingdom", or words to that effect, and that he discoursed upon what a tyrant might do or might not do in this kingdom, and added: thanks be to God we have a just and a pious king and no such occasion now.

Speaker takes his chair.

MR. HERBERT reports according to the resolution of the committee.

MR. MORE again excuses and explains himself, and withdraws.

MR. LITTLETON. I think we cannot go less than for these rash words that the gentleman be committed to the Tower [f. 35] during the pleasure of the House.

MR. GLANVILLE. I think there is no precedent that fines imposed by this House have been levied and rarely imposed, but exclusion and imprisonment have been most frequent. I move that this gentleman may be excluded the House and committed to the Tower.

SIR JOHN FINCH. That he be expelled the House, sent to the Tower, and referred to the King's further judgment.

CHANCELLOR EXCHEQUER. I am very willing with the House to clear this gentleman's intention and agree with the judgment proposed.

24. I.e., that More's words be read in the House, outside of the committee. See the other accounts of More's speech, below, which may be the only extant records; we have found no fair copies of the speech.

25. See Lowther, below.

MR. BANKES. If we punish him in part and leave him for further punishment to the King, we may infringe our liberties. Either let us punish him totally or refer him totally to the King. I think it fit we censure him entirely here.

SIR EDWIN SANDYS. Those things that are here offensive are common in books, and we may not speak here that which men may write. The prophet Iesus says, "Woe be to him that lays a snare for a man by a slip of the tongue. He is a perfect man that offends [not] in his tongue".[26] I think it not fit we should leave any of his censure to the King, but commit him to the Tower, which is a place [f. 35v] of punishment for offenses against the King. But I think it not fit we put him out of the House at this time. Sir Christopher Pickering's [*sic*] case was so carried.[27]

MR. WANDESFORD. That since he cannot rule his tongue, which is of most use in this House, I think it fitting he be therefore expelled the House as well as sent to the Tower.

MR. PYM. Let us advise upon this high punishment of putting him out of the House, and for the present only send him to the Tower. If we see cause, we may hereafter add to this punishment.

Resolved that for this offense by words spoken Mr. More shall be sent to the Tower, there to remain during the pleasure of the House.[28]

Mr. More, brought in by the Serjeant to the bar upon his knee, has this judgment pronounced against him.

III. DIARY OF SIR RICHARD GROSVENOR, MS 611, TRINITY COLLEGE, DUBLIN

[p. 144]

3 June

1. Lord Robartes's bill. An act for reversing of a decree made in Chancery on the behalf of Hester, Lady Lambart, complainant against Richard, Lord Robartes, and his Lady.

Tuesday morning appointed for the grand committee of evils, causes, and remedies.

SIR RICHARD WESTON reported the preamble of the subsidy, which was read.

MR. KIRTON moved to have the order for granting the subsidy which was that the bill should be brought in when our grievances were presented to the King.[29]

[p. 145] Tuesday afternoon appointed for committee for marshaling the grievances, in Court of Wards.

MR. CORYTON moved for a committee to consider of the heads of a conference with the Lords about our whole proceedings this parliament, which have gone so ill with us.

SIR DUDLEY DIGGES moved the same—presently to resolve the House into a committee—for he doubted matters were in so bad case above that if we desired a conference we could not have it. And where are we then when the whole business of the commonwealth is at a stand?

Resolved that the House should enter presently into a grand committee to consider whether there shall be a conference with the Lords and, if that be agreed on, then to consider of the heads.

26. See Ecclus. 19:16 and Jas. 3:2.
27. Sir Christopher Pigott's case. See HofC, 17 May, n. 12.
28. See above, n. 6.
29. For the order, see HofC, 27 March, OB.

The Speaker went out and Mr. Herbert called in.

[*Committee of the Whole House*]

Mr. Coryton. First, to decide whether there should be a conference with the Lords, and decide that by question.

Sir G. More. That first we should consider of the things for which we should desire a conference and then to agree whether a conference or not.

Mr. Browne. This conference touching and concerning our privileges, wished that to be the question.

Sir Walter Erle. The conference to be not only concerning our privileges, but concerning all other business[es] which retard our proceedings.

Mr. Wandesford. Fit for us to deal plainly with his Majesty what the causes are why we have not given that expedition to the business required. This in a mannerly way: either to do that which is required or give him reasons why we do it not. We have presented our greatest grievance to the Lords in that we have had many rubs. The Lords are so now, too. If we go on with the matter of the money and the Lords do nothing above in the business of the country, what account shall we give our country? That we draw together the heads of all our proceedings which have been done to the honor of the King. If they can not confer with us, we [p. 146] may resort to our own counsels again and/

By question, resolved that we should desire a conference with the Lords touching our privileges of parliament and the retarding of our business here, and such other heads as should be agreed on.

Sir John Strangways propounded a head, and that from common fame: that the University of Cambridge has chosen the Duke Chancellor, who now stands charged in the higher House of treason and from us of many fearful crimes. This is to the dishonor of this House. The Duke is a great favorer of Montagu; the whole frame of religion lies at the stake.[30]

Mr. Kirton. 2 things we charge the Duke with: one is plurality of offices.[31] Since when, this great Lord has been so insensible of the sense of this House that he has procured this place to himself. The 2d complaint: that honor was bestowed upon poor men, as now we see.[32] Since this complaint a gentleman called to be a baron forth of this House[33] who has not a place to be a baron of; and we may fear it is to make a party above, for we all here saw his affection to the Duke.

Mr. Coryton. There fell somewhat from Sir Dudley Carleton concerning new counsels which deserve to be a head of conference.[34] Nothing more dangerous to the commonwealth than when such things are spoken of.

By common fame reported that the Duke was cause of our going to Oxford and cause of our breach there, and the money desired was small, as not worth the labor thither.[35] If these have happened by him alone, nothing more dangerous.

30. See above, n. 10. Buckingham supported Richard Montagu, the Arminian whose books were under examination by the present parliament. See above, 17 April, OB.

31. Regarding plurality of offices, see HofL, 13 May, pp. 413–419.

32. Regarding honor, see HofL, 15 May, pp. 469–470.

33. I.e., Sir Dudley Carleton, see above, n. 12.

34. See above, n. 22.

35. In 1625, the crown's hope was that an additional subsidy bill could be passed in the Oxford session. See *PP 1625*, pp. 710, 713.

[p. 147] Mr. Long. A head: That here we sit to search out the grievances of the commonwealth which come now to receive a judgment. What success we can expect when some judges must be called up whose life, fortunes, etc., depend upon the Duke's favor? Some of their judges are kept away, as the B. of Lincoln; it may be because he will not give his voice with the Duke of Buckingham.[36] Now what success can we expect when they take hence judges to clear him there whose voices are involved in his condemnation in this House?

If the Duke be clear, I wish increase of honor to him; if not, I wish that his exceeding greatness does not only abate our edge to give to his Majesty, but God knows the issue.

The Duke is now made president of the Council of War.[37] In what case do we stand? How can we expect good from him who has employed our forces against our religion? This kingdom cannot subsist in that honor so long as this man thus stands and, in despite of this House, to aggravate the griefs of the kingdom. Assumes new honors when I expected he would rather have laid down his honors.

Mr. Wentworth. One of the 3 things that we found to be evils: our honor diminished. This conference may tend to much good, but I fear we shall have too much. We may think with joy that God has honored this island with light of His truth more than any other, so with strange deliverances and preservations. *Ergo* we have great cause to respect the honor of it, which the Lords will consider who are much risen in honor of late. Our wane of strength has been the cause of our loss of honor; must weed out all ill weeds and plant all good things.

[p. 148] 25 E. 3. In the statute setting down the true use of parliaments the King ought/[38]

That in parliament the King shall give law of redress for mischiefs found out by his people.

38 E. 3. The Lords and the Commons are bound to join together to procure the wealth of the people.[39]

To let them know that we have sought the redress of mischiefs, that religion may be kept secure. For, if we fall to Arminianism it will quickly turn to Bellarminism. That they will join with us to redress our [*illegible*].

Mr. Pym. That a member of the Lords House went to Cambridge to solicit this business for the Duke without their consent,[40] and that some others who have been agents to utter Montagu's book, as Dr. Cosin and Mr. Mason, have also employed themselves about this, so that it may be suspected a conspiracy to bring in Arminianism.[41]

Mr. Goodwin moved that the words spoken by the Lord of Imbercourt might not be committed, but that we might brand it with somewhat as not a fit speech for a parliament.

Sir Dudley Digges. Those words were but mistaken; I know his breeding at home and abroad. I do not believe he would not [*sic*] speak any such words to that purpose; for if any counselor should counsel any such thing, I hold him the greatest traitor that may be.[42]

Sir Walter Erle. He was sorry that he was gone forth of the House before he was called to answer it, for he deserved to be called to the bar as well as ever any did.

36. See above, n. 15.
37. See above, n. 11.
38. See above, n. 16.
39. See above, n. 17.
40. See above, n. 18.
41. See above, nn. 19 and 20.
42. See above, n. 22.

[p. 149] Sir Richard Weston. Those words were spoken out of a great fear lest matters would succeed ill between the King and his people. If such a disunion should arise, when it is to be feared, shall a counselor flatter and not to tell what has happened in other places to prevent?

Out of this arises other ill opinions against him who spoke faithfully. He did not flatter this House and I never heard him flatter the King when he gave him counsel in anything. Now how unhappy is he that, having spoken his mind freely here, having served the King 16 years abroad with good content,[43] no man more zealous to unite our neighbor princes and has returned with good applause, now he looks for the fruit and has received an honor from his master, that it must be said he is called up for other ends? I desire in this case that the House would not throw blemishes upon those who have served this House faithfully; that will discourage others to do the like. This man is not to be mentioned but with much honor; and the business to be let go to the ground, if you will have care of your own.

Mr. Coryton. That both his honor and words were fit heads.

Sir Thomas Jermyn. He dissented. That Sir D. Carleton was here questioned for 2 things: 1, for a speech here; 2ly, for his honor above.

Mr. Spencer. That that speech sounded ill but would not have it as a head because he had sat here many days after, not questioned. They proceeded by new counsels who had gotten the flowers of the crown and wore them in their hats and could not abide parliaments.

[p. 150] Mr. Kirton. That we have heard of new counsels and new projects.

Mr. Long. That we acquaint the Lords of these new counsels and desire to protest that such as shall give them might be declared traitors, and such also as should execute them.

Mr. More. It is impossible for a tyrant to bring this land to subjection, like that of France.

Here Mr. Chancellor interrupted him and said that he could not hear with patience such a supposition of a tyrant, etc.

Mr. Glanville. A conference already resolved with the Lords. Moved to consider whether they would join both together, or lay that aside, or have them apart.

Mr. Wandesford moved that Mr. More's words should be reported to this House.[44]

Mr. Chancellor said that the words offended him were that there could be no new ways, no new means of gathering money, "if the King meant to keep his kingdom".

Mr. More explained himself.

Mr. Browne did not remember the words so employed but that he cited the example of Louis the 11 who bragged that he brought his people, and that he conceived no hurt in it.[45]

Mr. Littleton. The words were offensive to him, for in that historical discourse of Louis 11, he spoke of those who gave new counsels. That by those the King could not/

[p. 151] Sir John Eliot. I confess the words are not only particular that offend me but the manner of the speech which ought not to be presented here to us. His speech was by way of supposition of a tyranny, which we no way fear; for our King is a pious prince and so will be still. For that

43. See above, n. 23.

44. See above, n. 24.

45. We have not found the source of the comment.

other part, he draws in upon that of new counsels: "that the King could not maintain his kingdom" and take the discourse as it was, it is fit for a censure. Moved to report it to the House.

Mr. More. That when he spoke of tyranny there was no such thing, could not be his words were exclusive.

Sir John Finch. There were words used, "if the King would keep his kingdom", as I think, with this connection after he had spoken the difference between the yeomanry and castles, etc., of this kingdom with other countries. He then said: we are born free, and must be free if the King would keep his kingdom.

Mr. Herris said that the words were: If we should have a tyrant (as we had none) yet he must have a free people if he would keep his kingdom.

Mr. Herbert reported what had been propounded:

1. If new counsels were followed, the King would not keep his kingdom.

2. That he discoursed upon supposition of a tyranny.

3. That we were born free and must be free if the King would keep his kingdom.

Sir John Eliot. That the last words are offensive of themselves. Let the inference be what it will be, for no act of the King can make him unworthy of his kingdom; it is against the tenet of our religion.

[p. 152] Mr. Griffith thought that those words, "if the King will keep his kingdom", had relation to foreign parts.

Mr. Glanville. If any man shall by way of argument deliver that there is any possibility that by any means the King may lose his kingdom, not fit for us to hear or for any man to make a possibility that there might be a tyranny in this kingdom. This is a hideous noise. Moved that it might be reported to the House.

Ordered that Mr. Herbert should report to the House that Mr. More spoke these words: "That we were born free and must be free if the King would keep his kingdom"; or words to that effect, and that he distrusted upon supposition what a tyrant might do or not do in this kingdom, adding as thanks be to God we have none occasion of that fear having a just and pious King.

Adjourned till Monday, 9 of the clock.

The Speaker came in and Mr. Herbert reported Mr. More's words as above.

Mr. More. I begin to accuse myself in mistaking some words. I commit myself to your favorable interpretation and upon my former protestation that it was as far from me to speak anything to the derogation of the honor of the King, this House, or kingdom as anything in the world. I spoke in heat, in zeal and in a religious zeal that I desired to have a free passage to the affairs of this kingdom. Which neither were, nor could be, which were impossible to be. He prayed that never greater sin lie upon his soul.

[p. 153] Mr. Littleton. No man but satisfied that his mind is right, but as fit that our language and words when we speak of kings should be so. It is against the tenet of our religion that there is any way that may make a king worthy to lose his kingdom. That we may do the King and ourselves that right we ought. I think we can do no less for these words but commit him to the Tower during the pleasure of the House.

Mr. Long concurred in part; he was satisfied in his intention. Thought fit to go to the Tower, but for the 2[n]d part he thought he meant that the King's greatest security was in the keeping of his subjects free, therein he acquit him.

MR. GLANVILLE. This House has sometimes fined, committed to the Tower, to the sheriffs, to the Serjeant, put out of the House. Moved that he that had transgressed our liberties here should be excluded the House and after sent to the Tower. He remembered the precedent of Mr. Shepherd who, for some words against a bill, was excluded.[46] Now he that speaks against him that calls us hither deserves it much more.

SIR JOHN FINCH. I conceive he was far from the intent which his words might import, yet he is beholding to the pious exposition of this House in his words. Remembered the case of Sir W. Stanley's words: if he be E. 4['s] son. That he be expelled this House, sent to the Tower, and referred to the King's further pleasure.[47]

[p. 154] MR. KIRTON. His intention not so bad as his words, yet to give a precedent and therein to condemn the words spoken by Mr. Vice [Chamberlain] who said that if the King did not punish he were unworthy his crown.

SIR R. WESTON. Intentions judge our actions, but words express our intentions. I agree with the sentence: he deserves no less than is laid upon him, but these are unlike those words spoken by Mr. Vice Chamberlain, who told the House they were words of the King himself.

MR. CORYTON. It behooves us how we speak of him to whom we owe ourselves. That he be put out of the House; and for his imprisonment, to put a time to it.

MR. SERJEANT TOWSE. Sequestered the House and committed to the Tower during the pleasure of the House.

SIR PETER HEYMAN. To put him forth and send him to the Tower, but not leave him to the King; for if we have power to punish let us limit it ourselves, not leave it to other hands.

MR. BYSSHE. To expel him, imprison him, and leave him to such further punishment as the King should please; for when we have discharged him of this House fit to leave him to the King, since the offense is against him.

SIR ROBERT PYE. To leave him to the King's pleasure for time of his imprisonment.

SIR NICHOLAS SAUNDERS. That we first send him to the Tower and then send for him out and dismiss him.

[p. 155] SIR EDWARD SPENCER. When his intention is clear, his words are only to be taken as one in a sleep; though that expulsion was punishment enough.

MR. BROWNE. For expulsion.

SIR H. ANDERSON. We have words and intentions. When words are out of the mouth, they are no longer his.

SIR JOHN ELIOT. I would be glad to put an end to this dispute and such as might tend to the honor of this House in respect of ourselves, House, the King, the cause. For the gentleman, I concur with those that go most ready to clear his intentions to mean no ill. And although words must expound our thoughts, yet I do acquit him in regard of his interpretation. But the words carried ill sense. At this time most necessary in re-

46. Thomas Shepherd, a lawyer, was expelled in 1621 for his offense to the House in a speech of 15 February that year, *CD 1621*, II, 82; IV, 53; V, 467. For the discussion of his punishment, see ibid., II, 95–96; IV, 62–65; V, 11–12, 467–468, 499–503; VI, 352, 376–377, 450.

47. We have not found the case.

gard of the many aspersions cast upon our proceedings. Neither would I aggravate or make it more than the justness of the cause requires, but make it a punishment in fact. For to exclude him is a punishment of disgrace, but not great enough in respect of the cause. That he be totally excluded the House and the liberties thereof; that he be imprisoned during the pleasure of the House. This will give satisfaction to his Majesty and our honor.

Mr. Bankes. When we go about to do right to the King let us not prejudice our own liberties as we shall do if we leave any part of punishment to the King; *ergo,* either totally leave him to the King or to ourselves. Imprisonment during our pleasure and expulsion.

[p. 156] Mr. Griffith. To be expelled the House is the greatest punishment; would have him committed, not expelled.

Sir G. More. If an eye or member offend, put it out. In Sir Thomas Parry's case,[48] a light offense to this, yet was he put out of the House and committed to the Tower. He was put out but not sent to the Tower upon a message from the King. That Mr. More be put out and committed to the Serjeant till Monday or Tuesday.

Sir F. Barrington.

Sir Edwin Sandys. We ought to be careful in all thing[s] that concern us. Solomon's advice: look right before you.[49] His speech gave offense, and nobly done to interrupt him in it. It is not fit to put an ill supposition upon a good king. I observe a great misfortune to men that are bookish, who put all suppositions in the world, but that which may be read in a book not fit to be spoken in a parliament.

The chief matter that aggravates a fault is the corruption of a man's heart. If his were so it lessens his fault, yet another instrument ought to be right. The tongue should be right, yet woe be to him that lays a snare to the slip of the tongue.[50] Yet this is such as must be punished.

I dissent from those who would refer anything to the King in this case. Let us not put him to right himself. To send him to the Tower and go no further because a slip of the tongue may befall any man; and not cut him off except his heart were rotten. Upon his petition and [p. 157] submission we may proceed to put him out if we please; mentioned Pigott's case.[51] To send him to the Tower and reserve the other to ourselves.

Mr. Wandesford. To put him forth and imprison him.

Mr. Pym. This offense not out of any ill intention. 2[n]d degree, out of a sudden intention, passion; cleared of both these. Degree that he spoke words subject to scandal. If he had not made a solemn protestation, I should more have doubted him. Now if we shall lay the highest punishment upon him for the lowest offense, I think we shall not proceed in justice.

To commit him to the Tower. Let us then see how his humiliation will work upon him. And thus shall we avoid a dangerous precedent in this House, since we are all subject to speak what we should not sometimes.

By question, resolved that Mr. More should be sent to the Tower, there to remain during the pleasure of the House.

The Serjeant sent for Mr. More who came to the bar. The Speaker delivered the judgment of the House, he kneeling on his knees; the Serjeant took him into his custody.

48. Sir Thomas Parry was put out of the House of Commons and suspended from the Privy Council in 1614. See *PP 1614,* pp. 202, 208, and 210.

49. Cf. 1 Kngs. 8:27.

50. See above, n. 26.

51. See above, n. 27.

IV. DIARY OF JOHN LOWTHER, ESQ., D/LONS/L, CUMBERLAND AND WESTMORLAND RECORD OFFICE

[f. 41v]

[3 June]

Saturday, after bills read and the order then to read engrossed bills read, some perceiving that the Lords not having the Earl of Arundel restored, then confined, nor the Bishop of Lincoln as I remember some mentioned/[52]

Moved to have the House turned to a committee (and so was) to consider of heads for a conference with the Lords because of our privileges. And reasons to be showed why we proceeded no slower.

[*Committee of the Whole House*]

1. How the Duke standing impeached before them of treason, and by us, etc., in contempt, was [f. 41a] made Chancellor at Cambridge. The actors and instruments to be considered. He now accumulating offices, it being before one of the charges.

2. How some employed that, etc., and Montagu that inclines to Arminianism, like to bring in half popery or Arminianism.

3. The interruption at Oxford. He being means to call us thither and dissolve us there when he touched.

4. The making Lord Imbercourt, that was a presenter, a baron, who had no estate in land, who was declared with us for him. As it were to make a party at this time. What justice could be expected?

5. The words he spoke of new counsels and the commoners' coats and clouted shoes. Other countries grown upon new counsels when parliamentary liberty was turned to tumultuary license or to that effect.

Upon which subject Mr. More speaking how impossible that was to [be] affected in England. How our yeomanry here, one would beat 10 of the slaves of France; and the King if he would keep his [kingdom] must preserve their liberty; and that, if a tyrant were, here is no forts, no cities, etc., to enthrall us, therefore impossible.

[f. 41av] Therefore he, being interrupted because he did bring such high points into supposition or doubt, was committed to the Tower, and after to be considered of if to be put out of House. But at first no more because all men did take he meant no evil; and he even in his speech commended the King his pious and gracious government, and showed these were but fanatical fears. Yet this slip of words thus censured; as if a man besides intention kill, etc. And, though madman, King is sacred, and so tongues to be wisely moderated.

Saturday, the King sent answer to the Lords how by many his great occasions he could not so ripen the matter for the Earl of Arundel as yet; but considering his great occasions he would haste as much as he could, and if before Wednesday sevennight he could, he would. But then upon the word of a King he would restore him or else show his causes to satisfy. That they might more cheerfully proceed in business.[53]

They notwithstanding, as I heard, adjourned until Wednesday or Thursday as/

V. NOTES OF LAWRENCE WHITAKER, SP 16/29:13[54]

3 June 1626

The House of Commons was resolved into a grand committee to consider of a con-

52. See above, n. 15.

53. For the King's message to the Lords regarding Arundel, see HofL, 3 June, p. 561.

54. The notes are endorsed: "Mr. Whitaker's note of what passed in the Lower House the 3 of June".

ference which was to be desired with the Lords, and of the heads whereof it was to consist.

[*Committee of the Whole House*]

Mr. Herbert in the chair.

Moved by Sir Walter Erle, and seconded by Mr. Wandesford, that this conference might be touching the privileges of parliament, which the House conceived to have been infringed, and touching the causes of the retardation of the proceedings in parliament, and such other heads as should be propounded and debated.

And so resolved by question.

Sir John Strangways first propounded for one of the heads the consideration of my Lord Duke's being chosen Chancellor of Cambridge, which he conceived to be a great contempt done to the House, it being done while he stood there impeached, etc.

Mr. Kirton seconded him in the same, and added to it that the Duke was also chosen president of the Council of War, and that he had lately procured titles of honor to be given to men of small estate, and one amongst others, that had been lately called out of this House, who had not so much as a place to call himself baron of; and he is now made a member of the Lords House—I will not say to help to make a party there, but it is worthy the consideration whether the calling of him thither, by the Duke's procurement, be not an affront given to this House.

Mr. Coryton. When that Lord was of this House he spoke of new counsels, and how by such counsels and by alteration of the form of government the people were in other countries brought to wear canvas clothes and wooden shoes; a thing not fit to be spoken in parliament. And then he proceeded to other things, as the breach of the parliament at Oxford, making some of the members sheriffs, sending Mr. Glanville with the fleet to Calais, etc.

Mr. Long. We have spent here much time in seeking out the causes of our grievances, and we have found out the cause of those causes and have sent him up to the Lords for judgment. And there we find that divers allied to that great man, that depend upon him and expect preferment by his favor, are called thither, and some members of that House kept from thence, as one amongst others whom we know of, the Bishop of Lincoln. And some called thither from hence, whose voices were involved in the censure which this House gave of that great man. And I think it not fit that a judge that has given his judgment once should now go into another place, there to give it again. And so proceeded to the disputations held at York House for the countenancing of Montagu's books, and to the other things formerly mentioned by others.[55]

Mr. Goodwin. Mr. Vice Chamberlain, that was Sir Dudley Carleton, and a member of this House, is now called up from hence and made a Lord, Baron of Imbercourt, the seigneury whereof is the King's; a circumstance not to be omitted. But, to let that pass, let us remember the words that he spoke in this House touching new counsels and alteration of government which were of so ill and dangerous a consequence that I hold them very fit to be mentioned in the conference.

Sir Dudley Digges excused my Lord Carleton, saying that certainly he meant not ill in that he spoke; neither did there to his apprehension any words fall from him to so ill a purpose as was conceived by divers of those that had spoken.

55. Regarding the conferences at York House, see HofC, 6 March, n. 48.

Sir Walter Erle said he could not excuse him, for he conceived that Lord deserved as well to be called to the bar for that he spoke in this House as ever any man did.

Mr. Chancellor of the Exchequer professed himself to dissent from those that took the words spoken by that noble Lord so heinously. I think, says he, they were spoken out of a great sense of his duty and respect to this House and out of a great fear he had of ill consequences that might happen by a dissension between the King and his people, etc. I hold him unhappy that having counseled this House faithfully and having as he never flattered this House so likewise never flattered the King in the affairs concerning this House, but having ever spoken his mind freely and served the King and his father 16 years abroad, with such approbation as no man ever served them and his country more faithfully, both in matter of state and of religion, and that now, when he comes to be rewarded here with honor for his service, it must be said in so grave and wise an assembly that he is called to his honor and to the Lords House for other ends. I am jealous of his honor, as of my own, and would have this House to be tender of throwing blemishes upon those that serve you faithfully; you will else give great discouragement to those that shall so serve you, etc.

Coryton. I hold it unfit either to give such counsel as that Lord mentioned to a king, or to mention it in parliament. I hold it to be such counsel as Jezebel gave to Ahab for the affecting of his desire in getting away Naboth's vineyard,[56] and, therefore, that it is very fit to be mentioned in the conference. Neither do I think it convenient for a man that has been here a presenter, and somewhat more (for he was in a sort a judge), to go and give his judgment again in another place; I think it ought not to be.

Sir Thomas Jermyn. The sense of that noble Lord's speech was only to show how some other kingdoms had heretofore enjoyed that happy manner of government which we now do, and how they came to have it altered, without giving any advice for setting on foot new counsels; and I think he therein committed no fault. And touching his honor, I hold it to be a deserved reward for his faithful, diligent, and discreet service of many years and, if a man may so speak, I think he has well merited what he has of his Majesty, etc.

Mr. Richard Spencer thinks it not fit to be spoken of as any head of the conference with the Lords. That alteration of government mentioned by that noble Lord proceeded rather from the insolency and misdemeanor of great officers in that kingdom who did much mischief, seized upon the King's revenue, and stuck some of the fairest flowers of the crown in their own hats, which forced the kings to look to their revenues themselves. It was no such alteration as that the mentioning of it could bear any ill construction amongst us, etc.

Kirton. It could not but bear an ill construction and be of dangerous consequence amongst us. He mentioned the King's betaking himself to new counsels with such a repetition of what had been done in another kingdom, as if he would teach the King new ways and to follow their example.

Long. Holds it very fit, notwithstanding all that has been said, to be a head of the conference, and moves that we may make a protestation that whosoever shall presume hereafter to give any such advice to the King for taking of such new ways and counsel shall be judged as traitors.

56. 1 Kngs. 21:5–15.

After him, Mr. More began his speech with the story of Louis 11 of France; who was interrupted and blamed by Mr. Chancellor of the Exchequer. And the House entered into some debate concerning the censuring of him. In which debate MR. KIRTON moved again that, in censuring of Mr. More, the speech of that member who was now gone from the House of Commons to the Lords (meaning my Lord Carleton) might also be censured. But he was not then seconded; so the Speaker went to the chair, and the House proceeded to the censure of Mr. More. And with that ended the day's sitting.

VI. NOTES OF SIR THOMAS BARRINGTON, SP 16/29:12[57]

1. The first that spoke[58] moved this: That my Lord Carleton's being called to the Upper House at this time was an injury to the House of Commons, his voice being first involved with the rest of the House against my Lord Duke, and though he were made a baron, he had no place to entitle his barony by, and we may guess which way he inclined.

2. Another moved[59] to make his speech of new counsels and the poverty of other kingdoms by reasons thereof (as he applied it) one head of our conference or declaration.

3. Another moved[60] the same that was before set on foot against him. That those that sat as judges among us against my Lord Duke being called to the Upper House must be judges the second time of the same cause.

4. The next whose speech I took[61] moved to this effect: That my Lord Carleton's mention of new counsels might be by the House censured as unfit language for parliament.

5. The next answered in my Lord Carleton's behalf[62]: That these words that are alleged for his part he heard not, and withal expressed his confidence that he spoke nothing with an ill intent, and therefore wished them to be charitable; affirming that he only made a relation to us of the condition of other countries.

6. Another answered:[63] That never man deserved better to be called to the bar while he sat among us, if he should intend in his speech as some understood it; but we must be careful in censuring.

7. Another[64] having expressed in general words the ill consequence of a quarr[el] (if any could be) between the King and his people, desired the House not to question any counselor of state that, out of a good meaning, had let fall somewhat freely to them to express that fear of his heart, especially such a counselor that never flattered us nor the King, and no man ever served better abroad, nor returned more honorable home. And now to suspect that he is called up for other ends, when he is only rewarded for his virtue, let us be careful how we throw such stains upon men when they have been faithful, for it will discourage others in the like employment. I have spoken what my heart dictates, and nothing but truth, and so concluded with a desire of having this debate laid aside.

57. The notes are endorsed, "For the Right Honorable the Lord Carleton", in a hand similar to Whitaker's in SP 16/29:13; in another hand is written, "Sir Thomas Barrington's notes of what passed in the Lower House concerning my Lord 1626".

58. I.e., Edward Kirton.

59. I.e., William Coryton.

60. I.e., Mr. Long.

61. I.e., Mr. Goodwin.

62. I.e., Sir Dudley Digges.

63. I.e., Sir Walter Erle.

64. I.e., Sir Richard Weston.

8. The next that spoke[65] said: That a presenter or a judge here should not be made a judge in the Upper House of the same matter.

9. The next moved[66]: That no personal complaint might be carried up to the Lords against him because he sat so long among us unquestioned, but that we should labor to prevent these new counsels.

Upon this Mr. More's words brought us into a new debate.

65. I.e., William Coryton.

66. I.e., Richard Spencer.

Order of Business Monday, 5 June 1626

MONDAY, 5 JUNE 1626

I. JOURNAL OF THE HOUSE OF COMMONS

[**CJ 866;** p. 84]
Lunae, 5 Junii, 2 Caroli Regis

L. 1a. An act to make Richard Pigott, the elder, liable unto the statutes touching bankrupts, to the intent that his creditors and sureties may be relieved against him for their just debts and engagements.

Sir Edward Fisher's bill, Friday next, in the afternoon, in the former place.

[*L. 1a.* Bul]keley.[1]

Astley his bill, tomorrow, 7 clock, Court of Wards.

Wagstaffe's bill, tomorrow, 2 clock, in the former place. Sir H. Poole, Sir William Strode, and the burgesses of Sussex, added to the committee.

Bill for marriages, tomorrow afternoon. All that will come to have voice.

L. 2a. An act for better vent and sale of white cloths.

Committed to

[col. 1]	[col. 2]	[col. 3]
Sir H[enry] Poole	Mr. [Henry] Sherfield	Sir B[aptist] Hicks
Sir Robert Poyntz	Mr. Rolle	Sir [Nathaniel] Rich
Sir H[enry] Whitehead[2]	Sir John Jackson	Sir George More
Burgesses 5 Ports	Sir Edward Peyton	Mr. Long
	Sir Richard Buller	

And all that will come to have voice; Wednesday, 2 clock, Exchequer Chamber.

Mr. Standish, being absent upon Friday and present on Saturday morning, spared, upon question; so Sir John Backhouse, being also here upon Saturday morning.[3]

Mr. Delbridge likewise, being here present this morning, is, upon special reasons alleged for his absence upon Friday/

Sir John Cutts has license to go into the country for his health.

Mr. Browne, sent for on Whitsun Tuesday for his wife's sickness, and returning again upon Saturday last, excused, upon question.

Mr. Owen,[4] stayed by attending Mr. Blonden, a member of this House fallen sick upon the way, and now present here, spared, upon question.

Upon question, whosoever shall be absent at the call of the House, not having asked leave openly in the House after 9 of the clock, to pay £10 at the least, for his default.

2ly. Upon question, all such members of the House, who by information to the House (without a call of the House) shall appear to absent the service of the House by so going out of town, to incur the like penalty. These penalties to be disposed as the House shall direct.

The House turned into a grand committee about the conference with the Lords.

Upon a report from this committee ordered, upon question, that this committee shall have power to take further into consideration of the things referred to the grand committee for righting our privileges, or of whatsoever was by them referred to any

1. The manuscript is frayed at the edge; what appears within brackets is supplied from the printed CJ.

2. *Sir M. Abbot* is crossed out in the MS following *Sir H. Whitehead.*

3. For the list of those absent at the calling of the House, see 2 June, Grosvenor.

4. I.e., probably Thomas Owen, returning from Shropshire. William Blonden sat for Bishops Castle, Shropshire.

subcommittees; and those subcommittees to make report to this grand committee.[5]

[p. 85] Upon question, this committee also has power to take consideration of the heads of the conference,[6] which was before agreed by the House; and to make such use thereof as they shall see fit. And this committee has also power to consider of heads and to frame a declaration to be made to his Majesty.[7]

Ordered, this grand committee shall presently sit; and so did.[8]

MR. HERBERT reports from the committee that it conceives this House has just cause of offense at the choice of the Duke to be Vice-Chancellor of Cambridge and do think fit that a letter be written to the corporation[9] of the University of Cambridge, to signify this dislike and require them to send some to the House to inform them.

Upon question, a letter to be written to the University of Cambridge, by name of their corporation, to signify unto them that this House has taken just offense at their **[CJ 867]** election of the Duke to be their Chancellor; and to require them to send some, instructed and authorized, to inform and give account to this House of the manner of their proceedings in the said election; and that if any other will come to give information they shall be heard. These to be here upon Monday next.

And further resolved, if any will in the meantime come and inform or complain, they shall be heard.[10]

II. DIARY OF BULSTRODE WHITELOCKE, ESQ., DD. 12.22, CAMBRIDGE UNIVERSITY LIBRARY

[f. 36]

June 5

The bill for better venting of white cloths debated.

SIR MAURICE ABBOT. That it is the custom of London and the inheritance of all the freemen of the City that none but freemen should buy any white cloths at Leaden Hall, and this bill takes away this their inheritance.[11]

SIR HENRY POOLE. That this bill enacts only that if cloth at Leaden Hall be not bought by the Londoners, but lies upon the hand of the clothiers, that then any stranger not a freeman of London may buy those cloths which the Londoners do not, paying those customs and duties that belong to the City.

This bill committed.

Ordered that such members of the House as shall be absent when the House is called without having asked leave openly after 9 a clock shall forfeit ten pounds at the least, or if the House be informed of any man's absence out of town without leave

5. A grand committee to consider a conference with the Lords was appointed on 3 June, see above. The grand committee for righting the privileges of the House had been appointed on 12 May and it resolved on the appointment of a subcommittee of twenty to frame a remonstrance to the crown. On 15 May that subcommittee was delegated to draw the heads for a joint conference. For the proposed heads for the conference with the Upper House, see 17 and 19 May.

6. The heads for the conference were discussed on 3 June, see above.

7. *Wherein a space to be left for the Lords to join if the peers' House shall think fit* is crossed out in the MS following *Majesty*.

8. *This committee adjourned till tomorrow morning, 9 clock, and Mr. Glanville, Mr. Littleton, and Mr. Rolle then to attend with their notes and the subcommittees for righting the privileges to meet at 2 of the clock this afternoon in the Court of Wards* is crossed out in the MS following *did*.

9. *Vice-Chancellor and proctors* is crossed out in the MS preceding *corporation*.

10. The names *Dr. Eden, Sir Nathaniel Rich, Mr. Pym, Mr. Selden* are crossed out in the MS following *heard*. Regarding the letter, see below, Grosvenor, and see 6 June where the King requested that the House forbear sending the letter. See also, 7 June, the declaration presented to the King.

11. See John Stow, *A Survey of London* (Oxford, 1908), I, 159–160.

asked after 9 a clock, the absent man to incur the penalty of ten pounds at the least.

[*Committee of the Whole House*]

Mr. Herbert in the chair.

[f. 36v] Mr. Wilde. Howsoever I wish that Cambridge may still retain the name of an academy, yet it shall be to me hereafter Asia Minor, the meaner university.

Sir Benjamin Rudyard. If a gentleman, out of his knowledge abroad, made a comparison between the miseries of other countries and the felicities of ours, with a desire of the continuance of our felicities, I think in this he offended not.[12]

Sir John Strangways remembers a part of a speech made by King James, 7 of his reign, viz.: All kings that are not tyrants or perjured, will[13] keep themselves within the bounds of the laws of the[ir] own kingdoms, and those that counsel them to other ways are vipers fitting to be cast out, and pests of the commonwealth. I hope our King that now is, and I am confident that he will, [will] inherit his father's virtues as he did the crown, and that if any persuade him to new counsels that he will cast them out.

Doctor Eden. I know nothing of the election of the new Chancellor in Cambridge but as I have heard here; but this I know, that the Chancellor is to be chosen within a few day[s] after the death of the old, and with as much freedom and more than any other officer of the University; and is the greatest office of honor that the University has to bestow, but it will take up no great time of a man. [f. 37] And the power of the Chancellor is in the Vice-Chancellor when the Chancellor is absent, and the office is but temporary, for every two years they may choose a new. Perhaps this may be a matter of obedience more than a matter of affront to this House. I desire you will leave a gracious ear open to hear what the University can say for themselves, and in the meantime suspend your judgment upon them.[14]

Speaker takes the chair.

MR. HERBERT reports from the grand committee their desire that the considerations of the grand committee for the righting of their liberties, and the committee for preparation of a conference with the Lords may be involved into that grand committee, and that they may have power to consider of a declaration to the King as well as a conference with the Lords, wherein there might be a place left for the Lords to join if it should be so thought fit.

Ordered that the grand committee that sat last shall have power to take further into their consideration those things referred to the grand committee concerning the liberties of the House and whatsoever was by them referred to subcommittees, those subcommittees to make their reports to this committee;[15] and to consider of those heads prepared before for a conference with the Lords and to make such use of them as they shall think fit; and to prepare a declaration to the King as well as a conference.

[*Committee of the Whole House*]

[f. 37v] Mr. Herbert in the chair.

A time appointed till tomorrow morning for the several committees to bring in their papers to this grand committee, and/

12. The reference is to Sir Dudley Carleton's speech of 12 May (see the fuller version of Wilde's speech in Grosvenor, below); see also, the debates of 3 June regarding Carleton's speech.

13. MS: *which.* See McIlwain, *Political Works of James I*, p. 309. The reference is to King James's speech of 21 March 1610.

14. Thomas Eden, Doctor of Civil Laws, was a Cambridge graduate. Regarding Buckingham's election as Chancellor, see HofC, 3 June, n. 10.

15. See above, n. 5.

Sir John Strangways desires some consideration may be had of the business of electing the Duke Chancellor of the University of Cambridge, for it is flown abroad that though we have condemned him yet the wiser and learneder sort and the University have chosen him their protector and Chancellor.

Sir Thomas Hoby. That there may be sent for Doctor Wren, Doctor Parsons, Doctor Beadle, Doctor Mawe, with the Vice-Chancellor of Cambridge.[16]

Sir John Strangways. That Doctor Eden may be enjoined by the House to write unto the University of the distaste of this House for their election of the Duke, and that they call a convocation and send hither some of both sides to give the House satisfaction.

Doctor Eden offers to undertake to have any here whom the House shall be pleased to nominate.

Mr. Noy. That the Speaker may write a letter to the Vice-Chancellor showing the distaste the House takes at their election and wishing him to send some to give the House satisfaction.

[f. 38] Resolved that Mr. Herbert shall report to the House that the committee do conceive that this House has just cause to take offense at the election of the Duke of Buckingham [as] the Chancellor of the University of Cambridge. And they think it fit that the House send a letter as from the Speaker to the University of Cambridge by name of their corporation and therein to let them know that the House takes offense at the election and that they send some to the House instructed from them to give information to the House about it, and that if any voluntarily will come that they may be suffered and that they be here by Monday next.

Speaker takes his chair.

MR. HERBERT reports the resolution of the committee.

Ordered according to the resolution of the committee.

III. DIARY OF SIR RICHARD GROSVENOR, MS 611, TRINITY COLLEGE, DUBLIN

[p. 158]

5 June

1. An act to make Richard Pigott liable to the statutes made touching bankrupts, to the intent his creditors and sureties may be relieved against him for their due debts.

1. An act for the settling, quieting, and estating of the manors, lands, tenements, hereditaments late of Sir Richard Bulkeley, Knight, the elder, deceased.

2. An act for the better vent and sale of white cloths made of the wool of this kingdom.

SIR MAURICE ABBOT. [1,] this bill takes away the freedom of London, which is the inheritance of those who serve for it. 2, it trenches upon the Merchant Adventurers obliquely. 3, in the bill, lawful for any man to ship cloth paying the duties, so that the King must lose his customs.

16. Matthew Wren, fellow of Pembroke Hall, Cambridge, he was appointed chaplain to then Prince Charles in 1622, received a DD from Cambridge in 1623, and became Master of Peterhouse in 1625 (*AC; DNB*). John Beadle, a Cambridge educated divine who became rector of Little Leighs, Essex, in 1632 (*AC; DNB*). Leonard Mawe, also a Cambridge divine, had been Vice-Chancellor in 1621, was appointed a chaplain to Charles, became Master of Trinity College in 1625, and in 1628 would be appointed Bishop of Bath and Wells (*AC; DNB*). John Goslyn (Goslin) was Vice-Chancellor in 1626 and Master of Gonville and Caius (*AC; DNB*). See below, n. 20. Both Dr. Mawe and Dr. Wren are cited as "His Majesty's chaplains" in 1626. See HofL, 10 June, p. 602. We are unable to identify further Dr. Parsons.

SIR H. POOLE. No intention to take away from the freedom of London or the merchants any liberty except in their defaults. The meaning of this is that the cloth shall not lie so long upon the clothiers' hands as formerly.

SIR G. MORE. The scope of this bill is neither unjust nor unreasonable; for if we cannot sell our cloth to the merchants, reasonable that others should buy it.

Committed, all that come to have voice, Wednesday, Exchequer Chamber.

Ordered by question that what member should be absent from the House when it shall be called, and have not leave from the House after 9 of the clock, shall pay £10 at the least; or if any shall be informed to be gone down out of the town, though it be not called.

MR. SPENCER moved to go to the business touching the rectifying of the King's revenue.

[p. 159] The House turned to a committee.

[*Committee of the Whole House*]

Mr. Herbert came into the chair touching the conference with the Lords.

Mr. Wilde. The purpose of this committee to confer with the Lords touching our privileges and to consider of some heads fitting. As touching privileges, I think it necessary that that be made one head, touching that particular upon misinformation which had been given to his Majesty against our members at the last conference. For other matter of privileges, not to insert them in this conference, only that because it concerned both Houses.

Next, concerning the retardation of our business, that is but the general. Some specials have been moved, as that of the University of Cambridge, which hereafter shall be the meaner academy in my opinion; in all their privileges and immunities have received their strength from this House and deserved a good return to this House.[17] This to be one head.

Next which was moved, the speech of Sir D. Carleton wherein there were many things that gave great cause of offense,[18] but I assure myself that he being now honorable could take it amiss that, being now in place of honor [he] should be compared to persons poor lying under a wall in the streets. We have great cause to be sensible of the blessings of God upon our kingdom which has excelled others. This not to be thought too much for us but rather as an argument to raise us up in thankfulness to God, having above all the sincerity of the gospel. *Ergo,* for any that shall speak of these things as thinking them too much for us, then it could not be defended; but if he spoke it, that we should be drawn to thankfulness to God, then, out of question, his speech could not be so offensive; and to the point of honor he said nothing, etc.

Sir Benjamin Rudyard said that it had been meet to have questioned him before and not since his [*illegible*] and, for his honor, he wished his honor and fortunes were answerable.

[p. 160] Sir John Strangways reported words of King James, 21 March, 7 *Jac.,* 1609, words: All kings that are not tyrants or perjured will suffer themselves to be bounded within their laws. They that shall counsel otherwise as pests and vipers.[19]

Dr. Eden. That he knew nothing but by common fame of the University's choosing of the Duke their Chancellor. Their customs in choice of this officer is to be made

17. The University was incorporated by act of parliament, *SR,* 13 Eliz. I, c. 29.

18. See above, n. 12.

19. See above, n. 13.

within a few days after vacancy; 2ly, with as much freedom and more than any other matter of elections there; for whereas they are tied to choose others such as their heads name, in this every man may propound. 3. It is the greatest office of honor they have, but withal a place of no great employment. And the power of the Chancellor is in the Vice-Chancellor when he is not there, so it is no matter of distraction. 4. It is a temporary office for 2 year[s], then a new one to be taken when they please. I speak not this to divert any to be sent for to give an account of their proceeding. There is among them many men of judgment; the Vice-Chancellor a man of judgment who has served here.[20] If please you to suspend your judgment till they be heard, they will make it appear to be no affront to this House but rather of obedience. There is no Bellarminism nor Arminianism.

Sir Thomas Hoby. It is apparent this is an affront to the House. I say no more. Moved that the heads of the remonstrance lately thought of should be considered, for that would afford 2 or 3 heads for this conference.[21]

Mr. Littleton. That he had no warrant to report the heads of the remonstrance, and this was not the committee.

[p. 161] Sir John Eliot. That Mr. Littleton would remember them of the particulars then thought on, that we might make use of it.

Sir Nathaniel Rich. That we are a little out of the way and foreclosed by our own order; for now we must only confer with them for those things which are partly in their knowledge as well as ours. We have sat lon[g] and done little; some things are fallen upon us that have blasted our hopes. That we shall do no good.

The Lords House is adjourned. Moved that the House should be moved that in the power of the committee might be enlarged that we might have power to make a declaration to the King of such heads as we shall like, and to leave a place for the Lords to join with us if they please, or else to present it ourselves to the King.

Mr. Pym. That our power may be enlarged to consider both of heads for a conference and a declaration, for the same heads will not be fit for both.

Sir Thomas Hoby. We have power enough already to make a declaration and offer it to the Lords.

Mr. Glanville. 2 grand committees on foot: the one how to right us in our privileges, and this is to consider of a conference with the Lords. Moved that the House would order that all these committees might be considered of together, that they interfere not.

The Speaker went into the chair. Where, upon MR. HERBERT's report, it was ordered that this committee, the grand committee for righting of our privileges, and the committee for drawing the heads of a conference, should be involved in this one, and their power enlarged; that they should also think of heads for a declaration as well, as well as a conference.

The Speaker went forth and Mr. Herbert went into the chair again.

[*Committee of the Whole House*]

[p. 162] Sir Walter Erle. To resolve whether you would proceed with first either a conference or declaration.

Sir John Eliot. To adjourn the committee with this: that Mr. Rolle, Mr. Littleton, and

20. John Goslyn sat for Barnstaple, Devonshire, in 1614. See *PP 1614*, p. 453.

21. Regarding the proposed remonstrance, see above, n. 5.

Mr. Glanville should provide their labors against tomorrow morning.

Adjourned.

The Speaker went in and MR. HERBERT reported that which was resolved in the committee.

Resolved by question that the Speaker should write a letter to the [University of] Cambridge [by the name of] corporation of Vice-Chancellor, doctors, proctors, and the rest of the masters, regents, and vice-regents of the convocation house, that the House takes offense at this manner of choosing of the Duke for their Chancellor and look[s] for some deputed from them with instructions to inform this House and give account of their proceedings in the election at which this House had taken just offense, and withal that such others as will come voluntarily to give information shall be heard.

By another question, resolved that they should be here upon Monday.

IV. DIARY OF JOHN LOWTHER, ESQ., D/LONS/L, CUMBERLAND AND WESTMORLAND RECORD OFFICE

[f. 42]

[5 June]

Monday, the House resolved to send to the Vice-Chancellor, doctors, proctors, regents *et non* to certify of the election of the Lord Duke, as an affront offered to the House and for the miscarriage and contempt to the House.

Order of Business Tuesday, 6 June 1626

TUESDAY, 6 JUNE 1626

I. JOURNAL OF THE HOUSE OF COMMONS

[CJ 867; p. 85]
Martis, 6 Junii, 2 Caroli Regis

Merton College bill, Thursday next.

MR. SPENCER reports Astley his bill, with amendments. *Engrossetur.*

L. 1a. Hackett.

Some exceptions being taken to the letter to be sent to Cambridge.

Master of the Wards	Sir D[udley] Digges
Mr. Chancellor Duchy	Sir Thomas Hoby[1]
Sir Thomas Lake	Mr. Dr. Eden
Sir John Eliot	Mr. [John] Pym
Sir B[enjamin] Rudyard	Mr. [Edward] Littleton
Sir Nathaniel Rich	

To[2] meet in the Court of Wards, 2 clock; and the House to sit at 5 a clock.

[p. 86] Bill for Canvey Island, Thursday next, in the afternoon, former place.

Leave given to Mr. Poynings More, for sickness, to go out of the town for a few days.

Thursday[3] next, for the report from the committee of privileges for Warwick and other business there depending.

A letter read from the inhabitants of Lincoln concerning articles delivered by the clerks of assize unto the high constables, etc.,[4] whereby great trouble and charge to the country.

This referred to the committee for grievances, and they to make a subcommittee to examine it and to report to the grand committee.

The petition against recusants in authority engrossed, read, and allowed to be presented to his Majesty. To be delivered by the Privy Council of the House, and Sir J. Fullerton.[5]

Sir Gervase Clifton has leave to go down, in respect of his wife's sickness, and to return with all speed.

The surgeons to be sent for to attend the committee for ships and shipping.

The report for the general fast to be tomorrow morning.

Bill for continuance and repeal of statutes, Thursday afternoon.

The committee for causes, evils, and remedies to sit upon Friday next.

The House turned into a grand committee about the remonstrance.

[*Afternoon*]

Martis, 6 Junii, 2 Caroli Regis

Bill against buying and selling offices, tomorrow in the afternoon, in the Exchequer Court.

Courts of justice, Saturday in the afternoon.

MR. PYM reports from the committee for the letter to Cambridge, about the election of the Duke of Buckingham.

Which, being 2 read, MR. CHANCELLOR OF THE EXCHEQUER delivers a message from the House [*sic*]: That the King, having taken knowledge hereof, has commanded

1. *Sir Thomas Lake* is crossed out in the MS following *Digges*.
2. *to go presently into the Committee Chamber* is crossed out in the MS following *to*.
3. *Friday* is crossed out in the MS and *Thursday* is inserted.
4. We have not found the letter.
5. We have not found a copy of the completed petition. See OBs for the dates of the reports made on the recusant list throughout the session, and HofC, 27 February, n. 35.

him to signify his pleasure that the House forbear to send this letter.

Resolved, to defer the further consideration of this message till tomorrow, 10 clock.

II. DIARY OF BULSTRODE WHITELOCKE, ESQ., DD. 12.22, CAMBRIDGE UNIVERSITY LIBRARY

[f. 38v]

June 6

The petition concerning those that are in office and place of government military or civil who are recusants or justly suspected to be so by acts of state read after engrossing, and appointed to be delivered to the King by the Privy Council and Sir James Fullerton.

[*Committee of the Whole House*]

Mr. Herbert in the chair.

Mr. Littleton reports from the subcommittee concerning the privileges of parliament a bill which they have framed for them and a remonstrance. And the desire of the subcommittee [is] that the messenger for Sir Dudley Digges and Sir John Eliot be sent for and examined why and by whose direction they came to the House of Commons and sent for them out and carried them to the Tower;[6] the writings of them seized and taken from them, the gentlemen being chairmen and their papers concerning the Duke. Thomas Meautys, upon the seizing of Sir John Eliot's papers, refused that a note should be taken of them.[7] The committee think fit that a general declaration be made, wherein all the world and the King may take notice of the proceedings of this parliament. And desire that therein may be a humble excuse that we cannot perform with the King as soon as we thought we should, and that all the interruptions in this parliament they conceive have been wrought by the Duke or on his behalf for his advantage. That some men have been made barons who have had alliance and dependence upon the Duke[8] and some barons that are indifferent are kept from parliament [f. 39];[9] and that in contempt of this House the University of Cambridge have chosen the Duke their Chancellor.

Whether you will take consideration [of] some speeches made by a gentleman of this/

That you will declare your opinions concerning any that advise the King for new counsels or any alteration of the established government of this kingdom.[10]

The bill concerning the privileges of parliament read.

The remonstrance read.[11]

Mr. Long. If any man will get preferment, it is a received opinion that it must be by him.[12] It is not so much the poisonous informations of those vipers that do us so much harm, only as that those who are good men dare not do right nor let the King know the truth, being kept from his presence, and hazarding their estates, their fortunes, and their beings if they offend one man.

I desire these things may be made known in our declaration.

Chancellor Exchequer. Out of my experience in parliament I believe such an unreasonable proposition as this might be made, but I cannot believe such an assembly will

6. I.e., on 11 May.

7. Meautys was a Clerk of the Privy Council and a client of Buckingham. See SP 16/27:100; *APC 1625–1626,* p. 4. See 1 June for the committee appointed to witness the return of Eliot's papers.

8. I.e., Sir Dudley Carleton, see HofC, 23 May, n. 11.

9. I.e., the Bishop of Lincoln and Lord Arundel, see HofC, 3 June, n. 15.

10. A reference to Sir Dudley Carleton's speech of 12 May.

11. See below, 13 June, OB.

12. I.e., the Duke of Buckingham.

agree to it or give any the least approbation to it. I do not think you will have such an opinion that those officers about the King dare not do their duties were the Duke ten dukes. [f. 39v] I will end with an entreaty that no calumnies may be suffered against those that serve the King wisely, faithfully, and honestly.

Sir John Eliot. I am confident that in the particular of that person, and so of the rest of the honorable persons of this House, they have done their duties. I will not accuse any, neither can I excuse all. I conceive the gentleman[13] went not to lay any aspersion upon the King's good officers, but only mentioned the Duke's greatness. Too many men have crept into places of authority by his means. There are misreports and misreporters who I doubt are about the King. I am confident there are many, and that honorable gentleman for one, that have done good offices; but their good deeds excuse not others' faults. I conceive that which was moved by the gentleman fit to be made a head for that declaration.

Sir Robert Mansell. This proposition concerning the power of this great man I think is not fit for this time but deserves a single consideration. If none had moved this, I would; for it will appear that the effects of his power be effects of dishonor, danger, shame. Whensoever they come to be anatomized, it will appear. [f. 40] I cannot justify any one thing done by this great man in his office of Admiral done with judgment.

Moves that this proposition may be reserved till our reply to the Duke's answer, at which time I shall have much matter to add to the aggravation of the Duke's charge.

Mr. Long explains and excuses himself.

Chancellor Exchequer. For any man to say that the best men when they are called to counsel dare not for fear of the Duke deliver their minds freely, I think this a calumny.

Sir Dudley Digges. If he that sits here shall forbear to say truth, he does not his duty; nor for that is he to be taxed. I will hazard all I have except my reputation and my soul—my life and all my fortunes—and say this man's power is too great.

Sir George More. That there may be no more of those words spoken by Mr. Long.

Mr. Goodwin. That since a worthy gentleman has been charged with having raised a calumny, he may be cleared by question.

Mr. Long. I do desire so much time may not be spent about me. I am clear in my own thoughts, and so I hope I am in the opinion of the House.

[f. 40v] Doctor Turner. I would willingly recommend you to a storehouse for more heads for this conference and declaration. Desires that those of the Council of War of this House that are discharged of that place may be added to the subcommittee for the conference and declaration.

Sir Henry Poole. That I have observed that nothing has been committed but first it has received a debate and consideration in the House or grand committee.

Mr. Kirton. That the subcommittee may have general power to consider of new heads,[14] which has been before done in this parliament.

Mr. Littleton. It is fit things should be first debated in this House before the committee meddle with them.

Sir Dudley Digges. It is only that which every member of the House may do that is desired. That those of the subcommittee

13. I.e., Mr. Long, above.

14. A subcommittee of twenty had been named on 12 May to draw the heads for the remonstrance.

may propose heads one among one another to be presented to the grand committee.

A subcommittee appointed to draw and prepare a conference with the Lords and a declaration to the King upon these heads that have been here debated, and to report to the House such new heads as shall be proposed to them.[15]

[f. 41]

Pomeridiem

The Speaker in the chair.

MR. PYM reports from the select committee for penning of a letter to be sent to the University of Oxford [*sic*] concerning their electing the Duke of Buckingham their Chancellor.

Which is read and approved.

CHANCELLOR EXCHEQUER. His Majesty understanding that this House has an intention to send a letter to the University touching the election of the Duke of Buckingham their Chancellor; his Majesty understands that the election was according to their charter; and if there be any error in the form of the election, his Majesty says it belongs to him to examine it and not to this House; and therefore his pleasure is that you forbear to send any such letter to the University.

SIR DUDLEY DIGGES. I wonder how his Majesty should take notice of this letter which was framed but just now. Moves that we may defer the consideration of this message till tomorrow morning.

Agreed that the Speaker shall forbear coming to the House till 10 a clock tomorrow morning.

III. DIARY OF SIR RICHARD GROSVENOR, MS 611, TRINITY COLLEGE, DUBLIN

[p. 162]

6 June

Dispatch about the heads of the conference with the Lords and declaration to the King.

A message from the King touching the Cambridge business; that if in their election of the Duke to the Chancellor's place they had done anything illegal it fitted him to take notice, not the House.

IV. DIARY OF JOHN LOWTHER, ESQ., D/LONS/L, CUMBERLAND AND WESTMORLAND RECORD OFFICE

[f. 42]

[6 June]

The King sent a message to stay the letter, holding it derogatory to his prerogative to intermeddle with the universities or the election which, if any error was in it, belonged to him to correct.

15. It is unclear whether this is the same subcommittee that was named on 12 May (see n. 14, above) or a new one appointed this day following the resolution on 5 June to merge the two grand committees for righting privileges and drawing heads.

ORDER OF BUSINESS WEDNESDAY, 7 JUNE 1626

WEDNESDAY, 7 JUNE 1626

I. JOURNAL OF THE HOUSE OF COMMONS

[CJ 867; p. 86]
Mercurii, 7 Junii, 2 Caroli Regis

A letter from Mr. More to Mr. Speaker, and a petition to the House, read.

And MR. CHANCELLOR EXCHEQUER delivers a message that his Majesty is graciously pleased to remit his further punishment, if this House so please.[1]

Upon question, Mr. More remitted from further imprisonment and restored to his place in the House.

Upon question, the report for the general fast to be made upon Friday next.

The House to be presently resolved into a grand committee to take consideration of the message delivered yesterday in the afternoon from his Majesty, concerning the letter to be written and sent to Cambridge.

[p. 87] *L. 2a.* An act for abbreviation of Michaelmas term.

Committed to
Sir Thomas Fanshawe
Mr. [Henry] Sherfield
All the lawyers of the House
Sir William Strode
Sir George More
Dr. [Samuel] Turner
Sir H[enry] Poole
Sir Thomas Grantham
Mr. Attorney Wards
Sir H[enry] Whitehead

And all that will come to have voice; Friday next, in the afternoon, in the Court of Wards.

Engrossed bills to be read upon Friday morning next.

The grand committee for tonnage and poundage and the Book of Rates to sit tomorrow, 8 clock.

A petition from Mr. Burlamachi read.[2]

The grand committee tender, in writing, the substance of a message to his Majesty in answer of that sent yesterday.[3]

This read and allowed; and ordered to be sent to his Majesty by Mr. Chancellor Exchequer, Chancellor Duchy, Sir James Fullerton, and Sir George Goring.

Upon question, the House to sit again at 5 clock.

Upon the question whether the money remaining in the treasurers' hands, to be presently paid in part of satisfaction of Mr. Burlamachi his warrants from the Council of War, the House, upon the question 2 put, divided. The yea went out.

Tellers for the yea:	Sir George More
	Sir John Eliot
Tellers for the no:	Sir W. Erle
	Mr. Coryton

With the yea: 148
With the no: 123
Difference: 25

1. We have found neither Mr. More's letter and petition nor the King's message. More had been sent to the Tower on 3 June for offensive words spoken in the House.

2. We have not found the petition. Philip Burlamachi had petitioned the Council in May for reimbursement for the monies he lent the English crown for their payment of £70,000 to Christian IV and Count Mansfeld. See SP 16/25:108; *APC 1625–1626*, pp. 472–473. Concerning Burlamachi, see HofL, 15 May, p. 475, n. 122. He had earlier petitioned the Commons on 21 February (see note 9) and 15 April (see note 5); and in the previous parliament, on 10 August (see *PP 1625*, p. 442, nn. 2 and 3). A warrant was issued the following December for partial payment of the charges he incurred for levying, clothing, and arming the footmen serving under Count Mansfeld. HLRO, Main Papers, HL, 8 December 1626.

3. For the substance of the message, see Whitelocke, below.

The grand committee formerly appointed to take consideration of the money disbursed by the countries,[4] for coat money, conduct money, and otherwise, to sit upon Monday next, afternoon.

[p. 88]

Mercurii, 7 Junii, 2 Caroli Regis
Post Meridiem

MR. CHANCELLOR OF THE EXCHEQUER reports back to the House his Majesty's answer to our message sent this forenoon.[5]

The letter read.

Resolved, to put off the further consideration and debate thereof till Friday morning.

The committee for purveyance for hawks' meat, and other hawks, and other purveyance, power to send for any to inform them.[6]

II. DIARY OF BULSTRODE WHITELOCKE, ESQ., DD. 12.22, CAMBRIDGE UNIVERSITY LIBRARY

[f. 41v]

June 7

Petition of Mr. More, committed to the Tower by the House, for his release.

CHANCELLOR EXCHEQUER. His Majesty is well pleased to remit Mr. More if the House shall think fit.

Resolved that Mr. More shall be released out of the Tower from his further imprisonment and restored to the House.[7]

SIR THOMAS HOBY moves that we may resolve ourselves into a grand committee for consideration of the King's message sent yesterday in the afternoon.

Ordered accordingly.

[*Committee of the Whole House*]

Mr. Littleton in the chair.

Sir Nathaniel Rich. I conceive that this, as well other matters, befall us through misinformation. For we intended not to question the power of their charter nor the errors in the election, but to examine of the contempt offered to this House.[8]

Why this should be offensive to his Majesty, I do not know. And I am persuaded if he be rightly informed he will commend us for going in this way and not hinder us. I conceive this message trenches much upon our liberties, and desire we may apply ourselves to give the King satisfaction.

Sir George More. That a committee may be appointed to make a declaration to the King and give him satisfaction for [f. 42] what we have done or intend to do.

Mr. Pym. I take it to be a public grievance that the government of the University should be committed to a man accused of great crimes in parliament,[9] and therefore within our cognizance. And by this election a contempt and affront is offered to this House, which we may take notice of and examine. Besides, some wrong done to us by a peer of the Lords House who with others solicited for the Duke.[10]

Moves that we may send a humble message to the King to give him satisfaction concerning this by the privy councillors presently, and in the meantime respite the sending of the letter.

4. I.e., the committee appointed on 21 February.

5. I.e., regarding the University of Cambridge, see Whitelocke, below.

6. I.e., the committee on Pitcairn's patent, see HofC, 25 May, and n. 12.

7. See above, n. 1.

8. See the King's message delivered the previous day (6 June) by the Chancellor of the Exchequer.

9. I.e., the Duke of Buckingham.

10. I.e., the Bishop of London, see HofC, 3 June, n. 10.

Chancellor Exchequer desires that the message may be set down in writing.

Sir Dudley Digges. That it may be set down in writing, but Mr. Chancellor Exchequer may deliver it by word of mouth.

A subcommittee named to pen the substance of this message to the King.

Mr. Speaker in the chair.

Petition of Mr. Philip Burlamachi for £4,800 disbursed by him for the conveyance of the soldiers beyond sea.[11]

[Committee of the Whole House]

Mr. Littleton in the chair.

[f. 42v] Chancellor Exchequer reports the substance of the message to be sent to the King: They do acknowledge they were about to write to the University because that the very election itself, whereby the University is committed to the government of one that is charged and publicly complained of by the House of Commons, is in itself a grievance.

Because they are informed that in the manner and carriage of the election divers abuses have been/

They desire your Majesty to rest assured that neither in this nor any other thing the House did or do intend to enlarge their own power or jurisdiction to the diminution of his Majesty's right and prerogative.

Mr. Speaker in the chair.

MR. LITTLETON reports the message.

And the House appoint Chancellor Exchequer, Chancellor Duchy, and others to carry it to the King.

Resolved that the House shall sit this afternoon.

Resolved that Mr. Burlamachi shall be paid presently from the treasurers' according to such warrants as he has from the Council of War.

Pomeridiem

[f. 43] CHANCELLOR EXCHEQUER. We attended his Majesty and presented the humble declaration.

That all corporations derive their right and privileges from him and he has most cause to be careful of the universities,[12] which he is resolved to maintain against any whatsoever that shall either willfully or negligently oppose them. Concerning the election, his Majesty holds it to be no grievance. Nor that any man is to lose his fame by an accusation. If anything be done against your privileges and in contempt of this House,[13] his Majesty is pleased that you may examine it and punish the offenders if there be any in that kind. For the election and the form of it, his Majesty does avow his former message.

The letter to the University is read.

CHANCELLOR EXCHEQUER. It is uncertain to me yet, for ought I have heard, whether the Duke be accused of High Treason or not, and I do not believe he is. Moves that a committee may draw a new letter; for if we send this, I shall protest against it, and think it will offend.

The debate hereof deferred till Friday[14] morning next.

11. See above, n. 2.

12. The act of incorporation of both universities (Oxford and Cambridge) was passed by parliament, 13 Eliz. I, c. 29, and signed by the Queen. Aside from other provisions the act specifically incorporated the Chancellor, masters, and scholars of each university.

13. *parliament* is crossed out in the MS and *House* is inserted.

14. *tomorrow* is crossed out in the MS and *Friday* is inserted.

III. DIARY OF SIR RICHARD GROSVENOR, MS 611, TRINITY COLLEGE, DUBLIN

[p. 163]

7 June

MR. SPEAKER presented a letter to himself and a petition to the House from Mr. More, being prisoner in the Tower.

MR. CHANCELLOR OF EXCHEQUER said that the King was pleased to remit him, if pleased the House, from any further punishment.

Ordered by question that he should be freed from the Tower and restored again to the House.

SIR THOMAS HOBY. That the House should be turned into a committee to consider of a mannerly answer to the King's message sent us yesterday.

Friday morning appointed for Sir Robert Harley to report the reasons of a fast concluded at the committee should be reported.

The House resolved into a committee to answer the King's message touching the letter to be written to Cambridge. Mr. Littleton called into the chair.

[*Committee of the Whole House*]

Sir Nathaniel Rich moved the message should be delivered again.

Sir Richard Weston read the message: His Majesty understanding/
That election has been made according to the powers and charters of that University, and if it has been otherwise done it belongs to him to take notice thereof. *Ergo,* commands the House not to send any such letter.

Sir Nathaniel Rich. This is the same fruit we have often tasted of: misinformation. For we meant not to question their charters nor the election, but to answer the contempt to this House in choosing this person at this time. We sent not for them as delinquents, but to inquire into the matter and to be informed in such things as we think we have just cause to be offended of.

[p. 164] Moved that we give his Majesty a dutiful answer, for this message trenches deeply upon our liberties. They are commons, and not to be excepted from us.

Dr. Eden. That he did not move to have the University sent for, but only told them the customs of the House, which he spoke not to divert the House from sending for them.[15]

Sir G. More. We sit here as dutiful subjects to the King and as faithful servants to the commonwealth, so it befits us to do our duty to both. This House, taking offense at this election and knowing the heads of house are commons,[16] subject to the jurisdiction of this House, we could not deal more judicially than to send for them by a letter that they might come, to hear them before we adjudged them.

Moved that this might be made known to the King by a declaration of our resolution, and forbear (till this were done) of any further proceeding in that business, and after resolve what to do, the rather because his Majesty says that reformation belongs to him.

Mr. Pym. It was never part of our intentions to examine the power of the University charter nor whether they had done according to the same, but to examine whether the University had not done this

15. See Eden's speech on 5 June.

16. I.e., the heads of the Cambridge colleges who, on 5 June were encouraged to come to the House of Commons voluntarily on Monday, 12 June. See the speech of Sir Thomas Hoby and the resolution of the House, 5 June, and see also, n. 16.

against the honor of the House, he being presented as a public grievance.

Moved to respite the letter till by a message we had acquainted the King with reasons of what we had done, etc.

Sir R. Weston liked the last motion but moved that what the message should be, should be penned down.

Sir Thomas Hoby. It was fit to put it in writing and to consider what to be put in writing.

[p. 165] Sir Dudley Digges. Not to set it down in writing, because the message was not delivered in writing.

Sir Peter Heyman. That we answer by writing without prejudicing our liberties.

Ordered that an answer should be presently sent to the King by Sir R. Weston, Chancellor of the Exchequer, by word of mouth. 9 gentlemen sent into the Committee Chamber to consider of the answer.

Till their return this committee was adjourned and Mr. Herbert called for into the chair, being the committee for to consider of the heads for a conference; but he came not in.

The Speaker went in and read bills.

2. An act for the shortening of Michaelmas term and more speedy passing of recoveries (the scope of it is to cut off the 2 first returns). Committed, Friday,[17] Court Wards.

MR. ROLLE motioned from the subcommittee about the Book of Rates in the Custom House:[18] that a petition should be made to the King to know whether he would receive such a Book of Rates and tie him to it as the House should agree upon.

SIR P. HEYMAN presented a petition from Mr. Burlamachi: that he has disbursed £4,700 for the entertainment of soldiers in the Low Countries and has no satisfaction; desired to have the said sum out of the treasurers' hands for the war.[19]

MR. CORYTON. That the country might be paid out of this money remaining that money which they had laid out for the soldiers pressed in their countries.

SIR H. MAY. That Burlamachi might be paid because he had an act of parliament for it.[20]

SIR FRANCIS GOODWIN. That the act gave authority also for the country to be paid.

SIR H. POOLE. That it was easier to bear the charge by many in the country than by one man; wished the stranger to be satisfied.

[p. 166] The committee to consider of the answer to the King's message returned, and Mr. Littleton came into the chair.

[*Committee of the Whole House*]

The message was read: They do acknowledge they were about to write to the U[niversity] because that the very election itself, whereby the U[niversity] is committed to the government of one that is charged and publicly complained of by the Commons in parliament, whereof the [*blank*] are a part.

By question, resolved that the substance of this should be the answer to his Majesty's message. This sent by Sir R. Weston, Sir H. May, Sir G. Goring, Sir James Fullerton.

They returned to Burlamachi's business.

MR. GLANVILLE. Two competitors for this money: Burlamachi and the country. Those

17. *Monday* is crossed out in the MS and *Friday* is inserted.

18. I.e., the subcommittee appointed 27 March.

19. See above, n. 2.

20. See *SR*, 21 Jac. I, c. 33, pt. 44, "Charge of foreign service shall be defrayed under this act".

that have warrant from the Council of War must receive their money from the treasurers. This House can give them no warrant.

SIR JOHN ELIOT. This business has been often here and referred to a committee which has not often met;[21] but when they did, considering how satisfaction might be given to all, there was a subcommittee to make ready the charge but could not yet find a number for the grand committee. Those who desire for their countries should have attended to make a committee, whereas Burlamachi has attended. Why then for our own faults we should put out Burlamachi I know not. There is enough also remaining to satisfy the country.

MR. ROLLE. That by the act[22] the Council of War ought first to have discharged the country and repaid the money laid forth by them.

[p. 167] SIR EDWIN SANDYS. The act of parliament has provided for both. Let us weigh well we gave 3 subsidies; the greatest gift considering the shortness of time. We told our countries they should not be charged with coat and conduct money. Where is now the act or credit of the parliament men if this be not looked to?

1. That Burlamachi be paid. 2. To send to the Council of War that they grant no other warrant till the country be paid their money. And next that the country make up their accounts.

SIR R. WESTON. That the armies in the Low Countries could not have subsisted without Burlamachi's credit. Let us not make a quarrel between him and some particular countries. This is just to be paid and cannot be denied. The Council Table do intend to pay this money to the countries.

MR. NOY. That he had viewed the act; that the Council were to issue money according to the ends in the statute. There is a negative clause, viz., that the charge of foreign employment shall be defrayed out of this money and not otherwise.

MR. SHERWILL. That there is need of a report because if the money paid by Burlamachi were before the warrant, then he has security; if after, then fit he be paid.

MR. STRODE. To commit it first. That the committee should consider what is in the treasurers' hand: how much due to the country, what expended by Burlamachi.

After very long dispute a question propounded whether Burlamachi's should be first paid or not. The House divided: the yeas 148; the nos 123.

So ordered, that Burlamachi should be paid so much of his money as was in the treasurers' hands.

[p. 168] Monday appointed in the House to sit a committee of the whole House touching the taking the accounts of the treasurers of the war, and to consider how to pay the countries' money for coat and conduct money.[23]

[*Afternoon*]

7 June, afternoon, the House sat at 5 of the clock.

SIR R. WESTON reported that the 4 messengers had presented the declaration of the House, to which his answer was: that all corporations derive their liberties from him; that he will defend the liberties of the University against all men.

21. Following the submission of Burlamachi's first petition in the present parliament (see above, n. 2) a committee was appointed to hear his cause (see HofC, 21 February) and was empowered to name a subcommittee.

22. I.e., *SR*, 21 Jac. I, c. 33.

23. *Ordered that the Speaker should write a letter to the Council of War* is crossed out in the MS following *money*.

Crimes objected not to be taken for proofs.

But his Majesty says that where we say there were many passages done in the contempt of the House in this election, he gives us leave to examine that and punish the offenders; though for the election itself his Majesty justifies his former message.

MR. KIRTON. That we may punish any misdemeanor from corporations. Moved that he might deliver this in writing as he had received the answer in writing, and that we consider of it till morning.

SIR JOHN HOTHAM. No cause to have this delivered in writing, but that we send away the letter and proceed to examine the matter.

The letter read by the Clerk.

MR. NOY took exception at a clause where it is said that he was accused in parliament of High Treasons, etc.

[p. 169] SIR R. WESTON. That to send this letter as it is, is against the King's message. This letter commands the Vice-Chancellor to give account of the election, which is expressly forbidden us by the King. Wished this letter to be forborne and that a committee might be chosen to think of such a letter as might maintain our privileges and not offend his Majesty, else this would offend his Majesty and he would protest against it.

Deferred to be treated of till Friday morning.

IV. DIARY OF JOHN LOWTHER, ESQ., D/LONS/L, CUMBERLAND AND WESTMORLAND RECORD OFFICE

[f. 42]

[7 June]

We by message answered him that it was done in a contempt to us as we conceived. We sent not for them as delinquents.[24] We desired not to encroach upon his prerogative. But he that so stood accused, and their burgesses being amongst us, and for them so accusing him, he ought not to have been chosen. Whereof his Majesty, being rightly informed how this was an accumulation of the things complained of, would give leave to proceed.

[*Afternoon*]

The King sent back answer by the same messengers, the Chancellor of the Exchequer and others, how all corporations were derived from him; he bound to maintain them, especially the universities. That he would and was resolved so to do against whomsoever that did purposely or by accident impeach them. He did think the election good, and would not have it questioned. But if any particular persons did miscarry themselves, he was content we should examine them. But he said a man accused was not condemned nor lost not his fame therefore, etc.

[f. 42v] Yet SIR JOHN HOTHAM thought we might proceed with the letter.

Which was read, reciting the affront that the Duke, accused in parliament of treason, should be chosen.

The CHANCELLOR OF EXCHEQUER protested against the knowledge of the accusation of treason.

So did NOY.

Nota: For they meant in the Lords House, but in our House they admitted there was none; and because the letter was so directly, it was then put over unto a new day, Friday, for debate.

24. I.e., Wren, Parson, Beadle, Mawe, and Goslyn. See above, n. 16.

Order of Business Thursday, 8 June 1626

THURSDAY, 8 JUNE 1626

I. JOURNAL OF THE HOUSE OF COMMONS

[CJ 867; p. 88]
Jovis, 8 Junii, 2 Caroli Regis

Greg his other patent to be brought in tomorrow to the committee for grievances.[1]

The House turned into a grand committee for tonnage and poundage.

MR. NOY reports from the grand committee for tonnage and poundage that this committee of opinion that **[CJ 868]** a remonstrance should be made to his Majesty, concerning/

2ly. That a committee should be named for framing hereof.

Upon question, such a remonstrance to be made.[2]

2ly. A committee to be named to frame heads for this remonstrance. To be:

[col. 1]	[col. 2]	[col. 3]
Mr. [William] Noy	Mr. [John] Glanville	Mr. [John] Pym
Mr. [Richard] Spencer	Sir M[aurice] Abbot	Mr. [Thomas] Wentworth
Sir Nathaniel Rich	Sir P[eter] Heyman	Sir George Fane
Sir William Spencer	Sir A[rthur] Ingram	Sir Francis Barnham
Sir Thomas Myddleton	Mr. Herbert	Master of the Wards
Sir D[udley] Digges	Sir Roland Cotton	Mr. Rolle
Mr. Secretary Coke	Mr. [Edward] Littleton	Mr. [William] Cage
Sir J[ames] Perrot	Sir Robert Pye	

Tomorrow in the afternoon, Star Chamber.

SIR FRANCIS FOLJAMBE tenders to make proof, by witnesses, the copy of the letter pretended to have been written by Sir John Savile to have been a true copy of the letter written by him, and interrogatories for them to be examined upon; which read.

But resolved, the Speaker not to be tied to those, but might minister any other interrogatories upon occasion.

Mr. Farrer brought in to testify herein,[3] testifies: Daniel Foxcrofte showed him that which he said was the original letter,[4] and that it agreed in substance and effect, as he verily remembers. That he thinks the superscription or letter was not Sir John Savile's hand, which he had formerly seen, but he took the subscription to be Sir John Savile his hand. [p. 89] That this was published as Sir John Savile's letter; and saw several copies of it; and saw divers hands subscribed to a writing which were gotten upon this letter; but what the substance of that writing was, or to whom it was directed, knows not.

SIR JOHN SAVILE acknowledges such a letter came down, whereunto his name was set.

Anthony Foxcrofte called in, confesses he has seen the original, whereof he takes this to be a copy, and had it in his own hands within this month, finding it in his father's countinghouse window, and thereupon read. Thinks the letter nor superscription written by Sir John but knows not whether the subscription such. That it was published as Sir John Savile's letter; and copies given out of it; and hands thereupon[5] gotten to a

1. The motion was made by Sir Richard Grosvenor, see his account, below. Regarding Edward Greg, see HofC, 24 May, n. 49. Greg's patent was regranted in 1613. See HofC, 28 February, n. 4.

2. We have not found the remonstrance for tonnage and poundage. See HofC, 6 March, n. 27; and 24 May, n. 20.

3. We are unable to identify Farrer. For the letter, see HofC, 22 May, OB.

4. Regarding Foxcrofte, see HofC, 22 May, n. 11.

5. MS: *hands thereupon hands.*

writing, which was sent to London, to one Key,[6] to be by him delivered to Sir John Savile. Thinks, Daniel Foxcrofte, his father, had this original within this fortnight; and saw it, within these 3 weeks, in the counting-house window. Saw it within this week, and had it within this week in his own hands, and thinks his father now has it, but knows not that certainly. Confesses he saw it yesternight, and had it in his hands, and delivered it to his father.

Daniel Foxcrofte called in, confesses he has seen the original whereof this a copy. Saw it within this fortnight. Being asked when the last time he saw it, says he is old, and his memory bad. Confesses he saw it within this week. Confesses he had seen it within 24 hours. And asked again whether he had it not last night, confesses he had. Asked where the letter is, confesses he has it about him. And delivered in the letter.

The original letter read; and SIR JOHN SAVILE, showed the name subscribed and demanded whether this be his handwriting or not, denies it absolutely.

MR. BEST. That Mr. Edmund Savile told him he did write the letter, by his father's direction.

SIR JOHN SAVILE denies he ever gave his son any direction to write[7] any letter to this effect, but confesses he gave direction to write a letter to Benson, for making a certificate, but not with any such clause.

Sir John Savile denies that ever he wrote, or directed, any other letter to be written to any such effect as this (without the offensive clause) except that written by Benson.[8]

Sir John Savile, demanded whether this letter be of his son's writing or not, answers: it is not his son's hand nor Benson's, nor knows whose writing it is, but would as gladly know as any man.

Sir John Savile, demanded where his son is, answers he well knows not; for has not seen him these 10 days.

[p. 90] MR. BEST. That [*blank*] his son 5 weeks before, and also after Sir Francis Foljambe delivered in the copy told him, he had written this letter.

And MR. GOLDSBURGH affirms Mr. Savile told him he knew best what was in the letter, for he wrote it.

SIR WILLIAM HERBERT relates some words spoken by Sir J. Savile about 5 weeks since, that he had given direction to his son to say he wrote this letter of purpose to discover the plot against him.

SIR JOHN SAVILE. That the letter, written by Benson, was to the same men, and of the same subject, but without the offensive clause.

Sir John Savile, demanded whether he subscribed the letter written by Benson, denies it, nor ever saw the letter written by Benson after he, by his direction, had written it; nor knows by whom that letter was sent; but says that letter was sent and delivered accordingly.

Sir John Savile. That this original letter not written with Benson's hand.

Daniel Foxcrofte, having retired into the Committee Chamber, and called in again, and demanded whether this original first delivered to him, says it was sent him opened, and as it now is, enclosed in a letter from Harrison; which read.

Demanded whether the name subscribed be Sir John Savile's, says he knows not, but

6. Probably John Key of Woodsom, described in Grosvenor, below, as a "clothier in London". *APC 1625–1626,* p. 355.

7. MS: *any direction to his son to write.*

8. Benson was a fellow Yorkshireman. *Wentworth Papers 1597–1628,* Camden Fourth Series, no. 12 (London, 1973), p. 251. The offensive clause was: "But they [the Commons] are so resolutely bent and with such eagerness upon the pursuit of a great man as rather than they will fail or surcease they are resolved to hazard the whole estate of the commonwealth, as I fear" (see above, 22 May).

has seen many of his subscriptions and never saw "John" written short, "Jo.", but, "John".

The words, "pretended letter", written on the backside of the original; he confesses he wrote those words presently after the receipt of it; he distrusting it, because of the difference of the subscription. Confesses this published in the country; and copies given out by himself of this, as Sir John Savile's letter; and procured thereupon divers hands to a writing to be sent up to Sir John Savile. That he received no letter about this time from Benson, nor saw any such, nor knows Benson's hand, nor whose hand it is. That he has kept the original letter ever since his receipt of it, never delivering it out of his own presence. That he received a letter from Harrison's wife,[9] as he remembers, on Saturday was 7night, and another from Harrison himself, which he has about him. That the writing with the hands was sent up to be delivered to Sir John Savile. That he received no other letter from Sir John Savile, or any other, but only one other letter from Harrison, dated 21 *Maii* last.

Mr. Farrer called in, affirms he never saw any letter to this effect, but only this original now shown him. Knows not whose hand the body or superscription of the letter, but thinks the subscription is Sir John Savile's. And this is (as he verily believes) is the same letter he saw. Never heard of any letter written by Benson, nor knows whether this written with Benson's hand.

So Anthony Foxcrofte.

John Harrison called in, confesses he had 2 letters to this purpose: one written on Saturday night, the other left at his house on Sunday after. [p. 91] One was written by Benson, written with his own hand and in his own name, but by Sir John Savile's direction; the other subscribed, "Jo. Savile". Knows not who or whether Benson's man delivered it him or not. The 2nd letter left at his house upon Sunday in the afternoon. That this was delivered him sealed, and he opened it. Knows not whether the letter he sent to Foxcrofte were the original or a copy of it; for he delivered that letter to some of his neighbors and they delivered that, or a copy of it, to him again upon Monday after. Confesses he did write to his uncle Foxcrofte that he had sent him a letter sent from Sir John Savile. Confesses he did send to have this letter kept safe by his uncle or else to be sent to his wife; and wrote to her to keep it safe. That this he did after he heard it was questioned in parliament. Knows not who wrote the superscription of the letter, but conceived it was Edward Smyth's[10] writing, but now knows it not. Thinks not the subscription to be Sir John Savile's handwriting, for better written than Sir John writes. Thinks the letter **[CJ 869]** he received with Sir John Savile's name subscribed to it was in half a sheet of paper.

Demanded who put wax to this letter said it might be he might put wax to it. Afterwards he said he thinks the wax upon the original was upon it when it came to him.

SIR JOHN SAVILE. That the letter was in a whole sheet, and was after half cut off by reason Daniel Foxcrofte was misplaced; and thereupon a new superscription was written, as he has heard.

[Harrison.] That he delivered the letter, subscribed "Jo. Savile", to his neighbors who delivered him back that or a copy, but knows not whether. Remembers not what seal upon this letter. That he delivered the letter he received from Benson, and delivered it to his neighbors; but had neither it, nor the copy thereof, from them.

Being asked why he sent not that to his

9. I.e., John Harrison's wife. See HofC, 22 May, n. 11.

10. We are unable to identify Edward Smith.

uncle as well as the other, says because that was not directed to Foxcrofte but only to himself, or to him and Metcalfe.

Upon question, John Harrison to[11] appear again upon Monday morning and Sir John Savile then to produce his witnesses; and Mr. Edmund Savile then also to attend.

The report from the committee of privileges to be upon Tuesday next; and the committee to choose another in the chair when Sir John Finch his own election shall come in question at the said committee.[12]

II. DIARY OF BULSTRODE WHITELOCKE, ESQ., DD. 12.22, CAMBRIDGE UNIVERSITY LIBRARY

[f. 43v]

June 8

[*Committee of the Whole House*]

At the committee for the bill of subsidy of tonnage and poundage.

Resolved that a remonstrance concerning the cause of tonnage and poundage and the incidents thereof shall be made to the King.[13]

Mr. Speaker in his chair.

MR. NOY reports from the committee for the bill of tonnage and poundage the resolution of the committee.

Resolved accordingly, and a committee named to draw the heads for this remonstrance.

SIR FRANCIS FOLJAMBE moves that the business concerning Sir John Savile's letter may be examined this day according to the order of the House, and prefers certain interrogatories to be asked of the witnesses.

Which are allowed of by the House.

MR. GLANVILLE. That the Speaker is to ask all those questions which are in the interrogatories, but may also ask other questions as he shall think expedient.

Mr. Farrer, brought in and showed the copy of the letter and examined,[14] says that about the beginning of March one Daniel Foxcrofte[15] showed him the original letter written by Sir John Savile, and thinks it agreed both in word and effect with this copy. And in his judgment he thinks the subscription [f. 44] was Sir John Savile's hand, but the superscription nor the letter was not. He often has before seen Sir John Savile's hand. He saw two or 3 copies of that letter to that effect as the original, and it was much spoken of in the country; and he saw many hands of clothiers gotten to a petition by reason of that letter.[16]

Anthony Foxcrofte, another witness, says, being shown the letter, that he has seen the original letter whereof he takes this to be a copy, and had it in his own hands within this month. That he has seen Sir John Savile's hands and that the letter nor the superscription was not Sir John Savile's hand, but whether the subscription was his hand or not he knows not. That this letter was divulged as Sir John's letter; and divers hands were gotten to a petition and sent to one Key, a clothier, to be delivered to Sir John Savile.[17] Thinks Daniel Foxcrofte had the original within this fortnight. That he had the original letter in his own hand within this week and thinks Daniel Fox-

11. *remain in the custody of the Serjeant until Saturday morning next he called in* is crossed out in the MS following *to* and the words printed here are inserted.

12. Sir John Finch was returned from Canterbury. The nature of the election contest is not clear. For background about Canterbury factions, see Peter Clark, "Thomas Scott and the Growth of Urban Opposition to the Early Stuart Regime", *The Historical Journal,* 21, 1 (1978), pp. 19–21.

13. See above, n. 2

14. See above, n. 3.

15. See HofC, 22 May, n. 11.

16. We have not found the petition.

17. See above, n. 6.

crofte has it now. It[em]. He says he saw the original last night in his father's hand.

Daniel Foxcrofte, shown the copy of the letter, says that he had seen the original in his own hands last night and had it in his own keeping, and it is in town now.

At last he confesses that he has it about him and delivers [f. 44v] it into the House, which, compared with the copy, agrees with it.

And it being showed to SIR JOHN SAVILE, he says that the letter, nor superscription, nor subscription is written with his hand.

MR. BEST. That Sir John Savile's son, Mr. Edmund Savile, told him that he wrote this letter by his father's appointment.

SIR JOHN SAVILE. That to bring this copy[18] to light he bid his son, if he were asked, not to deny the writing of the letter. Says that he gave all the encouragement he could for the bringing out of this letter. That he did not appoint his son to write or set his hand to any letter. But appointed one Benson to write a letter, which he did not sign nor knows well what was in it, but [it] was not with any such clause in it as concerns the House. That this letter is not his son's hand nor Benson's, nor he knows not whose hand. That after he had given Benson directions to write a letter, he did not see it.

Daniel Foxcrofte, reexamined, says that this letter came to him enclosed and unsealed in a letter from Harrison.[19] Which letter is delivered in and read. Says that he thinks the subscription to the original letter was not Sir John Savile's hand, for he having seen often his hand written "John", this was "Jo." only. That he did give copies [f. 45] of this letter abroad. That he procured many hands to be set to a petition to be sent to be framed by Sir John Savile at London.[20] That he received no letter from Benson but heard there was one from him, but he heard it not from Metcalfe nor Harrison. That he received a letter from Harrison's wife upon last Saturday for the sending back of this original, and another letter for Harrison for recalling of this original letter, wherein was that he should send it back as he wished well to Sir John and to himself, and that he knew who wrote the superscription.

Mr. Farrer, brought in and shown the original letter, says that he is verily persuaded that that is the same letter which he saw. That the subscription Sir John Savile's hand. Never heard of any letter to that purpose written by Benson.

Mr. Harrison, brought in and shown the original letter, says that he had 2 letters, one written by Mr. Benson with his name subscribed and the other with "Sir Jo. Savile" subscribed.[21] Benson's letter was sent by his man to him. Sir John Savile's letter was left at his house, he knows not by whom, which original he delivered to 3 or 4 who brought back either that same or another copy to him, which he sent enclosed in a letter to Daniel Foxcrofte, but he knows not well what it was, for, being market day, he did not look into it. That he does not know who wrote the superscription to that letter whereunto John [f. 45v] Savile was subscribed, but thinks he can call to mind by tomorrow morn who wrote the superscription.

MR. BYSSHE moves that, for the uncertain answers and abuses offered to the House and that he may the better recollect himself,

18. *letter* is interlined above *copy* in the MS.
19. Regarding Harrison, see HofC, 22 May, n. 11.
20. We have not found the petition.
21. See Grosvenor, below. The letters were read in the House this day. We have not found them.

Harrison may be committed close prisoner till tomorrow morning.

SIR JOHN ELIOT. That this witness has abused the House and makes him suspect in the cause. Moves that he may have time to answer further till Saturday morning, and in the meantime be committed to the Serjeant.

MR. GLANVILLE. That he may only be committed to safe custody to be forthcoming, not committed to prison lest it should be said we compel him to say what we would have him.

MR. BROOKE. That Harrison has said nothing that in my opinion deserves commitment as a delinquent. That he is a substantial man, an honest man, and of good credit in his country. Moves he may not be restrained.

CHANCELLOR EXCHEQUER. That he should not be committed.

MR. LITTLETON. That we should first hear out all the matter and after that pass our censure as we shall think fit, but in the meantime that he be not restrained of his liberty.

[f. 46] Harrison brought in, is told the House gives him time till Monday morning to give a clear and full answer.

III. DIARY OF SIR RICHARD GROSVENOR, MS 611, TRINITY COLLEGE, DUBLIN

[p. 169]

8 June

I moved for Greg's second patent to be brought in, which was ordered to be brought in tomorrow.[22]

The Speaker went forth of the chair and Mr. Noy in the chair for the subsidy of tonnage and poundage.

[*Committee of the Whole House*]

Mr. Rolle reported from the subcommittee for the Book of Rates who had resolved that a remonstrance should be made to the King:

1, because it is like to be a work of great labor and some fruit should come of it, better to be otherwise spent; 2, they are to call many merchants before them to know the value of commodities, which will be dangerous for raising of new impositions after the parliament. *Ergo*, they thought it fit to make a remonstrance for these reasons:

1. King James offered that if they would assure him of those customs then paid he would ever after bind the crown.[23]
2. That he would be pleased for avoiding of further questions; he would bind the crown for further impositions.
3. That these customs have been employed to other uses than they were granted for, and therein to petition him that hereafter those be employed as by the act shall be limited.

[p. 170] Sir Robert Pye. That of those particular sums £20,000 was by an act of parliament assigned to the household,[24] and that in time of peace there was no need of so much.

Mr. Spencer. That none of this tonnage was appointed for the household; and that if in time of peace there necessary to spare, it might be laid up to be ready against times of war.

By question, resolved that a remonstrance concerning the business of tonnage and poundage and the incidents to it should be made to the King.

22. See above, n. 1.

23. See King James's speech, 21 May 1610. *PP 1610*, I, 88–89, 106, 254; II, 146, and see index, *sub* impositions.

24. See *SR*, 1 Jac. I, c. 33, *An act of a subsidy of tonnage and poundage*. And see Spencer's speech, below. Income from tonnage and poundage was to be used specifically for the safeguard of the seas.

Mr. Speaker went into the chair and MR. NOY reported the resolution of the committee.

The same ordered in the House and a committee named to prepare the heads of a remonstrance.[25] Mr. Noy, Friday, Star Chamber.

SIR FRANCIS FOLJAMBE desired to have the order read whereby it was appointed to examine the letter of Sir John Savile formerly complained of, and presented interrogatories to be administered to the witnesses.

The Serjeant called in the witnesses. One Farrer, to whom the copy of the letter was delivered to read and he examined whether he had seen that letter subscribed with Sir John Savile's hand. He answered that in the beginning of March, talking with Daniel Foxcrofte about business, told him he had seen the contents of a letter from Sir John Savile, and repeated the contents. To whom Daniel answered: Here is the original; which he viewed. That neither the letter nor superscription was Sir John Savile's hand. But the name he took to be his hand; the reason he thinks so, he had often seen his hand before and did then conceive this to be his hand. That he had seen 2 or 3 copies of the said letter, all to the same effect; that he saw a note of divers hands gotten to a petition by reason of that letter. That he knows not to whom they were sent.

[p. 171] One Anthony Foxcrofte called in, who, first reading the letter, said that he has seen the original whereof he takes this to be the copy. That he had it in his hands within the month. He found it in his father's chamber window and read it. He saw not Sir John Savile write it and *ergo* knows not whether the letter or superscription was his hands, nor the subscription. That this was published as Sir J. Savile's letter; that copies were given forth of it. That by reason of this letter hands were gotten to a petition. That the paper to which the hands were was sent to one Key, a clothier in London, to be delivered to Sir John Savile. That Daniel Foxcrofte had the letter in his hands within this 3 weeks and thinks he had it within this fortnight. That he saw it in his own hands within this week; that he thinks his father has it; that he saw it yesternight and delivered it to his father.

Daniel Foxcrofte called to the bar, who also read the letter and said that he had seen the original letter, whereof this was a copy, in his own hands within this fortnight. Being asked whether he had seen it since, he answered that he was an old man and forgot many things. Then he said he had seen it within this week; that he had seen it within 24 hours. Then, he did see it yesternight. That he had the letter in his own keeping; that the letter was in the town. Then confessed that he had the letter about him. He was commanded to deliver the letter and was sent into the Committee Chamber.

The original was read, which appeared to be the same with the copy delivered into the House.

The letter showed to SIR JOHN SAVILE who said that he gave direction for the writing of a letter to one Benson. That this is none of his handwriting; that he had labored to bring this letter to light.

MR. BEST said that Mr. Edmund Savile, his son, had written this letter by command of his father.

[p. 172] SIR JOHN SAVILE said he bade his son not to deny the writing of it if he were asked by any man, and this he commanded him because he hoped by that means to bring this to light. That if his son were

25. See above, n. 2.

faulty, he marveled they sent not warrant for him. That he never gave direction to his son to write any letter to this purpose.

MR. GOLDSBURGH said he heard Mr. Savile justify he had written the letter.

SIR WILLIAM HERBERT reported the conference he had with Sir John Savile about this letter; that he told Sir John of the letter and the effect thereof, to whom Sir John said: You art a fool and a madman. I think thou art of the plot, and that if he would conceal what he told him he would reveal the truth, viz., such a letter is come to town and there is an original of it, father[ed] upon a son. There are many aim to bring a disgrace upon me but I may bring it upon them. I have talked with my son and have commanded him to justify the writing of it, that I may have a ground to examine the plot of it.

I told some that they would be deceived in it and wished them to suspend their judgments. I spoke it to Sir H. May, Sir Dudley Digges and others, that he had a plot to evade this business.

SIR DUDLEY DIGGES moved that the remembrance of private conference should not be spoken in this House.

Daniel Foxcrofte called to the bar again. He said that this letter was sent unsealed to him in a letter from [Har]rison; in that letter said that they should get 2,000 hands to 2 or 3 papers, and left to Sir John to put in what he please. [p. 173] On the back of the letter written: a letter from Harrison wherein the pretended letter from Sir John Savile. He said he wrote that presently after the receipt because it came in one side of a sheet, and he doubted the name. That he had given forth copies of this letter. That he has heard that Benson wrote a letter, but never saw it; that none of the parties to whom it was directed ever told him of it. That he never delivered the original to any out of his own hands. That Harrison's wife wrote to him on Saturday was sevennight for the letter back again, and another from Harrison.

The letters read by the Clerk. Harrison's had these words: There is such ado in the parliament about the letter which I sent you that as you love me and yourself keep the letter in your own hands till I see you, that you deliver it to him from whom you had it. A second letter, 21 May, from Harrison read, wherein were these words: The case so stands that as you wish well to yourself or me, that you send the letter to my wife. I know not who wrote the letter, but I know perfectly who wrote the superscription; as you tender my good or Sir John Savile's, send it presently.

SIR PETER HEYMAN observed that Harrison's wife's letter was for the original letter and Harrison's was that a supposititious letter should be put into the room.

Harrison called in and said that he had received 2 letters near together, both to one purpose for the substance. When I had read them, I gave them to some clothiers whom it concerned. They sent him either the letter or a copy, which he presently sent to Foxcrofte. That the letter was left at his house [*illegible*] copy.

[*Illegible*] if he had 2 letters, directed to Foxcrofte [*illegible*] a time he would have mentioned such a letter also when he wrote to his uncle.

[p. 174] He never looked on this letter after he received it from the clothiers.

Now he says this was not the letter itself he received from Sir J. Savile.

Whether the clothiers delivered back Benson's letter or a copy, as well as Sir John Savile's. Where that is.

MR. WANDESFORD remembered that Harrison's letter to his uncle was dated 6 March. He received the letter the 5th, so that there was no time to let the clothiers have the letters; as he said, that he received it again from the clothiers before he sent it to his uncle.

SIR JOHN SAVILE said that some had confessed to him that the letter was a whole sheet of paper but, Daniel Foxcrofte being placed out of his rank, the others cut off that part wherein the superscription was, and on the other side placed Daniel in his own rank and place.

Harrison called in again who, to questions propounded, answered: that upon Sunday he received the letter subscribed to [*sic*] "Sir Jo. Savile". He sent it to his uncle upon Tuesday. That his neighbors had the letter but one night. That some of his neighbors had changed the names on the back because Daniel Foxcrofte was not placed as he should have been, so they cut off one side of the letter. That he knew not who put wax to the letter.

MR. BYSSHE moved that to refresh his memory, and partly for abusing the House, he should be committed to prison lest he be deal[t] with in the meantime.

[p. 175] SIR JOHN ELIOT. The witness desires time to recollect himself; I would give it him. He has abused the House in his answers. I move to commit him to the Serjeant till Saturday morning, then take it into further consideration.

SIR WILLIAM BEECHER. I am ill satisfied with this witness and I speak not against the censure; but hearing Sir J. Savile say that such a man wrote the superscription, he would have Harrison asked whether he were the man.

MR. GLANVILLE. That Sir John's hand might be compared with other warrants or letters of his. To defer this till Saturday and to take notice of the carriage of this man and make use of it because we take no oath. This moves such men to speak they care not what. I remember R. Davenport's case who was committed 18 *Jac.* to the Tower for dealing doubly.[26] Moved that this Harrison should be committed to the Serjeant.

SIR PETER HEYMAN would have him committed to the Serjeant but so as none to speak with him or practice with him.

MR. BROOKE spoke in his defense in that he spoke nothing that might deserve a commitment. He said that he had delivered both these letters to his neighbors upon Sunday, etc.

MR. LONG. That this man had contradicted himself 6 several times, and how rich soever he was he did not believe he had any honesty. To be committed to the Serjeant.

SIR B. RUDYARD. He neither liked the answers nor liked that a witness should be committed so long before the full trial of the cause; witnesses should be free.

SIR ROBERT PYE. To set down the reasons why we did commit him.

SIR J. FINCH. To have him called in and examined whether he neglected his memory.

[p. 176] SIR H. MAY. Magna Carta should be remembered here. If this man be restrained he must pay fees. I have heard many men speak of contradictions. One man said he spoke 6, but named none. He said he delivered the letter to his neighbors who altered the superscription. Moved that he be not restrained, but give him command to attend here.

MR. WANDESFORD. That Sir John Savile

26. I.e., the case of Randolph Davenport, accused in both Houses of giving false testimony against Theophilus Field, Bishop of Llandaff (see *CD 1621*, index, *sub* Davenport) and subsequently committed to the Tower (ibid., IV, 416–417; V, 201–202, 397; VI, 479).

should give his word for his appearance, and he to go at liberty.

SIR JOHN STRANGWAYS. This man has abused the House. He answered that he could not tell whether this were the letter or no, a true copy or not. That he wrote to his uncle to keep the original for Sir John Savile's discharge and his own.

MR. WHITBY. Not to commit him or restrain him, for this was imprisonment.

MR. LITTLETON. It is dangerous during examination to put anything upon a man to terrify him. End the business first and then punish him if you see cause.

He was not committed but had time given him till Saturday [*sic*].[27]

IV. HARLEIAN MS 1601, BRITISH LIBRARY[28]

[f.1]

Thursday the 8th of June 1626

Mr. Farrer called in on Sir Francis Foljambe's part against Sir John Savile concerning the letter he sent into Yorkshire. He says he saw the original letter in Anthony Foxcrofte's hands and is persuaded that it was the same in effect in substance with the copy. The subscription in his eye was Sir John Savile's hand. He saw 2 or 3 copies in the country. He is persuaded these hands were gotten by reason of the letter.

Anthony Foxcrofte. He has seen the original of which he takes this to be the copy. It was published in the country as Sir John Savile's letter, and divers copies of it divulged. The [*illegible*] directed to one Key, a clothier. He thinks he had the original letter within this week in his own hands. He thinks his father has it. The last time he saw it was yesternight. He received no letter from Mr. Harrison last Whitsuntide. He delivered the letter last night to his father.

Daniel Foxcrofte. He has seen the original letter in his own hand the last night and has it now about him; which he left here in the House and then withdrew into the Committee Chamber.

Being called down again, he said he received the letter from Harrison enclosed in another letter of/

27. I.e., till *Monday*. See above, n. 11.

28. Harleian 1601 is a small anonymous collection of notes for five days at the end of the 1626 session. For a full description of the diary, see Introduction, *PP 1626*, I, 8–9.

Order of Business Friday, 9 June 1626

Committee for transmitting the charges against Richard **Montagu** to the Lords to meet this afternoon	404, *20/2
Committee on the bill for the mitigation of the sentence of the greater **excommunication** to meet tomorrow	404, *10/3
L.2a. An act for settling of a jointure upon the wife of Sir Thomas **Littleton:** committed	404, 407, *1/6
Sir John Eliot: moves for a message to the Lords desiring a copy of the Duke of **Buckingham's answer** to the **charge** against him [*see below*]	406, 407, *21/4
Resolved: as Eliot moved	404, 406
Message to the Lords (Sir Humphrey May, Chancellor Duchy)	404, 406, 408, 409
Committee for considering the cases of Sir Robert **Howard** and Mr. **More,** MP, to meet tomorrow; members added	404, *22/5
Report from the committee on the bill for **subscription** (Sir James Perrot)	404, 408, *15/2
Ordered: the bill for subscription to be engrossed	404, 408
Report from the committee on the bills for **arms** (Thomas Wentworth)	404, *14/3; 20/3
Resolved: matter of finding arms is committed to a committee of the whole House, to meet Thursday [15 June]	404, 408
L.2a. An act for reversing a decree made in Chancery on behalf of Lady **Lambart,** complainant against Richard, Lord **Robartes:** rejected	404, 408, *3/6
Report of the Lords' response to the message desiring a copy of the Duke of **Buckingham's answer** to the **charge** against him: the Lords will consider the message and send answer by their own messengers (Sir Humphrey May, Chancellor Duchy) [*see above*]	404, 406, 409
Sir Heneage Finch (Speaker): that he has received a letter from the King to be read in the House	406, 408
Letter from the King to the Speaker for speeding the **subsidy** bill: read	405, 406, 408, 410(2), *27/3; 12/6; 13/6
[*The King's letter is printed on p. 406*]	
Edward Littleton	406, 408, 410
Mr. Long	406, 408, 410
Sir William Strode	406, 408
Sir John Coke (Secretary)	406, 408
Sir Robert Pye	408, 410
Resolved: to consider the King's letter on Monday [12 June]; any MP may have copies of the letter	405, 407, 408, 410(2)
Report from the commitee about a **general fast** (Sir Robert Harley)	405, 407, 408, 410, *29/4
Reasons for a general fast: read	405, 407, 408, 410(2)
Sir Nathaniel Rich	408
Resolved: to petition the King to command a general fast	405, 407, 408, 410
Francis Rous	410
Resolved: a committee to be named for considering the reasons for the fast and framing a petition to the King	405, 407, 408, 410

FRIDAY, 9 JUNE 1626

I. JOURNAL OF THE HOUSE OF COMMONS

[CJ 869; p. 92]
Veneris, 9 Junii, 2 Caroli Regis

The committee for Montagu his articles,[1] in the afternoon, in the Exchequer Chamber; and the lawyers ordered to attend.

Bill of excommunication, tomorrow.

L. 2a. An act for the more convenient/[2]
Committed to

[col. 1]	[col. 2]
Mr. [Christopher] Wandesford	Sir D[udley] Digges
Sir John Strangways	Sir A[rthur] Ingram
Mr. [Edward] Littleton	Sir John Stradling
Mr. John Drake	Sir Thomas Denton
Sir H[enry] Poole	Mr. [Francis] Rous
Sir William Spencer	Sir John Lowther
Sir Roger North	Mr. Francis Finch
Sir Francis Barrington	Mr. [John] Fettiplace

[col. 3]
Mr. Whitaker
Sir Richard Grosvenor
Mr. [Philip] Mainwaring
Mr. [Christopher] Brooke
Mr. [William] Coryton
Sir Edward Peyton

Tomorrow[3] in the afternoon, in the Exchequer Court.

Upon question, a message presently to the Lords to desire a copy of the Duke's answer that so this House may upon consideration thereof make a reply thereunto with as much speed as may be, if there shall be cause.

This message to be delivered by the Chancellor of the Duchy; which sent away presently.[4]

The committee for examination of Mr. More's privilege, tomorrow in the afternoon.[5]Sir John Lowther, Mr. Dyott, Sir Richard Strode, and all the lawyers of the House, added to the committee.

SIR J. PERROT reports the bill concerning subscription, with some small amendments. *Engrossetur.*

MR. WENTWORTH reports from the committee for arms; many difficulties about the finding of arms and, in respect thereof, the committee has thought fit to refer it back to the House, and desire the opinion thereof.

Committed to a committee of the whole House; Thursday[6] next, 2 clock, in the House.

L. 2a. An act for the reversing of a decree made in the High Court of Chancery for and on the behalf of Hesther, Lady Lambart, complainant against Richard, Lord Robartes, and the Lady Frances, his wife, defendants.

1. Upon question, not to be committed.
2. Upon question, not to be engrossed. Rejected.

MR. CHANCELLOR OF THE DUCHY returns answer from the Lords: That they will take our message into consideration with all speed.[7]

1. I.e., Richard Montagu. For the report on Montagu's books, see HofC, 17 April, OB.

2. I.e., settling of a jointure on the wife of Sir Thomas Littleton.

3. *Monday 7night* is crossed out in the MS preceding *Tomorrow.*

4. For the message sent up by Sir Humphrey May, see HofL, 9 June, OB. For Buckingham's answer to the charges brought against him, see HofL, 8 June, pp. 566–585.

5. More, sent to the Tower on 3 June (see above), was remitted from further punishment and took his seat in the House on 7 June.

6. *Monday* is crossed out in the MS and *Thursday* is inserted.

7. For the answer given to the House of Commons, see HofL, 9 June, OB.

A letter from his Majesty to Mr. Speaker, read in the House, concerning the speeding of the bill of subsidy, dated this day.[8]

Ordered, every man that will may have copies of this letter.

Upon question, to take his Majesty's letter into consideration upon Monday morning next.

SIR ROBERT HARLEY tenders in reasons for a general fast to be desired of the King; which read.[9]

Upon question, to be petitioners to the King to command a public fast.[10]

[p. 93] 2ly. Upon question, a committee to be named to consider of the reasons to be given at the praying a conference with the Lords about their joining; and to draw a petition to his Majesty, wherein a space to be left for the Lords to join with us, if they please.

The old committee to stand,[11] with addition of:

[col. 1]	[col. 2]	[col. 3]
Mr. [Christopher] Wandesford	Sir H[enry] Wallop	Sir P[eter] Heyman
Sir Benjamin Rudyard	Sir M[iles] Fleetwood	Mr. Long
Sir A[rthur] Ingram	Mr. [Edward] Kirton	Sir Edward Hales
Sir Roger Palmer	Mr. [John] Rudhale	Mr. [Francis] Rous
Mr. [Christopher] Sherland	Sir John Strangways	Sir William Masham
Mr. L[awrence] Whitaker	Mr. [John] Carvill	Sir H[umphrey] Lynde

Tomorrow afternoon, in the Exchequer Chamber.

Upon question, Sir Edward Coke, standing *de facto,* returned a member of this House, to have privilege against a suit in Chancery, commenced against him by the Lady Clere.[12] A letter/

MR. NOY tenders a petition from many inhabitants of Norfolk.[13]

Ordered, the committee for continuance and repeal of statutes to take consideration of this petition and to hear counsel therein.

The committee concerning Sir Robert Sharpeigh enlarged to all burgesses of port towns and Sir Robert Pye.[14]

The committee for evils and causes to sit tomorrow morning.

The consideration of the King's message about the letter to Cambridge to be also tomorrow morning.

8. For the King's letter, see Whitelocke, below.

9. Harley's full report is not included in any of the accounts.

10. A public fast was proclaimed for 30 June, "moved thereunto the rather by the good inclination of the Commons House of Parliament". *Stuart Proclamations,* II, 97–99. See also, SP 16/31:18, instructions for a Book of Prayers for the fast (calendared for 5 July). For the authoritative printed work, see *A Form of Prayer, Necessary to be Used in these Dangerous Times of War and Pestilence for the Safety and Preservation of his Majesty and his Realmes* (London, 1626), *STC,* no. 16543.

11. A select committee "to consider of and set down the reasons which shall be used by the committee . . . about a general fast" had been appointed on 29 April.

12. Sir Edward Coke had been pricked for sheriff of Buckinghamshire but, notwithstanding, was elected to parliament from Norfolk. See the discussion of his case, HofC, 14 February. See also, App., II, D. No new writ was issued for Norfolk during the session and Coke was granted privilege of parliament in the case of Lady Clere. Regarding the case, see Coke, *Fourth Inst.,* pp. 47–48.

13. We have not found the petition.

14. I.e., the committee regarding Sharpeigh's patent for the surveyorship of Newcastle coals. See HofC, 24 May, nn. 16 and 17.

II. DIARY OF BULSTRODE WHITELOCKE, ESQ., DD. 12.22, CAMBRIDGE UNIVERSITY LIBRARY

[f. 46]

June 9

SIR JOHN ELIOT moves that, the Duke having put in his answer yesterday to the accusation of this House, we may send a message to the Lords desiring a copy of that answer, whereto we may make our reply if there be cause.

Resolved that such a message shall be sent presently to the Lords, and Chancellor Duchy appointed the messenger.[15]

CHANCELLOR DUCHY reports that having delivered the message this day resolved on to the Lords, they answered that they would speedily take consideration of this message and return their answer by messengers of their own.[16]

[f. 46v] MR. SPEAKER. That this morning he has received a letter from the King which is to be read in the House.

And [it] is read, a copy whereof follows:[17]

Carolus Rex

Trusty and well-beloved, we greet you well. Our House of Commons cannot forget how often and how earnestly we have called upon them for the speeding of that aid which they intend unto us for our great and weighty affairs concerning the safety and honor of us and our kingdoms. And now the time being so far spent that unless it be presently concluded it can neither bring us money or credit by the time which themselves have prefixed,[18] which is the last of this month, and being further deferred will be of little use, we being daily advertised from all parts of the great preparations of the enemy ready to assail us, we hold it necessary to give them by these our letters our last and final admonition and to let them know that we shall account all further delays or excuses to be express denials. And therefore we will and require you to signify unto them that we do expect that they forthwith bring in their bill of subsidy to be passed without [f. 47] delay or condition so as it may fully pass that House by the end of the next week at furthest, which if they do not it will force us to take other resolutions. But let them know that if they finish this according to our desire that we are resolved to let them sit together for the dispatch of their other affairs and, after their recess, to bring them together again the next winter. And if by their denial or delay anything of ill consequence shall fall out either at home or abroad, we may call God and man to witness that we have done our part to prevent it by calling our people together to advise with us, by opening the weight of our occasions unto them, and by requiring their timely help and assistance in those actions wherein we stand engaged by their own counsels. And we will and command you that this letter be publicly read in the House.

Given at our palace of Westminster the 9 of June in the 2nd year of our reign.

To our trusty and well-beloved
Sir Heneage Finch, Knight,
Speaker of our Commons
House of Parliament

[f. 47v] MR. LITTLETON moves a day may be assigned for consideration of this letter, and thinks Monday a fit day.

MR. LONG seconds that motion, and that we may have copies of the letter.

SIR WILLIAM STRODE. That we may sit morning and afternoon and prepare our grievances ready to be presented to the King before the end of the next week like-

15. See above, n. 4.

16. See above, n. 7.

17. The letter circulated as a "separate". For other manuscript copies see, for example, SP 16/29:54, 55, 56; NLW, Peniarth 410D, pt. II; Lansd. 491, ff. 174v-175; BL Add. 22,474, pp. 360–362; Harl. 161, ff. 137–138; and HRO, 44/M/69, xxxix, 15. A copy of the letter was sent to the Upper House, see HofL, 9 June, p. 593.

18. The subsidy bill had been introduced on 5 May and a select committee then appointed to prepare a preamble for the bill. On 3 June the bill and preamble were read together with the order of 27 March that stated that the bill would be brought in "as soon as we have presented our grievances and received answer to them".

wise, and so let the subsidy and that go on together.

SECRETARY COKE. That we may tomorrow take consideration of the King's letter.

Resolved that the contents of this letter shall be taken into consideration on Monday morning, and any that will to have copies of the letter.

SIR ROBERT HARLEY reports from the committee for the fast some heads for a conference with the Lords to join with us for a fast.

Resolved that this House shall petition the King to command a public fast, and a committee appointed to consider of the reasons and frame a petition, wherein the Lords may be prayed to join with us if there be cause.[19]

[f. 48] MR. GOODWIN. That Sir Edward Coke being chosen a knight for Norfolk and it being in doubt whether his election be good or not and not yet determined, that he forbearing in his own modesty to come to the House, a subpoena is served upon him. Moves that he may have the privilege of this House.

MR. LITTLETON. That this gentleman is a member of this House returned *de facto,* and till it be declared that the election be void he is to have his privilege.[20]

MR. SELDEN. That in this parliament it being a question whether an honorable gentleman, a baron of Ireland,[21] were capable of sitting here or not, yet before it were decided the House allowed him privilege. And as much reason is for privilege in this case.

MR. WANDESFORD. That the deciding of this question will be the determination of the case that has been so long debated here. Therefore moves we may put off the debate hereof.

MR. PYM. That our privileges are ours by reason of our attendance here; and since we dispense with his being here, that therefore we may forbear allowing him his privilege.

[f. 48v] MR. NOY. The question is whether Sir Edward Coke shall have his privilege in the Chancery, hanging the debate of his lawful or unlawful election. He is returned to us and his attendance is necessary to know the end and event of this debate, and is to expect it; and therefore is to have his privilege.

Resolved that Sir Edward shall have the privilege allowed him for staying the suit.

MR. SPENCER moves that a committee may be appointed to put into order those things which are under commitment and appoint what matters shall be handled.

III. DIARY OF SIR RICHARD GROSVENOR, MS 611, TRINITY COLLEGE, DUBLIN

[p. 176]

9 June

2. An act for the more convenient settling of a jointure upon the wife of Sir Thomas Littleton.

Committed, Saturday,[22] Court of Wards; I am one.

SIR JOHN ELIOT. We understand that the Duke yesterday put in his answer yesterday. In the conclusion of our charge we left a liberty to reply.[23] This is now necessary, for

19. See above, n. 10.
20. See above, n. 12.
21. I.e., the case of Lord Lambert (Lambart), arrested and imprisoned in the Fleet on mesne process. See HofC, 24 February, OB.
22. *Monday* is crossed out in the MS and *Saturday* is inserted.
23. The Commons in their charge prayed that the Duke would "be put to the answer of every one of these particular examinations . . . ". See HofL, 15 May, p. 463.

proof must carry that business. Moved for a message to the Lords that [we] might have a copy of his answer; and that in due time [*illegible*] might reply.

The message sent by Sir Humphrey May.

[p. 177] SIR JAMES PERROT reported the act concerning subscription. Passed to be engrossed.

Thursday afternoon in the House a committee to consider of the heads to draw a bill concerning the finding of arms.

2. An act for reversing of a decree made in Chancery for the Lady Lambart. The bill rejected.

The SPEAKER reported a letter he received sitting in the chair, from the King.[24]
It was read:

To our trusty/
Ch[arles],
Trusty and well-beloved, we greet you well. Our House of Commons cannot forget how often and how earnestly we have called upon them. Aid, unless presently concluded can neither bring us money nor credit/
Be of as little use, we being daily advertised of the enemy read[y] to assail us. Our last and final admonition: all excuses to be denials. *Ergo* we will you to signify that we do expect that they forthwith bring in their bill of subsidies,[25] which if they do not it will force us to take other resolutions. But let them know that if they finish this according to our desires that we are resolved to let/
If by denial of [*sic*] their delay/
We have done our part to prevent it by calling our people together to advise with us, by opening the weight of our occasions unto them.

MR. LITTLETON. That we show our loyalty to King and care to the commonwealth to assign a day when this may be debated and in the meantime to think of it. This to be Monday.

MR. LONG moved to have copies of the letter.

SIR WILLIAM STRODE. That we might sit morning and evening to dispatch [and] make ready our grievances and put them into the King's hand because of [an] order in this House.[26]

SECRETARY COKE. Consider the time, whether a day or two may not now [be] of as great consequence as the subsidies be worth. Moved [to] [be]gin tomorrow.

[p. 178] SIR ROBERT PYE. For tomorrow to begin. Action rather than words will join the King and us together.

Ordered to take this letter into consideration upon Monday, in the meantime to have copies of the letter.

SIR ROBERT HARLEY presented the reasons for a fast agreed on by the committee appointed for that purpose.
They were read.

SIR NATHANIEL RICH moved for a committee to draw a petition to the King and leave a space for the Lords to join with us.[27]

Resolved by question that the House should petition the King to command a public fast; 2, that we shall name a committee to consider of the reasons and likewise of the frame of petition to the King with space for the Lords to join with us.
The former committee named with some addition. Tomorrow, Exchequer Chamber.

MR. GOODWIN. That Sir Edward Coke was served with a subpoena being a member of the House as yet, the House not having determined the validity of his election,

24. See above, n. 17.
25. See above, n. 18.
26. I.e., the order of 27 March. See above, n. 18.
27. See above, nn. 10 and 11.

he being chosen a sheriff. Moved he might have his privilege.[28]

MR. WANDESFORD. That we neither deny it for wronging ourselves nor grant it because we then determine the business.

MR. LITTLETON. The country has declared him *de facto* and ought to have his privilege.

MR. SELDEN. However the law be that he being a sheriff is not capable, yet so long as the return of him remains unjudged he ought to have his privilege. We have this parliament adjudged the like in the L. Lambert's case,[29] it being questioned whether in respect of his person he be capable.

MR. PYM. There are rules of law and of wisdom; sometimes they meet, sometimes differ. Some privileges due to the member, some to the House itself, as no member to be sued. [p. 179] As we have forborne the privileges of the House itself, so let us that of this particular gentleman. That rule of wisdom should move us in this particular. Our privilege given us in respect of our attendance; if we have forborne his attendance we may forbear his privilege, which is incident unto it. Wished to forbear; and when we thought fit to send for him we may also yield him his privilege.

MR. CORYTON. In new found ways no true wisdom; so long as the choice stands it is good. I wish this had not been moved. If we refuse him his privilege, we judge the cause against him; that before he be made incapable we give him his privilege.

MR. NOY. We are not now disputing whether he be duly elected but whether he ought to have his privilege. Privilege in other courts are double: a necessary service, they are officers of the court. Others are bound to a necessary attendance though unwilling, as if a man be served with process so a sheriff appearing.

Sir E. Coke is returned, and complained of his election. He is bound to attend the issue of that debate. He ought to have his privilege as well here, and he should have in all other cases.

By question, resolved with one voice that Sir Edward Coke should have his privilege.

MR. SPENCER moved for a committee to consider of all our business and to think of what fit to proceed in that we be not at the other end forced to huddle up many things together and do nothing.

[*Illegible*] SPENCER. That we present our last grievances again and desire an answer from the King.

[SIR D.] DIGGES. That we should go on with our declaration and then to the whole business of the House.

[p. 180] MR. KIRTON. Our greatest grievance above with the Lords.[30] Now hasten to make ready these here till we hear what will become with that great man above. For if nothing be done with him, the country will be ill satisfied if he clear not himself.

IV. DIARY OF JOHN LOWTHER, ESQ., D/LONS/L, CUMBERLAND AND WESTMORLAND RECORD OFFICE

[f. 42v]

[9 June]

Friday, the House, having intimation of a letter from the King, sent a message to have a copy of the Duke his answer to which they might reply, it being put in yesterday.

The Lords sent word we should have answer by messengers of their own with all possible speed, but sent none that day. But proceeded against Earl Bristol, being all the forenoon in examining, as I heard, 2 wit-

28. See above, n. 12.
29. See above, n. 21.
30. I.e., the charges against Buckingham.

nesses for the King against him, the afternoon for him.[31]

Then the same day the King's letter to the Speaker, by the intimation in it to be publicly read, was read, showing how we could not be ignorant how time was delayed, how he had called us, represented the danger of the state by enemies, etc., and required advice and help in the things undertaken by our counsel. Called God and men to witness [he] had done his part whatsoever [f. 43] happened hereafter. Therefore required us to perfect our own promise to send up subsidy bill by the end of the next week without any condition, else he would take all delays and excuse for denials and take other resolutions.

After long debate the consideration of it was deferred until Monday.

Divers propositions then made to go on with the business of the commonwealth. Tonnage and poundage in Book of Rates, continuance of statutes, grievances first to be presented and the most material, as the naval war,[32] etc.; to be ordered by a committee which to proceed in first, but this denied.

Then the reasons for a fast to be desired were read, and we to desire the Lords to join; but, because they comprehended not *causa causarum* as seemed, they were recommitted.

V. HARLEIAN MS 1601, BRITISH LIBRARY

[f.2]

Friday the 9th of June 1626

A letter sent to the Speaker from the King which is to be read publicly by command. Wherein is mentioned that the subsidy bill be brought in and passed this House by the latter end of the next week at the furthest without delay or condition else he shall resort to new resolutions. This to be taken as his final admonition and he shall take all delays or excuses to be denial.

MR. LITTLETON. To have this business deferred until Monday next and then to take it into consideration.

MR. LONG. That we may have copies of this letter.

Which was granted, and we were informed by SIR JOHN COKE that it was the King's pleasure that we should have copies.

Resolved upon question that we shall take this letter into consideration on Monday next, in the meantime that any may have copies of this letter that will.

SIR ROBERT HARLEY brought in the reasons which were drawn for the fast, which he desired might be read.

Which was done.

Resolved upon question that we should petition his Majesty to command a public fast.

MR. ROUSE. There are some devils that cannot be cast out by prayer and fasting they are so powerful.

Resolved likewise that a committee shall be named to consider of the reasons and to draw a petition to the King for the fast, space being left for the Lords. To meet tomorrow in the afternoon in the Exchequer Chamber.

MR. GOODWIN. Moves that Sir Edward Coke may have his privilege, being served with a subpoena out of the Chancery in the case of my Lady Clere.

31. See HofL, 9 June, p. 592, OB.

32. MS: *materials*.

MR. NOY. He ought to have his privilege.

Resolved upon question that Sir Edward Coke should have his privilege.

Ordered that the business of this day concerning engrossed bills and the King's message concerning the letter to be sent to Cambridge should be debated tomorrow morning.

Order of Business Saturday, 10 June 1626

SATURDAY, 10 JUNE 1626

I. JOURNAL OF THE HOUSE OF COMMONS

[CJ 869; p. 93]
Sabbati, 10 Junii, 2 Caroli Regis

The committee for penning a remonstrance concerning tonnage and poundage to meet upon Monday in the afternoon; and Sir H[enry] Poole, all the merchants of the port towns, Mr. [Christopher] Sherland, Sir John Pickering, Sir H[enry] Anderson, Mr. Whitaker, added to the committee.[1]

Lady Dale's bill, Tuesday; and Sir John Pickering, Mr. William Whitaker, Sir Eubule Thelwall, Mr. Nicholas Jordan, and Mr. [Richard] Escott, added.

SIR GEORGE MORE informs the House that he was present at a High Commission court where seven bishops present; and knows that then all the proceedings against Sir Robert Howard from the first of February, 22 *Jac.*, were frustrated and made void.[2]

And SIR H. MARTEN affirmed that the order of the House there read and allowed; and all ordered to be there done accordingly.

Tuesday next,[3] for full satisfaction to be given to this House of the performance of the order concerning Sir Robert Howard; and then the order/

[p. 94] MR. PYM reports from the committee for religion concerning the schoolmaster of Abergavenny. That he was about 18 years since a recusant suspected, and convented since before the bishop, but cleared. His wife a recusant, and her friends, and has divers scholars, sons of popish recusants.

Affirmed by divers gentlemen of worth that he himself is very conformable; a very good schoolmaster; has brought his wife to church and to receive the communion; and has/

Upon question, Morgan Lewis, this schoolmaster, to be discharged from further attendance, only with an admonition from the committee for religion for catechizing his scholars; which he promises.[4]

[CJ 870]
L. 2a. Bulkeley.
Committed to

The knights and burgesses of Wales and Cheshire and Lancashire	Mr. Whitaker
Mr. [Christopher] Sherland	Mr. Nicholas Jordan
Sir George More	Mr. [John] Keeling
Sir H[enry] Poole	Sir Nicholas Saunders
Mr. [Edward] Bysshe	Mr. John Drake
Mr. Clement Coke	Mr. Francis Finch
Mr. [Humphrey] Newbery	

Tuesday next, in the afternoon; notice to the Lady Bulkeley and Serjeant Davenport, and counsel to be heard of all parts, if they will.

MR. CORYTON reports the bill for avoiding suspicion of partiality in any the members of the Commons House of Parliament,

1. For the committee named to frame the heads for the remonstrance concerning tonnage and poundage, see HofC, 8 June, CJ.

2. On 3 May the House ordered that the proceedings in the High Commission Court against Sir Robert Howard from 1 February, 22 Jac., be declared void.

3. I.e., on 13 June. On 14 June the House ordered the register of the High Commission Court to bring "the acts and proceedings and depositions against Sir Robert Howard" to the committee for that cause the following day, i.e., on 15 June, the day the session ended.

4. Regarding Morgan Lewis, see HofC, 1 May, n. 3.

with amendments; which 2 read. *Engrossetur.*

SIR H[ENRY] POOLE reports the bill for the venting of white cloths, with some amendments; which 2 read. Recommitted, presently, in the Committee Chamber.

Bill for nichills accounts in corporations, Tuesday next. Mr. [Christopher] Sherland and Mr. [Edward] Whitby added to the committee.

Bill for discovery of popish recusants and of church papists, Monday afternoon, Court of Wards.

The forfeited sums of £10 to be paid to the Clerk;[5] and to be paid before Thursday next, except they shall in the meantime make an excuse allowed by the House; and Wednesday next appointed for their excuses.

Mr. Whitson, upon question, spared his £10.[6]

The grand committee for the declaration to sit presently.

Mr. Rudhale licensed to go into the country, upon the sickness of his only brother.

Mr. Baron Trevor and Sir Charles Caesar bring with them from the Lords the copy of the Duke's answer; and further signify that the Duke has made a request to their Lordships, which they recommend to this House,[7] that we would proceed with all expedition in our reply to this answer, that so they might proceed on with the business. The messengers dismissed without any answer.

[p. 95] Ordered, the House shall sit again at 2 clock.

Ordered, all the gentlemen employed in delivering the charge against the Duke, with the aggravations, shall bring in all their parts in writing.[8]

Upon report[9] from the committee about the declaration, resolved upon question that the grand committee and subcommittee should have power to send for the roll of parliament[10] in the rolls concerning the declaration made from the Duke of Buckingham to both Houses of Parliament, 21 *Jac.*[11]

2ly. That this grand committee, or subcommittee, shall have power to send for the Lord Digby,[12] or his counsel, to make good, by proof, that point which concerns the abuse of this House.

The grand committee for the declaration to sit at the rising of the House.

II. DIARY OF BULSTRODE WHITELOCKE, ESQ., DD. 12.22, CAMBRIDGE UNIVERSITY LIBRARY

[f. 49]

June 10

After some bills committed, etc.

[*Committee of the Whole House*]

Mr. Herbert in the chair.

Mr. Selden reports some new heads from

5. I.e., for absence at the calling of the House on 2 June. For the order, see HofC, 23 May.

6. For the defaulters, see Grosvenor's list on 2 June.

7. For Buckingham's reply and request, see HofL, 10 June, p. 602.

8. I.e., those who spoke and assisted at the conference of 8 and 10 May; see HofC, 6 May for the names.

9. Printed edition: *upon the report.*

10. Printed edition: *parchment.*

11. I.e., the relation of the Spanish marriage negotiations and the journey of the prince and Buckingham into Spain. PRO C 65/186. Regarding the parliament roll for 1624, see Elizabeth R. Foster, *The Painful Labor of Mr. Elsing*, Trans. Am. Phil. Soc. (Philadelphia, 1972), p. 31.

12. I.e., John Digby, Earl of Bristol. See below, n. 19.

the subcommittee for the declaration to the King and conference with the Lords:[13]

1. That the Duke does often strive to excuse himself of such things as are laid to his charge by casting an ill odor upon the King that is dead and using likewise the King's name that now is for that end.

Resolved that this shall be used as a head for the conference or declaration, or both.

2. The subsidy of tonnage and poundage having been taken since the death of King James not being confirmed by parliaments.

Allowed.[14]

3. That there may be some good caution given in the declaration or remonstrance, or both, to those that shall either by contract or bounty meddle with the King's estate and revenue of the crown.

Allowed.

Mr. Speaker in the chair.

[f. 49v] Baron Trevor and [*blank*][15] bring a message from the Lords. That according to our desire, they have sent us a copy of the Duke's answer which is enrolled in their House. That the Duke in their House made a request which their Lordships thought fit to recommend to this House, that we would reply with all possible speed that they may go on with that matter.

Ordered that the House shall sit this afternoon at 2 a clock, and those gentlemen that were employed in offering the Duke's charge to the Lords shall bring in all their papers that may conduce to this business.[16]

[*Committee of the Whole House*]

Mr. Herbert in the chair.

Mr. Selden proceeds in his report, with a motion to the grand committee from the subcommittee that they may have power to send for some records and some persons. Some speeches made by the Duke concerning the state of Spain and this state very false, made at a conference [*blank*],[17] being enrolled, and concerning this House as well as the Lords. That this roll may be sent for. And that they may have power to send for the Lord Digby, either by himself or his counsel, to make good those things that were in his petition to that effect.

[f. 50] Mr. Spencer moves that it may be known who said that those things were false.

Mr. Selden nominates the Earl of Bristol.

Mr. Spencer. That King James said that whatsoever the Duke spoke at that conference, he spoke it by his commandment; and this King James said openly to both Houses at Whitehall.[18]

Sir Dudley Digges. That the debate is not now to be whether that in the record be true or false, but the desire of the subcommittee is that that record may be looked into and examined.

Resolved that the subcommittee shall have power to send for that record, and to send for the Lord Digby to be heard either by himself or by his counsel touching that

13. Regarding this committee, see HofC, 6 June, n. 15. The intended remonstrance (or declaration) is printed at the end of the day's proceedings, 13 June.

14. A committee had been appointed on 8 June to draw a separate remonstrance regarding tonnage and poundage.

15. Sir Peter Mutton. See HofL, 10 June, p. 602.

16. See above, n. 8.

17. 24 February 1624. For a description of the conference, held at Whitehall, see Ruigh, *Parliament of 1624,* pp. 162–167; for the report of the conference, see *LJ,* III, 220–233. Concerning the Parliament Roll, see above, n. 11.

18. See *LJ,* III, 232–234 and Ruigh, *Parliament of 1624,* pp. 167–168.

part of his petition which is concerning the abuse of this House.[19]

Speaker in his chair.

MR. HERBERT reports the resolutions of the committee.

Resolved that they shall have power to send for the record and the Lord Digby, accordingly.

[f. 50v]

Pomeridiem

The Speaker in his chair.

The/

The answer of the Duke of Buckingham to the Commons' declaration and impeachment against him to the Lords.[20]

The consideration of this answer of the Duke referred unto those 12 committees that drew the charge and those who were assistants to those that delivered the charge.[21]

MR. PYM reports the charges and articles framed against Mr. Montagu and his works, which he was by order of the House to deliver unto the Lords at the bar in their House.

Which are twice read and ordered to be engrossed to be left with the Lords at the delivery of his charge against him.[22]

The conclusion recommitted.

[*Committee of the Whole House*]

Mr. Herbert in the chair.

Resolved that this grand committee shall send for the Lord Digby to be heard by himself or his counsel concerning the abuse of this House mentioned in his petition, and that the roll shall likewise be brought hither.[23]

III. DIARY OF SIR RICHARD GROSVENOR, MS 611, TRINITY COLLEGE, DUBLIN

[p. 180]

10 June

2. An act for the quieting and settling of the lands late of Sir Richard Bulkeley, Knight.

Committed, self one, Tuesday, Exchequer Court.

MR. CORYTON reported the bill to avoid suspicion of injustice in any member of the Commons House of Parliament. Passed to be engrossed.

SIR H. POOLE reported the bill for the better utterance and venting of white cloth.

SIR P. HEYMAN. For recommitment. The Cinque Ports have a charter wherein they have liberty to buy cloth in Blackwell Hall.[24] Moved for a recommitment.

Recommitted. They went into the Committee Chamber.

Monday for bills for church papists and the conformity of recusants, Court of Wards.

Ordered that such as were absent upon the last call should pay their £10 to the Clerk by Thursday next.[25]

SIR THOMAS HOBY moved to proceed in that committee concerning the heads of the declaration to be made to the King.

Mr. Herbert came into the chair.

19. Presumably the petition submitted by the Earl of Bristol to the Upper House on 19 April (HofL, 19 April, p. 284) wherein he alleged that "the said Duke has abused their Majesties, the state, and both the Houses of Parliament".

20. For the Duke's responses to the articles of impeachment, see HofL, 8 June, pp. 566–585.

21. For the names of those who assisted at the conference of 8 and 10 May, see 6 May.

22. For the complaints against Richard Montagu, see HofC, 17 April.

23. See above, n. 19.

24. We have not found the charter.

25. I.e., absent on 2 June. See above, n. 5.

[*Committee of the Whole House*]

Mr. Selden reported the heads of the declaration and conference, etc., agreed upon by the subcommittee.[26] The most concern the Duke of Buckingham.

1. The Duke has often labored to excuse himself by casting foul odors upon his late Majesty, and does use his Majesty's name to excuse his offenses.

Sir Francis Stewart. That at the conference with the Lords he said that he was a suitor to King James that he should sell no more honors, and this was to cast an ill odor upon a good prince.[27]

Mr. Wandesford. That the Duke said King James made a benefit of sale [of] honors, not himself.[28]

[p. 181] Sir H. May. If a King command a thing to be done, the minister has done his duty when he has told him it is unfit. Unless you give leave to the King's servants to aver their master's commands, you do much prejudice them.

Secretary Coke wished to be careful lest the King might happily justify what the Duke said.

Mr. Wandesford. That he could not believe that King James sold honors.

Sir Robert Pye said that making of baronets was bought and yet under the Great Seal.[29]

Mr. Kirton remembered the £20,000 of the Earl of Manchester.[30]

Sir F. Stewart remembered the £20,000 had of Earl of Middlesex.[31]

Mr. Pym. That of baronets no sale of honor, being done *sub ratione boni,* on pretense of a service to the commonwealth—the keeping of 30 soldiers in Ireland.[32]

Mr. Newbery said that to say the King commanded it was not good, neither could justify the fact no more than to justify the taking away of life or goods by the King's command.

[*Illegible.*] To make use of the speech concerning new counsels as though parliaments should be altered by new counsels. The subsidy of tonnage and poundage never heretofore taken but by parliament; new, [of] late, this has been levied with parliament.

That the taking of the subsidy of tonnage and poundage without consent of parliament as an effect of new counsels.[33]

[*Illegible.*] A desire that some good caution may be given to those who shall deal by contract or by bounty with his Majesty's estate.

Sir Nathaniel Rich. The meaning was that none should be earnest to get states out of the King's estate.

[Sir D.] Digges. A great part of the crown lands by bounty and contracts carried away. A warning and caveat to all, that none dare hereafter by contract or bounty procure any of the King's ancient lands.

Mr. Spencer would not have it a head but rather referred to the regulating of [the] King's estate.

[Sir William] Beecher would not have the King tied from contracts of his [*illegible*] the

26. See above, n. 13.

27. Cf. HofL, 15 May, p. 480. We find no record of the remark as remembered by Stewart.

28. See Buckingham's speech on 15 May, HofL, pp. 479–480.

29. Regarding the baronetcies, see HofC, 27 March, n. 13.

30. See HofL, 15 May, p. 470, n. 85; and 8 June, pp. 576–577.

31. See HofL, 15 May, p. 456.

32. See above, n. 29.

33. The allusion to "new counsels" is a reference to Carleton's speech on 12 May. Regarding tonnage and poundage, see HofC, 6 March, n. 27; and above, CJ, 8 June.

lest necessity constrained it to be broken and then must be done upon worse condition.

[p. 182] Sir John Eliot. No way dangerous to the King's honor or bounty that there should be any preclusion in the will of any not to buy the King's land by way of contract or bounty.

Sir Edwin Sandys. No well-understanding subject but is grieved to see the diminution of the King's revenue. This has been an Italia[n] trick, that the prince should sell his own land to live off his subjects. This land has ever been tender of the King's revenue.

Wished that the King's book might be viewed again, for his revenue will grow by escheats and otherwise. I would have this both in the conference or declaration, and in that of the King's revenue. In this to give an intimation of it; in that to settle it. The bounty of the King should proceed from the fruit, not from the root whence it should grow.

3. That because there has been a diminution of the revenue of the crown that there should be a consideration of some caution or warning that men shall not be too busy by contract or bounty hereafter [to] waste the revenue of the crown.

The Speaker went in.

A message from the Lords:

Baron Trevor, Sir Charles Caesar. They brought from the Lords a copy of the Duke's answer to the charge of the Commons, and commended a request made by the Duke to them that we would proceed with all speed to a reply.

Ordered that the Speaker should come in the afternoon at 2 of the clock and then the answer to be read, and that the 8 gentlemen should bring all their papers and speeches.

Mr. Herbert returned into the chair.

[*Committee of the Whole House*]

Mr. Selden moved that the subcommittee might have power to send for some persons and records.[34] That the Duke of Buckingham made many speeches in 1 *Car.* in parliament which are entered of record in the Chancery,[35] being made at a conference. So many falsehoods expressed in that roll that not fitting should remain without examination of this House. The Earl of Bristol reported this to be so.

Mr. Spencer moved [to be] tender in this because the [*torn*] the Duke spoke all by his command.

[p. 183] Sir Robert Pye. That we plead not for the state of Spain. The/

Mr. Spencer. Those things which are done before both Houses, if ever entered of record, if the Clerk have entered otherwise than the Duke spoke, he may be questioned; but all the Duke said was justified for true both by the King dead and this King.

Sir Thomas Fanshawe. If my Lord of Bristol have said that this roll is false, he being now accused in parliament, let us consider how far we should take notice of the falsifying of a record testified by him now accused.

Sir D. Digges. I would know if all things spoken at a conference be entered. I would know if there be any ordinance there made and somewhat it is, and dispute no more.

Ordered that the subcommittee should have power to send for the record which is

34. See above, n. 13.

35. For the Duke's speeches in 1625, see *PP 1625*, Index, *sub* Villiers, George. The speeches are not entered on the Parliament Roll (C 65/189).

said to have many falsities in it and much to the prejudice of this House.

[*Afternoon*]

June 10, afternoon.

The House sat and the Duke's answer was read.

IV. DIARY OF JOHN LOWTHER, ESQ., D/LONS/L, CUMBERLAND AND WESTMORLAND RECORD OFFICE

[f. 43]

[10 June]

Saturday some bills reported.

[*Committee of the Whole House*]

New heads for declaration to be proposed.

The new counsels executed in taking tonnage and poundage without parliament.
1. His abuse of the parliament in his relation false from Spain, 21 *Jac.*, made a record, being but a conference, and entered as a parliament roll, now produced against Bristol as an accusation and labored to prejudicate it.[36]
[f. 43v] That the King shall not give nor make contract for his crown revenue under danger.
The Duke his casting all his excuses upon the King that was and is, as an evil odor of his government.
To protest God and the world we used no delay but proceeded parliamentarily for relief.

Sir Edward Coke, who was made sheriff of Buckingham[shire] and came not to the House nor no new writ went out, being served with a subpoena by the Lady Clere, was allowed his privilege, 9 *Junii.*[37]

V. HARLEIAN MS 1601, BRITISH LIBRARY

[f.2v]

Saturday the 10th of June 1626

An act for the avoiding of suspicion of injustice in any member of this House. This bill brought in from the committee with small amendments and passed by question for engrossing.

Ordered that those which cannot make such excuses as the House shall accept of for their absence at the call of the House by Thursday next are to pay ten pounds apiece to the Clerk.

[*Committee of the Whole House*]

Mr. Selden's report of the heads for the declaration and conference to the grand committee, Mr. Herbert in the chair.
First new head: that the Duke of B[uckingham] does strive to excuse himself by laying ill odors on Lord Digby to affirm the falsity of the rolls. This information came from my Lord of Bristol.

Sir Robert Harley. To know the particulars wherein the records are false and then to examine them.

[f.3] Resolved upon question that the subcommittee shall have power to send for the record and to send for my L. Digby if need be.

36. See above, n. 11.

37. See HofC, 9 June, n. 12.

Order of Business Monday, 12 June 1626

I.	Journal of the House of Commons,	423
II.	Whitelocke,	423–428
III.	Lowther,	428
IV.	Harleian 1601,	428–430

to the King and to insert in it an answer to the **letter from the King** [*see above*] 428(2)

[*End: Committee of the Whole House*]

Report from the committee of the whole (MR. HERBERT) 423, 428

Resolved: to proceed with the declaration (remonstrance) to the King and make an addition to it in answer to the letter from the King; the declaration is recommitted to the **subcommittee,** which is to draw the addition this afternoon [*see above*] 423, 428

Resolved: no other committees to meet this afternoon 423

MONDAY, 12 JUNE 1626

I. JOURNAL OF THE HOUSE OF COMMONS

[CJ 870; p. 95]

Lunae, 12 Junii, 2 Caroli Regis

The bill for venting of white cloths reported, after the recommitment, with a proviso for the 5 Ports. *Engrossetur.*

Mr. Browne has leave.

L. 1a. Privileges.

The grand committee about the declaration sat.

MR. HERBERT reports from this committee that there was a declaration there framed (which he tendered to the House) which in the opinion of the said committee was to be presented to his Majesty.[1]

Upon question, a committee of the whole House presently to take his Majesty's letter into consideration.

Ordered, MR. HERBERT shall now make his report from the committee.

And upon his report, ordered we should go on with the declaration, and an addition, comprehending an answer to his Majesty's letter.[2]

This addition to be made by the former subcommittee, to meet 5 clock this afternoon, in the former place. And the declaration recommitted to the same subcommittee. And all other committees this afternoon to be put off otherwise than to adjourn themselves.[3]

II. DIARY OF BULSTRODE WHITELOCKE, ESQ., DD. 12.22, CAMBRIDGE UNIVERSITY LIBRARY

[f. 51]

June 12

[*Committee of the Whole House*]

Mr. Herbert in the chair.

Mr. Selden reports from the subcommittee for drawing heads for a conference and for a declaration, the form of a declaration drawn, and desires Mr. Herbert may report it to the House.[4]

Sir George Goring takes exception to the first clause in the declaration concerning the dissolution of the parliament at Oxford, making of sheriffs, and sending away Mr. Glanville. That it trenches upon the King's honor more than upon the Duke's.[5]

Mr. Wandesford. It trenches not upon the King's honor at all, for he was misinformed by the Duke of the proceedings and intentions of parliament.

Mr. Glanville declares the manner of his sending away with the fleet, and that the Duke mediated with the King for his stay but the King would not. That he never declared himself against the Duke as is[6] set down in the remonstrance.

Mr. Long.[7] That he was at Oxford parliament and heard Mr. Glanville speak against things done by the Duke, and he brought in the protestation there which touched him.

1. The intended remonstrance (declaration) is printed at the end of the day's proceedings, 13 June.

2. For the King's letter, see 9 June, OB.

3. Regarding the subcommittee, see HofC, 5 June, n. 5.

4. The remonstrance (declaration) is printed at the end of the day's proceedings, 13 June. We have not found a draft of the document.

5. Regarding Glanville's foreign employment, see HofL, 15 May, p. 461, n. 65. See also, SP 16/6:132 for his arguments against such employments.

6. MS: *in.*

7. I.e., Walter Long, Robert did not sit in 1625. Regarding Glanville's speeches, see *PP 1625,* Index, *sub* Glanville. On 12 August 1625 he introduced a brief resolution in the Commons, ibid., pp. 475 and 478.

Chancellor Exchequer. I think there can be no proofs that the Duke was the cause of those things set down in the first clause of the declaration. For the bringing of the parliament together at Oxford, the King's necessities were the cause thereof. And for the dissolution of it, I heard the King say that the Duke earnestly and instantly besought the King not to dissolve the parliament.

Chancellor Duchy. I profess in the faith of a Christian that I do not know any one particular of that which has been last read to be true. And if they be not, they will return to our dishonor.

[f. 51v] Mr. Selden. That whatsoever is in that declaration was resolved on to be heads for this or a conference by the House.

Sir Dudley Digges. That if any will speak to the matter, he may in the House when it is reported. And moves we may in the committee only speak to the frame and expression thereof.

Resolved that this declaration shall be presented to the King and that Mr. Herbert shall report it to the House as the opinion of the committee.

Speaker in his chair.

MR. HERBERT reports the opinion of the committee.

The King's letter read.[8]

SIR HENRY POOLE. That is to be done which concerns the honor of this House and the satisfaction of the King. Let us consider our engagements upon the dissolution of the treaties with Spain[9] and our engagements this parliament. I desire therefore the bill of subsidy may be read.

SIR JOHN STRANGWAYS. Many things that are in the letter are very considerable. And therefore I desire we may resolve ourselves into a grand committee.

CHANCELLOR EXCHEQUER. Seeing the state of the question is known and that the King expects performance and not delay, moves it may be debated in the House.

Resolved that the House shall forthwith resolve into a grand committee to consider of the King's letter last sent.

[*Committee of the Whole House*]

Mr. Herbert in the chair.

[f. 52] Sir Thomas Fanshawe. If the King's letter had been to require subsidies for his own private occasions, I should not have moved to forward it; but since it is for the maintenance of the wars whereto so great sums are necessary, and that the time is so precious, and we shall hereafter perfect our work and win the King's favor by giving him satisfaction, I desire we may do it without any further delay.

Our religion is at stake and I am glad to hear that the Arminians shall be by proclamation cried down.[10] Since it is the first time the King has promised us, let us give him his request and God's blessing go with it.

Mr. Browne. I am of the same opinion that we should give satisfaction to the King. But we must have a care likewise to our liberties. And if we shall give away the people's money with[out] having redress of our grievances, the country will blame us. I doubt not but the King will be pleased to give us further time. And I think it fitting that we present our declaration to the King;

8. For the King's letter, see 9 June, OB.

9. I.e., in 1624.

10. See the remonstrance, 13 June. The King made no promise in the letter of a proclamation against Arminianism, but assured the House that if supply were granted he would continue the session. In his speech of 8 February (see HofL, pp. 27–28) he reminded the Houses of his answer to the petition concerning religion (presented in 1625) with the proclamation of 14 August that year for enforcing the laws against priests and jesuits. See HofL, 8 February, p. 28, n. 5.

which if he shall be pleased to hear and pass his royal word that we may proceed in a legal course against the great grievance and any other offenses, I think it will be a good way.

Moves that the King would hear our declaration before both Houses, promise to give us reformation of our grievances, and that so we may go on with the bill of subsidy and pass it by the end of this term.

Mr. Newbery. This letter lays a kind of necessity upon [us] to pass the bill by such a time[11] or the King shall be forced to other resolutions. When we engaged the King in this war it was not the intention of this House that we should send away our treasure and ships into other countries and pay £5,000 *per mensem* to I know not who beyond sea, but for a war as should be for our good and the weakening of our enemies.

[f. 52v] When our grievances may be redressed and the Duke either convicted[12] or acquitted according to the justness of his cause, subsidies will naturally come in; but before that I shall not willingly consent to the bringing in of the bill.

Sir Edwin Sandys. The House is a proper place to debate single questions that have no multiplicity of doubt in them. According to the day set down in our order[13] the King has designed his occasions; and if we break our day, he must break with his engagements. If a strong and hateful enemy come to invade the land and his Majesty have no money, he must take other courses to/

I have heard it said by great men and confirmed by oath [that] before the middle of August we shall have a great army of enemies in the kingdom.[14] The King says we shall sit still to dispatch our grievances. Our declaration is ready. And I have not seen a thing resolved in a great committee unresolved in the House. If there be nothing else to be said against the bringing in of the subsidies than has been, I desire we may grow to a resolution for passing it.

Mr. Coryton. I think that which comes from us is a willing and free gift, and the King's letter is little less than a requiring. I have never known the counsel of this House to ill purpose, if it were followed; if not, I think it a grief to King and kingdom. Before such course be taken as appertains to justice in the Duke of Buckingham's case, I think it not reasonable to pass the bill of subsidy. And I think many other are of that mind.

[f. 53] Sir Robert Pye. I think it fitting that after we have given this money we should tell him that if the occasions and charges of the foreign war be greater than this commonwealth can bear, we desire they may be looked into and lessened.

Sir William Strode. I think it is a reasonable good letter, and fear that the King will not retract from it.

Chancellor Duchy. It was neither the King's purpose nor his counsel's either to command this House or threate[n] them; but as he takes his liberty, so leaves us to ours. It was the counsel of the old men to Rehoboam: speak kindly to this people this day and you will win their hearts for ever.[15] I will say to you: speak kindly to the King this day and you will have his heart for ever. And it will conduce to all your ends. And therefore let the bill be read.

Mr. Coryton. If it please his Majesty to proclaim open war with Spain, I think it will be very beneficial to the kingdom. I think there is no danger of a foreign invasion.

11. I.e., "by the end of the next week at the furthest".

12. MS: *convinced.*

13. I.e., the order of 27 March.

14. There were rumors of the Spanish preparing for war. See HofC, 3 June, n. 4 and below, n. 17.

15. 1 Kgs. 12: 6, 7.

Sir George Goring. To give counsel without passion is no less commendable than to speak truth without flattery. Nothing adds more to a prince than the reputation that he has in his subjects' hearts.

Secretary Coke. More certain arguments of a speedy invasion at this time than there was in '88. I pray God I may be proved a false prophet. There is a great and imminent[16] invasion expected which requires more supply than is apprehended.

Sir Robert Mansell. The preparations in Spain are much greater than they were in '88.[17] I speak it upon knowledge. There may be good cause to doubt and secure Ireland. If anything do happen in Ireland or here, I can charge the Duke of Buckingham and those that had the charge of the sea businesses to be the cause of it. [f. 53v] And there has been no want of care and resolution in the King nor fault in this House. I hold this letter to be a very gracious letter, seeing it will gain reputation abroad and secure the kingdom, and that we shall have justice against the Duke. I desire that the bill may be appointed to be read on Thursday.

Mr. Carvill. Let us pass a bill for the first subsidy; and if our grievances be redressed afterwards, we shall go on cheerfully to pass the rest.

Mr. Richard Spencer. That we may read the bill of subsidy tomorrow and prepare our grievances to be answered as soon as we may.

Mr. Long. The expectation of justice against the Duke of Buckingham is that which sticks most with me. And in what state will the kingdom stand if this great improvident man be still in that great office? And I think he accounts this council as a spider's web which he can easily break through. If the House see justice passed against this man tomorrow, I think the bill would go on the next day.

Mr. Kirton. It is not the first time that we have heard of imminent dangers. We see what a company of diversions have been for the saving of one man. I do believe the wisdom of the council of state such that if there had been such danger they would not have suffered such interruptions. Moves that we may declare to the King where the fault lies and [f. 54] our willingness to supply the King if the fears and griefs by reason of the great power of this man may be removed.

Mr. Wandesford. It is the case of a common informer to cease when he has put in his information, but this House has cause to look further and see that justice be done. The power of a favorite is like the eye of the sun: the higher it grows, the more intolerable. I am sorry it is no more rather than so much that we intend to give. The necessities being so great, we ought to be the more careful in the managing of businesses that they be well done. The Duke's growing greater and greater in power is nothing but setting himself against the commonwealth. Let us deal plainly and tell his Majesty how the case stands with us, and I doubt not but his eyes will be open and he will yield unto our just desires.

Sir John Eliot. I shall/

There is not by any man the least purpose of any diversion from that course of justice which is already taken for the Duke's trial. That there is a hesitation with the Lords, it is too true. I have met with one jealousy/

That this eager prosecution of the Duke's follows upon particular respects or disrespects and private spleen or malice rather than [f. 54v] sincerity for the good of the

16. MS: *emient*, here and below.

17. See the minutes of the Council of War for late spring. SP 16/28.

commonwealth, which I desire to clear in this: that it was begun at Oxford and by those that are now absent.

It is but justice that we crave, which the King owes us, and I am confident we shall in time receive. That the King in his honor cannot forbear that protection of one so near him. In this we but desire that he may come to his trial. 5 H. 4, the King's confessor being charged in general by parliament,[18] the King returned his answer and protestation openly in parliament that he knew no faults he was guilty of, but because he was impeached by all the parliament he would not keep him from his trial but leave him. Thus much I am confident we shall have of our King. This makes the difficulty with me: that if we give our money now we cannot hope they shall be converted to those ends which we intend.

Mr. Littleton. That we may make ready our grievances and present them to the King with our declaration, and give bill a first reading with a reservation that it be not read the second time till we have answer of our grievances.

[f. 55] Sir Dudley Digges. We ought to give the King all possible satisfaction, but there is not one argument urged for the speedy passing of the bill but it is answered by this one argument: the Duke of Buckingham. That the King may be acquainted with our declaration, and I hope he that rules the hearts of kings will put it into our King's mind that shall be for all our good and comfort.

Chancellor Exchequer. We all confess we have an enemy diligent and potent, and yet we have not gone one step forward this parliament. What is the reason of this? It is urged the great grievance of the Duke of Buckingham. Have not we done our parts in that, and does not the King promise us redress? The King has given way to many of our proceedings which he did at first forbid, with a mind willing to be ever in league with his people. If we make a happy consultation this day, we make the King safe at home and feared abroad. If we do it not, I cannot tell that we shall have another day of consultation. I speak not to hinder the declaration, but let it go forward in its due time and let us rely upon the King's grace and favor, and let the bill be brought in tomorrow morn.

Sir Edwin Sandys. That we may insert in the declaration this clause: that in confidence of reformation in that great grievance, we have begun with the bill and given it a first reading. Which I wish we may do tomorrow.

[f. 55v] Sir John Eliot. I am confident that upon our declaration the King will be pleased to expect the event of these counsels, truly understanding both the Duke and us.

Sir Thomas Hoby. That the declaration may be presented and the reply to the Duke's answer may be perfected, and after that the bill of subsidy brought in.

Chancellor Duchy. This letter was written with a general consent of counsel. If you go on with the declaration and not with the subsidy, or so as the subsidy may go forward to the satisfaction of the King, I fear it will end your counsels. The beginning with the bill of subsidies will conclude no questions. The conclusion of the declaration will conclude your counsels, I am afraid.

Sir John Eliot. Where we are not guilty, we need not fear. I am confident of the goodness of our Sovereign and desire no more such arguments may be made of conclusions of counsels.

18. *Rot. Parl.*, 5 H. IV, no. 16.

Sir Robert Pye. I desire that there may be freedom of speech of both sides, and that you put the question for the bill of subsidies to be read.

Sir Nathaniel Rich. This declaration is a kind of presentation of our grievances. Moves that this, with some addition by way of answer to the King's letter, may be dispatched; and upon his answer we may resume the debate hereof and speedily give his Majesty satisfaction.

[f. 56] Resolved on question and division, that a question shall be put for the reading of the bill of subsidy before any question for the declaration.

Resolved that we shall proceed on with the declaration and in that declaration insert an answer to the King's letter.

Speaker in his chair.

MR. HERBERT reports the resolution of the grand committee.

Resolved by the House accordingly.

And the former subcommittee for the declaration to draw the addition by way of answer to the King's letter.

III. DIARY OF JOHN LOWTHER, ESQ., D/LONS/L, CUMBERLAND AND WESTMORLAND RECORD OFFICE

[f. 43v]

[12 June]

[*Committee of the Whole House*]

Monday, a declaration read[19] of all hindrances in parliamentary proceeding begun at Oxford and so till now, and all put on the Duke: the making of sheriffs, sending Glanville into Cadiz, denied by him, so the dissolution at Oxford by the Council.

Then the King's letter taken into consideration and, after dispute until four at clock, resolved by question not to proceed with subsidy, but to make a declaration as before, with this: that we may have justice of the Duke and then to proceed to read the bill, with show to pass it within the time (of the event).

IV. HARLEIAN MS 1601, BRITISH LIBRARY

[f.3]

Monday the 12th of June 1626

Resolved upon question that the declaration now read brought from the subcommittee shall be presented to the King. 2ly, that it shall be reported to the House.

SIR JOHN STRANGWAYS. Divers things in the letter considerable.[20] Therefore moves that the House may be resolved into a committee.

CHANCELLOR EXCHEQUER. The King expects a performance, not an answer. The question must be whether we will read the bill or no.

Ordered upon question that a committee of the whole House shall presently take the King's letter into consideration.

[*Committee of the Whole House*]

Mr. Herbert in the chair of this committee.

Sir Thomas Fanshawe. Most of his necessities descended from his father.[21] Moves that we may give the King his request and [God's] blessing go with it.

Mr. Browne. By this silence it appears some straights press us. His opinion to proceed with the declaration and to desire the King that we might in a legal manner proceed against the Duke or any other offender.

19. See above, n. 1.

20. I.e, the King's letter, see above, 9 June.

21. I.e., most of King Charles's financial necessities descended from the policies of James.

Sir Peter Heyman. Three things hinder the passing of the subsidy bill. First, the charge of the Duke depending in the higher House. 2ly, our grievances. 3ly, this letter moves that we may deal plainly with the King. If anybody knows any other things that they should speak them.

Mr. Newbery. Three things trouble him. First, that the monies should not be gotten from us by threats as we have had divers this parliament. They should come freely.

[f.3v] Sir Edwin Sandys. First, the setting of a day for the passing of this bill contrary to the course of parliament. 2, the threats—he conceives there is no threat in this letter. 3, that this will be a hindrance to our other business. Moves that if there be any other matters, some others would declare it.

Mr. Coryton. He conceives this kind of asking little better than requiring. He has never known the counsel of parliament do amiss. Before misinformations be cleared, the giving of subsidy will do no good. The declaration most necessary and may be made more full than it is. His opinion that it is not fit to pass this bill of subsidy before the business of the Duke be ended.

Sir Robert Pye. In this letter no threats nor time prefixed for everything in it has reference to his own resolutions and affairs.

Sir William Strode. More fear than is expressed. He thinks this is a reasonable good letter. Moves to go on and read the subsidy bill and doubts not but the King will give us leave to sit and end our other business.

Chancellor Duchy. The King had no purpose to menace or to prefix a time. Moves that the bill may be read; for please the King today and it will advantage all our other business.

Sir John Coke. There is now more certain information of a speedy, puissant, and imminent invasion than was in '88, therefore need to make haste to pass this bill.[22]

Sir Robert Mansell. He knows the preparations in Spain to be greater now than in '88, and they are brought into those parts of Spain which are nearest unto us. He charges my L. Duke to be the cause of bringing us into these dangers by misemploying the King's treasure. Moves to appoint a time for the reading of the bill on Thursday.

Mr. Carvill moves that there may be a bill to pass the subsidy to be paid at the end of this month presently.

Sir James Perrot. He conceives no danger to read the bill. [*MS torn*] the grievances were read.

[f.4] Mr. Spencer. [*MS torn*] We were told that if we speak kindly to the King today he will be ours forever.[23] So if the King speak kindly to us this parliament in our grievances we, as we now are, shall be his forever. Moves that the bill may be read tomorrow.

Mr. Long moves that the declaration may be made before the subsidy bill be read.

Mr. Kirton. He agrees with Mr. Long in all things.

Mr. Wandesford. There have been times when the Commons have protested against the judgment of the Lords. Did it please the King now with God that subsidies given should be more than conditional; and shall it be thought disloyalty in us to condition now with the King, being our own gift?[24] It

22. See above, nn. 14 and 17.

23. I.e., told by the Chancellor of the Duchy, Sir Humphrey May. See above, n. 15.

24. After the experience of the contract in 1610 James said he would not bargain or condition with the Commons. See, for example, *PP 1614*, pp. 17, 44.

is the Duke's power we complain of. Moves that we may go on with the declaration to inform the King what is the cause of our retarding this business.

Sir John Eliot. *Quinto* of H. 4, the King's confessor accused. Moves to have the declaration.[25]

25. See above, n. 18.

ORDER OF BUSINESS TUESDAY, 13 JUNE 1626

TUESDAY, 13 JUNE 1626

I. JOURNAL OF THE HOUSE OF COMMONS

[CJ 870; p. 96]
Martis, 13 Junii, 2 Caroli Regis

L. 1a.[1] An act for the better continuing of peace and unity in the Church and commonwealth.

L. 2a. An act concerning divers privileges of parliament.

Committed to

[col. 1]	[col. 2]
Mr. [John] Glanville	Sir Robert Crane
Sir P[eter] Heyman	Mr. [John] Pym
Mr. [Edward] Littleton	Mr. Herbert
Sir John Stradling	Sir Robert Bell
Sir Nathaniel Rich	Sir William Spencer
Mr. Francis Finch	Sir H[enry] Whitehead
	Sir J[ames] Bagg

[col. 3]
Sir Thomas Hoby
Sir H[enry] Poole
Mr. [Christopher] Wandesford

And all that come to have voice; this afternoon, Exchequer Court.

Upon question, a collection to be made of all the knights and burgesses for reward of officers, etc.

Upon question, this collection to be of 10s. a knight, and 5s. a burgess.

Sir Francis Barrington
Sir George More
Mr. [Robert] Bateman
Sir B[aptist] Hicks
Sir Nathaniel Rich
Mr. [Edward] Kirton

appointed collectors.

All men peremptorily to pay before Thursday next.

Upon question, the clause to stand, concerning the removal of officers.[2]

"And Scotland" to be left out.

"Only" stricken out, and "chiefly" put in.

Upon question, the several interlinings, "as we conceive" and "as we have just cause to believe", annexed to the dissolution at Oxford: making sheriffs, the adjournment to Oxford, the sending Mr. Glanville—to stand as in the declaration.

Upon question, the petition for removal of the Duke from the King's presence to stand.

Upon question, the word "enemy" to stand.

Upon question, the word "assured" put out, and "do fear" inserted.

Upon question, the declaration to stand in the misemployment of the supplie[s].

Upon question, the declaration in that point which concerns, "but no sooner", etc., not to be recommitted.

And upon question, that clause to stand without alteration.

Divers other amendments made.

Upon question, this allowed and ordered to be engrossed.

The committee for the replication to the Duke's charge to meet at [*blank*] clock this afternoon in the Star Chamber.

The business concerning Sir John Savile's letter to be heard tomorrow morning, after

1. Preceding the entry for this bill *The report from the committee for privileges* is crossed out in the MS.

2. Below are the resolutions on the proposed alterations in the remonstrance (or declaration) which is included following this day's proceedings. Copies of the remonstrance are printed in Cobbett, *Parl. Hist.*, II, 200–207; and Rushworth, *Hist. Collections*, I, 400–406. The remonstrance circulated as a "separate" and numerous manuscript copies are extant, for example, see: Cornell MS +H83, ff. 206–209v; Harl. 160, ff. 116–120; HRO, 44/M/69, Misc. Box 2; NLW, Cummings Papers; SP 16/29:86 (printed below).

the declaration to be engrossed be finished.[3]

Upon question, whether Sir John Savile's cause should be heard tomorrow, the House divided. The yea went out.

Tellers for the yea:	Sir John Strangways Sir John Hotham.
For the no:	Sir Francis Barrington Mr. Richard Spencer.

With the yea: 188
With the no: 121

II. DIARY OF BULSTRODE WHITELOCKE, ESQ., DD. 12.22, CAMBRIDGE UNIVERSITY LIBRARY

[f. 56v]

June 13

Upon the reading of the bill concerning the liberties of parliament.

SIR NATHANIEL RICH moves that the [bill][4] being presented to the House from a grand committee, it may now, having been twice read, be engrossed and not committed.

SIR PETER HEYMAN. That he never saw a bill engrossed but it was first committed; and desire this may.

SPEAKER. That by the orders of the House a bill may be engrossed without commitment.[5]

This bill committed.

SIR JOHN ELIOT moves that there may be a collection throughout the House for reward of those clerks and officers that have attended this parliament and that the sum may be as it was at Oxford: that every knight may pay 10s. and every burgess 5.

SIR CLEMENT THROCKMORTON. That seeing the knights have no more privilege here in parliament than burgesses, they should not pay a double sum.

MR. WANDESFORD. That the wages of knights are double the wages of burgesses, and this proportion has been ever in parliament.

Resolved that there shall be a collection of all the members of the House, and the pro[por]tion to be 10s. of every knight and 5 of every burgess.

Some appointed collectors; and the money to be paid by Thursday next.[6]

MR. SELDEN reports the declaration with the addition by way of answer to the King's letter.[7]

Which is read.

To the clause concerning placing and displacing of officers in England, Scotland, and Ireland, MR. MURRAY objects to the mentioning of Scotland [f. 57], saying that he knows not whether those offenses, if any such be, are within our cognizance.[8] If such things be done, the Scotchmen are ready enough to take exceptions to them and to complain thereof. And therefore moves that Scotland may be left out of the declaration.

3. After *finish* the following passage is crossed out in the MS: *Upon question, Sir John Savile to have Monday next to produce witnesses to prove who wrote the original letter, he now undertaking here to produce his proofs or else to show good reason why he cannot do it.* [p. 97] *Upon question, the cause concerning Sir John Savile to be heard tomorrow and the witnesses which shall be then produced on either part to be heard and if Sir John Savile shall then desire further time for any witness then to have time for it till [illegible]*.

4. MS: *the being being.*

5. "In the same manner the clerk reads the bill the second time. . . . Then if no man speaks against the bill, it is ordered to be engrossed, if begun with the Lords, or to have a third reading if brought from the Commons. If any doubt be conceived, which is often *pro forma tantum,* the bill is committed". Elsyng, "Method of Passing Bills", p. 227.

6. I.e., 15 June.

7. The intended remonstrance (declaration) is printed at the end of this day's proceedings. For the King's letter, see 9 June, OB.

8. See the remonstrance (declaration), below.

Ordered accordingly by the House.

MR. SPENCER takes exception to this declaration consisting of 3 parts: 1, a declaration; 2, an answer; 3, a request. The declaration is only our conceit. If the King say we conceive amiss, we must conceive better again. The request is to desire the sequestration of the Duke from the King, he standing now accused by us in the Lords House.

SIR JOHN ELIOT. Opinions so strongly fixed on reason and probable grounds, I think is a parliamentary way; and if any man laying his hand upon his heart do not believe that which is there laid down, I shall not believe him.

Tis nothing we desire but justice, and we see the power of this great man such that we can scarce come to accuse him, nor witnesses to testify against him. We do but desire he may be removed from the administration of affairs of state.

SIR HENRY MARTEN. It is a shrewd phrase to style a man an enemy to this commonwealth. I desire you would take consideration of that phrase.

SIR JOHN SAVILE. I desire to know what course or means the Duke has legally to come to make his answer and justification to this declaration. If there be none, I do protest against it.

[f. 57v] SIR JOHN STRADLING takes exception to a clause, viz.: that no sooner shall the Duke be removed from the King's presence but that we will with all possible speed hasten to the dispatch of that supply which the King desires. I take this as a condition: that if the King will do this, we will do that. The King has often admonished us from such kind of conditioning. And I desire that clause may be left out.[9]

SIR CLEMENT THROCKMORTON. That upon our conceits and conjectures, which are uncertain, we in this declaration desire a certain punishment: the removal of the Duke from the King. This course I never heard of in any court and desire it may not be used by us who are judges.

MR. PYM. We sit here as law makers, as counselors, and as judges. This declaration is our counsel to the King and may very well and parliamentarily be upon probable grounds and conjectures.

Resolved that those clauses concerning the meeting of the parliament at Oxford and dissolution of it, making of sheriffs, and sending Mr. Glanville in the fleet shall stand as they are in the declaration expressed.

Resolved that the request for the Duke's sequestration shall stand as it is expressed.

Resolved that the phrase that we hold the Duke to be an enemy to Church and state shall stand.

Resolved that the clause whereto Sir John Stradling took exception shall stand as it is penned in the declaration.

Ordered to engross the declaration.

[*Afternoon*]

[f. 58]

At the committee for purveyance.[10]

Offered unto them a copy of a report. In the Star Chamber 36 Eliz., Coke, Attorney General, did inform the court that a purveyor could not make purveyance of things of inheritance, as of trees growing, glass, or

9. King James was outspoken against bargaining or conditioning with parliament. See HofC, 12 June, n. 24. In the present session Charles spoke of "conditions" on 29 March (see above) with regard to the subsidy bill. Stradling's objection to the clause was overruled, see the resolutions, below.

10. The committee to examine purveyance was appointed on 25 May, see above. The report this day may be from Sir William Spencer, first named on the committee list.

other things annexed to the freehold.[11] Magna Carta, c. 21, and 11 H. 4, 28, Hill said that a purveyor could not take gravel without the consent of the tenant of the land.[12] But a purveyor may take victual without the consent of the owner, and that has been so used as long as the King has had purveyors by the allowance of the law. And the King has as good right to take victual by his purveyor as the subject has in the thing purveyed, so that it be disposed for the King's household. And he said that there are more than 75 statutes made against purveyors to redress their enormities and offenses by them committed by color of their commissions, but there is no statute made to declare their power or constitutions. And he said that purveyance is to the King a *proprium quarto modo sumptum, quia convenit sibi soli* and no other person can [have] it.

He said it appeared by the statutes of 28 Eliz.; 36 E. 3, c. 2; 23 H. 6, c. 4; 2 *et* 3 P. *et* M.,[13] that there are seven incidents to the office of a purveyor:

1. He ought to be a sufficient man and able to answer the King and his people for his misfeasance.

[f. 58v] 2. It is an office of trust and confidence and he cannot make a deputy.[14]

3. Purveyors ought to be sworn in Chancery to do their office truly.

4. A purveyor ought to make tables of things purveyed, to be there set down in certainty, so that his dealings may be notorious and known to the people.

5. They ought to make purveyance where there is plenty; and they must take things in their season and in convenient time and no more than is necessary for the King's service.

6. They ought to make purveyance of things in their kind and not to take money for them; for, he said, that purveyors for money trade at Shooters Hill.

7. They ought to have a patent under the Great Seal of England to endure for six months and no longer, for if the patent be for life it is void.

Nota. 33 Eliz., Nicholson, a purveyor, was hanged because he made purveyance for the Queen and sold the things purveyed for money to her Majesty's subjects and converted some part to his own use. The which case was cited in parliament, 19 *Aprilis* 1624, by Sir Edward Coke.[15]

III. HARLEIAN MS 1601, BRITISH LIBRARY

[f.4]

Tuesday the 13th of June 1626

Resolved upon question that a collection shall be made for the officers. The knights of the shire to pay 10s. And the burgesses 5s. The collectors: Sir Baptist Hicks, Sir Nathaniel Rich, Mr. Kirton, Sir Francis Barrington, Mr. Bateman. All to be paid Thursday next.

MR. SELDEN's report of the deliberation. My Lord of Arundel's confinement taken out of it.

The Speaker never goes with anything when it is delivered *in haec verba.*

Ordered that this declaration shall be engrossed by tomorrow morning.

Ordered that the committee for drawing of the Duke's reply shall meet this afternoon at 3 a clock in the Star Chamber.

11. See Coke, *Second Inst.*, I, 35.

12. 9 H. III, Magna Carta, c. 25; *YB*, 11 H. IV, Mich., pl. 53, a case heard by Robert Hill, justice of Common Pleas. (E. Foss, *A Biographical Dictionary of the Judges of England 1066–1870* [London, 1870]).

13. There is no statute of 28 Elizabeth regarding purveyance; perhaps *SR*, 28 E. I, c. 2 is meant. *SR*, 36 E. III, c. 2; *SR*, 23 H. VI, c. 1; *SR*, 2 & 3, P. & M., c. 6.

14. Marginal Note: "Quare 2 & 3 P. & M.". The statute relates to purveyors and their deputies.

15. The case was cited by Coke on 19 April 1624. See the diary of Edward Nicholas, SP 14/166, f. 133 (YCPH transcript). We have not found the source of the reference.

IV. THE INTENDED REMONSTRANCE OF THE HOUSE OF COMMONS, SP 16/29:86[16]

Most gracious sovereign;

We your most loyal and faithful subjects, the Commons assembled by your Majesty's most royal authority in this present parliament, having with all dutiful affection from the time of our first meeting earnestly endeavored to proceed speedily in those affairs that might best and soonest conduce for our dispatch of the intended speedy supply of your Majesty's great designs, to the enlargement of your support, and to an enabling of ourselves and them whom we represent to the full and timely performance of the same; having, notwithstanding, by reason of divers informations, interpretations, and other preventions of our proceedings been hitherto so retarded in the presentment of these affairs, that we now thought it a negative [*sic*] part of our most humble duties thus to declare both these interruptions and preventions, with the true, original, and continued course of them; as also, our own most earnest devotions to the parliamentary service of your Majesty. [And we most humbly, therefore, beseech your most excellent Majesty to] be graciously pleased here to cast your eye on some particulars that have relation as well to your [first][17] parliament as to this one, of which we cannot doubt but that your great goodness may receive an ample satisfaction touching our most loyal and faithful intent.

In the first parliament in the first year of your Majesty's most happy reign over us, the Commons then assembled, after they had cheerfully presented unto your Majesty as the first fruits of their affections two entire subsidies, were exceedingly pressed by means of the Duke of Buckingham (for his own end, as we conceive), to enlarge the supply; which, when he conceived could not there be affected he procured, for the same end, from your Majesty, an adjournment of the parliament to the city of Oxford, where the Commons, then taking into just considerations the mischiefs which the kingdom variously has suffered, and that chiefly by reason of the exorbitant power and frequent misdoings of the said Duke, were entering into a parliamentary way of examination of those mischiefs, power, and misdoing. But no sooner was there any motion made there of his name to this purpose but that he, fearing that his actions might have been too much laid open to the view of your most excellent Majesty and to the just censure of that which might have followed then presently, through his misinformations to your Majesty of the intentions of the said Commons (as we have just cause to believe), procured a dissolution of the said parliament.[18] And afterward, also the same year, through divers misreports made to your Majesty on his behalf touching some members of the said Commons who had more particularly drawn his name into question, he, as we cannot but conceive, procured the same members to be made high sheriffs of several counties for this year that followed, to the end that they might have been precluded from being chosen members of the present parliament lest they should again have therein questioned him.[19]

And by the like practice also (as we are

16. See above, n. 2. A proclamation was issued on 16 June prohibiting the "publishing, dispersing, and reading" of the remonstrance (or declaration). See *Stuart Proclamations,* II, 93–95. The sections within brackets in the remonstrance, below, have been supplied from the version printed in Cobbett, *Parl. Hist.,* II, 200–208.

17. I.e., the first parliament summoned by Charles I in 1625. In the first session of that parliament two subsidies were passed. See *PP 1625,* pp. 118, 121, 272. Here, above and below, the words in brackets are supplied from Cobbett, *Parl. Hist.,* II, 200–207.

18. The parliament convened at Oxford on 1 August and was dissolved on 12 August 1625.

19. See the Introduction, *PP 1626,* I, 3, n. 3.

likewise persuaded) he procured, soon after the said dissolution, another member of the same House, because he had justly professed himself against his ends, to be sent as secretary of your Majesty's last fleet,[20] thereby indeed to punish him, by such withdrawing him from the practice of the law, which was his profession, under color of an honorable employment.

It pleased your Majesty afterward, in February last, to call this present parliament wherein, though, none of those whom the said Duke had procured to be made high sheriffs have sat as members.[21] Yet we, finding in ourselves the like affection to the service of your Majesty and next to the good of the commonwealth, we took into our serious consideration several propositions how for the safety of your Majesty's kingdoms and allies we might enlarge our support, add to the military strength without charge to the poorer sort of your subjects, and give a larger supply to your Majesty for the instant and pressing occasions than have ever yet (but once) been given in parliament. Whereunto, for the enabling of ourselves and those whom we represent, we conceived it first necessary to search into the causes of those mischiefs which this your kingdom suffers, and divers of the grievances that over-burden your subjects without doing of which we could neither be just and faithful to your Majesty nor to the country that does trust and employ us, as your royal father, of blessed memory admonished the House of Commons in the 4th session of his first parliament.

In this consideration we found that the most pressive and comprehensive mischief and grievance that we suffered was fundamentally settled in the vast power and enormous actions of the said Duke,[22] being such, that by reason of his strange kind of plurality of offices, all gotten by ambition and some for money, expressly against the laws of your realm; his breach of trust in not guarding of the seas; his high injustice in the admiralty; his extortion; his delivering over the ships of this kingdom into the hands of a foreign prince; his procuring of the compulsory [*blank*]; waste of honor for his own gain; his unexampled exhausting of the revenues and treasure of the kingdom; his transcendent presumption of that unhappy application of physic to your most royal father of blessed memory [a] few days before his death; and some other of his affairs carefully and maturely examined by us. We made a parliamentary charge of the same matters and offenses against him to the lords, by your Majesty assembled in parliament, thence expecting some remedy by a speedy proceeding against him. But, may it please your most excellent Majesty, not only during the time of our examination of the matters and offenses of the same charge we were directly interrupted and diverted by messages procured through misinformation from your Majesty which, with most humble duty and reverence we ever received, whence in honor it so fell out that so much time was spent amongst us before the same charge was perfected but also, within two days next after the same charge was transmitted by us to the Lords, upon untrue and malicious informations, privately, and publicly, and against the privileges of parliament, given to your Majesty of certain words supposed to have been spoken by Sir Dudley Digges and Sir John Eliot, knights (two of the members of our House), in the service of transmitting the same charge,[23]

20. I.e., John Glanville. See HofL, 15 May, p. 461, n. 65.

21. Sir Edward Coke, pricked for sheriff of Buckinghamshire and returned to parliament from Norfolk, was apparently not turned out of the House nor was a new writ issued for his place. See HofC, 9 June, n. 12.

22. For the grievances against the Duke enumerated below, see HofL, 15 May, pp. 463–477.

23. Regarding Digges and Eliot, see HofC, 11 May, n. 15; 12 May, nn. 1 and 7; 13 May, n. 2; 15 May, n. 3; 19 May, n. 1; and 20 May, n. 7.

both of them having been especially employed in the affairs of countries, which is about examination of the said matters and offenses. They were both, by your Majesty's command, arrested and committed to close imprisonment within the Tower of London, and their lodgings presently searched, and their papers there found taken away by reason whereof not only our known privileges of parliament was much infringed, but we ourselves that upon full hope of a speedy course of justice against the said Duke, were preparing with all dutiful affection to proceed to the dispatch of the supply and other services of your Majesty, were wholly, as the course and privilege of parliament binds us, diverted for divers days to the taking only into consideration some course for the certifying and preservation of the privileges so infringed.

And we think it our duties, most gracious Sovereign, hereby rightly to inform your most excellent Majesty of the course held in the commitment of the said two members. For whereas, by your Majesty's warrant to your messengers for the arresting of them that were pleased to command that they should repair to their lodgings and there to take them, your Majesty's principal secretary, the Lord Conway, gave the said messengers, as they affirmed, an express command, contrary to the said warrant, that they should not go to their lodgings but to the House of Commons, and there to take them. That if they found them not there they should stay until they were come to the House, and not apprehend them wheresoever else they should find them. Which, besides that it was contrary to your Majesty's command, is an apparent testimony of some mischievous intention there had against the whole House of Commons, and against the service intended to your Majesty all which, with the several interruptions that preceded it, and the misinformations that have caused all of them we cannot doubt but were wrought and procured by means of the said Duke to his own behoof, and for his advantage, especially because the said interruptions have, through such misinformations, come amongst us only upon those times wherein we have had the matters and offenses charged against him in agitation. But your Majesty, out of your great goodness and justice, being afterward truly informed of the privileges and demerit of the cause that committed our said two members, graciously commanded the re-delivery of them out of the Tower of London, for which we render unto your Majesty most humble thanks.

And we again, by reason of the hopes of the dispatch of the proceeding with the Lords upon our charge against the said Duke, in a cheerful purpose, to go on with the matter of supply and other service to your Majesty, when again these hopes failed in us by reason of some new exorbitances now lately showed in the exercise of his so great power and ambition. For by such his power and ambition, notwithstanding our declaration against him for his so great plurality of offices, he then also procured to himself by the solicitation of his agents,[24] and of such as depended upon him, the office of Chancellor of the University of Cambridge. Whereas yet the same University, having two burgesses in parliament,[25] did, by the same burgesses a few weeks before, consent with us in the charge against him for his ambition to sue for it. Such was his power to make them give it him, contrary to what themselves had agreed in parliament with all the commons of England. And he procured also the same office by the special labors and endeavors of a factious party, as we are informed, who adhere to that most dangerous innovation of religion published in the seditious writings of one Richard Montagu, clerk, of whom it is then also, and

24. See HofC, 3 June, n. 10.

25. I.e., Sir John Coke and Thomas Eden.

heretofore, upon other reasons, it has been conceived the said Duke is and long has been an abettor and protector.[26] These actions of the Duke have thus among us hindered the service of your Majesty by reason both of the interruptions that have so narrowly accompanied them, and of the preventions of our cheerfulness which otherwise had long since been effectually showed in us that have nothing else in our cares next to our duty to God but the loyal service of your Majesty, the safety of your kingdoms, and subsistence of ourselves and those whom we represent for the continuance of that service and safety which we cannot hope for.

And we beseech your most excellent Majesty graciously to review this our humble and free protestation, which we cannot hope for so long as we thus suffer under the pressures of the power of this ambitious Duke and the divers and false informations so given to your Majesty in his behalf and for his advantage, especially when we observe also that in such his greatness he prevents the giving of true information to your Majesty in anything that may any ways reflect on his own misdoings to show unto your Majesty the true state of your subjects and kingdoms otherwise than as it may be represented for his own ends. Unto which purpose he has also procured so many persons depending on him, either by alliance or advancement to places of eminency near your sacred person. Through his misinformation also of that kind, and the like, we have seen, to our great grief, both in the time of your Majesty's royal father of blessed memory and of your Majesty, divers officers of the kingdom so often by him procured to be displaced and altered, that within these few years past, since the beginning of his greatness, more such displacings and alterations have by his means happened than in many ages before them. Neither was there in the time of your royal father of blessed memory any such course held before it was by the practice of the said Duke thus induced. And since that time divers officers of the crown not only in this your kingdom of England but also in Ireland, accordingly as they have been friends or adverse to the said Duke, have been either so commended or mispresented by him to his Sovereign; and by his procurement so placed or displaced that he has always herein, so much as in him lay, made his own ends and advantage the measure of the good or ill of your Majesty's kingdoms.

But now at length, may it please your most excellent Majesty, we have received a copy of the said Duke's answer to our charge transmitted against him,[27] whereunto we shall presently in such sort reply according to the laws of parliament. That unless his power and practice again undermine the proceedings we cannot doubt but that we, upon the same, shall have judgment against him. In the times, also, most gracious Sovereign, of these interruptions which come among us by reason of the commitment so procured by him of two of our members, a gracious message was formerly received from your Majesty wherein you had been pleased to let us know that if you had not a timely supply your Majesty would betake yourself to new counsels which,[28] we cannot doubt, were intended by your Majesty to be such as stood with justice and the laws of this realm. But these words, "new counsels", were remembered in a speech made among us by one of your Majesty's Privy Council, and lately a member of us who, in that same speech, told us that he had often thought upon those words, "new counsels", and that in his consideration of

26. See HofC, 3 June, n. 30.

27. For the Duke's answer to the charges, see HofL, 8 June, pp. 566–585. For emendations and corrections suggested perhaps by Bishop Laud, see SP 16/27:25.

28. I.e., in Sir Dudley Carleton's speech, HofC, 12 May.

them he remembered that there were certain nations where such kind of parliaments have been anciently used as now in England. That in England he saw the people live in happiness and plenty, but that in those other nations he saw them poor both in their persons and habits, or to that effect. Which state and condition happened to them, as he said, where such "new counsels" were taken, as that the course of parliaments ended.

This intimation, may it please your excellent Majesty, was such as gave us all so just cause to fear that there were some ill ministers near your Majesty's sacred person that in the behalf of the said Duke, and together with him who is so strangely powerful, were so much against the parliamentary course of this kingdom as they might, perhaps, advise your most excellent Majesty with such "new counsels" as these that fell under the memory and consideration of that privy councillor. And one special reason among others has increased that fear among us: for that the subsidies of tonnage and poundage which determine upon the death of your most royal father, our late sovereign, and were never payable to any of your Majesty's ancestors but only by a special act of parliament, and ought not to be levied without such an act, yet, ever since the beginning of your Majesty's happy reign over us, the said subsidies have been levied by some of your Majesty's ministers as if they were still due; although also a parliament has since been begun and dissolved by procurement of the said Duke as is before showed, wherein no act passed for the same subsidies.[29] Which example is so much against the use of former times and the known right and liberty of the subjects that it is an apparent effect of "new counsels" given against the ancient settled course of government of this your Majesty's kingdom, and chiefly against the right of your commons, as if there must be any subsidy, tax, or aid lawfully levied upon them without their consent in parliament or contrary to the settled laws of this kingdom.

But if any such do so ill an office as by any misrepresentation to the state and right of your Majesty's royal subjects to advise any "new counsels", as the levying of any aid, tax, or subsidy among your people contrary to the settled laws of this kingdom we cannot, most gracious Sovereign, but esteem them that so shall advise not only as vipers and pests to their king and commonwealth (as all such were to both Houses of parliament styled by your most royal father),[30] but also capital enemies as well to the crown and dignity as to the commonwealth. And we shall for our part in our parliament show, as occasion shall require, and be ready to declare their offenses of this kind such as may be rewarded with the highest punishment that your laws inflict on any offenders.

These were some of those things among many other, most gracious Sovereign, which have so much prevented a right understanding between your Majesty and us, and which have possessed the hearts of your poor people and loyal commons with unspeakable sorrow and grief, finding apparently all our humble and hearty endeavors misinterpreted, interrupted, hindered, and now, at last, almost frustrate by the interposition and ambitious power of one man, against whom we have just cause to protest not only in regard of the particulars wherewith he has been charged (which in a parliamentary way we were enforced to insist upon as matters which lay in our notice and proof), but also we apprehend him of so unbridled ambition, and so averse to

29. A bill for tonnage and poundage passed the Lower House in 1625 but was rejected by the Lords. See *PP 1625, sub* Tonnage and Poundage.

30. McIlwain, *Political Works of James I,* p. 309. Speech at Whitehall, 21 March 1610.

the good and tranquillity of the church and state that we verily believe him to be an enemy to both. Therefore, unless we would betray our own duties to your Majesty and to those for whom we are trusted, we cannot but express our infinite grief that he should have so great power and interest in your princely affections and under your Majesty in a manner wholly to engross to himself the administration of the affairs of this your kingdom which, by his means, are drawn into a condition most miserable and hazardous.

Give us then leave, most dear Sovereign, in the name of all the commons of this kingdom, prostrate at the feet of your sacred Majesty, most humbly to beseech you, even for the honor of Almighty God whose religion is directly undermined by the practice of that party whom this Duke does support; for your honor, and welfare of this kingdom which, by this means, is threatened with almost unavoidable dangers, and for the love which your Majesty as a good and loving father bears unto your good people (to whom, we profess in the presence of Almighty God, the searcher of all hearts, you are as highly esteemed and beloved as ever King was) that you will be pleased graciously to remove this person from access to your sacred person. And that you would not balance this one man with all these things, and with the affairs of the Christian world, which do all suffer so far as they have relation to this kingdom, chiefly by this means.

For we protest to your Majesty and the whole world, that until this great person be removed from intermeddling with the great affairs of state we are out of hope of any good success and do fear that any money that we shall or can give will, through his misemployment, be turned rather to the prejudice and hurt of this your kingdom than otherwise, as by lamentable experience we have found in those large supplies we have formerly and lately given. But no sooner shall we receive redress and relief in this (which, of all other is our most insupportable grievance) but we shall forthwith proceed to accomplish your Majesty's own desire for supply and likewise, with all cheerfulness, apply ourselves to the perfecting of divers other great things such as we think no one parliament in any age can parallel, tending to the stability, wealth, strength, and honor of this your kingdom and the support of your friends and allies abroad. And we doubt but through God's blessing as you are the best, so you shall be ever the best-beloved and greatest monarch that ever sat in the throne of this famous kingdom.

Order of Business Wednesday, 14 June 1626

Committee of the whole on the bill for the **continuance and repeal** of divers **statutes** to meet this afternoon 445, *23/3

Committee for framing heads for a **remonstrance** concerning **tonnage and poundage** to meet this afternoon 445, *23/3; 8/6

Ordered: Register of High Commission Court to bring proceedings against Sir Robert **Howard** to the committee for considering the case of Howard 445, *17/2

WEDNESDAY, 14 JUNE 1626

I. JOURNAL OF THE HOUSE OF COMMONS

[CJ 870; p. 97]
Mercurii, 14 Junii, 2 Caroli Regis

Thomas Winniffe, bailiff to Sir Harbottle Grimston, Knight, one of the members of this House, to have privilege, being arrested at Colchester upon mesne process.

[CJ 871] Upon question, ordered that this House shall not desire that the depositions in the Exchequer concerning Webbe's patent for sole making of rape oil may be sent from the Exchequer to the House or committee for grievances.

Mr. Whitby has leave to go down in respect of the sickness of his wife;[1] and Mr. Sherland to succeed in the chair of grievances, and Mr. Whitby to leave his instructions and notes concerning the grievances.

Committee for the fast to meet tomorrow in the afternoon.[2]

L. 2a. An act for the better continuance of peace and unity in the Church and commonwealth.

Committed to

Mr. [Humphrey] Newbery
Mr. [Francis] Rous
Sir George More
Sir A[lexander] Temple
Sir H[enry] Poole
Sir H[umphrey] Lynde

Sir Richard Grosvenor
Sir John Jackson
Mr. [John] Pym

And all that will come to have voice; Friday, Court of Wards.

Bill for hearing of preaching this afternoon, in the Exchequer Chamber.

Excommunication, tomorrow in the afternoon, in the former place.

[p. 98] *L. 2a.* Pigott.
Committed to

[col. 1]
Mr. Browne
Sir D[udley] Digges
Sir H[enry] Poole
Sir Thomas Puckering
Knights and burgesses of Buckinghamshire
Sir H[umphrey] Lynde
Sir Thomas Myddleton
Mr. [Thomas] Wise
Mr. Whitaker

[col. 2]
Sir John Stradling
Sir M[iles] Fleetwood
Sir George More
Sir O[liver] Luke
Sir G[ilbert] Gerard
Sir Roland Cotton
Sir Thomas Cheeke
Knights and burgesses of Bedfordshire
Sir Clement Throckmorton
Mr. [Christopher] Sherland

[col. 3]
Sir Thomas Dacres
Sir M[aurice] Abbot
Mr. [Robert] Bateman
Sir Nicholas Saunders
Sir Francis Barrington
Mr. [William] Strode

Monday next, Exchequer Court. And notice to be given the parties.

Monday next, to hear excuses of defaulters;[3] and the £10 defaulted to be paid in the meantime.

The conclusion of the articles against Montagu read, and allowed to be engrossed.[4]

1. *and the committees to name another in his place* is crossed out in the MS following *wife*.

2. Sir Edwin Sandys wrote to Sir John Coke on 17 June that, "the committee never met again . . . . It was the general desire that the fast might not be weekly but either monthly or once for all. And the reason was that frequency bred disreputation". HMC, *12th Report, App. 1*, p. 271 (Coke MSS).

3. I.e., those not present at the calling of the House. For the list of those absent, see Grosvenor, 2 June.

4. The final list of articles against Montagu is not included in the accounts for this parliament. For the report on Montagu from the committee on religion, see 17 April.

The committee concerning proofs against Montagu to sit tomorrow morning, 7 clock, in the Court of Wards.

The committee for taking consideration of the Duke's answer to have power to send for any records or witnesses, and to draw up the reply.

The engrossed declaration read and allowed to be forthwith[5] presented to his Majesty, upon question.

Much debate whether this should be delivered by the Speaker, in presence of the whole House, if the King yield the whole House access.

Upon question, by messengers to desire access to his Majesty, as soon as it may stand with his Majesty's pleasure, with the whole House and the Speaker.

The number to be 4: Sir James Fullerton, Sir George More, Lord Carey, Mr. Murray.

An introduction to be made by Mr. Speaker, with reasons for enforcing the declaration. The heads hereof to be set down presently by Sir D. Digges, Sir John Strangways, Sir John Eliot, Mr. Selden, Sir Thomas Lake, Sir Nathaniel Rich, Mr. Pym, Sir B. Rudyard.

The committee for evils and causes, to sit presently.

SIR JAMES FULLERTON. That his Majesty's answer to our message is: that we shall have answer to our message tomorrow morning.[6]

SIR JOHN HIPPISLEY tenders a warrant from the Council of War for £1,000 about the repairing of castles about Dover.

Continuance of statutes, this afternoon.

The committee for the remonstrance for tonnage and poundage to meet this afternoon in the Star Chamber.[7]

Ordered, to send for the register of the High Commission Court to bring with him the acts and proceedings and depositions against Sir Robert Howard, in state wherein they stand, unto the last committee appointed for that cause, tomorrow morning, 7 clock, Star Chamber.[8]

II. DIARY OF BULSTRODE WHITELOCKE, ESQ., DD. 12.22, CAMBRIDGE UNIVERSITY LIBRARY

[f. 59]

June 14

The declaration read after engrossing.[9]

SIR THOMAS HOBY. That according to a precedent, 18 *Jac.*, the Speaker and the whole House may go to the King and the Speaker present it to the King with a preamble of his own, as the Speaker of the Lords House did when both Houses of parliament joined in 18 *Jac.*[10]

SIR NATHANIEL RICH. In a declaration concerning religion the Speaker had liberty to make an introduction of his own and to use his papers in 18 *Jac.* before the King.[11] It is in the power of the House and agrees with the honor and precedents of both Houses. And therefore I desire that you

5. MS: *forthwith to be presented*. The remonstrance (declaration) is printed on 13 June, see OB. See also, Attorney General Heath's letter offering support to Buckingham, 13 June (SP 16/524:28).

6. The King dissolved the parliament the following morning.

7. On 8 June the House had resolved to draft a remonstrance regarding tonnage and poundage.

8. On 10 June the House ordered that the provisions of the order of 3 May be satisfied. See HofC, 10 June, nn. 2 and 3.

9. See above, n. 5.

10. The Lord Chancellor presented the petition regarding religion from both Houses to King James on 17 February 1621. See *LJ*, III, 22; *CD 1621*, IV, 69–75; V, 470–472, 512–513; VI, 282–283, VII, 576–577.

11. On 7 December 1621 it was ordered that the Speaker should not leave the House in order to present the remonstrance to the King (*CJ*, I, 661; *CD 1621*, VI, 229) although Rich had moved for his going (ibid., VI, 228; *CJ*, I, 660).

may make an introduction of your own and read the declaration to the King.

SPEAKER. 7 *Jac.*, the debate of impositions holding solemnly 10 days and being drawn into the form of a grievance, they did resolve that it being to be read and left in writing that therefore the Speaker should not go with it.[12]

SIR DUDLEY DIGGES. That the Speaker may press those 2 points as point of honor. That it is a greater honor for his Majesty to hear the just complaints of his Commons than the protection of any servant. And also to the point of justice, etc.

Resolved that messengers shall be sent to the King to desire access unto his Majesty for the whole House as soon as it may stand with his Majesty's pleasure.

8 named to go with the Speaker and consider of the heads for the Speaker's speech by way of introduction.[13]

[f. 59v] Speaker withdraws with the rest to frame the heads for his speech.

[*Committee of the Whole House*]

Mr. Wandesford in the chair.

Sir Thomas Hoby reports from the subcommittee concerning unexperienced commanders. Captain Cooke,[14] Captain Paramour, Captain Porter.[15]

Speaker in his chair.

SIR JAMES FULLERTON reports that having delivered our message to his Majesty for access, his Majesty's answer is that we shall have an answer tomorrow morning.

12. On 7 July 1610 a committee that excluded the Speaker (Sir Edward Phelips) carried a petition to the King. *CJ*, I, 447.

13. See CJ, above.

14. *Captain Moyer* is crossed out in the MS preceding *Captain Cooke*.

15. Following *Captain Porter* the names of Captains *Baller* (?), Latham, Rigby (?), and *Kerton* are crossed out in the MS.

Order of Business Thursday, 15 June 1626

THURSDAY, 15 JUNE 1626

I. JOURNAL OF THE HOUSE OF COMMONS

[**CJ 871;** p. 99]

Jovis, 15 Junii, 2 Caroli Regis

The examinations taken against the Bishop of Bangor, to be brought in to the Clerk.

Upon question, copies[1] of the declaration to be delivered by the Clerk to any member of the House.

Upon question, the Clerk, out of the collection,[2] to have £100.

The residue of the collection to be disposed as the collectors shall think fittest; Mr. Strode,[3] Mr. Smith added to them. And whosoever shall not now pay the 10s. and 5s., then to pay double [at] the next meeting.

The engrossed articles against Mr. Montagu/

The money remaining of the communion money to be distributed to the poor of the parish and to the officers of the Church.

Upon question, every knight and burgess of the House to pay 2s. more, besides the 10s. and 5s.

Mr. Maxwell came to let the House know the Lords desire the House to come up thither to hear the commission read for dissolution of this parliament.[4] Whereupon, after some speeches made, Mr. Speaker, with the House, went up accordingly.

II. DIARY OF BULSTRODE WHITELOCKE, ESQ., DD. 12.22, CAMBRIDGE UNIVERSITY LIBRARY

[f. 60]

June 15

Ordered that such members of the House as will may take copies of the declaration to be presented to the King.

Ordered that out of the collection for this session the Clerk shall have a hundred pounds.

Ordered that every knight and burgess shall pay 2s. a man more.

Serjeant brings word that Mr. Maxwell is without with a message from the King.

SIR JOHN ELIOT. I think it is sufficiently known with what affection, with what hearts we came hither. I need not remember you. Tis known to God and man, though we/

Many interruptions have caused that delay of that which the King so often put us in mind to do. The fear of him to come to a trial appears/

The particular sense of his own misdoing have occasioned those delays and diversions. Tis not without sense of grief that we have thus long sat. The particular of our expense amounts to almost a subsidy. But that we should fall in dislike with his Majesty and he be misinformed of us is our greatest grief.

That it may be by a general vote of the House that we retain a dutiful and loving heart and opinion towards the King, and likewise express it so in our countries. Moves we may make a general acclamation of this.

[f. 60v] Hereat many say such acclamation need not, for our hearts are all full of loyalty and love and good opinion of the King, and so every man will express in his country.

Mr. Maxwell, brought in, says that the Lords desire us to come up to their House to hear a commission read for dissolving of the parliament.

1. Printed edition: *the copies*. The remonstrance (declaration) is printed on 13 June.

2. I.e., the collection taken by the MPs, see 13 June.

3. *Sir Maurice Abbot* is crossed out in the MS following *Mr. Strode*.

4. For the commission for dissolution, see HofL, 15 June, p. 634.

The Commons and the Lords being together, the Lord Keeper says that he has received a commission from the King for dissolving of the parliament.

And the commission being read, the Lord Keeper pronounces: Be this parliament dissolved and determined by virtue of this commission.

Sic abeant omnes et cessat gloria regni.

Finis parlementi inchoati 6 die Febr. 1625, & determinati dissolutique 15 die Junii 1626.
Stante D.B.

III. DIARY OF JOHN LOWTHER, ESQ., D/LONS/L, CUMBERLAND AND WESTMORLAND RECORD OFFICE

[f. 43v]

[15 June]

The parliament then by message from King under Great Seal ended.

Provisional Index for Volumes II and III

Provisional Index for Volumes II and III

A complete index by volume and page will appear in the final volume of this series on the 1626 parliament. As an aid to the reader, the provisional index for the proceedings in the House of Commons includes the following two catagories (I) Bills; and (II) Speakers in the Lower House indexed by family name.

This index is based entirely upon the Orders of Business, and references are by date only (31/3 for 31 March). To find any item indexed, turn to the Order of Business for the day referred to in the index. The Order of Business will give page numbers for each mention of the item in that day's proceedings as well as cross-references by date to mention of the item on other days.

I. BILLS

II. SPEAKERS IN THE LOWER HOUSE